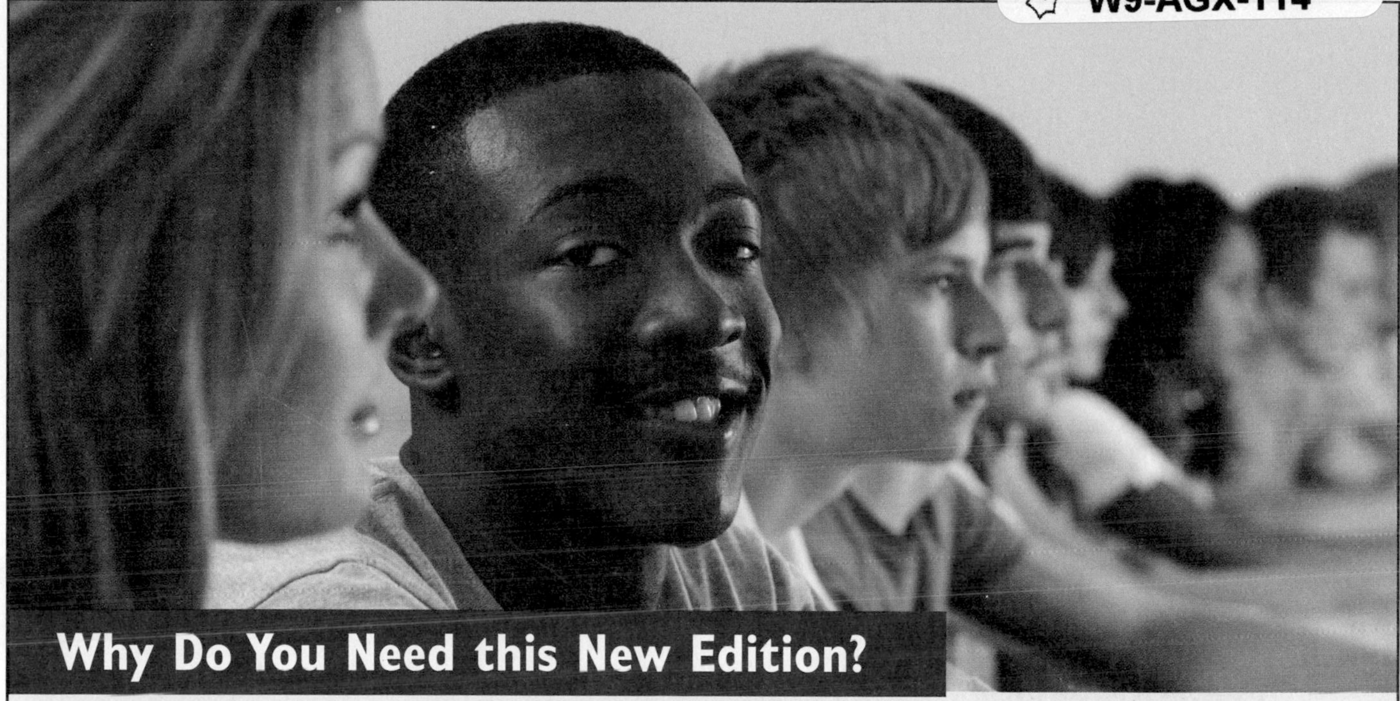

Why Do You Need this New Edition?

If you're wondering why you should buy this new edition of *The Art of Being Human*, here are 7 good reasons!

1. ***New Take a Closer Look* case studies** at the end of each Part II chapter help you **learn to analyze art, literature, and performances like a critic.** These new case studies explore select works in each discipline and challenge you to view the work critically by conducting your own analysis.
2. A **new *Chapter 15: Nature*** encourages you to view nature as one of art's basic themes and ends with an extensive, thought-provoking exploration of today's environmental crisis as reflected in contemporary art, literature, film, theater, and philosophy.
3. **Learning Objectives** at the end of each chapter provide you with a straightforward tool to review your mastery of the material.
4. **A timeline** inside the back cover of this text provides a concise chronological overview of major historical and artistic milestones.
5. **Discussions of fresh, new works from today's culture,** such as James Cameron's 2009 hit film *Avatar*, Tim Burton's 2010 visual spectacular *Alice in Wonderland*, the 2010 Broadway revival of Arthur Miller's *A View from the Bridge* starring Scarlett Johansson, Showtime's *The Big C* starring Laura Linney, and many, many more, help you make connections between contemporary art and the great works of the past.
6. **A crisp, modern, full-color format** allows you to see images in full color and makes key features [illegible] asier to find and read.
7. **A** [illegible] **pplement, M**[illegible] nable you to experi- en[illegible] ening to many of the mu[illegible] teractive tours of ma[illegible] scussed in the text.

PEARSON

PEARSON

myhumanitieskit™

MyHumanitiesKit offers a wealth of online resources to support student learning and comprehension, including chapter summaries, practice quizzes, essay questions, flashcards for studying key terms, and a rich array of interactive tools to engage students in learning. Throughout the text, you will see MyHumanitiesKit icons that alert you to available resources.

Explore on **MyHumanitiesKit.com**

Explore icons indicate the availability of a "Closer Look" interactive guided tour:

Warhol, *Marilyn Diptych*
Wren, Saint Paul's Cathedral
Monet, *Water Lilies*
Rivera, *Detroit Industry*
Degas, *The Rehearsal of the Ballet Onstage*
Manet, *A Bar at the Folies-Bergère*
Manet, *Le Déjeuner sur l'Herbe*
Manet, *Olympia*
Goya, *Family of Charles IV*
Goya, *The Sleep of Reason Produces Monsters*
Giotto, Arena Chapel
da Vinci, *Mona Lisa*
Duchamp, *Nude Descending a Staircase, No. 2*
Cassatt, *Woman with a Pearl Necklace in a Loge*
Picasso, *Collages*
Picasso, *Les Demoiselles d'Avignon*
Picasso, the History of *Guernica*
Raphael, *School of Athens*
Rembrandt, *The Anatomy Lesson of Dr Tulp*
Dali, *The Persistence of Memory*
Taj Mahal
The Bayeux Tapestry
The Parthenon
The Tale of Genji
van Gogh, *The Starry Night*
Blake, "The Chimney Sweeper" and "The Little Black Boy"
Wordsworth, "The Rainbow"
Mozart, Symphony No 40 in G Minor, First Movement

Listen on **MyHumanitiesKit.com**

Listen icons indicate the availability of an audio recording:

Beethoven, Ninth Symphony
Debussy, "Clair de Lune"
Homer, *The Iliad*
Shakespeare, Sonnet XXIX
Tchaikovsky, *1812 Overture*
Bach, "Toccata and Fugue in D Minor"
Beethoven, Symphony No 9
Stravinsky, *The Rite of Spring*
Joyce, *Ulysses*
Sophocles, *Oedipus*
Shakespeare, *Romeo and Juliet*
Mozart, *The Marriage of Figaro*
The Book of Job
Khayyam, *The Rubaiyat*
Strauss, *Death and Transfiguration*
Handy, "St. Louis Blues"
Joplin, "Maple Leaf Rag"
Shakespeare, *Othello*

Study and **Review** on **MyHumanitiesKit.com**

Study and Review icons remind students to visit the site after completing each chapter for:

Chapter Summaries
Practice Quizzes
Essay Prompts
Suggestions for Further Reading
Flashcards for the Key Terms

The Art of Being Human

The Humanities as a Technique for Living

TENTH EDITION

Richard Janaro
New World School of the Arts

Thelma Altshuler
Professor Emerita, Miami-Dade College

Boston Columbus Indianapolis New York San Francisco Upper Saddle River
Amsterdam Cape Town Dubai London Madrid Milan Munich Paris Montreal Toronto
Delhi Mexico City Sao Paulo Sydney Hong Kong Seoul Singapore Taipei Tokyo

Senior Sponsoring Editor: Virginia L. Blanford
Associate Development Editor: Erin E. Reilly
Executive Marketing Manager: Joyce Nilsen
Senior Supplements Editor: Donna Campion
Media Supplements Editor: Brian Hyland
Production Manager: S. Kulig
Project Coordination, Editorial Services, and Text Design: Electronic Publishing Services Inc., NYC
Art Rendering and Electronic Page Makeup: TexTech
Cover Design Manager: John Callahan
Cover Image: Auguste (René) Rodin, French, 1840–1917, Cambodian Dancer, 1906. Watercolor over graphite pencil, Sheet: 29 × 19.6 cm (11 7/16 × 7 11/16 in.). Museum of Fine Arts, Boston, Bequest of John T. Spaulding, 48.851. Photograph © 2011 Museum of Fine Arts, Boston
Photo Researcher: Jody Potter
Senior Manufacturing Buyer: Roy Pickering
Printer and Binder: Von Hoffman
Cover Printer: Lehigh-Phoenix Color

Janaro, Richard Paul.
The art of being human : the humanities as a technique for living / Richard Janaro, Thelma Altshuler. — 10th ed.
p. cm.
Includes bibliographical references and index.
ISBN-13: 978-0-205-02247-2
ISBN-10: 0-205-02247-2
1. Conduct of life—Textbooks. 2. Humanities—Textbooks. I. Altshuler, Thelma C. II. Title. III. Title: Humanities as a technique for living.
BJ1581.2.J36 2012
001.3—dc22

1 2 3 4 5 6 7 8 9 10—DJM—15 14 13 12 11

www.pearsonhighered.com

ISBN-13: 978-0-205-02247-2
ISBN-10: 0-205-02247-2

This book is dedicated to Micah, Josiah, and Samuel

Detailed Contents

PART II
Disciplines of the Humanities 67

Chapter 4
Literature 69

Chapter 5 Art 105

Chapter 6
Music 155

Preface

The tenth edition of *The Art of Being Human,* like its predecessors, introduces students to the joys of the humanities. As always, our aim is to communicate our enthusiasm for the humanities as experience for the mind and emotions. By becoming acquainted with the creative arts and learning to think critically about them, students will also better understand themselves and the world they live in.

The Art of Being Human tells the story of outstanding achievements in the humanities throughout history and across the world's many cultures. We acknowledge the contributions of the past because people very much like us lived there, and what they said and did can shed light on the present. We continue to find new reasons to rejoice, new stimuli for the senses in work from the past and the present, from different cultures and peoples around the world, and from women and men.

New Features of *The Art of Being Human*

This text has remained popular through nine editions because the humanities are alive and will be alive forever—and as a part of our daily lives, they must grow and change. Thus, the present text includes a number of important revisions necessary to keep our special approach to the humanities vital.

There is little throughout the tenth edition that has not been reexamined, revised, or rewritten for clarity. A wealth of new headings breaks up long passages of text, making the writing more accessible and inviting for students. A full-color design enhances the presentation of over 200 pieces of art and makes features more attractive and compelling.

- **New Thematic Chapter on Nature.** *Chapter 15: Nature* traces the relationship between the natural world and the humanities, ending with an extensive and thought-provoking section on the impact of today's environmental crisis.
- **New *Take a Closer Look* case studies in each chapter of Part II.** Appearing at the end of each of the discipline-focused chapters, new *Take a Closer Look* case studies offer in-depth looks at select works in each discipline and challenge students to view the works critically by conducting their own analyses.
- **New Color Design.** Inspired by contemporary magazine and web design, we offer a totally redesigned text with a modern, inviting look for today's readers. The switch to full color allows us to present over 200 images the way the artists intended them.

- **New Learning Objectives.** Learning objectives at the end of each chapter provide students with a straightforward tool to review their mastery of the material.
- **New Timeline.** A concise timeline inside the back cover offers a clear, chronological overview of the text, making relationships between historical events and the creation of great art more transparent.
- **New Headings.** In response to reviewer requests, we have added new headings throughout the text to break up long chunks of narrative and guide readers. These headings, along with the new full-color design, provide a much more inviting and accessible text for students used to a fast-moving, image-laden world.
- **Updated examples throughout offer coverage of contemporary works to help students understand the connection between the arts of today and the great works of the past.** New examples include George Clooney's 2009 hit film *Up in the Air,* the Broadway 2009 smash *Next to Normal,* and many others. Furthermore, diverse and global examples throughout the text help students better appreciate the worldwide reach and universal appeal of the humanities. For example, the music chapter acquaints students with Algerian musician Khaled Didi's performance at the 2010 World Cup.

Enduring Strengths

The tenth edition of *The Art of Being Human* retains the many strengths that have made it a highly respected and easy-to-use text.

- *Full coverage of the humanities*: *The Art of Being Human* discusses all the important disciplines and examines connections to issues that remain of vital importance. Students are encouraged to explore how the arts and social themes relate to their own life.
- *Individual treatment of disciplines and themes*: The book's topical organization allows students to explore one artistic mode or theme at a time, rather than having to cover multiple disciplines and themes in each chapter, often the case in chronologically organized texts.
- *Flexible organization*: Each chapter stands on its own, so the book can be taught in any sequence and can be easily customized to meet the goals of any number of introductory courses on the humanities in two- and four-year colleges.
- *Diverse range of traditional and contemporary examples of all the arts*: *The Art of Being Human* strives to familiarize students with the reach of the humanities by including many examples of literature and art from cultures around the globe. We include the work of women and people of color as well, and we address issues that remain of vital importance for an increasingly global society.
- *Accessible writing style*: The authors explore the world of the humanities in a contemporary idiom that students can easily understand.
- *An impressive visual program*: The more than 200 color photos provide students with a rich visual appreciation of the arts. All of the images and their captions are tied directly to discussions within the text.

Supplements

A rich array of supplements is available for *The Art of Being Human* for both instructors and students.

For Instructors

An Instructor's Manual and Test Bank (0205022480) includes hundreds of test items and questions, timelines, checklists of major concepts, and suggested teaching strategies.

For Students

- MyHumanitiesKit offers review and study materials that specifically support *The Art of Being Human*, 10th Edition. On MyHumanitiesKit.com, students can listen to performances of many of the literary works and musical selections referenced in the text. Students can interactively examine not only some of the artwork discussed in the text, but also additional works of art by these artists. Finally, the site offers both review materials for each chapter and suggestions for further reading. Throughout the text, you will notice MyHumanitiesKit icons in the margins that alert you to available resources. To package your text with MyHumantiesKit, ask your Pearson representative for ISBN 0-205-20738-3.
- *Evaluating a Performance*, by Michael Greenwald (0321095413), guides students through watching and reviewing theatrical performances with a critical eye. Available at no additional cost when packaged with *The Art of Being Human.*
- Add a classic or contemporary novel to your course by selecting from a variety of Penguin titles in our **Penguin Discount Novel Program.** To review the available choices, visit www.pearsonhighered.com/penguin and consult your local Pearson Arts and Sciences representative to set up a value pack.

Acknowledgments

Our fervent hope is that after reading this book students will have gained the assurance of discovering much about themselves and learned about features of the humanities that will prove rewarding in their ongoing development. If, as Katherine Mansfield once said, a great poet must first be a great poem, what shall we say of the fully realized human being? Won't such an individual be not only a poem but also a song, dance, painting, play, movie, or new idea? These are distant stars at which to aim, but a journey too easily accomplished may not be worth the effort.

The "we" of this preface includes not only the authors but others who have worked long and hard helping to improve the book. Ginny Blanford, our acquisitions editor, stayed diligently on top of the project from its inception and helped guide us through the complexities we faced. Erin Reilly, our development editor, provided us with useful text suggestions. Lisa Black adroitly handled our text permissions, as Jody Potter did our photo permissions. Lori Sullivan was our meticulous production editor, overseeing copyediting and design. All became part of a team, and through their efforts we discovered the true meaning of *synergy.*

Still others contributed to the emergence of the final product: the many dedicated employees at Longman who took care of thousands of details. Both Rebecca Gilpin, Ginny Blanford's assistant, and Joyce Nilsen, executive marketing manager played key roles.

We would also like to acknowledge the letters from students and teachers who support what we are doing and made valuable comments about how we could do it even better, and the detailed, thorough, caring reviews by those who saw the manuscript in various stages of preparation: Michael T. Adessa, Scottsdale Culinary Institute; Leslie A. Cline, Southside Virginia Community College; Richard Davis, Grayson County College; Sidney Ann Ramsden-Scott, Monterey Peninsula College; Jill Silos, Hesser College; Nancy A. Taylor, California State University, Northridge.

To write a humanities text is perhaps the best way to discover the humane characteristics of others and the secret of all meaningful endeavor, which is that *no one can work alone.*

Richard Janaro
Thelma Altshuler

PART I

Exploring the Humanities

> "He who works for machinery; he who works for hatred, works only for confusion. Culture looks beyond machinery, culture hates hatred; culture has one great passion, the passion for sweetness and light."
>
> —**Matthew Arnold**

Chapter 1

The Humanities: A Shining Beacon

Humanity will not only survive, it will prevail.

—William Faulkner

Overview of this Book

The humanities can no longer be defined in a simple statement. At one time they were said to be the best products of the best minds. The word "**humanities**" grew out of the term "**humanism**," which did indeed once mean the study of what great artists, writers, and philosophers had accomplished. During the Renaissance, that huge artistic and political revolution which swept over Western Europe beginning in the fifteenth century, there was a revival of interest in the culture of ancient Greece and Rome—a culture that had been left largely unexamined during the thousand-year span following the fall of Rome. The intelligentsia of the Renaissance believed that only through a study of classical art, literature, and philosophy could a person become *fully* human. Thus these **disciplines** became known as the humanities. In time, the term had to be extended beyond the study of Greek and Roman culture to include that of major Western European countries: first Italy, then France and Spain, then Britain, and, finally, Germany. As cultures multiplied, so did the disciplines people needed to study in pursuit of humanness. Music, theater, and dance began to flourish during the Renaissance, and scholars discovered that these disciplines were also part of the ancient world's legacy.

In this book the term *humanities* has been broadened still further. Yes, we still need to pay attention to extraordinary artistic and intellectual achievements that have been singled out for special praise and that now represent what is sometimes called the "humanistic tradition." All of us belong to the human race and should want to know as much as possible about the distinguished contributions of those who have gone before. Yet we also need to recognize that the "humanistic tradition" usually was limited to the contributions made by *men* of the classical and then the Western European worlds. Plato and Michelangelo and Shakespeare continue to deserve our admiration and reward our study, but think of those persons, both male and female, past and present, who may be little known or not known at all, who nevertheless left behind or who now offer a myriad of wonderful songs, poems, and provocative thoughts waiting to be appreciated.

The humanities are also the creative and intellectual expressions of each of us in moments of inspiration, whether they happen in the shower or just walking down the street on a balmy day when our spirits are lifted by the sheer joy of being alive. In these times of global fears and a future of uncertainty, in these times of dizzying technological advances that can be both marvelous and bewildering, when it can be hard to pinpoint our identity in time and space, the humanities offer a safe haven, a quiet harbor where we can moor our vessels and, at least for a time, confirm who we are.

Gaspesie La Martre Musee des phares Lighthouse, Quebec, built 1906

The humanities offer a way of life filled with moments of critical thought and aesthetic pleasure, and they are urgently needed in our world.

Cosmo Condina/SuperStock

Each of us is more than a gender, an age, an address, an occupation. Each of us is thoughts, expressed or not, the capacity to be moved, the need to laugh or cry, longings for things just beyond our reach. The humanities give us stories to stimulate our imagination, ideas to stimulate our intellect, musical sounds to excite our passions, and the knowledge that we can respond to the creativity and thought of others and look inwardly to see what *we* think and what creative impulses lie dormant and cry out to be released; all of this helps us confront our true identity. A major aim of this book is to show how a study of the humanities can be the starting point for the journey into self-knowledge.

The humanities are not only inspiring achievements in themselves but also the *study* of those achievements and the critical process by which professional critics and scholars interpret and then communicate their findings to others so that they will never be forgotten. And the humanities are the critical process by which we ourselves look squarely at and come to appreciate what is there for us to read, see, or hear. This process, often called *critical thinking,* is essential to being effectively human, especially as the world's tempo increases. In fact, so crucial is critical thought and so important are the humanities in developing it that the following chapter is devoted solely to the subject.

> *We are healthy only to the extent that our ideas are humane.*
>
> **—Kurt Vonnegut**

The humanities can also be called a technique for living accessible to every human being who wants to do more with life. They offer a way of life filled with moments of critical thought and aesthetic pleasure, and they are urgently needed in our world.

The humanities are addictive. Once you let song and story, music and dance, and words and ideas into your life, you can never live without them. And you should never *have* to. The humanities are best appreciated in our quiet moments, and quiet is also addictive in a noisy world. *If only everyone on earth would insist on these quiet moments, wouldn't the world be a happier (and a safer) place?*

In a world that has become a global village, in a world with all its hovering threats of terror attacks and dirty bombs, with so many who are more than willing to sacrifice their own lives to kill others, in a world of environmental woes, a world in which cynics wonder about the value of living—in such a world there are always the humanities to lift our spirits. Art and music and literature, stories and songs, all the marvels of the human mind, the architectural and engineering achievements, or just noticing the first robin of the year keep reminding us of what it means to be truly human.

Humanity will not prevail just because we are living longer. Genetic scientists expect to replace the gene responsible for aging and promise life expectancies that were once found only in literary fables. (Perhaps some of us may live to celebrate our "eleventy-first birthday," like Bilbo Baggins of *The Hobbit.*) Existing on and on without coming to terms with who we are and without knowing how to reach a safe haven inside when the world gets maddeningly chaotic about us maybe wouldn't be the best technique for living. The humanities help make longer life spans abundantly richer.

> *The bomb that fell on Hiroshima fell on America too. It fell on no city, no munitions plant, no docks. It erased no church, vaporized no public buildings, reduced no man to his atomic elements. But it fell, it fell.*
>
> **—Hermann Hagedorn**

The key to the richer life is to be as open-minded as possible. One of the dangers of living longer is becoming too firmly enclosed by the values many of us have held since our earliest days. The humanities cannot fail to inspire open-mindedness. Exploring the literature, music, art, and patterns of thought of other cultures is indispensable to our own development. Why? The answer is simple: The world has grown too small for us not to care what is happening all around us; and the world *is* just that—all around us. So we need to balance a sharper awareness of who we are with a broader understanding of who *they* are; for they are part of us, and we of them.

The cultural history of Western civilization, as traditionally presented, simply will no longer suffice. During the time of the ancient Greeks, for example, were there not many women who thought great thoughts and secretly wrote great poems? While the much heralded early civilizations, like those of Egypt, China, Japan, Rome, and Greece, have received abundant attention and been the subject of countless critical and historical studies, they do not tell the whole story of human genius. Rich cultures flourished in Africa; in South and Central America; in the North America that was inhabited long before Columbus "discovered" it; in the lands that produced Islamic art, science, and philosophy, lands once thought too mysterious for the Western mind to understand; in lands of the unknown people who built Stonehenge in England and the thirty-foot statues that stand in eternal attention on Easter Island. While owners were sipping juleps on plantation verandas, slaves in their humble shanties were weaving elaborate tales and singing complex songs to keep their heritage alive.

The primary mission of this book is, therefore, to show you that a wonderful, a magical world of human devising has existed for as long as humanity has existed and that it is still there, waiting each day to be discovered anew. It is the world of the humanities. The humanities are here. They are just outside your door, waiting. They are even inside *you* if you know where to look. All you have to do is open that door or get in touch with your creative self and extend a welcoming hand. If you do, your life will be changed very much for the better. And you will want to run out into the street and share the wonder with everyone you meet!

Gifts of the Humanities

Economics tells us that the wants of people are insatiable, but resources are limited. Because almost everything is scarcer than we would like, treasured possessions, as well as basics like food and shelter, come with a price tag. Do we have enough money to buy everything we want? The answer is usually NO!

The resources of the humanities are unlimited, but all too often our wants are meager.

With the humanities the problem is reversed. *The resources of the humanities are unlimited,* but all too often our wants are meager. In the economic world you can't always be rich by choice, but in the world of the humanities you can be "poor" by choice.

Several decades ago, during a severe recession, banks attracted savings deposits by offering gifts to those who would forego spending and open CD accounts instead. People were walking out with new toasters, blenders, steam irons, and luggage; and, of course, bank reserves swelled. Such incentives are cyclical in nature, but the humanities always have gifts that are there for us regardless of what the economy is doing. Here are some of them.

Beauty

The shiny new car stands in the driveway, attracting envious glances from the neighbors. The owner glows with pride. Is it that the newly acquired possession is a sign of the buyer's apparent prosperity? Is it simply that people are genetically prone to owning things and the more the better? Although the answer may be "Yes," isn't something else involved? Is it something we call **beauty**?

> *"The ancient Greeks . . . were convinced that an explanation of, and definition for, Beauty was as concrete and discoverable as the answer to why the days got shorter in winter . . ."*
>
> **—Bruce Maddox**

Ever since philosophy began, ever since thoughtful people started asking what makes life good, the answer often involved the beautiful. Its close connection with pleasure has always seemed apparent. It is pleasant and desirable to see beautiful things and beautiful people. People prefer to live amid beauty than amid ugliness.

Though people may debate whether a particular person or piece of music is beautiful, there is widespread agreement that something deserves to be called beautiful if the arrangement of the parts is pleasing, if it seems *right*. The rightness of the arrangement determines the pleasure that it gives us. When there is something in an arrangement that seems *not* right, we are less attracted, possibly even repelled.

Explore on **MyHumanitiesKit.com** da Vinci, *Mona Lisa*

Is judging an arrangement—of a painting, a person's face, a story, a dramatic moment—as right or not right entirely subjective? Yes and no. Leonardo da Vinci's *Mona Lisa* has earned the reputation as the world's most famous painting. Each week thousands flock to the Louvre Museum in Paris to see the portrait of the lady with the enigmatic smile. Since its creation in the years between 1503 and 1505, innumerable art historians and critics have given their opinions of what makes this a great work. They often differ in the specific elements they praise—such as the haunting face or the ambiguity of the gaze—but they tend to agree that the way the artist has assembled the various elements has turned a flat canvas into the illusion of a living, breathing, three-dimensional human being. They tend to agree that *Mona Lisa* is a beautiful work of art. (See p. 104).

The pleasure that beauty inspires in us is called **aesthetic**. Yet what kind of pleasure is it? One answer is that the beautiful inspires within us *a feeling of well-being that is its own justification*. True, the attraction of a shiny new car may have less to do with its pure beauty than with the pride we feel in owning it, or if it belongs to someone else, by the envy we feel. When a beautiful face passes by, we might long for closer contact with it, but we would not have such a desire if we did not first make an aesthetic judgment. The critics who have written volumes about the "secret" of the *Mona Lisa* have already made an aesthetic judgment and are now trying to find the words to describe why the arrangement of the parts is right. A universal definition

The attraction of a shiny new car may have less to do with its pure beauty than with the pride we have in owning it.

Helga Esteb/Shutterstock

Oprah Winfrey

Bob Rich/Shutterstock

Ann Curry

Two television personalities illustrating variety in the beautiful.

of beauty that fits every example may be impossible to find, but suffice it to say that few of us would deny that the beautiful does indeed exist.

The humanities are, in part, a catalogue of works which have tallied a host of positive votes from people who have spent their lives in pursuit of the beautiful and who hold up road signs for us in our own quest. Be advised, however, that the pursuit is endless, and the catalogue needs almost daily updating. The road signs often vary from one culture to another. If we are to expand our capacity for aesthetic pleasure, we need to experience many versions of the beautiful and try to see them from other points of view.

Study the two portraits of women on the previous page. The photo on the left is that of Oprah Winfrey, long a favorite commentator and interviewer. The photo on the right is that of Ann Curry of *The Today Show* and *Dateline*. Both women have differing ethnic and cultural heritages, yet share a reputation for possessing true female beauty.

Isamu Noguchi, *Water Stone*, 1987

Example of a beautiful arrangement of parts: the shape of the sculpture, the serenity of the water, and its soothing sound as it slowly trickles down the sides.

In the Asian wing of New York's Metropolitan Museum of Art, tucked away in a corner that the visitor can easily miss, is a sculpture called *Water Stone* (see photo) by the Japanese artist Isamu Noguchi (1904–1988). It is a gray stone fountain of uneven shape with a perpetual flow of water that, at first glance, appears to be a sheet of clear glass sitting motionless on top, but, in reality, trickles slowly down the side so that the escaping water is always equal to the new supply being pumped up from below. The trickle creates a soft sound that soothes and mesmerizes the visitor who takes the time to sit on the bench provided. One woman reported that she sat there entranced for nearly an hour.

> *"Though we travel the world over to find the beautiful, we must carry it with us or we find it not."*
>
> **—Ralph Waldo Emerson**

The arrangement of parts in *Water Stone* includes the shape and texture of the stone, the varying shades created by the falling water, and, most important, the sound itself. But you don't have to be in a museum to experience the beauty of similar arrangements. A woodland stream, flowing over rocks of different shapes, will create varied shadings, and if you shut your eyes and really listen to the water, you will discover that it has a variety of sounds, depending on wind and the different rocks over which it flows. In truth, all you need to do to experience in full how the humanities can take you to that quiet oasis we mentioned is find a stream in the woods, or study closely the different colors in rainwater gushing alongside a curb. When you search for the beautiful, you will be astonished to realize how close it is.

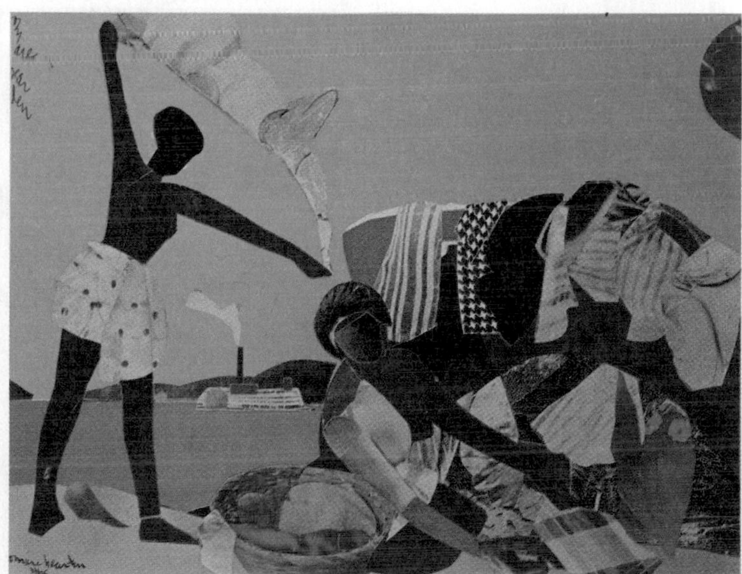

Romare Bearden, *Mississippi Monday*, 1941

Bearden claimed he was more concerned with aesthetics than with social commentary. What do you think engaged him aesthetically about this scene?

Of course, the arts can do more for us than provide an aesthetic moment. Sometimes they may convey a message the artist believes is important. In fact, some take the position that meaning is what we primarily look for in any work. Yet it does a disservice both to the artist and to us the viewers if we always insist upon looking for a message. (After all, what is the message in water slowly trickling down the side of a stone sculpture?) Many artists, as well as poets and novelists, object to those critics who analyze their work, evaluating it solely in terms of the important—or unimportant—meanings they find.

The painting *Mississippi Monday* by the American artist Romare Bearden (1912–1988) illustrates how an artist's intent can be misunderstood. By his own admission Bearden was interested primarily in creating aesthetic pleasure. Here he recreates a familiar scene: women hanging up laundry. What appears to be central to the painting is the color and design of the clothes themselves: that is, the *arrangement* of the parts. Doubtless the artist would say, "If you want to talk about what the standing woman is tossing from the bag or what the seated woman is doing with her hands, or to ask whether the painting is a commentary on the subservient role of women, go right ahead; but that's not what I'm up to."

The humanities can be enjoyed for both their aesthetic and communicative functions. Learning to distinguish one from the other is an important part of *critical thinking*, the subject of the chapter that follows.

Beautiful Movement

"*The best art always seems effortless . . .*"

—Stephen Sondheim

The perfection of movement cannot fail to inspire a sense of awe and admiration. Movement is as much a part of being human as breathing. Few of us, however, move in perfect synchrony, but almost all of us experience joy when we see it done right. Even though our own movements may lack the coordination of, say, the skilled dancer, there is also aesthetic pleasure for us in not just watching others, but in getting up and swaying, gliding, or shaking to a rhythm. We have patterned our lives to meeting deadlines and reaching destinations. Perhaps that's why people like, for a change, to be on the dance floor and simply move in rhythm. Are they trying to get somewhere in particular? No. The pleasure of the movement is its own reason for existing.

The French artist Edgar Degas (1834–1917) loved to paint dancers. He seems to have had no message to convey beyond the beauty of the women and the

Explore on **MyHumanitiesKit.com**
Degas, Rehearsal of the *Ballet on Stage*

Image © The Metropolitan Museum of Art/Art Resource, NY

Edgar Degas, *Rehearsal of the Ballet on Stage*, c. 1874

The ballet provided the artist with aesthetic pleasure, and the painting can offer us the same experience.

elegance of their movements. Ballerinas gave him aesthetic pleasure. His paintings give that same pleasure to us.

So do the serene gliding, graceful leaps, and the seemingly impossible spins of a figure skater such as the young South Korean star Kim Yu-na. Like all great skaters and dancers, she makes her body do what bodies seem never meant to do. In her leaps she defies gravity. In her spins she defies analysis. To the nonskater (most of us) it is difficult to see how two rigid blades attached to her shoes can seem to disappear as she twirls. In this respect figure skaters are akin to great magicians like David Copperfield. The arrangement of the parts in a given trick seem right if we don't see their function. Many of us are not as coordinated as a great magician or as strong and well-trained as a great figure skater. If we were, then their art might seem less beautiful.

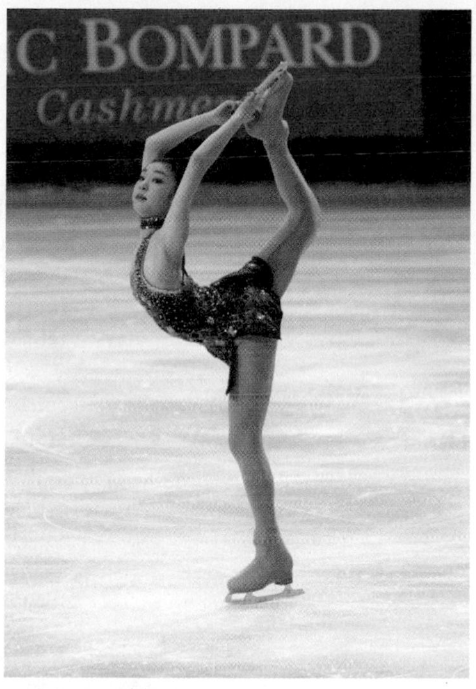

PCN Photography/Shutterstock

Kim Yu-na, Palais-Omnisports de Bercy, Paris, October 2009

Kim Yu-na, 2010 Olympic gold medalist, shows us that great dancers, as well as skaters, seem to transcend what nature enables the human body to do.

Language

Words in varied combinations are the means by which we communicate to ourselves and with each other. Through language we make ourselves understood to others, and we are able to understand what we read and what others are saying. The need for language becomes apparent at an early age; and we develop a love of language if we are fortunate enough to be around adults who talk to us (but not in baby talk), who enjoy reading, and who read to us.

Children develop through recognizable and documented stages. Most children between the ages of two and three become word-conscious. The need to attach a name to everything in sight appears to be an inborn instinct. Parents as well as older siblings can be annoyed at hearing the persistent "What's that?" throughout the day, even as they are happy that the insatiable demand for words is proceeding as it should. At this stage children like to repeat sentences and phrases they hear in their surroundings, even if they have no idea what they mean. Children like the sound and the "taste" of words. Unfortunately, the insatiable need to add to and replenish our vocabulary does not always stay with us.

How or when some of us lose the need for more words is a complex mystery. Unraveling it is perhaps less important than the awareness that *it does not have to happen*. That's where the humanities come in. Through reading, through listening to great language on the stage or screen—or, better yet, reading poetry aloud—we acquire models of how to say things in ways that make others sit up and take notice. People experienced in using the humanities as a technique for living sometimes make a point by directly quoting well-known lines, assured that their friends will catch the reference.

> *"True wit is Nature to advantage dressed:*
> *What oft was thought, but ne'er so well expressed."*
>
> **—Alexander Pope**

One of the most famous lines in all of drama is the beginning of Hamlet's third soliloquy: *To be or not to be: that is the question*. When people on similar wavelengths are discussing whether, for example, to stay home and watch television or go downtown for a costly evening of eating out and seeing a movie, the comment "Ah, that is the question" communicates instantly that the speaker is not leaning one way or the other but is wide open to suggestions. Directly quoting or providing variations on famous lines that you know others will recognize is not only fun but cuts down on the need for details and circular discussions.

The most popular work of the medieval English poet Geoffrey Chaucer (1340–1400), *The Canterbury Tales,* contains not only a collection of unforgettable stories but also famous descriptions of the people who tell them. Chaucer was a master at capturing the essence of his characters with swift strokes of his pen, many of which are part of the reservoir of language in the minds of people who read. One of the characters is a lawyer who is always in a hurry and apparently so busy that he could easily have been the envy of lazy people. After describing the man and his behavior in detail, Chaucer adds: "Yet he seemed busier than he was." Who knows how many thousands of readers over the last six hundred years have used this line as a reference to people who display the same kind of feverish but essentially meaningless activity? A high school student is asked why he is not doing his homework. His reply: "I'm very busy with other things." One parent then tells the other, "He seems busier than he is."

"Reading is to the mind what exercise is to the body."
—Joseph Addison

The sixth century B.C.E. Greek philosopher Heraclitus is famous for having said: "You cannot step twice into the same river." By this he meant that life is constant change, that the only thing stable in all the universe is the fact of change itself. A contemporary environmental expert, addressing a college graduating class and wishing to underscore the growing dangers of water pollution, echoed Heraclitus and remarked: "You cannot step *once* into the same river." Clearly, the versatile language derived from the humanities even increases the chance that an urgent cause may win more supporters.

The humanities help us to appreciate a variety of ingenious phrasing and offer us models of how language can be expertly manipulated. One of the greatest comedies ever written, Oscar Wilde's 1895 *The Importance of Being Earnest* (discussed in Chapter 7), is a storehouse of witty lines illustrating that one way of saying something is not necessarily as good as another. In one scene the hero, Jack Worthing, is being interviewed by his fiancé's mother, a social lionness with biting wit, who investigates his credentials as a suitor. At one point she asks the nervous young man whether he smokes. Sheepishly he admits that well yes, he does smoke. Her unexpected reply: "I'm glad to hear it. A man should always have an occupation of some sort." Not only is the lady staying one step ahead of him with her wit, but she is making an indirect statement about the indolence and lack of purpose of the upper classes.

Playing with language has evolved into a high art. Like the beautiful, language needs no further justification.

Playing with language has evolved into a high art. Like the beautiful, good language needs no further justification. A person characterized by others as someone with "a way with words" or "a flair for language" generally earns respect (unless, of course, it turns out that the person never has anything else to offer *except* words).

Yet just as a novel or play or movie can be spoiled when authors use words and idioms that have become so commonplace they are no longer effective, so too is the everyday language of most people littered with terminology employed over and over. "I'm so tired I could die" or "I'm so hungry I could die" belongs in the category of the no-longer-usable. Yet such hackneyed language keeps slipping from our tongues without our even noticing. "Like" has become the most frequently spoken word in our language, whether used appropriately or not. "I felt like a worn-out dishrag" might have been passable a long time ago (when dishrags were new), but, though it no longer makes any kind of impression, except boredom, it is at least grammatically sound. What, however, are we to make of "After she said she decided not to go to the dance with me, I was, like, this can't be happening"?

In addition to "like," ordinary speech is now littered with "y'know" and "go" in place of "said" (as in "I go . . . and then he goes . . ."). Hollywood and television perpetuate the idea that good dialogue is reproducing the way people actually speak.

But do we listen closely to that speech, whether it's in real life or on a screen? Does it startle us with its cleverness and its memorable turn of phrase? Does it help us grow? Listen carefully to the speech patterns of people with whom you are conversing. If their language tends to be fresh and interesting, chances are they spend a lot of time reading. Perhaps your own language reflects the same habit. We hope so.

Here is an excerpt from a poem by Taylor Mali, who has had a varied kind of life, having studied acting with the Royal Shakespeare Company and then becoming a poet and advocate of teaching literacy in the classroom. The poem is titled "Totally like whatever, you know?"

In case you hadn't noticed,
it has somehow become uncool
to sound like you know what you're talking about?
Or believe strongly in what you're saying?
Invisible question marks and parentheses (you know?)'s
have been attaching themselves to the ends of our sentences?
Even when those sentences aren't, like, questions? You know?[1]

Ideas

Language is not only the vehicle through which we can display our savvy in everyday dealings with others, it is also the means by which we formulate ideas. Still, all of us have flashes of ideas that we can't quite catch hold of because the words aren't there. A philosopher once said, "If you can't say it, you don't know it." When someone explains a complicated idea such as the theory of relativity and we nod to signify understanding, we are more or less guaranteeing that we would be able to deliver the identical explanation in our own words. Very often we cannot. Words are the means by which we think. If we have no words, we cannot have ideas. We *can* have intuitions without words, but they are not the same as ideas. Intuitions are, of course, vital human resources. We don't need words to find a piece of music exciting. Intuitions are necessary for a full appreciation of much that the humanities have to offer. But through our philosophers, novelists, and poets we derive a love for exciting ideas. After reading a stimulating passage that makes an explosive point, one often says to oneself, "Oh! I wish I'd thought of that!" (And don't we all glow with pride when we advance an idea that meets with approval, even admiration, an idea others wish *they* had thought of?)

> *"The most beautiful thing we can experience is the mysterious. It is the source of science."*
> **—Albert Einstein**

Thinking helps us keep our sanity—even in our world of rapidly accelerating change and technological marvels that are said to think *for* us. Fortunately, the brain can still be what makes us want to do more than just survive. Thinking keeps us in touch with ourselves and the world around us. Thinking comes in a variety of forms. Rigorous studies like mathematics, physics, and economics provide powerful exercise for the brain, but not all of us are adept at these disciplines. Yet happily, we have the humanities, which widen both our emotional range and our understanding of many things: the past, the present, human behavior, the workings of the creative mind, and the many unanswered questions that philosophers, scientists, and theologians have asked for centuries. The Society for Philosophical Inquiry movement is the brainchild of Christopher Phillips, author of *Socrates' Cafe* (2003), which describes various venues, all with that name, in which society members gather to discuss and share ideas. The format for the meetings is inspired by the teaching methods of Socrates (469–399 B.C.E.), mentor of Plato (427–347 B.C.E.).

> *"Difficult things of the world can only be tackled when they are easy. Big things of the world can only be achieved by attending to their small beginnings."*
> **—Lao-tzu**

Socrates and his young students would gather in an Athenian grove called Academe and discuss specific questions, such as "What is justice?" As recorded by Plato—since the master himself, as far as we know, wrote nothing down—the discussions took this form:

The question is posed by Socrates.

One student says:	*"Justice is whatever is in the best interest of the ruling party."*
Socrates answers:	*"Can the ruling party ever pass a law that is for some reason not in its best interest?"*
Student:	*"I suppose it could happen."*
Socrates:	*"If it did happen, would the people be justified in breaking that law?"*
Student:	*"I don't think so. A law is a law."*
Socrates:	*"In other words, it would be wrong to break a law just because somebody thought it was not in the best interest of the ruling party."*
Student:	*"Well . . . maybe it could be broken."*
Socrates:	*"If you thought the law could be broken and I said it couldn't, which of us is right?"*
Student:	*"I guess in that case we're both right."*
Socrates:	*"Is this your idea of a just society—one in which anyone can decide whether to obey a law or not? Would you want to live in such a society?"*
Student:	*"I . . . suppose I wouldn't."*
Socrates:	*"Then justice really has to be defined as something that is absolute and not only in the best interest of the ruling party or the individual who decides not to obey a certain law."*

The point of a discussion at a Socrates' Cafe is not to solve all the problems of the world. It is to adapt the technique of the ancient philosopher as well as those of other thinkers to puzzling questions of the past and present. Clearly "justice" is one. It has never been defined to everyone's satisfaction. Whether one agrees or not that justice is absolute and unchanging or that there is no applicable principle other than "might makes right," the discussion and defense of ideas are ways of strengthening our mental faculties. Like dancing, thinking needs no further justification.

Deeper Sense of the Past

The humanities allow us to see more than our personal past. Through the humanities we may immerse ourselves in the firsthand experiences of those who actually lived and often struggled in the past—lived and struggled with many of the problems that face us today. These experiences help each of us to better understand what living is all about. *The realized human being is an accumulation of what has gone before and how that affects the present.*

Through the humanities we can live more than once: here and now, and yesterday as well. Those who refuse to browse among the cumulative treasures of human expression have only themselves to blame if they find themselves trapped in one solitary existence.

Like all of us, the past has its right to be heard. It did not, we know, allow for the *full* representation of its genius, for the contributions of both men and women from a variety of cultures. Still, the past has its own glory, even as it stands. The statue of Venus de Milo has been around for many hundreds of years. It no longer has arms, but, gazing at it, we cannot help seeing the idealism, the adoration of the female form that must have motivated the unknown classical artist. Becoming familiar with treasures of the past brings us closer to those who came before us, inspires in us the pride of belonging to the continuity of our species. The love of beauty is timeless and universal, and the past, as reflected in the humanities, has more than its share of beauty, not to mention ideas and great language.

Some treasures from the past embody issues that still face us. *The Oresteia,* an epic tragedy by the Greek dramatist Aeschylus (525–456 B.C.E.), is based on a very ancient myth about the murder of a mother and her lover by a son seeking revenge for his father's death at their hands. In the final segment of the work, the playwright creates the world's first courtroom drama, in which the hero is acquitted on the grounds that his mother's crime had been greater than his. She had killed a man who was also a great warrior and leader of his people. The son, Orestes, has killed an adulterous woman and her lover. The decision to acquit the hero was made nearly 2,500 years ago and delivered from the stage at the Theater of Dionysus; the verdict is still discussed today. Theater history teachers often point out that while the acquittal does not sit well with everyone, especially feminists (who argue that it discriminates against the gender of the victim and ignores the fact that the murdered husband had a mistress), the work is nonetheless a milestone in the early history of democracy. There was, after all, a trial. Reading or watching a performance of *The Oresteia* can generate a discussion of whether the law, even in a democracy, judges all persons equally.

> *"In times like these, it's helpful to remember that there have always been times like these."*
>
> **—Paul Harvey**

Developing a profound respect for Socrates, Plato, Aeschylus, as well as the sculptor of the Venus de Milo, and others from the past does not mean that we choose to ignore the achievements of everyone else. At the same time, having profound respect for today and a wider vision of tomorrow does not mean that we ought to ignore what can be justly celebrated from yesterday.

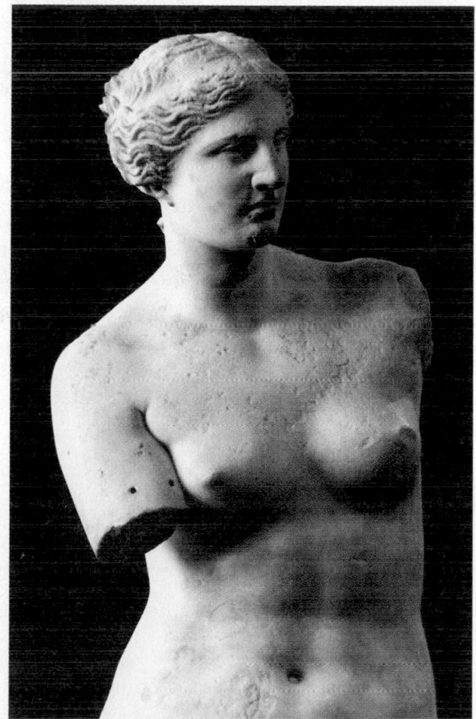

Clara/Shutterstock

***Venus de Milo*, c. 100–130 B.C.E.**

Becoming familiar with treasures of the past inspires in us the pride of belonging to the community of our species.

Becoming an "Infinite" Person

By sharpening our awareness of the present—the issues, the important themes and varied ways of presenting them—and by linking us to the past, the humanities provide a wider view of life. As this book unfolds, you will be learning much more about the humanities and what the various disciplines are and how they can deeply affect your life. Your view of the humanities and the world will continue to expand, and you will be on your way to becoming an infinite person.

Let us consider the very model of humanism, the very essence of the infinite person, Leonardo da Vinci (1452–1519). So broad was the range of his curiosity and creative genius that history has accorded him that rarest of titles: *uomo universale,* universal man. He is also called a **Renaissance man**, meaning a man of the broadest possible learning and a widely diverse range of interests and achievements. Since Leonardo's time that label has been given to many people, both the famous and the not-so-famous, who refused to be limited to just one field of endeavor, though it is doubtful that

Jakub Krechowicz/Alamy

Presumed to be Leonardo da Vinci, Portrait of a man in red chalk, c. 1510

Da Vinci: History has accorded him that rarest of titles, *uomo universale*.

many will ever match what Leonardo accomplished: plans for early versions of the airplane and the submarine; speculating about the human circulatory system long before William Harvey "officially" discovered the circulation of the blood; building the first hydrometer to measure the displacement of water; inventing the science of meteorology long before there were the proper instruments to make accurate predictions. And on top of all the scientific and technological contributions there are the works of art, including the world's most famous painting, the *Mona Lisa* (p. 104).

The example of Leonardo da Vinci suggests that, while few may hope to approach his genius, all of us can do more with our lives than we are doing at this very moment. There are so many books to be read, so much music to hear, so many plays to see, so many great films to view. We may not become Renaissance persons, but infinite choices await us. The more we absorb from the humanities the more we expand our knowledge, our capacity for understanding both ourselves and others. In a sense we become infinite, intertwining with innumerable lives in myriad combinations.

Here are just three advantages of becoming an infinite person. First, the infinite person commits no crimes against humanity. He or she is no longer narrowly preoccupied with self and its immediate needs, its sense of having been unfairly used, its desire to avenge wrongs against itself. Second, the infinite person is free of rigid prejudices and never works consciously to restrict others from exercising their right to assemble, speak their minds openly, practice their own religion, and follow their own preferences, as long as, in being free, they do not themselves limit the freedom of others. Third, the infinite person does not jump to quick conclusions but looks at all sides of an issue before making a judgment, recognizes that no judgment is final, and is always willing to reconsider in the light of new data. This person is therefore not constrained by family and social traditions and willingly seeks out the source of imposed or inherited beliefs so as to reevaluate them. "That's how we've always done it around here" is not the mark of the infinite person.

"The future is not some place we are going to, but one we are creating."

—Deborah James

The book you are about to read is thus not only a visit to the treasure house of the humanities, the stupendous creative and intellectual achievements of human beings. It has the underlying purpose of convincing you that you cannot fail to want to expand your life, to fill every moment with art and thought, once you realize that all it takes is the willingness to do it.

LEARNING OBJECTIVES

Having read and carefully studied this chapter, you should be able to:

1. Explain the origins of the humanities and how they need to be redefined today.
2. Explain critical thinking relative to the value of studying the humanities.
3. Briefly summarize the gifts of the humanities.
4. Explain why Leonardo da Vinci is cited as the perfect model of the "infinite person."

KEY TERMS

aesthetic an experience in the arts or in life, such as watching a sunset, that we value for no reason beyond itself.

beauty a pleasing arrangement of parts that affects us aesthetically.

discipline in the humanities, a given art form—literature, visual art, music, drama, dance, and cinema—as well as a field of academic study (such as "literary theory" or "history of dance").

humanism a movement begun in the early Renaissance that extolled and studied the creative and intellectual legacies of Greece and Rome, leading to the conviction that only through such study could one become fully human; a term that is now expanded to include the study of contributions from all cultures.

humanities once limited to "the best products of the best minds," narrowly defined as Greek or Roman, but later expanded to include Western European achievements and, more recently, the creative expressions of men and women around the world.

Renaissance man a label often applied to Leonardo da Vinci, indicating his display of genius in many areas from art to science; now used as high praise for anyone who has earned a reputation for high achievement in several fields (e.g. Albert Einstein).

TOPICS FOR WRITING AND DISCUSSION

1. The text states "Each of us is more than a gender, an age, an address, an occupation." Explain what this means and how it relates to the study of the humanities.
2. How do you define *beauty*? Give two examples, citing how you would use the term to describe a person and an object.
3. Reread carefully the section called "Ideas." Then restate Socrates' definition of justice in your own words.
4. What does it mean to be an "infinite" person? Describe either someone you know personally or a famous person in the news who seems to fit the label.
5. Briefly profile someone for whom the humanities function as a technique for living. OR profile someone who has no interest in the humanities.

Chapter 2

The Humanities and Critical Thinking

In the introductory chapter we said that the study of the humanities includes understanding the critical process by which professional critics and scholars interpret and evaluate cultural achievements and communicate their thoughts to others. In this chapter we will elaborate on the elements of professional criticism, presenting examples of what the critic notices in order to review a given humanities event. But we will also be dealing with ways in which most of us who are not professional critics can enrich our lives by using some of the same techniques: becoming objective in how we evaluate what we see, read, or hear; separating rational and emotional responses; and delaying a final judgment until we have all the data.

The critical thinking skill has a strong carryover into everyday life as well. We should not make snap judgments about other people or blindly accept opinions expressed in the media if we happen to be fond of the anchor or commentator, and—of vital importance to the conduct of our own lives—we should listen carefully to what others tell us before we make up our minds. All too often we are guilty of quickly deciding this is true or that is poppycock or he is not to be trusted or she always knows what she is talking about. Worse, we often place people in the wax museum of our mind, attaching labels that never change: bossy, lazy, dull, naive, and so on and on. From great literature and drama, we learn that people are far more complex than the stereotype labels we often attach to them.

Critical thinking sharpens the mind. If we start early enough in life and continue to exercise our critical faculties throughout our lives, chances are good that our mind will not desert us late in life. Toward the end of William Wharton's 1981 novel *Dad*, the main character, en route to his father's funeral, has a sudden glimpse of his own aging.

> *I'll become a bore to others,*
> *a drag in conversation,*
> *repeat myself, be slow at*
> *comprehension, quick at*
> *misunderstanding, have*
> *lapses in conceptual*
> *sequences. All this will*
> *probably be invisible to me.*
> *I won't even be aware of my*
> *own decline.*[1]

The older one gets, the more precious does the mind become. Many, early on, seek what they term "altered states," achieved through substance or alcohol abuse. A reason often given is that life is too complex: one has too many responsibilities—school, parental problems, relationship problems—so escape is not only pleasant but absolutely necessary. Even if the use of such escape mechanisms is relatively moderate and there are no lasting effects, the mind, that most fragile and wonderful commodity, is not being used— or is being ill-used.

◀ **Piet Mondrian, *Composition with Red, Yellow, Blue and Black*, 1921**

A modern painting, demonstrating careful geometric design—a visual parallel to critical thinking.

Peter Horree/Alamy

Those who miss the chance to develop critical thought may be too concerned with the specific details of everyday life to go beyond what seems most personally important at the moment. None of us can engage in thought to the exclusion of making practical decisions. There are times when "What shall I wear to the party?" becomes super-important. But the individual who is *solely* concerned with practicalities of the moment is a *noncritical thinker.*

Two friends are devoted sports fans. One, however, is a critical thinker; the other is not. They go to a baseball game together. After the last out, the noncritical person says, "OK, they won. Let's beat the traffic." The strategy doesn't work; they are stuck in a traffic jam. The noncritical friend does nothing but complain about the way the police are failing to manage the crowd or the rudeness of all the other drivers. The critical thinker might like to spend the time in a leisurely review of a crucial play or a team manager's bad decisions.

> *I love quotations because it is a joy to find thoughts one might have, beautifully expressed with much authority by someone recognizably wiser than oneself.*
>
> **—Marlene Dietrich**

Instructors of English comp classes, despairing over student unwillingness to write about general principles, as opposed to, say, what they did last summer or their favorite friend, often relent and assign a personal memoir. When well done, the memoir can result in a book like Frank McCourt's *Angela's Ashes,* about growing up poor in Ireland. It can also be self-indulgent and uninteresting. At their worst, memoirs can be, as Daniel Mendelsohn points out in an essay called "But Enough about Me,"

> *[U]nseemly self-exposures, unpalatable betrayals, unavoidable mendacity . . . memoir for much of its modern history has been the black sheep of the literary family . . . motivated, it would seem, by an overpowering need to be the center of attention.*[2]

Apollonian and Dionysian Responses to the Humanities

> *You miss all the fun if you obey all the rules.*
>
> **—Katharine Hepburn**

The German philosopher Friedrich Nietzsche (1844–1900) wrote a book in 1872 titled *The Birth of Tragedy from the Spirit of Music,* in which he revisits the great age of drama in fifth-century (B.C.E.) Athens. He points out that the art form had begun a century earlier as choral music and dance, without spoken dialogue. As it evolved, certain soloists became distinct from the chorus, and through their dialogue they told stories based on ancient myths. *The Oresteia* by Aeschylus, discussed in the previous chapter, is one such story. Most popular were the tragic myths, stories of powerful and rich men (often rulers) who, because of a fatal flaw of character, would fall from the heights of strength into the depths of despair and ruination. Not all of the tragedies, including *The Oresteia* itself, fitted this description exactly, but they are all filled with horror, suffering, and the extremes of human pain. They have scenes that are among the most shattering ever devised.

> *Music does not depict scenes or describe objects or tell stories, but it mysteriously embodies the continuous motion and emotion that we experience at the sight of objects and scenes and events.*
>
> **—Jacques Barzun**

What bothered Nietzsche was that, in lecturing or writing about tragedy, teachers and critics sometimes forgot that the roots of the art form were in dance and music. He believed the proper response to viewing a tragedy was to allow oneself to respond emotionally, the way we respond to music. He found that viewers and critics alike were focusing on the central characters' moral failings, on the consequences of breaking a moral law. As a result, Greek tragedies were evaluated and taught in terms of their lessons, not their strong emotional impact. Nietzsche believed it was wrong to encourage people to view tragedy through reason rather

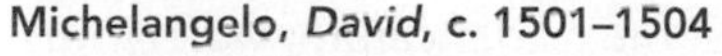
Brian A Jackson/Shutterstock

Michelangelo, *David*, c. 1501–1504

akg-images/Robatie-Domingie/Newscom

Donatello, *David*, c. 1440s

Michelangelo's *David*, left, illustrates Apollonian classicism, while Donatello's *David* exhibits another side of the Renaissance: the assertion of passionate individualism.

than emotion, wrong to insist on the moral philosophy behind a play at the expense of appreciating the force and the fury that drive it.

He then made a famous distinction between two ways of responding not only to drama but to events in real life. He identified as **Apollonian** that side of the human personality dominated by reason and disciplined analytical, rational, and coherent thought: in short, the side that responds to Greek tragedy by seeking its meaning. He dubbed as **Dionysian** that side of the human personality dominated by feelings, intuition, and freedom from limits: the side that responds emotionally to music as well as to the force and fury of tragedy.

> *"Music embodies feeling without forcing it to contend and combine with thought, as it is in most arts and especially in the art of words."*
>
> **—Franz Liszt**

Nietzsche derived these opposing terms from Greek mythology. Apollo was the god of the sun (hence of light and truth) and Dionysus was the god of the vibrant energy of the earth (hence of emotion, spontaneity, and intuition). Nietzsche believed the goal of life was to achieve a balance between reason and emotion: to be able to think clearly; to be steady, reliable, and responsible for one's actions; AND to be able to feel, to enjoy the fruits of the vine (so to speak), to express both love and hate (when necessary) unguided by a concern for rules.

We shall have occasion to refer many times throughout this book to Apollonian and Dionysian elements in the humanities. If critical thinking is a major goal of studying the humanities, the distinction between the two sides of our personality should be our starting point. It is impossible to study the humanities without seeing how one or the other, or sometimes both together, inform a given work. The symphonies of Beethoven, for example, are Dionysian in the effect they have on our emotions, but they are also Apollonian as our critical side learns to appreciate their monumental structures.

The Apollonian response also means looking at a work objectively before evaluating it. Critical thinking begins on the Apollonian side; writing a critical analysis is always Apollonian, even though a strong emotional response may have inspired the analysis. One can be enraptured by a musical performance *without* wanting to analyze it further. If this is the case, however, the comment "It was great; I was carried away by it" must not be confused with a full critical statement. It has to be recognized for what it is: a statement of a personal experience. "I liked it" is personal and Dionysian. "I liked it because it had . . ." may be introducing an Apollonian evaluation. Both are valid; but they must not be mistaken for each other.

The Popcorn Syndrome

"A wise skepticism is the first attribute of a good critic."
—James Russell Lowell

A word of caution. It is all too easy to give the critical mind a vacation, to surrender to the Dionysian excitement of the moment and decide that further considerations are not important. Doing so will not stretch our mental capacities and should be avoided unless a given work clearly does not warrant time and mental energy.

More seductive is the popcorn experience, usually felt at the movies. "This is strictly a popcorn movie" means that one should be able to sit back, munch on popcorn, and be entertained without having to think. A huge number of films and television shows belong to this category, as indeed do many popular novels called "good reads."

Dan Brown's *The Da Vinci Code* (2002), one of the most widely read novels ever written, topped the best-seller list for almost two years and sold well into the millions of copies. The story of a secret organization, oppressed by religious authorities because it can supposedly prove that Jesus was married and sired a family, is told in such fast-moving, cinematic prose that the reader cannot wait to turn the page. Exciting? Yes. Suspenseful? Indeed. A great novel? Here one must pause and reflect. Is the story totally believable? Is there any depth to the main characters? Does the novel leave the reader with what we may call "residual thoughts"? Or is it, like many others, just popcorn fun? Perhaps. Yet one may also decide that any novel *so* entertaining to read is certainly worthwhile. Popular music, films, novels, cartoons in newspapers and magazines—all that entertains and amuses us for even a short time—can be called, at the very least, the "temporary humanities." Like all emotional responses, fun is a legitimate way to spend some time. The non-critical stop there.

"Life is a moderately good play with a badly written third act."
—Truman Capote

For the critical, however, Dionysian enjoyment may also lead to a morning-after headache, what we can call the "popcorn hangover." The night before at the movies, the big bucket of popcorn, the pleasant company, the fast-moving plot, the nerve-jangling sound track that brings one into a la-la land of no stress. "What a great evening. What a terrific movie!" Then tomorrow dawns with a subliminal replay of the movie on the semiconscious screen of the half-awake mind. The sudden sitting up. The flash of truth: "*How could I possibly have liked that awful film?*" This can and often does happen, and it is, again, a perfectly valid response.

There is a deeper, more satisfying definition of "entertainment." Having enjoyed *The Da Vinci Code* as a "good read," a critical person might have looked forward to the film version of 2006, expecting to find not a work of high screen art but at the very least an engrossing, fast-moving thriller, especially since the author's prose had been more than once praised as "cinematic." But wasn't the action rather slower than expected? Didn't the slow pace lack the pulsating rhythm of popcorn movies? And didn't that pace bring to the surface some stilted dialogue of the sort that went unnoticed years ago (1973, to be exact) in Steven Spielberg's still celebrated thriller *Jaws*—unnoticed because of the director's sharp technique of dropping the sound level when he thought what was being said did not advance the plot?

The critical mind, perceiving that a response has been largely Dionysian, as when hearing a thrilling interpretation of Beethoven's Ninth Symphony in a concert hall, seeks in the later tranquility of musing on the exciting experience to consider those elements which caused the response: the beauty of the singers' voices? the unexpected shifts in tempo? the alternation between the majesty of the musical crescendos and the sudden silences that follow? No two analyses will be exactly the same; nor need they be. Critical thinking is valid as a process, not as the absolute determination of good or bad. The important thing is that the unexamined Dionysian response may be limited to "Gee, that was terrific!"—a suitable response as far as it goes but not likely to contribute much toward balancing the two forces in our lives. At best, the unexamined response ought to be restricted to experiences that defy words.

Listen on **MyHumanitiesKit.com** Beethoven, Ninth Symphony

Empathy and Alienation

Empathy, in this context the process by which we identify with a character or a performer so that for a short time we believe we are that person, is a Dionysian trick of our nature. Empathy is crucial to the entertainment process. If you, for example, should arrive late for a circus performance and sit down just as the tightrope walker's act has begun, what you would see is not only the death-defying performer higher up than you might ever care to be but hundreds of seated patrons swaying back and forth. They would be projecting themselves into the precarious journey, gasping each time the walker (as part of the act) appears about to fall. In similar fashion, you and your fellow audience members in a movie theater are in the passenger seat of a car careening wildly out of control, dodging the elevated pillars along Canal Street in New York. TV and movie directors know about Dionysian empathy and readily design opportunities for indulging in it. If the heroine, trapped in a mountain ravine with flood waters inching upward, attempts to scale the rock wall, she has to be successful at first and then *must* slip when she is halfway up and appear to be doomed. You give free reign to your empathetic imagination because deep down you know all will be well in the end, but you will feel cheated if all is well from the start.

"The gift of fantasy has meant more to me than my talent for absorbing knowledge."

—Albert Einstein

Just why empathizing with near-death experiences should qualify as entertainment has been debated for centuries. It may be traceable to the eighteenth-century shift away from the on-stage blood and gore of popular tragedies, including many of Shakespeare's, that featured hands being chopped off, tongues and eyes being ripped out, horrors that could rival the bloodiest slasher movie of today. The eighteenth century on both sides of the Atlantic introduced a more genteel way of life for the upper classes and those who imitated them. Shakespeare and his contemporaries went into a period of decline, or else their works were revised with all the horrors eliminated. But little by little, as society became more respectable, at least on the surface, stage entertainment began reintroducing melodramatic elements for audiences that enjoyed escape from their morally upright lives. In the nineteenth

Photos 12/Alamy

Scene from *Wolfman*, 2010

The greater the imminent danger, the more the audience feels it is being royally entertained.

century the circus was born with its empathy-inducing trapeze and high-wire acts and its wild animal encounters. All of this led inevitably to our present-day Dionysian orgies on film and television and, of course, to the perennial circus with its ever-more dangerous acts.

The flip side of the Dionysian coin when it comes to such entertainment can be called Apollonian alienation. The term **alienation** was coined by Bertolt Brecht, a major German playwright of the early twentieth century, about whom more will be said in Chapter 7. Brecht wanted to make sure audiences did not become so emotionally involved in plot and character that they failed to heed his messages. He often injected vaudeville slapstick, songs, and dances into very serious material. In this way he hoped to prevent empathetic responses.

> *"What is written without effort is in general read without pleasure."*
>
> **—Samuel Johnson**

The critical thinker is not so restricted. Attending a play or film with strong emotional undercurrents or reading a powerful novel filled with moving, tragic moments, we may appreciate the feelings evoked but also sit back and look objectively at the work. Questions raised might be: *Why is the hero's downfall so terrifying when he is not a very good person? How does the author make us care about what is happening to him?* When the author's technique becomes transparent, the viewing or reading experience becomes that much richer and we can seize the opportunity to expand our mind. Critical thinkers tend to retain stronger memories of their experiences and find enjoyment in discussing works with other critical thinkers who may have the same or sharply differing views. Mutual agreement doesn't matter. The process of building "brain muscle" does.

The Importance of Knowing When a Purely Emotional Response Is Appropriate

We are not, however, insisting that it is always better to analyze in Apollonian fashion. To enter the Sistine Chapel in the Vatican and gaze up at the magnificent ceiling created by Michelangelo is to be, quite literally, bereft of words. None necessary. Something inside tells us that these artistic arrangements are right, magnificently right. It is to experience what Plato would have called "pure beauty." Time stops for the viewer; practical concerns disappear. The experience doesn't have to be explained or analyzed. It is the quiet joy of being conscious at the highest level. When you get to a summit like this, you *know* it!

> *"Each day it is something new, fantastic and unbelievable. That is Bach, like nature, a miracle!"*
>
> **—Pablo Casals**

Great works like Picasso's *Guernica* or Michelangelo's *David*, the symphonies of Beethoven, and the tragedies of Shakespeare have powerful emotional effects on us long before we begin to exercise sober critical judgment. Even professional critics, whom we shall be discussing presently, no doubt allow themselves to be so affected before they stand back and begin a rational analysis of a work. Often there is no point to the rational analysis if the emotions have not first been stirred. What is unfortunate is that emotional appeal is often left out in formal lectures on the humanities.

Here is a poem by the American e. e. cummings (1894–1962) famous for not using capital letters, for dismantling standard English grammar, and for finding alternate ways to express feelings and ideas. In this poem, "somewhere I have never travelled," he delivers a clear Dionysian message but in off-the-wall language that can be intuitively understood without requiring further analysis.

somewhere i have never travelled, glady beyond
any experience, your eyes have their silence:
in your most frail gesture are things which enclose me,
or which I cannot touch because they are too near

Photos.com/Thinkstock

Michelangelo, *The Creation of Adam*, c. 1511

Seeing *The Creation of Adam*, the central panel in the Sistine Chapel ceiling, is to realize that there are summit experiences for which words are irrelevant.

your slightest look easily will unclose me,
though i have closed myself as fingers,
you open always petal by petal myself as Spring opens
(touching skillfully, mysteriously) her first rose
or if your wish be to close me, i and
my life will shut very beautifully, suddenly,
as when the heart of this flower imagines
the snow carefully everywhere descending;

nothing which we are to perceive in this world equals
the power of your intense fragility: whose texture
compels me with the color of its countries,
rendering death and forever with each breathing

(i do not know what it is about you that closes
and opens; only something in me understands
the voice of your eyes is deeper than all roses)
nobody, not even the rain, has such small hands[3]

Analysis here is not only irrelevant but unfair to the poet. What cummings is expressing all of us can feel. Does he not touch the depth of our Dionysian self that believes in the wonder of being truly and deeply in love without ever having the right words to say it? Don't we somehow know what it "means" for the voice of someone's eyes to be deeper than all roses? Read the poem aloud in case you're still in doubt.

The Importance of Responding Critically

Critical thinking carefully defines, describes, and analyzes something: an election, an important decision, a question that has puzzled or intrigued philosophers for centuries, a new electronic invention, a movie, a novel, Number One on the Top 40,

"*Take each man's censure but reserve thy judgment.*"

—**William Shakespeare**

or a decision about whether to move into your own apartment. Critical responses, as we have said, build our mental strength. They usually involve the following steps:

1. defining what we want to determine (e.g. *What made this film special?*)
2. putting aside instinctive, emotional responses
3. collecting information and considering all pertinent factors
4. evaluating the work or the topic in its proper context (*Don't dismiss a story because of customs and attitudes foreign to you.*)
5. being willing to understand characters unlike yourself (e.g. *I know it's good; the hero is young like me.*")
6. having now an informed opinion with evidence to back it up

Developing the skill of analysis and objective evaluation helps us to deepen our appreciation of the humanities and also to have a better sense of what seems to be truly worth our time.

Exercising the Mind

"Wonder, connected with a principle of rational curiosity, is the source of all knowledge and discovery."

—Samuel Horsley

Most of us get up and go when we feel the need to exercise our bodies, especially when something has prevented our moving about (such as being cramped for three hours in an airplane seat). Those who have suffered illnesses from a lack of exercise may be encouraged to alter the way they live and be urged to run, walk, take stairs instead of elevators, and participate in those activites to avoid that sluggish feeling well known to nonexercisers. Yet far too many have no trouble, and experience no guilt when they allow their minds to be sluggish. The critical responses we have discussed in the previous section come much easier to minds that are trim and fit. And getting there doesn't even involve a diet!

Critical thinking is enhanced as we engage in three important activities: solving problems, challenging assumptions, and recognizing contexts.

Solving Problems

Critical thinkers are always solving problems, even hypothetical ones. Try this one.

"Problems are only opportunities in work clothes."

—Henry J. Kaiser

> *Three salesmen traveling together in a blinding rainstorm spot a hotel and decide to get a room. The night clerk tells them the price for a triple room is $90. Accordingly, each man gives the clerk $30. After they go upstairs, the clerk double-checks the rate and realizes the room costs only $85 dollars. He gives the bellhop five singles and instructs him to give this money to the three salesmen. On his way upstairs, the bellhop stops and thinks, "They will be checking out early in the morning when the night clerk is no longer there. How would they ever know the true cost of the room?" He then decides to give the salesmen a $3-refund, and he pockets $2 for himself. The problem: After their "refund," each man has paid $29 for the room, bringing their total to $87 (29 × 3 = 87). Adding the $2 pocketed by the bellhop, the total is $89. What happened to the missing dollar?*

The error occurs in the way the problem is presented. The room actually cost $85, not $87. The men received $3 back, and the bellhop pocketed two. So now we are back to the original $90. A problem such as this one helps us to be careful about how we report an event and to listen carefully for inconsistencies and contradictions in the way others report.

Having developed the habit of critical analysis, we are prepared to confront a real problem in our own life. The family member who needs help is a problem thousands face each day. Suppose you have a brother who constantly overspends, is heavily in debt, and cannot curb his extravagance. One reason is that he always counts on being rescued by responsible relatives—for example, *you*.

The first step in solving such a problem is to determine whether a problem actually exists. Whether or not to pay off your brother's debts may not be a problem if you decide not to assume ownership of it. Whose problem is it? It's yours if you wish to avoid the pain of guilt you think you'll experience if you turn your back. But the problem belongs to your brother or to other family members if you decide to withdraw with a clear conscience. If the rest of the family also declines with a clear conscience, then only your brother has a problem.

Family bonds are likely to be pretty strong, but you have to weigh all the factors. Does your brother overspend very often? Is your brother capable of earning enough money to pay the debts? If not, will he listen to a rational argument in favor of spending within his limits? Merely paying off the debts to "avoid the hassle" may send the wrong signal.

> "*Other things may change us, but we start and end with family.*"
>
> **—Anthony Brandt**

No ultimate answer will be found here, but we have just engaged in the act of reasoning. Sometimes easy solutions evade us and we must settle on one, hoping for the best. Yet we are less likely to find a successful answer if we have not fully analyzed the problem—if we have not been critical thinkers.

Challenging Assumptions

Assumptions are a fact of everyday communication. They are the beliefs on which opinions are based and conclusions drawn. Often these are *buried*; that is, they lie underneath what people are saying without being acknowledged as assumptions, and often they are the real message that is being communicated. The critical thinker listens carefully, always seeking what is actually being said.

Suppose a newspaper reader turns to you and says that a convicted murderer has been released after being confined to a mental hospital for ten years. In the opinion of the staff, that person is no longer a menace to society. The reader then observes, "There ought to be a law against letting people escape the death penalty by pleading insanity and then releasing them so they can kill again."

The above statement makes no pretense to be factual. It is understood that the speaker is expressing an opinion. The buried assumptions behind the opinion, however, may not be recognized. Here are some possibilities:

1. The question of insanity should have no bearing on a court case.
2. The defendant was not really insane anyway.
3. The state or federal legislature should control how defendants plead.
4. Once a murderer always a murderer.
5. Those in charge of mental hospitals are not qualified to make accurate judgments about when to release a patient.

Noncritical listeners are likely to nod in agreement with the reader's observation because careful debate in this instance involves careful analysis of the buried assumptions. Many do not wish to invest the time needed for making this analysis.

Now suppose that the newspaper reader and the listener in the above example are both seasoned critical thinkers who exercise their mental faculties as often as possible, knowing how to balance their inner Apollo and Dionysus. A critically thinking reader would no doubt communicate a different version of the newspaper story, such as: "Abel Parsons has been released from the mental hospital where he has spent the last ten years. If you remember, he pleaded guilty by reason of insanity."

The critically thinking listener might then respond: "Does the article cite any reasons for his release?"

"One. The psychiatrist who has observed him for the whole time called in three consultants, and they all agreed that Parsons appears to be totally rehabilitated."

"Have they provided any sort of monitoring system to keep tabs on what he does at least for a while?"

"It doesn't say."

"I would think they'd *have* to set something up. Do you agree?"

The two people have not solved a thorny legal problem. What they *have* done in this hypothetical conversation is exercise critical thinking to get at the objective facts of the newspaper story rather than make assumptions about it.

Each of us lives within contexts: family, circle of friends, religious affiliation, political allegiances . . .

Recognizing Contexts

Everyone and everything exists in a **context**, a framework of circumstances and relationships. Knowing that nothing exists independent of one or more contexts, critical thinkers try to avoid making large-scale generalizations and absolute evaluations. Even so, like many others, they are, at times, not above simplifying, distilling contexts down to something manageable. People, including critical thinkers, can obscure the truth, not only of the past but of what happened just yesterday when the full context of an event is unpleasant or embarrassing to relate. Using the well-practiced skill of **rationalizing**, they tell others (as well as themselves) a convenient and palatable version of an event—say, a bitter argument with a sibling. In this version, the absent family member is usually the culprit and the speaker the victim. By the time the speaker is finished, the context within which the argument took place has become fixed in the speaker's mind exactly as it has been described, and chances are that it doesn't come close to what *really* happened. While dedicated critical thinkers are not immune to reinventing contexts or selecting those that can be comfortably dealt with, they are less likely, upon reflection, to feel good about substituting imagination for reality.

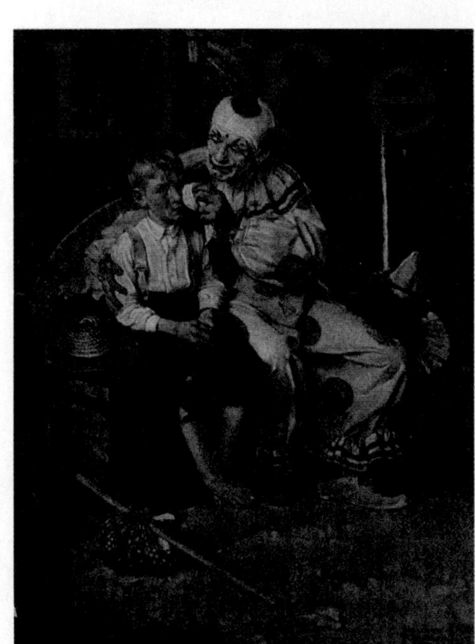

Norman Rockwell, *The Runaway*, Cover of *Life*, June 1, 1922

Would you be able to tell that this magazine cover by Norman Rockwell appeared almost ninety years ago?

One of the gifts of the humanities we described earlier is a sense of the past, which provides us with *historical context*. A casual browser in a secondhand store filled with attic discards might grow impatient because none of the items belongs to today. Those with a sense of the past, however, would be interested in examining toys, dolls, or clothing that reveal much about bygone periods. Examining pictorial records from publications of the past increases our interest in and knowledge of earlier times.

Norman Rockwell (1894–1978), the artist of the picture at left achieved fame as an interpreter of middle-class life. To see his work is to gain invaluable knowledge of how Americans lived almost a century ago. Study the picture closely. What dates it? What has been replaced by updated versions of the same items? Which, if any, are no longer in use? The title of the painting tells us what is happening. If the same thing happened today, how might it be handled? If nothing else, spending some time with old pictures like this adds to our critical-thinking skills.

The more we learn to recognize historical context, the less likely are we to evaluate everything in terms of today. In reading books or watching movies from the past, the critical thinker knows better than to judge them in terms of the present. *Gone With the Wind* (1939) is still recognized by professional critics as a milestone in movie making, even though a contemporary viewer may find some of it sentimental and dated. Without overlooking these failings, the critical thinker tries to view the film in the context of 1939 and enjoys what is still to be enjoyed, such as the marvelously advanced (for its time) use of color, the sweeping symphonic score, and the still believable performance of Vivien Leigh as Scarlett O'Hara. Whether a given work belongs to the past or the present, we can still appreciate its positive achievements without endorsing all of its ideas or techniques.

The ability to appreciate historical context makes one more tolerant of art forms in unfamiliar styles: for example, most operas.

Knowledge of historical context makes one more tolerant of outmoded styles, for example, nineteenth-century opera. The inexperienced viewer might easily lose patience with a three-hour performance in which arias often overshadow dramatic moments and performers may be chosen for the power of their voices rather than their physical appearance or acting ability. Critical viewers know that superb voices singing thrilling music more than compensate for outmoded conventions.

Sometimes a work from earlier times is rewritten for modern audiences, and sometimes contemporary "purists" prefer the way a particular story has always been presented. Here again, the dedicated critical thinker should be willing to accommodate either version. One such modernized update of a familiar and much loved work is the 1990 music drama *Miss Saigon,* based on *Madame Butterfly* (1904) by Giacomo Puccini (1858–1924). By modern standards, sentimentality, racism, and sexism abound in the original story of a Japanese geisha who falls in love with, marries, and has a child by an American naval officer. The latter, we discover, also has an American wife, and in 1904 audiences would have understood why his Japanese "marriage" was out of the question and a return to America was morally and socially necessary. They would have wept when Cho-Cho San, the abandoned wife, commits suicide in the presence of her son and applauded when she tells him to remember he is an American, places a flag in his little hands, and then dies a tragic but morally respectable death.

The context of *Miss Saigon* is the unpopular and divisive 1960s war in Vietnam. Many U.S. soldiers, finding themselves far from home for an indefinite period, consorted with Vietnamese women—a situation the French creators of *Miss Saigon,* Claude-Michel Schönberg and Alain Boublil, found strikingly parallel to the events in *Madame Butterfly*. This time the heroine is a Vietnamese prostitute, whose child a soldier fathers without marrying her. The soldier is already engaged to a woman in the States, and his betrayal of her creates intense feelings of guilt. In the liberal spirit of the 1960s, the financée is portrayed as a decent person who understands the anguish of her husband-to-be. As in Puccini's opera, the heroine commits suicide, but her death, though pitiful, is not made to seem morally respectable. Instead, the modern version is cynical, with no redeeming virtues for either the suicide or the war. The sacrifice is one more indication of war's inhumanity; nothing has been gained or proved.

Following a performance of *Miss Saigon,* critical viewers familiar with both versions of the story enjoy discussing the differences and similarities and defending a preference for one or the other. The post-play talk adds to the total pleasures of the evening.

SuperStock

Scene from Madame *Butterfly*, Royal Opera House

Cheol Joon Baek

Scene from *Miss Saigon*, Dancap Productions, 2010

Two versions of the same story—on the left, Puccini's *Madame Butterfly,* and on the right, Claude-Michel Schönberg's *Miss Saigon*—told nearly a century apart, show us the importance of engaging with each work in its historical context.

A Guide to Critical Viewing, Professional and Personal

Reading professional critics and seeing the kind of thing they notice as well as their reasons for evaluating an experience as worth our time or not is an excellent way to develop the skill of critical thinking.

Role of the Professional Critic

Criticism on the professional level is a career. The best critics earn high salaries for giving their widely respected opinions. Their work can be found on the pages of leading newspapers like the *New York Times* or the *San Francisco Chronicle,* magazines like the *New Yorker, Film Comment,* or *Opera News,* as well as Internet sites such as *Prodigy* and *Slate*. What professional critics have to say about something can help us decide among the many choices open to us. In the world of the humanities, with so much that is Dionysian to stir the emotions and, sometimes, to cloud our judgment, the professional critic is an Apollonian voice that can serve as a model for our own growing critical skills.

The noncritical viewer confronting a critic's panning of a film that breaks box-office records during its first weekend may be hostile, even if he or she hasn't yet seen the piece in question. A famous example involves the 1967 Academy Award–winning musical *The Sound of Music,* which has retained its popularity as a fixture on cable television. Most of the critics on the staff of prestigious magazines and newspapers disliked the film for a variety of reasons: its one-dimensional characters; its sugary sentimentality—as when the austere, military-minded father tearfully tells his children's governess, "You have brought music back into my house"; its predictability (the audience knows that the family will somehow escape the pursuing Nazis).

Pauline Kael (1919–2001), film critic for a women's magazine, wrote a **review** that was particularly scathing, quotes from which echoed throughout the country generating many angry letters. The critic called the movie "a sugarcoated lie that people seem to want to eat." This comment infuriated the film's ardent admirers, for it insulted them as well as the object of their adoration. (Kael was a dedicated crusader against the mass market's lowering the taste and expectations of the public.) The storm of protest caused the magazine to fire her, and the firing in turn ignited protests from other professional critics, among them Larry Devine of the *Miami Herald,* who recommended that the magazine "go back to the recipes and footcare."

Such putdowns from professional critics have given many of them a reputation for being arrogant snobs. The noncritical viewer may see no reason for such a person's existence. We suggest that there are two categories of professional critics: those who write for a popular audience and who are therefore likely to praise a work that will have mass appeal, and those who write for publications like the *New Yorker* (which hired Pauline Kael after she had been terminated) that appeal to the critical-thinking reader.

The latter enjoys such critics for their consistent philosophy of what constitutes a work of art and their ardent desire to live at a time when many such works are being created. The attitude of professional critics in a highly reputable publication is: Because we have such a limited stay on this earth, we want to be emotionally moved, intellectually challenged, and, above all, to be in the company of writers, directors, actors, and creative people, who respect the intelligence of their audience and readers. Robert Brustein, author, critic, and academic theater great, once wrote an unenthusiastic review of a play many theater-goers thought should be praised. He was accused of distancing himself from the "average" theater-goer ("*average*" often invoked as a genuine critical yardstick). Brustein wrote back that "I do not write in order to arbitrate your theatre going activities," adding his agreement with the poet T. S. Eliot that the function of a critic is to analyze a work of art. The presumption was no art, no analysis, no reason for a review. The prestigious critic writes far fewer reviews than those who like to connect to the "average" person, for he or she knows that there are not that many works out there with a chance to be judged works of art.

Then we have a professional critic like Alex Ross, the music reviewer for the *New Yorker* whose tastes in music range from Bach to be-bop. He is always looking for serious art even in works often denounced by other critics as beneath their consideration. He reviews chamber music at Lincoln Center, as well as bands like the Velvet Underground, which was given credit for spearheading the punk rock and alternative rock movements.

In 1965 the pop artist Andy Warhol, whose paintings now sell for millions of dollars, became the band's manager, guaranteeing that the Velvet Underground had an artistic underside. In urging his readers to keep an open mind about the dissonant atonal chords of contemporary concert music, Ross cites the fact that such chords "crop up in jazz; avant-garde sounds appear in Hollywood film scores; minimalism has marked rock, pop, and dance music from the Velvet Underground onward. Some times the music resembles noise because it *is* noise, or near to it, by design."[4] The word "design" alerts the reader who is still entertaining doubts that music sounding like nothing but noise may be well worth a close listen.

The professional critic is likely to bestow extravagant praise on something he or she considers to be a masterpiece, and such praise raises our level of interest.

The professional critic not only evaluates but serves as a teacher to those of us without substantial backgrounds in a particular art form. They get down to specifics about the work they are reviewing, and almost always their philosophy of what constitutes art in the form is evident.

In a review of the Joffrey Ballet Company's performance in *Cinderella* by the famous English choreographer Sir Frederick Ashton (1904–1988), the critic Alistair Macauley writes that the performance moves the audience

> *into a new realm of form, where Ashton's wealth of vocabulary and luxurious style expands the whole stage world immensely . . . And the greatest and most chilling of Ashton's many inventions are the strikes of doom that arrive at the midnight hour. . . . [The supporting dancers] all form into an impersonal machine, the workings of a gigantic clock in which Cinderella finds herself trapped. She is barred by one wall after another. . . . In few other ballets is the poetry drama of ballet so potent.*[5]

In these few sentences the critic has informed us that a great ballet performance is one that "expands the whole stage world immensely" by providing unexpected "inventions" like the brilliant use of scenic technology to tell us what midnight means to the heroine. It is not that we don't know this; it's just that the way it tells us the old story is new and thrilling. If the critic had said merely that the ballet is "fresh and really good," our knowledge of ballet would not have increased.

The Personal Critical Response

One does not have to be a professional critic to engage in the process of evaluation after a careful and fair viewing, listening, or reading. Here is "The world is too much with us," a poem by William Wordsworth (1770–1850), who lived in England's Lake District at a time when the Industrial Revolution was beginning to have an impact and many people were moving from the country to the cities seeking a more lucrative life style. The poem remains an iconic expression of the limitations of living for economic gain.

The world is too much with us; late and soon,
Getting and spending, we lay waste our powers:
Little we see in Nature that is ours;
We have given our hearts away, a sordid boon!
This Sea that bares her bosom to the moon;
The winds that will be howling at all hours,
And are up-gathered now like sleeping flowers;
For this, for everything, we are out of tune,
It moves us not.—Great God! I'd rather be
A Pagan suckled in a creed outworn;
So might I, standing on this pleasant lea,
Have glimpses that would make me less forlorn;
Have sight of Proteus rising from the sea;
Or hear old Triton blow his wreathéd horn.[6]

The first step in becoming an informed critic is not to jump to hasty conclusions.

The first step in becoming an informed personal critic is *not to jump to a hasty conclusion.* "I don't like it" or "I love this poem" is an irrelevant remark at this early stage in the process.

The next step is to determine what it is you have just read. Describe the poem as clearly and objectively as possible. A possibility: The poem contains (or appears to contain, which might be a more conservative, more cautious approach, at least in the beginning) a regretful realization that, in a concern for material welfare, we no longer live on close terms with nature; and from a current perspective, we are less and less likely to enjoy nature given what so many are doing to ensure their own profits.

But more than two centuries after its creation, the poem continues to remind us that the wondrous beauty of the natural world is its own justification. Noticing how the seasons affect the landscape, how plants and flowers will grow and bloom wherever they are given space, costs nothing and yields treasures that money cannot buy.

Wordsworth could not have known about environmentalism as such, but he is already aware that the commerce of everyday life, the "getting and spending," is creating a danger that the natural world would be ignored, uncared for. And so he thinks of an ancient time when mythology turned nature into a wondrous force to be dazzled by and always respected.

If you are adventurous and enjoy probing a little deeper, you can obtain information about the poet's life from the Internet. You would learn that, as Wordsworth grew older, he feared he was losing the inspiration he used to feel when he was out in nature. You would also learn that this poem was written in 1804, perhaps during a transition phase in the poet's development—that is, at a time when, in reaching full maturity, he might have begun to fear that, though he was profiting from writing, he was doing so at the cost of his inspiration. If you wanted to advance this idea, you would do well to tread softly, however. Though many literary scholars take the plunge and read autobiography into every work by an author, the poet in this case might have been making a general statement applicable to all people.

In any case, speculation about ideas in a work sharpens our critical faculties, even if it doesn't say the last word about what we are reading. The important thing is to separate probability from possibility. It is virtually certain that Wordsworth is upset about the pursuit of material gain, and it is possible that, at the age of 34, he fears that he might be losing the passion that fired his youth.

The next stage in the critical process is to look at the poet's *craft*—that is, the handling of language, **imagery** (the pictures in your mind that the poem communicates), and the way the requirements of the medium do not interfere with the poet's expressive needs. What makes poetry different from prose is that poets are able to compress a great deal into fewer words than prose requires.

> *"I do not feel obliged to believe that the same God who has endowed us with sense, reason, and intellect has intended us to forego their use."*
>
> **—Galileo**

"Getting and spending" in three words describes our whole economic system. That is compression of thought in a memorable sequence, one that has been used over and over, even by economists themselves. Wordsworth makes us see an ocean in the image of the sea baring its bosom to the moon. Just saying "the sea" would have served his purpose, but not equally well. The aptness of the phrasing in creating the picture in our minds extends our pleasure in reading the poem because the image allows for intricacies that even great paintings of the sea cannot provide. The reason? The image makes us find the intricacies for ourselves. A painting is what it is. We do not see beyond it.

Finally, the poem is a **sonnet**, a demanding literary form in which the poet is restricted to fourteen lines. In the past, poets challenged themselves by using rhyming lines and writing in a definite rhythm. Often rhythm and rhyme are forced, as in "Backward, turn backward, oh time in your flight, / And make me a child again, just for tonight." One suspects that anyone who would write such a line wouldn't mind being a child again for a longer period, but "just for tonight" allows for the rhyme. The rhythm of the lines makes it impossible for us not to see that the requirements of the form have totally taken over the poet's individuality. Rhythm and rhyme, not the poet, are the stars.

If you read Wordsworth's poem aloud to find the rhythmic pattern, you discover that unaccented syllables are followed by accented ones, that there never are two accented or unaccented syllables side by side. At the same time, when you read it without stressing the rhythm, the words flow naturally and manage to keep the rhythm unnoticed. The rhyming pattern is also quite regular. (The first and fourth lines rhyme, as do the second and third, the fifth and eighth, the sixth and seventh, and, finally, the ninth, eleventh, and thirteenth, and the tenth, twelfth, and fourteenth.) Yet in reading the poem aloud, following the natural progression of it, you don't find the rhymes jumping out of their context.

But, you may ask, so what if the rhythm and the rhyme are not obtrusive? One answer may be that when the poet works within rigid guidelines without having them dictate his content we admire his craft, his poetry-making skill. Being aware that the poet has carefully concealed the artistry behind the poem happens to be one of the pleasures of responding critically. When the pianist performs a complicated jazz solo or a sonata by Mozart, we should not have to think about the musician's years of practicing eight hours a day. When the ice skater glides across the arena in perfect sync with Debussy's "Clair de Lune," we should believe that we can strap on a pair of skates and do the same thing. *Art is the illusion that there is no art.* Only when the skater attempts a triple axel and falls do we then watch future leaps with apprehension, painfully aware of the difficulty involved. Of course, we don't forget that the art *is* there; but when we keep being reminded of it, strangely enough, the art isn't there anymore. You don't want the actor to let you know how great he or she is. Critical thinkers can discover that for themselves.

Listen on **MyHumanitiesKit.com** Debussy, "Clair de Lune"

Literalists and Figuratists

F: Only three things matter in real estate. Location, location, location.

L: That's only one.

If you first meet someone in a theater lobby and casual chitchat leads to comments about the movie just seen, you can usually tell whether you're talking with a critical or a noncritical thinker *by that person's use of language*. The noncritical relate all experience, whether at the movies or in real life, to themselves. "The movie was too gory for me. I prefer a nice love story." (Or it could go the other way: "*I hate gooey love stories; give me good old-fashioned horror any time.*") The critical speak in or imply general principles. This trait comes from involvement in the humanities: listening, viewing, or reading a great deal and thinking about the experience.

Noncritical thinkers may be called **Literalists**, a term derived from their habitual way of *not* seeing general principles. They are tuned into what is happening at the moment, and their opinions are often shaped by popular views expressed by friends who are just like them or by what a favorite commentator has been saying about issues such as global warming, homeland security, and the state of the economy. They prefer supermarket-type plastically wrapped ideas that can be taken in whole and never analyzed. Critical thinkers may be called **Figuratists**, a term derived from the fact that their language is colorful and suggests wide experiences in many fields, including the humanities. If they are talking about the present moment, the likelihood is that they will see it in broader terms. There is a vast difference between "The cream in my coffee looks sour" and "Looks as if the world was too much with this cow."

Responding to the literalist's "I know what I like," the figuratist in the lobby may begin with "This movie was riddled with clichés. Look. Here's a list of them." The general principle, which is implied and easily defensible, is: *Cliché-riddled dialogue is not the sign of a fresh new talent; it is visiting familiar territory, which is not worth the viewer's time.* An answer like "Well, I don't have anything else to do, so I don't mind what you call clichés" quickly identifies the speaker as a noncritical literalist.

Literalist Speech

Literalists are limited to what we may call the "everyday concrete." They are also likely to listen haphazardly to what a figuratist is *generally* saying, latching on to the very last thing that was mentioned.

F: *So many of the so-called professionals I run into don't seem to be what I would call experts. I'd love to meet one who could give me sound answers to important questions: where to live, whether to change jobs, what suntan lotion is most effective, where my children could get the best education.*

L: *I didn't know you had children.*

F: *I don't.*
(Blank stare)

The Figuratist is really saying that there is no certainty, not even when you're dealing with people who are expected to be experts. He or she is citing specific, hypothetical examples to arrive at general principles. The "F" person in the example above may well have asked a store clerk to recommend the best suntan lotion and received only a vague reply, or even worse, "You'd have to ask the manager, who's out to lunch."

Friends of "F" may have children, but not necessarily. Being broadly interested in what's happening in the world, "F" knows a good deal about educational systems, has read widely on the subject, has viewed panel discussions, and so on. Their conversation continues.

F: *I think my students don't know the difference between the classroom and their bedroom.*

L: *My neighbor says her son likes to sleep in class.*

F: *The least their parents could do is send them to school with pillows.*

L: *I don't think that would be wise.*

No further comment.

> *"One must be able to transcend the narrow confines of a self-centered existence and believe that one will make a significant contribution to life . . ."*
>
> **—Bruno Bettelheim**

Figuratist Speech

Figuratists, especially those who devote considerable time to reading great literature, use fanciful, often metaphoric language—that is, language that means something other than what is being directly said. They are quickwitted, and effective ways of communicating occur more naturally to them than to people who have spent less time in libraries. For example, at a recent opening of a bad play, a figuratist, talking to friends afterward in the lobby, was overheard commenting: "Watching this, I thought I was giving CPR to a statue." Somehow, "The play was boring" just doesn't have the same zing.

Figuratists are adept at twisting words, which in their original context were just mildly clever, and making them shine with brilliance. Many years ago the celebrated (and somewhat arrogant) British dramatist Noel Coward wrote a personal note to the then Prime Minister Winston Churchill, who was famous for cleverness and quick wit, inviting him to the opening night of his play. He ended the note this way: "Oh, and feel free to bring a friend if you have one." Not one to take an insult lying down, Mr. Churchill replied: "I won't be able to make the opening, but I will come the second night if there is one."

> *"Put all your eggs in one basket and—WATCH THAT BASKET."*
>
> **—Mark Twain**

Bettmann/Corbis

Yogi Berra, 1953

"It ain't over till it's over" just seems more effective than "There's always hope."

An added bonus for the avid reader of great writers is that clever remarks like Churchill's are in the public domain. They can be absorbed into one's own repertoire of shining comments. It is also fun for the figuratist to converse with other widely read friends and either quote from instantly recognizable sources or, even better, to come up with a personal variation. Shakespeare has probably penned more frequently quoted lines than any other writer in the English-speaking world, so many in fact that the figuratist feels obliged to allude to but not to repeat them verbatim one more time. The queen in *Hamlet,* tossing flower petals into the heroine's grave, cries, "Sweets to the sweet: farewell!" A figuratist, much addicted to chocolates, was heard to say, just before giving in to the temptation of one more delectable piece: "Sweets to the sweet: farewell, teeth!"

The most often repeated of the great lines are those which contain wisdom behind the wit, so that the critical thinker knows there is no way to improve upon them. The legendary Yogi Berra is credited with many now famous, if not always grammatically respectable, remarks. Much of his wisdom sprang from the observations of a folk philosopher thinking about his beloved game of baseball. "It ain't over till it's over" is now, despite the grammatical lapse, *the* best way to imply that there is always hope. There is, after all, always a ninth inning, with three outs.

Nor is every saying attributed to Yogi Berra the mark of an untutored philosopher with bad grammar. One suspects that, as he grew older and realized his comments were becoming famous, he gave them more depth and an entirely original style. "In theory there is no difference between theory and practice. In practice there is." This sly bit of wisdom sneaks up on us. It could be rephrased like this: "People who spend their lives talking theories really need to see what's out there." But it wouldn't have the zing of the seasoned figuratist that Yogi Berra really was. And the critical thinker is always looking for clever uses of language, whether from the libraries or from the baseball stadium.

> *"In this world there are only two tragedies. One is not getting what you want, and the other is getting it."*
>
> **—Oscar Wilde**

Critical thinking is indispensable to the art of being human, though the critical thinker is always going to run into an uncritical acquaintance who insists, "I'd rather not think about what I read or see, I'd rather just enjoy myself." Is there no way to convince the acquaintance that it's possible to both think and enjoy; that, in fact, thinking just *might* be the ultimate way to enjoy living? Those who think well speak well, and those who do both will remain avid lovers of the humanities, a perennial reservoir of inspiration that sharpens our critical faculties.

LEARNING OBJECTIVES

Having read and carefully studied this chapter, you should be able to:

1. Distinguish between Apollonianism and Dionysianism, using Michelangelo's and Donatello's *David* as illustrations.
2. Explain the "popcorn syndrome" and give an example from your own TV or film viewing experience.
3. Explain why the e. e. cummings poem is Dionysian, not Apollonian.
4. Summarize the major steps in solving a problem.
5. Bring to class an item (preferably a column) from a daily newspaper that contains hidden assumptions.
6. Study the Norman Rockwell illustration and indicate items that give away its age.
7. Summarize the steps in the personal critical response.
8. Distinguish between Literalists and Figuratists.

KEY TERMS

Apollonian term derived from Nietzsche's symbolic reference to the Greek god of light and truth; used to describe something or someone that is orderly and rational.

context as used in this chapter, the environment, background, or special circumstances in terms of which a given work is best understood. Historical context is the influence that the ideas, values, and styles of a particular time have on a society, work of art, or philosophy.

critical thinking the faculty of rational and logical analysis; looking at subjects objectively, gathering all information, and then drawing conclusions about the subject based on evidence; the opposite of jumping to hasty conclusions based upon a purely emotional response.

Dionysian term derived from Nietzsche's symbolic reference to the Greek god of wine and vegetation; used to describe spontaneity as well as a lack of order and structure, signifying the passionate and creative (often impulsive) aspects of art, society, or an individual.

empathy identifying with another actual person or a character in a book, film, or play; becoming, in a sense, that person and being totally involved in his or her problems.

Figuratist a critical thinker whose use of language is characteristically colorful, often playful, filled with metaphors that suggest a greater interest in the general than in just the particular.

imagery found especially in poetry, the pictures the poet creates in your mind that communicate in a few words what ordinary prose cannot, or at least not as economically.

Literalist the noncritical person whose language reflects a concern for the immediate moment, especially as what is happening or being viewed relates to the self.

Popcorn Syndrome an all-inclusive term for every aspect of the enjoyment of watching a movie or TV show strictly for pleasure with no desire to think about it afterward.

sonnet a 14-line poem that imposed on poets tight rules of length, rhythm, and rhyming pattern.

TOPICS FOR WRITING AND DISCUSSION

1. Write a two-page memoir in which you describe yourself and your experience with the humanities. Include your preferences—why you like this and don't like that.
2. Where do you see yourself in the seesaw conflict between Apollo and Dionysus? Which side of yourself needs work, and how do you propose to accomplish this?
3. It has been said "Wisdom is rooted in the figurative." Explain what this might mean.
4. Which of the following questions, if answered properly, would illustrate critical thinking? Explain why.
   a. Who wrote *The Da Vinci Code*?
   b. At what temperature does water boil?
   c. Which of this year's films has earned the most at the box office?
   d. Wordsworth's sonnet "The world is too much with us, late and soon" is said to illustrate what makes a classic. Using this poem as an example, define "classic."
   e. What provides a better vacation: whitewater rafting or cruising?
   f. Is living in the twenty-first century better in every way than living in an earlier century?
   g. Do you prefer to read fiction or nonfiction?
5. Samuel Barber's Adagio for Strings, op. 11, was used by director Oliver Stone behind a scene in the 1977 film *Platoon* in which a band of American soldiers burn a Vietnamese village. The performance of the work at London's Albert Hall on September 15, 2001, with Leonard Slatkin conducting, can be heard on YouTube. Listen to it, then decide whether Oliver Stone used the music appropriately.
6. Give an example of a "popcorn hangover" you have experienced.
7. How do you recognize when someone is giving an informed opinion?
8. Briefly indicate and describe the steps in the personal critical process.
9. Bring to class a review by a professional critic. (The text mentions some places where such reviews can be found.) Point out specific examples of what the critic noticed.
10. Write an imaginary conversation between a literalist and a figuratist.
11. Why do you think e.e. cummings refused to use capital letters or "proper" punctuation and grammar?

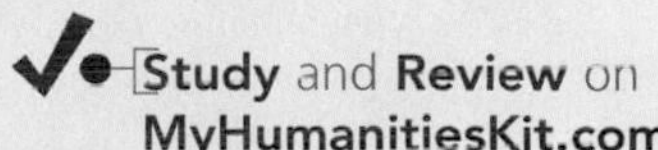

Chapter 3

Myth and the Origin of the Humanities

Long before there was print, before the formal arts existed, there were the humanities in the form of **mythology**. Music and dance probably began as rhythmic accompaniments to stylized movements in which people honored and appeased the gods and observed certain stages of life, such as the transition from youth to adulthood. Early forms of the drama occurred when people pretended to be brave hunters stalking wild animals needed for their survival or heroic warriors battling evil spirits. In Neolithic cave drawings, such as those found in Lascaux, France, our ancestors depicted both the animals on which their survival depended and themselves in the act of hunting those animals. In reimagining the hunt, they endowed their deeds unwittingly with mythic significance.

Early people in societies that were of necessity closely knit preserved their history by weaving stories of their past—stories about where they may have originated and their relationship to the gods; stories about great hunters, warriors, and leaders; and eventually, stories designed to illustrate the difference between right and wrong.

Though not a separate discipline of the humanities, mythology underlies much of the work created in *all* disciplines. Literature, visual art, music, drama, cinema—all may have roots in **myths** that are sometimes unique to a given culture, but in many instances are universal, found in one version or another in most cultures. For this reason, mythology is an appropriate starting place for our study of the humanities.

What, then, *is* mythology? Webster gives us two ways of defining it. One is "the science or study of myths." The other is "a collection of all the myths of a specific people or about a specific being." Myth can also be defined as "a traditional story of unknown authorship, ostensibly with a historical basis, but serving usually to explain some phenomenon of nature, the origin of humanity, or the customs, religious rites, and so on of a people." Thus we can speak about the mythology of a Native American nation or the mythology of a specific hero such as King Arthur. In this chapter we discuss the role mythology played in shaping the humanities. We'll conclude by sampling mythic elements in some famous literary works.

We also discuss the fact that all of us have our own personal mythology, which began in early childhood when we objectified our fears and our secret longings, divided the world into good and evil, and had our heroes that, for the most part, we identified with. Our myths stay with us for life and grow up with us, fulfilling psychological needs at every stage of our development.

In examining the mythic roots of many works in the formal disciplines of the humanities, we can see that Shakespeare's portrait of King Henry V is one of a nearly perfect hero, the champion and defender of a people, the one who seems indestructible. But so is Frodo, the tiny hobbit of *The Lord of the Rings,* who sacrifices home and security and ultimately his very life to save Middle Earth from the terrible Sauron.

◀ **Johnny Depp as the Mad Hatter, *Alice in Wonderland*, 2010**

Some childhood myths, such as *Alice in Wonderland*, stay with us for life.

Photos 12/Alamy

The hero is one of innumerable mythic *archetypes* or models by which we, individually or collectively, come to organize our understanding of the world, the nature and purpose of human life, and events that take place, such as a war between righteous and unrighteous forces.

We need, at the outset, to demolish some common misconceptions about myth. It has become a deceptively simple four-letter word used in a variety of ways not necessarily related to the humanities, though closely tied to our personal needs. In popular usage myth is *something erroneous yet widely believed*—something to be refuted by rational adults, such as "the Myth of Mental Illness," or MYTH OF CALORIES EXPOSED; EAT ALL YOU WANT AND GET THIN! Another misuse of the word is patronizing, in the sense of "old stories once believed by naive people in a prescientific age that didn't know better."

> *"Myths are clues to the spiritual potentiality of the human life."*
> —**Joseph Campbell**

If myths could be easily dismissed as just false and outmoded beliefs, they would not be the subject of this chapter. But mythology belongs to and affects large numbers of people. Knowledge of myth is basic to cultural literacy. Writers assume that readers will understand mythic references, such as the comment by *New Yorker* film critic Anthony Lane describing the film *Eternal Sunshine of the Spotless Mind* (2004) as "romantic." (Romance, love that goes far deeper than just sexual attraction, is an archetype we can date back to the Middle Ages.) The film, says Lane, suggests that "every one of us harbors an inextinguishable need, and that we helplessly swing back toward our soulmates...."[1] Intrinsic to the romantic love archetype is the belief that each of us is destined to meet the right person eventually. And who knows? Maybe some of us do. Myths are not necessarily untrue. They are stories containing beliefs and character types that remain with us for life and drive many of our ideas, our hopes, and our dreams.

If nothing else, myths can be interesting stories, unrestricted to literal facts, truthful psychologically and emotionally. They help us to understand how a given culture characterizes itself and other cultures with which it engages. They help us understand how individuals think and to be aware of their underlying needs. Above all, knowledge of mythology renders us less likely to make snap judgments about right and wrong because we realize that the sharp distinction between right and wrong is itself a mythic archetype. We must realize that the belief in right versus wrong is not necessarily false. All we are saying is that certain beliefs, certain ways of organizing our thoughts, are deeply ingrained and *true* in a certain sense of the word. Right from the start we must learn that "true" has more than a scientific laboratory definition.

Myths are almost as necessary for survival as breathing and eating. In addition to influencing both the humanities and, as we shall see, psychology, myth affects the behavior of people all over the world. This chapter examines basic myths about creation, birth, death, the afterlife, love, power, magic numbers, the importance of circles, the arduous journey, and the unspoiled garden. Some of these myths date back to very early people, but all recur in many forms. They are symbols in our culture and in our unconscious minds that help to shape the way we view ourselves and our world. They are vital to the study of the humanities.

Archetypes in Mythology

Even if myths were only a collection of stories about recognizable families, feuds, passion and revenge, they would be enjoyable as literature. Reading them, we are struck by similarities in stories and characters. We might ask ourselves why certain of these are found again and again and often influence the way we ourselves think and react to what others do. Scholars question even more. They seek in myth a common thread, a chance to learn if the stories tell us something important about the human condition. For this they turn to a theory of psychologist-philosopher Carl Jung (1875–1961), who maintained that all persons are born with an instinctive knowledge of certain **archetypes**, the models by which people comprehend experience and cope with the enormous and often baffling task of being human. Jung believed these models are shared by societies all over the world, though they may take different forms. Archetypes are mythic characters, events, symbols, and buried assumptions transmitted from one generation to another through what Jung labeled the **collective unconscious**.

> *From the unconscious emanate determining influences which, independently of tradition, guarantee in every single individual a similarity and even a sameness of experience, and also of the way it is represented imaginatively. One of the main proofs of this is the almost universal parallelism between mythological motifs.*[2]

Jung's theory is not accepted by all psychologists or scholars of myth, but without it or another comprehensive theory to replace it, we have a difficult time accounting for the continued appearance of certain myths and myth elements: tales of a terrible flood and the salvation of one good man; the stories about dangerous journeys into the land of death and darkness; and, above all, tales about the major stages in the life of a singular human being—sometimes partly divine—known as the *hero*. There are, however, some alternative explanations.

> *"These heavenly archetypes were felt to be true in the same way as the events and forms that inhabit our imaginations often seem more real and significant to us than our mundane existence."*
>
> **—Karen Armstrong**

One is the *external* theory, the most scientific of the possibilities. According to this theory, stories were spread along migratory routes. Myths originated in specific places and then were transported as people warred, traded, and intermarried with each other. In general, we do find myth similarities among certain cultures whose migrations can be traced.

An example of the migratory spread of old stories is the way the myths of the African Yoruba tribe were transported to Cuba, where they were modified and adopted by a whole new body of listeners. These stories gradually became systematized into both a religion and a philosophy known as *Santeria*, which offers an explanation of universal origins that combines Catholic monotheism with African polytheism. Santeria continues to be practiced in Cuba, and its pantheon of heavenly protectors includes both African gods and Christian saints.

Yet another explanation for the universality of myth is the predictable one that human beings share common needs, regardless of geography and level of cultural sophistication, and thus certain elements found in all myths must play their part in helping people cope with the conditions in which they find themselves. Similar needs do not necessarily imply contacts between cultures or a mandatory belief in a collective unconscious. If human needs are very much the same everywhere, why shouldn't myths be as well?

The Hero as World Myth

The hero is an archetype found in almost every culture; hence the label *world myth*. The Irish novelist James Joyce coined the term **monomyth** to convey his belief that the concept of the hero is pretty much the same everywhere. Regardless of how each culture views existence and its particular survival needs, stories of

The hero is an archetype found in almost every culture—hence the label world myth.

> *The human passions transform man from a mere thing into a hero, into a being that in spite of tremendous handicaps tries to make sense of life.*
>
> **—Erich Fromm**

heroes seem to be essential. As early as 1909, Otto Rank, a disciple of Freud, indicated the characteristics of the hero in Western mythology.

> *The hero is the son of parents of the highest station. His conception takes place under difficulty. There is a portent in a dream or oracle connected with the child's birth. The child is then sent away, or exposed to extreme danger. He is rescued by people of humble station, or by humble animals, and reared by them. When grown, he discovers his noble parentage after many adventures, and, overcoming all obstacles in his path, becomes at last recognized as the hero and attains fame and greatness.*[3]

Freud, a pioneer in the psychological interpretation of mythology, maintained that the two families in the monomyth—the noble and the common—represent the parents as they appear at different stages of the child's development. Jung argued that the components, or motifs, of this pervasive myth were primordial images, or archetypes. For Jung, they were a profound part of universal expectations of life. *Everyone* is prone to believe in and await the coming of a hero.

Birth of the Hero. The hero's birth occurs under wondrous circumstances: bowing trees; a shower of gold penetrating the ceiling of a room in which a young girl has been confined; the visit of a god in the guise of some other creature, animal or human; and mysterious prophecies. Usually the hero has been sired by a supernatural being.

From the beginning of human awareness, the phenomenon of birth has preoccupied and baffled people. Eventually they came to know the causal sequence that led to reproduction. But they must have marveled over the sequence that made such a miracle possible! Even for "ordinary" mortals, the birth of a child is a glorious event; announcements are mailed, friends offer congratulations, and a birthday remains a special day throughout life. In a real-life version of the prophecy that attends the birth of a hero or heroine, the parents are offered best wishes, a way of urging providence to take note of the infant, to destine the child for love and success. Those whose glorious future does not materialize may even believe themselves to have been cursed by fate.

> *The ultimate meaning of these stories is psychological rather than concrete, and the stories themselves serve only as metaphors for the myth, expressing something that is deeply felt but not easily said.*
>
> **—David Leeming**

Early Recognition of the Hero. The hero destined for greatness must be recognized early in life, often after accomplishing a spectacular physical deed—such as the young Arthur's removal of the sword Excalibur from the stone that had held it until the rightful owner should come along, or Theseus' superhuman ability to lift a heavy stone that covered a golden sword and sandals, evidencing he was a king's lost son. (One version of the myth, however, credits him not so much with strength as with ingenuity in lifting the stone by devising a lever!) Sometimes recognition comes through fulfillment of a prophecy, as when Jason arrives in the kingdom wearing only one sandal.

The theory behind the monomyth is that the theme of early recognition identifies a universal need for acceptance. In the painful stages of early adolescence, the child asks "Who am I?" and fears that the answer will be "You're nobody." Children are so small compared to the adults around them that it's no wonder they lack a sense of worth.

Many of us later admit that in childhood we harbored fantasies of secretly being children of a prominent, even royal, family, stolen from the cradle by thieves or given away by our true parents. This unknown identity allows the extraordinary child to live with such average people and to perform dreary domestic tasks unsuited for noble beings. One day, the child-turned-adolescent feels the recognition of special status will surely arrive. One only has to look at the popularity of the Harry Potter books for proof of the widespread appeal of such myths.

The Hero's Great Deed. It always occurs in young adulthood, at a time when the hero has left home and is separated from the parents. It is a mythical version of the universal rite of passage, the attainment of adult status at puberty. All mythologies recognize the importance of the transition to adulthood.

Almost every early culture required the accomplishment of an arduous task to signify the end of childhood: enduring bitter cold, surviving the wilderness, recovering a magic item from a ferocious guardian, conquering a predatory beast. Theseus destroyed the Minotaur of Crete, a creature with the head of a bull and the body of a man, which had demanded the regular sacrifice of the finest Athenian young men and maidens. In order to kill the Minotaur—an extraordinary feat in itself—Theseus had first to find the dreaded creature by making his way through a labyrinth, a series of deceptive passages, which Freud-oriented myth commentators have viewed as the journey through the maze of childhood sexual stages. According to Freudian interpretation, the ultimate discovery and killing of the Minotaur thus becomes the young adult's arrival into sexual maturity.

> *"The first condition that any mythology must fulfill is that of cleaning the doors of perception to the wonder of ourselves and the universe of which we are the ears and eyes and the mind."*
>
> —Joseph Campbell

Many of the great deeds in mythology are physical, but others are purely mental. Oedipus, the protagonist of the great Sophoclean tragedy (discussed in Chapter 7), achieved greatness by solving the riddle of the Sphinx—half monstrous bird, half-woman—who devoured and would continue to devour those who could not give the correct answer to this question: *What creature goes on four feet in the morning, two feet at midday, and three feet at twilight, and goes slowest when on the most feet?* When Oedipus arrived, Thebes was in a chaotic state of panic, for no one could solve the riddle. But Oedipus did. The answer is *man, who crawls on all fours as a child and therefore goes slowest, walks upright as an adult, and uses a cane near the end of his life.* The furious Sphinx killed herself, and Oedipus was made king, only to suffer disastrous consequences.

The need to celebrate a hero's successful and wondrous feat stays with us through life. We love to watch and empathize with milestone achievements: the inauguration of the new president; the Academy Award ceremonies; the placing of a ribboned gold medal around the neck of an Olympic champion. We mark the milestones in our personal lives: birthdays; graduation; the first date; the first kiss; a letter of acceptance; getting the desired job; marrying; becoming a parent. All too often, however, we prefer to identify with the publicized deeds of celebrities and downplay the importance of our own achievements, especially if we have deep-rooted feelings of unworth (about which much more will be said in Chapter 14).

The Hero's Loss of Power. Myths of the West seldom end when the heroes are happy and successful. Fairy tales do. (When the prince marries Cinderella, we never hear a word about the heroine's relationship with her family, in-laws, or children.) In adult mythology, however, the hero, like Oedipus, usually falls from greatness. King Arthur must live on to see Camelot destroyed, his noble kingdom shattered. In the West, the story of the hero tends to be tragic.

> *"When the best leader's work is done, the people say, "We did it ourselves.""*
>
> —Lao-tzu

If heroes lose their power, a possible compensation is that their death is usually glorious and their former greatness acknowledged. When Oedipus, who blinded himself so that he might never again look upon his misbegotten children, says, "I am the unclean one who has defiled this land" and makes his way to exile in the desert, the chorus asks the fearful question: Why does this happen? Why is Oedipus guilty of patricide and incest when he was doomed by a prophecy to perform these deeds? Why not blame the gods for his unkind fate? Yet in accepting full responsibility for his deeds, he retains his noble status. In Sophocles's play, the doomed hero walks *unbowed* from the city. The grieving citizens make a respectful path for him. A vast presence is departing, and he will be mourned for many years to come. In a sequel to the play called *Oedipus at Colonus,* the hero, nearing the end of his life, is suddenly visited by a brilliant light that he somehow is able to see, though still blind, and within which the mystery of human suffering is made clear to him, if not to us.

Great heroes fail, but their failures only testify to the bigness of their lives. It's almost as though mythology is saying "You can't have it both ways. You are either uncelebrated but perhaps content, or you take the risk of greatness, knowing that it doesn't last."

Recognition of the hero's nobility is seldom there during his lifetime. In fact, there is sometimes outright hostility toward him. Before he undergoes a violent death, Theseus is blamed by his once loyal subjects for the Spartan invasion of Athens at a time when he was gone from the kingdom. They even drive him out of the city, forcing him to seek the hospitality of the rival king who eventually kills him. But later the citizens realize the mistake they have made and erect an enormous tomb to honor his memory.

The history of Western civilization has recorded many instances of actual heroes, rejected or highly controversial during their lifetime but revered after death: Joan of Arc, Galileo, John F. Kennedy, to name a few. The Irish playwright George Bernard Shaw (discussed in Chapter 7) ends his play *Saint Joan* on a note of irony as church officials regret having burned Joan at the stake. To their surprise she suddenly appears, telling them that since she is now a spirit, she is free to come and go as she wishes. If they *truly* want her to come back, she has the power to do so. Whereupon, they turn away and leave the stage. Alone, Joan looks upward and speaks the final lines of the play: "O Lord who madest this beautiful earth, when will it be ready to receive thy saints? How long, O Lord, how long?" Perhaps the appeal of this myth is that, though we may have secret feelings of unworth, the fallen hero (or disgraced politician or celebrity) is no better off.

The Hero in Non-Western Mythology. Asian and Mideastern mythology have their hero stories, but they seldom concern the exploits of a singular mortal who is to be revered and celebrated to the exclusion of ordinary human beings. The Buddha himself (by birth a prince named Siddhartha) achieved great humility, never sought power, and discouraged his followers from looking upon him as a deity of some sort.

Joseph Campbell has pointed out that whereas

> *the typical Occidental hero is a personality, and . . . necessarily tragic . . . the Oriental hero is the monad [a simple indivisible unit]: in essence without character . . . untouched by . . . the delusory involvements of the mortal sphere. And just as in the West the orientation to personality is reflected in the concept and experience even of God as a personality, so in the Orient, in perfect contrast, the overpowering sense of an . . . impersonal law . . . harmonizing all things reduces to a mere blot the accident of an individual life.*[4]

Judaic and Islamic traditions contain many stories of Moses and Mohammed, respectively, and their feats of leadership, but both prophets are regarded as spiritual forces, not as mighty conquerors. Before his death Moses asked that his burial site be concealed so that no elaborate memorial could be built in his memory. The Islamic laws taught by Mohammed assume "the brotherhood of man . . . [the] equality of all believers . . . and absolute submission to the will of God [Allah]."[5]

In Chinese mythology great dynastic rulers are cited for their virtue and their social achievements, such as in the case of Huang Ti, the so-called "Yellow Emperor" who made agriculture possible and encouraged the development of a musical scale. He is celebrated for having driven out the barbarians, but his success came not from his unique superhuman valor but from the help of the gods, who looked with favor on his virtuous character. Confucius occupied himself not with metaphysical beliefs about the spirit behind the universe but with practical advice for those who would rule: Walk the straight and narrow and live for the good of society. In Western mythology, King Arthur comes close to the Confucian ideal, but he was also a brave warrior of consummate fighting skill and would have been less revered if he had not been. He certainly meets the Western "requirement" that the hero be a singular individual capable of astonishing physical feats.

> *"Dreams are private myths. Myths are public dreams."*
>
> **—Joseph Campbell**

The Special Someone. The archetype of the hero is still very much with us. Celebrities, today's demigods and demigoddesses, may not be the literal progeny of deities and mortals, but they are as vivid in the public mind as their bygone counterparts. Their exploits are followed in magazines, gossip columns, and television interviews, and they set the trend in clothes, hairdos, and language.

There are still those who perform Herculean tasks and win admiration: the new home-run king; the world's fastest runner; the first astronauts in space; the first woman to walk the length of Tibet on foot; the first blind climber to reach the top of Everest; actors who receive Oscars for their first screen roles; and Nobel-prize winners, often unknown before their achievements catapult them to celebrity status.

We keep looking for that special someone who solves all problems. The archetype of the mysterious stranger has been important in American mythology because of the early dangers encountered in settling so vast a land and the democratic structure of frontier societies in which leaders were not born into their roles but had to prove themselves.

> *"Heroes are people who rise to the occasion and slip quietly away."*
>
> **—Tom Brokaw**

A classic example of the "special someone" myth can be found in George Stevens's 1952 film version of Max Brand's popular Western novel *Shane*. The film (still available on DVD and television) features a retired gunfighter who rides out of the Wyoming hills on a white horse, rescues a group of peaceful farmers from the lawless cattlemen intent on driving them off their land, shoots the leader of the bad guys, and then rides back into the misty land of his origin.

Today, we continue to wait for the special person, such as the politician with no ties to lobbyists who will stand up for the right and the just regardless of what they might mean for a political future; who will finally be able to make all the industrial nations of the world understand that they cannot keep sending carbon atoms into the air; and who will "fix" ailing economies by convincing special interest groups that there is more to life than making as much money as they possibly can.

Archetypal special people have always been males in the past, perhaps because the humanities have a long history dominated by mythmakers who were not women. Females abound in myth history, but (as we shall see further on in this chapter) they have so often been portrayed (by men) as the troublemakers of this world. But just as mythology continues to be created, its heroes have been appearing in both genders.

Movies and TV shows are, of course, rich sources of myth. Weapon-brandishing women exist on equal terms with men and kill monsters with the best of them: think Sigourney Weaver in the *Alien* trilogy and Angelina Jolie in the *Tomb Raider* films. In both the film and television series *Charlie's Angels,* three fearless women chase crooks at the speed of light. The Chinese film *Crouching Tiger, Hidden Dragon* (2000) featured a beautiful heroine who was almost supernaturally adept at the martial arts and could even fly. Shu Lien became a worthy successor to the popular but once exclusively male traditions of kung fu and karate.

The Power of Words

One interpretation of word significance is male jealousy over female reproductive powers. In myth, the power of the uttered word could be supreme. Men could talk. Perhaps that is why men have traditionally insisted on having the last word.

Language of a special kind is another recurrent archetype. "In the beginning was the Word" begins the Gospel of John. "It is written . . ." is found in speech the world over to represent absolute authority. Cultural anthropologists theorize that our male ancestors, in jealous awe of women's reproductive powers, believed that language was literally manmade and that words uttered by men were more miraculous than birth itself. In early cultures, when birth was considered a magical event, men may well have sought ways to match or even surpass this phenomenon in which they seemed to play so small a part. In many myths the male hero is able to move heaven and earth because he knows secret words. Perhaps this myth helps explain the right that men have exercised: having the last say in all matters.

The words "Open sesame!" yielded wonders for Ali Baba, even as *Sesame Street* serves as a modern archetype—the thoroughfare that takes children from ignorance to knowledge through the magic of letters and the fantasy creatures that attend them. Rumpelstiltskin was an elf whose magic name had to be guessed to save the queen's firstborn child. And unless you are told "Simon says," you may not imitate the leader. A sneeze still receives the blessing of "Gesundheit!" from well-wishers. When two people happen to say the same thing at the same time, one immediately exclaims "Jinx! You owe me a Coke!" (the fee varies geographically). Presumably, bad luck will attend those who fail to carry out the verbal ritual.

For thousands of years the world of human affairs has counted on the reliability of someone's word, as when a pact is made over a handshake and the inevitable "I give you my word" is uttered. There are still places in which insisting upon a written contract instead of accepting a spoken promise is greeted with suspicion and hostility. Most of us have yet to dismiss as insignificant the giving of our word, or to minimize the disappointment when others break theirs. In fact, *break* is an interesting verb to use in conjunction with *word,* is it not? In myth, a broken magic wand can be disastrous.

Yoshikazu Tsuno/Getty Images

Scene from *Sesame Street*, 1969–present

Sesame Street is the long-running television program that shows children the magic of words.

The Power of Numbers

The belief in the magic of words is closely associated with the magic of numbers. Humanity long ago discovered that numerical units were basic to the design of both the earthly and the heavenly universe. In *The Divine Comedy,* Dante makes abundant use of the number 3 representing the Trinity. The poem is divided into three parts—*Inferno, Purgatory,* and *Paradise.* The last two parts contain 33 cantos, or chapters, corresponding to the age at which Jesus died; the first part has one extra canto to bring the total to what was considered the perfect number, 100.

In Hebrew tradition there are also mystic numbers. The letters of the Hebrew alphabet have number equivalents, and certain combinations of numbers are believed by some to hold the secrets of the universe. A school of Hebrew mysticism called Kabbalah studies the numerical complexities of Hebrew scripture. For example, some scholars have determined that there are 620, not just 10, commandments: 613 that were present in the five books attributed to Moses and seven that were added later by rabbis. Not by coincidence, these scholars observe, is the fact that the Ten Commandments contain 620 letters.

When the 999th person jumped off the Golden Gate Bridge, the authorities quickly announced that a mythical 1,000th had followed suit right away.

People still have mystic feelings about numbers and sequences, expecting, for example, that the news of two deaths will lead inevitably to news of another. The Golden Gate Bridge in San Francisco was a popular place for suicides, and, when authorities discovered that the nine hundred ninety-ninth person had leaped to a watery grave, they quickly announced the thousanth suicide as having already occurred, gave the person a fictitious name and occupation, and said services would be private. They knew all too well that a real thousandth would have shown up in no time at all—so powerful can numbers be.

The Circle

The circle is an archetype that affects our lives profoundly. Because the circle is an unbroken line without beginning or end that encloses a uniform space, people have used it to symbolize oneness, completeness, and eternity. In myth, it appears as a shield, a ring, a pendant, the sun, and the moon, as well as in markings on cave walls or on stones. Countless circular structures, some dating back many millennia, are found throughout the world: temples, stone circles, and, of course, that most intriguing of all ancient monuments, Stonehenge, a large circle of heavy stones on Salisbury Plain in southwest England, once thought to have been a place of human sacrifice, but now known to have almost certainly been the means of identifying the seasons of the year by the changing positions of the sun. A group of scientists waited all night on the eve of the summer solstice and were delighted when the sun's rays did indeed shine directly through the front portal. For mythologists, Stonehenge reinforces the myth that the universe is a finite circle.

Eastern and Western minds apparently came to similar conclusions about the universe. Both decided on the circular, geometrically perfect shape, which made the universe seem somehow *manageable*—that is, within the scope of human comprehension, if not control. Contemporary science continues to debate the

Laurence Delderfield/Shutterstock

Stonehenge, England, c. 2,500 B.C.E.

Science notwithstanding, Stonehenge continues to reinforce the myth that the universe is a finite circle, a myth that seems to be preferable to a belief in infinity.

> *Tomorrow, and tomorrow, and tomorrow,*
> *Creeps in this petty pace from day to day,*
> *To the last syllable of recorded time;*
> *And all our yesterdays have lighted fools*
> *The way to dusty death.*
>
> **—William Shakespeare**

> *. . . the idea of a universe existing without a Creator seems just as far-fetched as the idea that God created it, especially when you look up at the stars at night. We know they weren't always there. You can trace everything back to the Big Bang, but where did the ingredients for the Big Bang come from?*
>
> **—David Lodge**

nature and extent of the universe and indeed whether "circle" does or does not really apply. Is it a random collection of planets and suns formed in the aftermath of an original explosion? Does it extend infinitely? Yet, at the same time, physicists continue to seek uniformity in physical laws. Einstein's general theory of relativity maintains that space is both infinite and *curved* and that gravity so warps space that no object can travel in a straight line forever.

For the East the circle has traditionally been an appropriate symbol of the order behind *nature*. The *yin* and *yang* of Taoist philosophy, which represent the attraction of opposite forces that keep the universe in balance, are artistically depicted as a black and white circle. (See Chapter 10 for more on Taoism.) In Western views, the human mind is often seen as a self-contained circle. In Eastern views, consciousness is like a flowing river; thoughts and feelings come and go. The Western idea of the personal ego as a walled city is a strange concept to the traditional Eastern mind.

At the same time, for the East the circle is a symbol of the oneness of nature and the living beings who inhabit it. In the West the vocabulary of circles is often narrowly related to self. We have "holistic" medicine that treats the "whole person." When we feel unsure of where we want to go with our lives, we speak of trying to "get it together," and if we feel that we are losing control, friends might offer to help us "pick up the pieces."

Except for different images of the mind, East and West seem to have always liked the idea that everything makes sense; the circle does not suggest chaos. Universal humanity does not want to think of itself as adrift and abandoned, an existence that cannot be comprehended.

The circle also represents immortality. The Hindu and Buddhist concepts of reincarnation and the cycles of existence, shared by many Westerners, are obvious examples. What is the belief in an afterlife, found the world over, but the concept that existence has no end—like a circle?

The Journey

One of the major archetypes in Western mythology offers a noncircular view of the meaning of existence. The difficult journey is another way of depicting the course of human life. Life-as-a-journey implies both purpose and a final destination as opposed to a random series of disconnected happenings. We think of life as moving from one stage or "phase" to another; again, this implies that we can make sense of life.

The mythic hero usually sets out on a journey fraught with danger and has a challenging task that must be performed at the conclusion. Fearful obstacles usually threaten the hero as he goes: dense, maze-like forests; dangerous beasts; and magical potions that induce slumber and prevent motion. But sooner or later, the journey continues.

Our expectations thus formed by the myth, we look for progress in our own lives and in those of others. We expect the obstacles. We say, "No pain, no gain." We are sure the journey will prove worth the effort. Accomplishing the big task will mean recognition and approval. When others seem not to succeed in their journey, we say, "He is stuck in adolescence" or "She's still at the same old job!"

The mythical journey is also a quest. The hero searches for his homeland, a buried treasure, the Holy Grail. Attainment of the goal gives shape and purpose to life; and here we note a conflict in the two key symbols. Whereas the circle guarantees life without end, the journey is supposed to yield important results. We don't mind applying the circle to universal order or to the shape of the mind as a self-contained whole, but we resist thinking of life as just one thing after another without purpose, without direction. We hate to think of ourselves as "going around in circles." We like to think that, regardless of life's continual changes, its ups and downs (there are always mythical mountains to cross), life *does* come to something after all.

Life as a journey implies both purpose and a final destination, as opposed to a random series of disconnected happenings.

The journey in Eastern mythology is a series of happenings, not necessarily in a sequence and without a necessary final task. In the myth of Bodhidharma, the monk who supposedly brought Buddhism from India to China, the hero stops to meditate on a mountaintop for nine years, during which his legs fall off. But the story merely points out that this is what occurred; it does not call it a tragedy. For the East, life is indeed one thing after another, and each day has to be accepted for what it is. For the West, a journey without a successful destination is worthless. "She died before her time" is a Western mythic observation. So is "Here he is, thirty-five years old, and what has he done with his life?"

The Garden

In the West, as we have said, journeys are supposed to have successful destinations, but related myths question these destinations—myths that say we are heading down the "wrong path" and myths that look back to the past and say "Would that we had never embarked on this journey; we have lost too much."

Myths of a Golden Age, when things were better, extend far back in the Western tradition. In fact, the usual downfall of the hero implies that what was once good is now gone. With the death of King Arthur went all hope of another Camelot. Many myth scholars believe that the archetype of the Golden Age had its origins in the biblical account of the Garden, the earthly paradise Adam and Eve called home until they were cast out for eating the forbidden fruit from the Tree of Knowledge.

The Hebrew Bible also contains a countermyth with a countersymbol to the Garden. Adam and Eve are expelled from *their* Garden, but Abraham and his descendants are offered the hope for a Promised Land, Canaan, the fertile land of milk and honey. Moses leads the Children of Israel out of captivity in Egypt, but he does not live to reach his destination. His followers, however, find that Canaan is anything but a joyful paradise where they can live happily ever after. It is constantly attacked, conquered, and occupied. Yet the promise made by God to Abraham projects the Garden into the future. The Golden Age has yet to come, but come it will.

In the eighteenth century, writers in Europe and America revived the Garden myth as they mourned the shift from rural to urban living. They lamented the wretched lives of the urban poor, densely packed into crime-ridden, filthy slums. The teeming cities represented for these writers the antithesis of the Garden, and they celebrated the unspoiled countryside and the happy, unschooled innocents who lived there, uncorrupted by the greed and arrogance of cosmopolitan life. Literature and drama began to cast their eyes far afield, imagining the paradise of remote lands, where the sun shines warmly all year long, food is abundant, and inhabitants live in perpetual harmony.

"Ah happy hills, pleasing shade,
Ah fields beloved in vain
Where once my careless childhood strayed,
A stranger yet to pain!"

—Thomas Gray

This literary movement was inspired by the philosophy of *primitivism*, which held that those who lived far from cities in what was called the "state of nature" were happier, less apt to commit crime, and more willing to share the fruits of the land than their educated and wealthier counterparts. The key spokesperson for primitivism was the French philosopher Jean-Jacques Rousseau (1712–1768), whose contributions to the idea of freedom are discussed in the final chapter of this book. For now, we need to know that Rousseau restated the myth of the Garden, blaming government and social controls, both products of so-called civilization, for the corruption of humanity. In doing so, he created the archetype of the *noble savage* who is untutored but astute in the ways of nature, infinitely resourceful, and able to provide food and shelter for his family.

"I am pessimistic about the human race because it is too ingenious for its own good. Our approach to nature is to beat it into submission. We would stand a better chance of survival if we accommodated ourselves to the planet . . ."

—E. B. White

Primitivism led to the popularity on the stage and in fiction of this new mythic figure. In England, the "man Friday" of Daniel Defoe's Robinson Crusoe was far more adept at living without the comforts of civilization than the shipwrecked British gentleman who depends on him for survival. In America, Mark Twain (1835–1910) created Huck Finn and his wonderful raft and sent them floating down the Mississippi River, portraying a way of life representing a perpetual escape from civilization, its moral codes, its social demands, and its unhappy inhabitants. Sir James M. Barrie gave the world Peter Pan, who eludes the aging process and lives a boy's carefree existence in Never-Never Land. In our time, Steven Spielberg provided E.T., the extraterrestrial, an adorable, unspoiled being from outer space who manages to escape the clutches of humanity, which is—except for one tender and understanding little boy—unworthy of his purity. He waits somewhere "up there" for a true believer who will find a way out of the mess we humans have made of the once beautiful earth.

The "discovery" of America in 1492 gave rise to a new version of the Garden archetype—the New World—which continues to influence us today. First came the explorers, proudly planting their nations' flags on the "virgin" soil (while Native Americans watched). Then came boatloads of pilgrims seeking a new start in life. Then by the thousands came immigrants seeking prosperity in streets supposedly paved with gold. As the eastern half of the United States became densely populated and the dream of prosperity gave way to the reality of long hours of work and crowded tenements, the archetype of the Garden was moved out to the frontier, the wide-open West. Pioneers left their homes by the thousands, seeking a new Canaan. Some prospered, many did not. The promise of the New World still holds out hope for millions throughout the globe.

When they come to the promised land, modern immigrants, like their predecessors, bring with them a strong archetype—the family—as well as the customs, traditional beliefs, and rituals that hold families together. Sometimes the newcomers are received with enthusiasm, and sometimes they are rejected. Often members of the younger generation drift away, become part of the new culture. The elders sometimes intensify the traditional rituals, hold even more tightly to their customs, close themselves in for fear of losing their identity, self-respect, dignity. Disenchanted by the New World, they remember their old country, where things were better, where people were nicer, and the streets safer. Like Dorothy in the Land of Oz, they discover that maybe their original home wasn't so bad after all. The Garden always seems to be somewhere else. But if this archetype can cause disillusionment, it can also be the source of hope.

Gods as Human Beings

As an archetype the Greek god is written about and depicted in statuary as a larger-than-life mortal. Unlike most other early cultures, the Greeks had ambivalent feelings about their deities. They feared them because of their enormous power and because they could be unpredictable (the gods could strike down anyone they chose, at any time, and for any reason), and they also resented them. The

Greeks believed that nothing in the universe was as important as human beings. If there were to be gods, they must be made in the image of humanity (not the other way around as in Judaism, Christianity, and Islam).

In humanizing their gods, the Greeks in effect deified themselves.

The archetypal term "Greek god," describing a very handsome man, usually refers to Apollo, who was always portrayed as the epitome of physical perfection and whose name itself has become an archetype of male beauty. "Greek goddess" (or often just "goddess"), describing a woman of surpassing beauty, usually means Aphrodite or the Roman Venus. Despite the fact that we don't run into an Apollo or a Venus every day, the enduring myth is that such physical perfection, though godlike, *is* attainable by certain mortals.

Otherwise, the Greek deities were thought of as residing on Mount Olympus, which is a very real place, in much the same way that our own deities live high up in the Hollywood Hills or on the slopes of Aspen or along the Grande Corniche, the topmost road on the French Riviera and home to the wealthy (*and* "beautiful") people of this world. Zeus and Hera, the king and queen of the other deities, were married celebrities who held grudges against each other and fought bitterly. Many human woes were ascribed to the fact that Zeus and Hera were often on opposite sides in a war, each plotting against the other. *In humanizing their gods, the Greeks in effect deified themselves!*

Myth as Explanation

Mythology consists of much more than the archetypes that shape the way we interpret our world and what happens to us in it. For our ancestors two major aspects of being alive must have been very baffling. One was the mystery of natural phenomena. The other was how to account for all the trouble that seemed to be part of life. Mythology was their way of understanding the mystery of the universe and the pain and hardships of living in it.

If science had been at the disposal of our ancestors on either side of the world, they might have turned away from mythmaking in favor of observation and experimentation. Lacking science, they created stories to account for what they could not otherwise explain. We should be grateful that they did, for these ancient stories, along with the music and dances that must surely have accompanied group ceremonies, became the foundation on which the humanities now rest securely. The myths they wove made the natural world and its amazing phenomena seem less remote and frightening and helped remove the fear that life was innately evil, that bad things happened without cause.

"The sad thing is that most evil is done by people who never make up their minds to be good or evil."

—Hannah Arendt

The need for acceptable explanations for life's tragedies remains with the humanities. Often these explanations are at odds with scientific evidence. For example, in 1927 the American author Thornton Wilder, most well known for his innovative play *Our Town,* published the novel *The Bridge of San Luis Rey.*

The novel is about a footbridge built across a steep gorge in the Andes Mountains of Peru. Thousands had traveled across it for years, but on this particular day the bridge collapses and five unsuspecting travelers are suddenly hurled to their deaths. The novel then presents the story of each victim and poses the question, "Why this person?" Although scientific explanations are abundant, the author prefers to leave the door open for the possibility that divine intervention was responsible. Is it more comforting to believe everything happens for a reason instead of believing that life is a series of random, senseless occurrences? Our ancestors must have thought so and may have left explanatory myths as their legacy to us.

Creation

Even the greatest scientists have wrestled with the agonizing questions Why is there something when there might have been nothing? Is there an essential principle that requires existence to exist? Or did it spring accidentally from nothing? And if so, how and why? Why are *we* here? Why haven't we discovered intelligent life anywhere else in the universe—at least so far? Mythology supplies a number of different answers, and the quest continues.

One creation myth recounted in the *Upanishads* sacred books of India says: At first he was lonely and afraid but, above all, he "lacked delight (therefore, we lack delight when alone) and desired a second. . . . This Self then split into two parts; and with that, there were a master and a mistress."[6] But this first woman was afraid to be touched and so hid from her male Self. She turned into various animals, but he pursued her and mated with each of her manifestations until the natural world, as we know it, was formed.

The story does not explain where the Self came from, but once that is accepted, everything else follows in a cause-and-effect sequence.

Most Asian mythologies have no clearcut story of creation. The Buddhist Dharma constitutes the orderly principle that guides the universe, which had no beginning; therefore the natural world, which is the outer garment of this order, must have always existed. Confucianism, a major Chinese philosophy, stresses the social world and one's duties within it and avoids the question of how it began, which does not matter as much as how life is lived.

In a Taoist creation myth, the operation of the universe depends on the attraction of opposites—prophetic of the modern electromagnetic theory of nature.

In another major Chinese philosophy, Taoism (DOW-ism), we find a creation story that resembles those of non-Asian cultures, giving further credence to Jung's theory that early cultures developed similar myths without traceable communication with each other. In this story, the universe, as it is in the Hebrew Bible, was at first a dark formless void. Within this void a single egg came into being inside of which was the fetus of what would eventually become the giant Pan-Gu. After attaining colossal size, Pan-Gu stretched his arms; the egg broke and the lighter half floated upward to become the sky while the heavier part sank downward to become the earth. Ever since, the operation of the universe has depended on the attraction of opposites—astonishingly prophetic of the modern electromagnetic theory of nature!

In Greek mythology, pre-creation is depicted in a similar fashion. It is called the "formless confusion of Chaos" existing only in darkness. Chaos in some mysterious way gave birth to children: one was Gaea, or Mother Earth. Others were Night and Erebus, or Death. Night placed an egg in the depths of Erebus, and from it was born Love (though we are not sure how this love was defined). Love's first act was to create Light and Day.

Greek myths tell us that the gods came after the creation, but this order is not surprising when we consider that in the Greek myths the power of Fate appears to be greater than that of the gods. For the Greeks, the power of Fate always existed, was responsible for the coming of Night and Death, and must therefore be reckoned as *the* divine force.[7]

According to an Aztec myth, before the universe was formed there were gods. A fight developed over who would create which part of the world. Eventually a snake divided in half—one half to create the upper part, the other half to create the lower part. The half that created the earth felt she was less important and began to quarrel with the half that made the heavens. As compensation for her inferior position, the gods added to her importance by allowing different parts of her body to be the source of important elements—the rivers and streams coming from her eyes, for instance.

Many other cultures attribute the origin of the natural world to a divinity that preceded its existence. Judaism, Christianity, and Islam share a common belief that the world was brought into existence by an all-powerful and singular creator. Working within this tradition, the English poet John Milton (1608–1674) in his epic poem *Paradise Lost* assumes the preexistence of both God and a chaotic universe which was transformed into the orderly cosmos the poet knew. According to Milton's interpretation, in the beginning there was

the vast immeasurable Abyss,
Outrageous as a Sea, dark, wasteful, wild,
Up from the bottom turn'd by furious winds
And surging waves, as Mountains to assault
Heav'n's highth, and with the centre mix the Pole.
Silence, ye troubl'd waves, and thou Deep, peace,
Said then th'Omnific Word, your discord end.[8]

In the modern world, a debate continues between those who believe the universe had no known beginning and those who believe it cannot have always existed. Modern science is deeply committed to the law of cause and effect, yet when it comes to the question of whether there was a *first* cause, a deep division of opinion remains. The theory that the origins of the universe can be traced to a big bang, a huge explosion of a single particle, is widely held. Once this explanation is accepted, the theory manages to explain all that followed. But where, some ask, did the single particle come from? One answer has been that it came from nothing, but that we need not assume that "nothing" is necessarily empty.

It is interesting to note that one of the crucial unsolved questions is remarkably similar to those asked by our earliest ancestors.

The Natural World

That remarkable stone circle on the Salisbury Plain in southwestern England, Stonehenge, was erected, as we pointed out earlier in the chapter, as a means of predicting the seasons according to the position of the sun with respect to the stones at various times of the year. Yet Stonehenge could not explain why there *were* seasons. Why was it not always summer? Why the bitter cold, when people could freeze to death and food was scarce? Nature was surely something to inspire wonder, apprehension, and worship. Many early myths sought to explain nature, and early rituals—ceremonial dances as well as animal and human sacrifice—were efforts to control it.

> *"Every part of the earth is sacred to my people. Every single pine needle, every sandy shore, every mist in the dark woods, every meadow, every humming insect. All are holy in the memory and experience of my people."*
>
> **—Chief Seattle**

In Scandinavian communities, for example, the fertility deity was Freyr, who was thought to bring rich harvests to the earth. He did so by wooing a maiden, symbolizing the union of earth and sky. Rituals that honored Freyr and the abundance he gave were, Scandinavians thought, essential to survival. In almost all early cultures help from the gods was needed if crops should fail or were insufficient. If the weather did not cooperate, food could be found in the sea if the storm god could be appeased.

In Greek mythology, Apollo, the sun god, drove his chariot across the sky each day, thus accounting for the rising and setting of the sun, just as Apollo's sister Artemis presided over the moon at night. The king of the gods, Zeus, was responsible for hurling thunderbolts, and Poseidon controlled the sea. But these activities could be altered at the whim of the gods. Thus the sea might be made so calm that no ships could move when Poseidon wished to punish a fleet that failed to honor him. Or a sea monster might appear, sent by Poseidon in response to the prayer of a mortal as when Theseus prayed for the destruction of his son, who he believed had committed adultery with his stepmother.

Early peoples performed what was called "sympathetic magic," the acting out of ceremonies designed to affect the behavior of the gods. Thus people terrified by the darkness of the winter solstice, the longest night of the year, in countries throughout the world attempted to evoke the return of the sun through the lighting of candles, as if the sun—or the powers in charge of light—would imitate the lesser light below.

A Greek explanation for the seasons was the love of Demeter, goddess of the earth, for her daughter Persephone. So joyful was Demeter at the very thought of her daughter, that when Persephone was near, Demeter provided people with a superabundance of all the good things the earth could yield. One day, however, the girl was glimpsed by Hades, lord of the underworld, who captured her and took her to be his bride. Demeter so mourned her loss that the earth came to be covered with the ice and snow of perpetual winter.

If Zeus had not intervened, all human life would have ended, but he was so touched by Demeter's grief that he arranged for Persephone to live with her mother for all but four months out of the year; those she owed to her husband. That is why when Persephone is in the underworld the earth freezes over and when she returns her happy mother allows the earth once again to bloom.

> *"What more natural than if a beautiful boy had thus been killed, than to think when later the ground blossomed with Narcissus or hyacinths that the flowers were his very self?"*
>
> **—Edith Hamilton**

Another explanation occurs in the myth of Dionysus, the male deity who governed the abundance of the earth. Winter came about because he died and, in the underworld, was torn to pieces and eaten. Still, when he was somehow resurrected and became whole again, spring returned—but only temporarily. Each year Dionysus meets his terrible fate again.

The descent into the underworld of both Persephone and Dionysus can be regarded as sacrifices that ensured rebirth. This idea, that without sorrow or death there can be no springtime joy, was an early belief that has captured the minds of writers and philosophers ever since.

For the Greeks, vegetation could be connected to the involvement of gods with beautiful mortals. The blooms of the hyacinth and the narcissus celebrated the transformation of their namesakes from death to eternal life in nature. Hyacinthus was a beautiful young mortal dearly loved by Apollo, who was accidentally killed by him while they were playing a game of discus throwing. (Note that once again the Greeks attributed human failings to their gods.) Apollo then had the dead body transformed into the hyacinth.

Mythologist Edith Hamilton interprets such transformation stories in a somewhat ominous way. They are, she speculates, vestiges of ancient human sacrifice rather than of accidental death. Ancient people sometimes selected a number of handsome young people for sacrificial rituals designed to appease the gods. According to Hamilton, when the Greeks told their myths in later years, they revised the stories to rid themselves of this violent era in their past:

> *It might happen, if the fields around a village were not fruitful, if the corn did not spring up as it should, that one of the villagers would be killed and his—or her—blood sprinkled over the barren land. . . . What could be more natural then, if a beautiful boy had thus been killed, than to think when later the ground blossomed with narcissus or hyacinths that the flowers were his very self, changed and*

yet living again? So they would tell each other it had happened, a lovely miracle which made the cruel death seem less cruel.[9]

The sacrifice of animals was probably performed each year at the spring festivals honoring Dionysus to ensure the god's return and the renewal of the growing season. At the drama festivals, when the tragic protagonist fell from his high position he became a kind of symbolic sacrifice so order could return to the state.

From what is now Ghana in West Africa comes a story of how the country flourished and was prosperous because each year a beautiful girl was given to a devouring serpent. One year, however, when the girl was led to the pit where the serpent waited, rescue came in the form of a brave young man engaged to marry her. He stood by while the serpent appeared and twice spat venom on the girl because he knew that only on the third try could the reptile be destroyed. At the appropriate moment, the young man beheaded the serpent only to find that it kept growing new heads—seven in all. The girl was saved, but the serpent had its revenge. As the last head was cut off, it flew away, saying, "For seven years, seven months, and seven days, Ghana will receive neither water nor rains of gold." A drought ensued, destroying the populace and a once-great empire. In this myth we do not find the cycle motif of the Persephone and Dionysus stories but rather an unhappy explanation for a catastrophe that must have actually taken place.

In Native American mythology, human sacrifice was needed in order to make the heavens work properly. After four worlds that had not worked, a fifth world was revealed, but it was discovered that the sun and moon could be set in their courses only by the death of a Navajo each day and another each night. Later, when human beings claimed credit for the prosperity of the world, they were punished by plagues and monsters.

Human Suffering

Sometimes known as the *problem of evil,* suffering caused by natural catastrophes (such as the devastating tsunami of 2004 that took more than 200,000 lives in southeast Asia) and by the inhumanity of regimes such as that of the Nazis in the early twentieth century has been and continues to be analyzed by philosophers, theologians, and writers. Our ancestors asked the same questions we hear now. Why are some people consumed with hatred, envy, and greed? Why are there famines, plagues, and wars? Like many contemporaries, they wanted to believe there were reasons for the suffering people had to endure. The idea that terrible things happened without cause was unacceptable because it suggested a universe ruled by chaos, a universe in which humankind was powerless. In creating stories that explained suffering, our ancestors were able to reassure themselves that order did indeed prevail in the universe and that if they acted in an appropriate manner, they might escape misfortune.

> *"Evil enters like a needle and spreads like an oak tree."*
>
> **—Ethiopian proverb**

A common explanation for suffering was an early act of transgression against divine law: offending a god or disobeying a command. The Greek myth of Pandora explains how human misfortune came about because of a woman's curiosity. Beloved by Zeus, Pandora was given a magical box in which all of the other gods had placed something she is not to know. Frustrated by the gnawing desire to discover what treasures were concealed inside the box, she disobeys Zeus and opens the box, out of which fly death, sorrow, plagues, war, and every other calamity visited upon mortals ever since. Alarmed, Pandora slams the box shut, not knowing that trapped inside was the gift of hope.

In the Judeo-Christian tradition, God commands Adam and Eve not to eat the forbidden fruit growing on the Tree of Knowledge. (The fruit, often depicted as an apple, is not identified in Genesis, and apples are not native to the Middle East.) Tempted by the serpent, Eve eats the fruit, and Adam does the same. Genesis does not say that Eve prevailed upon Adam to follow her into sin, though later versions turned the story into a myth of woman's weakness. In Milton's *Paradise Lost,* God judges Adam more harshly than he does Eve because, even though Eve has sinned first, Adam, being a man, should have known better.

In an African myth of the Burundi tribe, a woman is again blamed for bringing about human suffering. At first, human beings are not touched by Death because divine dogs protect them. One day Death approaches a woman and promises to give her and her family special protection. When the woman opens her mouth to speak, Death jumps in. Questioned by the chief of the gods concerning the whereabouts of Death, the woman lies and says she has not seen him. The chief of the gods, being all-mighty and all-knowing, recognizes that the woman is lying and allows Death to dwell inside the woman and all of her descendants.

According to another tale found in the oral tradition of many African cultures, Kintu, the first man, and his wife Nambi are hurrying to leave the land of the sky in order to flee Death. They have been warned not to delay their escape, but Nambi decides to go back for grain. Death follows her as she attempts to rejoin her husband. As a result, death becomes the punishment for all future generations, a motif notably similar to that found in Genesis.

A legend found in Mexico and Central and South America is that of *La Llorona* ("The Weeping Woman"). So popular is this figure in oral storytelling that numerous versions of her persist. In one version, she is a phantom, never seen, but heard weeping at night, mourning her children, for whose deaths she is responsible. In another version, she is a spirit doomed to wander forever in search of the children she neglected during her lifetime. Still another version shows her to be blatantly evil, a woman who lures men to follow her only to suffer violent death. In this telling, the woman resembles the Sirens of Greek mythology, the sea maidens whose seductive singing lures sailors to their doom, and the Lorelei of Germanic lore, a lovely maiden who sits on a rock, combing her hair and singing so beautifully that sailors wreck their ships trying to reach her.

"Don't go backwards; you have already been there."
—Ray Charles

The La Llorona tales are often told as a warning to unmarried pregnant girls who, finding themselves abandoned, have no recourse but to give up their babies. Presumably, repeating the story of a mother mourning her lost children reminds young girls of what can happen when they indulge in practices forbidden by religion and family.[10]

The tragic results of curiosity and disobedience are also found in two other famous myths, one from the Greeks and the other from the Hebrew Bible. Both illustrate a universal belief that some things are better left unknown. In the Greek myth, an extraordinary musician named Orpheus, later the subject of the operas we discuss in Chapter 8, is in love with the beautiful Eurydice, who dies and is taken to the underworld. Orpheus follows her down and uses the gorgeous strains of his lute to convince the king of the underworld that Eurydice should be returned to the land of the living. His request is granted, with one condition: Orpheus must walk straight up the path without turning around to make sure that Eurydice is following. He almost keeps the pact, but at the last minute, unable to bear the suspense, he turns around, only to see his beloved being reclaimed by the powers of darkness, lost to him forever.

The prizewinning 1959 Brazilian film *Black Orpheus*, set during the night of Carnivale in Rio de Janeiro, tells essentially the same tale. A figure wearing the mask of death pursues the modern Eurydice through a crowded street, finally seizing her and carrying her into an empty building and down an endless spiral staircase. The modern Orpheus follows them, but instead of being given the chance to return to life with her, he dies also. The morning finds the two lovers, together, impaled on the sharp spikes of an aloe plant. In this modern retelling, death is not the result of curiosity or disobedience, but—more tragically—something that occurs without any purpose at all.

The story continues to fascinate writers and public alike. In 2000 there was Mary Zimmerman's fanciful stage adaptation of the Roman Ovid's *Metamorphoses*, itself an updating of Greek myths. Eurydice is now a modern, liberated woman who decides she is *not* going to follow meekly behind her lord and master, Orpheus. She pays the price, but the assumption is that her independence is worth it.

In a biblical tale, Lot and his family are allowed to escape the destruction of Sodom and Gomorrah, with one condition—that they flee the city without turning around to see what is happening. Lot's wife, however, cannot resist the temptation, and when she turns around, she is transformed into a pillar of salt.

The traditions of the East do not speak of human suffering as caused by disobedience to a divine command; rather, they blame selfish acts by individuals for the world's ills. In Hindu belief, what happens to a person is the result of *karma* (see Chapter 10 for a fuller discussion), a summation at death of how one's life has been conducted. If it has been less than morally satisfactory, the spirit is reborn into a new body and a less fortunate social position in which hunger and poverty dominate. If it has been mainly satisfactory but not perfect, the spirit is reborn with a chance to live a better life. Thus Hindus speak of "good karma," which means a life blessed by good deeds in a past existence, while "bad karma" is just the opposite.

Cursed by Fate

The Greeks introduced another way of accounting for human woes, and that was Fate. It was visually represented as three sisters, one of whom wove the thread of life, another stretched it out, and the third cut it. In addition to having a person's lifespan determined by the whim of Fate, Greek mythology also developed the concept that many people were followed throughout their lives by the unkindness of Fate because of a transgression they themselves committed in the past or one that was committed by an ancestor for which they are paying the price. Two of the greatest Greek tragedies are trilogies about noble families cursed by Fate because of past sins.

The Greeks personified Fate as three sisters, one of whom wove the thread of life, another stretched it, and the third cut it—presumably on a whim.

The Oresteia by Aeschylus (525–456 B.C.E.) consists of three plays about the doomed family of Atreus, who killed his brother's children and then served them to him as food. He committed this atrocity as an act of vengeance against the brother for having forced his wife into adultery. The two sons of Atreus, who must bear the consequences of their father's sin, are Menelaus, king of Sparta, and Agamemnon, a Greek warrior. Menelaus marries the beautiful Helen, who runs off with the Trojan prince Paris, thus precipitating the Trojan War. Agamemnon fights the ten-year war on his brother's side, returning home only to be lured to his death by his wife, whose lover stabs him. The two adulterers are in turn murdered by Agamemnon's son Orestes with the assistance of his sister Electra. The Furies, ferocious mythic women whose duty it is to haunt and terrify evil-doers, pursue

Orestes, taunting him demonically day and night until he is exonerated by the goddess Athena in the world's first known trial scene.

The doomed family of Cadmus includes his son Oedipus and the four children sired by him and borne by his wife, who is also his natural mother. Cadmus had been a wealthy citizen who offended the gods by bragging that, because of his business success, he was just as powerful as those deities. The disasters visited upon his offspring were punishments for his arrogance.

Greek myths and tragedies are of enduring relevance because the question of whether any of us really has free will is still very much alive.

The tragedy of the doomed Oedipus is told in three plays by Sophocles (discussed in Chapter 7): *Oedipus the King, Antigone,* and *Oedipus at Colonus.* By the fifth century, Athenians had developed a highly sophisticated urban civilization, and, though the old myths still formed the basis for many plays of the period, they were subject to question. In particular, the Oedipus plays dealt with the issue of whether the protagonist, suffering because he had long ago killed his father and then married his mother without knowing the truth of his parentage, should accept responsibility for his actions when he was doomed by Fate to commit them. Sophocles resolves the issue by having his protagonist willingly accept responsibility as a means of maintaining his dignity. "The gods willed that I should slay the man I didn't know was my father," he says, "but the hand that struck the blow was mine."

Greek mythology and the tragedies it inspired remain of enduring relevance because the question of whether any of us really has free will is still very much alive. It is at the core of many a court case involving dilemmas of responsibility. Inherited traits, family abuse, poverty, and a bad environment frequently enter into arguments for the defense. In Chapter 16, Freedom, there is more about this problem which crops up continually in the media, literature, and drama.

Myths of Childhood

Our earliest encounters with literature, the stories told or read to us, probably influenced our expectations of later life. Childhood tales—despite their frequent violence and terror—usually satisfy the child's (or even the parent's) need for security by bringing the action to a happy conclusion. ("And they all lived happily ever after.")

Adults like to escape from the demands of everyday life by giving in to their childhood love of magical kingdoms, witches, wizards, and perils that are inevitably overcome. Fables from distant childhood have been kept alive, particularly by the Disney company. Both the young and the not-so-young have made huge box-office successes of *Snow White, Beauty and the Beast, The Little Mermaid, The Lion King,* and Tim Burton's 2010 version of Lewis Carroll's *Alice in Wonderland.* This section deals with some childhood tales and their themes that are too important not to be considered as valid introductions to the humanities.

How We Get Our Values

Children who still hear about the Three Little Pigs learn that hard work and diligence, not fun and frivolity, pay off in the long run. The tale of the child on her way to Granny's house teaches children a lesson about disobedience. Red Riding Hood's journey would certainly have been a lot safer if she had heeded the advice about not speaking to strangers. Similarly, the mother goat in "The Wolf and the Seven Kids" goes off leaving her children home alone with the admonition not to open the door to anyone. Most of the seven goats pay for their disobedience by being eaten whole; of course, as often happens in fairy-tale land, they are rescued, none the worse for their ordeal. Sleeping Beauty, threatened with awful consequences if she pricks her finger on a spindle, cannot resist the temptation to explore a hidden spinning wheel and so suffers the inevitable wound. But like so many childhood myths, that of Sleeping Beauty contains not only dire warnings about disobedience but also the reassurance that nothing *really* bad is ever going to happen.

> *"The fairy tale takes a child's anxieties and dilemmas very seriously and addresses itself directly to them: the need to be loved and the fear that one is thought worthless; the love of life and the fear of death."*
>
> **—Bruno Bettelheim**

Not all childhood mythology is designed to teach. Many of the stories offer comfort and security, even as they reflect the stress of modern life. Characters can face very real dangers and frightening villains. Sauron, who guards the Mount of Doom in J. R. R. Tolkien's *Lord of the Rings,* is evil incarnate and ultimately conquered, but only after a furious battle sequence. Maurice Sendak, also known for his imaginative stage and opera sets, has written a number of children's stories, such as *Where the Wild Things Are,* in which a little boy sent to his room without supper flies out of his bedroom (without adult permission, of course) and encounters weird, fantastic, sometimes frightening creatures, all vividly illustrated by the author. But, despite the odds, the boy manages to return safely—and to find his supper waiting for him. The myth appeals to the need for escape from humdrum, sometimes burdensome, reality, as well as the need for reassuring safety and love.

The Importance of Being Attractive and Rich

The old fairy tales, still popular, reinforce stereotypical gender roles, class distinctions, and the notion that good and evil are based on physical appearance. People named Charming, Beauty, and Snow White are not only physically attractive but morally pure. The names Wicked Witch and Stepmother are given to unattractive characters who are up to no good. Cinderella is both breathtakingly beautiful and hard-working. By contrast, her stepsisters are selfish, ugly, and possessed of unfortunately large feet.

Fairy tales take place in magic kingdoms dominated by a class system, for, after all, they originated in a time when it was believed that nobility was inborn. People may not have believed literally in the blue blood of one small segment of the populace, but they were reminded time and again that "class will tell." The heroine of "The Princess and the Pea" is so innately sensitive, so clearly a member of the upper class, that she spends a sleepless night because one pea is under the pile of mattresses on which she has been lying. The pea has been deliberately placed there as a test of her true aristocracy. The values embedded deeply in these tales may ultimately

Stock Montage, Inc./SuperStock

Gustave Doré, *Little Red Riding Hood Meets the Wolf,* 1862

Red Riding Hood's journey would have been safer if she had heeded the advice about not speaking to strangers.

be harmful, but they also provide good stories, and who bothers to analyze them when children drift off to happy sleep?

The Importance of Names

> *"I confused things with their names: that is belief."*
>
> **—Jean-Paul Sartre**

In one folktale, a lower-class heroine, a miller's daughter, marries a prince on the strength of a false promise—that she can transform flax into gold. She is locked in a room and told to fill it with the precious metal, but of course she doesn't know how. Help comes from a little man who tells her he can perform the magic, provided she promise to give him her firstborn child. Since the poor girl is not yet married and is in danger of losing her life if she doesn't perform the task before morning, she agrees. The gold appears, the marriage takes place, and in due time a child is born. When reminded of her agreement, the queen begs for another chance, which she gets! The condition is that she must tell the little man his name. Her first guesses are not even close, but she eventually is victorious when she overhears him boasting "Rumpelstiltskin is my name."

The myth probably appeals to children at the age when language is becoming important. During dramatic presentations of the story, young audiences continually scream the name to the actress playing the heroine. Perhaps it helps children affirm their own identities, for they too have names, and names, as they are learning, are all-important, especially unusual names that make one unique.

The Dark Side

Though modern childhood mythology does not shy away from confronting real dangers, even the time-honored fairy tales can evoke multiple responses. Amid the magic kingdoms and beautiful characters lurk goblins, bats, and skulls. Through these and other dark elements, like the terrifying forest in *The Wizard of Oz,* children learned that life is not always sunny.

The beautiful Snow White appears to die from biting into a poisonous apple given to her by her jealous stepmother. She is even placed in a glass coffin, though in real life, children are generally shielded from close contact with death. Of course, the kiss of a prince restores her to life and leads to the usual proposal of a royal marriage.

Much emphasis is placed on the threat of being eaten. In *Hansel and Gretel,* still popular as children's theater and as opera, the wicked lady in the tempting gingerbread house warms her oven in dreadful preparation for roasting the two children. In the nick of time they are rescued and the lady herself consigned to a painful death.

In his 1983 musical play *Into the Woods,* Stephen Sondheim brings together all of the major characters from the fairy tales and puts them into small houses on the edge of the woods; they become symbols of the true dangers in the world. Mythical illusion is continually shattered in the play. After their marriage, Cinderella discovers that Prince Charming is having many affairs. When confronted, he explains: "I was raised to be charming, not faithful." Jack's excursion up the magical beanstalk nets no fortune, and the hand of the dead giant falls on and kills the baker's wife. Traditional myths help the makers of the humanities to communicate dark messages.

> *"There must be more to life than having everything."*
>
> **—Maurice Sendak**

Roald Dahl's *Charlie and the Chocolate Factory,* filmed twice in recent times, is not precisely the wholesome entertainment its title appears to promise. The 1971 Hollywood version, that seemed to be a delightful fable about a wondrous world of unbelievable candy, was turned into a dark story of how greed destroys.

The children who can't resist the many temptations drown in a chocolate river or are crushed in mixing machines. The purity and common sense of the young hero is, however, recognized by the factory's proprietor, and he is allowed to ride a magic elevator into a never-never land free of greed and corruption.

Some parents seek to avoid frightening their children (especially at bedtime) by eliminating all threatening motifs, by making sure that hungry wolves are not allowed to eat either little pigs or old ladies. One mother was distressed, however, when her child burst into tears at the bland ending by demanding to know whether the wolf was still hungry!

Is it important for each generation of children to be taught the old fables? A writer named Leonard Courier apparently believes so. His short story "A Christmas Morning" concerns a science-minded father who decides to eliminate all fairy-tale illusions in order to make sure his son will be able to face a harsh world. "The story of Santa Claus is nonsense," he says, and forces the child to stay awake all night so that he will observe the true source of his presents. The child, rubbing his eyes, watches as his parents assemble the gifts under the tree. At dawn he pleads to be allowed to sleep, but his father insists that he have breakfast and then play with his toys.

Before he may eat, however, the boy is required to show that he has learned his lesson. "Finish this sentence," says his father, "There is no—." When the boy keeps silent, the father becomes angry and threatens to beat the child if the correct answer does not come forth. "Well, what is it?" he repeats. "There is no what?"

Wearily, the little boy looks up and says, "There is no father."

Popular Mythology

Much of what we say and how we react to certain situations have roots in mythology, both past and present. Whether we know it or not, we keep creating and perpetuating myths. The fables of the Greek writer Aesop (sixth century B.C.E.) contain many stories and morals that stay with humanity from age to age, including the tortoise who wins the race against the swifter hare and the fox who decides that the grapes he is unable to reach are probably sour anyway. The latter story is the source of the term "sour-grapes" applied to anyone claiming "I didn't want it anyway." Aesop gave practical advice, but it was often contradictory. "Look before you leap" is the opposite of "He who hesitates is lost." Still, either moral can be a word of wisdom, depending on the situation.

Many popular beliefs are quoted without regard to their origins. Discovering the roots of popular mythology is not a plea for being more realistic. Its purpose is to encourage the *habit* of identifying certain thought and emotional patterns so they can be more readily evaluated as either still vital or no longer useful. In a sense it is also an introduction to the critical appreciation of the humanities.

Common Sayings

All of us hear them; nearly everyone uses them. Life would be different without them. They are expressions of beliefs that may have originated in ancient stories, religious teachings, or frequently repeated slogans. They may be considered misconceptions by some, but indeed most of them are not challenged at all. Even those who scoff, however, may not be analyzing why the belief has found such wide acceptance. The following is a selective listing of some common beliefs that constitute our everyday mythology.

> *"Truth is one, the sages speak it by many names."*
>
> **—The Vedas**

"What goes around, comes around." The saying helps many of us account for bad things that happen. It is easier for us to believe that bad things are not random like a lightning strike, but are the logical result of a misdeed. Thus, if we avoid such misdeeds in the future, all will be well.

"Mother Nature." As long as nature continues to be personified as a maternal force, many people will believe that, despite neglecting what is happening to the planet, somehow we will all be nurtured and protected by the mother of us all.

"They'll think of something." The ending of some Greek plays resolved terrible problems by having an actor dressed as a god come down to the stage. The device, as discussed in Chapter 7, was known as a *deus ex machina,* and it has become a standard critical term for plot contrivance. In popular mythology the *deus* is sometimes medical research. Like the cavalry riding to the rescue, like the mysterious stranger who appears just in time, science will solve every problem, find a cure for every disease in the nick of time. Because "they" have helped so often before, they can be expected to help every time. If rescue is inevitable, every rule of good health can be violated for our bodies or our cities while we wait for our rescuers.

> *"Love isn't finding a perfect person. It's seeing an imperfect person perfectly."*
>
> **—Sam Keen**

"All you need is love." Whether love is defined as the sweetest thing, whether it makes the world go round, or whether it's all you need, a popular belief is that love is as important as breathable air. Even the high divorce rate has not interfered with the belief that living alone is unnatural or that there is no happiness outside commitment to one other person. A first failure requires the search for the right choice next time, and a newly single person's claim of being happy is met with disbelief and offers of matchmaking. The myth is not only that there is someone for everyone but that love and talk of love can substitute for any other human concern.

"It must be fate." Also called destiny, fate plays an important role in Greek mythology and is one of its major legacies. It is still present in the way people react to events. The idea of destiny can offer comfort, relief, and freedom from responsibility because, if something is "meant to be," it will certainly happen, and no one is to blame. There is a positive side as well. If destiny can bring disasters, it can also bring good fortune, love, and happiness. It can be the source of perpetual hope. In a popular film of 1980 called *Somewhere in Time,* two lovers separated by a century finally meet because it was their destiny. The man, who is of the modern world, is at first restless and brooding, as if he knows that his life is incomplete. As soon as he finds himself in another part of time and sees the beautiful woman who seems to be waiting for him, he knows that all is as it should be.

"Just deserts." Early on, we learn that Santa Claus rewards only good children, while naughty ones receive a piece of coal, getting what they deserve. Life without the myth of deserving is unimaginable. It underlies our whole system of justice, for example. It probably acts as a deterrent to untold numbers of people who might otherwise commit crimes, or even provides secret comfort to people who are serving long sentences in prison: "After all, I *deserve* this."

"Us versus them." The desire to be part of a group and therefore at odds with people in another group is well established. It may encourage school spirit and often promotes family unity, but it can also lead to wars, mob violence, and a lifelong distrust and hatred of "the other." Coaches and sergeants urge their charges to fight more ferociously by reinforcing the "us/them" distinction, and in time of war it can help to bring about both national unity and inflexible mistrust of the enemy. Belonging to a privileged group underlies the racism implicit in films of the early twentieth century in which ethnic minorities are treated as inferior. The belief presupposes the superiority of one group over the inferiority or even nonhumanness of another.

"There's always room at the top." Belief that unlimited success should be possible for everyone is a spur to ambition as well as a cause for major disappointment in those who never achieve wealth or fame. The very word "*top*" is loaded with preconceptions and expectations. At the top are entertainers, athletes, corporation executives, and political leaders. The pervasiveness of the belief is indicated by sales of how-to books and enrollment in seminars promising a quick and guaranteed road up. (Of course, if the "*top*" is to have any meaning, there must be a lot of people "*below*.") Literature abounds with tales of those who buy into the mythology of upward mobility. The Horatio Alger novels of the early twentieth century all have heroes who start off poor and become wealthy either by hard work or accident. They were successful novels, and their counterparts were films based on performers who inevitably became stars after early disappointments. The myth is so deeply ingrained in Western culture that many believe it is their *duty* to move up.

"Isn't that just like a (man/woman)?" **Gender roles**—models of appropriate behavior and functions for men and women—were for a long time codified and unchanging. For many cultures these have been religiously defined, and failure to observe the rules can have serious consequences. Even among those who consider themselves enlightened, the old myth that men are this and women are that often lurks in the background. Men are expected to like adventure movies, while films about dating, marriage, and betrayal are called chick flicks. Men are accused of never asking directions when lost, while women are not supposed to pass a clothing store without examining the window display. In 2004 Martha Stewart, called the queen of the domestic divas, was arrested, then tried and convicted in a business scandal. Her supporters argued that she had been the victim of the masculine cultural mythology that resents a woman's success. In this mythology, they contended, the woman who gets ahead is called "pushy" and "unfeminine," while a successful man is called "assertive."

> *"God made man, and then said 'I can do better than that.'"*
>
> **—Adele Rogers St. John**

"Everybody does it." The equation that goodness equals weakness accounts for the cynical acceptance of cheating, or "cutting corners," as an understandably human practice at all ages and places: on the playground, in class, in a courtroom or personnel office. Using test answers dishonestly acquired is only one example, with "everybody does it" furnishing the rationale. It is, after all, the way of the world. To the victor belong the spoils, presumably, regardless of how the spoils are obtained.

Does anybody think mythology has no relevance to ordinary living?

How Myths Influence the Humanities

> *"I've always preferred mythology to history. History is truth that becomes an illusion. Mythology is an illusion that becomes reality."*
>
> **—Jean Cocteau**

Throughout the rest of this book, especially in Part II, which introduces you to the formal disciplines, we shall have many occasions to point out the myths, stories, and archetypes that underlie a given work. In this final section of Chapter 2, we want to offer some prominent uses of myth found in literature, drama, and cinema. You will see how a knowledge of mythology greatly enhances the appreciation of what is read or seen.

A reading of the poem "Leda and the Swan," for example, by the Irish poet William Butler Yeats (1865–1939) is more meaningful if we know the myth of how a woman named Leda was raped by the all-powerful god Zeus disguised as a swan. Leda bore him two daughters, one of whom was Helen, whose adulterous love for the Trojan prince Paris led, mythically at least, to the Trojan War. Literature comes alive through our understanding of how Venus, goddess of love, became obsessed with a handsome mortal, Adonis, and begged him not to go hunting, or how the young man disregarded her plea and was mortally wounded, leaving Venus to mourn. Shakespeare was inspired by their story and made it the subject of one of the world's great love poems.

"A thing of beauty is a joy forever."

—**John Keats**

We can read *Endymion* by the English poet John Keats (1795–1821) more easily if we know the fable about the handsome shepherd, who, while sleeping on a hill, so arouses the moon goddess with love for him that she casts a spell causing him to sleep forever. He will never wake up, but he will never grow old. The myth of eternal youth is universal for obvious reasons.

A reading of the poem *Prometheus Unbound* by the English poet Percy Bysshe Shelley (1792–1822) is enhanced by knowing the story of the mythical Titan who stole fire from the gods, giving it to mortals. Prometheus was punished for his transgression by being shackled to a gigantic rock; every day thereafter a huge vulture ate his liver, which would grow back the following day while the vulture waited to devour it once again, the cycle of torture repeated without end.

Even when death comes in mythology, there is always the question of what comes afterward. Two major kinds of afterlife are described: one sometimes known as paradise, the other a dark, often dismal—and in many stories, eternally painful—place.

In Greek mythology, the souls of brave warriors were believed to reside in an eternal paradise called the Elysian Fields after having been spared the pain of death. When it came time for them to die in battle, a benevolent god lifted them up and escorted them to a place of peace. In the medieval legends, after King Arthur is slain in battle, his body is placed on a magical ship that bears him to the faroff land of Avalon, where he will presumably live on forever. In the modern mythic trilogy *Lord of the Rings,* Frodo, the hobbit hero, embarks on a long and treacherous journey to destroy the magic ring which has caused so much pain and death. After bringing peace to Middle Earth, his world, he must die himself. In an ending that resembles Arthur's fate, author J. R. R.Tolkien describes Frodo's final seaward journey in unforgettable terms:

> *Then Frodo . . . went aboard; and the sails were drawn up, and the wind blew, and slowly the ship slipped away down the long dark firth; and . . . went out into the High Sea and passed on into the West, until at last on a night of rain Frodo smelled a sweet fragrance and heard the sound of singing that came over the water. And then . . . the grey rain-curtain turned all to silver glass and was rolled back, and he beheld white shores and beyond them a far green country under a swift sunrise.*[11]

In view of today's environmental concerns, the myth of a green afterlife has much appeal.

The Greeks also had Hades, or the Underworld, where the souls of nonwarriors had to live after crossing the River Styx that led from the land of the living to the land of the dead. While it was dark and cheerless, it was not, however, a place of torment.

Much of Asia's rich mythology is relayed in the form of parables, as in the story of Ryokan.

> *Once there was a monk named Ryokan living a simple life of poverty and meditation. One night a thief enters the monk's little hut and steals his food as well as the clothes off his back. Instead of being angry, Ryokan says "I only wish I could give you the moonlight on my floor."*[12]

Roman mythology is kept alive in a number of enduring tales, such as that of Baucis and Philemon. Rumors of their virtue reached the ears of Jupiter, king of the gods, who had become so disgusted with humanity's evil ways that he planned to destroy it and start over. But before doing so, he decided to see for himself whether there was any truth to the rumors. Disguised as a poorly clothed, weary and hungry traveler, he visits the neighborhood of Baucis and Philemon, going first from house to house. Everyone turns him away until he reaches the home of the reputedly virtuous pair. Poor as they are, they welcome him, build a fire for him, and give him all the food they have.

After the god finally reveals his true identity, he bids them name their wish. So they ask to be allowed eventually to die together. Jupiter grants the wish; and when they die, he transforms them into intertwining trees.

As we have seen, myths can become part of our everyday awareness. We can find mythology in films, television shows, literature—even comic strips. Who are Superman and Batman if not mythic characters? Surely we all know that no myth contains the full truth. Moreover, some mythology interferes with our judgment, and some is downright superstition. Even so, there are those dazzling mazes and those magic rings and the wonderful stranger who comes out of nowhere. We need a little mist in our gardens.

In one of the most haunting yet little known novels of the twentieth century, *Memoirs of a Midget* by British author and poet Walter de la Mare (1873–1956), the tiny heroine is at one point forced to earn a meager living in a carnival sideshow, watching as people either laugh or show cruel pity. After many nights of agony, during which she learns not to look at the crowd, a mysterious force suddenly compels her to raise her head:

> *. . . my eyes chanced to fall on a figure, standing in the clouded light a little apart. He was dressed in a high-peaked hat and a long and seemingly brown cassock-like garment, with buttoned tunic and silver-buckled belt. Spurs were on his boots, a light whip in his hand. Aloof, his head a little bowed down, his face in profile, he stood there, framed in the opening, dusky, level-featured, deep-eyed—a Stranger. What in me rushed as if on wings into his silent company? A passionate longing beyond words burned in me. I seemed to be carried away into a boundless wilderness—stunted trees, salt in the air, a low, enormous stretch of night sky, space; and this man, master of soul and solitude.*[13]

> *"Goodbye," said the fox. "And now here is my secret. It is only with the heart that one can see rightly; what is essential is invisible to the eye."*
>
> **—Antoine de Saint-Exupery**

Nothing is made of this incident for a long time. We forget about it. The story moves forward as if it never happened, until one night the midget disappears, leaving behind only this cryptic note: *I have gone with him*. The identity of the stranger is never revealed—or even whether there had been anyone there at all. We never know where the midget has gone or what fate befell her. Yet none of that seems to matter. Have we not wished, at least once, that a dreadful problem could be solved by the sudden appearance of an outsider who knew all about us and knew exactly what to do?

Real life has its outsiders, its strangers, such as the paramedics who respond to frantic 911 calls within minutes and who always seem to know exactly what needs to be done. The television series *Trauma* centered on these actual heroes rather than on the doctors who receive patients in the emergency room.

Mythology is alive and well. We can be thankful; we need it.

LEARNING OBJECTIVES

Having read and carefully studied this chapter, you should be able to:

1. Briefly explain Jung's theory of the archetypes.
2. Summarize the phases of the hero, or world, myth.
3. Contrast the hero in Eastern and Western mythology.
4. Explain the Circle as a major archetype.
5. Contrast Eastern and Western versions of the journey myth.
6. Discuss the myth of the Garden, indicating contemporary relevance.
7. Summarize the various creation myths in the chapter.
8. Summarize the various myths that account for human suffering.
9. Using one childhood myth, explain the values and expectations it leaves you with.
10. Add two more popular myths to the list given in the chapter.

KEY TERMS

archetype a model (e.g. the hero, the circle, the journey) which, through mythology, becomes part of our subconscious and an addition to the way we organize our thinking about ourselves, human beings in general, and the nature of the universe.

Collective Unconscious Jung's phrase for the universality of many myths and archetypes among cultures, some of which could not possibly have had any contact with each other.

gender roles the way acceptable male and female behavior and functions are defined in a given culture.

monomyth reference made by Irish novelist James Joyce to what he considered a fundamental myth of all cultures: that of the hero. Also known as the *world myth*. In Western mythology, the hero is a special individual ordained by fate to be the doer of wondrous deeds, often as the savior of a whole group of people. In many Western myths, the hero's power does not last.

mythology (1) the collective myths of a specific culture or group of cultures (2) the organized study of myths, either those of world cultures or of a specific culture.

myths tales and beliefs transmitted from generation to generation, or springing up as part of the popular mind in a current generation, many containing psychological truth or fulfilling some deep-rooted need.

TOPICS FOR WRITING AND DISCUSSION

1. The purpose of this chapter has been to encourage you to seek out myths that may underlie works in the humanities. It could be argued that the enjoyment of a given work should not depend upon knowing its mythic roots. What argument can you give in *favor* of knowing mythic roots? OR: support an opinion that knowing or not knowing mythic roots does not make any difference.
2. Write a short paper about three myths from your early childhood that helped shape your expectations of life. Do you still have them? If so, what role do they play in your life? If not, what happened to make you discard them?
3. Write a short fable about an animal hero who must undertake a dangerous journey to accomplish a task. Share it with the class and see whether they can grasp your meaning or perhaps recognize some contemporary issue in it.
4. Some myths have environmental subjects. In the stories of Demeter, grieving for her daughter Persephone, and Dionysus, descending annually into the underworld, we have an explanation of winter and the return of spring. Make up a fable to explain what is happening to the ozone layer, the rainforests, the polar ice caps, or the planet's nonrenewable resources.
5. Discuss a modern personality whose life more or less fits the pattern of the rise and fall of the hero, as described in the chapter.
6. As far back as the ancient Greeks, people knew that the lives of prominent personalities often are filled with tragedies or, at any rate, many troubles. There are contemporary examples one could cite. In many of the old myths, troubles beset those who offended the gods. What do you think accounts for the problems now?
7. Briefly write your autobiography in mythic terms. Describe your birth, your mission in life, the villains you must outwit, and your magic powers. If you want to be whimsical, who's to stop you?
8. Take an old fairy tale and rewrite it (seriously or comically) in terms of how it might fill a psychological need of today.
9. The section on "Common Sayings" is not and does not pretend to be exhaustive. Can you think of at least two others not mentioned and explain their purpose as popular mythology?

Study and Review on MyHumanitiesKit.com

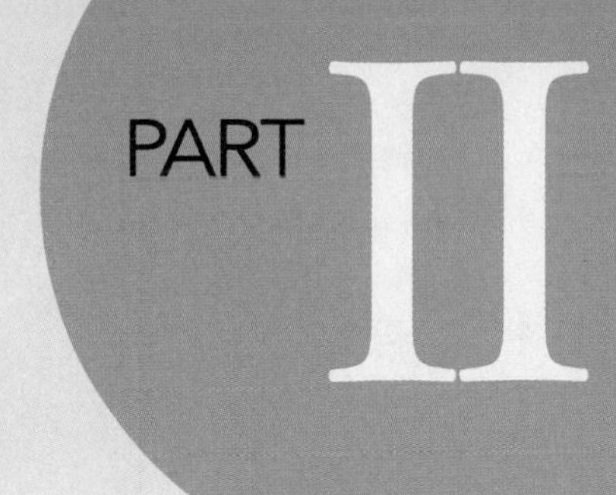

Disciplines of the Humanities

"The artist puts before him beauty of feature and form; the poet, beauty of mind; the preacher, the beauty of grace; then intellect too, I repeat, has its beauty, and it has those who aim at it."

—John Henry Newman

Chapter 4

Literature

Who has not greatly elaborated on an incident that occurred, embellished with more excitement, more color than it had? In this sense, we are all born story-tellers.

A few become professionals at it, but everyone can become involved in what others write and thus share *their* imaginations. Alas, however, some begin to lose interest and leave all that behind when they're out of school and going off to their daily jobs. To those people we issue an ardent plea. Go back and look for your imagination. You've left it somewhere. But you can't ever really lose it. Maybe it's hiding in a drawer along with the "missing" snapshots of you lying on a baby rug.

How did it all start? What was the first kind of literature? Our guess is that the literary impulse was being felt long before there were written languages to preserve the earliest expressions of it. In the visual arts, there are cave drawings that date back thousands of years prior to the beginning of history. Using our imaginations (which we just found in that drawer), we can suppose that early (*very* early) people were dancing, chanting, and pounding away with stones and sticks. And there music and dance! It is hard to imagine, however, that some form of literature did not happen along with these other arts.

Let's assume that people are natural-born poets and storytellers (and by natural progression, readers) and therefore there is no good reason to look upon literature as something locked away in libraries. We'll look at a few examples of the major types, or **genres**, of literature: the poem, the novel, and the short story. We'll see how they might have evolved, and the needs they may have served. We'll discuss drama, a major genre of literature, in Chapter 7.

Some of the works we shall study are **classics**, in the sense that they have outlived their time and continue to be relevant. Some have earned the right to be called **masterpieces**. The more recent must wait a bit for such classification.

A masterpiece is a work that in style, execution, and resonance far exceeds what other writers were doing at the same time. For example, though many sonnets were successful in Shakespeare's time, many of *his* sonnets tower above those of his contemporaries in profundity, sophistication of technique (handling of meter and rhyme), and the intricate use of words contained in what may be the largest vocabulary of any writer of the past or the present. Much of our wisdom springs from the memorable statements in his poems and plays.

Many classics are also masterpieces, but they don't always have to be. Time and circumstances give continuing relevance to a classic. A masterpiece can always stand on its own, and it will find admirers in any age. Sometimes a masterpiece such as Herman Melville's *Moby-Dick* (1850) is not recognized until much later. In the case of Melville, recognition came with a review published in 1924–thirty-three years after Melville's death.

This chapter addresses itself to literature of the past and present which springs from the soul of human beings and through which we come to understand ourselves and others with whom we share the amazing condition of being alive. We are going to discuss a few representative works that have achieved literary distinction, some well known, others less familiar but with much to offer.

◀ **Marc Chagall, *The Juggler of Paris*, 1969**

The imaginative world of great literature gives human life another dimension.

Literature as History

> "We are storytelling animals—who we are, what we are, and why. When we die we become part of other stories. This residue is our immortality."
>
> —Salman Rushdie

At some point—we don't know exactly when, except that it was many thousands of years ago—groups must have felt the need to identify, to *define* themselves. They knew they had common bonds that came from their strivings. Imagine how you would feel if you suddenly developed amnesia and had no clue about your past history. Wouldn't you become obsessed with the desire to locate yourself in time and space?

The Basic Literary Impulse: Identity

Early in *The Grapes of Wrath* (1939) by the American novelist John Steinbeck (1902–1968), a simple incident illustrates how important it is that people leave behind a record of themselves. Steinbeck saw the westward migration of dispossessed Oklahoma farmers of the 1930s as an example of how human society developed. Trying to get to California, the longed-for promised land of abundant work and prosperity, they were despised nobodies robbed of their roots and their identity and given the collective designation *Okies*. When a family pulled into a large orchard looking for work, the question was always "How many hands for picking?"—never "What is your name?"

During the arduous journey, Grampa Joad, patriarch of the novel's central family, dies and has to be buried by the side of the road in some desolate and nameless place. Tom Joad, a grandson, writes a brief note and puts it on the body. It says with all the simplicity of a folk poem:

> *This here is William James Joad, dyed of a stroke,*
> *old, old man. His fokes bured him becaws they got*
> *no money to pay for funerls. Nobody kilt him. Just*
> *a stroke an he dyed.*[1]

Leaving the body unidentified was unthinkable. If Tom had had a literary bent, he might have wanted to say more.

> "Literature transmits incontrovertible condensed experience . . . from generation to generation. In this way literature becomes the living memory of a nation."
>
> —Alexander Solzhenitsyn

The pharaohs of ancient Egypt spent most of their adult lives designing their own monumental tombs, which survive to this day. The great pyramids identify not only the rulers but the culture that bore them. Egypt established its past and present identity through art and architecture. Other cultures did it through literature, usually in oral form, and in some cases their efforts can be traced back thousands of years. The literary impulse was originally the same thing as the need to establish identity and a history.

The First Epic: *Gilgamesh*

In the days when literature was transmitted and preserved both orally or in some kind of written form, the **epic** was a genre that emerged as the literary heritage of early societies. An epic is a long narrative poem recounting the actions and adventures of a hero who exemplifies strength, courage, and cunning, but not necessarily moral virtue. When survival was the predominant concern of a people, their myth heroes had to seem unconquerable, as indeed they hoped their society was.

> "If you would not be forgotten as soon as you are gone, either write things worth reading or do things worth writing."
>
> —Carson McCullers

One of the oldest is the epic *Gilgamesh,* the story of a tyrannical king who lived around four thousand years ago in a land that is now Iraq. Inscribed on twelve tablets, it was discovered in the ruins of an Assyrian library dating from the seventh century B.C.E. Classical scholars believe the story has its origins in a cycle of songs and poems created to celebrate the deeds of a real person, Gilgamesh, a king in the city of Uruk in 2750 B.C.E. Over the course of a thousand years, the songs and poems became popular throughout Mesopotamia, and eventually Babylonian poets transformed them into a singular epic poem. It is believed the definitive version of the epic was compiled by a Babylonian priest named Shin-eqi-unninni.

Central to the poem are the swashbuckling exploits of a superman. So formidable did Gilgamesh become, so devastating to all who stood in his way, that even the gods were intimidated. So they created a gentler, more compassionate counterpart named Enkidu. Some scholars have interpreted Enkidu as Gilgamesh's other self, the side with humane principles. The climax of the epic is a tremendous wrestling match between the two superheroes, ending in a tie, suggesting that both aggressiveness and kindness are necessary for human existence.

Gilgamesh is one of the oldest of literary works, discovered in the 7th century B.C.E. but probably much older than that.

Enkidu finally dies in the story, but Gilgamesh lives on, undefeated, and still a mortal problem for the immortal gods. Was the author saying that even though kindness is a necessary element in the human personality it is less likely to outlast aggressiveness?

The *Iliad,* which we consider next, marks a considerable change in the nature and purpose of the genre. Like *Gilgamesh,* it has a climactic showdown between two supermen. It is a work intended, as usual, to provide its audience with a history and an identity. It did just that, but it also extolled the glory and the virtue of an enemy.

An Early Masterpiece: Homer's *Iliad*

The *Iliad* is not only a prime example of early literature but one of the treasures of human culture. It has been traditionally attributed to Homer, who may have lived anytime between 1200 and 850 B.C.E. For a long time classical scholarship tended to believe that the poem was composed over several centuries and therefore cannot be attributed to one poet. When it comes to very ancient works, assigning authorship is always a risky business, but as the traditional joke says, "If it wasn't by Homer, it may have been written by somebody else named Homer." Nothing is definitively known about him except that, according to legend, he may have been blind. More recent scholarship, in any case, suggests the poem is too unified *not* to have been the work of a single genius.

> *"Homer is new and fresh this morning, and nothing perhaps is as old and tired as today's newspaper."*
>
> **—Charles Peguy**

Epic as Cultural History. The *Iliad* seems to have been an ambitious effort to give the nation of Greece a cultural history, a sense of continuity. The epic describes events leading up to and then the waging of a ten-year war against Troy, known to Homer as Ilion, hence the poem's title, which means "The Song of Ilion." Why song? The answer may be that those who performed the poem could remember the lines better if they were sung.

The absence of written languages is a most important point to remember about much early literature. Even though *Gilgamesh* was discovered on clay tablets, it was set down in *cuneiform,* wedge-shaped characters that **symbolize** things; it was not a language as such, with words that stand for things. A minstrel—or rhapsodist, as he was also known—was a professional man hired and paid by powerful rulers and their court to present their "history." Naturally that history was about the exploits of ancestral rulers who were also brave warriors. Common people would not enter the literary scene in any major way for more than two thousand years.

Explore on **MyHumanitiesKit.com** Cuneiform Writing in Sumeria

The *Iliad* is subtitled "*The Wrath of Achilles.*" Achilles would have been recognized as one of the great myth heroes because of his prowess in battle and his reputation for being unconquerable. (In one myth, his mother dips him as an infant into the river Styx to make him immortal, but holds him by his ankle, which becomes vulnerable and eventually leads to his demise. Hence the term "Achilles' heel" to describe anyone's vulnerability.)

Homer's epic accounts for the ten years' duration of the conflict through a well-known story of how Agamemnon, one of the Greek generals, reluctantly surrenders his mistress, a Trojan captive, in a prisoner exchange but insists on taking Briseis, the mistress of Achilles, for himself. In retribution Achilles refuses to fight, and so the conflict grinds to a standstill. His withdrawal turns the tide in favor of the Trojans. Early listeners among the Greeks, hearing the story for the first time, would have been in suspense wondering how their ancestors managed a victory.

> *"When power narrows the area of man's concern, poetry reminds him of the richness and diversity of his experience."*
>
> **—John F. Kennedy**

According to one popular legend, the Greeks offered the Trojans a huge wooden horse as a peacemaking gift. Inside were Greek soldiers who crept out in the middle of the night, slaughtering both citizens and every royal prince they could find. Historians believe that the story of the horse was totally fictitious and that the war itself actually took place during the twelfth century B.C.E. At any rate, the story of the Trojan horse is not included in the *Iliad*.

Much later, the story was part of a great literary work, the Roman epic the *Aeneid* by Virgil (70–19 B.C.E.), which attributes the founding of Rome to Aeneas, a Trojan prince who manages to escape the slaughter. A Roman writer would have been only too delighted to depict the Greeks as devious, dishonorable warriors. If the seeds of the Roman empire were in Troy and Troy had been conquered, it is in the spirit of literature-as-history to show that the conquest was an inglorious one.

That the story of the horse is not found in the *Iliad* does not, however, mean that the work is written as a chest-beating rah-rah glorification of a Greek victory. Not that the Greeks are shown as cowards. Achilles was already established as a hero of titanic proportions, and Greek sympathizers would have eagerly waited for him to finally assert himself. The plot is complicated by the fact that almost all of the gods become involved. Some side with the Greeks, others with the Trojans; and the tide of battle flows both ways until Achilles and Agamemnon are reconciled and Achilles agrees to meet the gallant Trojan warrior Hector in single combat to determine the final outcome.

Had the victory over Troy been accomplished solely by Achilles's slaying of Hector, the *Iliad* might have been a prime example of literature meant to glorify a nation's past. We cannot know whether Homer intended it as such. But what emerged contains not only the Greek victory but the tragedy of the losing side.

Hector, a prince and Troy's most important defender, is treated so sympathetically that the true climax of the epic is Hector's death at the hands of Achilles, who ties the body of the slain warrior to his chariot and drags it ignominiously around the walls of Troy, afterwards selling it back to the Trojans. The *Iliad,* while rooted in Greek history, is essentially a tragic poem about a fallen hero—a hero who was not Greek! Virgil's *Aeneid* is a nationalistic poem. The *Iliad,* ultimately, is not.

Aeneas is portrayed as the perfect hero: strong, brave, and intelligent. Troy is shown to have fallen because the destiny of Aeneas was to found a city much greater than Troy. Yet, although the *Aeneid* is as thrilling and as wondrous as an epic should be, it is less gripping than the human drama of the *Iliad*.

***Iliad* as Tragedy.** There exists, of course, the possibility that the *Iliad* went through several centuries of change as a memorized poem, sung generation after generation by unknown minstrels. It may have been gradually altered to become a tragic epic. The Greeks, after all, developed the art of theater, and their dramas were originally tragic in nature, indicating that as a nation they loved to be moved by stories of noble people who suffer a downfall. In the plays, as we shall see in Chapter 7, the fall of the hero comes about because of a fatal flaw in an otherwise good person. The *Iliad,* as we have it today, anticipates the age of Greek tragedy.

Does Hector have a tragic flaw? In a sense, he does. He is characterized as a brave warrior who goes beyond what is expected of him because, like all warriors, he wants to be remembered for great deeds of valor. The ambition to be known for bravery is characteristic of a hero, to be sure, but it can also be a fatal weakness born of the pride that drives human greatness. Pride would become the major theme of the Greek—and indeed many later—tragedies. The *Iliad* may be said to be the first major work in the literature of the Western world, not only for its soaring poetry but for the *humanization* of its major characters, Hector in particular.

"Humanization" in this sense explains what makes certain literary characters stand apart from others. It is very close to a term that actors often use to define what they are looking for in a character they're going to play: *polarity,* or the binary extremes that exist in people's natures. In playing a role, the actor first determines major characteristics defined by the playwright—for example, *he is a jealous husband; she is a faithful wife.* Then the actor tries to locate the opposite of these characteristics—*he loves his wife very much and doesn't want to lose her; though faithful, she resents his jealousy and secretly wishes she could have a fling.* Great writers have always known that human beings are never just one thing or another. If characters are given certain unwavering traits instead of the contradictory natures we all share, the result is melodrama, rather than tragedy.

((•⊢Listen on **MyHumanitiesKit.com**
Homer, *The Iliad*

If characters are given certain unwavering traits instead of the contradictory natures we all share, the result is melodrama, rather than tragedy.

Like all tragic heroes, Hector has a blind side. Several times before his mortal combat with Achilles, his arch enemy, he has been warned that he almost certainly will die. His wife, Andromache, has pleaded with him not to leave her and their son. Her own father and seven brothers were slain by Achilles in earlier battles: there is, she tells him, no way to defeat this warrior who is surely favored by the gods. But Hector is resolute. He firmly believes that he and he alone has the strength and courage to defeat Achilles.

> *Nay, go thou to the house and busy thyself*
> *with thine own tasks, the loom and the distaff,*
> *and bid thy handmaids ply their work: but war*
> *shall be for men, for all, but most of all for me,*
> *of them that dwell in Ilios.*[2]

Most of all for me. This is not only courage, but pride as well. Here is the polarity in Hector's character; here is Homer's humanization of him. Hector *assumes* he is the only one who can save Troy, just as so many human beings close their minds to the possibility that someone else might be able to perform a difficult task better than they can. This supreme confidence in himself causes Hector to fight with reckless abandon against overwhelming odds—and to fail, weakening his city's defenses as well.

To create a great tragic figure like Hector is to create an ironic contradiction. The very thing that destroys Hector (and Troy) is his bravery, but bravery is also the source of human greatness. The suggestion—to be echoed over and over in many enduring literary works—is that *to be great is to be tragic.* Did Homer, or the creators of this masterpiece, make this discovery so many thousands of years ago?

In composing the *Iliad* he (or they) was apparently caught up with something more imposing than victory, more glorious: the realization that human beings in their finest hour always reach beyond their abilities; that they will never achieve the goals they set for themselves but must nonetheless pursue them only to fail. If this is a truth of existence, then the question is whether it is better to have failed at something tremendous than to have stayed within limitations and won trivial successes. Great literature inspires big, unanswerable questions like this.

The Iliad deserves its place of honor as the first literary masterpiece of the Western world. The poet establishes a fundamental principle of much great literature: real life is not a simple struggle between good and evil.

***Iliad* as a Masterpiece.** The *Iliad* deserves its place of honor as the first literary masterpiece of the Western world. The poet establishes a fundamental principle of much great literature: *real life is not a simple struggle between good and evil.* Hector may be the hero of the *Iliad*, but Achilles is not the villain. The subtitle of the poem is "The Wrath of Achilles," and the warrior's outrage against Agamemnon is indeed the force that drives the plot. Homer as historian presents, without judgment, the story of Achilles's anger as he knows it. If the author is less compassionate toward the Greek warrior than he is toward Hector, he duly recognizes the man's strength and courage as well as his place in Greek history.

What makes the *Iliad* not only a great epic but also a great tragedy is, however, the struggle inside Hector between his desire for glory and his understanding of his wife's anguish, his sensitivity to her ardent pleas born out of his deep love for her. As a reader, you will find that the impact of many masterpieces arises from conflict *within* the characters, not *between* them.

The Russian playwright Anton Chekhov (1860–1904) observed: "Evil flows *through* people, not *from* them." Hector's pride leads him into a violent battle in which not only he but many others are slain. Achilles' refusal to fight costs the Greeks many lives and a more honorable victory. Both men believed their cause was righteous. Neither man could be described as evil, yet their actions had disastrous consequences. That is the way of tragedy and, as the great writers such as Homer knew, the tragic way of humanity.

If Homer had lived in the modern world who knows how he might have responded to the Holocaust, the My Lai massacre during the Vietnam War, the 9/11 terrorist attacks, or the bitter fighting in Iraq and Afghanistan? Big questions, difficult answers. Great literature, whether from the past or the present, makes us feel, makes us think, and inevitably we are changed.

Poetry

"The poet speaks to all men of that other life of theirs that they have smothered and forgotten."

—Dame Edith Sitwell

Though classified in this chapter as a form of history, the epic is also narrative poetry that tells a story in rhythmic language. Narrative, as found in *Gilgamesh* and the *Iliad,* was probably the earliest genre of poetry; but as early societies grew in sophistication and produced artists who could be identified by their style, technique, and typical themes, poetry evolved into numerous forms. By the time of the Greek poet Sappho in the sixth century B.C.E., poets were highly trained and respected members of society. They worked in a written language expected to be elevated above everyday talk—that is to say, above *prose.*

Lyrical Poetry

The Romans inherited from the Greeks the desire to cultivate the arts of civilization. These included the pleasurable pursuits of good food, wine, mineral baths and massage, and all forms of sexual expression. But civilized pleasures also included historical writings such as the epic, as well as poems expressive of personal feelings. Especially popular among the Romans was **lyrical poetry**, so named because it was usually sung to the accompaniment of a *lyre*, a stringed instrument similar to but much smaller than the harp.

> *The stars about the lovely moon hiding their shining forms when it lights up the earth at its fullest.*
>
> **—Sappho**

Sappho may have been the first poet on record to write about deeply personal feelings, even referring to herself by name in poetic prayers to the gods. Sappho is known to have accompanied herself on the lyre and may have composed most of the music as well. She would have used the kind of musical notation that we know existed at the time, but so far none of the music has been discovered.

Among Sappho's favorite subjects are the joys and the sorrows of being in love. Apparently a woman of strong physical needs, she introduced into literature one of its most enduring themes: unrequited passion—a theme that, as we shall see, became wildly popular during the Renaissance and, indeed, can still be found in contemporary popular songs.

In one of her most famous poems, *Ode to Aphrodite*, Sappho implores the goddess of love to have pity on her as she languishes in the agony of romantic frustration:

Ode to Aphrodite

Then didst thou, Divine one,
Laugh a bright laugh from lips and eyes immortal,
Ask me, What ailed me—wherefore out of heaven
Thus had I called thee?
What it was made me madden in my heart so?
Question me, smiling—say to me, "My Sappho,
"Who is it wrongs thee? Tell me who refuses
"Thee, vainly sighing.
"Be it who it may be, he that flies shall follow;
"He that rejects gifts, he shall bring thee many;
"He that hates now shall love thee dearly, madly—
"Aye, though thou wouldst not."[3]

Other writers, especially William Shakespeare, would carry this theme to greater heights, but Sappho will always be remembered as a distinguished pioneer in poetic art (as well as the founder of the first known school for women).

> *Passion makes the world go round. Love just makes it a safer place.*
>
> **—Ice-T**

Lyrical poetry also flourished in Rome, and again the primary subject was love, a popular Roman pastime. Much of it is highly artificial: high-flown words that professional poets knew would please their public. Since in Roman society upper-class women acquired power and independence, the theme of unrequited passion was often expressed from the male point of view, as in this poem by the short-lived Catullus (87–54 B.C.E.), one of many written to and about a lady named Lesbia.

True or False

None could ever say that she,
Lesbia! was so loved by me.
Never all the world around
Faith so true as mine was found.
If no longer it endures
(Would it did!) the fault is yours.
I can never think again

Well of you: I try in vain.
But . . . be false . . . do what you will.—
Lesbia! I must love you still.[4]

To the theme of unrequited passion Catullus and other Romans added that of betrayal and infidelity, of a sworn lover's being false. Instead of swearing vengeance and wishing harm to befall his lady, however, Catullus merely suffers.

The lyrical poetry of Greece and Rome was forgotten during the early and late Middle Ages. Poetry became for Christians a way of expressing the mystic experiences of the devout as they tried to escape from worldly temptations and find God. But the classical themes of love were revived during the Renaissance (beginning in the fourth century) when women of the aristocracy again attained stature and claimed the right to reject men's pleas for their favors. The pain of scorned love reemerged as a popular subject.

The Sonnet

The **sonnet** is a fourteen-line poetic form invented by the Italians in the early Renaissance during the revival of interest in classical art and literature. While the form was modern in its time, the usual subject—the pain caused by unsatisfied love—was of classical origin. The poet Francesco Petrarca (1304–1374), known to the English-speaking world as Petrarch, played a large part in the classical revival. He recognized the genius of the *Iliad* and had it translated into Latin. He is best known, however, for having developed the sonnet. The demands of the form, the discipline of having to put all his thoughts and feelings into fourteen rhymed and rhythmic lines, challenged him, as it has challenged poets ever since.

The Petrarchan Sonnet. Over the centuries a number of variations on the sonnet have emerged, but the basic form is still the Petrarchan. The rhythm, called iambic pentameter, also became the fundamental rhythm of English poetry and is closely identified with the sonnets and plays of William Shakespeare, who was heavily influenced by Petrarch.

That the meter is there should be a happy discovery.

"Iambic pentameter" means that each line has five repetitions of an unstressed followed by a stressed syllable. Each pair of syllables is called a *foot,* similar to a bar of music. The word *decide* is an iambic foot. The line "Decide on when to go or not, my dear" has five repetitions of the pattern and is therefore an example of iambic pentameter. Read aloud, the line heavily accents every other syllable. The poet has the difficult task of writing fourteen lines following the rigid pattern of rhythm without its being heavily obvious. (A listener would soon grow very tired!) In good sonnets, the lines have a sense of inevitability about them and give no suggestion that the poet was straining to keep the rhythm going or to seek rhymes. When read aloud, the poem should not sound overly rhythmic, like a waltz being played for a beginner's dance class. That the meter is there should be a happy discovery. In the following lines from a mercifully obscure poem, the rhythm (not to mention the rhyme) hits you squarely in the face.

He writes to us most every day, and how his letters thrill us!
I can't describe the joys with which his quaint expressions fill us.

The English language falls easily into iambic patterns. (Ordinary English speech tends to be iambic.) Great poets in the language, like Shakespeare, know that rhythm has an emotional effect (as it does in music), but they don't want it to overwhelm the words. Compare the above lines with the opening lines from one of Shakespeare's most famous sonnets (XVIII). Note that to discover the iambic meter you have to distort the natural flow of the words.

Shall I compare thee to a summer's day?
Thou art more lovely and more temperate.

> *"Scorn not the sonnet: critic, you have frowned,*
> *Mindful of its honors; with this key Shakespeare unlocked his heart."*
>
> **—William Wordsworth**

The challenge to the writer of a Petrarchan sonnet grows more rigorous still. Not only must each line fit the rhythmic pattern, but the poet must find five or seven line-endings that rhyme. Though rhyme may have originated as an aid to memory, it remains an essential ingredient of poetry, still employed by many poets who like the musical resonance that rhyme can create, as well as the challenge of having the rhymes not seem forced. In Petrarchan and Shakespearean sonnets, rhymes are placed in certain sequences and cannot be varied. The great poets are somehow able to stay within the bounds of the rhyme scheme and still find freedom of thought.

> *Great poets are somehow able to stay within the bounds of the rhyme scheme and still find freedom of thought.*

Two of Petrarch's schemes can be outlined using letters of the alphabet to represent the rhyming line-endings: the first is *abbaabbacddcee;* and the second, *ababcdcdefefgg.* In other words, a poet writing in the first scheme must rhyme the final sound of the first line with that of the fourth, fifth, and eighth lines, the final sound of the second line with that of the third, sixth, and seventh lines, while there are two new rhymes at the end of the final two lines, represented as *cddcee.*

Shakespeare's own favorite was the second scheme, perhaps because it allows more rhyming options. In Spanish or Italian, for example, many words have the same endings, making rhyme that much easier. In English, however, fewer words have multiple rhymes. Perhaps for this very reason, much English and American poetry—most of the speeches in the *plays* of Shakespeare, for example—abandon rhyme altogether. **Blank verse** is poetic language that has rhythm but not rhyme. You probably wouldn't want to listen to a play in which the dialogue rhymed like an Italian sonnet. But one of the marvels of the Shakespearean play is that the rhythm is there underneath the dialogue—like a faint drum—but it too is seldom obvious.

Here is one of the famous sonnets written by Petrarch to the love of his life, a twenty-three-year-old married woman he called Laura. "Love's Inconsistency," translated by Sir Thomas Wyatt, captures the mixture of pain and joy well known to everyone who has fallen deeply into a love that is not returned.

Love's Inconsistency

I find no peace, and all my war is done;
I fear and hope, I burn and freeze likewise
I fly above the wind, yet cannot rise;
And nought I have, yet all the world I seize on;
That looseth, nor locketh, holdeth me in prison,
And holds me not, yet can I 'scape no wise;
Nor lets me live, nor die, at my devise,
And yet of death it giveth none occasion.
Without eyes I see, and without tongue I plain;
I wish to perish, yet I ask for health;
I love another, and yet I hate myself;
I feed in sorrow, and laugh in all my pain;
Lo, thus displeaseth me both death and life,
And my delight is causer of my grief.

Many of the rhymes are not exact, but we may assume the translator had a difficult time being faithful to Petrarch's original words in Italian. "Done" and "seize on" are stretching verse conventions quite a bit, as are "prison" and "occasion" and "life" and "grief" in the concluding couplet.

Shakespeare's Sonnets. Among the glories of literature in our language are the 154 sonnets penned by William Shakespeare (1564–1616), universally acknowledged as the master of English verse not only for the complexity of his thought but for the unsurpassed manner in which he handles both rhythm and rhyme.

Shakespeare's plays are written for the most part in blank verse, unrhymed iambic pentameter. When Shakespeare ends a scene with a **couplet**, two lines that rhyme, he is using a poetic scheme that might seem obvious and undramatic in lesser hands, but he manages to make the rhymes seem perfectly natural. Here is Hamlet's famous couplet spoken after he learns that his uncle murdered his father, whose ghost has demanded vengeance, a violent crime that the young man is afraid he may not have the will to commit:

The time is out of joint: O cursed spite,
That ever I was born to set it right!

"Shakespeare, with his open candid nature, laid bare his soul."

—A. L. Rowse

Though Shakespeare takes rhyming liberties in his sonnets from time to time, one aspect of his genius certainly has to be an extraordinary vocabulary (said to have included over 30,000 words) from which he was able to draw forth words that perfectly fit rhythm, rhyme, and meaning. The sonnets are generally expressions of love, sometimes obsessive adoration, which is not always returned.

The identity of the person (or persons) to whom these poems are addressed has aroused considerable debate among Shakespearean scholars. However, poetry was popular during the Elizabethan age (sixteenth-century England) and the subject matter was generally love in both its positive and negative guises. In this respect Elizabethan poetry was for its time similar to the popular songs of the 1930s and 1940s with **lyrics** that either extolled the beauty of the beloved or the heartbreak of a broken romance. Like the songwriters of those times, Elizabethan poets did not always write from personal experience. Writing good poetry was a profitable business, and the youthful Shakespeare, who came to the big city of London from the small town of Stratford-upon-Avon without a great deal of money, realized he might be able to support himself with his skills as a writer of both plays and poems. In Sonnet XXIX he speaks of the joy that love can bring.

Listen on **MyHumanitiesKit.com**
Shakespeare, Sonnet XXIX

Sonnet XXIX

When, in disgrace with fortune and men's eyes,
I all alone beweep my outcast state
And trouble deaf heaven with my bootless cries
And look upon myself and curse my fate,
Wishing me like to one more rich in hope,
Featured like him, like him with friends possess'd,
Desiring this man's art and that man's scope,
With what I most enjoy contented least;
Yet in these thoughts myself almost despising,
Haply I think on thee, and then my state,
Like to the lark at break of day arising
From sullen earth, sings hymns at heaven's gate;

For thy sweet love remember'd such wealth brings
That then I scorn to change my state with kings.

The meter of the poem cheats only here and there. "And trouble," for example, is an iambic foot with an extra, unstressed syllable, but the rest of the line follows the rhythmic pattern. Of course, the rhythm of a poem is often apparent only through **scanning**—that is, by exaggerating the meter. Shakespeare does not want his lines to sound *overly* rhythmic. The secret of Shakespearean verse is to read it as if it were prose. Meter and rhyme are often only quietly there. They function like subtle background music in a well-directed film. The genius of the poet is his ability to merge form and content into a unified whole.

Shakespeare uses only two semicolons in Sonnet XXIX. Other lines (except for the final line, of course) use either commas or no punctuation at all. In either case, the thought extends beyond the rhyming word, as in lines 9–12. The rhyming of "despising" and "arising" is glossed over because there is no pause after "arising." Shakespeare writes prose while adhering to the rules of poetry. He does, as we have said, take liberties here and there, as in "myself almost despising" because clearly a rhyme for "myself" would have posed more of a challenge than a rhyme for "despising." For the most part, however, his fertile mind was able to make rhythmic and rhymed lines fit together logically and inevitably. Larks *do* arise!

In Chapter 7 we look at examples of how Shakespeare's mastery of poetry is overwhelmingly evident in his plays.

> *"His vocabulary was large–almost 30,000 words—but he usually chose small, common words—although in shocking juxtaposition, to describe Juliet, Harriet, or anything else important."*
>
> **—Jaronde Lanier**

Metaphors and Conceits. A **metaphor** is a form of expression in which an abstraction such as "justice" or "love" is explained in terms of something that is visual and concrete. It is the soul of poetry. To say "There is no justice" is less effective than a poet's telling us that "Justice is the blind lady dropping her scales."

Shakespeare, as we have said, possessed an enormous vocabulary. He lived in an age when the English language was bursting with words taken over from the various cultures with which England had interacted: German, Scandinavian, and, of course, French. The linguistic resources stored in his brain and always readily available for his pen gave him the power to express and investigate complex ideas for which verbal abstractions were not adequate vehicles. So Shakespeare also experimented with metaphor.

The most famous metaphoric expressions of love ever penned can be found in the balcony scene from *Romeo and Juliet,* in which the two young people declare their devotion in language that has become the very icon of romance. When Juliet emerges from her bedchamber, Romeo wonders "what light through yonder window breaks?" Then he answers his own question: "It is the east, and Juliet is the sun." In a *Discover* magazine article on metaphor, Jarond Lanier considers the appropriateness of comparing a beautiful young woman to the sun and how such a metaphor illustrates the poet's ability to establish a connection between an inner feeling and its outward manifestation.[5]

Later on in the scene, Juliet indicates that she is not altogether happy about the feelings they are expressing. She is afraid that their infatuation with each other is "too swift, too like the lightning/ Which doth cease to be ere one can say it lightens." But there is no going back. They are committed to each other. They must part for the moment, yet "parting is such sweet sorrow/ That I shall say goodnight till it be morrow." "Sweet" is a time-honored metaphoric alternate to "nice," but it was Shakespeare who used it in an unexpected context and gave the metaphor a complexity that casual usage rarely captures.

Moviestore collection Ltd/Alamy

Olivia Hussey and Leonard Whiting, *Romeo and Juliet*, 1968

The famous lovers exchange famous metaphors in Franco Zeffirelli's film version.

A generation younger than Shakespeare, John Donne (1572–1631) is famous for special kinds of metaphors called metaphysical **conceits**, extremely elaborate and extended associations between two dissimilar things. The varied life Donne led helps to explain his unique manner of communicating complex feelings and ideas with references to widely separate human experiences. In his youth, he served as a soldier in English expeditions against the Spanish. In later life, he became an Anglican priest and eventually the dean of St. Paul's Cathedral in London. The development of his poetic works reflects his contrasting modes of living. The poems of his youth express sensuality, cynicism, and a humorous approach to life, while those of his later years exhibit a fervent spirituality. The deeply religious older man, however, retained a strong undercurrent of the younger man's sexual urges, and in the following sonnet, one of his most celebrated, the two sides of his nature merge. The struggle to achieve mystic exaltation and free the self from sin is described in sexually explicit terms.

"Donne's poems furnish a curious record of his emotional, intellectual, and spiritual progress through life. He brings all the resources of a mind rich in learning to a focus in his poetry."

—Alexander M. Witherspoon

Holy Sonnet XIV

Batter my heart, three person'd God; for you
As yet but knock, breathe, shine, and seek to mend;
That I may rise, and stand, o'erthrow me, and bend
Your force, to break, blow, burn, and make me new.
I, like an usurpt town, to another due,
Labor to admit you, but Oh, to no end,
Reason your viceroy in me, me should defend,
But is captiv'd, and proves weak or untrue.
Yet dearly I love you, and would be loved fain
But am betroth'd unto your enemy:
Divorce me, untie, or break that knot again,
Take me to you, imprison me, for I
Except you' enthrall me, never shall be free,
Nor ever chaste, except you ravish me.

Donne expands his conceit to include not only a violent sexual encounter ("except you ravish me") but a startling plea to God to divorce him from Satan or else to "untie" him, suggesting a kind of mystical adultery. Donne seems to have been deeply in love with his wife, perhaps explaining why it may have been natural for him to associate the sexual and spiritual bonds between two people. But only a great poet would have had the creative audacity to make God one of those people.

John Donne has fascinated critics and scholars for centuries as a writer of great complexity with a hidden self that may never be completely understood apart from what he wrote. Poetry is the key that unlocks the door to the hidden self, which has no language until a poet finds a way to liberate it.

A Modern Love Sonnet. Shakespeare's sonnets may or may not be personal. Donne's certainly are, and as the sonnet form has continued to develop over the years, the content has become almost always an expression of a poet's deepest feelings. At least such expression is characteristic of sonnets by Edna St. Vincent Millay (1892–1950), an American poet who lived a free-spirited life in Greenwich Village. Many of her sonnets are about lost love. Here is one of them:

> "After her graduation, Miss Millay became a resident of Greenwich Village and symbol of "flaming youth."
>
> **—Norman Foerster**

Time does not bring relief; you all have lied
Who told me time would ease me of my pain!
I miss him in the weeping of the rain;
I want him at the shrinking of the tide;
The old snows melt from every mountain-side,
And last year's leaves are smoke in every lane;
And last year's bitter loving must remain
Heaped on my heart, and my old thoughts abide,
There are a hundred places where I fear
To go,—so with his memory they brim.
And entering with relief some quiet place
Where never fell his foot or shone his face
I say, "There is no memory of him here!"
And so stand stricken, so remembering him.[6]

Note that the poet adheres closely to iambic pentameter and has a definite rhyme scheme: *abbaabbacdeecd.* Note also that, here again, meaning comes first. The first sentence of the second stanza is five lines long, not stopping to punctuate the rhymes; and, as is true of the Shakespearean sonnet, the strict rhythm does not intrude on the thought.

Haiku

The Japanese **haiku** is founded on oneness with the natural world. It is a short poem (no more than seventeen syllables, distributed over three lines—five, seven, five—) in which the writer captures an incisive thought or an image derived from direct observation of nature, but in words that ordinary language cannot match. The thought or the image becomes fixed forever in the reader's memory. Its nearest counterpart is Zen painting, in which the artist captures the essence of an object in a few brushstrokes.

Much of this poetry springs from the Buddhist tradition, which discourages lengthy rational sequences in favor of sudden intuitive insights. Many poets use haiku as a vehicle for exploring their inner self, for bringing them into closer contact with nature; and for the delight of children, many of whom learn to love poetry from the apparent simplicity of the form.

Almost a contemporary of John Donne was Matsuo Bashō (1644–1694), who pioneered in the development of the haiku.

Detestable crow!
Today alone you please me—
black against the snow.[7]

Here is another haiku, this time by a later poet, Kobayashi Issa (1763–1827):

Oh, don't strike the fly!
See? With knees bent and hands clasped
he prays for his life.[8]

Burstein Collection/Corbis

Miyamoto Ninten, detail from *Shrike*, early 17th century

Much Japanese art is, like the haiku, apparently simple, but conveys a depth of meaning.

The first poem illustrates the Japanese art of capturing both an image and a thought at the same time, and the second imparts a moral admonition to understand, not harm the natural world.

Contemporary poet Campbell McGrath (b.1962) is fond of expressing his own sudden insights through this ancient genre.

5 a.m.: the frogs
ask what is it, what is it?
It is what it is.[9]

Going from a translation of a frog's croak to the wisdom of Buddhist and Taoist philosophy is no mean feat, but haiku allows the poet to do just this.

Parallels to the haiku are abundant in the world of visual art, especially among artists who like to create a scene or express a thought using as few details as possible. In the painting shown here, *Shrike*, by the Japanese artist Miyamoto Masashi (pseudonym, Niten), who was also a Samurai and Zen Buddhist (1585–1645), the focus is on just two central objects: a bird and a caterpillar crawling up the tree branch apparently unaware that the shrike perched atop the branch will soon end its life. Like many haiku, the painting says more about life than a great abundance of words could match.

Simple Forms, Profound Meaning: William Blake

In the centuries that followed the tremendous literary and dramatic achievements of Shakespeare's age, many different poetic forms became popular. Poets still wrote sonnets but they also expressed themselves in a variety of other ways. One poet in particular, William Blake, was fascinated by what a serious writer might do with nursery rhymes. Blake (1757–1827), who was both an artist and a poet, shows in some of his verse how a simple, popular form becomes, in the hands of a master, an unforgettable way of expressing a truth that is both personal and universal.

> *"To see a world in a grain of sand*
> *And heaven in a wild flower,*
> *Hold infinity in the*
> *palm of your hand*
> *And eternity in an hour."*
>
> **—William Blake**

Unlike today when modern poets can set down their thoughts and feelings in whatever form they deem suitable, in Blake's time it was still customary for a poet to choose among available verse models and adhere closely to their requirements. In two of his most famous achievements, collections known as *Songs of Innocence* (1789) and *Songs of Experience* (1794), Blake met the challenge of simple, childlike verse, heavily rhythmic and forcefully rhymed (unlike the Shakespearean sonnet). But underneath their sing-songy music lies Blake's sorrow over the inevitable loss of childhood innocence and the adult's unavoidable confrontation of what life holds.

The most famous poem in *Songs of Innocence* is called "The Lamb," and it is paralleled in *Songs of Experience* by another, equally famous poem, "The Tiger." Taken together, the pair make a powerful statement. Both poems speak to religious themes, but their contrasts could not be greater.

The Lamb

Little Lamb, who made thee?
Does thou know who made thee?
Gave thee life and bid thee feed,

By the stream and o'er the mead;
Gave thee clothing of delight,
Softest clothing, wooly, bright;
Gave thee such a tender voice,
Making all the vails rejoice.
Little Lamb, who made thee?
Dost thou know who made thee?

Little Lamb, I'll tell thee,
Little Lamb, I'll tell thee.
He is called by thy name,
For he calls himself a Lamb.
He is meek, and he is mild;
He became a little child.
I a child, and thou a lamb,
We are called by his name.
Little Lamb, God bless thee!
Little Lamb, God bless thee!

Even though the poem suggests a nursery rhyme and is written in a childlike style, lurking behind the surface innocence of the poem is the knowledge that lambs were sacrificial animals and also that Christ, who "calls himself a Lamb," was himself a sacrifice. The poem suggests the darker world of experience that is to come.

Explore on **MyHumanitiesKit.com**
Blake, "The Chimney Sweeper" and "Little Black Boy"

In the *Songs of Experience* Blake uses the same childlike verse but expresses emotions that come to us as we grow and begin to experience the world's evil. Here is the companion piece to "The Lamb."

The Tiger

Tiger! Tiger! burning bright
In the forests of the night:
What immortal hand or eye,
Could frame thy fearful symmetry?

In what distant deeps or skies
Burnt the fire of thine eyes?
On what wings dare he aspire?
What the hand dare seize the fire?

And what shoulder, and what art,
Could twist the sinews of thy heart?
And when thy heart began to beat,
What dread hand? and what dread feet?
What the hammer? what the chain?
In what furnace was thy brain?
What the anvil? what dread grasp
Dare its deadly terrors clasp?

When the stars threw down their spears,
And water'd heaven with their tears,
Did he smile his work to see?
Did he who made the Lamb make thee?

The Art Gallery Collection/Alamy

Henri Rousseau, *Tiger in a Tropical Storm (Surprise!)*, 1891

"Did he who made the Lamb make thee?"

Tiger! Tiger! burning bright
In the forests of the night:
What immortal hand or eye,
Dare frame thy fearful symmetry?

The poem combines simple language, childlike patter, and *huge questions*. Blake was thirty-seven when he wrote this poem. The child's narrative viewpoint of "The Lamb" is now that of a grown up, sobered by the world. "Did he who made the Lamb make thee?" is as electrifying a line as exists in the entire range of the humanities and will always speak deeply to anyone who has ever asked the awful question: "If God is good, why is there evil in the world?" Philosophers have pondered this question, and millions of words in complex prose have been written in answer to it. But it took poetic genius to ask it in eight short words that echo through time, defying an answer.

As with all great literature, explanations only scratch the surface. Just as the innocence of "The Lamb" is tempered by the dark reminder of sacrifice, so too is the fearfulness of "The Tiger" tempered by the recognition of the animal's magnificence: "burning bright." Is this a compensation? Does evil fascinate even as it terrifies? Or do the two poems, taken collectively, hint at a divine order behind the universe that is beyond our ability to understand? Great literature unsettles, disturbs, makes us wonder, even as it thrills us with its power.

Religious Poetry

Religious rituals with their rhythmic chantings provided the foundation for much poetry.

The urge to communicate with and sing the praises of a deity is as old as humanity itself and, like dance and music, an early component of the humanities. The key word here is "sing," for much prayer was and continues to be sung or at least *intoned* (defined as a prolonged monotone or chant). The precise kind of intonation varies from religion to religion as well as among the different sects within a particular faith. Buddhist monks, Roman Catholic clerics during a mass, the cantor in a synagogue, priests in a tribal ceremony, worshippers in the mosque all chant in their own styles.

What is chanting but intoning words in rhythm and often in rhyme: in short, poetry? Protestant believers singing a hymn are putting poetry to music. Great composers like Mozart and Beethoven adapted prayers and chants into enormous symphonic works requiring full orchestras and large choirs. Words in rhythm, the building blocks of poetry, are integral to human religious experience.

The Native American version of the familiar psalm shows the universality of the theme as well as its simple power.

The psalms in the Hebrew Bible, attributed to King David, contain many personal expressions of joy in God's creation and faith in the transcendent power of God's love. One of the most enduring of the psalms in the King James version of 1611 is "The Lord Is My Shepherd," and the metaphor describing the relationship between a loving God and his cared-for flock has been a cornerstone of Western religions. A Native American version of the poem begins "The Great Father above is a Shepherd Chief." But the metaphor presupposes a separation between God and creation, which is not true of all religions.

The poet Gerard Manley Hopkins (1844–1889) was an ordained Catholic priest who, after years of conflict between his urge to put poetry first in his life and his belief that giving into poetic inspiration was self-indulgent, finally convinced himself that his inspirations came from God. He dedicated the rest of his short life to poetry that paved the way for **modernism** while at the same time reaffirming God's glory. In the following poem, one of his greatest, he views God and the natural world as being one, a concept that was prevalent during the latter half of the nineteenth century.

God's Grandeur

The world is charged with the grandeur of God.
It will flame out, like shining from shook foil;
It gathers to a greatness, like the ooze of oil
Crushed. Why do men then now not reck his rod?
Generations have trod, have trod, have trod;
And all is seared with trade; bleared, smeared with toil;
And wears man's smudge and shares man's smell; the soil
Is bare now, nor can foot feel, being shod.

And for all this, nature is never spent;
There lives the dearest freshness deep down things;
And though the last lights off the black West went
Oh, morning, at the brown brink eastward springs—
Because the Holy Ghost over the bent
World broods with warm breast and with ah! bright wings.

The best way to study this poem is to read it aloud a number of times. There is no need to break it down into images, metaphors, and possible meanings. Like Hopkins's world, it is a unity that cannot be divided, only appreciated. This much-heralded revolution in poetic language stems from the poet's immersion in Welsh poetry and its influence on the development of what he called "sprung rhythm," the sudden interruption of the poetic flow. This interruption is illustrated in the famous last line, when Hopkins, after giving us the powerful image of the Holy Ghost exclaims "with ah! bright wings." Sprung rhythm is also found in the line "Why do men then now not reck his rod?" Many of the poet's contemporaries, not accustomed to "sprung rhythm," were probably horrified by the juxtaposition of "men then now not reck." But the purpose of sprung rhythm is to make us trip over the words and thus see with new eyes—something poetry has always tried to do and works unceasingly to find better ways to do it.

Premodernism

Poetry is called "modern" if it has been written within the last hundred years (or so). Modern can also mean "less accessible than poetry used to be." The fear for many is that modern poetry, like modern art and music, will prove too difficult to understand. Though some poets of the modern era may be obscure on first reading, most of them *are* approachable if the reader is patient—and, above all, if their work is read aloud. Difficulties readers often face is that many modern poets, abandoning traditional forms such as the sonnet, do not use strict rhythm and rhyme and, like e.e.cummings (discussed in Chapter 1), distort standard grammar. We need, however, to grant poets the right to create their own forms and their own way of using language.

> *"If I feel physically as if the top of my head were taken off, I know that is poetry."*
>
> **—Emily Dickinson**

The American poet Emily Dickinson (1830–1886), an introverted, reclusive woman, found in poetry an outlet for the thoughts and feelings she kept locked away inside her. Only three of her poems were published during her lifetime, but many of them were found after her death in little packets hidden away in a drawer. She is now considered one of the greatest poets of the nineteenth century.

Dickinson had the uncanny ability to take simple, universal experiences and translate them into their final form, as in:

After great pain a formal feeling comes—
The nerves sit ceremonious like tombs;
The stiff Heart questions—was it He that bore?
And yesterday—or centuries before?
The feet mechanical
Go round a wooden way
Of ground or air or Ought, regardless grown,
A quartz contentment like a stone.
This is the hour of lead
Remembered if outlived,
As freezing persons recollect the snow—
First chill, then stupor, then the letting go.

Dickinson is on the very threshold of modern poetry, except that she, unlike some of our contemporaries, anchors her feelings in traditional iambic meter with half of the lines rhyming in couplets. Her premodernism is suggested by the fact that the other half do not rhyme and there is no consistent pattern. That is, the poem begins with two consecutive rhyming couplets, followed by a nonrhyming couplet, followed by a rhyming, followed by a nonrhyming, concluding with a rhyming couplet. To have a pattern, Dickinson could have alternated rhyming with nonrhyming, but there is something magical about the coupling of "snow" and "go." "Letting go" so obviously follows after chill and stupor that it seems almost by accident that "go" should be a rhyme. Try thinking of a nonrhyme that would work as the final line. As we have said before, art is the illusion that there is no art. The words of a great poem just seem to have fallen into place by their own accord. Behind a bad poem we can detect the poet's hard work.

We might call Dickinson a transition poet. She has one foot in the world of the lyrical poem and the other in the coming world of modern poetry, in which rhythm and rhyme schemes, if indeed they exist at all, are not allowed to get in the way of what the poet wishes to express. Many modern poets turn increasingly to an almost proselike sentence structure, but they can suddenly do a grammatical about-face, as Dickinson does in "The feet mechanical/ Go round a wooden way/ Of ground or air or Ought, regardless grown. . . ." Here the old Apollonian-Dionysian split is evident. The sentence has a standard grammatical structure of subject and verb, but note that the poet uses the adjective "mechanical" instead of the expected adverb form "mechanical*ly*"; and then we have the three nouns, "ground," "air," and "Ought" (the latter a verb used as a noun and then strangely capitalized). No matter how much great pain has numbed us, there are duties we have to perform whether we want to or not. The poem is both simple and complex, proselike and poetic in the highest sense of the word. The pairings are Dickinson's signature style, making much of her work instantly recognizable as hers.

To move beyond the strangeness of some of the words is to realize that the poet is crystallizing the universal experience of grief. Anyone who has felt the pain of losing a loved one or the agony of rejection or defeat knows about the numbness that follows the shock. Dickinson makes the numbness seem normal, reassuring those who share her thoughts that they are part of the human fellowship. Here we join forces with a poet who is sharing her very soul.

Poetry of the Harlem Renaissance

"Black Woman" shows us that a good modern poem is never over until we reach the final, enlightening line.

From time to time there emerge conscious literary movements, brainchildren of people drawn together by the common aim of bringing their culture, their statements, to the attention of a wider audience. One such movement was the Irish Renaissance of the early twentieth century. Another was the Harlem Renaissance, which from the mid-1920s to the mid-1930s launched the careers of dozens of African American artists, including a number of poets.

On the night of March 21, 1924, Charles S. Johnson, editor of the literary magazine *Opportunity,* invited a number of distinguished white literary figures, including playwright Eugene O'Neill, to attend a celebration of African American literature. The poet Georgia Douglas Johnson (1886–1966) was among those who presented work. Now considered the first major female African American poet of the twentieth century, she adapted the traditional style of the lyric poem while communicating anything but lyrical images of the painful hardships endured by a neglected but crucial sector of America. "Black Woman" illustrates how a modern poet makes the reader see life with a different set of eyes, as Hopkins had done half a century earlier.

After you read the poem, look at the painting by Elizabeth Barakah Hodges (p. 88). The two artists complement each other in that the painting intensifies our understanding of the poem mother's sorrow.

BLACK WOMAN

Don't knock at my door, little child,
I cannot let you in,
You know not what a world this is
Of cruelty and sin.
Wait in the still eternity
Until I come to you,
The world is cruel, cruel, child,
I cannot let you in!
Don't knock at my heart, little one,
I cannot bear the pain
Of turning deaf-ear to your call
Time and time again!
You do not know the monster men
Inhabiting the earth,
Be still, be still, my precious child,
I must not give you birth![10]

Although Johnson gives her theme away early in the piece, the poem is not really complete until the shock of the final line in which she suddenly abandons

Elizabeth Barakah Hodges/SuperStock

Elizabeth Barakah Hodges, *Black Madonna IV*, 1998

A modern version of the Madonna and Child theme.

the metaphor of someone knocking and confronts us with the reality of the woman's plight. Johnson's structure almost defines modern poetry, which is intended to move, startle, and give sudden insight, and it does so with ever-increasing complexity. Having to compete with other linear media and, more particularly, with visual media requiring little thought, a good many modern poets go their own ways knowing they will reach a small, understanding audience, one that is accustomed to seeing with new eyes and will work, if need be, to grasp what can be the mystery of that last line.

Johnson's poem is a direct appeal for greater understanding of the pain many women endure. Much modern poetry is far less direct.

Poetry in Our Time

Though some poets, such as John Ciardi (1916–1986), have argued for a return to the days when people read poems aloud, the fact is that poetry has become a largely silent language. For this very reason modern poetry need not be grasped immediately; it can be read and reread, studied, thought about, returned to days later. It occupies its own space, its own corner of the world, into which the reader is invited, a space where a private dialogue takes place between the poet's thoughts and the reader's mind. Such dialogue creates a special kind of bond that exists nowhere else but in the humanities.

Because they consider their work accessible to the patient reader, modern poets usually prefer that their work not be analyzed and translated into a prose equivalent that cannot do justice to the whole. The American poet Archibald MacLeish (1892–1982) wrote his own manifesto for poetry; and, in so doing, has provided us with a few metaphors that rival Shakespeare's.

> *"If the poem can be improved by its author's explanation, it never should have been published."*
> **—Archibald MacLeish**

Ars Poetica

A poem should be palpable and mute
As a globed fruit

Dumb
As old medallions to the thumb

Silent as the sleeve-worn stone
Of casement ledges where the moss has grown—

A poem should be wordless
As the flight of birds

A poem should be motionless in time
As the moon climbs

Leaving, as the moon releases
Twig by twig the night-entangled trees,

Leaving, as the moon behind the winter leaves,
Memory by memory the mind

A poem should be motionless in time
As the moon climbs

A poem should be equal to:
Not true

For all the history of grief
An empty doorway and a maple leaf

For love
The leaning grasses and two lights above the sea—

A poem should not mean
But be[11]

Taking Ciardi's advice and reading this poem aloud, slowly, tasting the words, leads to an immediate understanding of why a poem is a "globed fruit." Here's a prose translation: *Poetry is an experience; it is not reducible to its prose meaning.* How's that? Does that do justice to the poem? We hope the answer is NO!

What is amazing about this poem is that it becomes the very thing it talks about: a poem that is equal to itself and nothing else. Analyzing it further is like asking what a bird means, or a sunset, or a Louis Armstrong jazz improvisation. The American philosopher Ralph Waldo Emerson anticipated modern poetry in the early nineteenth century when he said that the function of the poet is to adorn nature with a "new thing." You can ask, "What is it?"—not "What does it mean?" There is a difference.

> *"Collins is often very funny—but more startling than the wit is the way his mind makes unexpected leaps and splices."*
>
> **—The Boston Globe**

Another poet whose work illustrates complex simplicity is Billy Collins (b.1941), who served in 2001 as Poet Laureate of the United States. He is fond of using colloquial American idiom—the language of everyday speech—as a way of inviting the reader in. Once there, however, we realize we are not reading straightforward prose after all, and we have to adjust our consciousness, precisely what the modern poet wants.

My Number

Is Death miles away from this house,
reaching for a widow in Cincinnati
or breathing down the neck of a lost hiker
in British Columbia?

Is he too busy making arrangements,
tampering with air brakes,
scattering cancer cells like seeds,
loosening the wooden beams of roller coasters

to bother with my hidden cottage
that visitors find so hard to find?

Or is he stepping from a black car
parked at the dark end of the lane,
shaking open the familiar cloak,
its hood raised like the head of a crow,
and removing the scythe from the trunk?

Did you have any trouble with the directions?
I will ask, as I start talking my way out of this.[12]

In addition to its colloquial style, the poem is filled with details we are all familiar with: a hiker, car brakes, garden seeds, a roller coaster, and the death figure so common in Halloween decorations. The final two lines also suggest a familiar situation: trying to persuade the nice police officer not to write a ticket. Billy Collins is one of us, isn't he? Not some lofty genius perched inaccessibly above our heads. Oh, and the title. Straight out of the colloquial way of talking about death with its suggestion of a lottery. In a lottery only a few people win, most lose, except that *perhaps* in this case it's turned around. Most of the time we win, and only a few don't. There is hope after all. But on the other hand, the random nature of death cautions us against overconfidence. The tendency is to think always that it happens to that widow in Cincinnati or that hiker in Canada, who had no business hiking alone anyway. Still, there's always the chance, slim though it may be, that the car at the end of the lane is *not* there by mistake.

> "*The poet is the priest of the invisible.*"
>
> **—Wallace Stevens**

What, then, is the final answer? Shall we go through life worrying that any moment might be our last? Or do we keep a sense of humor, as in trying to talk our way out of a ticket? Chances are when your number is up there's not much you can do about it. But look! Maybe the driver of that black car *will* realize he's got the wrong house. On the other hand . . . we don't need to say it. Billy Collins already has.

Campbell McGrath, whose haiku about the frog you have already read, is yet another modern poet who, like Collins, writes in seemingly straightforward, proselike verse, except that he is far less idiomatic than Collins. His language is rich and often mesmerizing, and his work needs to be read aloud several times, then read silently, as the light begins to emerge. Here's an example:

THEN

What happens then, after the stars explode, after the
universe expands to the limit of possibility,
after the bones of the last animals disappear into the
plains, and melt into the dirt, and rise up as corn,
rise up as grass blowing in the autumn winds that carry
the soil back to the sea as the oceans boil away
and the galaxies recoil into swirling matter, and the
earth becomes a single ripple, a single integer in the equation?

What happens then, how does the story turn out, the
social narrative in many languages, the striving cultures,
new definitions of justice, new plans for a rebuilt city,
leaders and followers, a championship season,
plots and dramas we each have played our small part in,
our domestic sentence, our phrase or motif,
our single character—& or q—whichever shape our
being has pressed into the ledge of time?

What happens after our works have all been forgotten,
the paintings lost, the architecture collapsed,
when the last books have fallen into the sea to be
consumed by whales, digested by shrimp and minnows.
when our music no longer echoes, and lampreys alone
read the poetry of humanity in the dim library of the deep?

What happens after the body fails, after the noise of the
blood falls still, the lungs grow stiff.
after the white bird ascends from the marsh at dawn to
escort the soul to the borders of this realm,
the day, the hour, the moment after—what happens then,
what happens then?[13]

McGrath, like all modern poets, has the advantage (if the word is indeed apt) of living in an era when science has discovered more and more about our world. Scientists just investigate and report. Poets react. When Einstein speculated that the universe is expanding, he asked the question: Will it do so indefinitely? Many who followed Einstein said it would appear to be so, and they went on with their investigations. In this powerful poem, Campbell McGrath asks What happens when it does? Then his subtext adds: What happens if it is all true and all life forms, including us, go out of business? Herein lies the mystery at the core of this poem. Just as there was the big bang and scientists and philosophers wondered what was there before (forgetting that Augustine asked the same question a thousand years ago), we may be faced with a second big bang. We—and the poet—are left with the question Does everything start again, only in a different way? The poem cannot be called nihilism—the most extreme form of pessimism that denies all hope—because it does in fact end with the word "then."

The Novel

Explore on **MyHumanitiesKit.com** The Tale of Genji

The emergence of the novel as a literary form was inevitable. The novel is essentially a long narrative, and the great epics discussed earlier are long narratives of adventures, battles, conquests, and complicated human relationships—all the stuff of fiction. In this respect, the *Iliad* and the *Aeneid* could be considered forerunners of the novel, and they certainly are not the only examples. Throughout the world every culture has produced stories, either written or communicated orally. Much of the Hebrew Bible contains narratives: for example, the story of Moses leading the children of Israel out of bondage and the story of the patient Job whose faith is put to a severe test.

Between 400 B.C.E. and 400 C.E. India produced its great Sanskrit epic *The Mahabharata,* a vast tale of family struggles over inherited lands and fortunes, with more episodes than any novel that can be precisely dated. The eight hundred years of its development tell us that an enormous number of writers were involved. Similarly, both China and Japan have literary traditions that preceded Homer, indicating that the storytelling instinct developed along with human communication skills.

Many literary historians believe that the world's first "official" novel was *The Tale of Genji* written by a Japanese aristocrat, Lady Murasaki Shikibu, over a thousand years ago. Though filled with brave deeds and heroes, it is classified as fiction because it is written in prose.

akg-images/Newscom

Scene from Mursaki Shikibu's *The Tale of Genji* featuring Torii Kiyomasu "Prince Genji," color woodcut, date unknown

Many credit Lady Murasaki with writing the world's first true novel, *The Tale of Genji,* some 1,000 years ago in Japan.

France in the late Middle Ages produced a number of prose tales called **romances**. These were stories of knighthood, chivalry, and love affairs between brave knights and their fair ladies (often married to other men). From England came the tales of King Arthur and the knights of the Round Table. Not only were they artful narratives but they created a whole mythology that continues to influence the human dream. In addition to Camelot, these tales gave prominence to the search for the Holy Grail, which has become a lasting symbol of the elusive prize for which human beings keep searching.

In Western literary history, the word "*novel*" comes from the Latin *novellus*, meaning new and unfamiliar. Early in the Italian Renaissance the author Giovanni Boccaccio (1313–1375) used the Italian word **novella** to describe the short prose narratives he wrote. It is very possible that the sense of "novelty" contained in the term was intended to distinguish fictional stories from those that supposedly had a basis in truth.

Early Western Novels

Early Western literature, especially the picaresque tale, flourished in Spain. These often quite long stories narrated the adventures of a carefree soldier of fortune living the free life on the open road and getting involved in all sorts of intrigues and love affairs. The Spanish also had tales similar to the King Arthur legends, dealing with the adventures on the road of brave and dashing knights who were superheroes; tremendous in battle and noble and chivalrous toward their true loves.

"The storyteller takes over to recount the event, and this is the one who survives, who outlives all the others. It is the storyteller in fact that makes us what we are."

—Chinua Achebe

The first known major novelist of the Western world was Miguel de Cervantes Saavedra (1547–1616), whose life span closely parallels Shakespeare's. His *Don Quixote* (written between 1612 and 1615) remains one of the most popular and beloved of all novels. The central character is an old man who has read so many stories of brave knights that he has gone mad and believes himself to be one of them. Riding a broken-down old horse named Rocinante and attended by his faithful squire Sancho Panza, he goes off in search of glorious adventure. Intended originally as a satire on the ridiculous excesses of the wandering knight story, *Don Quixote* became, in the opinion of many, a tragic tale of an idealist who sees the world not as it is but as it ought to be: a world in which people are driven by the noblest of motives, chivalry prevails, and love means forever. As an adventure story, *Don Quixote* influenced the work of many novelists who followed, setting the pattern for long, loosely structured yarns which would find a home in the magazine serials of the eighteenth and nineteenth centuries. The serial was a publishing gimmick, each episode ending with the hero or heroine in a perilous strait and thus keeping the reader coming back to purchase more issues.

The English novel had its true beginnings in the eighteenth century. The coming of the magazine fostered a passion for fiction that had potential novelists busily scribbling. But the period was also one of a passion for science and its search for truth. Those who dictated the taste of the reading public insisted that a lengthy published work, to be worth the time spent in reading it, must be a true story. Consequently, much fiction was passed off as biography or autobiography, and this meant that the author's real name was often omitted. For example, *Gulliver's Travels* by Jonathan Swift (1667–1745) and *Robinson Crusoe* by Daniel Defoe (1659–1731), two enduringly popular works of fiction, pretended to be nonfictional accounts of actual adventures.

The Novel in America

American writers were slow to gain recognition and respect abroad. In the early nineteenth century British critics were asking, "Who reads an American book or goes to see an American play?" These questions incurred the wrath of native authors, who promptly responded. There was Washington Irving (1783–1859) and his satiric novel masquerading as nonfiction, *A History of New York, by Dietrich Knickerbocker* (1809), which took an irreverent swing at Thomas Jefferson's democratic ideology. Irving became the first American writer to win the long-awaited praise from abroad. His achievement was followed closely by that of James Fenimore Cooper (1789–1851), who romanticized the American wilderness in such novels as *The Last of the Mohicans* (1826) and *The Deerslayer* (1841).

Then came Nathaniel Hawthorne (1804–1864), who, with *The Scarlet Letter* (1850) and *The House of the Seven Gables* (1851), won almost unanimous praise in England. In 1851, Herman Melville's *Moby-Dick* also appeared, though Melville was not hailed as a great novelist until many years after his death in 1891.

By the end of the nineteenth century, American novelists William Dean Howells and Henry James were making their presence felt on both sides of the Atlantic. Mark Twain had already written *Huckleberry Finn*. Serious American writers no longer had to play catch-up with their European counterparts. Important novels could return a publisher's investment. That's why an eager young writer named F. Scott Fitzgerald (1896–1940) could sit down with great deliberation and resolve to write "the great American novel." We are all familiar with that phrase, which has become for many the great American myth, something to be aspired to but never quite realized. In fact, the pursuit of the great American novel became itself a theme for many American writers whose novel-writing heroes usually shed their youthful idealism, confront a harsh world, and realize that the perfect novel can never be written.

Two novelists of the early twentieth century, F. Scott Fitzgerald and Ernest Hemingway, exemplify two kinds of writers, different in their style and themes, but both representatively American nonetheless. Fitzgerald wrote in rich, complex prose, evoking a still classic portrait of the 1920s: the **Jazz Age** of short-skirted flappers, bathtub gin, sleek roadsters, and endless rounds of wild parties—a carefree period that would come to a crashing end in 1929 when the stock market dropped through the floor and countless investors jumped out of windows.

Fitzgerald was an observer and critic of this careening culture. His *The Great Gatsby* (1925) is the tragic story of a man who dedicates his life to the pursuit of wealth (derived from sources outside the law), gives lavish parties which are the talk of affluent Long Island society, and seems to have realized the American dream. But when he makes love to a woman he knows is married, and allows her to drive recklessly in his Rolls Royce, causing the death of another woman, his actions lead to his own predictably violent death.

> "The Great Gatsby *does not proclaim the nobility of the human spirit; it is not politically correct; it does not reveal how to solve the problems of life; it delivers no fashionable or comfortable messages. It is just a masterpiece.*"
>
> **—Matthew J. Broccoli**

The final passage of the novel illustrates Fitzgerald's frequently imitated, never matched, style as well as provides a glimpse into Jay Gatsby, one of the few truly tragic figures in American literature:

> *He had come a long way to this blue lawn and his dream must have seemed so close that he could hardly fail to grasp it. He did not know that it was already behind him, somewhere back in that vast obscurity beyond the city, where the dark fields of the republic rolled on under the night.*[14]

Vastly different from, but of equal stature to, Fitzgerald is Ernest Hemingway (1899–1961) who recreates the rugged individualist hero of earlier American fiction such as *The Deerslayer* and *Huckleberry Finn* but places him in a number of different locales where he is tested for courage. In *A Farewell to Arms* (1929) he appears as Frederick Henry, an ambulance driver in World War I, who falls in love with a nurse only to see her die. Bitter and angry at the civilization that has ruined his life, not to mention the world, he deserts the army and thus becomes the first in a long line of alienated American heroes who drop out of society.

As he grew older, however, his sensibilities and values changed. Some Hemingway scholars believe that he became obsessed with maintaining his physical conditioning as well as his magnetic appeal to women. His heroes were transformed into strong, silent, intensely masculine figures, stoically able to experience and conquer extreme dangers, always falling in love with, then losing, strong women. Biographers see the Hemingway hero as a portrait of the man he longed to be.

Perhaps the alienation of Frederick Henry in *A Farewell to Arms* weighed heavily on Hemingway's conscience. The death of Catherine as well as the futility of war motivate his running away, but to the later Hemingway, it would have been an act of cowardice. The theme of the mature Hemingway novels and stories is the attainment of a courageous stand against not only war but all of life's brutalities.

Hemingway's 1940 novel about the Spanish Civil War, *For Whom the Bell Tolls,* has what many critics have regarded as the author's most memorable portrait of the stoical, courageous hero, one who is willing to die for a cause that is not his own. The American Robert Jordan joins a band of Spanish guerillas battling a repressive government. When the superior forces seem to have them trapped in the mountain, Jordan orders them to escape while he mans a machine gun to hold off the advancing army long enough to ensure the guerillas' safe exit. The scene includes a moving farewell to Maria, a woman with whom he would have gladly lived for the rest of his life. Like all of Hemingway fiction, this novel cannot have a traditional happy ending; yet it does have his characteristic take on what constitutes happiness. For Ernest Hemingway, happiness is having conquered the coward who lives inside each of us. One literary historian has observed that Robert Jordan is Frederick Henry redeemed. Henry saves himself when he deserts the army; Jordan, who might have saved himself, chooses not to.

The Coming-of-Age Novel

Children do not exist as central figures in fiction prior to the nineteenth century. They are usually ghostly presences in families. Charles Dickens (1812–1870), painfully conscious of the abuse of minors in schools and in factories, gave the world several memorable young heroes, including David Copperfield and Oliver Twist. Yet we do not see the world through their eyes. They are treated as victims of a crumbling social order. The novels that bear their names in the title are not stories of the development of a young person's psyche through experience.

> *"Fiction was invented the day Jonah arrived home and told his wife that he was three days late because he had been swallowed by a whale."*
>
> **—Gabriel Garcia Márquez**

At the beginning of the twentieth century—and very much owing to the influence of Freud's unveiling of the inner world as well as the growth of the new science of developmental psychology—writers invented the coming-of-age novel, which centers on the early stages of youthful consciousness and the often painful transition to maturity. In some respects, *Huckleberry Finn* was a pioneer in the new genre. It is, after all, told in the first person, and the novel concludes with Huck's now mature decision to remain permanently alienated from civilized society. He has in fact come of age.

Huck foreshadows Holden Caulfield, the hero of one of the most widely read coming-of-age novels in American literature: *The Catcher in the Rye* (1951) by J. D. Salinger (1919–2010). Often classified as a "loss of innocence" novel, usually an apt description of most coming-of-age books, *Catcher* actually has a hero who is pretty disillusioned from the start, finding the adult world full of "phonies," of inauthentic people. He searches for at least one adult he can respect and emulate as a role model, finally deciding on one of his teachers. Spending the night on this man's sofa, he is awakened by the teacher's efforts to abuse him, thus confirming Holden's earlier opinions. Like Huck before him, he will remain convinced that civilized society is a poisonous place.

The novel came along just as America was regrouping itself after the devastation of World War II and economic forecasts were for a brighter and more affluent future. But Holden sees that the price will be a sharp decline in morality, as the limitless pursuit of affluence blinds human beings to the virtues that once defined true humanness: compassion, understanding, nonaggression, and unselfish love.

Five years earlier, in 1946, there had appeared another now classic coming-of-age novel, *The Member of the Wedding* by Carson McCullers (1917–1967), this time with a young female named Frankie struggling to find herself in a world still marked by a huge global conflict. A small town in the American South, where the novel is set, is seemingly quite far away from gunfire and bombs, except that the war comes close to Frankie's home when her older brother, about to be married, is now a soldier and will be shipped off to battle following the wedding.

Not the war per se, and not her brother's having to leave for war, is causing Frankie's unhappiness as the novel begins. She is extremely precocious but has no friends her own age. She used to sleep next to her father, until he told her she was too old, and now she must sleep either alone or with six-year-old John Henry West, a neighbor's child who is always at her house. If only she could be elected to a club, but she never is, a fact highlighted in the brilliant opening paragraph, surely one of the most efficient bits of exposition in all of literature:

> *This was the summer when for a long time she had not been a member. She belonged to no club and was a member of nothing in the world.*[15]

Her restless loneliness is duly noted by Berenice, a black cook, housekeeper, and nanny, who is indeed an integral part of the family but not really appreciated as such by Frankie. Berenice is the voice of quiet wisdom in the novel, someone who watches over the children and plays cards with them because they have nothing else to do. But Frankie, who is 12 and much too tall for her age, wants to free herself from the "same old same old" routine of her life but doesn't know how to do it, hitting on one idea after another.

> *She decided to donate blood to the Red Cross; she wanted to donate a quart a week and her blood would be in the veins of Australians and Fighting French and Chinese all over the whole world, and it would be as though she were close kin to all of these people.*[16]

In her search for belonging, Frankie's thoughts eventually turn to the imminent arrival of her brother and his soon-to-be bride and the wedding she will be attending. She realizes that they could be the "we of me," and so she resolves to be a member of the wedding party and to leave with them on their honeymoon. To celebrate her

The Everett Collection

Julie Harris, Ethel Waters, Brandon de Wilde, *The Member of the Wedding*, 1952

Frankie, Berenice, and John Henry in a tight family grouping in a screen version of *The Member of the Wedding.*

resolve, she changes her name to F. Jasmine Addams and soon embarks on a remarkable odyssey through the town, feeling like an adult.

The odyssey calls to mind classic day-long journeys, such as Leopold Bloom's in James Joyce's *Ulysses* and Mrs. Dalloway's in Virginia Woolf's novel of that name. Frankie wanders into parts of town she would once not have dared to enter, even venturing into the Blue Moon Café, a notorious hangout for soldiers looking to pick up girls and take them to a hotel room upstairs. In fact, she meets a soldier, who takes her for a much older person and makes a date with her for that evening, a date Frankie keeps until she finds herself upstairs with the soldier and experiences for the first time panic of a possible sexual encounter she doesn't want or understand. She flees the hotel and runs back home.

Frankie's coming of age cannot be attributed to a particular moment, such as Holden Caulfield's realization that the teacher he has idolized is intent on abusing him. It is more subtle, an accumulation of all that she experiences during her day-long odyssey, climaxed by the bride and groom's gentle amusement over her "we of me" fantasy and their quick departure. Reality, it seems, does not cooperate with our fantasies.

In the painful final pages of the book, John Henry, the child neighbor who has always been taken for granted as being present in the kitchen, where Frankie has spent most of her life, dies from meningitis, the house is sold, and Berenice must face life without them. But sad as these things are, Frankie, now almost an adolescent, rises above them and is excitedly making plans to travel all over the world with a newfound best friend. "I am mad about Michelangelo," she tells Berenice, who hides her sadness and inevitable loneliness with the knowledge that Frankie is coming of age. There are no tear-filled goodbyes. There cannot be. *The Member of the Wedding* is a novel about the seasons of life, and one of them must be the letting go of summer.

The Short Story

A case could be made—in fact, *has* been made—for the argument that the short story is essentially an American invention, along with jazz, which we discuss in Chapter 6. We have to be cautious, however, because much depends on what we mean by the short story. If we simply mean a brief tale featuring one central action, then we'd have to concede that the Bible got there long before there *was* an America. The stories of Cain and Abel, Joseph and his brothers, Ruth, Abraham's near sacrifice of Isaac, not to mention the Garden of Eden itself, must be considered literary masterpieces as well as religious writings, models of tales that waste few words; and that is precisely what great short stories do.

Magazine Fiction

> *A woman is sitting in her old, shuttered house. She knows that she is alone in the whole world; every other thing is dead. The doorbell rings.*
>
> **—A short tale of horror attributed to Thomas Bailey Aldrich**

The form itself gained recognition and respectability early in the nineteenth century on both sides of the Atlantic with the growing popularity of the magazine. Along with weekly or monthly installments of long novels, magazines printed pieces of short fiction that could be read in one sitting, presumably because writers could not produce lengthy fiction fast enough to meet the demand. Besides, large sums of money awaited those who could devise a fantastic story, especially one involving murder and ghosts in eerie castles and building to a shattering climax. Financial returns on a novel came much more slowly.

When we think of such stories, the name Edgar Allan Poe (1809–1849) immediately comes to mind. With his dark and brooding atmosphere, his old castles with their locked doors and cobwebs, his ghostly voices echoing down dark hallways, Poe made enough money to support his two tragic habits, drinking and gambling. Though he appears never to have been very happy in his brief lifetime—something that may explain the fantastic world of the imagination into which he continually escaped—he left behind a treasury of short fiction, such as "The Goldbug" and "The Murders in the Rue Morgue, that clearly established American preeminence in this field.

Later, in France, the short story became swept up with a literary trend known as *realism*—a strong reaction against the earlier novels and stories of sheer fantasy. Character became as important as, if not more important than, plot in the novel; and the short story was expected to climax in a revelation, offering an insight into some aspect of human nature or life itself. The revelation was often an ironic one.

> *"Filled with mingled cream and amber,*
> *I will drain that glass again.*
> *Most peculiar visions clamber*
> *Through the chambers of my brain."*
>
> **—Edgar Allan Poe**

Epiphany

The sudden insight into life or human nature which short stories often give us is called an **epiphany**, a term borrowed by Irish novelist James Joyce from its biblical meaning: the sudden appearance of Jesus to his disciples after the resurrection. Joyce and subsequent literary critics used the term to mean an action or a line of dialogue that reveals a truth.

One story that has achieved international renown largely because of its shattering epiphany is "The Lottery" by Shirley Jackson (1919–1965), who often combines the chilling aspects of Poe with climactic meaningfulness. "The Lottery" exists on a number of levels. While it rewards the discerning reader with an epiphany that widens and deepens with each reading, it also offers a suspenseful and realistic surface tale of an annual prize-drawing ceremony in a typical, peaceful small town, with the nature of the "prize" carefully withheld until the horrifying climax. As townspeople gather for the drawing, each one takes from a black box a small scrap of paper. All of the scraps are blank, we later discover, except one, which has a black mark on it. The one who draws this is declared the "winner," but the prize is death.

A literary epiphany is an action or line of dialogue that reveals a truth.

Early in the story, the symbolic nature of the events is hinted at. There are rumors being discussed that some towns are thinking of abandoning the lottery. Then an elderly denizen comments that this is a bad idea: "Lottery in June, corn be heavy soon." We realize that the author is showing us the survival of an ancient sacrificial ritual in which one person is slain so that the gods will provide an abundant harvest. The story is not about an agricultural ritual. It is about the survival of many primitive instincts we believe are long buried.

The Short Story Today: John Updike

Many stories published in recent years have dispensed with the once required epiphany. Increasingly popular—and critically praised—are stories about believable people and complex relationships with which the reader can identify. This literary trend parallels what is happening in novels and dramas. Contemporary writers are reflecting the *zeitgeist* (or general outlook) of our age: there is no overarching theory that applies to people and their cultures the world over.

But sometimes there is a monumental occurrence that absolutely requires a response from our literary sentinels. The event that will most likely define the early part of our century took place on September 11, 2001, just before nine o'clock in the morning. So devastating was this event that we knew our lives were changed forever,

"*The consequences of slavery only artists can deal with. There are certain things only artists can deal with, and it's our job.*"

—Toni Morrison

and all of us would forever remember what we were doing when the planes struck the World Trade Center. Not surprisingly, writers were slow to gather their thoughts and feelings together enough to compose poems or dramas or fiction about the disaster. And, not surprisingly, one of the greatest short story writers of our age was among the first.

John Updike (1932–2009), prolific almost to the end of his life, published his response to 9/11 in *The Atlantic* under an intriguing title that does not give away the subject matter, "Varieties of Religious Experience," borrowed, of course, from the great work by William James. Though Updike was an ardent believer for most of his life, his use of "religious" here represents a broad spectrum of how people reacted and what interpretations, if any, they could muster. (James's book makes the point that there is no one universal religion or one way to define religious experience.)

The story shifts focus from one set of characters to another, each in entirely differing circumstances—from a Cincinnati man visiting his daughter in Brooklyn and able to see the disaster from the terrace of her penthouse, to a pair of parking garage attendants, who represent the least affected, "carrying on a joshing conversation," to a businessman in a plush office high up in one of the towers, to the pilots of the planes, getting drunk the day before on unfamiliar hard liquor and watching pole dancers in a sleazy Florida bar, to the thoughts running through the mind of a plane-fearing woman on the ill-fated flight out of Newark on which a group of passengers overpowered the hijackers and forced the plane to crash in a Pennsylvania field. The Cincinnati man on his daughter's terrace may well represent Updike's own reaction on that never-to-be-forgotten day, beginning with one of the most powerful opening lines in recent fiction: "*THERE IS NO GOD*: the revelation came to Dan Kellogg in the instant that he saw the World Trade Center South Tower fall." But then he finds himself in a vortex of conflicting attitudes that finally resolve themselves.

> *Heartland religiosity, though its fundamentalism and bombastic puritanism had often made him wince, was something Dan had been comfortable with; now it seemed barbaric.*[17]

Like most modern short story writers, Updike draws no conclusions (how could he?). At the same time, his rich imagination and humanity allow him to empathize with so many kinds of people. The story ends, not exactly on a note of hope, but from the perspective of innocence. As Dan and his granddaughters look at the lights later shining up from Ground Zero, the older girl refuses to go onto the terrace. She says, "Children shouldn't see what you're looking at. It's scary."

> *"Don't be scared," her younger sister told her. . . . "My teacher at school says the lights are like the rainbow. They mean it won't happen again.*[18]

We know Updike had his doubts.

This chapter has offered an introduction to a very complex subject by focusing on particular examples from major genres of literature. It makes no claim to being an exhaustive study. We have sampled a few important works by way of encouraging you to make the reading of literature an ongoing part of your life. We hope you will take it from there. Once you open the pages of literature, short or long, prose or poetry, you will discover infinite worlds and dimensions of reality that can carry you to a place only the humanities know about: your own private island of imagination.

LEARNING OBJECTIVES

Having read and carefully studied this chapter, you should be able to:

1. Define *classic* and *masterpiece*.
2. Explain the difference between the two epics considered in the chapter.
3. Define lyrical poetry, using that of Sappho as your example.
4. Describe the characteristics of the Shakespearean sonnet.
5. Distinguish between a metaphor and a conceit, using the balcony scene from *Romeo and Juliet* and Donne's "Batter My Heart."
6. Summarize the Harlem Renaissance.
7. Define *modernism* in poetry using the Campbell McGrath full-length poem.
8. Briefly indicate the contributions to the American novel of Cooper, Fitzgerald, Hemingway, Salinger, and McCullers.

KEY TERMS

blank verse poetry that has rhythm but not rhyme.

classic a literary work that continues to be read for years, even centuries, after its initial appearance because it remains relevant.

conceit as a literary term, an elaborate description of something in terms of something else; example given was Donne's sonnet "Batter My Heart," in which mystical exaltation is expressed in sexually charged language.

couplet two lines of poetry that rhyme consecutively; used by Shakespeare to conclude a sonnet.

epic a genre of literature; a long narrative poem recounting the actions of a hero who exemplifies strength, courage, and cunning, but not necessarily moral virtue.

epiphany a sudden insight into life or human nature that often serves as the climax in a work of fiction, particularly a short story. The author James Joyce adapted this term from its original religious context.

genre broadly in the humanities, any distinct category within a discipline, such as in literature the epic, the sonnet, the novel, or the short story; generally imposes certain requirements and limitations on the writer: e.g. a sonnet must have fourteen lines; a haiku must have seventeen syllables.

haiku traditional Japanese poetic genre in which the poet presents one image, usually derived from an observation of nature, which may also contain an underlying thought; usually limited to three lines: 5 syllables/ 7 syllables/ 5 syllables.

iambic pentameter classical rhythmic scheme widely used in English verse; consists of five repetitions in a poetic line of an unstressed followed by a stressed syllable, as in the line "When in disgrace with fortune and men's eyes."

Jazz Age phrase coined by F. Scott Fitzgerald to denote the decade of the 1920s; connotes a free style of life among affluent youth preoccupied with partying, heavy drinking, fast cars, and sexual promiscuity.

lyric literally "of a lyre," which was an ancient musical instrument, hence words sung to music.

lyrical poetry rhythmic, often rhymed, music-like poem; usually deals with the poet's feelings, especially of love.

masterpiece here, a literary work acknowledged to tower above others of its time because of its style, execution, memorable characters, or profound meaning; not necessarily recognized in its time.

metaphor widely used literary device; offers writers a way to describe something highly abstract in terms of something else that is more concrete.

modernism term frequently employed by literary critics and historians to categorize work that breaks with traditions and conventions of the past.

novella a work of fiction that is shorter than a novel but longer than a short story.

romance here, a literary genre popular in the Middle Ages revolving around the exploits of a brave and handsome knight and his love for a beautiful lady, often married to someone else.

scanning reading a poem, aloud or silently, exaggerating its rhythm so as to determine whether it has a definite rhythmic pattern, such as iambic pentameter.

sonnet genre of poetry invented by Renaissance Italian poets and brought to perfection by Shakespeare; a rigid and challenging form requiring the poet to express a thought in fourteen lines, controlled by a strict rhythm and rhyme scheme.

symbolism a way of communicating meaning that goes beyond the "surface meaning" of a story or novel; of expressing a thought that cannot be directly stated because of its complexity.

TOPICS FOR WRITING AND DISCUSSION

1. Achilles and Hector are the co-heroes of the *Iliad,* but they couldn't be more different. Describe the characteristics of each one, then indicate why they are heroes in the context of the age that produced the epic.
2. Write your own sonnet using iambic pentameter and the rhyme scheme of "When in disgrace with fortune and men's eyes." Try to make your sentences flow from line to line rather than stop at the end of each line. In other words, try to make your rhyme scheme as low-key as possible.
3. Write a poem, not necessarily observing strict rules of rhythm or rhyme, using one of the following themes:
   - **a.** a romantic involvement you want to break off
   - **b.** a romantic involvement you would like to have
   - **c.** advice to someone who is depressed over a lost love
   - **d.** a verse letter to someone who has stolen your love
   - **e.** a verse letter to the loved one who has been stolen

   It would be interesting to have the poems read aloud to the class by people other than the poets, then ask the class whether the writer was male or female.
4. Reread Blake's "The Lamb" and "The Tiger." With or without rhythm and rhyme, write a short poem about another animal using it as a symbol for something else you should not name directly. Share the poem with the class and see whether anyone catches your meaning.
5. Traditional *haiku* presented an image derived from an observation of nature, but modern poets often have fun with the genre. Write some *haiku* of your own on one or more of these subjects: pollution; a rock concert; an after-school job; a shopping mall. Your poem must be written in three lines and observe the 5/7/5 syllable format See p. 81 for examples.
6. What do we mean when we say that in good poetry the rhymes seem to be there by chance? Illustrate, using Shakespeare's "When in disgrace with fortune and men's eyes." Be sure you make it clear what you mean by "chance."
7. Reread the material on the conceit. Write a short poem in which you describe something (falling in love, breaking up with someone, wishing you had not made a promise that you do not want to keep but feel you must) using an extended metaphor. Hint: The entire poem could focus on one situation or action that is clearly something else.
8. Explain the original religious context of "*epiphany,*" then indicate why James Joyce thought it an appropriate way to define the most important element in a short story.
9. The text indicates F. Jasmine Addams comes of age at the conclusion of *The Member of the Wedding.* What has she left behind? What do you see her doing as a fully mature young lady?
10. Does Updike give "The Varieties of Religious Experience" a happy ending? A cynical one?

TAKE A CLOSER LOOK: Exploring a Short Story—John Collier's "The Chaser"

Born in England, John Collier (1901–1980) was a master of the type of magazine fiction discussed in the chapter, with many of his stories publishing in the *New Yorker.* "The Chaser," printed below, was later adapted into an episode of the *Twilight Zone,* a landmark series of early television that first exposed many Americans to science fiction writing.

The Chaser

Alan Austen, as nervous as a kitten, went up certain dark and creaky stairs in the neighborhood of Pell Street, and peered about for a long time on the dime landing before he found the name he wanted written obscurely on one of the doors.

He pushed open this door, as he had been told to do, and found himself in a tiny room, which contained no furniture but a plain kitchen table, a rocking-chair, and an ordinary chair. On one of the dirty buff-coloured walls were a couple of shelves, containing in all perhaps a dozen bottles and jars. An old man sat in the rocking-chair, reading a newspaper. Alan, without a word, handed him the card he had been given.

"Sit down, Mr. Austen," said the old man very politely.

"I am glad to make your acquaintance."

"Is it true," asked Alan, "that you have a certain mixture that has—er—quite extraordinary effects?"

"My dear sir," replied the old man, "my stock in trade is not very large—I don't deal in laxatives and teething mixtures—but such as it is, it is varied. I think nothing I sell has effects which could be precisely described as ordinary."

"Well, the fact is . . ." began Alan.

"Here, for example," interrupted the old man, reaching for a bottle from the shelf. "Here is a liquid as colourless as water, almost tasteless, quite imperceptible in coffee, wine, or any other beverage. It is also quite imperceptible to any known method of autopsy."

"Do you mean it is a poison?" cried Alan, very much horrified.

"Call it a glove-cleaner if you like," said the old man indifferently. "Maybe it will clean gloves. I have never tried. One might call it a life-cleaner. Lives need cleaning sometimes."

"I want nothing of that sort," said Alan.

"Probably it is just as well," said the old man. "Do you know the price of this? For one teaspoonful, which is sufficient, I ask five thousand dollars. Never less. Not a penny less."

"I hope all your mixtures are not as expensive," said Alan apprehensively.

"Oh dear, no," said the old man. "It would be no good charging that sort of price for a love potion, for example. Young people who need a love potion very seldom have five thousand dollars. Otherwise they would not need a love potion."

"I am glad to hear that," said Alan.

"I look at it like this," said the old man. "Please a customer with one article, and he will come back when he needs another. Even if it is more costly. He will save up for it, if necessary."

"So," said Alan, "you really do sell love potions?"

TAKE A CLOSER LOOK: (Continued)

"If I did not sell love potions," said the old man, reaching for another bottle, "I should not have mentioned the other matter to you. It is only when one is in a position to oblige that one can afford to be so confidential."

"And these potions," said Alan. "They are not just—just—er—"

"Oh, no," said the old man. "Their effects are permanent, and extend far beyond the mere casual impulse. But they include it. Oh, yes they include it. Bountifully, insistently. Everlastingly."

"Dear me!" said Alan, attempting a look of scientific detachment. "How very interesting!"

"But consider the spiritual side," said the old man.

"I do, indeed," said Alan.

"For indifference," said the old man, "they substitute devotion. For scorn, adoration. Give one tiny measure of this to the young lady—its flavour is imperceptible in orange juice, soup, or cocktails—and however gay and giddy she is, she will change altogether. She will want nothing but solitude and you."

"I can hardly believe it," said Alan. "She is so fond of parties."

"She will not like them any more," said the old man. "She will be afraid of the pretty girls you may meet."

"She will actually be jealous?" cried Alan in a rapture. "Of me?"

"Yes, she will want to be everything to you."

"She is, already. Only she doesn't care about it."

"She will, when she has taken this. She will care intensely. You will be her sole interest in life."

"Wonderful!" cried Alan.

"She will want to know all you do," said the old man. "All that has happened to you during the day. Every word of it. She will want to know what you are thinking about, why you smile suddenly, why you are looking sad."

"That is love!" cried Alan.

"Yes," said the old man. "How carefully she will look after you! She will never allow you to be tired, to sit in a draught, to neglect your food. If you are an hour late, she will be terrified. She will think you are killed, or that some siren has caught you."

"I can hardly imagine Diana like that!" cried Alan, overwhelmed with joy.

"You will not have to use your imagination," said the old man. "And, by the way, since there are always sirens, if by any chance you should, later on, slip a little, you need not worry. She will forgive you, in the end. She will be terribly hurt, of course, but she will forgive you—in the end."

"That will not happen," said Alan fervently.

"Of course not," said the old man. "But, if it did, you need not worry. She would never divorce you. Oh, no! And, of course, she will never give you the least, the very least, grounds for—uneasiness."

"And how much," said Alan, "is this wonderful mixture?"

"It is not as dear," said the old man, "as the glove-cleaner, or life-cleaner, as I sometimes call it. No. That is five thousand dollars, never a penny less. One has to be older than you are to indulge in that sort of thing. One has to save up for it."

"But the love potion?" said Alan.

"Oh, that," said the old man, opening the drawer in the kitchen table, and taking out a tiny, rather dirty-looking phial. "That is just a dollar."

"I can't tell you how grateful I am," said Alan, watching him fill it.

"I like to oblige," said the old man. "Then customers come back, later in life, when they are better off, and want more expensive things. Here you are. You will find it very effective."

"Thank you again," said Alan. "Good-bye."

"Au revoir," said the man.

After reading the story above, the following questions will help you explore "The Chaser" as a critical reader.

1. Describe the old man's sales strategy. Why does he keep talking about the poison when the young man is trying to buy love potion? Why is the love potion so affordable and the poison so expensive?
2. What are the old man's views on love? The young man's?
3. What lies ahead in the young man's relationship with his beloved? Does your idea align more closely with the old man or the young man?
4. Collier was noted as a science fiction writer. What elements of science fiction do you detect in the story?

Chapter 5

Art

In August of 1911, in the midst of the worst heat wave in Parisian memory, the year when the supposedly unsinkable *Titanic* was being built, amateur painter Luis Beroud arrived at the Louvre Museum ready to set up his easel and continue copying the *Mona Lisa.* With the proper credentials, amateurs were allowed such privileges so long as their canvas was not the same size as the originals. When Beroud finally looked up at the space usually occupied by da Vinci's masterpiece, he saw that it had been removed from its place between two much larger paintings. The guard on duty, who had been napping, seemed undisturbed by Beroud's alarmed reaction. Someone must have taken it to be photographed; that was not uncommon. Yet such proved not to be the case: *Mona Lisa* had obviously been stolen. Even though it was eventually found and a confession was obtained from Vincenzo Peruggia, an impoverished Italian who said he wanted to restore the work to Italy, its rightful home, subsequent investigations have doubted that he acted alone. The mystery of the audacious theft has never been completely solved. Early in the investigation, no less an august figure than Picasso was under suspicion.

The heist shook the art world. Everywhere people were wondering how this could have happened to one of the most precious works ever created by a human being. The question was, and still is, what makes art "precious": its intrinsic aesthetic value or the sum of money it can bring either at an auction or on the black market? Suppose the painting that was eventually returned to the Louvre turns out to be a marvelous fake but worth much less than, say, an original van Gogh. Would it make any difference?

If some creators provide us with works on canvas or three-dimensional stone or marble that do not resemble anything immediately identifiable, do we refuse to call them artists? Who decides? Sometimes the judgment of history does, as in the case of Vincent van Gogh. Sometimes acclaim comes during an artist's lifetime: witness Michelangelo, Leonardo, and Picasso. Sometimes judgments vary during and after an artist's lifetime. The jury is still out when it comes to Andy Warhol, a pop artist who stirred up a controversy when he unveiled a painting of one hundred cans of Campbell's soup. They *do* look so real they might have come straight from a supermarket shelf, but many have asked, "Why would anyone want to paint cans of soup?" So perhaps intense realism cannot be the sole criterion for determining what is or is not *art.*

This chapter offers a brief introduction to the visual arts: painting, sculpture, architecture, photography, and computer art. We encourage you to approach the subject without bias, without defined expectations. Be open to what may at first seem unfamiliar, even crazy. Above all, do not expect a neatly packaged definition of art that can apply to every work by every artist. As Robert Thiele, a contemporary avant-garde painter, once said, "Art is what the artist does."

◄ **Leonardo da Vinci, *Portrait of Lisa Gherardini, wife of Francesco del Giocondo (Mona Lisa)*, c. 1503–1505**

The most famous work of art in the world. What is its mystery?

GL Archive/Alamy

What makes a true artist? Who decides?

The Need to Imitate

Astonishing cave paintings dating back to the days of primitive cultures teach us that even the earliest humans expressed themselves through art. While the artistic technique is hardly polished, we can recognize the subject—usually animals, such as a wild horse, familiar to the cave dwellers. The exact motivation of the artists cannot be known, but one thing about the work speaks for itself: *the early artists developed a technique for imitating what they saw*. Some of the paintings seem to express feelings as well, such as fear of the animal's power, or perhaps a sense of mastery over that power. A good bet, however, is that early artists must have enjoyed imitation because they had an instinctive knowledge of how to do it. *They liked to transfer to a two-dimensional surface what they saw in their three-dimensional world.*

"Art is what the artist does."
—Robert Thiele

All visual art, regardless of when it was produced, is imitation. Some of it—and only some of it—strives for a **likeness** of the world out there—the familiar world. Some of it imitates the world of imagination inside the artist, and often it is rejected because it is *not* familiar.

"A good spectator also creates."
—Swiss proverb

Imitation is also a key factor in music and dramatic art. Music can imitate the sound of birds chirping, the wind whistling through a forest, or waves crashing against a shore, though we know that these effects are created by instruments. Aristotle called the art of acting *mimesis,* or imitation, even though Greek actors wearing masks and walking on stilts could not have *looked* like real people, nor could they have sounded like real people when they intoned their speeches. The actor's art of imitation, from the Greeks to the present, involves the truth, not necessarily the appearance, of human beings.

Imitation, therefore, needs to be broadly defined and understood. The term does not refer exclusively to what looks absolutely real and authentic. In the humanities, imitation means that the artist uses reality as a starting but not necessarily an ending point. Sometimes, though a work of art has the external appearance of reality, it may actually be making a comment about life. Yet we need to be cautious if we find we like a certain work because we know what it is "saying."

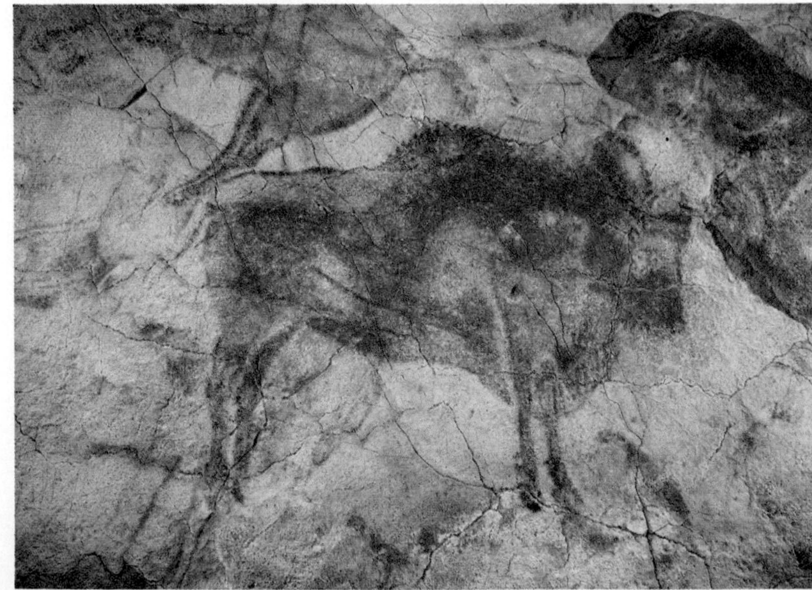

Gianni Dagli Orti/Corbis

Cave painting of a bison, Santander, Spain, c. 25,000 to 35,000 B.C.E.

Early cave painting demonstrating the attempt to imitate the familiar world.

The painting *The Bar at the Folies Bergère* by the French artist Édouard Manet (1832–1883), whom we discuss later in the chapter, does not represent photographic realism, but its likeness to reality is clear. The expression on the barmaid's face suggests either boredom with her necessary job or quiet dissatisfaction with the disparity between her own circumstances and those of her affluent customers. One *could* therefore say that the painting is making a social comment, but that is probably not the intent of this artist, who is famous for being primarily interested in imitating the shapes, colors, and the light of the world around him. At any rate, social commentary is unlikely to be the reason for the work's enduring fame.

Album/Oronoz/Newscom

Édouard Manet, *The Bar at the Folies Bergère*, 1882

Social commentary is probably not the intent of Manet, famous for being interested in imitating the shapes, sounds, and colors of the world around him.

Explore on **MyHumanitiesKit.com** Manet, *The Bar at the Folies Bérgere*

We miss out on a great deal if we demand strict **realism** in every work we view. The artist may be imitating things we have never seen and never will see except on that canvas or in a bronze shape. Visual art, as Ralph Waldo Emerson said of poetry, "adorns nature with a new thing." In all its myriad forms, realistic or not, art enhances our world.

Let Me See!

An artist's need to imitate grows out of a particular way of seeing: seeing intensely, noticing details, shapes, and colors. Unfortunately, most of us tend to see selectively, except in isolated moments when a landscape or a sunset calls us sharply to attention. Children tend to see as the artist sees, and perhaps that is why Picasso urged people not to grow up, to come to the world each day as the child does.

> *Every child is an artist. The problem is how to remain an artist once he grows up.*
>
> **—Pablo Picasso**

Though we saw more intensely as children than as adults, most of us probably did not imitate what we looked at—at least not very accurately. Remember what you did when the elementary school teacher asked you to draw a house? Unless you were an instinctive artist, you were content to make the generic two-dimensional house (three rectangles and a triangle), just as you made stick figures to represent people. You made the *symbol* of a house because by now you were acquiring language and the inner world of symbolism was taking over your life.

The generic house and the stick figure got the job done for most of us. We assumed everyone knew what we meant when we drew that skeleton of a house. We were drawing the *idea* of the house. Why bother to imitate a real house? Isn't that what cameras are for?

Some artists can produce an astonishing likeness of the original. The Dutch masters of the seventeenth century were so good at faithful rendering that many artists who came later decided it was unwise to compete and began to experiment with other techniques and other goals.

What are such goals? One is the imitation of inner reality. Just think of your dreams. Every object, every location is made up of bits and pieces of other things. If you could hold onto a moment of a dream long enough to draw it, you would be, at least for a time, a modern artist. In a sense, the imitation factor is still there, except that a strange new world is being imitated. When the artist's production offers unfamiliar stimuli to us, we need to look at it nonjudgmentally, trying to absorb all that is there to behold.

The treasure of art, however, is that its reality lives on after its subjects die. The final product is an addition to reality, not simply a way of reproducing it. The artist always contributes something new, something that never before was put together in precisely that way. Leonardo's *Mona Lisa* is not Mona Lisa. The latter left the earth long ago; the former will never die.

Styles and Media

Now that we know all visual art is imitation but that imitation does not always mean creating a direct likeness, we can talk about the varied styles and methods—or **media**—of imitation. Imagine a school where everyone else is drawing rectangles and stick figures, except for one pupil who wants to be different, to make a drawing that looks like the real thing. Already we have a *style* decision.

The young artist, however, feels confined by the sheet of paper handed out for the assignment. A two-dimensional surface does not offer enough freedom or originality, so the artist brings a bar of soap to school and proceeds to carve a tiny three-dimensional model of a real house. Not only is this a departure from the *style* of the others, but soap is a different *medium* from paper.

The medium of imitation can be just as exciting as the act of imitating itself. Standing close to Michelangelo's statue of David or Moses, we are astounded at how lifelike the artist was able to make the marble seem. A painting of David is not the same as the statue, even though we might recognize that both imitate the same character. The medium enters strongly into the experience of art.

If the basic urge of the artist is to imitate the appearance of people, places, and things, the basic style is therefore *Art as Likeness,* though there are different versions of that style. Artists differ widely on how they define and create that world. Though a myriad of artists claim to be reproducing reality, we nonetheless find in their work a variety of styles and approaches.

Creating Likeness in Different Styles

Even when the ultimate aim is to create something that looks very much like the real thing, artists can greatly differ in the kind of likeness transferred from the external world to a medium. The head of a man sculpted in marble by an Athenian artist of the fifth century B.C.E. might in no way resemble the head of a man molded in clay by a contemporary artist living in Fiji, though both artists might have said their intention was to create the likeness of a man.

In this section we investigate *Art as Likeness*, looking at major achievements and styles in its long history. We shall then be prepared to understand when and why artists began to consider other possibilities of artistic expression.

> *"Art is essentially the affirmation, the blessing, and the deification of existence."*
>
> **—Friedrich Nietzsche**

Classical Art

Early in the history of Art as Likeness is the **classicism** of Greece and Rome. But first, let us look again at the term "classic," as defined in Chapter 4 and then consider *classicism* as the style of a specific era in the history of the humanities.

A classic, as we pointed out in Chapter 4, is a work of literature, drama, film, or song that continues to be read, performed, seen, or sung long after it was created. Critics will sometimes become so enthusiastic about a new work that they label it an "instant classic." The implication is usually that the work will endure, will still be relevant many years from now. Of course, when that label is given to a recent work, no one can really know how long it will survive. Generally it is safer before applying the label "classic" to glance backward and make sure that a given work has indeed outlived its time. The irony is that the creators of acknowledged classics seldom knew their works would live on. History is also filled with would-be artists who were confident they had created a "classic," only to have their work forgotten.

In the visual arts, "classical" refers to a historical period when a culture's distinct artistic styles and media first flowered. Because cultures evolve on their own time lines, their classical periods date to different historical eras. Classical Islamic art, for example, generally dates from the time of the prophet Mohammed (570–612 C.E.) through the eleventh century. It is highly abstract and geometrical in nature, imitative not of the familiar world but of the artist's vision of the spiritual world. Islamic classical art was primarily decorative, used on tapestries, rugs, holy buildings, and the residences of high-ranking persons.

The ancient period of Indian Classical art extends from about 3,500 B.C.E. to 1,200 C.E. Some of it is, like Islamic art, abstract, but much Indian art is amazingly lifelike. Sculptures of nude males show painstaking effort to duplicate in stone the soft textures and muscles of the human body.

Classical Chinese art dates from around 500 B.C.E. to the fall of the Han empire in 220 C.E. Ancient pottery displays lifelike figures of men and animals, similar to those in the cave drawings, suggesting the central importance of the successful hunt. There are also many fantastic masks meant to depict the faces of gods, who, of course, could not resemble human beings.

Ancient Japanese art has the oldest history, for there is evidence of human settlements in Japan 30,000 years ago. Pottery and household utensils unearthed by archeologists cannot be precisely dated but are assumed to be older than almost any other comparable artifacts. Findings suggest that ceramic art was highly advanced, combining form and function. Jugs and plates served not only for practical household needs but for aesthetic pleasure as well. They tend to have unusual shapes and are often elaborately decorated with abstract designs indicative of a style of living that required the beautiful as well as the useful.

Dogu with Goggles, Final Jomon period (1000-400 B.C.E.), Kamegaoka site, Tsugaru-shi, Aomori, Tokyo National Museum/DNP Archives

Dogu (clay figurine), c. 1000–400 B.C.E.

A statuette wearing snow glasses shows how classical Japanese art reveals a culture that required the beautiful as well as the useful.

In Western culture, classical art means the sculpture, wall carvings, **frescoes** (wall paintings), mosaics, and architecture of Greece and Rome. It spans the sixth century B.C.E. through the fifth century C.E. Although the statues and buildings of many tourist-visited ruins are white or gray, the popular image of this art is of stone shapes that lack color. In fact, classical artists were fond of color and had methods for making paints, which have, unfortunately, faded over the centuries. Most of the gleaming white

The ratio of the Golden Section, found all over the world, is 1 to 1.68. No one knows how it originated beyond the fact that Euclid was fond of asking people to divide a stick at the most pleasing point and the relationship of the two divisions was often 1 to 1.68.

columns found on the Acropolis of Athens, for example, were originally painted in bright colors.

Stone and marble were abundant in this classical world and artists made generous use of these media. The artists responsible for decorating the city of Athens in the fifth century B.C.E. liked to work in marble, but they left it for the most part in an unpolished state. The Romans, who incorporated Athens into their empire in 146 B.C.E., were intent on rivaling or, if possible, eclipsing that city's monumental achievements in art. Hence Roman sculptors vigorously polished their marble, establishing the process that has been followed ever since.

Classical Athenian buildings were designed and constructed with mathematical precision in keeping with the Greek love of numerical and geometric harmony. The statues were mainly depictions of gods and goddesses cast in human forms. They were likenesses of noble, heroic beings, larger than life and thus not direct likenesses of particular human beings. In this sense they represented the perfection of *humanness,* which the artists apparently considered the appropriate way to imitate the appearance of the divine. By depicting their deities as human beings, the artists were also elevating humanity to a godlike level.

A statue known as the Artemision Bronze, named for Cape Artemision in Greece, has been traced back to 460 B.C.E., early in the classical period. A near perfect likeness of a human being, art historians believe its subject was either Zeus or Poseidon, the god of the sea (Neptune in Rome). It is sometimes called *The God from the Sea.*

"Man is the measure of all things."

—Protagoras

One of the best preserved of all the great works from the fifth century B.C.E. is *The Charioteer*. Also cast in bronze, it shows that classical Greek artists did indeed

Mervyn Rees/Alamy

Artemision Bronze, c. 460 B.C.E.

The Artemision Bronze marks the beginning of the Athenian classical period. Supposedly the statue of a god, it also represents the perfection of the human form.

Alionaz/Dreamstime

The Charioteer of Delphi, c. 474 B.C.E.

The Charioteer, a bronze statue from the fifth century B.C.E., shows that classical Greek artists also imitated real people. Or it shows that they may have seen no difference between gods and ordinary folk.

imitate real people. The likeness is that of a young man, a chariot driver, who was certainly not a god. Yet his features are without flaw. His face is noble. He could well be a god, even as the Artemision Bronze could well be a perfect human. *The Charioteer* is clearly the work of a sculptor who knew anatomy. The veins of the young man's right arm (the left is missing) as well as his feet are rendered with painstaking fidelity to life, and the folds of his garment are so believable that they suggest the genius of Renaissance artists.

The classical Greek world is typified by the Parthenon, built as a temple for the goddess Athena. But it also represents the Athenians' passion for the ordered world of mathematics. The floor of the Parthenon was for a long time believed to embody a particular formula discovered and expressed mathematically by Euclid (c. 300 B.C.E.), one of the early founders of geometry. Legend has it that Euclid was fond of handing friends a stick and asking them to indicate where they would divide it that was aesthetically satisfying to them. He found that nearly everybody divided the stick in about the same place, which was not the center. So he began to measure the ratio between the two sections and discovered that it tended to be 1 to 1.68. Expressed verbally, Euclid's law states that the most pleasing relationship between two connecting sections is such that the smaller is to the larger what the larger is to the sum of the two. Euclid called it the law of the **Golden Section**.

Fascinated by the theory, mathematicians and art historians have sought—and claim to have found—the Golden Section in a variety of places, including, in addition to the floor of the Parthenon, the foundations of many Roman ruins, the floor plan of medieval cathedrals, the pages of medieval illuminated manuscripts, and in much Renaissance art and architecture. There is some doubt that the exact Euclidean ratio exists in all the places claimed for it, but researchers say many come astoundingly close.

Beginning in the fourth century B.C.E., there was a movement in Greek art toward greater realism and less idealization. It is known as the period of Hellenistic Art. Whereas the chariot driver is an ordinary mortal with the appearance of a god, Hellenistic statues depict gods with the more defining features of mortals. There is less geometry and more genuine likeness, suggesting that actual models may have been used. By the third century and following, even more ambitious attempts at realism were to be found. The new artists chose subjects that were far less serene than those of their predecessors, more dynamic, with strong appeal to the passions. They often captured moments of sensuality and the agony of death throes for

ollrig/Shutterstock

The Parthenon, 447 B.C.E.

The floor of this great symbol of Athenian glory appears to exemplify the Golden Section: a ratio of 1 to 1.68 between the shorter and longer sides.

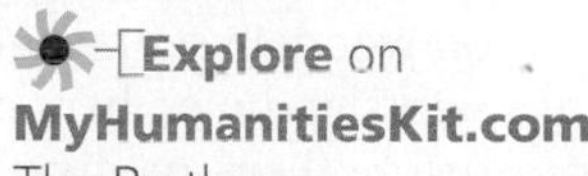

Explore on **MyHumanitiesKit.com** The Parthenon

Asier Villafranca/Shutterstock

The *Laocoön*, c. 200 B.C.E.

The Laocoön, showing a father and his sons being attacked by serpents, is a prime example of Hellenistic art. Gone is the serene formalism of the classical period.

a new kind of public, one that demanded excitement from art. The *Laocoön* is a first-century sculpture depicting in graphic detail the anguish of a father and his two sons as they are being strangled by sea serpents. The figures are not idealized, unless their agony represents the "perfection" of pain! The Romans would imitate the quieter classicism of the fifth century, but they were also heavily influenced by the vivid realism of the later period.

Despite the endurance of certain Hellenistic works like *the Laocoön,* Greek and Roman art, however, leaves the general impression of a civilization that valued balance and harmony. In fact, the classical music that emerged in the middle to late seventeenth century is linked to a revival of interest in that aspect of the classical world demonstrating such order.

Medieval Art

Christianity, which dominated Western civilization from the fifth to the fifteenth centuries, turned its back on what it considered the pagan world of classical art. Visual art mainly had one purpose: to remind the faithful of the life and death of Jesus, Mary, the saints, and the disciples. Artists who were selected by the church devoted their talents to the sacred adornment of church interiors. With a limited number of available paints (often made from the juice of berries), they created art on wood, in stained glass, and on church walls. Sculptors made marble statues of saints and members of the Holy Family. Like the Greeks and Romans centuries before them, medieval artists imagined spiritual beings in human terms, though their work is not very lifelike. Medieval art generally presents the *idea,* not a faithful imitation, of its subjects. Some of it, however, such as the famous Bayeux tapestry of the eleventh century, does indeed indicate that, when dealing with earthbound subjects, medieval artists attempted to be realistic.

Explore on **MyHumanitiesKit.com** The Bayeux Tapestry

Nearly all of the professional art was done by males. One exception was the art of embroidery, which flourished in both France and England during the period. The Bayeux tapestry is thus not really a tapestry at all but a series of panels embroidered in colored yarn on a linen background. It stretches 203 feet and tells the story of the Battle of Hastings in 1066, in which Normans under William the Conqueror defeated the Saxon army of King Harold. The tapestry is believed to have been commissioned by

Photos.com/Thinkstock

Scene from the Bayeux tapestry, c. 1070s

A panel from the Bayeux tapestry, an example of medieval art produced by women.

William's half-brother and was once attributed to Queen Matilda, William's wife. But subsequent research reveals it was more likely made years later by English embroiderers.

In the twelfth-century painting of the Madonna reproduced here, the artist has made an effort to duplicate the look of a real woman, but the nose is improbably extended, and there is a definite masculinity about the face. The face of the baby Jesus in no way suggests that of an actual infant. It belongs to an adolescent, as it does in nearly all such paintings. Medieval artists thought of the infant Jesus as being already wise. Once again we see the *idea* of the divine child, not the appearance of a real-life baby.

Yvan Travert/akg-images/Newscom

Fresco, Roshen monastery in Bulgaria, c. 12th/13th century

The maturity of the child was characteristic of medieval religious art.

Classicism was, however, by no means completely dormant during the Middle Ages. Medieval cathedrals, built during the eleventh and twelfth centuries, utilized classical principles of mathematical order. They were, of course, strongly reflective of the Christian religion, and their floor plan—a central aisle called the *nave* and a smaller chapel on each side—was shaped like the cross. They are considered the finest examples of the *Gothic* style. A sixteenth-century Italian art historian named the style after the "barbarian" Goths, the Teutonic invaders who had conquered Rome. The label was meant to connote a barbaric departure from classicism, perhaps because of the demonic-looking gargoyles—statues of ugly, evil monsters designed to frighten away malevolent spirits. But there was nothing barbaric about the plan of construction. With their soaring towers reaching up to heaven and their stone buttresses, the cathedrals were so finely engineered that no mortar was originally used to attach the stones to each other.

Giotto. The work of a thirteenth-century Florentine artist Giotto di Bondone (1266/67–1337) introduced revolutionary new techniques and prepared the way for the artistic realism of the **Renaissance**. Along with a number of colleagues, Giotto sought to bring new life to what had become the workmanlike craft of decorating church interiors. A contemporary called him a sovereign master of painting, who drew all his figures and their postures according to nature.

Artists of the Renaissance, influenced by Giotto, experimented with an imitation of how the eye actually sees.

Giotto was concerned not only with *what* the eye sees but *how* it sees. If you look, for example, at railroad tracks stretching ahead of you for miles, you will see that they do not appear to stay the same distance apart. The distance gradually *shrinks* until, at some point, they would converge. An illusion of sight, it is known in the art world as **perspective**, and Giotto was, if not its inventor, certainly the first artist to create masterworks in which figures and objects are painted larger or smaller depending on where they stand relative to the viewer.

Most art historians regard the frescoes on the wall of the Scrovegni Chapel in Padua as Giotto's masterpiece. There are thirty-seven scenes from the life of Christ and that of the Virgin. One of the most powerful of the scenes depicted is *The Kiss of Judas*, shown on the following page, in which the figure of Christ in the foreground is slightly larger than the figures in the background, while the background is smaller still. In earlier medieval work, figures and objects all seemed to be on the same plane of reality.

Explore on **MyHumanitiesKit.com**
Giotto, Arena Chapel

akg-images/Cameraphoto/Newscom

Giotto di Bondone, *The Kiss of Judas*, 1304–1306

The Kiss of Judas, one of the thirty-seven scenes painted by Giotto on the walls of the Scrovegni Chapel in Padua, Italy, showing how adept the artist was in achieving perspective.

Giotto, like many artists of the Renaissance to come, created frescoes, an art that would come into its own a century after his death. Art scholar William Fleming explains the nature of the art:

> *The artist must first make his drawing on the dry plaster of the wall. Then, taking an area he can finish in a single day, he spreads a thin coat of wet plaster over the dry, making it necessary to retrace the lines underneath. Earth pigments are then mixed with water, combined with white of egg as a binder, and applied directly to the fresh plaster—hence the term fresco. The pigments and wet plaster combine chemically to produce a surface as permanent as that of any medium in painting.*[1]

The fate of Leonardo's *Last Supper*, a fresco painted on the wall of the refectory in Santa Maria del Grazie in Milan, showed that all fresco art did not create permanence.

Renaissance Art

The *Renaissance*, meaning "rebirth," began in Italy as early as the fourteen century. Giotto is sometimes categorized as "early Renaissance." He certainly had much to do with the transition from medieval two-dimensional art. The full-bodied Renaissance would become a vast movement encompassing art as well as politics.

The movement would then spread throughout western Europe, finally reaching the British Isles late in the sixteenth century. At first a revolution in art, bringing the world a vibrant, pulsating realism never before known, it led to a political and social revolution against the tight controls of religion. It deemphasized the next world as the sole concern of human beings and began to focus on leading the good life in *this* world. It reinstated science as a legitimate source of knowledge and held a greater respect for individual achievement.

In the humanities, the term "renaissance" signified a renewed interest in the knowledge and art of the classical world—in part because that world had been ignored for so many centuries, but also because classical artists and thinkers were concerned with making sense of and bringing beauty to the only life they knew for certain.

Renaissance artists combined classical discipline with something new: the demand for freedom of individual expression. The Renaissance constitutes the greatest single revolution in the history of Western art and thought, though centuries earlier the Arab world had kept alive the teachings of Greek philosophy, especially those of Aristotle with his desire to analyze the human condition and his anticipation of the scientific method.

> *What gives us surer knowledge than our senses? With what else can we better distinguish the true from the false?*
>
> **—Lucretius**

At first the artistic revolution was a quiet one: artists experimenting with more lifelike representations of the human form. As the years went by, however, the revolutionary fires grew more intense. Artists began to react boldly against religious traditionalism and demand the right to practice their craft without constraints and fear of censorship.

Fillipo Lippi. Better known as Fra Lippo Lippi (1406?–1469), largely because of Robert Browning's famous poem about him, Lippi typifies the Renaissance spirit. Forced into monastic orders at the age of eight, he had a hard time suppressing his desire to escape from the confines of his cell. Finally he lost the battle and began to sneak out at night, roaming the countryside, drawing people and objects that caught his eye. A forerunner of the great Italian Renaissance artists of the sixteenth century, Lippi was recognized for his genius at a very young age and commissioned to paint biblical scenes in the chapel. So astonishingly real were his figures that he was accused of using forbidden human models. There were even rumors that he hired prostitutes to pose for his depictions of the Virgin Mary.

> *And I've been three weeks shut*
> *within my mew*
> *A-painting for the great man,*
> *saints and saints*
> *Again, I could not paint all*
> *night.*
>
> **—Robert Browning**

Of particular interest to the artists of the Italian Renaissance was that in classicism the human body was depicted in the nude—something prohibited by the church. True, the nude human form as displayed in ancient times had been made geometrically perfect and thus not truly lifelike, but classical art set in motion the interest of the new artists in realistic anatomy. Leonardo da Vinci is said to have stolen cadavers from graves so that he could learn more about the human body and eventually depict it exactly as it was.

One theory of the near-perfect classicism of Michelangelo's *David* is that the young artist had only classical statues to work from and knew little about the actual human body. *David* is a work in the purely classical style, depicting a human being in heroic, godlike terms, physically perfect in every respect. A widespread belief is that there must have been a model for the sculpture, but even if the suspicion is well-founded, Michelangelo still idealized his model in classical style. Eventually, however, he and many of his colleagues *would* work directly and realistically from models, causing considerable scandal among the clergy and political conservatives.

The new art had two dominant characteristics. First, continuing in Giotto's tradition, it tried to make the eye of the viewer see things and people as they appeared in real life, continuing to use perspective to achieve the illusion of three dimensions. Second, it invited an *emotional response* from the viewer. Compare the *David* (image found in Chapter 2) of Michelangelo, which is the epitome of the Apollonian in art, to the *David* of Donatello (also found in Chapter 2), which depicts, in Dionysian style, a young man who is surely not idealized, a young man who typifies the respect for individualism and personal differences that would be fundamental in the Renaissance. The sensuality of Donatello, who died a century before Michelangelo, anticipates a new emotional style that is a long way from suggesting classical repose. Yet despite the classicism of Michelangelo's *David,* the Florentines did, after all, react emotionally to it. It is Renaissance in subject if not in form. The subject—the boy about to take on the giant Goliath—was not only biblical but also contemporary and political. The townspeople saw David as a symbol of relatively tiny Florence challenging mightier Italian cities such as Venice or Rome for supremacy in art and urban sophistication, perhaps challenging the Vatican itself in the name of individual freedom.

The obsession of Renaissance artists with imitating life as precisely as possible owes something to the general spirit of the age. The new realism, with its charged emotions, its sense of the dramatic, and its introduction of new ways of seeing and imitating life, brought together an astonishing array of great artists, most of them located in or near Florence. Many of these artists have achieved places of honor in the history of the humanities, but Leonardo, Michelangelo, and Raphael were accorded almost instant immortality. Each is generally referred to by his first name only, an honor bestowed on them in their lifetime and retained ever since.

> *Iron rusts from disuse; stagnant water loses its purity and in cold weather becomes frozen; even so does inaction sap the vigor of the mind.*
>
> **—Leonardo**

Leonardo da Vinci. The oldest of the three giants of art, Leonardo came to Florence from the nearby town of Vinci. He excelled in so many fields—as a painter, sculptor, architect, inventor, and at least *conceiver* of such astounding marvels as the submarine and the airplane—that he richly deserves the label bestowed upon him in his lifetime, *uomo universale*. The label has been translated as "Renaissance man."

At least two of Leonardo's works stand out as definitive examples of their respective genres: the mural *The Last Supper* and the portrait *Mona Lisa*. Commissioned in 1494 as a sacred fresco for the refectory (dining hall) of Santa Maria del Grazie in Milan, *The Last Supper*, which shows the final gathering of Jesus and his twelve disciples before his arrest and crucifixion, took three years to complete. *The Last Supper* is celebrated for a number of reasons. First, it is a triumph of perspective. Designed to occupy the entire far wall of the dining room, the mural presents the illusion that the room actually extends into the painting, continuing on into the natural world glimpsed through the windows behind Jesus and the disciples.

Second, Leonardo introduced a technique known as **chiaroscuro**, in which the contrast between light and shadow shows how people and things look to us in the real world. The technique of blending light and shadow was quickly copied by other artists, but except for Rembrandt, the great seventeenth-century Dutch master, Leonardo's handling of the technique has not been equaled or surpassed. The introduction of perspective contributed to the illusion of reality, but the interplay of dark and light was necessary for a totally authentic experience of vision.

Leonardo is also master of subtext, a way of showing what may be happening behind a human face, though just what it is can be debated.

Third, the mural is a notable example of Leonardo's genius for capturing the endless complexity of human beings, reproducing not just physical but *psychological* likeness. Jesus has just said: "One of you which eateth with me shall betray me" (Mark: 14:18). While he remains the calm center of the group, his pronouncement creates an emotional storm among all the others, save one. Only that one knows the betrayal has already taken place.

Does the painting show which one is Judas, the betrayer? Look carefully. From the viewer's perspective, Judas is third to the left of Jesus, his arm leaning on the table, and he appears to be holding the bag of coins he has received for pointing Jesus out to the Romans. The magic of Leonardo is nowhere better illustrated than in the fact that we do not need to see the bag to identify Judas. He is not looking directly toward Jesus.

Art Directors & TRIP/Alamy

Leonardo da Vinci, *The Last Supper*, 1494–98

Leonardo da Vinci created chiaroscuro and psychological realism and knew exactly how to direct the viewer's eyes to Judas.

Leonardo is like a stage director. By his placement of the characters and the direction of their eyes, he controls the manner in which the viewer watches the scene. And *watch* is a more appropriate word than *see;* though a painting is a static object, depicting a moment frozen in time, *The Last Supper* unfolds as a drama being witnessed on a stage.

Leonardo's complex faces, especially that of Jesus, are the parallel in visual art to what modern theater calls *subtext,* a technique whereby the playwright lets the audience know what is happening below the surface by having a character remain silent or else speak a very few words. Given the author's skill at creating the proper subtext, great performers on the stage can provoke thoughts and pique the curiosity by a slight glance or by the silences that precede or follow their words. Similarly, a great artist like Leonardo is able somehow to show what is happening inside a subject's mind. In Christ's face we can read sorrow, because he knows who the betrayer is and knows that the deed cannot be undone. There is resignation to his imminent death on the cross. And, astonishingly, we see understanding and forgiveness too.

Through both the placement of his figures—Judas and Jesus, for example—and his ability to suggest the inner life, Leonardo greatly influenced the development of dramatic art. Max Reinhardt, one of the great theater directors of the last century, counseled his students and apprentices to study Leonardo if they wanted to learn how best to stage a scene. Konstantin Stanislavsky, who founded the modern school of truthful acting, was known to have spent many hours in his classes analyzing the dramatic elements in works like *The Last Supper.*

Leonardo also goes far beyond surface realism in another masterpiece, the *Mona Lisa* (1503–1505). The work has become the most famous single work of art in the world, still attracting huge numbers of visitors each day to the Louvre Museum in Paris.

Explore on **MyHumanitiesKit.com** da Vinci, *Mona Lisa*

What is all the fuss about? How do we account for the extraordinary stature of a canvas measuring 30 × 21 inches? A reason, of course, may be that widely discussed mysterious smile. One does not find many complexities in portrait paintings because artists customarily were and are still hired to render both a realistic likeness *and* an idealization in the classical mode. Her expression, still a source of debate and the subject of many volumes of interpretation, will probably elude definitive understanding forever.

A close look at the painting, however, reveals that the mouth is shown with only the faintest trace of a smile. Just as interesting is the fact that Signora Gioconda, the wife of a Florentine merchant, is looking at something or someone not shown in the painting—just *what* we can never know. But this adds to the mystery.

The following experiment, suggested by one art critic, can be performed right at this moment. Cover the left side of Mona Lisa's face, using your hand or an index card. Presumably you will see a warm, sensuous woman, gazing provocatively—at *you.* Now cover the right side, and presumably you will see an aristocrat who finds something (not you, of course) mildly amusing. Many have said that Leonardo in this work has revealed the essential ambiguity of all human faces and personalities. If we agree, then we could say that the *Mona Lisa* accomplishes what many artists rarely achieve: its creator has both particularized and generalized his subject. What should stand out in our mind, however, is that the portrait is a supreme example of the Renaissance movement toward individualism, an organic part of the rebellion against the medieval emphasis on the oneness of all people in the eyes of heaven and the promise of everlasting life in the hereafter rather than on the rich diversity of life in this world.

Michelangelo. What Shakespeare is to theater and Beethoven is to music, Michelangelo is to sculpture. Before he came upon the scene, sculpture was thought to be a skill at best, ordinary decoration at its least. Michelangelo helped to change the reputation of sculpture, making it an art form of the highest order. He did it through an effort of will and physical strength that are almost unimaginable.

> *"That in thy holy footsteps I may tread:*
> *The fetters of my tongue do thou unwind,*
> *That I may have the power to sing of thee,*
> *And sound thy praises everlastingly!"*
>
> **—Michelangelo**

As a youth, Michelangelo learned from masters of the classical style, but the artist soon realized he wanted more than what they were teaching. He wanted to create figures that were totally his, that bore his unmistakable mark. In fact, he was so confident that no one would confuse his style with another artist's that he signed

Afagundes/Dreamstime

Michelangelo Buonarroti, *Pietà*, 1498–99

Digital Press/Newscom

Michelangelo Buonarroti, *Pietà Rondanini*, c. 1550s–1564

A youthful *Pietà*, left, in its classical serenity, is in sharp contrast with the *Pietà* by the aging Michelangelo, who has known the pain of living.

his name to a work only once—and that was the *Pietà* in the Vatican, created when he was just twenty-two somewhat less self-assured than he would become in a short time.

> *We must recognize the emergence of Michelangelo as one of the great events in the history of man.*
>
> **—Sir Kenneth Clark**

As Michelangelo matured, his work shows a tension between classicism and the expression of passion. The Vatican *Pietà,* however, viewed by the thousands who daily visit St. Peter's, shows the crucified son lying across the lap of his grieving mother. Since its creator had come so recently from the studio where he first learned his craft, a craft that was essentially classical, the sculpture, as we should expect, contains more of the *idea* of pain than the *essence* of it. There is a serenity about the work that is uplifting indeed, but a little removed from an effort to capture in marble a most extreme human emotion.

> *No one has mastery before he is at the end of his art and his life.*
>
> **—Michelangelo**

In contrast is the *Pietà Rondanini,* created when the artist was in his eighties. The sculptor attempted to destroy the work before anyone could see it, so convinced was he that it was unworthy of his most severe critic, whom he believed to be God. Presumably it was originally intended for his own tomb, but now we are left with only fragments. Most clearly seen is the face of Mary, on which Michelangelo indelibly chiseled the pain missing in the youthful work. This sculpture is intensely personal art, a personal statement by a genius who is not happy with what he has done, a genius who has felt the sorrow unknown to most human beings: the sorrow of having not quite ascended to the very highest level possible for a mortal. Of course, the judgment of the ages has been that Michelangelo did indeed attain this level, but he never enjoyed the knowledge of what he had achieved. A story repeated over and over in the humanities!

Michelangelo's restless, unceasing quest for perfection helps explain why he was not content to stay only with sculpture. He also aspired to be the greatest painter the world had ever known. His biggest challenge—even greater than that of the seventeen-foot block of marble that became the *David*—was a task given him by Pope Julius II: to paint the ceiling of the Sistine Chapel inside the Vatican. Michelangelo's imagination was immediately stirred. There was the height itself, as close to heaven as his art was ever likely to take him. There was the huge expanse of the ceiling, allowing for a series of paintings on religious themes that would at the same time present to the viewer a totally unified effect. And there was the challenge that fresco posed, for the plaster had to be applied to the ceiling and painted before it was completely dry. Legend has it that the artist worked almost single-handedly for four long years, lying on his back for hours at a time while plaster continually dripped down on his face. But Michelangelo was both passionate and businesslike in his work. He had assistants, and the project was carefully planned—and kept secret even from the pope until the gasp-filled unveiling. Never for a moment did the artist fear that the pontiff would be disappointed, but Michelangelo may still have harbored the fear that the work had not satisfied God.

That Michelangelo not only sought perfection but did so in such challenging media as marble and fresco tells us why he has come to symbolize the Renaissance itself. The unending quest for greatness is surely a sign of an enormous human ego, quite consistent with the period's stress on individualism and human achievement. At the same time, to offer up that ego in the service of God was to renounce worldly fame as well as the self.

Sometimes losing the struggle against ego added further to his anguish. He was adored by a huge public. Prospective patrons offered incredible sums for his services. How could he not have felt a measure of pride when he saw on all sides confirmation of his greatness? His letters reveal someone who was always at odds with himself, always fighting to suppress his ego. On the other hand, some critics have suggested that to believe God was the only audience suitable for one's work constitutes arrogance of cosmic scope.

His style—sometimes referred to by the word *terribilità*, which means "awesomeness"—reflects the need to challenge the medium in the way that the matador challenges the bull. But Michelangelo cannot be the only artist whose creative process was inspired by the difficulty of the medium. All artists—to be artists—have overcome obstacles that would stop most of us in our tracks. The medium cannot surrender willingly; otherwise it is not worth conquering. Referring to the permissiveness in modern poetry and modern theater, where great liberties are allowed in language and structure, the critic Andrew Sarris has made the telling observation, that where everything is possible, nothing matters.

> *I'm sure marble puts up a good fight too. It's dead, and it resents being hammered into life.*
>
> **—Henrik Ibsen**

Yet great art must hide the effort that goes into it. Try never to sit in the front row at a ballet. You should not hear the heavy breathing or see the drops of perspiration falling to the stage. Still, we have to know the passionate striving is there, underneath it all. We've said it before, but it bears repeating: *Art is the illusion that there is no art.*

Raphael. The youngest of the three great artists of the Florentine Renaissance, Raphael died only a year after Leonardo and nearly half a century before Michelangelo. This fact is important to remember, for when we consider how much Raphael achieved in a relatively short lifespan we can only speculate on what he might have done had he lived longer. Raphael had the advantage of observing the techniques of his two predecessors, and his work clearly shows their influence, their carrying art toward more and more intense realism, especially Leonardo's characteristic interplay of light and shadow, a technique Raphael employs in the *Alba Madonna* of 1510.

> *I know an artist who spent a dreadful morning comparing himself to Raphael.*
>
> **—Bertrand Russell**

The Art Gallery Collection/Alamy

Raphael Sanzio da Urbino, *The Alba Madonna*, 1510

In contrast to the medieval *Madonna and Child*, on page 113, Raphael's Virgin looks more like a real woman with real children.

The painting also illustrates how far the technique of realistic perspective had progressed from the time of Giotto. The hills in the distance, painted near the top, are much smaller than the figures of the infant Jesus and his playmate. Moreover, the Virgin Mary looks like a real woman, while both children look their appropriate age. The divine nature of mother and child is suggested by the adoring, almost worshipful, look on the face of the other child; otherwise this could be a study of an ordinary family.

The chiaroscuro effect comes from the light Raphael gives to his sky and from the dark interior of the cloak from which the Virgin's arm extends, as well as from her right sleeve. The background also shows a contrast between light and shadow, and there is shade in the foreground, suggesting that the figures may be near a tree.

In 1508 Raphael, already famous, had been called to Rome by Pope Julius II, who commissioned him to paint four frescoes for the Vatican Palace illustrating theology, philosophy, poetry, and justice. The most famous of these is the fresco celebrating philosophy, *The School of Athens* (on the following page). In the work we see, again, a highly sophisticated use of perspective, with the many, many figures all painted in accurate proportion relative to the two arches in the background and the two statues that tower over the participants. In addition, each figure is painstakingly detailed despite the fact that, in order to recreate so large a scene, the artist had to paint with extremely minute strokes on the wet plaster.

The work of Raphael and the other great artists of the Italian Renaissance has made Florence and Rome art centers attract many thousands of visitors yearly and millions more through the magic of virtual tours on the Internet. Eventually you will want to see the originals up close; life offers few comparable experiences.

Two Women of the Post-Renaissance. Until relatively modern times—say, the last hundred years—women were largely excluded from artistic production by the societies in which they lived. Unfortunately, this was true during both the Renaissance and the *post-Renaissance,* a term sometimes used to describe the art of the late sixteenth century. A few women, however, defied the restrictions of their time and managed to produce great art. Two of the most renowned of these women are Sophonisba Anguissola and Artemisia Gentileschi.

Overlooked in art histories for centuries, the works of Sophonisba Anguissola and Artimisia Gentileschi are now being recognized, not just because they were done by women, but because of their brilliance.

Sophonisba Anguissola (c. 1532–1626) and her five sisters were all trained artists, but she was the first female to achieve an international reputation for her art. So precocious was her talent for realistic portraiture that the great Michelangelo agreed to teach her and later expressed admiration for her work. Georgio Vasari, the first major critic and art historian of the Italian Renaissance, author of the male-dominated *Lives of the Artists,* credited Anguissola with having produced "rare and beautiful" work and placed her above all other female artists. This suggests that she was probably one of many women who practiced the art of painting.

Several generations younger was Artemisia Gentileschi (1592–1652), whose reputation has eclipsed Anguissola's. Art historians now consider her the most

Richard Osbourne/Alamy

Raphael Sanzio da Urbino, *The School of Athens*, 1510

Raphael's *School of Athens*, a triumph of perspective and minute detail. The two central figures on the upper level are Plato and Aristotle.

Explore on **MyHumanitiesKit.com** Raphael, *School of Athens*

important female artist of the post Renaissance, though only thirty-four of her works have survived. In her time, she was scorned by both critics and male colleagues as too aggressive—that is, "unfeminine"—in promoting her work. As a youth she showed as much promise as Anguissola had shown years earlier, but, unlike her predecessor, she was denied the chance to study with an established artist like Michelangelo.

Scorn for her spread to the public sector when she was involved in a sex scandal that became the topic of gossip in Florence. She accused a fellow artist, Agostino Tassi, of raping her and demanded that he be arrested and brought to justice. The trial lasted seven months, during which several of Tassi's male friends testified that Gentileschi was generally known as promiscuous. Another witness saved the day by testifying that Tassi had, in his presence, openly boasted of the rape. Her reputation somewhat restored (though still a bit tarnished from all the negative publicity), Gentileschi persevered. Feminists and art historians have debated the effect of the trial on her paintings, citing in particular their frequently violent themes. One of her most acclaimed works, *Judith Beheading Holofernes,* depicts the biblical heroine Judith, who seduced the Assyrian general Holofernes, then beheaded him with his own sword in order to protect her community from invasion.

akg-images/Robatie-Domingie/Newscom

Artemisia Gentileschi, *Judith Beheading Holofernes*, c. 1612

Considered Gentileschi's masterpiece, *Judith Beheading Holofernes* is a superb example of late Renaissance intense realism. The chiaroscuro effect adds depth and horror to the scene.

akg-images/Newscom

Rembrandt Harmenszoon van Rijn, *Old Woman Praying*, 1629

One of Rembrandt's masterpieces of psychological realism, the extraordinary illumination on the woman's face is a technique duplicated by no other artist.

Rembrandt: The Perfection of Likeness. From Leonardo on, the demand for portraiture increased in Europe. As years passed, rich and powerful households began to decorate their halls with the watchful eyes of departed ancestors. Perfect likenesses, which might also doctor up an unattractive wrinkle here or a weak chin there, brought newfound riches to artists who could master the skill of faithful—or nearly so—imitation.

The master painters of the **Dutch school** of the seventeenth century were able to reproduce faces, figures, and landscapes with the greatest accuracy possible until the invention of photography two centuries later. In fact, many casual and infrequent visitors to museums still respond most favorably to their work because of its startling realism.

Of all the Dutch masters, none surpassed Rembrandt Harmenszoon van Rijn (1606–1669). Like the great Italian masters, history has accorded Rembrandt the honor of being known by his first name only. While he can be said to have mastered the art of perfect likenesses, he was also, like Leonardo, interested in what we may call **psychological realism**. Like many artists, Rembrandt often worked on commission, but he almost always looked for the challenge in his subject: the character behind the face, the pain suffered (even if he didn't know the cause), the longing for that something else that might have compensated for a disappointing life. He was fond of painting old people, whose faces bore the marks and burdens of many years of hardship and loss.

In seeking ways to further the technique of intense inner realism, Rembrandt was aided by the chiaroscuro effect that Leonardo had used so eloquently. So painstakingly did Rembrandt practice the effect that he, rather than Leonardo, has come to be identified with it. In the work reproduced here, only the face matters, bathed in light from a mysterious source. To look at many paintings by Rembrandt is to see such a contrast between light and darkness that it is tempting to believe the source of light must be external to the painting. Though the amazing light dominates this picture, we must not suppose that the darkness is unimportant to the total effect; for the artist uses it to enhance the quiet drama of age and weariness.

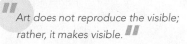

> *Art does not reproduce the visible; rather, it makes visible.*
>
> —**Paul Klee**

A visit to a major museum will afford you the opportunity to look at many conventional portraits which have their nearly perfect likenesses, but *only* of surface realism: expressions seem devoid of emotion; they offer no clue to what sort of life the person has led. It takes a supreme genius to accomplish that.

Explore on **MyHumanitiesKit.com** Rembrandt, *The Anatomy Lesson of Dr. Tulp*

Rebellion Against Perfect Likeness

The art world was well aware that Rembrandt and other masters of the Dutch school of intense realism had taken the imitative aspect of visual art about as far as it could go. So, as one would expect, new generations of artists would attempt to emulate their work. Well into the eighteenth century, on both sides of the Atlantic, landscape and portrait painting tended to be technically proficient—and, with rare exception, generally unexciting. One of the chief characteristics of art, however, is novelty, so sooner or later this trend had to run its course. Someone was bound to come along and rebel against the tradition of perfect likeness. Francisco Goya (1746–1828), Spain's major artist of the late eighteenth century, was a decisive leader of that rebellion.

Goya. His early work, it is true, is characterized by realistic landscapes depicting the natural beauty of the Aragon countryside in which he was nurtured, as well as portraits of considerable vitality with finely detailed, nearly photographic likenesses of his subjects. The young Goya proved he could do what the Dutch had done—well, almost. Though he was little known when he came to Madrid, the cultural center of Spain, he quickly became a star, gaining great favor among the aristocracy because of his talent for flattering portraiture.

Then something happened he had not counted on: The lifestyle of Madrid's fashionable elite became unbearable to him. He was appalled by the greed, hypocrisy, and constant jockeying for social position, realizing that, if his success were to continue, he would have to race through life churning out portraits for the aristocracy. Fortunately for posterity, the demands of artistic integrity were too great for Goya. Instead of doing the hack work of a money-grubbing portrait painter, he wanted to paint what he *felt* about this society, in a style that would mock the pretentiousness of the lazy, unproductive, yet arrogant aristocracy. The negativity may have been partly influenced by a serious illness which left him totally deaf in 1792.

The artist became a thorough-going cynic, developing a hatred for the privileged and the things they did to hold their power. His "portrait" of royalty, *The Family of Charles IV*, completed in 1800, is outrageously satiric in nature and intent. Instead of surface or psychological realism, it is caricature.

The family is standing in a gallery: the king, the queen, and the others, of varying ages and sizes. In Rembrandtian style, there is light coming into the

Interfoto/Alamy

Francisco Goya, *The Family of Charles IV*, 1800

The painting is far from an idealization of the royalty found in traditional portraiture; it is almost a caricature.

Explore on **MyHumanitiesKit.com** Goya, *The Family of Charles IV*

Peter Barritt/SuperStock

Francisco Goya, *The Third of May*, 1814

The statement about war is Goya's main purpose in *The Third of May.*

gallery from some undefined source beyond the canvas, just enough light to illuminate the faces. They are far from the idealization of royalty that artists were normally paid to create. The youngest children have bizarre, almost paranoid expressions. Perhaps for the very first time an artist captured the less-than-enviable lives of children who are not so much spoiled and pampered as enslaved to certain behaviors. The queen seems insensitive to them—and indeed, to just about everything. She is posing foolishly, as though she has a naive conception of what regal bearing is all about. The king is just as silly-looking, but there is also a trace of sadness in his face, a fleeting memory of happy times long-ago? We know that the children will grow up to be like their parents. Goya has turned art-as-likeness into art-as-commentary. The theme is not the inner life of the subject, as in Rembrandt, but the pessimistic inner life of the artist.

The fact that the royal family must have been pleased with the portrait—after all, they did accept it and did not throw the artist out of the palace—remains one of the ironies of art history. Were the king and queen so vain or so blind to reality that they never noticed Goya's insulting approach? If so, then Goya was probably right in his assessment of the Madrid court. And his style would become even darker, often verging on madness.

The invasion of Spain by Napoleon during the first decade of the nineteenth century did not help Goya's disposition. The ravages of war, the brutal acts human beings were capable of committing depressed him further. In two of his masterpieces, *The Second of May* and *The Third of May,* Goya used art once again to make an intense statement by dramatizing war's cruelty. In the latter work, reproduced here, we see the execution of several Spaniards by Napoleon's firing squad. The artist's focus is on the pleading looks in the faces of the condemned and frightened men. The figures are recognizable as men, but they embody the artist's powerful statement about war that gives the work its enduring relevance. Notice, too, Goya's

A modern perspective is that art by virtue of its activity is beautiful, no matter what the subject matter or technique.

superb handling of chiaroscuro, as well as Rembrandtian influences, like the contrast between light and shadow.

Many of Goya's later works seem downright unpleasant, if not hideous, to many viewers. They raise even now, as they surely did then, questions about the sanity of the artist and the legitimacy of art that is intended to disturb, to externalize its creator's dismal view of existence—art that seems anything but aesthetic and provokes feelings of outrage and horror.

Still, contemporary art that intentionally disturbs the viewer is so commonplace that many of Goya's descendants would regard as impertinent the question of whether art always has to be beautiful. Or they would contend that art by virtue of its artistry always *is* beautiful regardless of subject matter. If one of the criteria for determining that a given work should be labeled as "art" is that the artist has conquered a challenging medium, breaking through steel-like limitations, then Goya's astonishing feat of capturing humanity's elusive passions must be called beautiful.

Explore on **MyHumanitiesKit.com**
Goya, *The Sleep of Reason Produces Monsters*

Impressionism

While Goya and others opened the door for the intensely personal in art, realistic landscapes and portraits continued to be popular. Although in some countries there were rumblings among younger artists that the days of perfect likeness had run their course, in art meccas such as France and England art had come to mean "the imitation of likeness in fine detail." Would-be artists were judged on how proficiently they abided by the rules. In Paris, particularly, new artists aspired to have their work exhibited at the annual Salon, a vast exhibition held at the Champs-Élysées Palace. The jurors who selected the works to be shown were by and large drawn from the ranks of so-called experts who had governed popular taste for decades. Paintings in unfamiliar styles were seldom welcome, and the few that slipped by were generally crucified by the critics.

Édouard Manet. One such regularly rejected artist was Édouard Manet (1832–1883). Intent on painting in a style that was wholly his own, he did not follow the strict guidelines established by the panel of experts who selected the pieces for Salon showing. Accustomed to rejection, Manet nonetheless went ahead, convinced that eventually his methods would be recognized as legitimate. In 1862 he submitted the work that is now acknowledged as an early masterpiece of the Impressionist movement but was at the time the subject of scorn and derision, *Le Déjeuner sur l'Herbe* (*Picnic on the Lawn*), which features three figures seated on grass: two well-dressed men and a nude woman. Another nude woman is in the background, probably drying herself off after a skinny-dip in the lake. The nude on the lawn may or may not have been skinny-dipping, but it really doesn't seem to matter. The picture was intended to be a study in the way the eye sees. It is a sort of realism, but perfect likeness is not its aim either.

Explore on **MyHumanitiesKit.com**
Manet, *Olympia*

Manet advanced a comprehensive rationale for the new style. A painting, he said, should not imitate the superficial appearance of things. Nor should it be valued because it makes a statement. Instead, a painting should be an event, equal to nothing but itself, existing for itself—not for an issue and not as a souvenir of how someone looked. It should be an experience of color and light. The familiar world is the starting point for Manet, as it would be for many who followed in his footsteps, but it becomes a world transformed by some of the most brilliant colors ever applied to canvas, a world in which the outlines of human beings and natural

> *"Right now a moment of time is fleeting by! Capture its reality in paint! To do that we must put all else out of our minds. We must become the moment."*
>
> —**Paul Cezanne**

Explore on **MyHumanitiesKit.com**
Manet, *Le Déjeuner sur l'Herbe*

Peter Horree/Alamy

Édouard Manet, *Le Déjeuner sur l'Herbe*, 1862

One of the paintings, now priceless, that was rejected by the Salon judges and is now regarded as an early masterpiece of Impressionism.

shapes are softened, less boldly distinguished one from the other, each playing an integral part in the total unity that is a subjective vision of the world at each moment.

Those who were affected by Manet's rationale were also greatly influenced by the science of optics, investigating the phenomenon of sight which had originated during the Middle Ages in Islamic countries, notably Egypt. The new artists wanted to go further than their Renaissance predecessors in the attempt to recreate true visual experience. They wanted to experiment with how color strikes the eye. Philosophers were beginning to ask questions like "Is color inherent in objects, or is it something that happens within the viewer?"

> *It is for the artist . . . in portrait painting to put on canvas something more than the face the model wears for that one day.*
>
> **—James McNeill Whistler**

The artist, for example, sees a family enjoying a picnic by a lake and decides to paint the event. But what is seen and must therefore be duplicated on canvas is a rush of light falling upon the eye in various hues and shadings, blending in with each other, and with brightness blending in with shadows. Rembrandt and Leonardo had done wonders with the effect of light on their subjects, but their technique was a way of giving drama to those subjects. For the Impressionists, light *itself* should now be central to art: the colors of the world carried to the marveling eyes of an artist by the amazing phenomenon of light. It would be many years before physicists would discover that light was made up of tiny particles call photons, but Impressionism revolutionized art by instinctively perceiving that light wasn't just *there*: it was somehow a physical thing.

Explore on **MyHumanitiesKit.com**
Monet, *Water Lilies*

Claude Monet. The new style found its name in a haphazard manner. Claude Monet (1840–1926), whose name was often confused with that of Manet, had also been rejected for years by the experts, but he began to sell after many of his

SuperStock

Claude Monet, *Impression: Sunrise*, 1872

Impression: Sunrise, the painting that gave Impressionism its name. Monet avoids photographic realism in favor of depicting the subjective experience of light and color.

contemporaries, working in similar styles, gained recognition. Edmond Renoir, son of another Impressionist, Auguste Renoir, was in Monet's studio one day, browsing through some of Monet's new works, when he came upon an intriguing scene of fishing boats in the harbor at Le Havre. What attracted him was the vibrant color of sunrise flooding the canvas and the hazy indistinctness of the boats, the entire scene forming a subjective experience capturing a glorious moment in time. He asked Monet what he was going to title the painting. The artist merely shrugged and said, "Oh, you can just call it *Impression*." Renoir, thinking the work deserved a less generic label, wrote *Impression: Sunrise*. From then on, Monet and all of his close allies were identified (and not always with a positive connotation) as the *Impressionists*.

> *"For us artists there waits the joyous compromise through art with all that wounded us in daily life."*
>
> **—Lawrence Durrell**

Berthe Morisot. The Impressionist revolution in visual art fostered the careers of two major female artists of the nineteenth century: Berthe Morisot (1841–1895), Manet's sister-in-law, and the American Mary Cassatt (1845–1926). Morisot was

Nimatallah/Art Resource, NY

Berthe Morisot, *The Psyche*, 1876

Morisot combines Impressionism with domestic realism.

B Christopher/Alamy

Mary Cassatt, *The Boating Party*, 1893–94

One of Cassatt's finest works, it shows a strong influence of both Manet and Japanese art.

the first woman admitted to the tight circle of French Impressionists, and her work, like theirs, shows an intense concern with the way light is seen. Interested in creating nearly true likenesses, she remained throughout her life on the outer rim of the circle.

In *The Psyche*, shown here, the figure of the woman dominates the work. Morisot takes great care to transfer to the canvas a faithful depiction of the woman and her reflection in the mirror. At the same time, muted light and shadow give the painting the soft glow characteristic of Impressionism. Morisot combines domestic realism with Impressionist techniques.

Mary Cassatt. Mary Cassatt was influenced by the Impressionist use of light and by the Impressionist philosophy that, in painting, content is subordinate to the artist's technique. Because of her affluence, she was instrumental in keeping the movement alive and gaining acceptance for it in the United States. Her father, a wealthy businessman of French ancestry, who recognized his daughter's artistic talent, sent her to the Pennsylvania Academy of Fine Art and after graduation to live in Paris. There the young woman met many of the important artists of the Impressionist movement and fell under their influence.

The painting shown here, *The Boating Party*, shows clearly that influence, especially Manet's, who painted a similar scene. Cassatt also came under the spell of Japanese art, an exhibition of which she had viewed in Paris. Japanese painters were fond of using bold shapes and fewer details. The darkness of the oarsman's coat is in sharp contrast to the soft light on the figures of the mother and the child on her lap. These figures, much like Morisot's, are representative of Cassatt's interest in domestic subjects. *The Boating Party* was created in 1893/94, a time believed to be when the artist's powers were strongest.

Post-Impressionism: Van Gogh

The Impressionist movement took hold so strongly on both sides of the Atlantic that it eventually became as authoritative as the traditions it replaced. Newer artists emerged who began to resist slavish imitation. The label *Post-Impressionism* has been coined by art historians as a convenient way to refer to the work of the artists who came after the heyday of Impressionism and whose work, though influenced by it, does not clearly belong to the earlier school.

Of this group, Vincent van Gogh (1853–1890) was surely the most original and the most intense.

He differs from the Impressionists in a major respect. He had no real theory of art. He simply loved color, especially yellow. He had no interest in consulting the science of optics so that he could accurately imitate the experience of seeing. For him, imitating the bright colors of the world was his way of expressing the uninhibited feelings of pleasure they aroused in him. And if he were painting a scene that had less yellow than he liked, he would splash yellow onto the canvas without restraint. No one gives us as much yellow in a starry night as van Gogh does.

Van Gogh is the prototype of the artist who creates entirely for himself. His style was so strange in its time that the few critics who ever took notice of his work were generally baffled, having nothing with which to compare it. If his devoted brother Theo had not handled most of his expenses, chances are he would have been hungry and homeless most of the time. But Theo believed in his genius and stood by him even when his paintings were denounced and ridiculed. Only one of the artist's paintings was sold during his lifetime. Tragically, he committed suicide before he reached the age of thirty-eight.

Van Gogh's life reinforces the romantic concept of the starving artist for whom art is the last outpost of being. Totally alienated, totally misunderstood by almost everyone except his brother, rejected twice as a suitor (once with a vehement cry of "No, never, never!"), hovering much of the time on the thin borderline between functional rationality and insanity (eventually to cross the border, never to return), he survived as long as he did only because of an often childlike delight in his private way of seeing and imitating the world.

Peter Horree/Alamy

Vincent van Gogh, *Sunflowers*, 1888

Against a yellow background, the plant seems alive and bursting with energy. Note the stabbing brushstrokes, unmatched by any other artist.

Sunflowers and *The Starry Night* have become priceless since van Gogh's death. (His work can bring $30 million or more.) These and his many other paintings show a brushstroke method that has become utterly identified with its creator: a short, stabbing technique, as opposed to a flowing line, that makes the entire canvas seem to be throbbing with energy. Despite the indifference of the art world, van Gogh abandoned himself to the sensuous impact of life's forms and colors, absorbing them fully and converting them into a heightened reality—an explosion of pure feeling transferred to color, shapes, and paint textures. Van Gogh's lines and bright colors virtually scream from the canvas.

We began this chapter by discussing the *Mona Lisa,* indicating that it is the world's most famous painting. Van Gogh's *The Starry Night* may well deserve the honor of being regarded as second only to da Vinci's masterpiece in popularity and critical adulation. Ironic for a man who took his own life before he was forty, never knowing what posterity had in store for him!

Brian Jannsen/Alamy

Vincent van Gogh, *The Starry Night*, 1889

The artist's most famous work and probably second only to the *Mona Lisa* in popularity and critical adulation. As you study the painting, can you think of a reason it doesn't fit within the Impressionist school?

Explore on **MyHumanitiesKit.com**
van Gogh, *The Starry Night*

Art as Alteration

Though they painted the world as *they saw it*, the Impressionists do not represent so startling a departure from reality that we cannot recognize on their canvases any trace of the familiar world. What we see is that world drastically changed. Looking at van Gogh's *The Starry Night*, we *still* recognize a sky, albeit a yellow one. At the same time, his work is moving in the direction of what has come to be called **modernism**. Many schools, movements, and techniques dating from about the last quarter of the nineteenth century to roughly the last quarter of the twentieth century have been linked by critics and art historians under that broad term. The style of the literature and visual arts from the late twentieth century to the present is often called **postmodernism**. What unifies modern and postmodern artists and makes them different from, say, van Gogh is *intention*.

Both van Gogh and the Impressionists give us the familiar world as altered by the emotions and the subjective experiences of light, color, and form. But when we speak of the later art as **alteration**, we are speaking of artists *who do not even start with the familiar world*. They want to impose something new on that world, some secret part of themselves. With such an intent, they have no reason to be bound by an artistic tradition unless it suits their personality, unless it can be adapted to their imagination.

> "*Art comes to you proposing frankly to give nothing but the highest quality to your moments as they pass.*"
>
> **—Walter Pater**

Entering the world of modern art can be confusing at first. There may seem to be no rationale at all, no clear overall purpose, no rules.

When Marcel Duchamp (1887–1968) bought a urinal and submitted it, untouched, for an exhibition in 1917, he challenged all definitions of art. Critics of such "found art" ask: "How much work does an artist have to do? What is off-limits for an artist?" Modern artists impose their own rules upon their own work. They are out there creating new traditions, and most of the time they feel alone. Small wonder that they sometimes, like Duchamp, develop a sense of humor.

Some modern art—in fact, a good deal of it—does in fact resemble people, places, and things. But that is usually where its traditionalism ends. Francis Bacon (1909–1992), for example, offers canvases with *some* recognizable reality, but that reality might be somebody sitting on the toilet, or a slab of meat bleeding. You know what it *represents*, but you may ask: "Why would anybody want to paint *that*?

The Sixty-ninth Regiment Armory Show, 1913

Modern art made its way to the United States at the tail end of the *Gilded Age*, a name given to the last two decades of the nineteenth century. Some Americans who had made their fortunes in railroads, coal, or steel, for example, were becoming intensely art conscious. This was the time of elaborate mansions, incredibly luxurious ocean voyages, and the accumulation of what became priceless art collections. New York in particular had a burning need to be respected as a hub of modernism in art. It wanted to see all that was new and exciting. It had already opened its arms to the Impressionists long before they were fully respected in Europe.

In 1913, the Sixty-ninth Regiment Armory in Manhattan was the site of an exhibition of new works by European artists that is still considered the most important single art show ever held in this country. Many American viewers saw for the first time the startling paintings of van Gogh, as well as the work of other artists whose styles seemed downright puzzling, if not laughable.

> "*The true function of art is to edit nature and so make it coherent and lovely. The artist is an impassioned proofreader.*"
>
> **—H. L. Mencken**

One of these artists was Wassily Kandinsky (1866–1944), whose work also provides an excellent introduction to modern art. Though as a young artist he achieved technical competence in drawing the human figure, he set his eyes on other goals. Kandinsky came to believe that what mattered in a work of art is *form,* the pleasing arrangement of lines and color, existing for no purpose other than aesthetic experience. In other words, a painting should provide an experience of the beautiful. Kandinsky delved into his imagination, found a new world of pure shapes and forms, and imitated those in a style that came to be known as **abstract art.** However, "What's that supposed to be?" is often the first question viewers ask.

Like many other modern artists, Kandinsky distinguished between beauty and anything else one might see in a painting.

> *He argued that in order to speak directly to the soul and avoid materialistic distractions, it was preferable to use an art based solely on the language of color. Free from references to a specific reality, color could become like music, beautiful for its interrelationships of tones and intensities.*[2]

Explore on **MyHumanitiesKit.com** Duchamp, *Nude Descending a Staircase*

Kandinsky's rationale made perfect sense to him, as well as to other exhibited artists, but not to all of the art critics and potential collectors who came to the Armory show in droves hoping to pick up some real bargains. In fact, not much of the show was received with open arms by either critics or the public. The shock of so much alteration was simply too devastating, confined as it was to one building. Canvases by Picasso, who would become the century's most celebrated artist, were widely denounced. The room in which they were displayed was nicknamed the Chamber of Horrors.

The work that caused the biggest uproar and controversy, however, bringing instant notoriety to its creator, was Duchamp's *Nude Descending a Staircase.* One critic called him "the biggest transgressor" in modern art. Duchamp could not have expected to be warmly welcomed after a newspaper published his observation that "the only works of art America has given are her plumbing and her bridges." Four years later, in 1917, Duchamp would further arouse the amused hostility of critics by submitting an actual urinal for an exhibit (and he was promptly rejected). The artist did in fact start a movement known as "found art," which has won (perhaps grudging) acceptance.

In *Nude Descending a Staircase,* shown here, Duchamp developed his own brand of abstractionism by which he moved from an actual model through successive stages of reduction until all that was left from reality was the sense of descending movement and the hint of a human figure. Duchamp, in other words, abstracted from a real scene only those elements that interested him as an artist, excluding everything else because he had signed away his responsibility and obligation to make his work resemble something a viewer could instantly recognize. The controversy might have been less heated had the painting, with such a promising title, not disappointed viewers by giving them no reality they were expecting. Abstract art remains a popular form of expression among contemporary artists. Sometimes we can gain subject matter clues from the title, but more often the artist will be altogether casual and call the painting or sculpture *Study* or just *Line and Color.*

Marcel Duchamp, *Nude Descending a Staircase*, 1912

At its first showing in this country, the painting probably confused viewers by not showing what its title promised.

Explore on **MyHumanitiesKit.com**
Picasso, *Les Demoiselles d'Avignon*

Cubism: Picasso and Braque

The enduring fame of the Armory show owes much to its having introduced America to the work of the most baffling, the most controversial, yet easily the most innovative of all modern artists. His work, displayed in the "Chamber of Horrors," drew thousands who came to laugh, but many came away in admiration. Picasso was to exercise more influence on a whole century of artists than any other we can think of, and he transcended his age so completely that some art historians rank him among the three or four greatest artists of all time.

Pablo Picasso (1881–1973) lived the entire length of the modernist movement in art. Anyone seeing only his work and none by his contemporaries would nonetheless know what modernism is all about. In his youth, he came under the heavy influence of the Impressionists and their decision that, with the emergence of photography, imitative realism was dead. During the incredible span of his artistic existence, he worked steadily and impeccably in more modern styles than any other artist of his time. Classically trained, he could bring to the canvas a lifelike portrait, but he could also duplicate subjective visual experience, or create a wholly new style that was neither realistic nor abstract but derived from yet another way of seeing the world. This style, which Picasso invented with strong help from a fellow artist named Georges Braque, was **Cubism**.

> *Painting isn't an aesthetic operation; it's a form of magic designed as a mediator between this strange hostile world and us; a way of seizing the power by giving form to our terrors as well as our desires.*
>
> **—Pablo Picasso**

Picasso was just nineteen when he visited Paris for the first time and there saw and marveled at the colors of the Impressionists. He was particularly drawn to the color blue and quickly developed extraordinary skill at both imitation and alteration by painting mostly indigent types—such as prostitutes and homeless wanderers—all in distinctly blue tones.

From the outset, Picasso wanted to show more than a "mere" talent for perfect likeness, which he possessed in abundance. As he intended to mark the world with the stamp of his unique genius, so too did Picasso want to alter its reality. And indeed he did, working not only on two-dimensional flat surfaces but in sculpture, architecture, and scenic design for the theater. (He also wrote poems and plays in his spare time!)

His joy in using colors has something of the child about it, the child who refuses to grow up; as a matter of fact, as he aged, he was fond of advising young artists to do everything possible to avoid growing up.

The child in Picasso led him into an obsession with the circus, where—still in his twenties—he embarked on a new period dominated by pink, orange, yellow, and gray and did portraits of clowns, trapeze artists, and other performers—portraits lifelike enough to be recognizable, but beginning to show the distortions of real forms that would characterize most of his mature work.

At an exhibition of African masks in Paris, he became excited by their colors and distortions of the human face. The influence of these masks was overpowering and immediate, leading him to his first major triumph, *Les Demoiselles d'Avignon* (1907), a portrait of five prostitutes in which features and body parts form a geometric design. Early viewers found the painting startling if not amusing because while pure geometric design might have been a *little* acceptable, designs made from figures that were expected to look like people would have been not only radical but smile provoking.

> *Art is meant to disturb. Science reassures.*
>
> **—Georges Braque**

Georges Braque. Georges Braque (1882–1963), a year younger than Picasso, saw *Les Demoiselles* in its initial showing and admitted that it changed his life and his artistic plans for the future. He made it his business to meet the genius who had opened his eyes to a wholly new way not only of painting but of *seeing*. Acting on

African mask, Lega culture, Democratic Republic of Congo, date unknown

Pablo Picasso, *Les Demoiselles d'Avignon*, 1907

The strong influence of African masks can be seen in Picasso's *Les Demoiselles d'Avignon.*

advice from his "older" mentor, Braque began working in the new style. He would look at a scene that appealed to him for some reason, then leave it, allowing himself to forget the realistic details until he was ready to *deconstruct* it in his memory, then *reconstruct* it on the canvas as geometric blocks in bold, unshaded colors. He did a series of landscapes in this style, causing one critic to complain that Braque had taken beautiful subjects and reduced them "to cubes." After the critical article appeared, the label *Cubism,* meant derogatively at first, was applied to the work of both Braque and Picasso. In 1909 the two artists formed a close association and consciously devised a Cubist movement, providing for it a clearly articulated rationale.

In thinking critically about their art, the two friends discovered that nobody ever really sees an object or a figure. Rather, what is seen is an event extending over a period of time, no matter how rapidly. The eye, moreover, is in continual motion and observes from continually shifting viewpoints. From where we sit or stand at a given moment we are looking from one particular and fixed vantage point. Both realistic paintings and photographs foster the misconception that such a thing exists as a stable field of vision. Our language suggests that we see reality, but in truth what we really see is fragments reassembled by the mind.

Georges Braque, *Harbor in Normandy*, 1909

One of the cornerstone works of Cubism, it has some ties to the familiar world, but there are also Cubist geometric designs so that the result looks like no place on earth.

Braque was just twenty-seven when he painted *Harbor in Normandy,* yet it remains one of his most famous works and indeed one of the signature works of Cubism. There are enough ties to the familiar world to orient the viewer: the lighthouse on the left and the boats at bottom right. But above them there are Cubist geometric pieces that may be the sky and a dock, but maybe not. The picture exists as an illustration of the fragmented world of vision—and *that,* not the likeness of a harbor, is the point.

Explore on **MyHumanitiesKit.com** Picasso, *Guernica*

Guernica. In 1937 Picasso was invited to do a large painting for the Spanish Pavilion at the Paris World's Fair. Instead of simply choosing a visual event and breaking it into geometric shapes in the style that made him famous, Picasso made an impassioned statement against war. *Guernica,* shown here, is now considered not only Picasso's masterpiece but one of the great artworks of all time. Among other things, it silenced critics who were saying that modern artists were too wrapped up in their technique and their innovations to pay attention to what was happening in the world.

"The cubist wished to present the total reality of forms in space, and since objects appear not only as they are seen from one viewpoint at a time, it became necessary to introduce multiple angles of vision and simultaneous presentation of discontinuous planes. This of course shatters the old continuity of composition imposed by the Renaissance single viewpoint."

—Helen Gardner

Using Cubist techniques, though he had abandoned the movement earlier when he and Braque went their separate ways, Picasso was able to deliver a message with one swift visual impact, a message that elsewhere had required thousands of words from reporters and innumerable pictures from photographers. The painting describes an event that caused worldwide revulsion: the German air force's infamous saturation bombing of Guernica, the cultural center of the Basque region in northern Spain and a stronghold of the Republican Army fighting against insurgent forces, who would ultimately win the Spanish Civil War. Francisco Franco, leader of the antigovernment army, had appealed to both Germany and Italy for support. The United States backed the Republican government that had been duly elected, while Hitler sided with Franco. The bombing of Guernica was also a way for Germany to demonstrate its military strength to the world.

The bombing took place on April 26, 1937, and numbered among its casualties not only hundreds of Republican soldiers but 2,500 civilians, including hundreds of

Pablo Picasso, *Guernica*, 1937

Supreme example of Cubism, turning the bombing victims into a wild fragmented scene of atrocities. One of the most powerful antiwar statements ever made.

children. Newspapers around the world published graphic images of the dead. Picasso, who had been undecided about whether he wanted to do a work for the Spanish Pavilion, saw the pictures and was so moved that he rushed home and immediately began sketching out what would become his masterpiece.

When it was unveiled at the New York World's Fair in 1939, *Guernica* received nearly unanimous critical acclaim and established Picasso's supremacy among living artists. There were, of course, detractors. The Marxist government in Russia said that only realistic art could bring about significant social change, and the Nazi regime, as expected, denounced it as "degenerate art."

Without Cubism, a style that can present simultaneously things that happen over a period of time, how could an artist have captured such a scene of total devastation? Few artists have attempted anything of the scope Picasso was able to achieve, for most paintings are essentially static, freezing a single moment in time. What Cubism does in *Guernica* is to place on a two-dimensional plane the dynamic motion generally found only in films.

Like a true masterpiece, *Guernica* continues to be frighteningly relevant. Wars like those in Vietnam, Iraq, and Afghanistan, which also have scarred national and world consciousness, come to mind whenever one looks closely at the painting. It is not a historical record of an event long past, but a living conscience. As such, it continues to generate profound emotional responses. The United Nations headquarters in Manhattan has on display a tapestry reproduction of the work. When in 2003 Colin Powell, then the U.S. Secretary of State, addressed the UN Security Council to advocate military action against Iraq, the tapestry, which would have been in full view, was covered.

Picasso's work became simpler in his later years, reflecting a childlike innocence that makes as strong a statement in its own way as *Guernica* does. This is a statement of hope for the future in a world tamed by peace and love, a statement that will be needed as long as the horrors of a Guernican bombing repeat themselves. The artist painted childlike doves on the ceiling of a tiny chapel in the southern French town of Valauris, near his home in Nice. With his friend and neighbor Henri Matisse, he developed **collage** into an art form, spending hundreds of hours cutting out tiny designs and pasting them onto large and colorful backgrounds. The ninety-year-old Picasso was not "losing it"—as has been suggested by a few cynics—but was showing that he had managed to do what few of us can: he had kept alive the child inside him. The art of being human needs the spirit of children.

Explore on **MyHumanitiesKit.com** Picasso, Collages

"Unreal" Realism

One reason for any artist's huge critical reputation is the degree to which the work influences other artists. Future artists viewed Picasso as a revolutionary leader, encouraging others to follow their own bent, regardless of how the public might react.

Surrealism. A popular style during the first half of the twentieth century, surrealism employs recognizable shapes and forms put together in unrecognizable contexts. The best way to define it is to say that it imitates the world of dreams and the unconscious mind. It owes much to the psychological theories of Freud and Jung. Their explorations into the strange regions below consciousness excited visual artists, writers, and philosophers. Inner space was proving to be just as fascinating as recent discoveries regarding the physical universe.

Dalí question: Was the artist painting from a deeply disordered mind or giving the public the Freudian subjects it wanted?

Dalí. The art surrealists wanted to imitate the geography of inner space, to make the unconscious mind a tangible part of the external world. At least this was the stated purpose of the movement, the major exponent of which was the Spanish

Salvador Dalí, *The Persistence of Memory*, 1931

Was Dalí lost in the maze of the unconscious, or was he giving the public what it wanted? Even so, where did his strange images come from?

painter Salvador Dalí (1904–1989). Unlike Picasso, who gives us fragments of things, Dalí creates a dream world made up of recognizable images that do not fit rationally together.

Dalí became as famous for his neurotic behavior as for the bizarre world of his canvas. His paintings are objects of fascination for psychiatrists and those art critics who interpret an artist's work in terms of psychological disorders. Some cite Dalí's maladjusted childhood as responsible for both his behavior and his art. Some call him as mad an artist as ever lived, but, citing van Gogh, add that madness is often the price of genius. This observation may well be made of van Gogh, and future generations of critics may confirm that it applies to Dalí. Yet many will argue that surrealism as practiced by Dalí was a highly commercial, carefully calculated artistic oddity, designed from the outset to capitalize on the popularity of Freud, to make the artist a center of widely publicized controversy, and thus to increase the price of his paintings.

If nothing else, we can say that there is little subtlety in Dalí's style, which is sometimes so obviously Freudian that students of Psychology 101 would have no trouble with it. Dalí seems especially obsessed with the popular Freudian belief that many of our actions are a result of two drives: the constant need for sex, which we are forced to hide, and the death wish, which comes from the pain of our neuroses. A good example is his *Inventions of the Monsters* with a naked upper torso, disembodied bare buttocks, and skeletal death figures all suggesting wicked thoughts and death longings that have been repressed and filed away, thus rekindling the neuroses which caused the misery in the first place.

Explore on **MyHumanitiesKit.com**
Dalí, *The Persistence of Memory*

Dalí's most famous work, shown here, is *The Persistence of Memory* (1931), an obviously, and perhaps consciously, Freudian work. It shows a tree branch over which hangs a wristwatch distorted because it is made of a soft, rubbery material. A rubbery watch hangs limply from a table on which rests a pocket watch that is not rubbery. Yet another limp watch is draped over what ought to be, but is not, a wrist. Those who insist on a Freudian interpretation, as Dalí perhaps hoped they would, may recognize the limp watches as symbols of unresponsive male sex organs, and the nondistorted pocket watch as a symbol of a happier sexual past. Was the artist forced to hide his sexual attitudes? Or was he deliberately giving his public the controversy he thought it wanted?

Even if we grant the possibility that Dalí was giving the public what it wanted—*shock*—and doing it for the money, we still have to ask ourselves where his strange images, figures, and landscapes came from if not from his innermost self. Whether tortured artrist or clever businessman, Dalí, with an entire museum in St. Petersburg, Florida, devoted to his work, remains an important figure in modern art and the one most likely to be central to any discussion of surrealism.

"*Where I was born, and where and how I lived is unimportant. It is what I have done and where I have been that should be of interest.*"

—Georgia O'Keeffe

Georgia O'Keeffe. The paintings of Georgia O'Keeffe (1887–1986) present another form of "unreal" realism. She gives us likeness that is also abstraction, and perhaps a glimpse into her unconscious as well. The artist appears to have worked from deep impulses inside her which led her to reinterpret the familiar world. She maintained resolutely that all art can be analyzed only in terms of what is happening on the canvas, of what the artist is *doing,* not saying.

What O'Keeffe *does,* then, is usually to imitate one or two striking and colorful forms in the familiar world and transfer them to canvas with many details left out. O'Keeffe sees the world not as the Cubists did—broken down into geometric shapes—but as a place in which certain shapes leap out at the artist for whatever reason: the colors, the aesthetic appeal of the form itself, the textures, or, as some critics have said, the unconscious sexual significance to the artist of the form—what it *looks* like or *suggests.* Freudian critics have had even more fun with O'Keeffe than they have with Dalí!

In 1905, at eighteen years of age, O'Keeffe left her home in Sun Prairie, Wisconsin, to study at the famous Art Institute of Chicago. Like other young artists at the turn of a new century, she was brimming with exciting ideas about what constitutes art and what an artist has the right to do. Today, young people from a later generation of artists may be standing exactly where O'Keeffe stood. Perhaps one or two of them will be thinking it is time to rebel against "traditionalists" like O'Keeffe.

Christie's Images Ltd./SuperStock

Yun Shouping, *Peony,* c. 1633–1690

This work exemplifies the simplicity of Asian art that so intrigued Western artists like O'Keeffe.

> *"She brought to the big city her love for simple shapes and extremely bright colors," one biographer notes; "she recalls seeing light on a red, white, and black patterned quilt before she could walk, and, as a toddler, the soft, smooth shapes made by buggy wheels in the dust—they looked good enough to eat!"*[3]

When she was twenty, O'Keeffe moved to New York. There she met the most fashionable artists of the day, whose work was shown in the studio of photographer Alfred Stieglitz, whom she was eventually to marry. But Stieglitz and his sophisticated circle were not able to influence the maturing artist as much as did the simplicity and sensuous beauty of Asian art.

In Asian art O'Keeffe found a style she could immediately understand, respond to, and imitate. The simplicity of a painting such as the one shown above, appealed to her love of color and shapes that convey an instantaneous image. Asian influence is clearly evident in O'Keeffe's *Purple Petunias,* also shown here. Later, when her aesthetic and emotional differences with Stieglitz made their marriage seem less idyllic than it had once been, O'Keeffe moved to New Mexico, a land of bright color and bold shape. In the undulating hills, the orange craggy rocks, the snow-tipped mountains, and the exotic flowers, she found a constant visual stimulation she had never experienced in drab (by comparison) New York.

Georgia O'Keeffe, *Purple Petunias,* 1925

This work typifies the Asian influence on O'Keeffe, but it also suggests sexual symbolism.

Much of her most famous work dates from after this move, as she developed her unique style: flowers bursting from their stems; mountains, canyons, the infinite sky with its continually changing colors; the bleached skull of a dead animal. All of these forms she transferred to canvases that were first painted stark white so that the electric colors and the proud shapes would stand out in sharp relief. As colorful as the Southwest surely

AFP Getty Images/Newscom

Edward Hopper, *Nighthawks*, 1942

The three hunched figures in Hopper's *Nighthawks* tell us as much about the Great Depression as the literature of the period.

is, O'Keeffe altered the landscape, giving it an electric vibrancy, giving as much as she took from this land, something all artists claim the right to do.

Edward Hopper. A contemporary of O'Keeffe and exponent of a simplified realism that leaves out unimportant details was Edward Hopper (1882–1967), who emerged out of the Great Depression of the 1930s. Hopper, like so many artists and writers of the period, could not help being touched by the belief that the art should not only appeal to the aesthetic sense but make a strong social commentary as well.

Hopper's forms come from the streets of urban America and the forlorn, despairing souls who walk them: the homeless, the abandoned, the chronic poor, the newly poor, the alienated drifters who move from one place to another seeking not only decent jobs but meaningful communication with someone else, and people whom we suspect came from good backgrounds and now find themselves displaced. Among his lonely, unhappy Americans are the three hunched figures sitting in a late-night diner in one of his best known paintings, *Nighthawks,* shown here. In a few bold details Hopper shows us what American writers have devoted hundreds of pages to describing: American loneliness. Hopper does not give us a perfect likeness of a diner in *Nighthawks,* but the few figures are all he needs to tell his sad stories.

Aaron Douglas. While Dalí, O'Keeffe, and Hopper were honing their craft, a young African American artist named Aaron Douglas (1899–1988) was traveling from Kansas City for a stopover in New York before heading to Paris. During the 1920s and 1930s the French capital was a magnet, luring artists from every country in the world and with every imaginable style. Ever since the heyday of Impressionism it was recognized as *the* place to be for those intending to make a name for themselves in the art world. However, the stopover took far longer than he expected, for while Douglas was in New York, he discovered Harlem.

Douglas, born in Kansas of middle-class stock, and a visual arts graduate of the University of Nebraska, at first lacked a sense of connection to African roots. The eventual discovery of an African heritage made a deep impression on the young artist looking for a style and a statement. What Douglas responded to in Africa was something he had not found in the quiet, uneventful life of midwestern America: a sense of being able to express emotion without restraint, whether it was joy and exaltation or bitterness and sorrow. All around him Harlem voices were giving vent to their feelings in poetry, jazz, dance, and drama. Some were seeking an appropriate visual arts language and encouraged Douglas to join them.

Douglas knew he wanted to go beyond art as strict likeness, but he hadn't an idea of *where*—and why. In the Harlem Renaissance and Cubism he found that idea. Douglas liked the fact that Cubist paintings forced the viewer to reconsider how reality was viewed. He also knew that he did not agree with those African American leaders who urged artists and writers to use their talents to make protest statements. He believed passionately that African American art should be its own movement and stand on its own merit. It too could show the world a new way to see.

The art of ancient Egypt gave Douglas his first encounter with Africa. What both shocked and excited him was that ancient Egyptian artists stylized the human figure in a way he knew Picasso would have understood. In the pen-and-ink drawing shown here, an African drummer expresses himself ecstatically; but the figure is drawn in what Douglas called "Egyptian form." The drummer's left hand is recognizable as a hand, but it is drawn in a Picasso-like cube that also reflects the stylization of Egyptian art. Douglas explains that, if he drew the hand the way you would see it in real life, "you wouldn't understand that that was a hand. It's only when it's done this way. . . . I used that hand all the time . . . got it from the Egyptians."[4]

Douglas's style is the result of a philosophy, a deep-rooted belief that in trying to imitate the actual world, art as likeness was really falsifying the way we see that world. Figures such as the drummer enabled him to transfer to visual art the excitement he found in the African American spirit, an excitement that was part of the way he saw things. Thus he was an imitator of both reality and his own emotions.

Schomburg Center, New York Public Library

Aaron Douglas, *Invisible Music, The Spirit of Africa*, 1926

Douglas fuses Picasso and Egypt into a unique style that has never been imitated.

Superrealism

During the last half of the twentieth century, a sculptor named Duane Hanson (1925–1996) took the banner of revolution and turned his back on modernists who had forsaken realism, perhaps because he suspected what they were doing with their excursions into fancy was taking the easy way out. What he gave the world was *superrealism*—a method of creating life-size figures that look so real you would expect them to answer if you talked to them. Some critics have compared his sculptures to the figures in Madame Tussaud's famous Wax Museum, a comparison that always infuriated the artist.

Hanson's superrealism does not exist just to astonish us with its lifelike appearance, but to make a definite statement about our society.

For one thing, Hanson's "people" are far more lifelike than the wax replicas of famous personalities at Madame Tussaud's. Yet the artist's aim is not solely to render a likeness so perfect it startles us; he also insists on our seeing the violent, sordid, and comic elements of our society. Hanson is a commentator on what he believes we have become as a nation. His figures are not celebrities we would recognize. They are social (and very often *antisocial*) types. Look, for example, at

Art © Estate of Duane Hanson/Licensed by VAGA, New York, NY. Photo: Smithsonian American Art Museum, Washington, DC/Art Resource, NY

Duane Hanson, *Woman Eating*, 1971

Superrealism, to make us painfully aware of middle-class vulgarity, as well as obesity and consumerism.

his *Woman Eating*, shown here. She is superreal in order to make us painfully aware of the obesity and the vulgar value system of the American middle class.

Hanson burst upon the art scene in the 1970s with a show that almost redefined sculpture. Neither classical nor abstract, his figures offered the somewhat frightened (and relatively few) visitors to his first studio—an old garage—their startling first experience with superrealistic three-dimensional art. Entering the studio through a rusty and squeaking door, which only added to the ghoulish scenes inside, the visitor was greeted by the life-size figure of a young woman hanging from a cross, the victim of a savage rape. In an adjoining alcove, one gasped at the horrifying sight of a young woman lying nude on a bed, a pair of blood-stained scissors thrust into her stomach, her open eyes still showing the terror she experienced before death came. Across from this sculpture lay the bloody figure of a dead young man, the twisted wreckage of a motorcycle beside him.

As if believing the shock of the exhibit was still not strong enough, Hanson capped off the evening with the piece that brought him to the attention of the Whitney Museum, New York's premier showcase for what is new, controversial but significant in contemporary art: bloody corpses of young soldiers strewn across a Vietnamese battlefield. A visitor was heard to whisper: "The technique is marvelous, but would you want this in your *house*?" It was clear from the outset that the sculptor was not primarily interested in selling to private collectors. His fame has come from exhibitions the world over.

With Hanson's statement about violence and America, notoriety was instantaneous, and the artist, perhaps believing no more need be said on the subject, embarked on a second phase in which his sculptures were superrealistic but not as frightening—at least not overtly so. With figures like the lady in the supermarket Hanson also reminds us of the soulless accuracy with which human-looking robots are constructed in the Disney theme parks, figures that smile vacuously at us and deliver electronic life-affirming platitudes with all the warmth of the computerized phone voice that says, "Sorry, but I did not understand you. Press or say 'one' again."

> *"While there is a province in which the photographer can tell us nothing more than what we see with our own eyes, there is another in which it proves to us how little our eyes permit us to see."*
>
> **—Dorothea Lange**

While O'Keeffe and Hopper simplify reality, Hanson details it, as in the woman's sloppy posture, the empty ice cream glass, the unread newspaper, the napkin holder with the thin napkins, the salt and pepper shakers, the two bags of groceries tossed against her leg, and the dangling handbag—startlingly real, yet there for a purpose other than the likenesses themselves. The sculpture encourages the question of whether this is how life should be. Something seems wrong, but what? Art that makes viewers question the life all of us may come dangerously close to living needs no further justification.

> *"It's admirable, I think, to be open to the new, and willing to learn; I submit, however, that once one has adjusted to the new, it must give pleasure or it will not be art."*
>
> **—Richard Wilbur**

In order to achieve such likeness, Hanson covered a live model with wire to form a "dummy," which he then immersed in plaster of Paris, allowing it to harden enough for him to sculpt the lifelike details and apply the many necessary paints. He finished the process by coating the statue with "fixative," a substance that makes paint or dye permanent. Fixative, highly toxic if breathed in an enclosed space, eventually proved fatal to the artist. He was in the process of changing his style and his medium when his life ended, and we can only speculate on the further riches his legacy might have contained.

Camera Art

With the increasing popularity of photography since its invention in the nineteenth century, the roles of portrait painting and realistic landscape art were diminished. People argued that if they wanted something that looked like the real thing, why not go to a medium that could better provide it? Creative artists, fascinated by the new invention, almost immediately experimented with and greatly expanded its possibilities.

Alfred Stieglitz. One of the finest photographers working in the early twentieth century was Alfred Stieglitz (1864–1946), who was obsessed with the desire to establish photography as a distinctly American art form. Some of his most famous works are camera images of his wife, Georgia O'Keeffe. He became famous both for his portraits, in which he was bent on proving that the camera could capture the inner person as well as, if not better than, the eye of the painter, and scenes of big-city life, which provide us with a photographic record of what urban life in America looked and *felt* like. The New York of Stieglitz is already showing signs of the congestion and frenetic pace that would become signature characteristics. In 1902 he founded *Camera Notes,* the first periodical devoted to studying the art and science of photography.

In that same year, Stieglitz sailed to Europe and was struck by the disparity in the accommodations provided for upper- and lower-class passengers. *The Steerage* is not only photographic art at its finest but also biting social commentary as well.

Jerry Uelsmann. Born in 1934, Jerry Uelsmann makes full use of camera technologies from a much later period. These allow him to take multiple images on each other, then link them together in the darkroom to create a world akin to surrealism on canvas. Reproduced here is *Homage to Duchamp* (2000), in which two images of the French abstractionist overlap in a frame that overwhelms the strange room in which it is placed. This is truly photography as alteration.

Library of Congress

Alfred Stieglitz, *The Steerage*, 1907

Considered Stieglitz' masterpiece and, still, one of the greatest examples of photographic art ever produced.

Courtesy Jerry Uelsmann

Jerry Uelsmann, *Homage to Duchamp*, 2000

Using photography to create a surreal world.

Pop Art

Influenced by comic books, movies, television, commercials, and billboard advertising, *Pop Art* inevitably arose as a phenomenon of the mid-twentieth century that brought fame to a few artists. It has been described as "fun" art, for its exponents all seem to have a sense of humor about much of what they do. They

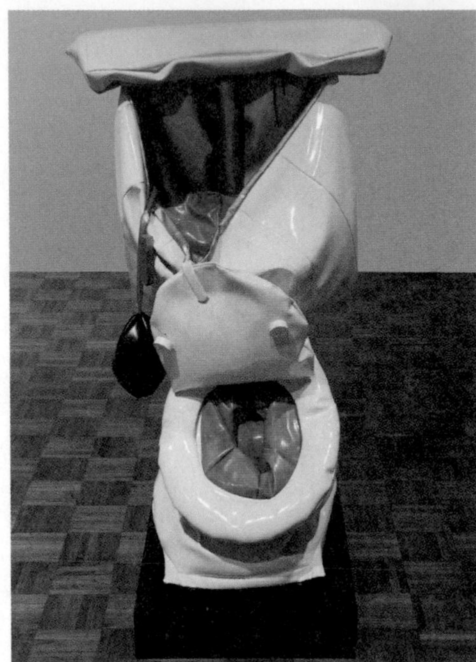

Claes Oldenburg, b. 1929, *Soft Toilet*, 1966. Wood, vinyl, kapok, wire, plexiglass on metal stand and painted wood base, Overall: 55 1/2 x 28 1/4 x 30in. (141 x 71.8 x 76.2cm). Whitney Museum of American Art, New York; 50th Anniversary Gift of Mr. and Mrs. Victor W. Ganz 79.83a-b. © Claes Oldenburg. Photograph by Sheldan C. Collins

Claes Oldenburg, *Soft Toilet*, 1996

One of Oldenburg's soft vinyl sculptures, showing the humor in Pop Art and the theory that anything can be turned into a medium for art.

© 2011 The Andy Warhol Foundation for the Visual Arts, Inc./Artists Rights Society (ARS), New York. Photo: akg-images/Newscom

Andy Warhol, *Marilyn Monroe*, 1962

Warhol's portrait of a modern Aphrodite is ambiguous, displaying both his satiric take on Tinsel Town and his love for it.

are sometimes, like Hanson, making a statement about the endless fads and superficiality of American culture. It has a link with the second phase of Hanson's art in its focus on ordinary objects and sometimes the sly suggestion that American life has nothing more important to offer.

Claes Oldenburg. A Swedish-born, naturalized American exponent of Pop Art, Claes Oldenburg (b. 1929) finished a cardboard and wood mural in 1961 called *The Street,* showing people, buildings, automobiles, and other objects seen in everyday life, but drawn in comic-book style, which is his artistic domain. The following year he achieved notoriety with *Giant Ice-Cream Cone* and the first of his soft vinyl sculptures, *Giant Hamburger*. These were followed by *Giant Tooth Brush* and inevitably by a piece called *Soft Toilet,* shown here, as well as *Giant Ice Bag,* which was made for the Osaka World's Fair in 1970, a sculpture that inflates and deflates as the viewer watches. With *Soft Toilet,* Oldenburg may have been thinking whimsically of Duchamp's still notorious urinal.

Andy Warhol. Probably the biggest name in Pop Art, Andy Warhol (1928–1987) earned his reputation with a painting mentioned earlier, *100 Cans,* containing stark likenesses of row upon row of Campbell's beef noodle soup. The inspiration for this kind of art is clearly the popular ad, but the excessive repetition of the can is both amusing and frightening. Is Warhol, like Hanson, ridiculing the stultifying conformism in American culture and its lack of imagination?

Yet Warhol is also in *love* with our culture he finds so tawdry, as we can see from this portrait of glamorous movie star Marilyn Monroe, which is a heightening of what used to grace the covers of tacky movie magazines. The colors are brilliant, suggesting the unreality of "tinsel town." But the artist, like so many others, was unable to resist the flashy sensuality that turned Monroe—once an unremarkable young woman named Norma Jean Baker—into a modern Aphrodite. Yes, Warhol knows that the star was a studio-manufactured product, but he himself was a filmmaker who manufactured a whole bevy of unreal types for his bizarre movies, including a fleshy transvestite named Divine and an entourage that was a walking Pop Art statement.

Warhol's films were central to his art, and *Chelsea Girls* (1966) ushered in a new cinematic phenomenon, the "underground film," popular for a time with young people who opposed almost anything connected to established American culture. The film lasted more than three hours and was shown on two screens that appeared unconnected. The "plot" comprised fragmentary sequences but also strangely haunting images. In one five-minute sequence a young woman is shown standing in front of a mirror, cutting her hair. Nothing else happens, yet the intense camera focus on her face and the sound of scissors create a mesmerizing effect.

Warhol's films were usually shown on special nights in art houses—theaters that cater to alternative tastes. Most of his film art, however, is hard to track down. Even so, it remains an important link between what we might call "stationary" art that is available in museums and galleries and "impermanent" art that is not meant to last, that occupies a brief moment in time—a new kind of art that may have been an inevitable development in America, a land of short attention spans and people always on the move.

Explore on
MyHumanitiesKit.com
Warhol, *Marilyn Diptych*

Performance, Prank, and Installation Art

Performance art is art as event. Its exponents are looking for ways to be different in an art world that changes all the time: a very tall order indeed. Or perhaps they believe that art is more beautiful to the extent that it doesn't stay around very long. Performance artists ignore the goal of one day having their work part of a permanent collection in a prestigious museum; they prefer to do something that will create a momentary stir, even a storm of controversy, and then be seen or heard no more.

"Prank" artists often cite Orson Welles, the great film director (more fully discussed in Chapter 9), as the founder of their movement. In the 1930s, Welles and his Mercury Theatre Company performed a radio adaptation of a famous science fiction novel, *The War of the Worlds* by H. G. Wells, about an army of Martians who invade the United States. Because the radio play was written in the style of a news program, many people—especially those tuning in late—believed the invasion was the real thing. Chaos erupted as people ran from their homes seeking safe hiding places. Welles insisted the program was not meant as a prank, but some performance artists insist that it *could* have been, and that anything generating this much excitement still counts as legitimate art.

An M.I.T. student spent her summer regularly sneaking into Soldiers Field, the Harvard football stadium, wearing a black-and-white striped shirt like that of a referee. On each visit, as she scattered bird seed over the field, she blew a whistle. At the opening football game of the season, when one of the real referees blew his whistle, hundreds of birds swooped into the stadium ready to eat. Since prank art is necessarily private, the perpetrators might advertise their successes only later on the Internet, provided their pranks are not exactly illegal.

Edward Kienholz. Superrealist Edward Kienholz (1927–1993) created a computer-generated performance art piece called *Still Live,* which included an armchair positioned in front of a black box said to contain a rifle and a timer set to fire it once within the next 100 years. According to one art critic, after eight years it still hadn't gone off. Visitors who sit in this "hot seat" had to sign a waiver. Kienholz reported, with some amusement, that at the opening almost a dozen people did.

No doubt many have sat in the armchair since the work's installation in 1974, but its title, *Still Live,* suggests a possible appeal to hidden Russian roulette impulses. If the artist had expected no one to sit there, why did he compose the piece at all? In any case, the performer here was not the artist, but the actual or potential viewer willing to risk all for a momentary thrill. Perhaps the work existed so that

Ilja Hulinsky/Alamy

Christo and Jean-Claude, *The Gates*, 2004

The photograph of Christo's huge installation in Central Park is all that remains for posterity.

those who sat in the chair could look deep within themselves and ask why they came.

Christo. Christo Javacheff (b. 1935), who as an artist uses only his first name, does not imitate or perform; he literally alters the world briefly, creating a huge and highly publicized event. He claims the natural environment as his medium. Among his projects were wrapping over a million square feet of Australian coastline in plastic, installing a gigantic curtain between two mountains in Colorado, constructing a twenty-four-mile fence made of twenty-foot-high nylon panels across hills in northern California, surrounding an island in Biscayne Bay, Miami, with enormous sheets of flamingo-colored plastic (a feat that struck terror in the hearts of environmentalists, who attempted, unsuccessfully, to halt the proceedings), and an enormous installation of 7,503 wooden frames, from which hung orange sheets, six years in the making, which went on display in Central Park for 16 days. Titled *The Gates,* the last event was said to be the largest art project since the Sphinx.

Architecture

"Architecture in general is frozen music."

—Friedrich von Schiller

Performance art is transitory by nature, limited to the time of presentation. This final section is concerned with a more permanent component of society: architecture, which serves a dual purpose. It provides for our many human needs: shelter, work, play, religious worship, and education. Of all the arts, architecture alters reality most noticeably. It gives many cities their distinctive look; and it adds an aesthetic dimension to life. Not all of it, of course, can be considered art. There has to be an aesthetic intent on the part of the architect. Major architects Frank Lloyd Wright and Frank O. Gehry have approached the design of buildings as a painter or sculptor would contemplate beginning a new work—that is, as a contribution to the aesthetic well-being of society.

The fundamental issue in determining whether a given architectural work can be labeled "art" is the interplay of *form* and *function*. The function of a building is to accommodate the needs of the inhabitants. An office building should provide employees with pleasing surroundings that will make working less of a chore, and it should allow employees easy access to spaces they will have to visit throughout the day. It must make doing business there simple and enjoyable, and it must be wheelchair accessible. A religious edifice such as a cathedral or a temple should be imposing and awe-inspiring both inside and out, so worshippers or meditators can believe for a time that they have left the familiar world and entered a different, some might say higher, mode of consciousness.

The form of a building—the general impression that it makes as a pleasing presence in a certain space—can be as important as its function. If designed by an architect-as-artist, it can also make a personal statement: *This form is what I consider beautiful, and I offer it for your use and your aesthetic pleasure.* Like all visual artists, architects seek to project themselves into space. They want to know that, because of them, a public area has been altered in some way that reflects their identity and may ensure them lasting honor. They know that architecture is art that alters for very long periods of time, and in some cases forever. The Taj Mahal in India, Saint Peter's basilica in Rome, and the Hagia Sophia in Istanbul have endured for centuries and have become symbols of their culture.

Explore on **MyHumanitiesKit.com** Taj Mahal

The debate over which is more important, form or function, has continued for centuries and will probably never be resolved. Those who want architecture primarily to serve a useful purpose argue famously that *form follows function*. Others, often called architectural purists, elevate form and the aesthetic experience it provides over what they call "mere utility." Still others ask, "Why can't we have both?"

Religious Architecture

Buildings created for religious worship or meditation are among the finest achievements in world architecture. The Parthenon in Athens, built to honor the goddess Athena, is one of the world's oldest architectural marvels and remains for many the symbol of Western classical civilization (see photo page 111). Angkor Wat, the largest of seventy temples in a complex in Cambodia, is not only a place of meditation for thousands of Buddhists but, as one of the wonders of the world, the main tourist attraction in that nation. Each year many thousands come for inspiration and an aesthetic experience that has been described as nearly without parallel.

Explore on **MyHumanitiesKit.com** Wren, St. Paul's Cathedral

Not many edifices have been cornerstones of two religions, but Angkor Wat, still the world's largest religious building, has been home to both Hinduism and Buddhism. Built originally in honor of the Hindu god Vishnu (see Chapter 10), it became in 1177 C.E. a Buddhist shrine after the Cambodian king was converted to Buddhism. With five pineapple-shaped towers rising close to 200 feet against the sky, Angkor Wat became the most imposing temple in the holy city of Angkor. The temple contains innumerable passageways and alcoves, the walls of which boast ornate facades depicting both mythic stories and scenes from everyday Cambodian life.

Few works of architecture have cast the same sort of spell as Angkor Wat. The English novelist W. Somerset Maugham once observed that the vast temple "needs the glow of sunset or the white brilliance of the moon to give it a loveliness that touches the heart." Many have noted that merely walking its nearly three-mile expanse is a transforming experience, leading to distinct (and for the better) changes in mood and attitude.

Modern cathedrals and other places of worship frequently break with tradition, and the results vary from praise in architectural journals to condemnations by the faithful. St. Louis Catholic Church in Miami looks like a flying saucer about to take off. The Crystal Cathedral in Garden Grove, California, has a neo-Gothic form, except that it is made entirely of glass and, according to some detractors, looks more like a luxury hotel than a church. A Lutheran church in Helsinki, Finland, was carved into the side of a hill and gives the illusion that one is entering a cave rather than a house of prayer.

Among the most admired and time-honored of religious buildings is the Blue Mosque in Istanbul (p. 343), built between 1609 and 1616. Its function, like that of other religious buildings, is to make worship spiritually uplifting in a splendid setting. Its interior is made up of more than 20,000 ceramic tiles that lend a bluish

Neil Setchfield/Purestock/Shutterstock

Jorn Utzon, Sydney Opera House, 1973

At one time the subject of critical controversy and public derision, the Sydney Opera House is now a source of civic pride and opera-lovers' aesthetic pleasure.

aura. It also serves as a hospice for the dying. But the magnificence of the architecture and the extraordinary light inside have made it a must for tourists.

Secular Architecture

Whenever the desire is to combine function with the form that only a great artist can bring to architecture, conflicts inevitably arise between those who create and those who pay for or use the structure. The architect-as-artist often runs into difficulties with both the general public and the specific person or group that has commissioned a given structure. The artist's irresistible urge to self-expression can be accused of subordinating a building's primary purpose.

Even where architecture is viewed as a public art, those who finance it can only speculate on how to define the public interest. When a private corporation or city planners underwrite an expensive structure such as a performing arts center, they will expect (for their millions of dollars) one that satisfies both functional and aesthetic needs, but not exclusively the desires of the architect. They know their investment is going to result in an edifice that will be around for a long time, and they are in trouble if it meets with public disapproval! They suspect it is going to define their city—for better or worse—as Sydney, Australia, is identified by its daring but internationally admired opera house.

> *We shape our buildings: thereafter they shape us.*
>
> —**Winston Churchill**

With its gleaming white, sharply pointed gables looking like monks' hoods, the Sydney Opera House opened in 1973 after sixteen years of construction. The design was to allow for excellent interior acoustics and to create for the audience a pleasant environment that would heighten the pleasure of the music being heard. The building was also intended to symbolize the city, so that people on ships entering Sydney Harbor for the first time would know they were about to visit a progressive, young metropolis very much involved in the arts and the new. An intense contest for the architectural commission resulted in the choice of a celebrated Danish architect, Jorn Utzon, who insisted on being able to express himself as an artist—to shape a certain space so as to embody his vision of the beautiful, not only to obey the functional requirements set forth by the city planners. The opera house, in short, was intended to be a meeting of the civic and the personal.

Not every taxpayer in Sydney agreed that the structure met either practical or aesthetic needs. As always happens when an environment is altered by a forward-looking artist who breaks with established tradition, there were many who decried his efforts and predicted that their city would be a laughing stock. World opinion, however, has been on the side of Utzon; now the Sydney Opera House is often singled out as one of the great architectural achievements of the twentieth century, an edifice that perfectly marries form and function.

Frank Lloyd Wright

There is by now widespread agreement over the innovations of a man considered the outstanding American architect of the twentieth century, Frank Lloyd Wright (1867–1959). He was born and raised in the relatively small Wisconsin town of Richmond Center. Accustomed to open spaces, air to breathe, and panoramic landscapes, he must have become aware of a growing urban America with huge buildings beginning to reach for the sky and densely crowded city neighborhoods where residents seldom interacted with nature. The writings of American philosopher Ralph Waldo Emerson and his vehemently anticity friend Henry David Thoreau also had a strong impact on Wright's architectural vision. Early on, Wright developed a strong rationale for his work: to link the functional demands of large buildings with the environmental demands of his own heart. His mission would be to provide for the practical demands of big business without the claustrophobia of crowded industrial complexes.

"No house should ever be on any hill or anything. It should be of the hill, belonging to it, so hill and house can live together each the happier for the other."

—Frank Lloyd Wright

At the outset of his career he designed what he called his "prairie house," a rambling one-story structure with plenty of windows and a low, overhanging roof. The idea was that it should blend into its surroundings, unlike the huge nineteenth-century mansions with their ornate external carvings, statues, and stained-glass windows designed for the blatant display of wealth. Wright's aim was to create a balance among function, form, and the environment.

During the first decade of the twentieth century, Wright designed the Larkin Building in Buffalo, New York, and its distinctively sleek look brought him to the attention of European urban planners. By the 1930s the term "streamlined" became fashionable and international in its appeal, and Wright was the acknowledged exponent of the new style, with its use of glass, including glass brick, curved surfaces, spacious interiors, and absence of unnecessary, purely decorative frills. He believed strongly that form follows function. With Wright leading the way, many modern architects said that no building could be considered beautiful if its basic function was impaired by "artistic" aims—such as installing a fountain ringed by statues to block its entrance.

In 1936 Wright designed the administration building and in 1944 the research tower of the Johnson Wax Company in Racine, Wisconsin, achievements hailed as masterpieces of modern architecture. One architectural historian proclaimed them "the most profound work of art that America has ever produced."[5]

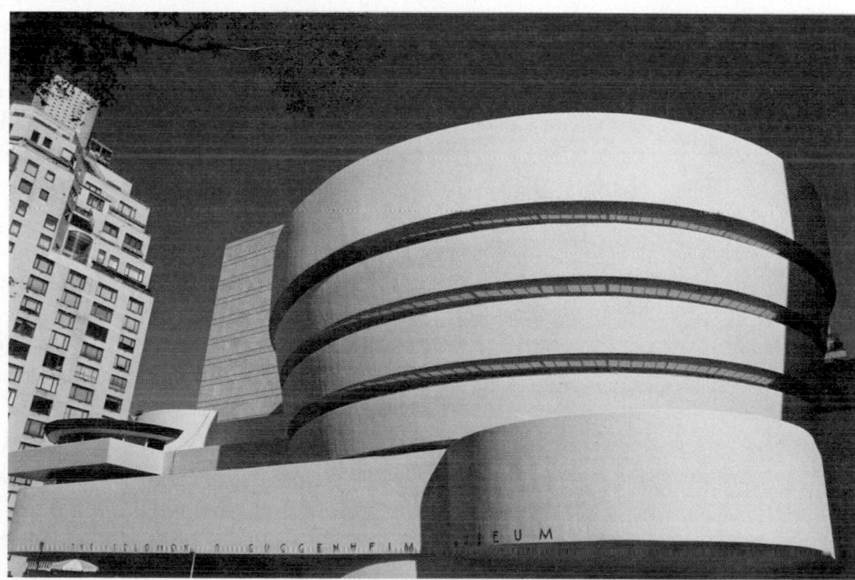

Grace Davies/Shutterstock

Frank Lloyd Wright, Guggenheim Museum (New York), 1959

Not as in his design for the Johnson Wax buildings, Wright wanted to shut out light to the Guggenheim Museum in New York, so that visitors could enjoy art in a peaceful oasis.

Money was never Wright's primary consideration. He wanted, first, to shield employees and visitors from the growing ugliness of the urban scene. Although he loved light and made extensive use of glass, he placed windows so that users of the buildings would not have to look out on parking lots and decaying streets. Instead they were enclosed by solid brick walls at street level while light was provided from overhead. He wanted users to feel as though they were "among the pine trees, breathing fresh air and sunlight." Wright was a visionary who helped create the look of the modern world, and he was an archenemy of overbuilding in that world.

Wright's final work—and for many, his crowning achievement—is the Guggenheim Museum on Fifth Avenue in New York. It is admired by some as the best possible example of modern architecture, and scorned by others who say it looks like a parking garage. The building is a series of circular stone ramps, which ascend in great swirls and serve as a thick barrier to the noise of the city. There are no windows this time. Instead, light enters through the small spaces between the ramps. Inside, art works are illuminated by soft indirect lighting. The artist's first thought was to shut out as much light as he could and provide visitors with a quiet oasis, another world of human creativity.

Frank O. Gehry

"I don't think it's very useful to open wide the door for new artists; the ones who break down the door are more interesting."

—Paul Schroeder

Another American who has taken modern American architecture to new levels is Frank O. Gehry (b. 1929). His work tends to put a great deal of emphasis on form without ignoring function. Gehry's genius lies in the ability to make form seem an inevitable result of function. Some of his critics call his style impractical, accusing him of subordinating function in the interest of artistic self-expression. A good many artists, however, defend his right to do just that.

Like many of his fellow Southern Californians, Gehry enjoys the *funky* in modern art—those elements that incorporate whimsy into serious aims. He is fond of fish, for example, and is apt to put a fish sculpture where one would least expect it—in front of an elevator perhaps. He makes furniture out of corrugated boxes, and he uses chain-link fencing unsparingly and, again, unexpectedly. He will stretch a chain-link fence across a courtyard where it serves no useful purpose except to be an object of art, similar to what Christo might do, except that Gehry's installations are permanent. To those critics who call such installations "frivolous" and "ugly," he replies that he is not sure "what is ugly and what is beautiful." Such a retort, a denial of absolute aesthetic standards in architecture, defends the right of artists to make personal statements with their work.

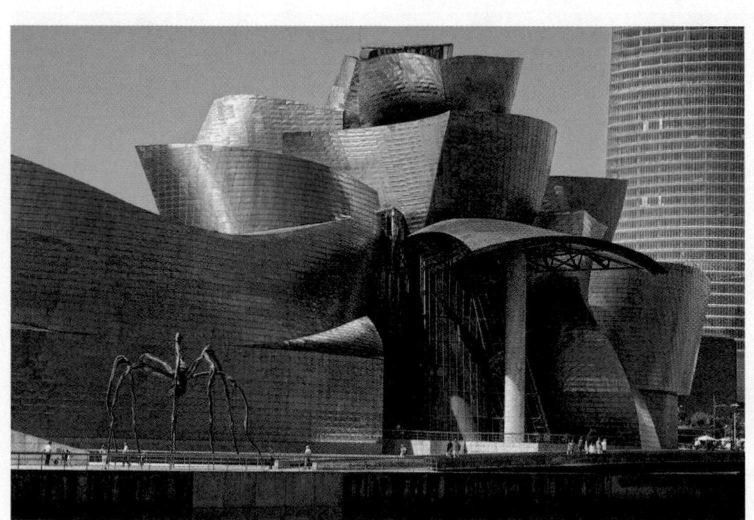

Matthi/Dreamstime

Frank O. Gehry, Guggenheim Museum (Bilbao, Spain), 1997

Gehry's Guggenheim Museum was designed not only to house great art but to stand as a work of art in itself.

By almost universal consent, Gehry's masterpiece thus far is the Guggenheim Museum in Bilbao, Spain. Here he was commissioned by people who were already on the side of art, people who knew and loved the innovative, however daring and controversial, and people who wanted to call worldwide attention to the city they loved. This time there was no room for the frivolity that often characterized some of Gehry's other works.

The structure, like the new Gehry concert hall in Miami Beach for the New World Symphony Orchestra, stands as a giant work of art in itself, and then the visitor enters to find more and more art, in spacious galleries lighted for the maximum enjoyment of each work on display, since its waterside venue had nothing like the Fifth Avenue traffic that Wright wanted to protect art lovers from.

If you never visit Bilbao, you may be fortunate enough to live in a city large enough to support a museum or gallery where, in addition to its permanent collection, traveling exhibits can be shown. Seize the opportunity whenever it presents itself. You will be delighted at how much your range of consciousness will expand and grow. If museums are not available, public libraries and the Internet have the astonishing capability of taking you to galleries and museums all over the world. You can relive the classical past in Greece and Rome, the magnificence of the Florentine Renaissance, the Holland of Rembrandt and other seventeenth-century artists who perfected the imitation of likeness, or visit the world of van Gogh and see the treasures he left for us. You can virtually travel to the Louvre in Paris with its multitude of antiquities, or to the Jeu de Paume with its priceless collection of Impressionist paintings. You can discover the rich legacy of American artists like Cassatt, Douglas, O'Keeffe, and so many others. The world of art belongs to you, and it is our hope that this chapter has encouraged you to browse in it whenever your spirits need uplifting. Art never fails you if you come to it with an eager curiosity and an open mind. The visual effects can be stunning. Look carefully.

Explore on **MyHumanitiesKit.com**
Cassatt, *Woman with a Pearl Necklace in a Loge*

LEARNING OBJECTIVES

Having read and carefully studied this chapter, you should be able to:

1. Explain what is meant by *classical art* and give three examples.
2. Describe *medieval art* and give one example.
3. Justify the label "Renaissance Man" as applied to da Vinci.
4. Relative to Michelangelo, explain the statement "Art is the illusion that there is no art."
5. Contrast Giotto and Raphael relative to their use of perspective.
6. Defend Goya's later style and subject matter from the charge that the artist abandoned the beautiful.
7. Define Impressionism as a rebellion against Art as Likeness.
8. Relative to Picasso, explain Art as Alteration.
9. Describe the architectural art of Frank Lloyd Wright and Frank O. Gehry

KEY TERMS

abstract art art that takes from reality only what the artist wants or that renders a visual depiction of concepts in the artist's mind; the result is a work of art that in no way resembles the familiar world.

alteration how the modern artist changes reality by adding to it shapes, lines, and even colors not found in nature.

chiaroscuro Italian term denoting a way of reproducing in a work of art the interplay of light and shadow in the real world.

classicism the balanced, harmonious, often mathematical characteristics of art and architecture in fifth-century Athens and those aspects of Roman art that were heavily influenced by artists of that period; also used for all subsequent art and architecture created in that style.

collage a work of art in which a variety of materials such as newsprint, magazine pictures, crepe paper, even glass and wood are glued together, forming a new whole, expressive of the artist.

Cubism movement in modern art, epitomized by Picasso, in which the artist breaks down the field of vision into discontinuous segments or in which the artist shows a number of visual events taking place simultaneously (as in *Guernica*).

Dutch school group of painters producing intensely realistic art, centered in Holland during the seventeenth century, with Rembrandt the outstanding example.

fresco artwork painted on the walls of churches and public buildings, popular in the Renaissance, in which the artist applies paint to wet plaster.

Golden Section aesthetically pleasing relationship between the two sides of a plane (like a rectangle), such that the shorter is to the longer as the longer is to the sum of both. The ratio is 1 to 1.68.

Gothic an architectural style of the late Middle Ages featuring high pointed spires and pointed arches; label coined by a critic of the style who called it barbaric "like the Goths who destroyed the Roman Empire."

imitation the transference of what is experienced either outside or inside the artist to a medium of art; it can mean an idealized reproduction (as in classicism), a faithfully realistic one (as in the Dutch school), or an externalization of what exists in the artist's mind (as in abstract art).

Impressionism mid-nineteenth-century art movement wherein the attempt to be realistic is abandoned and instead the artist projects onto the canvas a subjective experience of the world as color and light. In Impressionist art, forms tend to be less sharply divided from each other than they are in, say, landscape painting.

likeness the reproduction by an artist of a person or landscape with the aim of being as close to reality as possible; popularity began to diminish with the invention of photography in the nineteenth century.

media the particular materials in which a given artist works, such as paint, acrylic, charcoal, stone, or even tires, mufflers, broken pieces of glass, etc.

modernism refers less to a particular art movement than to art produced in the late nineteenth to late twentieth centuries.

performance art art as an event that generally exists only for the time it takes for the presentation or installation. The wrapped buildings, surrounded islands, and other installations of Christo may be kept for longer periods of time, but not indefinitely.

perspective technique of rendering, on a plane or curved surface, objects as they appear to natural vision; developed and refined during the early Italian Renaissance.

Pop Art style of mid-twentieth-century art influenced by comic books, movies, television commercials, and billboard advertising; can be just plain fun or satiric.

post-Impressionism broad term used by art historians for art of the late nineteenth- and early twentieth centuries that resembles but is not strict Impressionism; it is neither realistic nor abstract. The work of van Gogh belongs to this category.

postmodernism art produced from the late twentieth century to the present; less a specific movement than a broad umbrella term for the many innovative techniques.

psychological realism the manner in which such artists as Leonardo and Rembrandt are able to convey the inner life of their figures.

realism as used in this chapter, art as likeness.

Renaissance the period of artistic, political, and social movements that began in fourteenth-century Italy, then spread throughout western Europe in the fifteenth and sixteenth centuries; characterized by renewed interest in the classical world, and also marking the end of medievalism and the emergence of the modern world.

superrealism modern style made famous by sculptures of Duane Hanson that are so lifelike they seem about to move; this art form also can make biting social commentary.

surrealism modern style associated with work of Salvador Dalí, among others, in which recognizable objects are put together in bizarre contexts that seem like visualizations of dreams.

TOPICS FOR WRITING AND DISCUSSION

1. The theft in 1911 of the *Mona Lisa* caused an international stir. When the original was supposedly restored, art experts validated it as the real thing. What if it were now discovered to be a magnificent fake? Would that make any difference?
2. Discuss how the term *terribilitá* describes the qualities in the paintings of Michelangelo.
3. Go to an art gallery or museum in your area or on the Internet, choose a painting, and then carefully describe what attracts you about the painting to someone who tends to be uninterested in art.
4. Since, by definition, installation art is not meant to be permanent, what makes it "art"? When would an installation *not* qualify as art?
5. Write a short paper based on either of these statements: "I would rather be a stable, moderately successful, happy, if obscure person than a genius like van Gogh"; or "I would rather be a genius like van Gogh, even if the price were lack of recognition, than a moderately successful, happy, and obscure person."
6. You and a friend are standing in front of Duchamp's *Nude Descending a Staircase*. The friend asks, "What is that supposed to be? It doesn't look like the title." You reply that it doesn't matter. The persistent friend asks, "Then how can it be any good?" What is your learned response?
7. What did Picasso mean when he said we should all go through life like children?
8. An office building that was designed to resemble a huge snail may have amused a number of people, but over the years a committee was formed with the intent of having the building condemned as an eyesore, so far without success. A counter-committee has been working to preserve it on the grounds that it is "Pop Art." Which committee do you think has the stronger argument?
9. In the last century, a government-subsidized French panel of "experts" had the power to prevent the Impressionists from participating in the annual Salon, maintaining it was their responsibility to preserve the integrity of French artistic tradition. Even in the United States, there are subsidized groups such as the National Endowment for the Arts which have the power to withhold grants from art of which they do not approve. If all such groups were abolished, would there be any standards? Does it matter if there aren't any?
10. Historical periods are often defined and characterized by the kind of art (or music or literature) that, in the opinion of historians of the humanities, best summed up the spirit of their time. For example, the Florentine Renaissance is summed up in the work of the three immortal artists it produced. When future generations look back upon our age, which artist do you think would best represent what our time was like?

TAKE A CLOSER LOOK: Exploring Frida Kahlo's *Self-Portrait on the Border Between Mexico and the United States*

Christie's Images/Corbis

Frida Kahlo, *Self-Portrait on the Border Between Mexico and the United States*, 1932

Frida Kahlo was born in 1907 in the outskirts of Mexico City, just before the outset of the Mexican Revolution in 1910, which was to provide the background for her childhood. Health issues plagued Kahlo from an early age. At 6, Kahlo contracted polio affecting the development of her legs and then, at 22, she survived a serious accident when a bus she was riding on crashed into a trolley. Kahlo suffered serious injuries in the crash including a broken spinal column and a permanently damaged reproductive system. She recovered from the accident, but pain would follow her for the rest of her life, necessitating numerous surgeries and more pain. Turning her attention to her art, Kahlo met acclaimed artist Diego Rivera. The two married in 1929 and continued a rocky relationship (including a divorce and remarriage) until Kahlo's death in 1954. While the official cause of death was pulmonary embolism, many questioned if she may have accidentally or purposefully overdosed.

Explore on **MyHumanitiesKit.com** Rivera, *Detroit Industry*

Primarily known as Diego Rivera's wife during her lifetime, Kahlo's work became widely recognized in the late 1970s and has grown ever since with prominent exhibitions, several films depicting her life story, and even a U.S. postage stamp. Her work is often noted for its combination of Mexican indigenous influences and surrealism. With 55 of her 143 paintings being self-portraits, it is also intensely personal work.

Examine the painting closely; the following questions will help you explore *Self-Portrait on the Border Between Mexico and the United States* as a critical viewer.

1. Kahlo painted this self-portrait during a prolonged stay in the United States while Rivera was working on a series of murals he had been commissioned to paint there. What parts of the painting represent Mexico? The United States? How do these two depictions differ?
2. Kahlo once said, "I paint myself because I am so often alone and because I am the subject I know best." What parts of herself does Kahlo seem to be exploring in this self-portrait?
3. What elements of surrealism (p. 135) do you see in the painting? What elements of indigenous art do you see? How do the two work together?
4. Frida Kahlo was first exhibited as Mrs. Diego Rivera. How do you think being married to a famous man affected Kahlo's life?

Chapter 6

Music

We live within an audio environment that is most of the time unplanned. That is, we hear what happens to be around, whether it is a jet taking off, the squeal of auto brakes, a hair dryer, or an approaching train. Noise has been around forever. Mammoths were probably sending forth bellows at the moment human awareness was first forming. The majority of the world's population still exists at the mercy of unwanted noise.

Without music, we exist at the mercy of audio pollution as damaging to mental health as air and water pollution are damaging to physical health. Created by instruments or human voices, music can be defined as *the shaped sound between silences*: the better the shape, the richer and more pleasing the sound. Just as visual art offers a wide variety of shapes and forms to provide an enriched visual environment, music has many sounds: Bach, Mozart, Gershwin, Armstrong, Sinatra, the Beatles, Maroon 5. Limiting ourselves to one kind of music is as detrimental to growth as if we were never to set foot outside our house and discover the unlimited life experiences waiting out there.

Many sounds in the natural world are like music: the song of birds, a mountain stream, gently falling rain, wind over the prairie. The desire to imitate pleasing natural sound seems to be intrinsic to our species. Whistling can remind us of bird song (and note how we refer to the sound of birds in musical terms). The soothing sound of a flowing brook has inspired many composers. The Finnish composer Jan Sibelius wrote *Tapiola,* an orchestral work in which the strings recreate the sound of wind in a forest. In *The Birds,* the Italian composer Ottorino Respighi has the orchestra imitating the various songs and calls of different species. Composers recognize the affinity between nature and music.

Most ancient cultures shared the belief that music was a vital component of the natural world, a gift from heavenly beings. One theory is that for very early people natural sounds were the voices of the gods, and human song was developed to imitate their voices. In popular idiom, we sometimes hear comments such as "She sings like an angel."

Whether or not one believes the mythology of musical origins, music appears to be vital to the human spirit. Is it possible to imagine what life would be like without it? Music is one of the endless treasures bestowed upon us by the humanities, and we are fortunate that, as this art form developed over the millennia, it divided into endless varieties.

The purpose of this chapter is to encourage you to explore the wide range of musical sound. Some of it is recognized as part of the world's artistic heritage. Some of it is still very new and may achieve that distinction one day. (It's fun to predict what *will.*)

We will first separate music into its component elements, then describe some of its major, and widely differing, forms, together with some suggested works from the past and present as well as from other cultures that may offer us a more well-rounded musical life. As in any introductory text, the process is necessarily selective. We attempt to open the door of musical recognition a little wider.

◀ **Pablo Picasso, *Three Musicians,* 1921**

Pablo Picasso, the most famous artist of the twentieth century, has given us a Cubist portrait of people giving us music.

The Basic Elements of Music

Credit for the development of formal music goes to the ancient Egyptians and their belief that the god Thoth gave humanity seven basic sounds, perhaps much like the seven-tone scale that would come later. Ancient Chinese philosophy, which believed all nature was ruled by a divine principle of order, saw music as the human connection to that order.

> *"In a world of peace and love music would be the universal language."*
>
> **—Henry David Thoreau**

Along with laying the foundations of Western thought, art, and literature, the Greeks also created a profound theory of music. In *The Republic,* Plato writes about "the music of the spheres," a concept that has endured for many centuries. He describes the heavens as divided into eight spheres, on each of which a siren sings a note of astounding sweetness. The sirens in Greek mythology were long-haired, beautiful women who lured sailors to their deaths with glorious sounds; but, apparently, the sirens in Plato's heavens had no such destructive motives. Instead, their song represented the eternal order, or *armonia,* of the universe. That Greek term, which became the English word **harmony**, indicates a connection between music and the structure of the universe. Religions of the world have long claimed that through music one achieves union with the divine.

We see that music existed in many guises long, long ago. It became an art form in the West with the development of rules and guidelines.

Tone

The basic element of music is the **tone**, or note, a sound produced by the human voice or by a musical instrument that maintains the same frequency of vibration regardless of duration. Perhaps the imitation of a natural sound was then shaped to become pure and sweet. Or perhaps that pure and sweet tone just came from someone's imagination, and people nearby were astounded when they heard it. However it happened, the discovery of tones marked the beginning of the human victory over the unplanned audio environment. True music began when someone experimented with a variety of tones, some higher, some lower.

The Scale

People in the ancient world who discovered different tones through a natural instinct for song or a way to accompany dances and rituals could not have known that tone was caused by the frequency of sound-wave vibrations: the higher the frequency, the higher the tone, and vice versa. After a time, someone must have happened upon a distinct progression of individual tones from low to high, and that was the beginning of Western music as *we* know it. This orderly progression of frequencies from low to high is the **scale**. All cultures that developed music used a scale, though they did not necessarily happen upon the same sequence of tones.

At first, the dominant scale in both non-Western and Western music consisted of five tones, known as a **pentatonic scale**. It remains the basis for most traditional Asian music. The Western scale was expanded to six tones by the sixth century C.E. and was first written down (or notated) by an Italian monk. With the later addition of a seventh tone, the Western, or **diatonic**, scale was complete. Notes were also given letter designations—ABCDEFG—and each sequence of seven could constitute a scale. The addition of sharps and flats—or **half tones**—expanded the number of scales possible. Over time, the first note of each scale became the identifying **key** in which a given piece of music was composed. The basic scale in Western music begins with the note C (hence CDEFGAB); and these notes also acquired the names *do, re, mi, fa, so, la,* and *ti.*

Imagine that you are sitting at a piano. Beginning with C, your finger travels up the seven-tone progression using only the white keys. You are in the key of C. There are also the five black keys, or half-tones, such as C-sharp and E-flat. When you play the white keys plus the black keys, you are using the twelve-tone, or **chromatic** scale. To the list of musical keys we may thus include C-sharp, B-flat, and so on.

When we play or sing a seven whole-tone progression, except for that which starts with A, we are using a *major* scale. A *minor* scale is more complicated. The *natural* minor scale begins with A and goes up seven whole tones. The *melodic* minor scale substitutes G-sharp going up but the whole-tone G coming down. The *harmonic* minor scale substitutes G-sharp going up and also coming down. Though the verbal definitions are complex, music in minor keys is easily recognized. Many songs of heartbreak and loss are written in minor keys, as is instrumental music that seeks to create a somber mood.

> *I know that the twelve in each octave and the varieties of rhythm offer me opportunities that all human genius will never exhaust.*
>
> **—Igor Stravinsky**

Traditional symphonic music is usually identified in terms of the key and type of scale in which it begins (composers can change either or both within a given work) and the *opus* number (that is, where it occurs in the composer's repertoire). Thus one might see this on a program: Beethoven, Symphony No. 9 in D Minor, Op. 125. Combined major and minor keys can be found in blues music (discussed later in the chapter).

The music of most non-Western cultures is based on a scale of five tones that do not necessarily correspond to Western sounds. The Western preference for seven tones may have to do with the fact that Western listeners are accustomed to the narrower frequency intervals between the seven tones of the familiar scale. Hearing traditional Asian music for the first time and expecting the familiar scale, they are likely to find the sounds quite strange.

Africa has a long musical tradition without a formalized scale at all. Tones were, of course, fundamental as in other cultures, but these could change to suit the emotion of the musician or singer. Traditional African music has always made strong use of the human voice, and, when the voice is the primary way of preserving melody, much variation was and continues to be the rule. The music of Africa made possible the evolution of jazz and blues, two art forms that allow for maximum freedom of expression.

Rhythm

Early music throughout the world was probably monophonic—that is, limited to just the melodic line and sung or played without harmony. But rhythmic accompaniment would have been provided when appropriate, such as at ritual events like a funeral or a rite of passage celebrating the arrival of puberty.

We know rhythm was the underlying factor in early Greek ceremonies because we have written accounts of it. Certain rhythms were held appropriate for inspirational ceremonies because of their uplifting effect on the soul, while other rhythms—certainly those involved in the orgies held annually in honor of Dionysus—were deemed conducive to uncontrolled, licentious behavior.

Formal music might have begun with the discovery of tones, but rhythm by itself might well have preceded tone, scale, and the earliest instruments. Most likely, a rat–a–tat pounding of sticks and stones was an early factor in human development, used to mark occasions of great joy or solemnity. The early instincts are still with us. We often see very young children rat–a–tatting with blocks or just with their hands, the beat becoming more pronounced and regular as they grow older. Rap and hip-hop today give clear indication that people are just as attracted to the hypnotic effect of steady rhythm as their ancestors were.

Moving to a beat—or, as it is better known, *dancing*—may be even older than singing. Even without specific tones to sing, people must have found pleasure in letting out their feelings at the insistence of loud beats from any number and kinds of sources. Recall that Chapter 2 analyzed contrasting aspects of human culture and human personality: the Apollonian and the Dionysian. The Apollonian half of human beings enjoys order; the Dionysian half exults in unrestrained expressions of feeling. Neither side is sufficient by itself. Civilization advances with Apollonian order, but without Dionysian spontaneity, it can become rigid and uncreative.

Rhythm in music, as in poetry, is an alternation between stress and unstress. It acquires its different forms according to the pattern of alternation used. A once popular rhythm in Western music is that of the waltz, created from a stressed beat followed by two unstressed beats. Also described as a "stately" rhythm, it is far more Apollonian than it is Dionysian, and was thus suitable for the aristocrats of nineteenth–century ballrooms, though it had its Dionysian side in an era when touching someone of the opposite sex in public was otherwise frowned upon. Popular among aristocrats of the eighteenth century, the minuet was also based on Apollonian (that is, rigid and repetitive) rhythms. So are the marches used for funerals and graduation.

Plato approved of stately rhythms, which for him lent gravity to public occasions, affirming order in the state. He disapproved strongly of rhythms that were there only to excite the emotions. People of today who enjoy letting go on a dance floor to the beat of rock bands evidently find Dionysian liberation a satisfying escape from the Apollonian demands of household duties, jobs, or schoolwork. Rhythm is the mortar that holds a work together, that gives coherence to a collection of sounds. A change in rhythm can be a major event, often very exciting to the listener. It opens up new possibilities, new directions.

When musical tones joined the ancient human passion for rhythm, a new force was born that provided a way for emotions to be expressed, released, and controlled. Once rhythm was discovered, it never left musical art. Even the plainsong, a chant sung by medieval monks and clerics, has a rhythm, though it is hard to detect because there are so many stressed tones, and those not stressed tend to be delicately sung. In the famous *Bolero* by Impressionist Maurice Ravel, the underlying rhythm is so pronounced that it takes over the entire piece.

Desiring to free themselves from the restraints that traditional rhythms impose, some composers attempt to be totally arrhythmic; that is, they avoid all regular alternations of stress and unstress, seldom repeating a pattern. The listener is kept off guard, presumably on edge, and the piece aspires to create a mood of agitation and emotional instability.

What is the magic that rhythm weaves inside us? We can speculate at great length, of course. Children are conceived in rhythm, born in rhythm; parents clap their hands in rhythm to keep them from crying. The universe itself throbs with rhythms: the rotation of the earth, the alternation of the seasons, incoming and outgoing tides, birth and death. How about order and disorder, Apollo and Dionysus, belief and doubt, joy and sorrow? Anthropologists studying early rituals have suggested that rhythmic effects were used to express the heartbeat of Mother Earth.

Rock percussionist Mickey Hart of the Grateful Dead once said, "Rhythm is at the very center of our lives." If you were to ask a number of people which musical element they could most easily dispense with, rhythm would probably not be the answer.

Melody

The art of music began with differentiated tones played or sung in certain patterns that might or might not have been repeated. One might have flowed into another. These patterns were melodies. **Melody** is the part we remember of a song or a symphonic movement. If we remember nothing beyond a "babble" of instruments and a great deal of percussion, chances are many of us would ask, "What happened to the melody?"

The discovery of tone made melody possible. Melody can be defined in two ways: one, most familiar to Western ears, as *a significant sequence of musical tones that form a unity, like a sentence of prose, and are usually repeated later in the exact order or as a recognizable variation of the original;* or two, as found in many non-Western cultures, *an arrangement of tones in a flowing sequence that may or may not have a definite end.* Certain melodies were used over and over because they were pleasing, and a method was needed for preserving them. Musical instruments such as flutes were invented for this purpose.

"Music was my refuge. I could crawl into the place between the notes and curl my back to loneliness."

—Maya Angelou

Opera-goers, hearing a new work in its premiere performance, may at first find that "there are no melodies in it." Someone accustomed to only Western symphonic music may wonder why, at first hearing, there is no beautiful melody in sitar music from India, or may denounce a rock band for pounding out "just noise." Not every melody is beautiful in the sense of being played or sung often enough to be remembered.

Many are understandably drawn to what may be termed *romantic* melody, the melodic line that falls soothingly and repeatedly on the ears. Much of its emotional impact has to do with the instruments which play it: often, the violin, the piano, the guitar, and the flute, instruments that produce delicate sounds. Romantic melody tends to be "gentle," befitting the tender emotions it calls up. It is almost always slow.

A romantic musical style was dominant during the nineteenth and early twentieth centuries. Composers such as Brahms and Tchaikovsky were, and still are, called "masters of melody"—that is, they provide lush sequences of tones that are easily recalled and that evoke emotions within the listener. Brahms's *Cradle Song,* or "Lullaby," is known throughout the world and has become almost synonymous with treasured memories of an infant's earliest days. The main theme in Tchaikovsky's *Romeo and Juliet Overture* reminds people of the joys of first love. Translated into a popular song called *Our Love,* it contributed to Tchaikovsky's reputation as the king of melody.

Rhapsody on a Theme of Paganini by Sergei Rachmaninoff (1873–1943) offers excellent examples of romantic melody. The main theme is introduced at the beginning—a sprightly and graceful melody written by Nicolò Paganini, an Italian violinist and composer who lived a century earlier. Though Paganini's work has long been popular with violinists because of its intricate challenges to the instrument, Rachmaninoff's variations on his theme have become immensely more popular with audiences than the original—especially his 17th Variation, in which, after a dramatic

"Music is the arithmetic of sounds as optics is the geometry of light."

—Claude Debussy

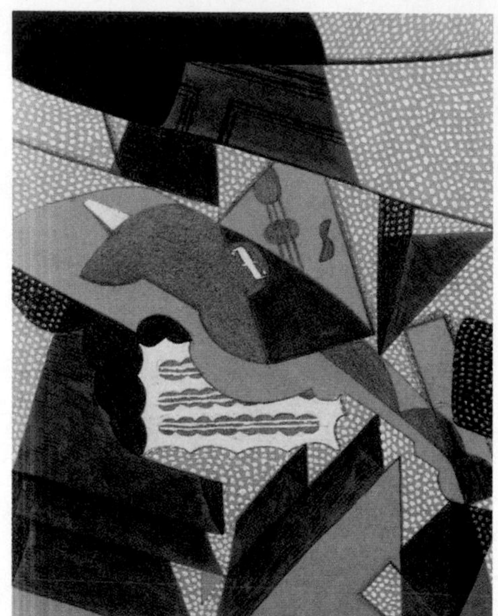

Christie's Images Ltd./SuperStock

Juan Gris, *Le Violon*, c. 1915–1916

Capturing the mood of new musical sounds.

silence, the piano enters and plays a melody that is Paganini's lively theme turned around and performed at a much slower tempo. When the string section passionately repeats the theme, the listener cannot help experiencing a surge of emotion.

Among jazz musicians melody usually means the theme that begins their performance and on which the remainder of it is based. By the conclusion of the piece, the original theme is usually different from the melody we heard at the outset—*very* different. Jazz is complex, requiring an initial willingness to devote the time needed to explore its many treasures.

An effective way to increase your appreciation for what is often considered nonmelody is to become a more attentive listener to jazz. In doing so, you will find variations on a melody performed by different instruments throughout a piece. From jazz move on to **chamber music** (concert music written for a few instruments rather than a symphony orchestra). Once again you will hear clearly defined themes that are then developed through variations into ever more complex patterns of sounds. By extending your definition of melody, you will find yourself enjoying a broader range of musical experience.

Sometimes melody is a sequence of tones that seems to go on indefinitely without repeating itself. During the 1960s sitar music achieved popularity in the West because of its extended melodic lines and its clearly non-Western, hence "anti-Establishment," sound. Some modern composers are drawn to non-Western sound in an effort to break away from the traditional. Philip Glass, a contemporary American composer, writes melodic lines that keep repeating a single pattern. Some have called his work monotonous and endlessly repetitive, while others find it pleasantly hypnotic. Director Martin Scorsese recruited Glass to write the Asian-sounding score for the film *Kundun* (1997), the story of the Dalai Lama. Although Glass is Western, the music was authentically Tibetan, and therefore unfamiliar to most Western ears. Listening to this music is a good way to explore alternative kinds of melody. We should remember that the so-called "beauty of melody" is a matter of historical period and cultural heritage. Not that all melody is beautiful—or that no melody is beautiful; rather, beauty in music has a lot to do with familiarity and the kind of instruments popular within a given cultural tradition.

Extreme departures from tradition have characterized modern Western music since the earliest years of the twentieth century, when composers reacted strongly against the romantic conception of melody. The aggressive **dissonance** in their music has had much to do with its deliberate lack of appeal to those who wanted music to sound romantic and were unwilling to tolerate anything else. Throughout the twentieth century composers kept experimenting with nontraditional scales and sounds. Sometimes they invented new kinds of musical notes that were not in any scale anyone knew but had to be half-sung and half-spoken. Composers have even included long stretches of silence in their music.

In recent years a significant number of composers have reacted against modernism, especially what they consider "noisy jangling and crashing," a fierce determination to sound like nothing that ever came before. The new music can be called, like the new visual art, *postmodern*. The most frequently performed works of this genre come from a group of composers calling themselves *minimalists*. Their goal is to divest music of modernism's unnecessary trappings and return to the basic elements, particularly rhythm. Minimalist music, such as that by Philip Glass and John Adams, is sometimes dismissed as coldly formal and unemotional, as well as monotonous, by unsympathetic listeners who also find it unmelodic. But, like all unfamiliar music, minimalist compositions can reward those willing to take the time to listen.

It has been said that music is what emotion sounds like. The emotional life of an individual is exceedingly complex, is it not? To insist that music sound only a certain way is like saying that people can feel only a certain kind of way. We can turn away, just as we don't have to welcome any stranger we think we don't want to know. But we also have the freedom to make friends.

Harmony and the Orchestra

In Asian music, tones are usually played by themselves, that is, without *harmony,* which is the simultaneous production of tones by voices or instruments. So accustomed are Westerners to hearing simultaneous tones that they tend to take harmony for granted, but like melody, harmony has historical and cultural roots.

During the first millennium, Christian churches incorporated music into the private services of monks and priests as well as public masses. Emphasis was placed on song as a means of communicating with God. Greatly influenced by ancient Hebrew chants, these sung prayers became known as *plainsong.* They were performed in unison by clerics acting as one voice praising God's glory and asking for mercy and forgiveness. Harmony created by units of voices singing different tones would have been out of place, a violation of the belief that all people were the same in the eyes of God.

> "Music provides a kind of pleasure which human nature cannot do without."
>
> —**Confucius**

During the sixteenth century, as the Renaissance, with its rebirth of classical culture, moved from one European country to another, bringing with it a celebration of life on earth, music—secular music—was eagerly sought. Since the Renaissance emphasized enjoyment during one's brief stay on earth, music could fill leisure hours with many pleasures. The royal courts all had musicians on hand, and new instruments were invented to explore the richness and sensuality of secular music. In these venues scarcely an hour of the day went by without the sounds of lute, recorder, or oboe, playing sometimes alone but often in small groups. Renaissance composers explored the harmonious interweaving of instruments and voices, as if to say that music should be the contribution of a number of individuals, each adding to life's enjoyment, each with a musical statement to make. The Renaissance also celebrated the uniqueness of each human being. No longer need music be limited to plainsong, delivered in unison to obscure the differences among the singers. Harmony allowed for a variety of interweaving musical themes, each with its own melody, played or sung by individualized instruments or voices. Eventually the development of harmony would lead to the complexities of the **baroque** style that flourished in Europe during the seventeenth century.

The invention of harmony also made possible the art form known as *opera* (the plural of *opus,* a Latin term meaning "work"), a collaboration of many distinct individuals—composers, orchestras, singers, poets who wrote their words, dancers, and that new species of artist, the scenic designer—with the whole becoming a rich and complex visual tapestry and festival of sound, all working together to give added meaning to the concept of harmony. (A fuller discussion of opera is included in Chapter 8, The Musical Stage.)

Orchestras grew in size and complexity; and, as they did, composers eagerly explored the range of the new instruments. By the eighteenth century the **symphony,** a musical form in separate units, or movements, became a concert staple. Major aggregations of musicians became known as symphony orchestras; these steadily increased in numbers as Haydn, Mozart, Beethoven, Brahms, and, late in the nineteenth century, Mahler wrote works that required more and more instruments. One of Mahler's major works is titled *The Symphony of a Thousand* because it involves literally that many musicians and singers. Tchaikovsky's *1812 Overture* requires, in addition to a massive orchestra, numerous cannons fired as the music reaches its climax. Beethoven's Ninth Symphony is now performed by an enormous orchestra of at least 150 musicians in addition to a chorus of perhaps 200 voices.

Listen on **MyHumanitiesKit.com**
Tchaikovsky, *1812 Overture*

In 1990 Leonard Bernstein, an American composer and conductor, was invited to present the Ninth Symphony at the site of the newly fallen Berlin Wall, which had, since the ending of World War II, separated East and West Berlin. On this occasion more than 200 musicians and singers from the United States, the Soviet Union, Great Britain, and France participated. The theme of the final movement, a choral setting of the poet Schiller's *Ode to Joy*, heralded a new dawn of freedom and friendship between the previously separated citizens of Berlin and also gave ringing hope that all oppressed peoples would triumph in their struggle against tyranny.

To open the 1998 winter Olympics in Nagano, Japan, conductor Seiji Ozawa led a performance of the "Ode to Joy" using choruses from four locations around the globe joined together by satellite. This time the music represented global unity, as athletes from diverse nations, unable to communicate with each other through words, could find in Beethoven's music a common bond.

Musical harmony, especially in the glorious complexities of the great symphony orchestras, has become a model of human society at its most ideal. It requires every musician to pull together for one common purpose. No one sound can be any more important than another, yet each one has its moment of prominence. If one tone is flat, the entire enterprise suffers. The ultimate product is a testimony to the genius of the individual.

Silence

"After silence, that which comes nearest to expressing the inexpressible is music."

—Aldous Huxley

Silence is the unpublicized ingredient that makes music possible in the same way that the empty space around a sculpture makes the sculpture possible, or the judicious use of wall space can make or break an art exhibit. Just imagine twenty-five original van Goghs crammed together: "Where is *The Starry Night*? Oh, there it is. I almost missed it. Funny, but somehow it's just not as exciting as I thought it would be." Fast-forwarding a DVD destroys all dramatic value. The acceleration erases the pauses, which are as significant as the words themselves. After all, if characters talked nonstop, how could a dramatic situation develop? In music the spaces—or silences—between notes can be equally important.

To deepen an appreciation of music, it is necessary to hear and enjoy silence. Silence has been an integral part of many works. The pauses in the second movement, the "Funeral March," of Beethoven's Third Symphony (analyzed later in the chapter) are as famous as the themes that precede and follow them. They make possible the dramatic effect when the main theme of the movement returns for the last time. There is silence, then part of the theme, then more silence, then more of the theme. The effect reminds the listener of someone trying valiantly to hold back tears.

Think of the last time you were in the presence of someone struggling for self-control while obviously overcome by a powerful surge of emotion. Weren't the silences full of meaning? Great composers handle silences in the same way that great artists since Leonardo da Vinci have known how to handle shadows. Great stage actors owe something of their greatness to the mastery they have achieved over the words that they do *not* speak and to the silences before and after the words they do speak.

A famous solo theme for French horn occurs soon after the opening of the fourth movement of Brahms's First Symphony. The moment is heralded by a tympani roll, which is followed by the introduction of the French horn theme. Some conductors, recognizing the musical benefits of silence, make the orchestra pause for several measures before the theme is heard. This silence dramatically intensifies the significance of what follows. The French horn enters like an actor making an appearance for which the audience has been eagerly waiting. In some interpretations, however, there is almost no pause at all, perhaps losing an opportunity for creating a thrilling moment.

The composer John Cage (1912–1992) is famous for having incorporated silence into his work and making it as important as the actual notes he wrote down for musicians to play. One of his compositions, *4'33,"* named for the four and a half minutes it takes to perform it, asks the artist to sit at the piano for that length of time and, with his gestures, maintain the required tempo. Cage insisted that the "notes are silent," but that they are there all the same. One of his longer pieces for the piano combines both played and silent notes, and in yet another, the pianist performs a series of complex chords and difficult runs up and down the keyboard, and then sits perfectly still for about fifteen minutes. Audiences, according to one critic, seem "almost afraid to cough." A strong influence on Cage's work was Zen Buddhism (discussed in Chapter 10), an extremely austere and disciplined form of Buddhism, demanding long hours of meditation in absolute silence.

What ultimately distinguishes one musician from another is not only the ability to play the notes as written but the musical intuition that manifests itself. One way in which the critical ear can detect the presence of this intuition, or this "feeling for the music," is to listen to how the performer manipulates the silences that surround the tones. Three world class pianists might record Beethoven's *Pathétique Sonata,* and though each plays exactly the same notes, the interpretation by each will have subtle touches unique to that musician. In almost every instance the telling factor is the handling of silence. Here a pause is elongated; there, foreshortened. As with the space surrounding a sculpture, silence in music helps to define, to single out, to create individuality.

The most evident gift from great music is its sound. But the very absence of sound is just as important. Remember: *Music is the shaped sound between silences.*

The Varieties of Musical Experience

There are so many styles, so many musical forms that singling out a few is difficult indeed. Within those parameters, however, certain kinds of musical experience—musical genres of the past and present—illustrate what music has to offer.

A Bach Fugue

Johann Sebastian Bach (1685–1750) was born in a Germany that did not regard music as an art form, but considered it either as court entertainment composed and performed for upper-class amusement by hirelings paid to do a job or as a

Bachhaus Eisenach

Johann Sebastian Bach, 1746

Bach, considered a mere employee hired to play the church organ and compose a few hymns, ended up revolutionizing the art of music.

subordinate adjunct to religious services. The music with which Bach is associated, which indeed he came to epitomize, grew out of religion but went beyond religion in its impact and influence on the future of music as an art. It became the very epitome of the **baroque**, a highly complex style not only of music but of art and architecture as well. Historians of the humanities usually date the baroque period from the middle of the seventeenth century to 1750, which happens to be the very year in which the composer died.

The baroque period was characterized by architectural grandeur and an elaborate use of color and ornamentation. Civic buildings, such as those that still line the Ringstrasse, the main street of Vienna, were adorned with gilt, statuary, and other forms of embellishment, none of which was intended to be purely functional. The term *baroque* was taken from French and Portuguese words that meant "imperfect pearl" and applied to the new style, which was far from classical simplicity. Architecture made abundant use of curved rather than straight lines, and baroque music is exceptionally intricate.

Catholicism found in baroque architectural splendor one means of bringing people back to the fold. The German monk Martin Luther (1483–1546) had rebelled against Catholicism for what he considered its moral corruption. With other reformers, he had started a revolutionary movement known as the Protestant Reformation, which aimed to divest religion of its Catholic sensuality. In contrast to the stark, wooden churches of the Protestant Reformation, the Catholic baroque houses of worship, especially in Italy and Poland, reintroduced the marble, brilliant colors, and statues of the Renaissance churches, perhaps in an effort to encourage defectors to return to a reinvented religion with an appeal to both the spirit and the senses. These churches dating from the seventeenth century are adorned with flying angels suspended from brightly painted ceilings and smiling gold cherubs resting near the top of marble columns. They were for their time the epitome of opulence, offering both dramatic and aesthetic appeal without apology.

> *"Classical music is stereotyped as an art of the dead, a repertory that begins with Bach and terminates with Mahler and Puccini. People are sometimes surprised to learn that composers are still writing at all."*
>
> **—Alex Ross**

Despite the many reforms instituted by Luther and his followers, Lutheranism remained closer to Catholicism than would be true of the multiple Protestant sects which were to develop. While Lutherans generally shunned the impetus toward elaborate visual ornamentation of the churches, they felt differently about the ornamentation of their music. Music became especially important in the Lutheran service, for which Bach composed many of his works. As the era progressed, composers, both religious and secular, sought to outdo one another in the intricacy of their compositions. They made strong use of **counterpoint**, playing one melodic line against another, with both melodic lines being given equal value and dominance.

Harmony, of course, had been standard in music since the early Renaissance, but Bach's counterpoint carried complexity a step further. Nonetheless, even though he had achieved considerable recognition for his music during his lifetime, after his death his church still considered him as primarily a great organist rather than a composer. When they first began to hear his compositions, congregations may have been slightly confused, if not overwhelmed by what they heard.

When Bach was hired to play the organ, he was welcome to compose little pieces to accompany the service, which fed his insatiable appetite for experimenting with organ sound. Seeking to expand his musical horizons, Bach took a leave of absence and went in 1705 to study with the famous Swedish organist and composer Dietrich Buxtehude, returning with new works of such intricacy and virtuosity that the church choir often could not sing them. By this time, however, word of the new music began to spread. Eventually he became musical director and choir director at St. Thomas's Church in Leipzig, where he remained for most of his productive life, scarcely traveling more than a few miles from the city.

His reputation expanded and blossomed, then began to fade as he grew older, even though the complexity of his work deepened. In some quarters he began to be called old-fashioned. He had almost single-handedly brought baroque music to its pinnacle and then was accused of not being modern enough. By mid-century Franz Josef Haydn (1732–1809) was learning his craft and soon would give birth to 104 symphonies, earning him the reputation he still enjoys as father of that musical genre. Haydn returned to the relative simplicity of classicism, and his tremendous influence helped to make baroque complexity obsolete. In Bach's declining years, younger composers were already experimenting with the style that Haydn would make famous.

Through the new works, German music was attaining stature as an art form, and thus the great repertoire of Bach—the cantatas, the oratorios, and the magnificent displays of counterpoint known as **fugues**—were considered dated even before they were ever really discovered. Bach's music would have to wait a full century before it would take its place among acknowledged masterworks.

Confined both geographically and professionally, Bach found liberation in exploring the possibilities of musical language. The baroque style required not only long, highly fluid melodies and countermelodies but also **improvisation**—a spontaneous variation or set of variations on a given theme. Through improvisation Bach could take wings and soar into the endless skies of inner space.

Music in the time of both Bach and Haydn was not expected to express a composer's innermost emotions; and indeed Bach's music is frequently labeled intellectual. It is, for example, greatly admired by mathematicians, who see in it a musical parallel to higher calculus. Nonetheless, there is indeed an emotional side to it. The great *Toccata and Fugue in D Minor* draws the listener into a vortex of sensations that are almost indescribable. The ear discerns the many melodic strands that play against each other, and the inner eye translates the sounds into patterns of light and lines that crisscross, engulf each other, and continually change into shapes never before seen or imagined. Surrendering to this music, we the listeners find ourselves visiting strange inner landscapes flooded with both thoughts and feelings.

Listen on **MyHumanitiesKit.com**
Bach, *Toccata and Fugue in D Minor*

A **toccata** is a freestyle musical form designed to allow the performer of Bach's day to display virtuosity; it is frequently, as in the case of the D Minor work, followed by a fugue, which is more strictly controlled by established musical laws. In a toccata the composer or performer may improvise on the stated themes, taking them in a variety of directions.

We need only listen to the D Minor performed on an organ to be astounded that one pair of hands could master so difficult a composition.

This practice has definite counterparts in jazz. It is no coincidence that jazz players often acknowledge a strong debt to Bach, particularly for his genius at improvisation, and often include variations on Bach melodies in their repertoire. The fugue allows for the simultaneous hearing of different melodies played or sung; it is a swift-moving form, stabilized by the laws of counterpoint—that is, the melodic lines heard simultaneously must complement, not conflict, with each other.

We need only listen to the D Minor performed on an organ to be astounded that one pair of hands could master so difficult a composition. The idea behind the fugue is to demonstrate that what for the average person would be an impossibility is indeed well within the capabilities of the performer. It allows both composer and performer to display their virtuosity. At the same time, the intricacies of the form require strong guidelines as well as enormous technical skills. The result may sound free and unrestrained, but in actuality the music is rigorously disciplined. The major jazz composers and performers of our time are often highly trained musicians whose flights of improvisation follow definite rules, similar to the fugues of Bach.

A Beethoven Symphony

> *I heard one evening a symphony of Beethoven's. I thereupon fell ill of fever; and when recovered I was—a musician.*
>
> **—Richard Wagner**

Explore on **MyHumanitiesKit.com**
Mozart, Symphony No 40

Sometimes the history of the humanities lopes along for many years, even decades, without producing an artist who rises to the highest levels of creative achievement. It can also happen that many artistic geniuses appear at or around the same time. The late fifteenth century in Italy, for example, saw three visual artists, acknowledged to be perhaps the world's greatest, all contemporary with each other: Leonardo, Michelangelo, and Raphael. Germany can boast that it gave the world Mozart and Beethoven during the late eighteenth century.

In the baroque musical tradition, which Bach epitomized, composers worked in a limited range of musical forms to find their own way through the music. Bach achieved greatness by making the forms accommodate his tremendous musical intellect and imagination. Mozart (more fully discussed in Chapter 8) easily rivaled Bach with his phenomenal output—and in a much shorter life span (1756–1791)—composing not only operas but symphonies, chamber music for inexhaustible combinations of instruments, several huge masses, a long list of songs, and concertos for both violin and piano. Mozart expanded the capabilities of the symphony orchestra and, in so doing, prepared the way for Beethoven, who would take it to new heights. In order to provide emotional release from a tormented life in which he gradually lost all of his hearing, Beethoven composed in new or greatly expanded musical forms. It is not an exaggeration to say he reinvented the music of the West.

Library of Congress

Ludwig van Beethoven, painted c. 1870

Beethoven expanded the range of many musical forms including the symphony.

Beethoven composed for churches, concert halls, small salons, private performances, royal chambers, and, above all, for himself. When he lost his hearing during the peak of his musical career, Beethoven turned inward, and out of his complex and anguished soul came sounds no one had ever heard before. Even today, more than a century and a half after the composer's death, when every note written by him has been played and interpreted by thousands upon thousands of musicians and heard by millions, new listeners and new performers can find in the music some as yet undisclosed aspect of Beethoven's gigantic personality.

This new tradition combined secular, religious, and nationalistic trends into one, making the music of northern Europe the equal of Italian music, which had been for centuries the dominant musical tradition of the West. In particular, it created and then quickly broadened the scope of the symphony, which became for Germany what the opera was for Italy.

The development of the symphony cannot be measured in terms of quantity alone. Haydn wrote 104 symphonies, Mozart 41, and Beethoven "just" 9. (Later, Johannes Brahms, intimidated by the majestic symphonic creations of Beethoven, would spend twenty years working on his first symphony and would leave the world "just" four!)

In 1804, Beethoven, after having given the world two symphonies in the tradition of Mozart, who had already stretched the limits of the form beyond anything yet known, came forth with his Third or E-flat Major Symphony, which is called *Eroica* ("Heroic"). The premiere proved to be an occasion for which the music world was still not completely prepared, even though the work had been preceded by Mozart's last symphony, the titanic *Jupiter*. After all, a symphony was originally a twenty-minute concert diversion, consisting of four movements: the first moderately paced, the second slow and lyrical, the third rapid and light-hearted, and the fourth rousing and climactic. The four movements were related only in terms of a composer's characteristic style, but they were not expected to make a unified statement of any kind.

The *Eroica* was twice the length of the *Jupiter*. It was a work so huge in conception, so complex in execution, and so overwhelming to experience that by all rights it should have invited immediate comparison with Michelangelo's *David*, the Sistine Chapel ceiling, or the great tragedies of Shakespeare. Unfortunately, many of the first listeners could not accommodate the work's heroic dimensions or its daring innovations, particularly its heavy use of seventh chords, up to that time a musical taboo, considered barbarically dissonant, unfit for civilized ears.

In the opinion of music historians, the most astonishing aspect of the *Eroica* is that it is not just big for the sake of bigness. One critic sums up the matter:

The Art Gallery Collection/Alamy

Jacques Louis David, *Napoleon Crossing the St. Bernard Pass*, 1800

Beethoven is believed to have dedicated his Third Symphony to Napoleon, depicted in Jacques Louis David's portrait, then rescinded the dedication when word reached the composer that Napoleon had declared himself emperor.

> *We are used to the scale of the Eroica, but what is forever new is a musical substance which requires every second of the vast time expanse which Beethoven organized to contain it. In its size it is wholly efficient, as fine an example of economy of structure as any four-minute Bach fugue.*[1]

In the *Eroica* not only do the four movements constitute a unity but each succeeding movement sounds like a perfect complement to the one before it. It is clear that Beethoven did not finish one movement and then tack on another as though the preceding one had not existed.

The first movement is on a grand, heroic scale, an epic style with noble themes and huge orchestration to be rivaled only by the composer's own fifth and ninth symphonies. The story is that Beethoven was inspired by the heroic image of Napoleon as the liberator of Europe. He created in the opening movement music that paralleled his feelings, and then dedicated the entire work to the man he perceived as savior of the free world. It is also widely believed that when word reached the composer that his hero had demanded to be crowned emperor, Beethoven rescinded the dedication.

Instead of glorifying an imperial leader, the work came to be identified with the common man movement hailing the heroism of ordinary citizens. It has the same fist-shaking thunder we find in the work of Michelangelo. A musical rebel, defying all tradition, plagued by illness that would eventually rob him of his hearing, misunderstood and criticized by many, Beethoven could readily identify with revolutionary movements in his native Germany, as well as in America and France.

One is tempted to hear in the second movement a musical parallel to Beethoven's profound disillusionment with Napoleon.

One is tempted to hear in the second movement a musical parallel to Beethoven's profound disillusionment with Napoleon. Profound sorrow is certainly there, as indicated by the tempo notation: *marcia funebre* (funeral march). It is the slowest of all slow movements, dirgelike and heartbroken. We have already spoken of it in the section on silence as a musical element. Whether Napoleon was the direct cause of the sorrow or whether Beethoven, having exhausted the range of noble emotions, found himself exploring the depths of sadness, we cannot know; but we can say that the first two movements of the *Eroica* strongly suggest an experience common to nearly everyone: the passage from heroic, idealistic youth to maturity and its awareness of tragedy.

The third movement, by contrast, is almost shocking with its galloping pace and precise horns, all of it sounding like nothing so much as a hunting party. Out of place? Surely not. Listening carefully to every note of the funeral march shows that there is only so much emotional wrenching one can sustain. Life must go on. The depressed spirit must pull itself up from despair.

The finale begins with a graceful, dancelike melody suggestive of polite society: civilization restored, so to speak. This melody leads through an intricate development back into the same heroic mood that opened the symphony. We have passed from romantic illusion to the depths of tragedy and, through struggle, upward again to a more mature, sober, and deliberate affirmation. The composer of the *Eroica* captures the human soul in full range. It would not mark Beethoven's last glimpse of paradise.

Listen on **MyHumanitiesKit.com**
Beethoven, Symphony No. 9

Beethoven's Ninth, and final, symphony was composed around 1818, when he was totally deaf. It is easily four times the length of a late Mozart symphony, and twice that of even the *Eroica*. Not the journey of a young man's soul coping with the sobering realities of life, the Ninth Symphony is rather the final statement of a gigantic mentality that has struggled for years with both physical and creative suffering—of a person who has labored to find and capture it all, as Michelangelo, two centuries earlier, had sought perfection in marble, and as Einstein, a century later, would seek the ultimate equation for unifying the interactions among all the forces in the universe.

During the first three movements of the Ninth, Beethoven gives us one haunting melody after another, complex rhythms, intricate harmonies, and bold dissonance. He seems to be striving to find a musical equivalent to every feeling that can be experienced. By the fourth movement he appears to have concluded that the orchestra alone was not enough to express the sounds he must have heard in the far recesses of his silent world. He needed human voices.

Other composers before him had written large choral works: Bach's *Passion According to Saint Matthew,* Haydn's *Creation,* and Mozart's *Requiem,* to name three supreme examples. But Beethoven pushes the human voice farther than many have believed possible.

There remains considerable controversy about the final movement of the Ninth. Some critics say it takes us as close to the gates of heaven as we can get in this earthly lifetime. Some have called it a musical embarrassment, totally unsingable. One soprano, after attempting it, vehemently declared that Beethoven had no respect whatever for the female voice. Others have suggested that in his deafness Beethoven heard extraordinary sounds that were not contained within the boundaries of music and for which there were no known instruments, not even the human voice. Perhaps such sentiments over-romanticize the work. But perhaps not. No one will ever know what Beethoven was hearing.

The musical setting for Friedrich von Schiller's "Ode to Joy," the main theme of the fourth movement, has attained the stature of an international hymn. By far, the majority opinion about this music is that it transcends its own "unsingability" and any breach of musical taste it may commit. Asking whether one "likes it" seems beside the point. One can only feel humbled by its majesty. Listening to Beethoven's Ninth Symphony is discovering what human creativity really means.

The premiere performance of the work in Vienna, at that time the capital of European music, was attended by every Viennese musical luminary. By now fully convinced of the composer's genius, they were eager to discover what new sounds the great man could possibly bring forth from an inner world that was barred forever from the real sounds of humanity and nature. Beethoven was the co-conductor.

Witnesses to the event have left behind stories of the performance, especially of how the maestro conducted with sustained vigor, hearing his own orchestra no doubt; for when the "other" orchestra had finished the work and the enthusiastic applause began, Beethoven had not yet put down his baton. When at last he realized what was happening, he started to walk from the stage, perhaps feeling his music had not communicated. The other conductor caught up with him and turned him around in time to see the huge audience on its feet, shouting, crying "Bravissimo!" Beethoven simply bowed his head. No one will ever know what it was he had heard, just as he could not have known what *they* had heard. Nonetheless, that moment lives on in the history of the humanities as a rare meeting of souls in that strange space where the spirit of art lives.

Art Songs

So far we have discussed possible origins of music, the basic elements of music, two major musical forms, and composers who achieved distinction through making glorious musical history. For many of us, however, everyday musical experience comes from songs, much shorter compositions with easily remembered melodies and rhythms.

An art song is written as part of the concert repertoire of great singers.

As children, we had nursery songs to teach or lullabies to soothe us. Most of us learned the alphabet by singing the letters. Nonsense songs with refrains like *Nikkity Nakkity Noo Noo Noo* gave us an outlet for feelings we could not always understand or find words for. Some kind of song-making—if only the spontaneous chanting of a child—is innate to the growing-up process at every time and in every place. Like poetry and the other arts, song evolved into evermore sophisticated styles. Eventually it reached a point at which the composer's choices were rigidly defined by the rules of music.

The birth of song as art probably dates back to the classical period when epic poems like the *Iliad* (see Chapter 4) were sung by minstrels as a means of being more easily remembered. In the early Middle Ages monks sang their prayers as a regular part of the worship service. By the later Middle Ages, however, wealthy aristocrats demanded song as part of court entertainment, and the subject almost always was love. By the time of the great composers we have discussed, song was a recognized art form, expected in concert programs and performed by highly trained professionals. Their works have come to be known as art songs, as distinct from popular songs, which are not originally written as concert pieces.

> *"Our sweetest songs are those that tell the saddest thoughts."*
>
> **—Percy Bysshe Shelley**

A genius of the art song was Franz Schubert, who, in his tragically brief life (1797–1828), composed more than 600! He wrote painstakingly for both singer and accompanist, his musical settings precisely suiting the words and fitting the mood of the poem. An excellent introduction to Schubert songs is "The Trout," with its sprightly melodic line and rippling fishlike accompaniment, and also "Death and the Maiden," with its agitated melodies and strangely peaceful accompaniment. The maiden of the title sees Death, a savage-looking skeleton, approaching and pleads with him to pass by and not touch her. But Death turns out to be friendly and promises that she will sleep gently in his arms.

Among Schubert's most famous works is the musical setting he gave to "Ave Maria." There is a legend that the composer, chronically poor, wrote the piece rapidly on a napkin or tablecloth and sold it to someone for the equivalent of fifteen cents. True or not, the story does suggest what we know about Schubert: namely, that he was unsuccessful in his lifetime, though, unlike van Gogh, he had a small circle of friends who recognized his genius.

Belated recognition for her art songs came to Austrian composer Alma Schindler Mahler (1879–1964). Early on, she was a wealthy Viennese socialite and hostess of glittering salons. Her warmth and nurturing spirit attracted numerous male artists to her. When only seventeen, she fell in love and married one of them, who neglected to mention that he already had a wife. Undaunted, and driven by her creative passion, she enrolled in a music school where she inspired fellow student Arnold Schoenberg, who would become a twentieth-century pioneer in the avant-garde, to compose music he heard inside him rather than what audiences would immediately accept. Alban Berg, another avant-gardist, also became a close friend and dedicated to her a masterwork, the opera *Wozzeck*.

Much given to amorous infatuations, she fell in love with Gustav Mahler (1860–1911), one of the great conductors and composers of the late nineteenth century. Her expectation was that they would nurture each other's careers, but he had other plans, demanding that she give up writing her little songs and live for him alone, as wives were expected to do. Mahler was already a recognized genius as both a composer and the conductor of the Vienna Opera, answering to no one except the emperor of Austria and God, to whom he dedicated his final symphony. Twenty years her senior, as her first near-husband had been, Mahler assumed the role of protective father, treating her as was expected of fathers in this time and in no way interested in encouraging her to develop her own considerable talents.

Exerting the same dictatorial attitude with which he directed the Opera, Mahler instructed his wife that she must nurse the children, create a quiet home with well-prepared meals, and, in her spare time, copy all of his manuscripts. But Alma was secretly in rebellion, writing to a friend that "the man who had to spread his peacock train in public wants to relax at home" and that this "after all is woman's fate. But it isn't mine!"

Finally, feeling perhaps a slight twinge of guilt, Mahler spent an afternoon with Sigmund Freud and admitted his marital problems. Freud's answer was to encourage him to look into his wife's work. After the session, Mahler returned home, played some of Alma's songs, then cried out, "What have I done? These songs are good," and insisted they would be immediately published. Unfortunately, Mahler died before he could follow through on his promised support. Alma lived to be 84, with a reputation only for being the nurturer of male genius. Belatedly, her songs have been rediscovered.

Folk Songs

Unlike many art forms that have established traditions within the humanities, the folk song has followed few aesthetic rules. Some folk songs originated centuries ago, perhaps as a way of spreading news in isolated areas, perhaps as musical improvisations by people who had little else to entertain them. Folk songs didn't require expert musical accompaniment or trained voices. They were likely to be handed down from generation to generation and changed every time they were sung. That's why there are many versions of the same song.

Folk music in recent times has often attained the status of the art song, especially when sung by accomplished singers like Joan Baez, Joni Mitchell, Bob Dylan, Willie Nelson, Judy Collins, Greg Brown, and more recently, Ani Difranco and Ferraby Lionheart. Yet it can still be a participant's art, an affirmation of group identity. In certain parts of the country, let a fiddler introduce the first few notes of "Turkey in the Straw" and almost immediately people are clapping their hands or dancing. During the civil rights movement of the 1960s the song "We Shall Overcome" created—and even now can create—instant bonding among people who may never have seen each other before.

Songs sung spontaneously at rallies or sporting events are not exactly folk music, but they fulfill a similar purpose in promoting group solidarity. For example, during the 1980s a widely popular rock group called *Queen* released a CD containing the song "We Will Rock You" that is now sung by students all over the country, especially during football games.

Genres of Folk Music. The history of folk music includes the *commemorative song*, which derives from times before people had written records of important events. During the Middle Ages, for example, troubadours kept people informed of heroic actions in battles and skirmishes. Maritime lore abounds with songs commemorating events that took place at sea, such as atrocities committed by a pirate captain or the sinking of a ship to its lonely, watery grave. The narrator of the commemorative song is never identified. A typical opening line is: "My name is nothin' extra/ So that I will not tell." One such song winds up in this self-effacing manner: "Now to conclude and finish/ Too far my lines have run." The group and the event are always more important than the singer/reporter.

The commemorative song does not belong just to the past. A modern American folk classic is Don McLean's "Bye, Bye, Miss American Pie," composed in 1971. Its mystifying refrain following the singing of the title tells how the narrator drove his "Chevy to the levee/ But the levee was dry." Like all folk music that continues to be sung, its tune is infectious, even though the meaning of the lyrics is not clear. A popular interpretation is that McLean wrote the song to commemorate the deaths of pop stars Buddy Holly and Richie Valens in a 1959 plane crash. That it *does* indeed make reference to a disaster is suggested by the final line, which speaks of "the day the music died."

The *work song* is also highly durable, for it is hard to imagine a time when work will not be central to most people's lives. In some cases the work song reflects great hardship and a state of tension between management and labor. Often, however, the music is jolly and full of bounce and joy, as though to help the original creator forget his tired limbs and meager salary.

I've been workin' on the railroad
All the livelong day;
I've been workin' on the railroad
Just to pass the time away.

The nineteenth-century folk ballad "John Henry" reflects the conflict between worker and machine at a time when the steam drill was about to replace hammers swung by human arms. John Henry became a folk hero, mythologized as a superhuman individual who was stronger and smarter than a machine, for a while. In his effort to beat the steam drill through the mountain with his hammer and steel pike, John Henry's great heart finally failed him.

He hammered so hard
He burst his poor heart
And he laid down his hammer and he died.
Lord! Lord!
He laid down his hammer and he died.

Another such worker was Joe Hill, a Swedish-born immigrant who, like so many others, came to the United States in the early twentieth century with dreams of success, only to be swallowed into a vast labor force, toiling for forty or more hours a week and trying to survive on a minimum wage. A born folk poet and singer, Hill began to compose songs about the hardships endured by the workers and the obstinate refusal of management to meet their demands or even to offer a compromise. He became a modern folk minstrel, and his songs, simple, easily sung, and remembered, soon spread from union hall to union hall, adapted to many kinds of labor problems.

> "Action is the antidote to despair."
>
> —Joan Baez

Hill was also an activist, traveling throughout the country, speaking to larger and larger gatherings of workers; and he inevitably acquired the reputation of troublemaker and rabble-rouser. While he was in Salt Lake City addressing a union meeting, a murder took place and Hill was arrested and charged with the crime. In a still famous trial, the prosecution produced witnesses that placed Hill at the scene of the crime. After a short jury deliberation he was found guilty and sentenced to die by firing squad. While awaiting his execution, he wrote his final song in which he said that some people could find justice in Salt Lake City "but not Joe Hill."

Joan Baez, a folk singer who epitomized the human rights movement of the 1960s and 1970s, wrote a commemorative ballad about Joe Hill, one that has already achieved the status of genuine folk art.

From San Diego up to Maine,
in every mine and mill,
where working-men defend their rights,
it's there you find Joe Hill,
it's there you find Joe Hill![2]

The *accumulation song* is deliberately drawn out, with verse after verse and a refrain repeated after each one. Songs like "The Twelve Days of Christmas" and

"Old MacDonald" start off with one detail (one gift, one animal) and then add more and more as the song continues. Accumulation songs extend group solidarity for longer periods, prolong the high spirits of the gathering, and keep loneliness at bay.

The *scoundrel song* celebrates the Dionysian personality—the perennial favorite of our hidden selves—the lawless, irresponsible, but charming rogue you couldn't trust or marry or put in charge of an important operation but who is always fun. An Irish favorite is "The Wild Rover," which upholds a life of drinking, carousing, gambling, and avoiding work. The narrator proudly sings that "if you don't like me, you can leave me alone." Who can argue with that premise? He intends to

> *... eat when I'm hungry and drink when I'm dry,*
> *And if moonshine don't kill me,*
> *I'll live till I die.*

To be sure, society would perish if it depended upon wild rovers, but the singer of scoundrel songs was usually a loner who could not, *would* not, adapt easily to the demands of organized society and so could hardly have been expected to celebrate the morally upright, the hard-working, and the pious.

> *"Believe it or not, there are places in the world where music is important. There are places in the world where all the arts are a matter of national pride."*
>
> **—Frank Zappa**

The *narrative song*, as its label implies, tells a tale, often at great length, answering, like the accumulation song, the need of listeners to stay together as long as possible. It was the folk version of the epic, usually filled with accounts of wondrous and miraculous events. The Scottish ballad "Binorie" recounts the sad story of a miraculous harp that was fashioned from the breastplate of a murdered girl and that sings as it plays. The harp reveals the events leading up to the girl's murder, then comes to the shocking climax: "My sister it was who did me slay." Quite possibly the song, like many others, was based on an actual event.

Country and western music has carried on the narrative tradition of folk music, adding its own unique tales to the repertoire. During the late 1960s "The Ballad of Billy Joe" was popular as a crossover song, topping country charts as well as the Top 40. Fans listened intently to the tragic story of a teenage boy who jumped to his death from the Tallahatchee Bridge. What was unique about the song was that it gave subtle suggestions about the "why" of the incident but never actually told us in so many words. Radio talk shows had hundreds of callers who gave their opinions, but the composer, Bobbie Gentry, refused to divulge the secret.

Bob Dylan and John Lennon are two of the great folk minstrels to protest the war in Vietnam.

The 1960s, a period of widespread alienation in the United States, saw a significant revival of folk music. Young people, often far from home, got together for the night in hastily improvised camps or in communes with ever-changing members and became instant—if temporary—friends through the common bond of singing. Joan Baez, composer/singer of "Joe Hill," and Judy Collins attained huge popularity by reviving old songs, particularly those that still spoke to the rebellious spirit seeking freedom from restraint. But the main thrust of the folk revival was the tightness of the group. It could have a distinctly spiritual side. At concerts Judy Collins sang the old hymn "Amazing Grace" and soon had 10,000 voices joining in with hands interlocked in a show of community. The hymn, once revived, has remained an integral part of our culture; it was sung during the funeral of President Ronald Reagan at the National Cathedral in 2004.

New folk minstrels emerged, using *protest songs* to make statements against war, pollution, and the corruption of the establishment. Bob Dylan's "A Hard Rain's Gonna Fall" and John Lennon's "Give Peace a Chance" were written and sung in protest, originally against the Vietnam War, but since then against other wars, or all wars. They are modern folk songs that attain the level of art. Lennon

Christie's Images Ltd./SuperStock

Grandma Moses, *We Are Coming To Church*, 1949

The grass-roots simplicity of the artist, Grandma Moses, is a visual parallel to folk music.

summed up the dream of a world without war, hunger, and hatred in what may be the most important folk song of the last century: "Imagine." Though composed and sung by a master musician, "Imagine" has all the simplicity and the passionate honesty of the folk tradition. These three songs will probably endure as long as there are troubled times. And when will there *not* be?

The protest song is very much alive, especially in the work of Ani Difranco, who began playing the guitar when she was nine years old. Before she had even reached her teens, she was singing songs by the Beatles in the coffeehouses of her native Buffalo. By the time she was 20 she had released her first CD, which instantly established her prominence in the field of folk rock. She has since sung in venues ranging from small clubs to Carnegie Hall.

Difranco's songs are socially oriented, dealing with a wide variety of issues, especially sexism, racism, domestic abuse, homophobia, the rights of people to determine whether they want to reproduce, the plight of the poor and homeless—and most particularly, the idiocy of fighting wars to solve problems. She has campaigned for independent presidential candidates, believing that what America needs is a leader who is not tied to the philosophy of a particular party.

Difranco is a superb musician. Her guitar work is characterized by staccato rhythms, rapid fingerpicking, and constant changes in tuning. Her lyrics are those of a poet, using complex metaphors, alliteration, and irony. She delivers her words in a half-spoken intonation, with heavy rhythmic stress. With her, folk music has traveled a long road from its grass roots in work songs and nonsense songs intended for community bonding; yet Difranco never forgets that her sophistication ultimately springs from the same heart that produced "Joe Hill."

Folk music has inspired concert composers of the past and present. Beethoven was charmed by the Gaelic folk tradition and composed song cycles based on both Irish and Scottish melodic patterns.

The American composer Aaron Copland (1900–1990) was so delighted by his country's folk music, especially songs of the Old West, that his music has come to define America in sound. *Billy the Kid,* one of Copland's many ballet scores, utilizes the folk song "Goodbye, Old Paint" (sung by a cowboy to his horse) in a stirring theme and variations. *Rodeo* interweaves themes and rhythms from the Saturday night barn dances. *El Salón México* is an orchestral suite woven out of traditional Mexican folk material and exuberant Latin rhythms, set against Copland's unique dissonance. Perhaps the composer's most famous score was written for the ballet *Appalachian Spring,* which employs a number of folk themes, notably the old Shaker hymn "Simple Gifts." The ballet itself celebrates time-honored rituals like the raising of a barn by everyone in the community.

American folk themes found their way into the concert hall in the symphonic music of Aaron Copland.

Folk themes such as those incorporated into this ballet often came from other cultures. Appalachian music, for example, has deep roots in the Gaelic folk music of Ireland and Scotland as well as the British folk tradition. The Israeli *hora* and the Italian *tarantella* are folk dances known throughout the world. *Polka* music was originally derived from Polish folk themes. We encourage you to pay attention to the many folk cultures brought to these shores from other countries and the rich musical experiences they provide.

The Spiritual

The spiritual had its beginnings in the need of African Americans to articulate and preserve their roots, to give meaning to their suffering, and to demand a rightful place in society. Taken—stolen—away from their homeland as far back as the seventeenth century, with no future except slavery, pain, and death, they took comfort in their relationship with God and an ultimate reward in a paradise where everyone was free.

Deep river,
My home lies over Jordan.
Deep river,
I want to cross over into campground.

Spirituals emphasize God's personal concern for each person, however obscure that person may be in the eyes of other mortals. For instance:

I sing because I'm happy,
I sing because I'm free
For His eye is on the sparrow,
And I know He watches me.

As the spiritual genre grew and developed, it was made more and more complex by church choirs and soloists, each of whom would add the mark of their individual interpretations. Often transported by religious ecstasy, they created the new genre of *gospel* music. Over the years this genre, while remaining as an indigenous part of church services, has also moved into the arena of popular music. It is characterized by giving the singer free reign to add enough notes to allow a fuller emotional expression.

Gospel Songs

Mahalia Jackson (1911–1972) became the best-known and highly influential exponent of the gospel genre. Born in New Orleans, when that city was bursting at the seams with new music—ragtime, jazz, and blues—she grew up next door to a church in which music played a vital role. She heard traditional hymns played and sung with many rhythmic variations. In addition, the sounds of Mardi Gras music, street vendors, and the songs belted out from the barrooms with wide-open doors and windows seeped into her blood. Devoutly religious, Jackson blended spirituals and aspects of the New Orleans secular style into religious songs that became nationally famous when she moved to Chicago and married a businessman, who recognized her potential and launched her career. In 1954 Columbia Records signed her to a long-term contract, and gospel music was soon on the charts.

A civil rights activist, Jackson took part in the historic March on Washington in 1963, singing before thousands assembled on the Mall to hear Martin Luther King Jr.'s epoch-making "I Have a Dream" speech.

> *"Blues are songs of despair, but gospel songs are the songs of hope."*
>
> **—Mahalia Jackson**

> *"Do not play this piece fast. It is never right to play Ragtime fast."*
> —**Scott Joplin**

Ragtime, Jazz, Blues

Ragtime dates back to the turn of the twentieth century, to a period when the legendary fortunes of the Rockefellers, Vanderbilts, Goulds, and Astors were being amassed and when the American moneyed aristocracy, their acquaintances, and all those who emulated their Victorian manners were entertaining guests with salon orchestras playing stately waltzes. The aim was to establish European elegance on this side of the Atlantic.

Some of the less privileged, eager to take advantage of the freedom to pursue upward mobility, wanted to gain the social recognition already enjoyed by wealthy families, and they wanted to show everyone they were capable of creating elegance of their own. Ragtime emerged from the African American community and its musical traditions, transformed by the influence of European styles. African American musicians wanted to do more than play the minstrel-show type of music with which white audiences had come to identify them. Ragtime came along at just the right moment. The acknowledged master of the new genre was Scott Joplin (1868–1917), who began his career in backrooms and honky-tonks but became a national celebrity with the publication of "Maple Leaf Rag" in 1899.

Listen on **MyHumanitiesKit.com**
Joplin, Maple Leaf Rag

Joplin heard the original ragtime tunes played by small African American combos on riverboats. They may have been variations on old plantation songs, minstrel-show cakewalks, and banjo melodies, played at lively tempos. White audiences expected African American music to be high-spirited, but **ragtime** would be different. Its label was coined to identify the syncopation that was the trademark of the new genre. **Syncopation** occurs when the melodic line of a piece is played against, not with, the accented beats of the rhythm accompaniment. Syncopated pieces are usually difficult to play because the left hand and the right hand follow different beats. (For a perfect example of syncopation, listen to George Gershwin's "Fascinatin' Rhythm.")

> *"Jazz came to America 300 years ago in chains."*
> —**Paul Whiteman**

Joplin was captivated by the new sounds, but he wanted to turn them into a legitimate, recognized genre which would be associated with African Americans but also prove the equal of the foreign imports. This meant imitating or at least coming close to European rhythm. He slowed down the pace to make the music even more stately. On the sheet music of his "rags" he would write: "Do not play this piece fast. It is never right to play Ragtime fast."

Culver Pictures

George Gershwin, date unknown

George Gershwin's *Rhapsody in Blue* put jazz on the international musical map.

The waltz is always played in three-quarter time. Ragtime, played almost exclusively on the piano, is written in *two*-quarter time, its tempo also never changing. The primary influences on Joplin's music, in addition to riverboat songs, were the popular European marches as well as the waltz and the quadrille, a dignified French square dance.

The enormous popularity of "Maple Leaf Rag" and other Joplin hits made African American musicians sit up and take notice, especially in New Orleans, which was a stronghold for the liberal acceptance of new music. Jelly Roll Morton (1885–1941) introduced Joplin to New Orleans but played him at a faster tempo, an innovation that would be integrated into yet another American musical genre: *jazz.*

Jazz. The musical roots of jazz are African. The music brought to this country by slaves was marked by what is known as a "call and response" pattern. Participants would sing or play a particular combination of tones, and this combination would be answered by singing or playing a variation on it. The original purpose was similar to that of the folk song: community bonding.

During the late nineteenth century, African American musicians went to New Orleans where they studied European genres and rhythmic patterns. But they brought with them a knowledge of their own traditional sounds, derived from what were called "field hollers" as well as rhythmic songs sung by slaves as they rowed, and the spirituals that were a profound part of African American religious life.

The typical scale used in African music contains five tones instead of the European scale of seven. The New Orleans musicians tried to combine the two without sacrificing the African scale. The result was that they added half-tones, called *blue notes,* to the five-tone scale. From ragtime they borrowed syncopation. The synthesis of all these strains made possible the evolution of jazz.

As the decades of the twentieth century rolled by, the form attracted a range of musical geniuses, some self-taught, some classically trained. They had—and continue to have—one thing in common: knowing how to maintain a balance between control and the need for soaring release. The call and response form had required that the responders change the original theme, adding their own variation. Even when jazz became a sophisticated art form, improvisation continued to be its major characteristic.

Whatever their training, jazz instrumentalists and composers admire Bach because he more or less invented improvisation, the art of taking flight from a set theme. A typical jazz piece follows a disciplined pattern. The group, or the soloist backed by the group, will play the main theme once through, sometimes a well-known song, sometimes an original tune composed for the group. Then one instrument after another performs a variation of the theme.

Duke Ellington did the most to bridge the gap between the concert hall and the intimate jazz club.

Original jazz works have deliberately offbeat titles like "Take the A Train," "One O'Clock Jump," and "Stompin' at the Savoy"—titles that deliberately do not relate to anything beyond themselves. Jazz often shapes and defines the "cool scene"—a late-night coming together of sophisticated people who want to lose themselves in the music and escape, if only briefly, from their problems, just as the performers seek to lose themselves in the music.

Following in the footsteps of Jelly Roll Morton, great jazz soloists like Charlie Parker and Louis Armstrong became famous for going off on lengthy variations, often improvising for ten or fifteen minutes before returning to the theme. One motive behind jazz improvisation was to explore the potential of one's instrument and take it to places that no one else had ever found. In a life tragically interrupted when he was only 28, a phenomenal cornet player named Bix Beiderbecke is said to have been obsessed with the desire to find the perfect note beyond the normal range of other players. Presumably, he did not live long enough to reach his goal. Some who were fortunate enough to hear him report that, as he pushed his instrument beyond the ordinary limits of its capabilities, his face turned almost scarlet and all of his facial muscles threatened to break loose from his skin.

Bettmann/Corbis

Duke Ellington, c. 1910

Ellington captured in his suave elegance.

Musical histories that deal with jazz as a serious and major art form give preeminence to Edward Kennedy Ellington—known universally as Duke

(1899–1974)—the person who did the most to bridge the gap between the concert hall and the intimate jazz club. A bandleader who had Manhattan society driving to the Cotton Club in Harlem during the late 1920s, Ellington sought to expand the range of jazz through continual experimentation

> *with what he called his "jungle effects." When the sounds of "growling" trumpets and trombones, sinuous clarinets and eerie percussion were recorded, the originality of the orchestration was immediately grasped internationally by music critics and record buyers. . . . As a jazz arranger his great gift was in balancing orchestration and improvisation.*[3]

Ellington brought jazz to Carnegie Hall, where it could be played and evaluated in a setting built for the performance of classical concert music. In so doing, he wrote out elaborate and complex orchestrations—something no one had done before him. He did leave room for solo flights (or else it would not have been jazz), but his own compositions, like "Mood Indigo," "Satin Doll," and "Sophisticated Lady," display a classic sense of discipline and musicianship, usually performed when he was wearing elegant evening clothes.

> *"His [Gershwin's] genius, like all genius, was unique, but his all embracing artistic vision still resonates powerfully today in a world where music is sometimes the only benign avenue of communication between antagonists."*
>
> **—Paul Simon**

Another major American composer who brought jazz to Carnegie Hall in the early years was George Gershwin (1898–1937). He started his career as a Tin Pan Alley songwriter, but Gershwin, who had been classically trained, was hungry for greater things. He moved on to compose the scores for Broadway musicals of the 1920s and the opera *Porgy and Bess* (discussed in Chapter 8).

In 1924 he found his chance. Paul Whiteman, a bandleader also hungry for serious recognition, commissioned him to write a concert jazz piece. The result was *Rhapsody in Blue*, which combined the textures of romantic works for piano and symphony orchestras with the pulsations, dissonance, and syncopated rhythms of jazz. Gershwin thus put an American art form on the international musical map. The *Rhapsody* became an overnight success and has sold millions of recordings. It remains in the standard concert repertoire of nearly every major orchestra.

Jazz has remained a major art form, studied in almost every school and performed regularly in concert halls throughout the world as well as in annual festivals devoted exclusively to both jazz classics and the very newest styles and musicians. The Newport Jazz Festival in Rhode Island and Jazz at Lincoln Center in New York are two notable examples producing important artists who are at ease in both the classical and jazz scenes.

One such performer was trumpeter and pianist Miles Davis (1926–1991), whose versatility led him to the forefront of innovators in many genres of jazz, including *bebop* and *cool jazz*. By the time he was 18, Davis had shown so much talent that The Julliard School offered him a scholarship, but he proved too impatient to wait for The graduation. When he was 19, he made his first recording and joined the jazz quintet of Charlie Parker, the premier saxophonist of the period. Because of his youth and lack of professional experience, Davis was used as a *sideman*—a nonsoloist who played back-up to the stars. It was not long before he stepped into the solo spotlight. In 1955 he created the Miles Davis Quintet, which took jazz to new heights.

Craig Lovell/Eagle Visions Photography/Alamy

Wynton Marsalis, 2002

Wynton Marsalis, trumpeter extraordinaire in both jazz and classical concert music, "potentially the greatest trumpeter of all time."

In his earlier work, Davis experimented with bebop, which had become the rage in the 1940s. An offshoot of the parent form, jazz, bebop was almost totally improvised and therefore greatly favored by soloists who wanted the music to serve their unique showcase needs. The more mature Davis of the Quintet gradually eased away from the eccentricities of bebop and moved toward what became known as cool jazz, a form more disciplined, more faithful to the music, and less given to wild flights of musical fancy. By the late 1950s Davis, who also played Carnegie Hall, was presenting jazz versions of concert music. One of his classic albums is *Sketches of Spain* featuring works by Joaquin Rodrigo and Manuel de Falla.

Since the early 1980s, trumpeter Wynton Marsalis (b. 1961) has distinguished himself as a performer and a composer, crossing over freely from jazz to symphonic music. Classically trained at The Julliard School, he was just 20 when he assembled his own band. His love of classical concert music—notably Bach, Mozart, and Beethoven—has earned him an enormous reputation in both fields. He has won nine Grammy awards. In 1983, he won in both the symphonic and jazz categories, the first artist ever to do so. In 1997 he became the first jazz composer ever to win the Pulitzer Prize for music. The prize-winning work was *Blood on the Fields,* commissioned by Jazz at Lincoln Center, which has an international reputation as an outstanding venue in which the finest jazz musicians in the world perform. Marsalis, who became its artistic director, has been called by famed classical trumpeter Maurice Andre "potentially the greatest trumpeter of all time."

World History Archive/Alamy

Billy Holiday, c. 1940s

Billie Holiday excelled in blues and jazz, singing with passion, and often sorrow.

Blues. The term *blues* derives from the melancholy mood produced by music that made liberal use of the half-tones in the African scale, the so-called blue notes. The genre has permeated our vocabulary to such an extent that "blue" seems always to have meant "down in the dumps." Many jazz tunes are bouncy and lively, but the jazz repertoire includes its share of blues.

"I've been told that nobody sings the word "hunger" like I do."

—Billie Holliday

The genre had its origins, as did ragtime and jazz, in the songs sung by slaves after a grueling day in the fields. While they sometimes desired an upbeat mood, the workers must have, just as often, sought an outlet for depression. As the form became caught up in the entertainment industry of jazz, sophisticated composers and singers turned the old songs into haunting expressions of sadness that found ready listeners among audiences of varied backgrounds.

Blues songs are almost always about the empty aftermath of a once burning passion. They are written from either a male or a female point of view. Men sing of women's faithlessness, and women return the compliment about men. Probably the most famous of all blues songs is "St. Louis Blues" by W. C. Handy (1873–1958), who also composed "Beale Street Blues." If jazz is associated with New Orleans, the headquarters of the blues was Memphis, and it is on Beale Street that many of the great blues clubs are located, attracting visitors from all over the world.

Listen on **MyHumanitiesKit.com** Handy, St. Louis Blues

Many of the soloists who elevated the form to a high status had tragic lives themselves, caused by bad relationships, social discrimination, or substance abuse.

"If it wasn't for bad luck, I wouldn't have no luck at all."

—Bessie Smith

Famous was Bessie Smith (1894–1937), believed by many to have developed the blues style imitated by countless others. She has immortalized many lines from blues lyrics, including "If it wasn't for bad luck, I wouldn't have no luck at all."

One of the most versatile of all the blues singing greats—as well as one of the most tragic—was Billie Holiday (1915–1959). Singer and songwriter, she excelled in jazz, jazz blues, torch songs, and swing. Nicknamed Lady Day, she was strongly influenced by jazz instrumentalists, developing a style that has never been imitated. The most famous of her own songs is "Lady Sings the Blues," and she is also remembered for a dramatic rendition of "Strange Fruit," a song about lynching. The photo on the previous page exhibits the passionate intensity of her singing.

Popular Songs

During the 1930s through the early 1950s, the so-called "big bands" were all the fashion. To escape the downbeat mood of the Great Depression and then the World War II years, people flocked to supper clubs to hear and dance to the well-orchestrated music of full-scale orchestras led by Glenn Miller, Tommy and Jimmy Dorsey, Benny Goodman, and numerous others. Miller developed a whole new style, featuring tight harmony serving as background for his own trombone solos. Goodman became the leading clarinetist of the day, crossing over easily from the night club to Carnegie Hall. Many songs that have since become standards were written for these aggregations, and many singers, including Frank Sinatra, made their debut with the big bands. Sinatra was soloist with the Tommy Dorsey orchestra.

"Through songs we find out things about ourselves. We say, "Oh yeah. I've felt that way.""

—Lois Walder

The big-band song, such as "This Love of Mine," the piece that vaulted a thin and wispy Sinatra into public prominence, had a very specific pattern. Usually about three minutes in length, it would be played once by the orchestra, then a solist—or group—would sing it through once. Until Sinatra became a sensation and the main reason people came to hear the Dorsey band, most of the orchestras played so that couples could dance. But the lyrics to the songs were extremely important also because phonograph records (78 speed) were hot items in music stores.

The period was also the heyday of the movie musical (see Chapter 9) as well as the Broadway show, which featured songs meant to be recorded and popularized as so-called hits. This necessity imposed stiff restraints upon lyricists who had to develop and conclude an idea in the usual three minutes, with words vaguely applicable to the film or stage context but able to tell their own story apart from any other context. A classic among these songs is Jerome Kern's "Smoke Gets in Your Eyes," with lyrics by Otto Harbach, who really deserves to be labeled a poet. Harbach develops a very common theme, dating at least as far back as Roman poetry: that of love lost. At first, the narrator believes the beloved is faithful, though friends think otherwise, advising that "when your heart's on fire" you must realize that "smoke gets in your eyes." But the narrator scoffs, only to discover that his love has left him. The friends are now the ones who scoff, but the narrator, in an absolutely brilliant repetition of the song title in a different context, points out that tears come when the flame of a beautiful romance is dying out and "smoke gets in your eyes."

Irving Berlin (1888–1989) could not read or write down a note of music but compiled the greatest number of enduring twentieth-century popular works. His songs generally express simple, honest, and universal emotions. While he could define the everlasting joys of love, he had no peer at providing the bittersweet happiness of nostalgia. It's all over, but one is left with fond memories all the same. The nostalgia of "White Christmas" elevated a popular song written for a sequence in a movie to the status of a Christmas carol.

In 1938 the popular singer Kate Smith asked Berlin to compose a patriotic song with which she could conclude her broadcast celebrating the twentieth anniversary of the armistice that ended World War I. After several attempts proved futile, the composer remembered a song he had written for an Army camp show during that conflict, a song rejected for being "too jingoistic." He found "God Bless America" buried in an old trunk, polished it a bit, and then offered it to Smith. Its first performance on the broadcast of November 20, 1938, electrified both the studio and the vast national audience. The song contains ten short lines and, sung once through, probably takes less than three minutes. No one has to be told about the song's impact in all times and on countless occasions since. When Jerome Kern was asked to indicate Berlin's place in American music, he answered tersely: "Irving Berlin *is* American music."

The reputation of Frank Sinatra (1915–1998) not only outlived the big-band era but expanded until it may very well be claimed that he was the greatest vocal stylist of popular songs. Composers and lyricists jumped at the chance to write for him because he was without peer in delivering a song's message through his vocal flexibilities and his acting talent. Many of the songs with which he was associated have become classics, though almost no contemporary singer has been able to duplicate the power of the original performance, which crystallizes emotions all of us share and gives us comfort in the knowledge that we are not alone.

Hulton-Deutsch Collection/Corbis

Frank Sinatra, 1953

Possibly the greatest of all vocal stylists.

A Sinatra classic is "One for My Baby," in which the narrator is sitting at a bar very late at night with no one around except a bartender who may be, but is probably not, listening, having heard the story so often. Nonetheless, the narrator pours out his heart. He has been abandoned by his one true love, though he does not deny having been responsible for the breakup, now there is only the effort to escape the pain through drink. The refrain to which he keeps returning asks the bartender to give him two more drinks: "one for my baby" and "one more for the road." As both poems and songs do when they achieve art, this one captures a certain moment, an image in the flow of time with universal applicability—that of the loner in a bar late at night with no clear future and, obviously, no one to comfort him.

The Beginnings of Rock. Rock is the most pervasive musical phenomenon of our time, having endured in its many forms for more than half a century. It is a major way of defining our culture in sound. **Rock** is a fusion of rhythm and blues, gospel, country and western, and rap styles. It has many complex facets, ranging from the conscious artistry of serious musicians to the out-of-control, body-bending shouting by athletic musicians prancing around a stage. Rock is first and foremost a celebration of the Dionysian spirit let loose and often exulting in a total disregard for rules. Such lyrics as can be deciphered sometimes denounce the establishment (*any* establishment) and glorify the strident life of total freedom.

Some historians of popular culture trace the origins of rock to 1955, the year in which the film *Blackboard Jungle* leaped onto the screen with an explosion of music titled "Rock Around the Clock." With its overly pronounced and rapid beat, the song had film audiences jumping in the aisles and dancing—even as the rock concerts would be doing in a few years. The band that arranged and played the piece was Billy Haley and the Comets, and to them is given the credit for introducing the musical movement first called **rock 'n' roll.**

". . . we note the glazed stares and numb, expressionless faces of youthful dancers at the great rock auditoriums where light shows, split screen movies, high decibel screams, shouts and moans . . . create a sensory environment characterized by . . . extreme unpredictability."

—Alvin Toffler

The incessant rhythmic beat of "Rock Around the Clock" may have been derived from the rhythm and blues music of small African American dance clubs in the South. Because of their confined spaces, they could accommodate only small combos, which made a big sound in compensation. The new sound spread quickly in popularity wherever small clubs were located. The polite dances of the big band era no longer suited a postwar generation bogged down in academic studies or nine to five jobs and in need of weekend release. The beat of rock 'n' roll accentuated by the strings of a twirling bass fiddle met the new needs.

Little Richard and Elvis Presley. Audience excitement generated by rock groups and rock concerts within a few years was foreshadowed in the frenetic energy of Richard Wayne Penniman, who called himself Little Richard (b. 1932) and claimed that he was the founder of the entire movement. He was certainly one of early rock's most outlandish performers, dressing usually in formal attire that was a bit disheveled, or it became so as he accompanied himself on the piano, without sitting down, frequently jumping on top of the instrument, never letting up on the crashing chords. His style anticipated that of the Beatles, who would also don unusual attire. Rock historian Nik Cohn agrees that Little Richard was the true father of rock:

> *Dressed in shimmering suits with long drape jackets and baggy pants, his hair grown long and straight, white teeth and gold rings flashing in the spotlight, he stood at, and sometimes on, the piano, hammering boogie chords as he screamed messages of celebration and self-centered pleasure.*[4]

Library of Congress

Elvis Presley, 1957

Often hailed as the King of Rock, Elvis fused musical elements from rhythm and blues, gospel, and country-and-western traditions to create his unique brand of rock 'n' roll that remains popular decades after his death.

In 1957 Little Richard, once more known as Richard Wayne Penniman, abruptly left the music world to become an evangelist preacher. But he did not find spiritual ecstasy incompatible with the music for which he was famous; and so he has gone back and forth between the two main areas of his life.

One year before Penniman's departure, a young singer from Mississippi named Elvis Presley appeared on television's popular *Ed Sullivan Show*, the premier venue for showcasing new musical talent. Elvis (1935–1977) quickly became a cultural phenomenon, scandalizing older audiences with a gyrating pelvis while simultaneously making rock wildly popular with younger audiences.

The immediate musical influence on Elvis was gospel, particularly its exuberance. With his guitar, Elvis added the beat and chord progressions of the rhythm and blues being played in Memphis. He incorporated elements from country and western songs, injecting them with a high-powered aggressiveness that remains the signature of all rock. In some circles, his music became known as *country rock* or *rockabilly*.

In the opinion of rock historian Charlie Gillett, Elvis's peak as an artist was reached in the early years when his songs delivered the passionate themes of the country-and-western genre—usually broken romance or condemnation of infidelity—as well as rock's liberation of the spirit. His first hit song was titled, characteristically enough, "Heartbreak Hotel," which achieves near poetry in its metaphors, such as the hotel of that name located on Lonely Street.

In Gillett's opinion, however, becoming a superstar so quickly was the worst thing that could have happened to Elvis. He signed a multimillion dollar contract with RCA, which insisted on putting a high-powered slick gloss on the music. The singer's former emotional directness became lost against a background of "vocal groups, heavily electrified guitars, and drums . . . more theatrical and self-conscious as he sought to combine excitement and emotion, formerly generated without any evident forethought"[5]—in other words, with honest spontaneity. Other singers and combos followed this trend, and the simple term *rock* was given to a variety of styles, many with the ear-splitting amplification of Presley's later work.

> *"A hundred years from now, people will listen to the Beatles the same way we listen to Mozart."*
>
> **—Sir Paul McCartney**

The Beatles. By the early 1960s, rock 'n' roll had become popular throughout the Western world and would soon spread even further. Now there is scarcely a corner of the globe where it cannot be heard. In England, particularly, it beckoned to a younger generation that was tired of the rigid mores and traditions of that country. They liked what they were hearing from this side of the Atlantic. Yet what music historians consider rock's most important band did not emerge from the United States, where the genre was born, but in the economically depressed northern English port center of Liverpool. In 1964 the Beatles made an indelible mark on American consciousness the moment they were introduced on *The Ed Sullivan Show* (where else?), which had showcased Elvis Presley eight years earlier. The name they gave themselves was whimsical and their hair was long but precisely cut. (In an interview, when Ringo Starr was asked what the group called their hairdo, he answered "Alfred," a response that encapsulates the band's studied eccentricity.) They were immaculately well-groomed, and, though their songs were bouncy and exuberant, the performers remained disciplined. They moved back and forth as they sang (except for Ringo Starr, their drummer), but never gyrated or bounced around the stage. And their lyrics were clear and well-articulated. Their harmony was complex, but the clarity of the lyrics made it seem as though they were singing with one voice. That night and that show have been considered the greatest debut of any singers, anywhere.

The Beatles caught on as no group ever did—before or since. Young women proved to be their most enthusiastic fans, some even fainting from sheer ecstasy. They were mobbed wherever they went. Sales of their records hit the stratosphere. Older audiences, as with Elvis, shook their heads in despair over the decline of not only music but of an entire generation. The Beatles knew perfectly well they were performing for a young audience who wanted the *new*. The well-groomed foursome—John, Paul, George, and Ringo—with the unfamiliar new style, not to mention a repertoire destined to take its place among the all-time classics, appealed almost uncontrollably to a rising subculture of "hippies," young people who championed freedom from all social and moral restraints. In all of its phases since the 1950s, rock has retained its revolutionary social battle cry, becoming the ultimate Dionysian music of our time.

The Beatles were admired for their honesty and a certain purity of heart. Their well-manicured physical presence was so powerful, in sharp contrast to the disheveled formal wear of Little Richard, that they might have attained enormous popularity even if their music had been second-rate. Of course it was not. Paul McCartney and John Lennon created songs of such originality and beauty that some are considered among the best popular songs in Western culture. "Yesterday," "Eleanor Rigby" (a model of syncopation), and "Michelle" have been performed by major symphony orchestras. Their album *St. Pepper's Lonely Hearts Club Band* ranks among the two greatest popular recordings ever made, the other being Michael Jackson's *Thriller.*

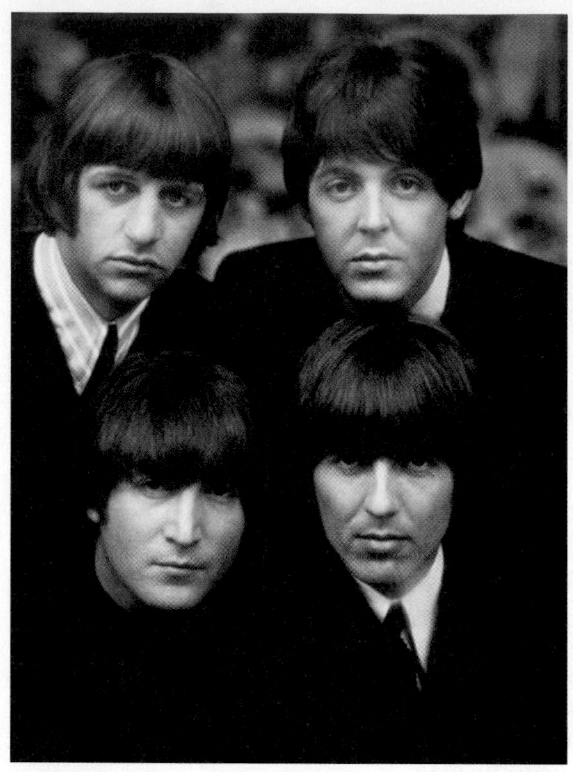
MARKA/Alamy

The Beatles, 1960s

Honesty and a certain purity of heart, The Beatles.

Both Lennon, whose life was cut short in 1980 by a deranged fan's bullet, and George Harrison, who played guitar for the group and who died in 2001, were strongly influenced by the culture and religion of India. All four Beatles briefly studied meditation at an ashram. Harrison studied the sitar with Ravi Shankar, a master Indian musician. His own songs, less well-known than those of Lennon and McCartney, are deeply felt poems set to very mystical, spiritual musical sounds. Ringo Starr and Paul McCartney, both now in their early 70s, continue to perform.

The Rock Concert. Despite the enormous sums of money the top rock groups earn from their recordings, they tend to go on worldwide tours, earning an incredible fee for just one performance that can attract as many as 50,000 fans. The rock concert has become one of the cornerstones of modern musical culture and at times can be an art form in itself, using the most advanced multimedia technology.

By far the most famous rock concert ever held took place in Woodstock, New York, over forty years ago when bands and soloists from both sides of the Atlantic gathered to celebrate togetherness and to protest the war in Vietnam. Unexpectedly, monsoon rains cascaded down upon the thousands of screaming fans, who joyfully rolled around in mud, some oblivious to the hardships and indignities they were enduring. Not only was much memorable music performed, but the collective experience made a powerful statement that war as a means of settling human problems was not an acceptable expression of humanity.

Local residents, horrified by what was happening to their once pleasant neighborhood, denounced the concert as a blight on American history. In all probability, however, the annual rites in honor of Dionysus, which gave birth to the great era of Greek tragedy (see Chapter 7), also got out of hand. Dionysian revelry and human creativity are often closely paired (see Chapter 2).

In 1965 another British combo, the Rolling Stones, came into a prominence they still enjoy, combining the exuberance of the Beatles with the free-spiritedness of Little Richard. In the words of rock singer, critic, and poet Patti Smith:

> *By 1967 they [the Stones] all but eliminated the word guilt from our vocabulary . . . I never considered the Stones drug music . . . they were the drug itself . . . thru demon genius they hit that chord . . . as primitive as a western man could stand. Find the beat and you dance all night.*[6]

To the Stones must go the credit for having originated the multimedia big-time rock concert, which can fill Yankee Stadium or the Los Angeles Coliseum. Enthusiastic fans are known to camp out days in advance in order to buy tickets, and that ritual continues undiminished. The rock concert began where polite society left off. It cut through the many layers of so-called civilized behavior that evolved to put a lid on untrammeled expressions of feeling, and it demanded from the audience shouting, stamping, gyrating on their feet with cries of ecstasy—a return to the pleasures of the sheer act of living, unverbalized, unanalyzed, uncensored. Smith describes the historic Madison Square concert of July 25, 1972, as a ritual "like any ancient ceremony," adding "pass the sacred wafer."

In 1980 another of the great rock bands, this time from Dublin, took center stage with their debut album *Boy*. They were four musicians who grew up nestled in a strong Celtic tradition in which people learned to sing when barely old enough to leave the cradle. In keeping with the customary practice of using offbeat names, they discarded their first two, Feedback and The Hype, before settling on U2. They became best known for their political and social themes, exemplified by their 2006 Grammy-winning album *How to Dismantle an Atomic Bomb*. For more than three decades now, the band has toured the world, driving home their pleas for peace, equality, and tolerance. The lead singer, Bono (born David Paul Hewson), has been nominated for the Nobel Peace Prize and has been knighted by Queen Elizabeth II.

Almost every country has given birth to a rock group of varying importance. Many are proponents of *progressive rock*, which includes an endless variety of experimental genres and subgenres. They tend to attract smaller legions of devoted fans and are glad they don't have to play the kind of music demanded by a mass market, thus freeing themselves to go in many new directions.

Hip-Hop

While it is too early to predict whether hip-hop will last as long as rock has, the genre has become a significant part of contemporary society, especially among younger audiences always seeking new ways to express their identity. **Hip-hop** is a broad term that defines an entire way of being (as rock really doesn't), and it has differing musical expressions as integral components. As one hip-hop critic points out, it "encompasses rap, baggy clothing, break-dancing, graffiti, vocabulary, and a general life style." The latter can be described as freewheeling and centered on the rights of individuals to declare their identity in any way they choose.

Rap, a major subgenre of hip-hop culture, is half-sung, half-spoken music with a pronounced and steady beat supporting rapid-fire rhyming words performed by singers with great verbal dexterity and extensive vocabularies. The subject matter is frequently social protest, but it can also range from philosophical cynicism about life to frank descriptions of sexual encounters. Rap enthusiasts insist that much of the material is sheer poetry.

Rap had its origins in the urban setting of the Bronx in the late 1970s with toasts, dub talk, and improvisational poetry delivered over music at weddings, proms, and other celebrations. Reminiscent of the call-and-response characteristic of the plantation songs, it would begin with a DJ, band leader, or master-of-ceremonies shouting in rhythm something like "Now throw your heads in the air/ And wave 'em like you just don't care/ And if you got on clean underwear/ Let me hear you say 'Oh yeah!'" The excited crowd would then scream "Oh yeah!" The first broadly successful rap album, *Rapper's Delight* performed by the Sugarhill Gang, appeared in 1979.

> *"We're all spokes in a wheel, going to the point, getting the ball rolling. Have you ever seen a wheel with one spoke? It's not a wheel. You got to come from different directions to get to the same point. And roll."*
>
> **—Ice Cube**

There is still considerable debate over whether rap has evolved—or will *ever* evolve—into an art form, but some of its exponents have been called folk poets, notably Lonnie Rashied Lynn (b. 1972), better known as Common (previously, Common Sense). His debut album *Can I Borrow a Dollar?* won him an almost instant cult following, and in the late 1990s he went mainstream. In 2003 he won a Grammy for his song "Love of My Life (An Ode to Hip-Hop)," and in 2006 was awarded a second Grammy for "Southside," a rap song performed with Kanye West. He has performed all over the world and is now embarked on a film career, which may bring rap and its social messages to an even wider audience.

The rapper Eminem (b. 1972) is so cynical he inspired a rock musician to say, "He is not a very nice person, but you can't deny the brilliance of his songs." It is doubtful that most rappers are asking to be considered "nice." They believe they can best express themselves creatively through this particular musical form. Rap has also been criticized for glorifying violence and drugs and expressing intolerance toward women and homosexuals. Defenders counter that an artist is an artist and the history of the humanities is filled with examples of works that are not "nice" but gripping and exciting nonetheless. They defend rap by pointing out that it does not exist to promote antisocial values, but instead honestly depicts the realities of urban life.

At its best, as in the work of Common and Eminem, rap represents a virtuoso use of language and an incredibly spontaneous kind of poetry, an exercise in exciting creativity.

Contemporary Non-Western Music

The diverse contemporary musical scene includes contributions from many other cultures, and we must always remember that one of the goals of humanities study is to raise our awareness that there are alternative modes of human creativity. A Chinese composer may be experimenting with new scales and new sounds on a synthesizer; a Cambodian equivalent of Lady GaGa may be recording her first CD with an equally crowd-pleasing verve but singing music that is not based on notes familiar to the West; an Islamic pop singer may be thrilling a café audience with a love song in a plaintive vibrato to the accompaniment of an instrument that is akin to but not the same as a mandolin or guitar; a vocal group in Ghana may be swaying as they chant an updated version of a much older song of welcome. Many non-Western sounds can be heard on the Internet and, because of today's rapid-fire communication, they will influence tomorrow's musical styles in both hemispheres.

In China, popular music is no longer limited to the marches and patriotic songs approved by the communist government before it opened its doors to the outside world. Some Western influences were there during the early twentieth century, but some musical forms, including rock, were judged to be a threat to the government because they encourage freedom of expression and were banned. A singer/composer named Cui Jian emerged during the student demonstrations of 1989, exuberantly singing daring lyrics denouncing government tyranny. Defecting to the West, where he found a strong welcome, he performed before thousands in a 1999 Central Park concert. Almost as popular in both East and West is the Tang Dynasty, a Beijing rock band that blends the sounds of the Asian five-note scale with the more familiar diatonic, or seven-note, Western scale.

Traditional Chinese music is still prevalent, making liberal use of percussion, especially drums, timpani, gongs, cymbals, bells, xylophones, and triangles. String sections include the two-stringed violin, the dulcimer, the lute, and the harp. The woodwind section comprises flutes, pipes, and Chinese trumpets, which look but do not sound like oboes.

Islam has supported a variety of musical forms, including jazz. The highest selling Arab albums come from an Algerian musician named Khaled, whose output has gone diamond, platinum, and gold. In 2009 he was a featured performer at the Montreal Jazz Festival. In 2010 he performed his piece "Didi" at the World Cup opening ceremony in South Africa. Khaled has had to move to Paris because Islamic fundamentalists objected to his portrayal of women both dancing and dressed provocatively.

An afternoon can be well spent in the exploration of these sounds, now so profusely available on the Internet.

The Musical Avant-Garde

Like their counterparts in visual art, innovators in concert music do not want to sound like anything that has gone before them; they do not wish to be confined by time-honored guidelines but seek to forge new directions. They are the **avant-garde.** Translated, the term says *advanced guard,* but this is a military phrase. Applied to the arts, *garde* can also mean *guardian* or *watchman.* In other words, the avant-gardist is one who looks after our best interests by protecting us from what has become dull, overly familiar.

The need to be free from restraint has always been a key factor, especially in works of genius. Beethoven, for example, expanded the range of music in creating his Third Symphony, forcing the music to accommodate his mighty passions. Gershwin's *Rhapsody in Blue* combined jazz and symphonic music as had never been done before. When the Beatles arrived on the scene, audiences could not have been prepared for the style and musical expertise the band brought to the rock genre. The four young men with long hair probably did not suspect, at least not in the beginning, that they were lifting rock to the level of high art. All of these composers did what they had to do: *express themselves in ways congenial to their temperaments regardless of conventions.*

The need to rebel is thus the need to be who you are, and if you happen to be an artist, your art will be rebellious. Today there are concert composers who are tired of the diatonic scale—sometimes *any* scale. One composer attacks a grand piano with her fists, then climbs up onto the instrument, stands upside down inside it and plucks the hammers, thus combining performance art with prank art. Many others have found in the synthesizer the key to uncharted inner worlds that enable them to produce sounds no one has yet heard.

Igor Stravinsky (1882–1971) is regarded by many as the father of the modern avant-garde in music. His revolutionary score for the 1913 ballet *The Rite of Spring* introduced sounds so unfamiliar that, combined with the provocative movements of Vaslav Nijinsky as well as his choreography, they sparked a riot at the Paris premiere (discussed more fully in Chapter 8). Though denounced by audience and critics alike (one critic called the music a "barnyard come to life"), Stravinsky would eventually win the day, and his **atonality**—music with less regard for key—encourage other avant-gardists to break away from bondage to familiar harmonies and structures.

One of his followers was Arnold Schoenberg (Alma Mahler's one-time classmate), born in Berlin and musically educated in Vienna. For his large-scale concert works, he reduced the size of the orchestra to fifteen instruments, for which he provided dissonance in dizzying counterpoint and bizarre harmonic progressions. Embracing Stravinsky's atonality, he abandoned key altogether in many of his early works, notably *Pierrot Lunaire,* using human voices that don't always sound like human voices to produce the intended musical equivalent of mental disturbance. In this work Schoenberg replaced the standard musical notes with notations requiring the "singers" to speak, but not always in recognizable words. At times they sound like lost souls seeking release from solitary confinement. In 1925, Schoenberg moved back to Berlin, where he came under the influence of the German avant-garde, which had strong counterparts in theater and visual art. This Berlin art scene was brimming with postwar cynicism, and had an audience that saw only deteriorating civilization for its future. Here, Schoenberg composed his opera *Moses und Aron,* in which characters sing-speak of their inability to communicate with each other. Both *Pierrot Lunaire* and *Moses und Aron* remain

"I love the development of our music. How we've tried to develop, y'know? It grows. That is why everyday people come forward with new songs. Music goes on forever."

—Bob Marley

Listen on **MyHumanitiesKit.com**
Stravinsky, *The Rite of Spring*

stern tests of one's willingness to entertain the *extremely* unfamiliar. But this final section of our chapter on music encourages you to give it at least a fair try. To no surprise, there are contemporary avant-garde composers who consider Stravinsky and Schoenberg old-fashioned.

Much of the music of the avant-garde, as we have said, is produced on synthesizers. Leading the way was the French composer Edgard Varèse (1883–1965). Starting out as a mathematics student, he found himself unable to resist the excitement of creating new musical sounds on a machine that seemed to be able to do anything the user desired. He declared boldly that he refused to submit to sounds that had already been heard, which could really be the battle cry of the musical avant-garde. Then he added that rules do not make a work of art. Encouraged by his friend and admirer Claude Debussy, he explored non-Western sounds, eventually combining them with his own reconfiguration (or discarding) of Western scales and tonal patterns.

In 1923, his *Hyperion* premiered, and, like *The Rite of Spring*, it caused a riot in the theater. Some of the instruments he employed were sleigh bells, rattles, crash cymbals, an anvil, Chinese blocks, Indian drums, and a washtub with a hole in the bottom that allowed the player to reproduce the sound of a lion's roar.

At the age of 71, Varèse created *Deserts*, his response to atomic energy and the dangers it posed for the world. The piece, using both taped and synthesized sounds, drove the audience into a frenzy and nearly led to another riot. One critic observed that Varèse deserved the electric chair for composing such noise.

Another dedicated user of the synthesizer to enhance the possibilities of musical sound was Karlheinz Stockhausen (1928–2007), noted for extremely long works, including an orchestral poem called *Light*, which celebrated the seven days of the week. If all seven movements were performed nonstop the audience would find themselves sitting in their chairs for 29 hours. One of his most remarkable achievements was designing a sphere-shaped auditorium built for the 1970 World's Fair in Osaka, Japan. Within this sphere, orchestra and chorus performed all of Stockhausen's work five and a half hours daily for 183 days.

Stockhausen is most often identified with *serialism*, a musical technique in which the composer disregards all theories of pitch, harmony, and key, creating his own version of musical notes and writing them down in quite nontraditional ways. Stockhausen enthusiasts insist that his structures, while strange at first to the ear, are geometric and logical within their own set of rules.

Relatively more accessible at first hearing is the work of Ellen Taaffe Zwilich (b. 1939), whose Symphony No. 1, premiered in 1983, was the first musical composition by a woman to win the Pulitzer Prize. Zwilich's repertoire is wide and varied, and her musical style ranges from a latter-day romanticism to the contemporary avant-garde. She is not known to be dedicated to a particular way of composing, nor is she an advocate of avant-garde theory, like Stockhausen. Zwilich has composed for particular performers, such as Doc Severinson, the long-time orchestra conductor for the *Tonight Show*, or for particular venues, such as the Circle Theatre in Indianapolis, which commissioned her to compose a work for the inaugural concert of the Indianapolis Symphony in its new home. Zwilich said that she wanted to challenge the acoustical possibilities of the hall.

She has written for choral groups and soloists as well. This versatility and flexibility more than qualify her as an avant-gardist. She will use all manner of instrumentation and musical sounds to suit whatever occasion requires her services. Much of her work falls easily on the ear—but not all of it. As long as her compositions satisfy her unique expressive needs, she doesn't seem to care whether they are broadly accepted, an attitude shared by countless other modern composers.

There is not space enough here to discuss all of the strange and wondrous new sounds that are being produced in both East and West by both men and women. In this chapter our goal has been to suggest how your life can be infinitely enriched if you are willing to listen—listen to the great classics of the past and the perhaps great-one-day experiments of the present. Don't forget Beethoven was often considered too "modern" by some of his contemporaries. But with all the sound that is there for you to hear, don't forget to spend a little time with your silences.

LEARNING OBJECTIVES

Having read and carefully studied this chapter, you should be able to:

1. Briefly describe the major elements of Western music.
2. Briefly contrast Eastern and Western styles of music.
3. Indicate characteristics of the baroque, using a Bach fugue as your example.
4. Using the *Eroica* symphony as your example, show how Beethoven unified the symphonic form, something his predecessors did not do.
5. Describe folk music, using three of its genres as examples.
6. Briefly trace the evolution of ragtime.
7. Explain why jazz musicians admire Bach.
8. Briefly trace the evolution of rock music, discussing three of its genres.
9. Indicate how the Beatles revolutionized popular music.
10. Cite three examples describing the musical avant-garde.

KEY TERMS

atonality a characteristic of much avant-garde music composed without regard for key.

avant-garde art forms that defy traditional guidelines; avant-garde music employs much dissonance and atonality.

baroque term applied to the artistic style of the mid-seventeenth to mid-eighteenth centuries; marked by elaborate ornamentation and complexity; original meaning: *irregular pearl.*

chamber music composition for small ensembles, such as four violins.

chromatic scale consists of twelve tones; if played on a piano, a consecutive run using both black and white keys.

counterpoint two melodic lines played against each other; characteristic of Bach's work.

diatonic scale consists of seven tones; white piano keys only; the fundamental but not the only scale in Western music.

dissonance in music, two or more uncongenial notes sounded or sung at the same time, producing an unfamiliar and, for some, unpleasant effect.

fugue lengthy musical composition or section within a larger composition in which two melodic lines are played against each other.

half-tone half of one interval between two notes in the diatonic scale; on a piano, half-tones are produced by the black keys.

harmony two or more tones, congenial or otherwise, sounded or sung at the same time.

hip-hop contemporary style of music that includes rap; a lifestyle marked by baggy clothes, idiomatic speech, graffiti, and break-dancing.

improvisation spontaneous set of variations on a stated musical theme; once performed, it may be written down and repeated by other performers.

key a particular scale that dominates a musical composition, identified by the first note of that scale and whether the scale is major or minor: e.g. C major, B-flat minor.

melody any arrangement of tones in a definite sequence that constitutes a unity.

pentatonic scale five-tone musical scale that preceded the familiar seven-tone scale dominant in the West; remains the basic scale of much non-Western music.

ragtime musical genre, forerunner of jazz, invented in the late 1890s by African American composers, notably Scott Joplin; strongly influenced by slow and stately European dances.

rap major subgenre of hip-hop in which rhyming lyrics are half-sung, half-spoken rapidly.

rhythm alternation of stress and unstress in music, usually created by a percussion instrument.

rock generic name covering a variety of styles that have a loud and insistent beat.

Rock 'n' roll style of music introduced in the 1950s and popularized by Elvis Presley; grew out of a fusion of rhythm and blues, gospel, and country and western styles.

scale the orderly progression of sound-wave frequencies, from low to high.

symphony a major orchestral form from the late eighteenth century to the present, usually consising of four separate sections, or movements, with contrasting tempos, sometimes constituting a unity, often not.

syncopation a form in which the melodic line of a piece is played against, not with, the accented beats of the rhythmic accompaniment, as in Gershwin's "Fascinatin' Rhythm" and the Beatles' "Eleanor Rigby."

toccata musical form perfected by Bach making liberal use of improvisation and allowing for an overpowering display of musical virtuosity by the performer.

tone a single sound produced by a musical voice or instrument; also called a note.

TOPICS FOR WRITING OR DISCUSSION

1. Explore the role of music in your own life. For example, what songs do you sing spontaneously? What music can you hear over and over without tiring of it? Can you say why?
2. Many people wear earphones on public transportation, while waiting in line, jogging, or just sitting on a bench somewhere. Go to some place in which you expect to find people with earphones. As politely as possible, ask them what kind of music they are listening to and why. Make a report to the class on your findings. Were there any surprises? Give your opinion of why people wear earphones: for aesthetic reason or something else?
3. Write an imaginary speech made to a friend in which you describe a concert you have just attended, comprised of five selections, each from a different period and composed in different styles. Make sure your vocabulary contains musical terms from the chapter.
4. The chapter covers many classic works and performers in rock and hip-hop forms. Single out at least two contemporary groups or soloists you think may one day achieve the stature of some of those mentioned as having earned a place in humanities history. Explain your choices.
5. Find a CD containing ragtime music. (Libraries usually have a lot of Scott Joplin.) Write a report presenting (and backing up) your opinion on why ragtime is no longer being written today.
6. Wynton Marsalis is the first composer to win the Pulitzer Prize for a jazz composition. He also serves as artistic director for the prestigious Jazz at Lincoln Center series. In your opinion, does jazz belong in the same venue that houses the New York Philharmonic Orchestra and the Metropolitan Opera House? Explain.
7. Bach and Beethoven are frequently found at the top of the World's Greatest Composers list. Since their time, many composers have attained considerable distinction, yet the two giants still retain their ranking. What did you learn about their musical accomplishments that might justify their hold on the title "the greatest"? If you think they no longer deserve this honor, explain why.
8. Do a little research and present a report on an all-female rock group. Present your opinion on why such groups tend to have fewer fans than the male groups. Is rock a male-dominated scene? If so, why? And if it is, do you think the popularity of female groups will grow?
9. Read through the section on avant-garde music. Find a composer you think might interest you. (Libraries or the Internet are always good resources.) Listen to selections of the composer's music and then present a report on why such music deserves wider hearing or why it does not.
10. From what the chapter has to say about non-Western music, do you believe it has anything to offer Western ears? Should one bother listening? Find an example of this music and listen to it. (Again libraries and the Internet are good resources.) Present a report on your findings.

Study and **Review** on **MyHumanitiesKit.com**

TAKE A CLOSER LOOK: Exploring Claude Debussy's "Clair de Lune"

Claude Debussy (1862–1918) was a French composer. His harmonies were regarded as revolutionary in his day and have been largely influential on modern-day composers. "Clair de Lune" is the third movement (and most noted) of his *Suite Bergamasque,* a piano suite published in 1905. "Clair de Lune" means "moonlight" in French. The title was taken from a poem by Paul Verlaine, a French poet of the Symbolist movement.

Listen to Debussy's "Clair de Lune" on MyHumanitiesKit.com. If you do not have access, you can find various performances available online. The following questions will help you explore "Clair de Lune" as a critical listener.

Listen on **MyHumanitiesKit.com** Debussy, Clair de Lune

1. Describe Claude Debussy's "Clair de Lune" analytically using the terms introduced in the "Basic Elements of Music" (page 156).
2. Would you describe "Clair de Lune" as Apollonian or Dionysian? Why?
3. Debussy's "Clair de Lune" belongs to a musical school known as Impressionism. After listening to "Clair de Lune," how would you describe the similarities and differences between Impressionism as an artistic movement and as a movement in music?

Chapter 7

Theater

Drama has always been a natural activity. Without being told to do so, children play-act, pretending to be people other than themselves. Often the players are divided into the totally good or totally bad, characters rarely found in real life. Yet drama *is* closely related to real life. It is a way of clarifying experience, a way of making sense out of life by imitating it; it is also a way of enhancing and intensifying certain occasions, as in a parade, a ceremony, or an imposing entrance to signal an important event. Drama gives shape to events, adds spice to life, quickens the pace. It is as though the dramatic instinct was invented to charge our lives with electricity and give us the need to project ourselves into make-believe action, as well as the wisdom to accept pretense as reality. To become involved in theater is to have a greater share of experience.

Theater exists in every culture, but it takes many different forms. Like visual art, drama does not always pretend to be an exact replica of real life. (In fact, realistic staging was absent throughout most of the history of theater.) Even plays that seem to mirror real life as we know it, really do not. The scenery is not real, and actors are saying lines that have been scripted for them. They may talk in verse or use language in an unusual, bizarre way. What happens on the stage depends on the *conventions* of theater, and these are not always the same. In Shakespeare, characters talk in verse. In musical theater people sing their feelings. Conventions also reflect the period of time in which the play was written or is being performed. Many of Shakespeare's works are performed in modern dress in a naturalistic style of acting not characteristic of the Elizabethan period.

Ever since theater began, audiences have had to accept the conditions governing the staging and performance of every play. These conditions are known as theatrical **conventions**, or *the conditions which the audience agrees to accept as real.* Granted that the stage may be totally bare or clogged with furniture, and granted that the actors may look nothing like the characters they are portraying (for instance, Juliet played by a boy or, as in a modern production, King Lear played by a woman), habitual theater-goers cooperate by playing along, by suspending their disbelief. Conventions have changed throughout history, and modern directors often like to add flavor to a production by surprising audience expectations. Habitual theater-goers adjust immediately to the new rules. Indeed, doing so is part of the fun of going to plays.

Brian Bedford, *The Importance of Being Earnest*, 2009

The formidable Lady Bracknell in a production of Oscar Wilde's *The Importance of Being Earnest* at the Roundabout Theater in New York.

Joan Marcus

Major Tragic and Serious Plays in Theater History

We begin with a contrast between the classical theater of ancient Greece and the very different Elizabethan theater of England. In classical theater, the playwright is Sophocles, author of *Oedipus the King* (430 B.C.E.) and *Antigone* (440 B.C.E.). In the Elizabethan theater, the representative playwright is Shakespeare.

The vast difference between the theaters for which Sophocles and Shakespeare wrote their plays strongly influenced the conventions governing them. In the classical period of Greece, audiences would have been sitting on stone benches in an outdoor stadium accommodating 14,000 to 20,000 people. They would be seeing plays shown only once during an annual three-day festival, part of a religious celebration sponsored by the state.

Javarman/Shutterstock

The theater at Epidaurus, Greece

The theater at Epidaurus, well-preserved and still functioning.

In the Elizabethan theater of London, audiences would have been sitting or standing close to the stage. Plays would have been available at almost any time of the year, and plays would have had no religious purpose. Entertainment and commercial success were the goals.

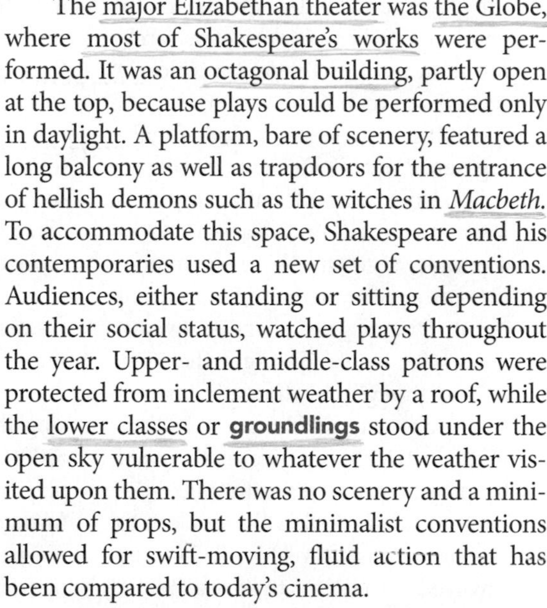

The major Elizabethan theater was the Globe, where most of Shakespeare's works were performed. It was an octagonal building, partly open at the top, because plays could be performed only in daylight. A platform, bare of scenery, featured a long balcony as well as trapdoors for the entrance of hellish demons such as the witches in *Macbeth*. To accommodate this space, Shakespeare and his contemporaries used a new set of conventions. Audiences, either standing or sitting depending on their social status, watched plays throughout the year. Upper- and middle-class patrons were protected from inclement weather by a roof, while the lower classes or **groundlings** stood under the open sky vulnerable to whatever the weather visited upon them. There was no scenery and a minimum of props, but the minimalist conventions allowed for swift-moving, fluid action that has been compared to today's cinema.

Travelshots.com/Alamy

The Globe Theater, London

The new Globe Theater in London, built in 1997, said to be a nearly exact replica of Shakespeare's theater, built circa 1598.

Greek Classical Theater and Elizabethan Theater: A Comparison

In the early days of classical theater, there were no plays as such. Instead, those who attended the festival saw a Chorus of masked men singing and dancing to hymns in praise of the gods, especially Dionysus, who provided the harvest. During the sixth century B.C.E., a soloist named Thespis stepped out of the **Chorus** and engaged in some form of sung dialogue with them, much as a priest celebrating a high mass might interact with the choir. Gradually the emphasis shifted from the Chorus to the actors—no more than three at any one time. Familiar myths were retold as transformed by the creativity of the writer. Emphasis was on what could happen if the gods were not obeyed. Drama was born.

A number of theories have been advanced to account for the convention of the mask, the most prominent among which is that, since actors whose voices could be heard in the open air by 20,000 people were not all that common, one masked actor could play many roles.

In the smaller Elizabethan theater, however, masks were not required; but males continued to play all the parts. Greek tragedies were based on well-known myths, though many in the audience must have assumed the stories were historically true. Elizabethan plays were not all based on myths, though Shakespeare took dramatic license with history in works such as *Julius Caesar* and *Antony and Cleopatra.*

Classical Greek theater had a Chorus of twelve or fifteen men praising the gods and providing background information and making moral comments on the consequences of the central character's tragic mistakes.

No Chorus was required for the Elizabethan theater, although Shakespeare chose to use an actor to perform the same function as in the opening of the fourth act of *Henry V.* Standing on a bare stage in daylight, he made the audience believe they were watching a tense encampment of soldiers on the night before a great battle.

> *Now entertain conjecture of a time*
> *When creeping murmur and the poring dark*
> *Fills the wide vessel of the universe.*
> *From camp to camp through the foul womb of night*
> *The hum of either army stilly sounds.*
> *That the fix'd sentinels almost receive*
> *The secret whispers of each other's watch:*
> *Fire answers fire, and through their paly flames*
> *Each battle sees the others umber'd face. . . .*
> *The poor condemned English,*
> *Like sacrifices, by their watchful fires*
> *Sit patiently and inly ruminate*
> *The morning's danger, and their gesture sad*
> *Investing lank-lean cheeks and war-worn coats*
> *Presenteth them unto the gazing moon*
> *So many horrid ghosts.*[1]

In the plays of both periods the elevated verse language was in keeping with the gravity of issues involved. Shakespeare, a poet known for the quality of his verse, occasionally included prose dialogue for characters of lower rank.

In the Greek theater, violence occurs offstage, never in front of the audience. We hear blood-curdling cries from the wings, then a Messenger enters to describe horrifying moments taking place elsewhere. In the original productions actors wore not only masks but stilts to make them truly larger than life, especially for so vast a space. Such outfits would have made onstage violence difficult.

Roman tragedies, performed in smaller venues, showed violent scenes such as multiple stabbings in full view of the audience. Sometimes slaves were substituted for actors at the last moment and actually killed. The phrase *Greek elements* is sometimes used now to describe a play with much dialogue and limited action, while *Roman elements,* staples of the film industry, mean that a work is full of violent action.

Classical conventions:

- *verse*
- *masks*
- *all-male cast*
- *the messenger*
- *the chorus*
- *Unity of time, place, and action*
- *Greek: violence off-stage only*
- *Roman: much on-stage violence*

> "Think, when we talk of horses, that you see them
> Printing their proud hoofs i'the receiving earth;
> For 'tis your thoughts that now must deck our kings,
> Carry them here and there, jumping o'er times,
> Turning the accomplishment of many years
> Into an hour glass . . ."
>
> **—William Shakespeare**

Elizabethan conventions:

- *all-male cast*
- *verse except for prose given to servants*
- *the aside*
- *the soliloquy*
- *no scenery*
- *unities discarded*
- *subtext*

Although the Elizabethans on all levels of society were fascinated by poetry and intricate wordplay, they too adored action—lots of it—and the more violent the better. Shakespeare gave them unceasing action: simulated battles, sword fights, multiple stabbings, and poisonings. He wasn't even afraid to violate the gravity of a tragic work by injecting scenes of low-life comedy, combined with sexual humor, in the midst of great tragic moments. Just before her suicide, Cleopatra has an encounter with a clown in which both engage in what can only be described as suggestive "gags."

Acting styles were very different, as would be expected by the design of the buildings. In Greek and Roman amphitheaters, gestures were broad rather than subtle. Actors used exaggerated, sweeping movements to accompany their words, just as officials at an athletic event indicate penalties by using hand gestures as they shout the nature of the offense and penalties imposed. In Shakespeare's theater, far more naturalistic acting was beginning to be seen, no doubt because of the complexity of the characters.

Another classical convention is *unity of time, place, and action.* Unity of time means that everything happens in the course of a single day. There is no shift of scene in classical tragedy, and there are no subplots. Audiences could concentrate on the single conflict unfolding before them, with no side issues involving minor characters.

The **unities** were not required by the conditions of the Elizabethan theater. Although Shakespeare in *The Tempest* did have all the action take place in one day (as if to prove he could do it!), he was able to have as much time pass as he chose. He was also able to write plays with subplots showing the fortunes of more than one character. In *King Lear,* the protagonist's relationship with his three daughters is paralleled by that of the Duke of Gloucester with his son.

Listen on **MyHumanitiesKit.com** Sophocles, *Oedipus*

Sophocles, *Oedipus the King.* Classical **tragedy** revolves around a central character, or **protagonist**, in terms of whose fortunes we follow in the story. Plays and movies of today continue to have this character, often called the *hero,* but this term can be misleading. *Hero* suggests a person of virtue and courage, who usually triumphs over forces of evil. In the great tragedies, however, the protagonist seldom has these qualities. A flaw in his character leads to his tragic downfall. *Oedipus the King,* one of the masterpieces not only of Greek theater but of all time, has a central character who can serve as the very model of a tragic protagonist.

The play begins with relative peace (as tragedies often do—the calm before the storm). The state of Thebes is in good hands, or so it is believed. King Oedipus is powerful and wise, able to solve problems as no one else can. In the past he has saved the citizens from being devoured by a horrible monster. Now, years later, Thebes faces another threat. There is a plague, and the Chorus, representing the people of Thebes, entreats their king to find out why. The oracle sends word that the plague will continue until the murderer of the previous king is found and brought to justice. Oedipus confidently agrees to solve the mystery, without realizing that he himself is the killer. A blind prophet tells him the truth, but Oedipus becomes enraged and denounces the man. He has saved the kingdom and cannot be a murderer. By the end of the play he is forced to recognize that the man he killed years before in an unplanned skirmish had been the former king of Thebes—and his own father as well.

For Aristotle, tragedy was about the downfall of a human being of noble and virtuous qualities, except for one weakness: hubris, the misguided assumption that worldly power placed one on the level of the gods.

Disaster follows disaster. As if this news were not bad enough, he realizes he is married to that deceased king's wife, Jocasta, who has borne him four children, and who is in actuality his mother. After discovering the horrible truth of his past, he tears his eyes from their sockets. We hear bloodcurdling cries from offstage, then the messenger enters to describe the terrifying moment. So vivid is his telling of it that we feel we are actually *there.*

Sophocles, *Antigone.* In a work written in 440 B.C.E., ten years before his masterwork, Sophocles told a later part of the myth as the basis for *Antigone.* It deals with the tragedy visited upon the children of Oedipus after he has blinded himself and gone off to wander in the desert in perpetual exile. In what has taken place before the action of the play, the two sons of the king, fighting a war on opposing sides, have slain each other in battle. Creon, brother-in-law of Oedipus, has succeeded him as king and given an order that one of the brothers cannot receive the burial rites required by the gods because he fought on the side of Creon's enemy. Antigone, a strong-willed woman, defies Creon's order, buries her brother properly, and is walled up in a cave to die for her disobedience. What the audience knows—and Creon doesn't—is that his own son, in love with Antigone, will hide in the cave and die with her.

Tragedy rewards audiences willing to look beyond the action itself. In Greek tragedy there is usually a philosophical theme, a commentary by the Chorus on why things happen or the cause of the downfall of someone who began with good fortune and ended with great loss. The tragic protagonist, not necessarily dead by the end of the play, must be much worse off, having descended, in Aristotle's words, "from prosperity to adversity." Oedipus, for example, is blind and left to wander aimlessly, unloved, uncared for. The Chorus pronounces sadly the final two lines of the play:

> *We may count no man happy*
> *Until he has crossed life's border, free of pain.*

It is not the message we would like to hear, but it offers a view of life—a *tragic* view—that must be faced, must be considered, and, if possible, transcended.

The Recognition Scene in Sophocles and Shakespeare

The great tragedies usually have a **recognition scene**, a moment when the protagonist fully understands what has brought about the disaster. First, there is a search for the meaning of what has occurred. This search may be followed by the attempt to justify the action, and finally, the acceptance of responsibility.

Is Oedipus responsible for what has happened? The fact that he would kill his father and marry his mother had been prophesied at his birth. The Greeks believed that fate ruled human life, so nothing could have changed Oedipus's destiny. Yet he *does* accept responsibility, perhaps wishing to show that he was a powerful man to the end.

A famous recognition speech is that delivered by Creon in *Antigone.* Having inherited the throne of Thebes after the downfall of Oedipus, Creon has become a powerful and arrogant ruler. In the speech he realizes his arrogance has caused the death of not only his

AP Photo

Christopher Plummer, *Oedipus the King,* 1967

A modern production, without masks, shows vividly the suffering of blinded Oedipus.

son but of his wife, who commits suicide because of it. He has lost those who were dearest to him and his life now lies in ruins. He cries:

Lead me away. I have been rash and foolish.
I have killed my son and my wife.
I look for comfort; my comfort lies here dead.
Whatever my hands have touched has come to nothing.
Fate has brought all my pride to a thought of dust.[2]

Listen on **MyHumanitiesKit.com**
Shakespeare, *Othello*

Although Shakespeare rarely followed classical conventions, he did include a speech of recognition in *Othello*, generally considered his most classically constructed work. In the final act, the protagonist has realized that he was tricked into believing his wife was unfaithful and he has murdered her without cause. At the point of his arrest he says to his captors:

Soft you; a word before you go.
I have done the state some service and they know 't.
No more of that, I pray you, in your letters.
When you shall these unlucky deeds relate.
Speak of me as I am; nothing extenuate.
Nor set down aught in malice. Then must you speak
Of one that lov'd not wisely but too well.[3]

At the conclusion of the speech, he removes a concealed dagger and stabs himself. The protagonist, having taken full responsibility, holds onto his dignity. Freedom to choose his own death is all that is left.

In all theater there may be no scene to match the recognition scene in *King Lear*, when the king, close to death, finally understands the terrible mistake he has made when he exiled his only loving daughter from his kingdom. Because of his prideful blindness to reality, he has supported his evil daughters, only to have them turn on him. The innocent daughter is captured and executed, and the old man, not always with full knowledge of who and where he is, finally understands what he has done and knows that he will never see his loving daughter again.

The moment is unrivaled. Instead of vast eloquence, Shakespeare uses relatively few words—and silence.

Why should a dog, a horse, a rat, have life.
And thou no breath at all? Thou'lt come no more
Never, never, never, never, never.[4]

The last line is said to contain the five most tragic words in all of drama. Actors who perform Lear are often unable to say them all before dissolving into tears.

Aristotle on the Nature of Tragedy

Thus far this chapter has dealt with the work of playwrights and the conventions of performance. We now introduce the world's first critic of theater, Aristotle (382–322 B.C.E.), who long ago set down his famous analysis of the purpose and the elements of tragic drama.

Playwrights of today, attempting tragedy, often have difficulty providing recognition scenes, because of a common belief that people are seldom responsible for their actions.

Looking around the amphitheater where the plays were performed, Aristotle wondered what moved people, *why* they were moved, what were the essential elements all tragedies must have, and finally, why some plays were more successful than others. He wrote his observations in *The Poetics*, which contains his famous and intact essay on tragedy and, it is believed, an essay on comedy of which all but the first line has been lost.

Aristotle analyzes how experiencing a make-believe story could have the same effect as it would if people were witnessing an actual tragic event. He realized that spectators were identifying with the characters and feeling almost the same pain as the actors, who pretended they were suffering. For this reason he decided that the ideal protagonist for a tragedy must be someone who is mainly virtuous (otherwise people wouldn't care what happened to the character) but is not totally innocent either. The character has a tragic flaw that leads to his or her destruction. If a bad fate befell an innocent person, the audience would reject this outcome as being too cruel.

Aristotle divided tragedy into six parts, arranged in order of importance: *plot, character, thought, poetry, spectacle,* and *song*. He then gave his famous definition of tragedy, which is

> *the imitation of a good action, which is complete and of a certain length, by means of language made pleasing for each part separately; it relies in its various elements not on narrative but on acting; through pity and fear it achieves the purgation of such emotions.*[5]

By "action" Aristotle is referring to the forward motion of the tragedy, which, through what the characters do, brings about a change of circumstances—a change for the worse—and thus the emotions of the audience grow more intense as the play leads to inevitable catastrophe. The aim is to stimulate an emotional response not for the sake of the emotion, but for the aftermath of emotion: the feeling of calm that follows it.

This calm, called **catharsis**, comes after undergoing other kinds of aesthetic experience: after listening to Beethoven's Third Symphony, for example. To the question "Why put oneself through such a wrenching ordeal?" the Aristotelian answer is that *one derives strength from reacting to make-believe pain as if it were real.* The spectator slowly returns to the life that was left outside the theater, but with the rational calm that would follow an actual catastrophe.

The flaw of Oedipus is **hubris**, or arrogance. It is universal. Everyone knows people who insist that there is no other truth but theirs. Aristotle's analysis holds. Tragedy, he said, requires audience identification; only then will the downfall of the protagonist be emotionally devastating, and no one can achieve catharsis who is not profoundly moved. Small wonder that playwrights have continued to reach for the heights of tragedy. No other theatrical art form has so much power to reach the viewer.

> *"The bad ended unhappily, the good unluckily. That is what tragedy means."*
>
> **—Tom Stoppard**

Underscoring dramatically the passing of the golden age of classical Greek tragedy, the deaths of Sophocles and Euripides (484–406 B.C.E.) occurred in the same year. Although the plays of Euripides seldom illustrate completely the principles set forth in Aristotle's *Poetics,* although they lack the concluding speech in which protagonists recognize their responsibility for the catastrophe, and although his plots generally lack the tight structure Aristotle so admired in *Oedipus,* Euripides was nevertheless called by Aristotle "the most tragic of all." Perhaps the philosopher meant that Euripides saw most deeply into the pain of being alive. This pain is his subject. In fact, the *Medea* of Euripides has proved to be, for modern audiences, the most persistently stageworthy of the Greek tragedies. Euripides is closer in spirit to the modern temper than were his contemporaries.

Euripides's *Medea*. What makes the plot structure of the *Medea* so tight and a principal reason for the work's popularity with modern audiences is the diminished role of the Chorus. The tragedy is driven by the terrifying inevitability of a jealous wife's revenge on her husband by murdering their sons. Scene after scene shows the wife's hatred growing more bitter and her decision becoming more irreversible at the same time that her maternal love intensifies. Euripides is more interested in the emotional and psychological turbulence that drives the work than in the moral and philosophical issues raised by a character's actions.

The play tells only the last part of Medea's story. We learn, though, that in the past Medea has used her magical powers to help her eventual husband, Jason, find the famous Golden Fleece and gain the stature of a hero. He has married her out of gratitude. As the play begins, Medea is living in Jason's country, finding herself among people with little regard for either foreigners or women. Jason tells Medea of his plans to marry a princess so that their sons will have the advantage of living in a royal household and be half-brothers to the royal children Jason will sire. He expects her to be pleased at the thought of their children's future. She is not, but pretends approval so that she can take revenge. After using her powers to design a poisonous gown that kills her rival, she is not yet satisfied that Jason has suffered enough. In one of the theater's most powerful scenes, Medea struggles against what she knows would be the ultimate revenge: the death of Jason's sons.

As the innocent children play, their mother tries to stem the force that is driving her to do the unspeakable, but she cannot do so. She takes them inside and, after a terrifying moment of silence, we hear their agonized cries. Their throats have been cut.

The ending of the play lacks the moral completeness of *Oedipus*. For Sophocles, though the fate of Oedipus was prearranged, his arrogance was really a defiance of divine law; for this arrogance he pays a tragic price. The suffering of Medea, however, does not spring from the violation of a moral law, but rather from the fact that as a loving mother she should not have been brought to such a state by an insensitive husband and that her passion for revenge has torn her apart. Nor does Medea go forth in ruins, as Oedipus does. With Jason grieving over the bodies of his slain children, Medea rides off in triumph on a chariot sent for her by a sympathetic neighboring king. Her last line as she looks up at the "unfriendly stars" is "Not me they scorn." If she will feel the pangs of guilt for the rest of her life, her grief will be private and no business of the gods—if indeed there *are* gods.

Hubert Williams

Lorna Haughton, *Pecong*, 2010

Lorna Haughton as Mediyah in Steve Carter's *Pecong*, an updated version of *Medea* set on a mythical Caribbean island.

Euripides gives every indication that he has abandoned the effort to find meaning in obedience to the laws of the gods. There is a pervading cynicism in his plays, a fear that humanity is abandoned in a godless universe, or at least one in which the gods, if they exist, are cruelly whimsical and justice is never carried out. As if to underscore his cynicism, many of his plays have contrived, unbelievable happy endings. He seems to be saying that in an amoral world, a happy ending is a random accident. In the world of Euripides moral responsibility does not exist; pain does.

Shakespeare and Dramatic Verse

Whether or not he intended to, Shakespeare nonetheless created characters that would achieve immortality and be better known than those of any other playwright. He was certainly interested in making money, and indeed was very successful at it. Almost despite himself, he rose far above the level of the others, although he might never have thought his works would live through the centuries.

Because the Elizabethan audience was so close to the stage, they could see the faces of the actors and could also hear quiet speech. One of the foremost Elizabethan conventions is the **soliloquy**, in which an actor, alone on stage, speaks his thoughts aloud. Though it was widely used in other plays by Shakespeare and his contemporaries, the most famous soliloquy in all of drama is Hamlet's, which begins "To be or not to be."

In contrast to the Elizabethan soliloquy, the **aside** is a remark made by an actor when other actors are present. The audience hears what is said, but other actors are not supposed to. Sometimes it is a shortened version of the soliloquy, as when Hamlet, after listening to his treacherous uncle's insincere rhetoric, comments to the audience, "A little more than kin, and less than kind." In ten words Shakespeare defines how Hamlet feels about the man who has married his father's widow almost immediately after the man's death. Serious drama stopped using the *aside* by the eighteenth century, but it was used in comedy well into the nineteenth and in musical comedy well into the twentieth century.

In Shakespeare, even epic battles are fought, but Elizabethan conventions allowed the wounded to make an eloquent speech before dying. Except for lower-class characters, who spoke in prose, most of Shakespeare's characters speak in elaborate poetry, revealing deep feelings. No effort was made to have them speak the way ordinary people, including those in the audience, would actually speak. No one complains, "Haven't had a thing to eat since last night" or "This rain is a nuisance." Everyone has a speech appropriate to the situation. *That* is a timeless and universal convention. Only on a stage do people always have the right words when needed!

The verse is written in iambic pentameter, a line of five feet (or poetic units), with rhythm sounding like this: da DAH, da DAH, da DAH, da DAH, da DAH. When skilled actors perform Shakespeare, the rhythm is often hard to detect, because the master somehow—miraculously—fits the rhythmic words to the scene so precisely that audiences seldom know the rhythm is there. Except for the more obviously rhythmic ending of some scenes, the dialogue sounds like elegant prose. If it did not, just think how monotonous the play would be!

An amazing example of Shakespeare's genius for tying together iambic pentameter and the precise words for a dramatic situation is found in the final act of *Othello*. The protagonist, maddened by suspicion that his wife is unfaithful, smothers her to death. Immediately after the deed, he hears a knocking on the door and an entreaty from Emilia, his wife's attendant, asking that she be allowed to enter. Othello shouts to Emilia that he will open the door soon, and then speaks to himself as the full horror of his deed becomes clear to him.

The Everett Collection

Lawrence Fishburne and Kenneth Branagh, *Othello*, 1995

Othello offers a wonderful example of Shakespeare's genius for tying together iambic pentameter and the dramatic demands of a scene.

Part of Shakespeare's genius was his ability to write lines that scan almost perfectly but allow the actor to explore the full range of emotion.

Yes: 'tis Emilia. By and by. She's dead:
'Tis like she comes to speak of Cassio's death,—
The noise was here. Ha! No more moving?
Still as the grave. Shall she come in? Were 't good?—
I think she stirs again:—no. What's best to do?
If she come in, she 'll sure speak to my wife:
My wife! my wife! what wife? I have no wife.[6]

The lines *scan* almost perfectly: that is, they can be read so as to exaggerate the iambic pentameter. But they cannot be spoken that way by an actor. Consider the first line. "Yes" is directed to Emilia in a loud voice. "'Tis Emilia" is spoken to himself in a soft voice. "By and by" is loud and to Emilia again. Then an absolutely essential pause before "She's dead."

The word "no" in the fifth line stands all by itself, demanding that the actor speak it between two pauses; otherwise the line is exact iambic pentameter. In fact, the entire passage compels the actor to hesitate wherever Othello's manic thought processes require it. Shakespeare's genius allows the actor to have it both ways: to have a rhythmic underpinning to the poetry as well as the freedom to explore the character's emotions.

Shakespeare's poetry is filled with **images**, words that create pictures in the mind of audience and reader. Perhaps he was trying to compensate for the fact that the plays were performed on a stage with no scenery. Lighting and sound systems would not come for hundreds of years. Perhaps no more famous dramatic image exists than the first two lines of the balcony scene from *Romeo and Juliet*:

Listen on
MyHumanitiesKit.com
Shakespeare, *Romeo and Juliet*

But soft, what light through yonder window breaks?
It is the east, and Juliet is the sun.

The moon, by contrast, is "sick and pale with grief/That thou her maid is far more fair than she."[7] In the famous scene in Act III of *Hamlet*, taking place in the bedroom of his mother, the adulterous Queen and accomplice in the murder of his father, there are some bold and violent images in the exchange between mother and son. After he has renounced her for her crime, she cries out: "Oh, Hamlet, thou hast cleft my heart in twain." Hamlet answers with a really powerful image:

Oh, throw away the worser part of it,
And live the purer with the other half.[8]

The lines also illustrate the use of *verbal dynamics*, moving from slow to fast, from loud to soft. Hamlet's famous speech to the actors who have come to perform at the castle indicates that Shakespeare was highly critical of the melodramatic acting styles of the period and sought a more natural kind of delivery.

Speak the speech I pray you, as I pronounced it to you,
trippingly on the tongue.... Nor do not saw the air too much
with your hand, thus, but use all gently; for in the very torrent,
tempest, and, as I may say, the whirlwind of passion, you must
acquire and beget a temperance that may give it smoothness.[9]

Shakespeare wrote the words for Hamlet to say, and it is likely that Shakespeare himself agreed with the advice. Still, it is a speech in a play, not in a handbook written for aspiring actors. This speech, like those of many other characters, may not represent Shakespeare's own beliefs after all. He loved words, he loved ideas, and he seems to have enjoyed creating characters adept at both. Scholars have been tempted to discover a consistent Shakespearean philosophy that runs through all of his plays. Indeed many passages, especially in *Hamlet, King Lear,* and *Macbeth,* contain profound wisdom about the human condition, wisdom that will always stimulate thought, whether or not it represents Shakespeare's personal philosophy.

Unlike classical plays, Elizabethan drama was under no obligation to deal with universal themes. Shakespeare may have been primarily interested in giving his diverse public a rich, many-layered entertainment. The profundity of the major characters also suggests that he was fascinated by human psychology (though the word did not exist in his time) and the challenge, in Hamlet's words, to "hold... the mirror up to nature."

If tightness of plot is generally not Shakespeare's strength, in his greatest plays character and thought are without equal in the entire realm of theater, whether he was educated in the formal sense or not. His major characters go from the particular to the general, finding broad moral principles that offer profound insights into the meaning of human life. These insights are often cynical. Many of his characters entertain a bleak vision of life. When Hamlet is challenged to a fencing match in which, unknown to him, his opponent's sword is dipped in poison, his friend Horatio has a grim foreboding and urges Hamlet to decline. Hamlet will not.

> *Speak the speech, I pray you, as I pronounced it to you, trippingly on the tongue; but if you mouth it, as many of your players do, I had as lief the town crier spoke my lines.*
>
> **—Hamlet to the Players**

> *... we defy augury: there's a special providence in the fall of a sparrow. If it be now, 'tis not to come; if it be not to come, it will be now; if it be not now, yet it will come: the readiness is all: since no man has aught of what he leaves, what is't to leave betimes?*[10]

Macbeth, whose kingdom lies in ruins and whose enemies are closing in on him, responds to the news of his wife's death in lines that could be the pessimist's manifesto.

> *She should have died hereafter;*
> *There would have been a time for such a word*
> *Tomorrow, and tomorrow, and tomorrow,*
> *Creeps in this petty pace from day to day*
> *To the last syllable of recorded time,*
> *And all our yesterdays have lighted fools*
> *The way to dusty death. Out, out, brief candle!*
> *Life's but a walking shadow, a poor player*
> *That struts and frets his hour upon the stage*
> *And then is heard no more; it is a tale*
> *Told by an idiot, full of sound and fury,*
> *Signifying nothing.*[11]

Shakespeare's audiences were challenged in another way, for the only way to tell night from day was to hear what the actors said. Plays were performed in daylight, so "night" occurred when actors mentioned it. Audiences saw the ghost of Hamlet's father wandering in the dark provided by their imaginations.

The Elizabethan theater was free from the burden of moving heavy scenery about, and playwrights realized that a bare stage could be any place as long as their words could describe it vividly. Scenes could move from indoors to outdoors or from garden to palace or the imaginary tomb in which Romeo and Juliet meet their deaths. Elizabethan audiences quickly adapted to the rules governing their theater.

Neoclassic Tragedy

In the years following the Elizabethan era, theatrical conventions changed once again. In the latter half of the seventeenth century, drama, poetry, painting, and architecture saw a general return to classical principles of order and balance. The ensuing century and a half period of the arts is appropriately called **neoclassicism.**

Neoclassic theater moved indoors. For the first time, plays no longer were performed in a vast amphitheater or confined to a courtyard depending on lighting from the sun. Instead, plays could be staged in elaborate rooms within a great house and could be shown at night through the use of lighting from elegant chandeliers.

Neoclassic conventions:

- *indoor theaters*
- *chandelier lighting (candles)*
- *upper-class audience*
- *return of unities*
- *artificial language in couplets*
- *classical myths retold in terms of neoclassic behavioral codes*
- *emotion described, not shown*

Audiences changed, too. Instead of the many social levels that attended the Greek and Roman theaters and the Elizabethan playhouse, audiences were now made up of well-educated, beautifully dressed aristocrats, whose preferences had to be considered. The demand was strong for a return to a theater less violent than Shakespeare's, with subject matter based on myth as it had been during the classical period, but the stories altered to reflect the issues and moral values of the age. A nonclassical element was the appearance for the first time of women playing female characters. The new convention allowed playwrights to focus on tragic myths about the destructive effects of sexual passion and other dramatic conflicts between men and women.

Playwrights returned as much as possible to the classical unities of time, place, and action. If the plot demanded scenes in different places, the problem was solved by having one lavish but neutral set, such as a large room that could represent a number of locales. Furniture and props were carried on and off by stagehands.

In addition to the unities, neoclassical dramatists, like their ancient predecessors, employed a highly stylized, elevated stage poetry. The verse was even farther removed from natural speech than the iambic pentameter of Shakespeare. Language was ornate, geared to aristocratic taste. The word "air," for example, was avoided in favor of "ozone," and "cat" became "feline creature."

Phaedra by Jean Racine (1639–1699) was by far the major tragedy in either England or France during the approximately hundred-year span of neoclassical theater (1650–1750). The dialogue is elevated in accordance with the acceptable style, and characters speak elegantly of their intense emotions without actually demonstrating them.

The protagonist is married to the mythical hero Theseus but feels a burning lust for her stepson Hippolytus. She knows she must conceal that lust, but it builds to such intensity that the actress performing this challenging role is forced to find ways to externalize the torment she is suffering.

Phaedra thus adds to the theater the element of the inner life. In recent years, writers and directors have created characters who feel more than they speak, forcing the audience to focus on their sparse words, their facial expressions, and their body language in order to understand them fully. A theatrical experience is less satisfying the more emotions are verbalized and more satisfying when less is said.

Governed by the conventions of its time, *Phaedra* takes place entirely in a civilized drawing room, and, although the characters have Greek names, they look and sound like aristocratic contemporaries of the audience. Should Phaedra reveal to her stepson her burning desire for him? Of course not, it isn't done; strong feelings don't belong in public.

Phaedra's tragic flaw is stepping over the bounds of appropriate behavior by revealing to her stepson how much she desires him.

Phaedra steps over the bounds, however. She tells her stepson that the only way she can even bring herself to look at her husband is to see the facial resemblance to his son. She does the unthinkable by revealing her true feelings.

Her stepson's response would be more suited to a mild dispute about an assigned seat in a theater: "Madame, I fear there has been some mistake." He is, of course, playing the game. His manners are impeccable, but they set off lethal rage in Phaedra, who takes revenge for her humiliation by reversing the situation. She tells Theseus that she has been the victim of unwanted sexual advances by his son. Her husband impetuously pleads with one of the gods to whip up a storm and a sea monster along the shore and so have his son killed. That violent death is, of course, reported by a messenger.

Before our eyes vomits a furious monster.
With formidable horns its brow is arm'd,
And all its body clothed with yellow scales,
In front a savage bull, behind a dragon
Turning and twisting in impatient rage.
Its long continued bellowings make the shore
Tremble; the sky seems horror-struck to see it;
The earth with terror quakes; its poisonous breath
Infects the air. The wave that brought it ebbs
In fear. All fly, forgetful of the courage
That cannot aid, and in a neighbouring temple
Take refuge—all save bold Hippolytus.
A hero's worthy son, he stays his steeds,
Seizes his darts, and, rushing forward, hurls
A missile with sure aim that wounds the monster
Deep in the flank. With rage and pain it springs
E'en to the horses' feet, and, roaring, falls,
Writhes in the dust, and shows a fiery throat
That covers them with flames, and blood, and smoke.
Fear lends them wings; deaf to his voice for once,
And heedless of the curb, they onward fly.[12]

The return to classical myths told in their own aristocratic language impressed writers for the English as well as the French stage. The Messenger, above, is describing a scene of unspeakable horror that he has actually seen, yet he does so elegantly and unemotionally.

Shakespeare, whose work is rife with passionate outbursts, had died in 1616, and, although he had been admired during his lifetime, his work was rather too uncontrolled for neoclassic audiences. Within half a century, efforts to "improve" him had already begun; his plots were acceptable, but his emotional directness was considered vulgar. Playwrights had no hesitation about rewriting his work. For example, John Dryden (1631–1700) turned *Antony and Cleopatra,* Shakespeare's tragedy of tempestuous middle-aged lovers who destroy each other, into *All for Love*, "a polite" tragedy of aristocrats who overstep the bounds of propriety. A neoclassical play, like a neoclassical building, exalts balance, harmony, order, and it shuns out-of-control passion. Characters talk brilliantly—and in rhyme—about their emotions but do not *show* emotion except in death scenes.

Realism and Naturalism

During the nineteenth century, commonly known in the West as the "Victorian Era" in recognition of England's powerful and long-reigning monarch, a change took place in both society and the theater. An increasingly prosperous middle class patronized the theater and demanded to see their own lives and times portrayed as they were. Instead of classical myths, they wanted contemporary themes and characters very much like themselves. This held true on both sides of the Atlantic because the American middle class wanted to imitate the good manners and polite language of the English middle class.

In the Victorian theater, the audience sat in the dark and looked up at a stage lighted first with gas lamps, then electricity. People on the stage moved and talked to each other without noticing that what they did and said was being seen and heard by a large number of eavesdroppers. Their job was to pretend the audience was not there, and the audience's job was to pretend that they were not watching actors moving about a set made to look like a real interior. They walked up and down real stairs, opened a door and exited through it, presumably to go outside. The actor was only going backstage, but this was the era of **verisimilitude**, the convention of making everything look and sound like the real world.

> *"The lights go down and the pulse goes up."*
>
> **—Judith Anderson**

The front of the stage—or **proscenium**—was supposedly the fourth wall of the room in which the action takes place. Actors were not supposed to "break" that wall—that is, to look at the audience. The convention, or rules, were clearly established. The play contained itself and only itself. These conventions are still

Jeff Quinn

Set for *A Doll's House*, 1980

Jeff Quinn's realistic set for a production of Ibsen's *A Doll's House* at the Green Room Theatre, Lancaster, Pennsylvania.

with us. Despite all of the experimentation that has taken place in the last hundred years or so, realism is by far the dominant mode of much theater; and actors are trained in the techniques of realistic acting.

Still, a certain amount of license was taken in Victorian times and is still taken now. If the open proscenium is supposed to be the fourth wall of a room, why is furniture often facing that wall? Why do actors, talking to each other, frequently turn their faces casually toward that wall when the audience isn't supposed to be there? Is their dialogue *actually* what we would hear outside the theater? The answer is that the convention is one of "as if," to use the famous two words of Konstantin Stanislavsky (1863–1938), founder of the Moscow Art Theater. Actors were meant to act "as if" they were really in that situation, and their language was "as if" real people really talked like that.

Yet when reading plays of the period, we are apt to wonder how on earth audiences of the time could have actually believed the dialogue was authentic. Up to a point it was—for a time middle class people observed the niceties of language that were stringently taught at home and in school. In today's theater and in films or on television, we still accept the "realities" of dialogue, except that by now actors often talk in short, sometimes incomplete, sentences about food, trains, money, and sex. Much dialogue is not allowed to be more insightful or profound than ordinary conversation. Even at moments of great love or great loss, characters can be as inarticulate as people without a gifted scriptwriter to tell them what to say. Sometimes instead of words there are grunts and sighs. This too is authentic—up to a point.

In Victorian theaters time intervals were explained by a program handed to the audience, as is still the case. Lighting now indicated time of day or night. With the coming of electricity in the 1880s, actors were artificially lighted and their features heavily emphasized or even disguised by stage makeup. If a younger actor was cast as a middle-aged person, every effort was made to conceal the actor's youth; but, as theater companies grew and spread about the country on both sides of the Atlantic, actors began to be cast as they physically and vocally suited the part. Versatile actors, suitable for many roles, were able to demand high salaries. In today's theater the big stars tend to be those who have made their reputations in film but return to the stage from time to time, working for far less but believing that only in the theater, before a live audience, can they develop their craft.

The director became a major figure also. Before this period, plays were put together by the actors. Often the theater's manager would star in a production and inform cast members to give him center stage at all times. In the theater of verisimilitude, however, both movement and interpretation of lines were carefully supervised by a director.

The convention of verisimilitude gave rise to a new genre which proved to be (and continues to be) a great audience pleaser: the tricky mystery play, in which the audience is kept in suspense about the identity of the murderer until a clever detective reveals surprises just before the final curtain. Phone lines have been cut, a raging storm prevents escape, everyone looks suspicious, with dubious movements and alibis for the time of the crime. The victim was disliked by any number of suspects. *Whodunit*? and *How*?

"The structure of a play is always the story of how the birds came home to roost."

—Arthur Miller

Nineteenth-century realism is the ideal convention for the puzzle play because, if characters are trapped within a limited space, intensity builds quickly. Audiences also know that the murderer is one of the cast. Although a surprise ending is a must in this genre, verisimilitude prohibits improbability. The playwright is not supposed to introduce late in the play information that solves the puzzle. There can be no surprise wills or marriage licenses or incriminating letters. There should be just the audience and the playwright in a duel of wits. The solution in the very best mystery plays is arrived at through logic, not a chance happening There have to be tiny details the audience is meant not to notice at the time, but they add up to a believable and clever revelation. The theater-goer thinks, "Oh, I should have known!" but is delighted at having been tricked. When there is no surprise, the experience is less satisfying.

> *"If a gun is hanging on the wall in the first act, it must fire in the last."*
>
> **—Anton Chekhov**

If theater of verisimilitude were completely true to the claim that it was mirroring real life in the most honest way possible, its stories would not be as tightly knit as they are. Something else is at work, popularized by French playwrights earlier in the nineteenth century, something known as the **well-made play**. In this genre, objects and people mentioned in Act One *must* be important later on. Guns are mentioned and someone will be shot; someone who coughs slightly will be revealed to have a fatal illness; the casual mention of a letter having been mistakenly sent will lead to devastating consequences. Almost nothing is wasted as everything advances the plot. Even the set has to observe the rules of this convention. Every chair on the set has to be occupied by one or another character at some point; a lamp must be lighted; a door must be opened; stairs have to be used. The latter convention still dominates in today's theater.

> *In the hands of a great playwright like Ibsen, exposition not only provides background for the audience, but, more important, promises what will eventually happen.*

Important to the well-made play was **exposition**, the revelation through dialogue of necessary background material, such as the past history and relationships among the characters. It remains vital to all realistic theater and has become a major problem for modern dramatists. In the hands of an inexperienced playwright attempting to sound realistic, exposition can sound silly. Families and friends in real life don't need to identify the people in a conversation. You already know that your best friend has a brother named Eddie who has been overseas in the Army. You therefore would not dream of asking, "How's your brother Eddie, who's in the Army?" Playwrights dealing with new characters, unknown to the audience, have to introduce information without sounding overly obvious, and they have to depend on dialogue alone—no narrator, no chorus, no interior monologue to help explain.

Henrik Ibsen (1828–1906) revolutionized the theater of verisimilitude by writing plays about controversial social issues (discussed more fully later in the chapter). Here we see how, influenced by the well-made play tradition, he adeptly and economically handles exposition—in this case, the nature of the relationship between husband and wife in the 1879 work *A Doll's House,* which exposes the sham that was, for Ibsen, the Victorian marriage.

HELMER: (from the study) *Is that my little lark twittering out there?*

NORA: (busy opening packages) *Yes, it is.*

HELMER: *Is that my squirrel rummaging around?*

NORA: *Yes!*

HELMER: *When did my squirrel get in?*

NORA: *Just now.* (Putting the macaroon bag in her pocket and wiping her mouth) *Do come in, Torvald, and see what I've bought.*

HELMER: *Can't be disturbed.* (After a moment he opens the door and peers in, pen in hand) *Bought, you say? All that there? Has the little spendthrift been out throwing money around again?*

NORA: *Oh. But Torvald, this year we really should let ourselves go a bit. It's the first Christmas we haven't had to economize.*

HELMER: *But you know we can't go squandering.*

NORA: *Oh yes, Torvald, we can squander a little now. Can't we? Just a tiny, wee bit. Now that you've got a big salary and are going to make piles of money.*

HELMER: *Yes, starting New Year's. But then it's a full three months till the raise comes through.*[13]

"Lark," "squirrel," "spendthrift," "Christmas," a busy husband, a change in income in three months—we've learned a lot in those few lines of exposition. This exposition also hints at the wife's revolt that is to come. In the hands of a great playwright exposition not only provides background for the audience but, more important, promises what will eventually happen. In a sense, most of the play is exposition. The past is exposed little by little and so is the shaky foundation of a Victorian marriage once thought ideal.

Modern Genres and Conventions

The neatly plotted Victorian play, set in the well-furnished living room, inevitably struck younger writers as a cliché. Modern playwrights wanted to create theater that was not limited by the back-and-forth dialogue of fourth-wall drama and the pretense that the audience was not there.

In the early twentieth century, German theater exerted universal influence with a new genre known as **expressionism**. Sets were no longer realistic, but symbolic. An American play called *The Adding Machine* (1923) had for a set a giant, early version of the calculator, on which the main character, named Mr. Zero, was eventually crucified. Stage sets were designed so as not to disguise their unreality, but often to convey a metaphor, representing society as a zoo, or a prison. Even in otherwise realistic drama, sets sometimes contained several rooms and levels all visible at the same time. Through increasingly sophisticated lighting techniques, audiences were trained to believe that, when a scene took place in a lighted part of the stage, the darkened part was not supposed to be there.

Theaters-in-the-round allowed audiences to feel closer to the actors and inspired playwrights to create works in which the visible presence of the audience was taken for granted. Even in proscenium theaters, stages could be bare of scenery to encourage audience imagination, a component of theater which many believed had been lost in the Victorian era.

In 1940, *Our Town* by Thornton Wilder (1897–1975) had a narrator walk out on an empty stage and create a small New Hampshire village in the audience's mind. Like other modern playwrights, Wilder wanted to return to the fundamental premise that audiences will accept anything as long as the rules are clearly spelled out in the beginning.

The theater introduced one innovation after another, sometimes more than one in the same play. American playwright Eugene O'Neill (1888–1953) wrote a modern tragedy called *Desire Under the Elms (1924)* in which a dramatic encounter between a son and his stepmother is taking place in an upstairs bedroom, while down below townspeople are doing a folk dance. So as not to detract from the intensity as the scene above nears its climax, the dancers are required to

> *"But most importantly of all, the theater allows both silence and physical movement to come to the fore in a way they cannot on the page. A blank space between paragraphs simply does not deliver the anxiety of a hiatus in a stage dialogue."*
>
> **—Tim Parks**

> *Masterpieces of the past are good for the past; they are not good for us. We have the right to say and even what has not been said in a way that belongs to us . . . corresponding to present modes of feeling . . .*
>
> **—Antonin Artaud**

"freeze," though the audience is asked to assume the dancing is continuing. The climax of the scene shows the stepmother murdering the child sired by the stepson. Although the "frozen" dancers are in one sense not there, the still-visible figures serve as an ironic contrast: normal life going about its business even as tragic lovers are committing an atrocity.

O'Neill also reinvented the Shakespearean soliloquy in *Strange Interlude* (1928), a six-hour-long drama that meticulously and tirelessly dissects the complex thoughts of the characters. The play combines naturalistic dialogue, a realistic set, and monologues spoken directly to the audience.

Even verse reappeared as playwrights sought ways to reach the heights achieved by the Greeks and Shakespeare. Except in a few instances, modern verse plays were ponderous and pretentious. Maxwell Anderson's *Winterset* (1935), for example, is about the son of an executed immigrant and his love for a girl who lives in a tenement; both speak improbable poetry. The playwright was more successful with historical dramas like *Elizabeth the Queen* (1931) and *Mary of Scotland* (1936), characters for whom complex poetry was more believable.

That there are many new conventions does not mean that the older ones have been cast aside. Verisimilitude in setting, costumes, and makeup continues to dominate the professional theater. But *dialogue is evermore naturalistic* as writers and actors work to approximate the way people actually do talk. There will always be an element of artificiality, however, since both drama and comedy are intensifications of reality.

Moments of silence often replace lengthy conversations. Instead of telling each other how they feel, characters are made to be as inarticulate as most of us can be. For one reason or another, there are constraints on expressing our deepest thoughts and emotions, and many of the new writers have become adept at writing dialogue that isn't saying what characters are really talking about. British playwright and winner of the Nobel Prize for literature Harold Pinter (1930–2008), is a master of pauses and silences and is frequently baffling to audiences. At his best, however, Pinter is able to turn his characters inside out. His audiences may leave the theater discussing the play and its true theme long after other audiences have forgotten what they saw.

Stories can be told in reverse rather than chronological order. More common is the *flashback*, in which scenes from the past are dramatically enacted rather than merely spoken about as in the well-made play. With the emergence of so many convention options, writers can have a set that resembles a real place but is lacking in just enough realistic detail to permit characters to move back and forth in time. Arthur Miller's *Death of a Salesman* (1949) makes brilliant use of the flashback. We first meet his sons as they are in present time, not having fulfilled the dreams their father had for them. Frequent flashbacks to earlier and happier times make the contrast painful to see, yet necessary for Miller's intent.

Some modern conventions:

- *bare stage*
- *return of the narrator*
- *continued use of verisimilitude*
- *flashback*
- *one actor in multiple parts*
- *transgender casting*

A relatively new convention is *having two or three actors playing all the parts*—perhaps the result of rising production costs and actors' salaries. Audiences are now willing to believe that Actor A is an old man in one scene and a teenager in the next or that Actor B is a man in one scene and a woman in the next.

Modern Tragedy

Except for a few plays, Greek, Elizabethan, and neoclassical tragedies focus on fatal mistakes made by protagonists of high stature. Aristotle had been quite clear about the matter. The downfall of a nonaristocratic person was just not big enough to lead the audience to an emotional catharsis. Shakespeare was interested in the inevitable fall of the noble and powerful because he viewed power as a curse, something that corrupts and leads to ruin. Ordinary people had no power and so could not be brought to disaster on a grand scale.

Beginning in the nineteenth century, a new kind of tragedy evolved, first in Europe and then in the United States. Because most of the audiences were no longer well-educated aristocrats, a different sort of tragic protagonist was necessary, along with a different philosophy about the cause of the downfall. Playwrights seeking tragic themes turned to people with ordinary occupations.

Moviestore collection Ltd/ Alamy

Klaus Kinski and Eva Mattes, *Woyzeck*, 1978

Scene from a modern production of *Woyzeck*, an 1836 tragedy of a common man victimized by class distinction and his own irrationality.

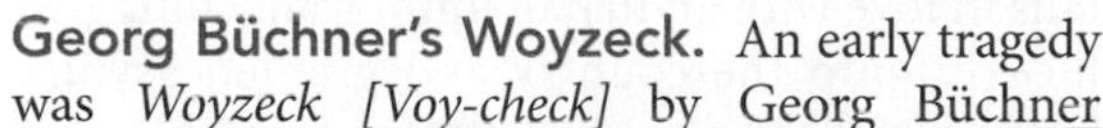

Georg Büchner's Woyzeck. An early tragedy was *Woyzeck [Voy-check]* by Georg Büchner (1813–1837), written in and left incomplete just before his death at 23. The play revolves around a lowly worker and his obsessive love for a girl who has given him a son but whom he suspects of infidelity. In a violent confrontation, he plunges a knife into her throat then later drowns when he attempts to retrieve the murder weapon. Büchner wanted to write for the theater but thrust aside all previous traditions. He pioneered in the movement known as **Expressionism**, which used nonrealistic scenery and abandoned naturalistic dialogue. Büchner was a profound pessimist who believed that ordinary human beings were victims of a class-conscious society that denied them education and forced them to live in poverty, conditions that filled them with uncontrollable rage.

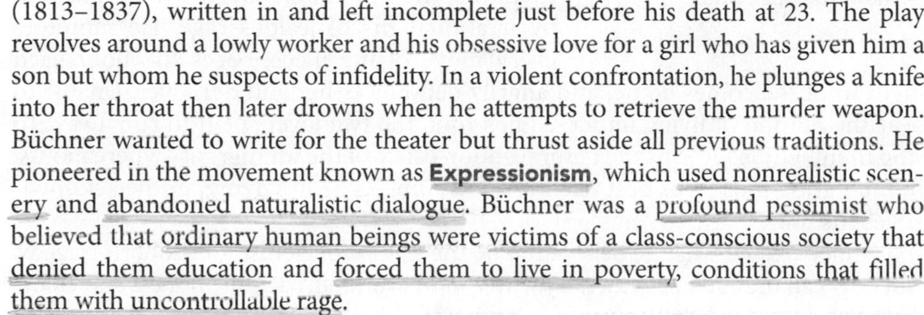

The manuscript of *Woyzeck* was lost until the early twentieth century. Long after his death, Büchner influenced whole generations of tragic dramatists who share his view that the tragic protagonist does not have a flaw of character causing a catastrophe for which he or she is morally responsible. The real tragedy, for them, is that no moral order exists to be overthrown.

Arthur Miller. A century later after Buchner, however, the American playwright Arthur Miller (1915–2005) would attempt to elevate lower-middle-class characters to the stature of tragic protagonists in a true classical tradition. Miller's intent was to replace Aristotelian requirements for tragedy with new standards appropriate for his middle-class subject matter. He gained international recognition with *Death of a Salesman* in 1949, the title of which suggests the ennoblement of a common man. Willy Loman, a "low man," not a king or prince, is a generally decent husband and father with a glaring weakness: He accepts the American Dream wholeheartedly and cannot face his own failure or that of his favorite son. Like a modern Oedipus, he insists on gilding reality with his own delusions, and when they fail, he commits suicide, mistakenly believing that his son will use the insurance money to become a financial success. While praising the work for its lyricism and dramatic intensity, many critics have insisted it falls short of tragedy because the protagonist remains deluded to the bitter end, never realizing his mistake. Playwrights of today, attempting tragedy, often have difficulty providing

> "Death of a Salesman *is a play about a man who for years has mistaken personality for merchandise. It stages the last crisis of his life, the day he realizes he no longer has a marketable product and decides to die.*"
>
> **—Otto Reinert and Peter Arnott**

Joan Marcus

Scarlett Johansson and Liev Schreiber, *A View from the Bridge*, 2010

An early moment from the 2010 revival of *A View from the Bridge*.

recognition scenes because of a common belief that people are seldom fully responsible for their actions.

In 1955, however, Miller wrote *A View from the Bridge*, with a protagonist who does not fall from a position of power but who nevertheless is aware of the mistake that has led to catastrophe. Without that awareness the audience would not be able to share the character's pain and feel the intense pity that leads to catharsis.

Eddie Carbone, a middle-aged longshoreman, is fairly happy at the beginning of the play. He and his wife have an uneventful life, free of financial worries. But when his wife's attractive young niece moves in with them, the picture changes. Eddie is attracted to her, at first in a protective, fatherly way. When the girl falls in love with an Italian immigrant smuggled illegally into the country and granted asylum by Eddie, the protagonist begins to be plagued by irrational fits of jealous rage. He monitors every move of the niece, paces the floor each night until she comes home, and angrily denounces her and her lover. Unable to bear the tension of living under Eddie's roof, the two lovers plan to run away. To stop them, Eddie informs the naturalization office of the immigrant's whereabouts. In retaliation the lover's best friend shoots him. As he lies dying, Eddie acknowledges his folly.

Miller created what he believed to be the ideal protagonist for modern tragedy. Not only can the audiences identify with a hard-working, basically honest and charitable human being but they can also understand his human weakness. If a modern tragedy is to succeed in the classical tradition, two factors must be involved. First, *we have to feel that the mistake could have been avoided.* Eddie is advised to curb his passions: gently by his understanding wife, and firmly by his lawyer, a character who serves a function similar to that of the Greek chorus counseling the protagonist. Eddie, in short, knows better. Second, *the mistake not avoided must have been caused by a believable character flaw.* Eddie is defensive about a sexual attraction which his conscious mind believes to be morally unacceptable. Consequently, he buries it deep inside, a suppression that only makes the situation worse.

The influence of Sigmund Freud is clearly evident in many modern tragedies. The father of psychoanalysis has given playwrights insight into the hidden sexual causes of anxiety and irrational behavior. Unsatisfied lust and unshakable feelings of guilt over forbidden sexual encounters are believable ways to explain character actions and motivations. Eddie's anger toward the young immigrant might also have been a sign of buried homosexual curiosity. Ultimately, then, the play is the tragedy of a decent man who refuses to acknowledge things about himself that he does not like and therefore denies.

Some critics have complained that both the wife and the lawyer go too far in attributing nobility of character to Eddie after his death, as though the author were overly intent on persuading the audience that he has indeed written a tragedy. Others have found the tributes moving and poetic, and the means by which Miller elevated the story to be on the level of classical drama.

Melodrama and Tragedy: A Contrast

Melodrama is often considered tragedy because it usually has scenes of suffering or death. In its basic form, it was highly popular with nineteenth-century theater audiences and early twentieth-century filmgoers. It is still very much with us, though in slicker modes.

In tragedy the protagonist, as noted by Aristotle, is mainly virtuous but not totally innocent; in nineteenth-century **melodrama**, the hero or heroine *is* innocent and is beset by problems from external forces, never from an inner flaw which leads to destruction. Melodrama made no huge demands on the mind, and, though it could be highly suspenseful, there was always the knowledge that everything would turn out as it should. Aspects of the genre are still with us, mainly in film or on television.

If he had lived into the early twentieth century and seen popular films like *The Mysteries of Mary* and *Orphans of the Storm,* Aristotle would have said these were not tragic. Tragedy is not about a helpless heroine tied to a railroad track by a sinister villain or poor people seeking shelter from the elements. The characters were easily separated into the totally good and the totally bad. When the villain was, inevitably and predictably, punished, the audience cheered because "it served him right." Traditional melodrama was not (and still isn't) big on examining the motives of a character. The stereotypical nineteenth-century villain who threatened the virtue of a pure heroine was simply bad because, well, that's what he was. When the heroine was rescued by the equally pure hero, again there was no troubling ambiguity. Melodrama is the triumph of the righteous over the once powerful but finally defeated bad guys. It can also be lots of fun: a night out, popcorn, and going home untroubled by any new ideas.

One element of melodrama is a holdover from the Greeks: the **deus ex machina**—literally, the **god from a machine**. Not all the classical playwrights created characters like Oedipus heading for an unavoidable doom because of a tragic flaw. Sometimes they wanted to provide a happier ending, so they invented the device of having an actor, playing a god, come down from the stage in a cart attached to a pulley, a god who would straighten everything out. The phrase *deus ex machina* is now used to describe any plot contrivance that violates the probabilities of human behavior and is introduced by the author for an expedient but implausible resolution: for example, a convenient bolt of lightning to kill the evil-doer.

In melodrama . . . characterizations are thin, and the search for overarching meaning is unrewarding.

Audiences became so accustomed to the suspenseful thriller formula that they stopped caring whether the artificial separation of people into good and bad violated their sense of what was real. The melodrama lives on as a source of pure entertainment, enjoyed by those who want to escape from the storm and stress of reality.

Yet Aristotle knew thousands of years ago that the cathartic effect of watching a profound tragedy was the best way to deal with storm and stress. Theater-goers who want to be profoundly moved still love the theater of true tragedy.

Comedy in Theater History

At the opposite end of the theatrical spectrum from tragedy is **comedy**, which finds little audience identification with the protagonists, for otherwise how could we laugh at their foolishness? *We* are not foolish, *they* are. We must remain separate from them in order to enjoy the spectacle of their troubles, which are comparatively trivial and temporary.

> "The world is a comedy to those who think, a tragedy to those who feel."
>
> —Horace Walpole

In addition to presenting three tragedies in a single afternoon, the Greeks invented the comic afterpiece, a fourth play designed to send the audience home in a happier state of mind. Though the plays contained mythical elements like the costumes of the Chorus, the stories were not based on myth but made fun of greed and corruption in Athenian society. After a time they became so popular that audiences wanted to go to the theater only to laugh. Thus was born the still thriving institution of comic drama.

The only surviving sentence from Aristotle's essay on comedy is this: "*Tragedy is life seen close at hand; comedy is life seen from a distance.*" It remains as valid as ever. Many disasters in *slapstick* comedy—someone falling through an open manhole; an arrogant man who has insulted the hero turning and suddenly tumbling down a flight of stairs—could turn dark if we were allowed to see the characters suffer; but we do not, and so we are able to enjoy ourselves at their expense. Our own lives don't seem so bad anymore.

Comedy is often about situations in which trivial mistakes lead to hilarious consequences. A secret must be concealed at all costs. A couple is really married but their parents don't know; or there's a mix-up in identities. Unknown to him, a man's identical twin is in town but the other twin's fiancée thinks she is being betrayed when she sees her supposed lover in the arms of another woman.

A chronic liar makes a vow that he will tell nothing but the truth for a full week and, of course, loses his friends who cannot bear his honesty. A really neat man becomes the roommate of a slob, and they fight unrelentingly. The people a family is trying to impress arrive for dinner on the wrong night, when the household is in utter chaos.

Comedy has evolved into many forms enduring through the ages, and more than one kind of comedy can exist in the same play. Historical periods examined in this section parallel the periods described in the previous section. Therefore we begin with comedy as in the Greek classical theater.

Satire

> "Experience is the name everyone gives to their mistakes."
>
> —Oscar Wilde

The comic afterpiece required of the Athenian playwrights was known as the *satyr* play because it was performed by actors in costumes identifying them as the mythical creatures who were half man and half goat. The plays made fun of the tragedies the audience had just seen as well as events and personalities in society the playwrights considered ridiculous. **Satire** has come to mean a species of comedy that ridicules such things as corruption in government, inequality, war as a solution to human problems, injustice, and hypocrisy. The satirist of the theater is both a comic writer, interested in getting audiences to laugh, and a reformer, dedicated to the betterment of society. Serious criticism of society can be communicated in other ways, such as newspaper editorials or sermons, but people prefer to laugh, and the satirist obliges—writing with a stiletto.

The Greek playwright Aristophanes (445–385 B.C.E.) used the stage both for comedy and as a plea for the improvement of the human condition. One of his enduring works is *Lysistrata*, with its perennially viable antiwar message and a basic situation that never fails to delight its audience.

During the unpopular war between Athens and Sparta, which lasted from 431 to 404 B.C.E., the women of both sides, tired of the senseless conflict and foolish loss of life, take matters into their own hands by uniting and establishing an all-female outpost on the Acropolis, the hill that dominates Athens. Not only are men barred from entering but the women under the leadership of the title character go on strike. There will be no lovemaking for the men until hostilities cease.

In addition to the foolishness of war, the play satirizes the frailties of human nature, in that the lovelorn men and women in both camps have difficulty living up to the terms of the oath. The play is both comical and serious. One scene has a soldier disguising himself as a woman to be near his beloved. Another depicts a frustrated husband attempting to embrace his wife, who appears willing but keeps delaying until finally she retreats to the fortress on the Acropolis where she and the other women are in charge. Then she tells him that they can get together once the war is over. An antiwar play in the midst of war? For the Athenians it was no problem. Although some political leaders argued it was not the right time or place for such an unpatriotic attitude, most believed that the ability to express a point of view was more important than automatic obedience.

One of Aristophanes's satiric targets was Socrates, the first major Greek philosopher, in a play called *The Clouds*. The dramatist portrays him as a foolish old man whose feet are never on the ground and who insists, for example, that rain is the result of natural forces rather than being sent by the Olympian gods. Since the prevailing view favored gods over meteorology, Socrates was depicted as an idiotic charlatan running a school called The Thinkery, which led pupils astray with ideas about natural causes and teaching them to debate so well they could win arguments against their own fathers. When the real-life Socrates was on trial for, among other things, corrupting the youth of Athens, it is possible that the unflattering characterization by Aristophanes may have influenced the votes of more than one juror who had seen the play. Considering his conviction and eventual execution, Socrates could have seen that the satire by Aristophanes was not exclusively a laughing matter.

Satiric plays continue to be written, but their appeal is usually limited to an appreciative audience that already agrees with the author. A prospective producer concerned about box-office receipts is wary of writers who "preach to the choir." Politics and the foibles of politicians offer convenient targets of ridicule. But advocates for the targets may fail to find any humor in the work.

Shakespeare's Comedy of Character

Aristotle listed *character* as second in importance only to plot. It is not clear, however, that he and the Greek audience in general thought of *character* as we do today. He may have meant simply the actor playing a certain role, defined by certain traits. Thus Oedipus, for example, is a king, a man of power, arrogant about his power, and unyielding in his convictions.

Today's writers have been strongly influenced by psychology, a pursuit unknown as such in Aristotle's day. A contemporary Oedipus might be shown as paranoid and defensive. His inner turmoil might be at least as important as the details of the story. In contrast, Euripides is probably the Greek tragic dramatist most accessible to modern audiences. In *Medea* he concentrates on the inner passions of his central character and thus develops something much closer in spirit to the modern concept of character as a component of theater.

Thus we can say there is a big difference between character as a figure in a play and character as a combination of traits we remember about a person, traits that make that person unique. All plays have characters of the first kind; not all plays have the second. Though the scientific study of the human mind that we call psychology was nonexistent in Shakespeare's time, the playwright nonetheless created more memorable characters than any writer before or since. Indeed, many of his works continue to hold the stage less for plot than for memorable characters, many of whom are the standout figures in his comedies.

"Comedy is the clash of character. Eliminate character from comedy, and you get farce."

—William Butler Yeats

One such character is Sir John Falstaff, whose comic portrait enlivens the history plays *Henry IV, Parts I and II*. A drunkard, a liar, and a con man, Falstaff's outrageous disregard for propriety makes Prince Hal—soon to become King Henry V—adore the company of this man who urges him to sow his wild oats as long as possible. Shakespeare gave Falstaff so many identifiable human weaknesses that his audience must have adored him as much as the prince, laughing *with*, not *at* him. Falstaff is not only a rogue but also the great philosopher of fun and corruption—the perfect Dionysian. He scandalously praises the sins of excess most of us commit but hate ourselves for. Nothing is worth repenting over, as far as he is concerned. Nothing is to be taken too seriously in this all-too-brief existence.

Falstaff not only consumes too much food and drink without concern for the morning after, he encourages the prince to do the same. Nor is he honest or patriotic. Given the assignment to buy uniforms for a group of recruits, he spends the allotment on himself. On the battlefield, when an enemy soldier expects to have hand-to-hand combat, Falstaff puts away his sword rather than fight and delivers a famous speech on the dubious value of honor. He observes that it "hath no skill in surgery" and cannot be felt or heard by those living or dead. He may be dishonest in misappropriating public funds meant for uniforms, but he is certainly honest about his own disinclination to be a wartime casualty.

He is poignant, too, in his misunderstanding of what he thought was the prince's friendship for him. Pretending to be dead, Falstaff hears the prince deliver a "eulogy" by making unflattering comments about his size. Even worse, when the prince finally does become king, Falstaff tries to benefit from their old friendship, only to be totally rejected with these words:

The debate goes on. Was Falstaff Prince Hal's rejected father substitute or a dishonored mentor? In great drama, there is never a final answer.

I know thee not, old man; fall to thy prayers;
How ill white hairs become a fool and jester!
So surfeit-swell'd, so old and so profane;
But, being awaked, I do despise my dream.[14]

AP Photo

Orson Welles, *Chimes at Midnight*, 1965
Orson Welles as Falstaff, beloved philosopher of fun and excess.

Do we then side with the new king and dismiss Falstaff? Literary scholar Harold Bloom, who has spent his life writing about and teaching Shakespeare, reports that one of his students denounced Falstaff by claiming that "the transformation of Prince Hal into King Henry V was exemplary... that Hal represented rule and that Falstaff was a lord of misrule, and I could not persuade her that Falstaff transcended her categories, as he transcends virtually all our categories of human sin and error."[15]

Professor Bloom's admiration for Falstaff was so great that he briefly deserted the classroom to play the role in a stage production. He sees Falstaff as being complex, not merely a coward or a jester. In his encounter with the king, he is courageous, aware that "Hal's ambivalence has resolved itself into a murderous negativity . . . Time annihilates other Shakespearean protagonists, but not Falstaff . . . "[16]

In this analysis, Bloom is at odds with his student and with other critics who have argued endlessly about the relationship between Falstaff and the prince. Was he a rejected father substitute or a dishonored mentor, as some have claimed? The critical fights continue, just as they have about countless other Shakespearean characters. To those who argue that "it's just a play" and wonder how there can be so much dispute about characters who never lived, theater lovers know: Shakespeare's characters did—and do—live.

One way of allowing the characters to "live" is by use of the **subtext**, through which characters reveal what is going on in their minds by speaking words that clearly mask their true feelings, or eloquently by silence. In *Twelfth Night* (1601), a comedy written when Shakespeare was reaching the summit of his genius, a young woman named Viola, shipwrecked and cast upon a foreign land, disguises herself as a boy for safety. Hired as a page by a handsome duke, she falls madly in love with her master but cannot tell him directly: instead she resorts to subtext as she describes the unrequited love of her "sister."

> *Love sought is good, but given unsought is better.*
>
> —**William Shakespeare**

She never told her love,
But let concealment, like a worm i' the bud,
Feed on her damask cheek: she pined in thought,
And with a green and yellow melancholy
She sat like patience on a monument,
Smiling at grief. Was this not love indeed?[17]

By the end of the play, Viola has revealed her true identity, complications have been sorted out, and couples who love each other embrace as the audience applauds. But through the use of verse and the subtext, Shakespeare presents not only an intricate situation but character as well. He may also be credited with having given the theater world its first clear example of subtext.

Farce

Farce is a genre of comedy that draws laughter from outrageous physical actions and improbably chaotic situations. Its characters are two-dimensional stereotypes easily described in a word or two. They are superficial, like dolls or animals in a cartoon. Many are derived from the **commedia dell'arte**, an Italian pantomime street theater originating in the middle of the sixteenth century. Its plays were usually improvised from bare plot outlines developed by the actors, each of whom was assigned to a certain character, often for life. Some of the comic types—or stock characters—were so universal they are still around (for example, the doddering old man who really believes a beautiful young girl loves *him*, not his money). Each age adds its own types: characters who are foolish because they do not fit the definition of a normal, rational human being.

> *Frivolity is the species' refusal to suffer.*
>
> —**John Lahr**

In the *commedia*, a central theme usually concerned the interaction of two young lovers trying to get together but thwarted by a miserly father, or by another characteristic type, the pretentious boor who used unnecessarily long words and thought himself a suitable mate for the girl, only to have scheming servants aid the lovers. Actors wore costumes and masks that immediately identified the type portrayed. Audiences loved the repetition of familiar stories with minor variations and the pratfalls and physical abuse visited upon the fools, who were, after all, so silly that they could be safely laughed out of existence.

> *If it were not for the company of fools, a witty man would often be greatly at a loss.*
>
> —**François de la Rochefoucauld**

Here is a partial list of fools inspired by the *commedia*; they have peopled the farcical stage for centuries:

the rich but stingy old man
the old man who tries to marry a beautiful young girl
the nerd
the bragging coward
the bigot
the clumsy, unpolished social climber
the brat
the completely self-absorbed actor (or beauty queen)
the drunken, irresponsible husband
his (understandably) nagging wife
the innocent "hick" or "rube"

We can add to the list any number of modern examples, including people who are excessively concerned with their health and will speak of nothing else; jocks; airheads—there's almost no end to it, is there?

Molière. The *commedia* exerted strong influence on the work of the major neoclassical comic dramatist, Molière, whose real name was Jean-Baptiste Poquelin. Monsieur Jourdain, the protagonist of one of his greatest comedies, *The Would-Be Gentleman,* is rich but still without the rank or social skills that would make him an acceptable guest at the court of King Louis XIV. His clumsy efforts to look like a titled gentleman, to learn fencing and the minuet, provided a hilarious target of ridicule for aristocratic audiences. When he rejects as a prospective son-in-law the man his daughter loves, he is tricked into believing that the disguised suitor has a title and so delightedly allows the wedding to take place. As the curtain falls, everyone onstage and in the audience is aware of the trick played on Jourdain, except the foolish social climber himself.

Courtesy KML Gallery of Fine Art

Maurice Leloir and Géry-Bichard, *Tartuffe* Act III, Scene II, 1669

Pretending to be deeply shocked, Tartuffe gives the maid a handkerchief so that she may dress more modestly.

In farce, there is no such thing as a recognition scene. Imagine if, before the curtain fell, the foolish M. Jourdain had realized he had been tricked, had realized he was not a titled lord, and his daughter had just married a man of her own class. Audiences might have begun to feel sorry for the duped Jourdain, and the laughter would have stopped.

Molière was a neoclassic playwright, contemporary of the tragedian Racine, mentioned earlier. His audiences would have included well-educated aristocrats, eager to laugh at the social climbers M. Jourdain as well as the title character of *Tartuffe,* his play about religious hypocrisy, controversial at the time in strongly Catholic France. In the scene pictured to the left, Tartuffe, pretending to be a dedicated evangelist so that he may bilk his host, Orgon, out of thousands, is scolding the maid for showing too much cleavage. He hands her a handkerchief to cover herself. Of course, his eyes help themselves to what is being revealed by the cleavage.

Moliere wrote in the neoclassic style of using rhymed couplets. Here Cleante, Orgon's brother-in-law, who serves as the voice of reason in the play, tries to communicate his doubts about Tartuffe's authenticity.

Brother, I don't pretend to be a sage,
Nor have I all the wisdom of the age.
There's just one insight I would dare to claim
I know that true and false are not the same;
And just as there is nothing I more revere
Than a soul whose faith is steadfast and sincere,
Nothing that I more cherish and admire
Than honest zeal and true religious fire
So there is nothing that I find more base
Than specious piety's dishonest face—
Whose impious mummeries and hollow shows
Exploit our love of heaven and make a jest
Of all that men think holiest and best.[18]

At about the time Molière's plays were appearing in France, the English stage entered a period labeled the Restoration, for it was in 1661 that monarchy was restored to the government after twenty years of domination by austere Puritans, who had dubbed theaters palaces of sin and closed them. Theaters, dubbed palaces of sin, were closed. With the ascension of entertainment-loving Charles II, theaters were reopened for the pleasure of a more permissive society.

Wycherley. A British minister turned playwright, William Wycherley (1640–1716), was allegedly shocked by the new freedom of the stage and wrote a farce comedy to make fun of it. The play, *The Country Wife,* was ironically a big hit, largely because it was itself as daring as the work it purported to condemn.

The Country Wife contains a comic technique that has endured through the centuries, *double entendre,* or "double meaning," whereby characters appear to be innocently talking of one thing, while audiences can infer less innocent goings-on from what they say.

One of the most famous examples of the technique is the china scene in which virtually all of the dialogue can be taken two ways, one of them so socially offensive that the play was banned in many places right up to the middle of the twentieth century!

The setting is the apartment of a scoundrel named Horner, a character with no moral scruples whatever but whose charm and cleverness delight audiences anyway. He is pretending to have suffered an accident that makes him unable to have sex and who therefore is considered safe by gullible husbands. The pretense allows the wives to visit Horner without causing gossip. A group of these ladies have been given permission by their husbands to go shopping with Horner, who has been entertaining them one by one in his boudoir, where he claims to have a rare and delicate collection of fine china. In this scene, Horner is entertaining Lady Fidget, while Mrs. Squeamish listens jealously as she hears Lady Fidget marveling at the china. When they reemerge, Lady Fidget is holding a china teacup and thanking Horner for the gift.

Mrs. Squeamish comes forward, urging Horner to allow her to go with him into the room: "O Lord," she says, "I'll have some china too. Good Mr. Horner, don't think to give other people china and me none; come in with me too." He refuses, saying, "Upon my honor, I have none left now . . . This lady had the last there." Lady Fidget agrees: "Yes indeed, madam, to my certain knowledge he has no more left."

When Mrs. Squeamish suggests that he may "have some you could not find," Lady Fidget retorts, "What; d ye think if he had any left, I would not have had it too? For we women of quality never think we have china enough."

Husbands betrayed by their lusty wives were called cuckolds and treated as figures of fun. The period introduced any number of cuckolds who took their place in the growing repertoire of comic types. Usually the cuckold was the subject of derision, whereas Horner and other characters like him were cheered. London upper-class audiences in the seventeenth century were quite sexually liberated. Because many women were sold into financially advantageous marriages with older, unromantic husbands, audiences could sympathize with Horner's female companions and the infidelities that they believed overbearing and stupid husbands deserved. (The clergy and some conservative audience members were less pleased, however, and eventually London plays had to pass the scrutiny of a censor.)

Oscar Wilde. Victorian comic playwrights, like their noncomic counterparts, often dealt with real issues as well, and they also did so within the convention of verisimilitude; but often the realism was one of scenery and costumes, not speech. The dialogue of Oscar Wilde (1854–1900), so witty and elegant, is rarely found except on the stage. In Wilde's plays, dialogue is an idealized version of how civilized people *should* talk. It is far from being a transcript of everyday speech, and when a play is as consistently witty as *The Importance of Being Earnest*, we are grateful. We can hear plenty of familiar speech *outside* the theater.

Wilde's play, which has entertained audiences ever since it was written in 1895, has as its premise a familiar story: the effort of a suitor to win the approval of his girlfriend's mother. In the play the young man is living a double life, being called Jack Worthing when he lives at his country estate and Ernest Worthing when he goes to London to court the young lady, Miss Gwendolen Fairfax. What stands in the way of the mother's approval is Mr. Worthing's inability to prove who his parents were. As a baby he had been "found" in a checked handbag at a London train station.

The story revolves around his identity and the need to meet the requirements of Gwendolen's mother, the formidable Lady Bracknell. When Jack as Ernest tells her about his bizarre origin, she answers curtly that neither she nor her husband would "dream of allowing our only daughter . . . to marry into a cloakroom and form an alliance with a parcel." In both its wit and its farcical elements, *The Importance of Being Earnest* is one of the funniest plays ever written in English.

In one of the many famous scenes, Gwendolen has discovered that Jack is not actually named Ernest, her main reason for having promised to marry him eventually, and has broken off their engagement. Jack's friend Algernon, who has just been rejected by his own fiancée, is helping himself to the muffins left on the tea table.

JACK: *How you can sit there calmly eating muffins when we are in this horrible trouble I can't make out. You seem to be perfectly heartless.*

ALGERNON: *Well, I can't eat muffins in an agitated manner. The butter would probably get on my cuffs. One should always eat muffins quite calmly. It is the only way to eat them.*

JACK: *I say it's perfectly heartless your eating muffins at all under the circumstances.*

ALGERNON: *When I am in trouble, eating is the only thing that consoles me... At the present moment I am eating muffins because I am unhappy. Besides, I am particularly fond of muffins.*

Wilde chose comedy. Another playwright might have chosen to deal with the "horrible trouble" of the situation and allowed his characters to go on and on about what to do about it. Other characters could have been introduced to give their own opinions. The rejected suitors might have been given sentimental speeches. Instead, there are muffins. Because it is a comedy, everything turns out all right in a series of improbable coincidences and the curtain falls on the lovers happily embracing.

The play is farce, enhanced by wit that continues to cause audiences to howl with laughter, even at Lady Bracknell's insensitive remark on hearing about Mr. Worthing's background: "To lose one parent may be considered a misfortune. To lose both looks like carelessness."

Contemporary Anti-Middle-Class Comedy

Characters who would resist the expectations of middle-class life abound in many twentieth-century plays. In *You Can't Take It with You* by George S. Kaufman and Moss Hart (1936), a family of extraordinarily unconventional characters live happily together. The daughter dances ballet badly, the grandfather makes illegal fireworks, and the mother is writing a play that will never be finished because she doesn't know how to get her characters out of a monastery. Except for one rational daughter who goes to work, the rest of the family does everything except hold down a nine-to-five job. Conflict arises when the one employed family member falls in love with the son of a banker. They would like to marry, so decide to get their families together for dinner. In order to pretend respectability, the hosts decide to conceal their idiosyncrasies. There is a mix-up about the date and the banker and his wife arrive on the wrong evening, during which the grandfather's fireworks explode in the cellar and everyone is arrested. Their encounter with another side of life (a very Dionysian side) makes them more tolerant.

The clash between upright middle-class Apollonianism and Dionysian lack of organization is brilliantly chronicled in the Tony Award–winning *The Odd Couple* (1965) by Neil Simon. In this case, a carefree and disorderly sportswriter named Oscar Madison allows his friend, an overly neat Felix Unger, to move in with him. The roommates have very different ideas about how the apartment should be maintained and clash in hilarious ways, including one scene in which Oscar, frustrated to the breaking point by Felix's unyielding neatness, dumps a whole plate of linguine on his head. While most audience members would probably not want Oscar as a houseguest, he is clearly the sympathetic focal point of a work that proved to be a hugely popular movie, as well as a long-running television series, proving, if nothing else, that an audience that observes the rules of the workplace as well as the family circle likes its entertainment a bit on the frivolous side. *The Odd Couple* continues to be popular.

Both the play and the film are important dramatic history. Felix and Oscar have become archetypal names for their respective characteristics. If someone says to you, "You're a regular Felix Unger," you need to take a good hard look at yourself.

Moviestore collection Ltd/Alamy

Walter Matthau and Jack Lemmon, *The Odd Couple*, 1968

Walter Matthau as Oscar Madison and Jack Lemmon as Felix Unger in a scene from the movie *The Odd Couple*.

Contemporary Serious Comedy

In *The Country Wife*, the cuckolded husbands are ridiculed, but all the characters, including the cuckolds, are treated much more sympathetically

> *"Two things people throughout history have had in common are hatred and humor. I am proud that, like Mark Twain, I have been able to use humor to lessen people's hatred."*
>
> **—Richard Pryor**

than in *The Real Thing* (1982) by Tom Stoppard, a serious comedy which is anything but farce. The husband in the play suspects that his wife has been unfaithful, but he is not like the husbands in *The Country Wife,* who are such absurd fools that they deserve our laughter. Nor is the wife a flirtatious, empty-headed deceiver who pretends innocence and is finally denounced. In Stoppard's play, the husband talks rationally about why she might be attracted to someone else—in this case a political activist just out of prison who has written a bad play about his cause.

Stoppard is a philosopher as well as a dramatist. Most of his plays, even the comedies, deal with serious issues. Frothy in some spots, *The Real Thing* never lets you forget that you are watching characters with depth talk brilliantly. In one scene, the betrayed husband tells his wife that her real sin is loving a bad writer.

> *I don't think writers are important, but words are. They deserve respect. If you get the right word in the right order, you can nudge the world a little, or make a poem children will speak for you when you're dead.*[19]

"Serious" comedy may sound like a contradiction in terms, but comic dramatists are very often not only deep thinkers but wry observers of human folly as well. They vent their distress through dialogue that is sometimes witty, but sometimes deeply felt. All comedy, even farce, tells us we must be flexible, we must adapt to the changes life brings our way. To stay rigidly fixed in one mindset is to go against nature and therefore to become laughable, as well as to be a continuing social menace. Unlike tragedy, comedy urges us to keep laughing, have perspective, and allow happiness to happen without rigid rules.

Parody

Stoppard is also an inspired parodist. **Parody** makes fun of a particular work or genre—a film, a song, a painting, or a commercial—a work the author believes has been unjustifiably successful. The technique of parody is that it pretends to be the work it is ridiculing, except that the basic elements of the original are laughably exaggerated so that the audience (or reader) will see the absurdity of taking it seriously.

The Real Inspector Hound (1968) makes fun of the melodramatic thriller popular since the nineteenth century—and Stoppard fears is still rather too popular. His play has the familiar plot of multiple murders in a remote English country house, complete with storms raging outside, a cast of characters, all of whom look suspicious, and plot entanglements impossible to understand.

What sets this work apart from the usual parody, however, is that Stoppard uses the tired old format to say something serious about the nature of reality. Two critics, sitting in a box and loudly denouncing the play, shatter the fourth-wall convention by climbing onto the stage when it appears the cast has deserted it. One critic answers the incessantly ringing telephone and thus becomes a character involved in the sinister proceedings. Soon he too disappears, and the other critic is murdered. Meanwhile, two of the characters, who have been previously killed, take their seats in the box and become the critics. Stoppard thus investigates the often nonexistent difference between illusion and reality.

Parody tends to be of only temporary interest, unless the target continues to be relevant. As long as people flock to creaky melodramas, *The Real Inspector Hound* will be funny. But more likely its serious theme of illusion versus reality will keep it alive. When watching a parody, we need to ask ourselves whether it offers something besides passing entertainment.

Theater of Ideas

Related to satire in terms of dealing with social issues but generally presented in the convention of verisimilitude, *theater of ideas* came into prominence in the late Victorian period in the work of two playwrights who would use the stage to raise the consciousness of their audience. One was Henrik Ibsen of Norway, whose opening scene in *A Doll's House* was mentioned earlier as an example of adroit handling of exposition; the other was his Irish-born champion, George Bernard Shaw (1856–1950).

> *One should never put on one's best trousers to go out to battle for freedom and truth.*
>
> **—Henrik Ibsen**

Ibsen

At first this journalist-turned-playwright scandalized his staid Norwegian audiences with frank exposés of hypocrisy in all the major institutions of his time: marriage, business, government, the clergy, education. Although *A Doll's House* is now credited with having changed the whole course of Western theater, at the time of writing it was considered shocking, even obscene. One critic commented: "No self-respecting man would take his wife to see this play."

Sara Krulwich/The New York Times/Redux Pictures

Janet McTeer and Owen Teale, *A Doll's House*, 1997

Janet McTeer as Nora, a woman who has just discovered that her marriage is built on lies, in a 1997 revival of Ibsen's *A Doll's House*.

The husband and wife of *A Doll's House* are Torvald, a recently promoted bank manager, and Nora, the "doll" of the title. The secret in Nora's past is that she has forged her father's name on a promissory note in order to borrow money to take her sick husband to a warmer climate and thus save his life. The man who holds the promissory note is an employee in her husband's bank. He has threatened to make her crime public if she does not persuade her husband to give him a promotion.

So far this man fills the role of the villain in melodramas already familiar to audiences. The stereotypical villain often wore a black cape and twirled his mustache as he uttered threats to the helpless heroine, whom he called "my proud beauty." (In *Bullwinkle,* a television cartoon series that made fun of just about everything, the names identify the villain as Snively Whiplash and the hero who rescues the girl as Dudley DoRight.)

Ibsen is more subtle. His villain is a complex character with a need for love and acceptance. Ignoring efforts to intervene, Torvald has fired the man, an action that leads to a letter exposing her crime. Rather than rush to Nora's defense or take the blame himself (as she had assumed he would), Torvald denounces her, saying she is no longer a fit mother to their three children. However, she may continue to live in the house, giving the appearance of respectability.

Meanwhile, the blackmailer has found a woman willing to marry and nurture him. His spirits uplifted, he returns the promissory note to Nora's angry spouse. In a moment that stirred up a huge controversy, Torvald cries joyfully, "Nora, I'm saved!" There is a profound silence, and then Nora asks quietly, "And what about me?" Eager to return the marriage to its former state, the husband tries to explain the rules of society: "No man sacrifices his honor for the one he loves." Nora's comeback shocked Ibsen's audience and remains one of the stirring lines in modern theater: "Millions of women have done so."

She has seen the truth, has seen the hypocrisy underlying their codified society, and now refuses to go back to where they were. Instead, she announces that she no longer consents to live a lie. Ignoring his protestations and promises to change the way he treats her, the newly liberated Nora quietly but resolutely informs him that she must first discover who she really is. She packs her bags, returns the wedding ring, and leaves, slamming the door behind her.

The slamming of that door is one of the most significant sounds in the history of Western theater. It caused a scandal so great that guests at dinner parties in respectable society were requested not to mention it. An actress playing Nora in Germany refused to play the final scene as written, so Ibsen wrote an alternate ending in which Nora realizes a mother cannot abandon her children.

A critic denounced Ghosts *as "an open garbage can."*

Encouraged by critical acclaim in more open societies, Ibsen returned to work, more resolved than ever to rip the mask from social respectability. In *Ghosts* (1885), he again horrified local audiences with a play that had venereal disease as a central issue, supported the idea of free love in preference to a marriage built on lies, and raised the question of whether euthanasia could be a valid solution to a hopeless medical condition. The "ghosts" of the title are secrets from the past which the respectable heroine has desperately sought to hide but which come back to haunt her in yet another now famous final scene when the curtain falls as she is facing the awful choice of whether to kill her son or allow him to live on in an unresponsive state. One of the critics who had denounced *A Doll's House* now called *Ghosts* "an open garbage can." While the critic's name is mercifully forgotten, Ibsen's powerful ideas have survived the hostility.

George Bernard Shaw

Although attacked on both sides of the Atlantic wherever theater audiences were comprised mainly of genteel middle and upper classes fighting to hold onto moral absolutes they feared were slowly vanishing, Ibsen gained much stature with the publication of Shaw's *The Quintessence of Ibsenism*, which recognized in Ibsen a kindred spirit who also wanted to use the theater as an agent for significant social change. Shaw's own plays were aimed at shaking audiences loose from dangerous preconceived ideas, but for the most part his vehicle was comedy.

In *Pygmalion* (1912), he attacked the rigidity of the class system in Britain with an amusing story about the transformation of a Cockney flower seller into a well-dressed, well-spoken lady accepted by the very highest levels of British society. On the surface it is a Cinderella story: the poor grubby lass who can't speak English "properly" is eventually passed off as a highborn lady because she speaks so well. Underneath the surface, however, the play criticizes the sins committed by the British to preserve respectability at all costs. If Eliza Doolittle, it asks, can rise above her inherited lowly place in society by showing evidence of education, why are so many denied that privilege?

"Do not do unto others as you would that they should do to you. Their tastes may not be the same."

—George Bernard Shaw

Eliza's father, a ne'er-do-well with a love of alcohol and a phobia against gainful employment, suddenly comes into money. Yet he is shrewd enough to know that if money also determines a person's social standing, it says nothing about the moral principles of the one who possesses it. He also knows that belonging to a higher class incurs certain unpleasant obligations, such as the need to be respectably married, which would deprive him of the pleasures that were his before anyone took notice of his existence. In *My Fair Lady* (1956), the Alan Jay Lerner–Frederick Loewe musical version of the play, Doolittle has two now classic songs: "With a Little Bit of Luck," a celebration of life without responsibility for upholding middle-class standards, and "Get Me to the Church on Time," in which he pleads for one more night on the town with his cronies before settling into a dull life of respectability.

Neither Shaw nor Ibsen belabored one issue from play to play, nor did they have one speech per play which would have sent a too explicit message to the audience. Plays designed as propaganda do that. Propaganda lacks subtlety and is less interested in character than in producing a desired action: to vote, to protest, to revolt. The playwright as propagandist belongs only nominally to the theater of ideas, but at its most intense, the *agit-prop* (agitation propaganda) play can stir an audience to an emotional frenzy, as happened at the final curtain of Clifford Odets's *Waiting for Lefty* (1935), a play about the plight of underpaid cab drivers in New York. On opening night, as the actors made the crucial decision "Strike!", the audience rose to its feet and echoed the call. Overcome with emotion, they rushed to the stage to embrace the actors.

In the more subtle Theater of Ideas, playwrights tend to present more than one side of an argument. Nora's final speech before slamming the door may be—and has been—taken as a rallying cry for feminism, but does Ibsen really recommend abandoning marriage and children as the only possible solution? Some scholars who have studied the play carefully maintain that it also can be presented as the tragedy of other human beings trapped in a social system that blinds him to the truth.

Naturalism

During the latter half of the nineteenth century, while Ibsen, Shaw, and their followers were forcing audiences to confront social problems once swept under the rug, other writers were experimenting with a new genre called **naturalism**. As its name implies, theatrical naturalism was an attempt to show life as it really was—without artificial-sounding stage dialogue or the well-made play structure. Nor were (are) these plays concerned with conveying ideas or effecting changes in society. Their premise: this is life, this is human nature, it's all there is.

Chekhov

The pioneer in naturalistic theater was a Russian playwright and former physician, Anton Chekhov (1860–1904), who abandoned the play of one central figure in favor of the play which deals with a group of persons, their actions, and interactions. Almost every character in a Chekhov drama is at one point or another an object of sympathetic understanding. The plays are plotless in the usual sense of the word, without carefully crafted exposition or a relentless drive toward a climax. They reflect a dedicated physician's insights from having observed and listened to many patients, and his unwillingness to make moral judgments.

> *"In the creative process there is the father, the author of the play; the mother, the actor pregnant with the part; and the child, the role to be born."*
>
> **—Konstantin Stanislavsky**

Chekhov's works were discovered in the first decade of the twentieth century and staged by Konstantin Stanislavsky at the Moscow Arts Theatre. The director noted that, since the plays lacked heroes and villains, there was no question of endorsing this character's behavior or condemning another's. It was really a matter of trying to understand why things happened. The author had spelled nothing out for the director. He seemed to have created certain individuals, set them in motion in certain situations, and allowed them to proceed according to mysterious laws of their own being. In order to present this new form of theater, Stanislavsky had to reinvent the art of acting, and his technique still pervades theater today.

Stanislavsky realized that an in-depth understanding of people in real life was the starting point. One had to know that when people did anything obvious reasons were not always accurate. Real people seldom behaved as one would expect, because all too often people were observed not as they were but in terms of preconceived notions. He came to see that Chekhov was being true to his own observations and knowledge of human nature, rather than to time-honored clichés that would be instantly understandable to theater audiences. If in real life a man were seen sitting by himself at a party, speaking to no one, someone might say of him, "He is antisocial." Someone else might observe, "Now there's an introvert" or "See that man? He feels guilty about something." Stanislavsky would say that we cannot ever fully understand another human being. We can only infer what is going on inside them by *what they are not saying.*

> *"Acting is being truthful in imaginary circumstances."*
>
> **—Konstantin Stanislavsky**

In developing his technique, Stanislavsky required his actors to use their imagination and project their characters into other times and places, determining what they might do or say under changing conditions. Gradually, he believed, the actors would put themselves inside the people they were playing, the only path to discovering the truth of a character; they would react to a given situation as if it were happening to them. The rehearsal process involved the actors' exploration of themselves—their past and present. In a very real sense, actors and playwrights were collaborators, and the director's function was to distinguish between what seemed true and believable and what did not. Hence the famous Stanislavsky definition of acting as *being truthful in imaginary circumstances.*

Chekhov's characters are often trapped inside their own feelings and longings, and his plays often deal with the gap between human desires and what reality provides. For this reason he knew that, though enormous social changes were underway in his native Russia, they would have no effect on people's behavior or their search for happiness. Yet he is compassionate toward those who delude themselves into insisting that progress is inevitable and that life will get better.

Three Sisters (1901), believed by many to be his masterwork, is also the most complex. Each of the characters, who create a tight ensemble on the stage, is dependent on what the others say and do, yet each is an individual whose inner drives must be explored by the actor, believed in totally, *lived.* No two performances of *Three Sisters* is ever exactly the same because to play Chekhov actors must continually seek new corners in their characters' inner lives.

The sisters in question are daughters of a general who had once lived in Moscow, a place to which they long to return, a place where they are certain happiness lies. Unfortunately, lacking the money to move from the country, they must endure the monotony of their everyday existence, finding brief moments of joy only in thinking of Moscow.

The oldest sister, Olga, is an unmarried school teacher who manages the household. She is afflicted with frequent headaches and fatigue from unrewarding work. Irina, the youngest sister, loves neither of the two men who want to marry her, but realizes she must settle for one of them and try to lead a life of useful work. The middle sister, Masha, is unhappily married to a dull and pedantic Latin teacher who probably would have been a good match for Olga. Their brother, at one time expected to have a brilliant career, has married a young woman from a lower-class family that enjoys living as if they were rich.

The arrival of a company of soldiers brings a brief excitement into their lives; then it departs. Other characters come and go. From time to time, small crises erupt: a fire, gambling debts, a duel in which one of the men who love Irina is slain. The brother's spendthrift wife begins to dominate the house. She dismisses a beloved family servant; she has an affair with a local official. Neither her husband or his sister know how to confront her. Their gentility has not taught them how to fight and win. Nor is Chekhov suggesting that they *should* know. They do what they must. Events are beyond their control. They react, they try, they cope. That is all anyone can do. Chekhov once remarked in a letter that it was a beautiful thing for people to hope that life will change and improve, but he knew it could not, because life just flows through and around people; and they have no way to control it.

"Drama is action, sir, action, and not confounded philosophy."

—Luigi Pirandello

In the hands of a romantic playwright, there might have been more overt drama, complete with impassioned speeches of love or denunciation. Far from romantic, Chekhov recorded reality as he found it, making riveting drama out of the everyday world.

The Family Theme

Chekhov's naturalism influenced many subsequent dramatists, especially in the focus on the tensions that trap people within a family. One who acknowledged this influence was Tennessee Williams (1914–1983), though his plays belong to the school of naturalism only in terms of their probing the psychological depths of their characters. Williams's dialogue is a blend of stark naturalism and poetic prose.

At the outset of the play that established his reputation, *The Glass Menagerie* (1945), the narrator, Tom, all but apologizes for the artless kind of experience about to unfold. He calls it a "memory play" and admits that in memory things are not seen exactly as they were. His play will consist of relatively few scenes, most of which develop some aspect of family conflict. The work does not unfold as a chronicle of a lifetime crammed with incident, but it does remind us once again that the capacity for sharing the feelings of others is a major gift that great playwrights of today can offer their audience. It also makes us keenly aware that family ties creating obstacles to happiness all but impossible to surmount are the rightful descendants of Chekhovian drama. In the best of such plays there is never a happy, never a clear, conclusion.

The family theme has led to tragedy of a high order that differs in kind, but not emotional intensity, from the plays of Aristotle's time. The intensity that can be achieved from the often bitter confrontation between parents and children or between siblings becomes more profound and moving as the playwright delves further and further into the past, into the darkness that threatens to engulf and bring down the characters involved.

Modern tragedies about how family bonds tear people apart are enduringly popular with audiences.

Admitting that *Long Day's Journey into Night* (1941) was a personal document "born out of an old sorrow," another American playwright Eugene

O'Neill (1888–1953) tells the story of a family torn apart by the mother's drug addiction, the father's bitterness over the passing of his glory days as a famous Shakespearean actor, the older brother's alcoholic compensation for his failure to equal his father's success on the stage, and the younger brother's futile efforts to make the family understand he needs treatment for consumption. The play, in fact, is *about* how people who love each other do not and cannot help each other.

Though O'Neill relives his painful youth in the character of the consumptive Edmund Tyrone, he does not make himself the central character. In Chekhovian fashion, each member of the Tyrone family shares that honor. In the fourth act, the mother, upstairs in her bedroom where she retreats from the world in morphine-induced fantasy, is heard walking back and forth. She will eventually surrender to her addiction and totally withdraw from all contact with reality.

Downstairs, the men confront each other in one scene after another of unbearable intensity. The father, a lifelong miser, is now hopelessly drunk and insists Edmund does not need to go into an expensive sanatorium. The older brother, Jamie, comes home, also drunk, having spent all his money on prostitutes, hating himself for his wasted life, confessing how jealous he is of his younger brother's genius and his secret wish that he will fail as a writer. In a powerful speech, he shows us how closely connected are love and hate.

> *Never wanted you to succeed, and make me look worse by comparison.... Always jealous of you. Mama's baby.... And it was you being born that started Mama on dope. I know that's not your fault, but all the same, God damn you, I can't help hating your guts.... But don't get me wrong, kid. I love you more than I hate you... you're all I got left.*[20]

Photofest

Florence Eldridge, Bradford Dillman, Jason Robards Jr., and Fredric March, *Long Day's Journey Into Night*, 1956–58

The delusional mother drags in her wedding dress to the sadness of her family.

The play reaches its climax with the mother's sudden appearance, now lost in her fantasies, wearing her yellowed wedding gown believing this is the day of her wedding, her happiest day. The three men look at her with infinite sadness. The curtain falls on the four members of the doomed family in what has been hailed as a work that scales the height of tragic drama, not equaled in its profound effect on audiences since the days of the Greek masters.

A Theatrical Century of Dynamic Change

During the twentieth century, beginning with World War I, the world seldom enjoyed prolonged periods of peace, and now the closing of the world into a global village has only intensified the unrest. Economic ups and downs have created social upheavals. The climate is changing rapidly and radically. It has become a world almost unrecognizable to people who have lived through the past half-century and longer. The endless problems of the twentieth century and beyond have had a huge impact on the theater. Many new genres emerged as playwrights struggled to approach the challenges of a modern world and reduce them to the size of a stage and to a few hours' duration. For many of them, it became clear that the realistic theater of the previous century was too confining. They also had to contend with competition from the new entertainment form, cinema, with the kind of storytelling that would make total realism possible.

Naturalism, the Theater of Ideas, and both classical and neoclassical drama continued to be respected and performed, especially by repertory companies and on university campuses. But audiences, growing accustomed to the continued acceleration of change, have been and continue to be eager for fresh approaches. In addition, gradual changes in the fabric of society—minorities and women demanding equal recognition, for example—quickly made obsolete the kind of problems Victorian writers had wrestled with. The theater has had to reflect the new reality.

The Modern Theater of Ideas

Early on new playwrights realized that if they wanted to use the theater as a platform for their ideas they could no longer rely on the established traditions of Ibsen and Shaw.

A German playwright who came to prominence in the 1920s, after his disillusioned nation had lost World War I and was drifting into chaos, Bertolt Brecht (1898–1956) had a lot to say to audiences about a socialistic system he believed would stabilize his country. He believed deeply that the theater could be an important instrument of social change. Yet he recognized that audiences have a way of becoming so involved in a story being enacted that they overlook the ideas behind the story. His solution to the problem was **Theater of Alienation** designed to wrap ideas in a sparkling package, often resembling musical comedy, a highly popular genre attracting huge audiences on both sides of the Atlantic. In doing so, he believed he could prevent the viewer from identifying too strongly with the characters, thus missing the point being made. The undisguised unreality of the play would thus "alienate" the audience from the story and allow the playwright's message to be plainly heard.

> *Brecht . . . thought the greatest pleasure is to be found in "productive participation," which involves the active judgment of the spectator and his application of what he sees on the stage to conditions outside the theatre. To make him critical and capable of watching productively, the spectator must be "alienated" from the play's events.*
>
> —**Oscar G. Brockett**

In *The Caucasian Chalk Circle* (1944), written in America after Brecht had fled a Germany he perceived as cruelly suppressing human rights, he creates a fairy tale about a fabled kingdom in which a servant girl saves and cares for the child of a ruler during an uprising. After the conflict is over, the child's birth mother returns, expecting to be reunited with her offspring. The servant has, however, become to all intents the true mother. To resolve the issue, a wise judge draws a chalk circle on the ground, places the child inside, then informs the onlookers that whichever woman is able to pull the child from the circle will be declared the official mother and granted full custody. Each takes one of the child's arms and begins to tug, causing excruciating pain. The servant loves the child too much to continue and allows the other woman to win. The judge surprises everyone by announcing that the loser in this case has the rightful claim and gives the child to her. Legal rules about property and kinship by blood are, he says, less important than the willingness to care for the child.

The History Boys is modern Theater of Ideas, investigating whether education that seeks only to get applicants into the best schools has any real learning validity.

A recent play about educational ideas is *The History Boys* (2004) by English playwright Alan Bennett (b. 1934), originally produced by the National Theatre of Great Britain. This work communicates complex ideas in memorable language galloping along at a dizzying pace and challenges audiences to perk up their ears and listen *very* closely. The central theme is education—or specifically, whether education any longer has any validity. The setting is an English prep school for boys whose families hope to have them accepted into either Oxford or Cambridge. The headmaster is also obsessed with that one goal and therefore runs a tight ship with rigid curriculum guidelines that, when followed, should result in the longed-for success.

To guarantee that the majority of his charges will pass the qualifying exam for the prestigious colleges, the headmaster turns to a teacher cleverly adept at teaching students how to write entertaining essays and give amusing answers on entrance applications. The headmaster admires the glibness and sophistry emphasized by this teacher and cares not at all that the boys will learn little else.

In stark contrast to this self-confident mentor who supposedly knows all the angles is the play's central character, Hector, an overweight homosexual literature

Sara Krulwich/The New York Times/Redux Pictures

Richard Griffiths, *The History Boys,* 2006

The teacher in *The History Boys* loves teaching but not school regulations.

teacher for whom closeness to the boys is his reason for living. He is extremely popular with them, but for reasons that are suspect. He doesn't exactly teach specifics and is so easy-going that his classes are always "fun." What he *thinks* he is teaching is respect for great language and thoughts. He hopes his boys will so admire the literary greats that they will become role models. Of course, the boys take advantage of his illusions. Some of them will, of course, get into the big schools, but how much will they really know—or care? Bennett is posing questions about education that apply to all countries that pretend to be providing a liberal education for every citizen.

The work has a kinship not only with Ibsen and Shaw but to Chekhov as well. The history boys, so-called because the qualifying exam is notoriously heavy on history questions, are not a generic group of two-dimensional characters who might be, in the hands of a lesser playwright, just "The Class." Each one has a carefully developed persona and a past history that makes them real to us. We come to like them as human beings, and by the end of the play we think they deserve much more from education. Then we ask: *But where are they going to get it?*

Theater of Cruelty

Often closely related to Brecht's theater of alienation is a movement theater historians have labeled **Theater of Cruelty**. Like Brecht, many of its playwrights want audiences to absorb the ideas they are setting forth, but they do it by pulverizing the viewer's emotions through shocking scenes. Unlike other innovative genres, Theater of Cruelty has grown in popularity, probably influenced by the violence in movies and on television and by conflicts the world over in which thousands of innocent people have died. Some of the plays speak indirectly to these conflicts by weaving violence into their plots.

A mental institution, but with sympathies clearly on the side of inmates seeking freedom from oppressive authority, is the setting of Dale Wasserman's adaptation of Ken Kesey's 1962 novel *One Flew Over the Cuckoo's Nest*. It centers on the conflict between a power-hungry nurse and a young troublemaker, who, though obviously not mentally ill, has been branded an activist dangerous to society. To the audience the young man is a hero, rightfully angry at the cruel treatment of patients who get out of line. In the climactic scene he is given punitive shock treatment as a means of making him passive and controllable. The electric currents shooting through the head of the strapped-down victim make the audience think they are in a room watching an execution.

Theater of Cruelty continues to attract audiences. It is an abundant element in the works of Martin McDonagh (b. 1970), a playwright who learned his art by buying a "How to Write for the Stage" book. Identifying with no previous theatrical tradition and highly influenced by film violence, he struck out boldly on his own, writing dark comedies about Irish men and women who refuse to suppress their wild Dionysian natures. He is less interested in communicating ideas than in extending the possibilities of on-stage violence.

The Lieutenant of Inishmore *illustrates more Theater of Cruelty; its stage was drenched in six gallons of fake blood and littered with dismembered corpses.*

His first success, *The Beauty Queen of Leenane* (1999), is, however, far less violent. It is a family-theme comedy about a cowering, unattractive daughter who finally works up the courage to murder her dominating, abusive mother as the audience cheers. The most shocking aspect of the play is the fact that the daughter is apparently not made to pay for her crime.

McDonagh's works have since become more "edgy," as some critics have labeled them, with blood and gore splashed all over the stage, causing some audience members to cringe and even cover their eyes. *The Lieutenant of Inishmore* (2001), produced by the Royal Shakespeare Company, is about a young terrorist

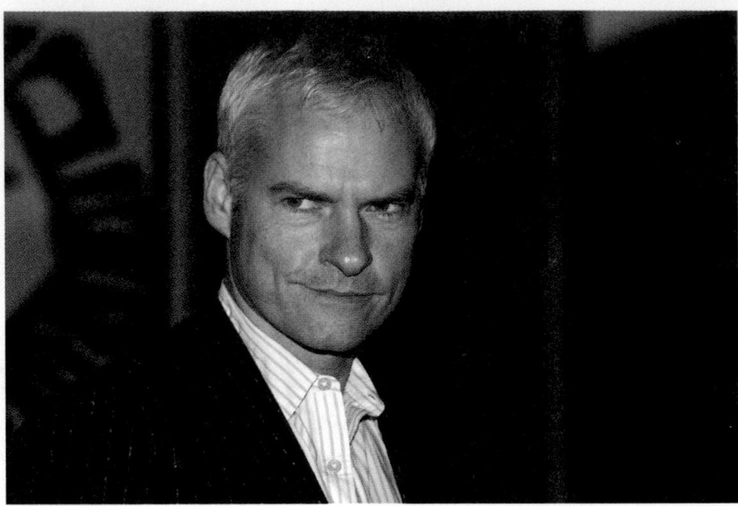

AP Images

Martin McDonagh, 2010

Irish playwright Martin McDonagh, who has made a career of splattering the stage with blood and gore.

thrown out of the Irish Republican Army because of his dangerous and irrational behavior. The only living creature he loves is his cat. Upon returning home, the former lieutenant is led to believe that the pet has been accidentally killed by his brother. This news unhinges the man, who embarks upon a killing spree that is both horrifying and, because of its excesses, funny at the same time. (In the Broadway production the stage was drenched in six gallons of fake blood.) But yes, behind the blood and a stage littered with dismembered corpses there *is* a serious message: the impulse to murder your fellowman is absurd and irrational no matter how you try to justify it.

His recent work is *A Behanding in Spokane* (2010), the only play he has ever set in America; but a change of scene has not softened the violence. The protagonist is a man who has lost his hand and turned killer because of it. The "idea"—if indeed McDonagh can be said to be at all concerned with ideas—is that violence will continue to erupt whether there is any motive for it at all. The impulse for it is deeply imbedded in human nature; and, of course, nothing in today's headlines ever disputes that belief. The suspicion, however, is that the playwright, enjoying one critical and box-office success after another, may justify the excessive violence of his work by citing humankind's savage nature, while at the same time enjoying the fame and fortune it has given him.

Racial Themes

> *"The plague of racism is insidious, entering our minds as smoothly and quietly and invisibly as floating or airborne microbes enter into our bodies to find lifelong purchase in our bloodstreams."*
>
> **—Maya Angelou**

A groundbreaking play depicting the lives and experiences of African Americans is *A Raisin in the Sun* (1959) by Lorraine Hansberry (1930–1965). In it a mother and her grown children argue over the best use of money received from an insurance policy. They have the opportunity to buy a house in a previously segregated white neighborhood. Both the son and daughter, however, want to use the money to advance their own careers, but the mother insists on moving out of their crowded apartment. She strongly maintains her convictions against pressure from a white man who offers her money not to move into "his" neighborhood. Despite their earlier opposition, the children rally around her strength, and the family moves, ready to stand up to the hostility of their new neighbors.

In 1976, the South African playwright Athol Fugard (b. 1932) wrote *Sizwe Banze Is Dead*, an impassioned play condemning apartheid, the now outlawed segregation of the races. An illiterate man, seeking employment but finding he his unable to use the identity card issued in his own town, is persuaded by a friend to use one found on a dead man. Without a card he will be sent back to the township restricted to his tribe. In a powerful speech he demands the right to use his own name ("Am I not a man?"). But his determination to cling to his own identity, a mark of personal dignity, is thwarted. By the end of the play he has been forced to accept the dead man's name. In return he is given a job and a little money to send home to his family. He will survive if he can continue to be deferential to white authorities. Fugard's play stands as a stern reminder of racial prejudice and its destructive effects.

A subtle question of identity for African Americans is posed in *Fences* (1987 and revived in 2010), which won the Pulitzer Prize for its author, August Wilson (1945–2005). The ideas in this complex work touch on past and present racial inequities as well as the tangled relationships within a family. Wilson prefers not to deliver a direct message. Instead, he focuses on the psychology of his main character, who becomes a symbol of the African American lost in a changing society. Born into a sharecropper's family in the Deep South, victimized and forced to adjust to a white-dominated world as he grew up, the character finds himself unprepared for a new world that demands liberation for everyone. He had found ways to survive prejudice, but now he feels lost. Wilson's theme is the tragedy of the semiliberated people who are tolerated without being welcome and who therefore suffer inwardly from a loss of identity—people who live behind the fences that separate them from each other and from themselves.

Gay Rights

Only in relatively recent times has theater addressed a subject that was once just whispered about. In the past, gay characters were not associated with the issue of rights but were more often given a comic treatment. Or, as in Tennessee Williams's *A Streetcar Named Desire* (1947) and *Cat on a Hot Tin Roof* (1955), homosexuality was made the unnamed source of failed marriages. The statement that homosexuality is tragic because of the suffering inflicted on gays by society had to wait for a more congenial social climate, a time when audiences were willing to confront once taboo subject matter.

A very early treatment of that theme was found in a 1934 play, *The Children's Hour* by Lillian Hellman (1905–1984), which dealt with a woman's slow realization of her passion for another woman. Audiences accepted the shocking theme, probably because the friend does not feel the same way, and thus the play treats the woman's "condition" as a pathological tragedy. The play makes no plea for acceptance of a homosexual lifestyle; rather, it shows the pernicious effects of scandal as a malicious student deliberately spreads rumors about the women. The gay woman commits suicide, as would have been expected at the time, while the heterosexual woman is granted a happy ending in which she marries the man she loves.

> *"I cannot and will not cut my conscience to fit this year's fashion."*
>
> **—Lillian Hellman**

Far and away the most stirring work to emerge from the newly found freedom of the stage has been *Angels in America* by Tony Kushner (b. 1956), a seven-hour production divided into two plays—*The Millennium Approaches* (1992) and *Perestroika* (1993). The first play was awarded the Pulitzer Prize before it ever opened in New York, and the second, soon after its opening.

Subtitled "A Gay Fantasia on National Themes," *Angels* is a significant work of theatrical art both for its epic scope and its dazzling innovations in technique. Adopting a fast-moving, razzmatazz style clearly influenced by the plays of Brecht, popular musical comedy, music videos as well as the pacing of quick-action films, and requiring minimal scenery, the work is ultimately much more than a gay rights statement. The author touches on gay rights, of course, but also political and religious corruption, the decline of the family, deterioration of the environment, and the need for a true spiritual awakening.

Despite its grim subject matter, the work is not pessimistic. As the title suggests, a miraculous turn of events is on the way, and this is foreshadowed through *The Millennium Approaches* by feathers falling from the sky when least expected.

Photo by Joan Marcus/Courtesy Everett Collection

Ellen McLaughlin and Stephen Spinella, *Angels in America: The Millennium Approaches*, 1993

The angel has only one line—the very final one in *The Millennium Approaches:* "The great work begins."

At the conclusion of the play, the promised angel finally appears, descending in resplendent fashion, her white wings covering half the stage, and declares, "The great work begins."

Beckett

For a play in such a totally unfamiliar style as *Angels in America,* table work and much discussion are essential. There are examples in theater history of initial misinterpretation that led to a disastrous opening. Stanislavsky's first production of Chekhov's *The Sea Gull* is one. Another, much closer to home, is the 1956 American première of Samuel Beckett's *Waiting for Godot.* The play, advertised as "the laugh sensation of two continents," starred two comic actors who had starred in popular films: Tom Ewell of *The Seven-Year Itch* and Bert Lahr, the Cowardly Lion of *The Wizard of Oz. Waiting For Godot,* since hailed by many as the greatest play of the twentieth century, bewildered the Miami critics and the opening night audience that clearly had never witnessed a play in which nothing ostensibly happens.

The play deals with two tramps in a park; they do not enjoy being there but for some reason they cannot leave until they have seen a mysterious man named Godot. After the successful second American production, one critic observed that the play was about "the anguish of waiting," but actually it is the thing itself. They wait. Nothing really happens. One decides to hang himself, but all he can use is the rope that holds his trousers up. When he removes the rope, the trousers fall. The bit was common in vaudeville many years before, but in this play it is poignant, not funny. They decide that perhaps they can hang themselves tomorrow. And perhaps Godot will come tomorrow. And perhaps, if they finally get to meet Godot, they will understand why they have been waiting. Or perhaps not. Or perhaps they ought to leave right now. The final stage direction is: *They do not move.*

As its critical reputation grew, the work was and continues to be revived and always serves as the topic for post-performance conversation and, sometimes, heated debate. It is studied in college courses. Scenes are popular in performing arts schools. The difference between *Godot* and other plays that have bewildered audiences is that the former is filled with possible meanings; and probing for meaning is part of its aesthetic appeal. In fact, the search for meaning can also be said to be the play's true theme. Does life in fact make any sense? And what do we do if it does *not* make sense? Like the tramps, who have only each other, maybe we are all abandoned in the park that is our world, hoping that somewhere there is someone named Godot.

This introduction to one of the world's most enduring art forms may encourage you to seek the pleasure of watching drama wherever it is found. Broadway is not the only place to look. Schools and colleges revive classic works, present new plays, and compensate for their limited budgets with innovative approaches. Many important theatrical productions have been recorded on DVDs and shown on television. These media now offer a library of nearly all the modes and genres of theater discussed in this chapter, from tragedy and comedy to naturalism, the Theater of Ideas, the Theater of Cruelty, and **avant-garde** masterpieces like *Waiting for Godot.* You can readily become a critical viewer if you choose.

Waiting for Godot is just about that: waiting. The two tramps know they must wait for the mysterious Godot but have no idea who he is or why they must wait. The play becomes a powerful metaphor for the confusion amid which we live.

LEARNING OBJECTIVES

Having read and carefully studied this chapter, you should be able to:

1. Give three examples defining *theatrical convention*.
2. Contrast Greek and Elizabethan theater conventions.
3. Briefly summarize Aristotle's description of the nature of tragedy.
4. Contrast Shakespearean and neoclassic tragedy.
5. Indicate why Ibsen is generally considered the father of modern drama.
6. Describe modern tragedy using Miller's *A View from the Bridge*.
7. Briefly define satire, comedy of character, and farce.
8. Cite three examples describing schools of contemporary comedy.
9. Define theatrical *naturalism* using the work of Chekhov as your example.
10. Define Theater of Alienation using *The Caucasian Chalk Circle*.

KEY TERMS

aside popular in Elizabethan drama, a remark made by an actor to the audience that other actors on the stage do not hear.

antagonist a character whose function in a play is to oppose the central character's actions; most often found in melodramas.

avant-garde French word meaning "vanguard" or "advance guard." In the arts, a movement constantly striving to break with convention and experiment with new forms. Used here to discuss theater, but also applicable to art, music, and literature.

catharsis according to Aristotle, the purging of pity and fear that comes from these emotional responses to a tragedy.

Chorus in Greek tragedy, a group of masked actors who sing and dance as well as comment on the moral implications of the play; can be found in much contemporary theater in different forms and with different functions.

comedy one of two major genres to grow out of Greek theater. Originally, it was a short piece that followed a trilogy of tragic plays, the purpose of which was to lighten the mood of the audience. Now, any theater work with the primary intent of promoting laughter. Farce, satire, parody, and comedy of character are forms of comic theater.

commedia dell'arte professional acting and pantomime troupe that performed in Italian streets beginning in the Renaissance; famous for its stock repertoire of comic types, such as the doddering old man who pursues a beautiful young girl.

conventions rules governing a given style of theater, such as fourth-wall verisimilitude or bare stage. These rules should not be violated, but often are, as when actors "break" the fourth wall by delivering a line directly toward the audience.

deus ex machina in Greek theater, an actor impersonating a god who descends to the stage on wires and resolves the action to the audience's satisfaction. Now, a contrived ending tacked onto a play (or story), intended to create a happy—or at least satisfying—ending.

exposition dialogue in a play that gives the background of the story and the relevant past history of the characters; problematic in the theater of verisimilitude, in which characters are supposed to talk as people do in real life—that is, without such statements as "As you know, dear, we have been married for twenty-five years."

Expressionism form of avant-garde drama introduced by German theaters during the 1920s, in which characters and sets are symbolic. Best example of American Expressionism is the play *The Adding Machine,* with a giant calculator for a set and a central character named Mr. Zero.

farce genre of comedy involving the actions of two-dimensional stock characters, improbable situations, much slapstick, and improbable resolutions of plot complexities.

groundlings relatively poor people who loved theater in Elizabethan times and paid a penny for the privilege of standing on ground level to watch the plays; they were vulnerable when the weather was inclement.

hubris Greek term meaning "arrogance"—the common tragic flaw of Greek tragic protagonists.

image poetic technique, used to great effect by Shakespeare, in which something that would otherwise need many words of explanation is communicated swiftly by being called something else that is easily understood and is usually visual as well.

melodrama form of theater that resembles but is not legitimate tragedy dealing with a conflict between two-dimensional characters, often the very good and the very bad.

naturalism technique of acting and writing based on the imitation of people as they actually are and talk in real life; naturalistic plays, like those of Chekhov, very often do not have well-structured plots, on the grounds that real life does not structure what happens.

Neoclassicism a style of theater (as well as art, music, and architecture) which reinvents the pure geometric formalism that characterizes early Greece and Rome; abundant in the seventeenth century.

parody exaggeratedly funny imitation of a person (usually a public figure or celebrity) or work of theater or literature that, according to the parodist, deserves ridicule; often it masks serious criticism.

proscenium in modern theaters, the front of the stage, usually framed and sometimes containing a curtain that can be raised and lowered, or drawn.

protagonist central character in a drama (or literary work), the person in terms of whose fortune we view and respond to the action; not to be confused with "hero," who is generally someone without flaws, who triumphs over bad people.

recognition scene in tragic drama, especially that of the Greeks and Shakespeare, when the doomed protagonist understands that he or she is responsible for the disaster; often lacking in modern tragedy.

satire genre of comedy that ridicules such things as war, political corruption, and religious hypocrisy. Tends to be less wildly exaggerated than parody.

scanning reading a line of verse and exaggerating the rhythm so as to determine whether it underlies, without intruding upon, the words. Scanning helps us better appreciate a writer's skill when we see that a strict rhythmic pattern is maintained while the speaker or actor is also free to explore the emotions within the verse.

soliloquy theatrical convention of Elizabethan drama in which an actor, alone on stage, voices private thoughts.

subtext what is implied but not spoken in a dramatic line or scene.

Theater of Alienation dramatic genre associated with the work of Bertolt Brecht; its intention is to highlight the artificiality of the theater so as to prevent the audience from becoming too emotionally involved in the story and the characters and instead concentrate on the play's ideas.

Theater of Cruelty dramatic genre that affects the audience through emotional shock; in recent years it has become increasingly "edgy"—that is, overwhelming the audience with blood and gore, as in The Lieutenant of Inishmore.

tragedy one of the two major forms of drama focusing on the downfall of a protagonist due to a serious character flaw. In Greek and Shakespearean tragic drama, the protagonist is a high-ranking noble person, but not so in modern tragedy.

unities convention of classical and neoclassical theater requiring the playwright to set the action in one place, have it occur during the time the audience is actually sitting in the theater, and limit the action to one central plot.

verisimilitude technique of making scenery and dialogue look and sound like real life; developed during the latter part of the nineteenth century but still dominant in today's theater.

well-made play developed in the nineteenth century and using verisimilitude in scenery and dialogue, but the tight, carefully crafted plot structure does not resemble the flow of real life.

TOPICS FOR WRITING AND DISCUSSION

1. Greek playwrights based their works on well-known myths. Discuss two famous events or persons of our time that you believe have acquired mythic status and would be appropriate subjects for a modern tragedy.
2. Of the six dramatic elements Aristotle discusses, he found plot most important. Explain what he means by *plot* and indicate why he believed it would be more important than even character, which he places second.
3. Both *Oedipus* and *Medea* are considered supreme examples of tragedy, but, even though they have in common the survival of the main character, they are vastly different. Explain this difference, then tell why each is a tragedy.
4. "Comedy," wrote Aristotle in the only sentence surviving from his essay on the subject, "is life seen from a distance." Explain what this means relative to Moliere's *The Would-Be Gentleman*.
5. Farce comedy depends on stock or stereotyped characters whose foolish antics are laughable. Create three stereotypes from contemporary life and provide a brief summary of a play you could write about each one.
6. Try your hand at parody. Make fun of a recent work (stage, screen, or television) you think has been overpraised and should be held up to ridicule to protect the consumer. Remember: pretend your parody is the work itself.
7. An early Theater of Cruelty play was *One Flew Over the Cuckoo's Nest*; the most (literally) shocking scene involved an electroshock treatment performed right on stage. But plays such as those of Martin McDonagh go far beyond that. Do you think McDonagh is unique? Or does the popularity of his work indicate a trend?
8. Review briefly the works we discussed from Theater of Ideas, both past and present. Single out one with ideas you believe are most relevant today and one with the least. Explain why in each case.
9. Television is closely related to theater; each has influenced the other over the years. Discuss one kind of television program with roots in the theater, or discuss a recent theater genre which strikes you as having roots in television. Explain either choice.
10. Shakespeare is frequently called the greatest writer in the English language. Review what you have learned about him from this chapter, then indicate why he does (or does not) deserve the honor.

TAKE A CLOSER LOOK: Exploring a Scene from Arthur Miller's *Death of a Salesman*

The Everett Collection

Dustin Hoffman, Stephen Lang, and John Malkovich, *Death of a Salesman*, 1985

The confrontation scene in a film production of *Death of a Salesman.*

First produced in 1949, Arthur Miller's *Death of a Salesman* (also discussed on p. 211) won the Pulitzer Prize that year and launched Miller's career as the premiere American playwright. The play centers on Willy Loman, a salesman with aspirations of grandeur. Set while Willy is in his early sixties, the play frequently shifts through time with Willy to show scenes from his past. Slipping in and out of these daydreams, Willy's grasp on reality is tentative from the first scene and degrades throughout the play. Through his flashbacks, we see that Willy has long related the idea of success in the business world with popularity, and has always forced his aspirations onto his sons, but mostly onto his oldest, Biff, who was a popular football player in high school. The climax of the play occurs in a series of confrontations between Biff and his father. Having discovered Willy in an extramarital affair, Biff had become disillusioned with his father's idea of success at an early age. With time, his annoyance and frustration with his father's habit of incessantly (and falsely) boasting of Biff's successes grows. Biff and Happy meet their father for dinner, and while Biff is trying to gently explain the reality of his failures in the business world, Willy interrupts to inform them he has been fired. In reaction, Happy, who takes after his father and has always been more eager to play along with Willy's delusions, tries to comfort Willy with promises of Biff's success. Back at home, the confrontation re-erupts, ending with Biff in tears and Willy driving away to commit suicide convinced that with the $20,000 insurance payoff,

Biff will finally achieve the success he is destined for. Below are a few lines from the final scene of the play, Willy's funeral.

CHARLEY: *(stopping Happy's movement and reply. To Biff.):* Nobody dast blame this man. You don't understand: Willy was a salesman. And for a salesman, there is no rock bottom to the life. He don't put a bolt to a nut, he don't tell you the law or give you medicine. He's a man out there in the blue, riding on a smile and a shoeshine. And when they start not smiling back—that's an earthquake. And then you get yourself a couple of spots on your hat, and you're finished. Nobody dast blame this man. A salesman is got to dream, boy. It comes with the territory.

BIFF: Charley, the man didn't know who he was.

HAPPY: *(infuriated):* Don't say that!

BIFF: Why don't you come with me, Happy?

HAPPY: I'm not licked that easily. I'm staying right in this city, and I'm gonna beat this racket! (He looks at Biff, his chin set.) The Loman Brothers!

BIFF: I know who I am, kid.

Read the summary here and on page 211, and the excerpt from the play above. The following questions will help you explore *Death of a Salesman* as a critical reader.

1. Why is Happy so angry with Biff?
2. What is Willy's tragic flaw? How does it lead to his downfall?
3. How does *Death of a Salesman* fit the traditional definition of a tragedy? Compare *Death of a Salesman* to the traditional tragedies described in this chapter. How does *Death of a Salesman* expand the definition of tragedy?
4. *Death of a Salesman* has often been described as a commentary on the American dream. What do you think Miller is trying to say? Do you agree? Why or why not?

Chapter 8

The Musical Stage: Opera, Music Theater, Dance

In days gone by—say, the late 1930s—going to a Broadway musical aroused expectations of beautiful dancing girls, men and women in virtuoso dance patterns, and tuneful (referred to by critics as "toe-tapping") scores. No one needed—or wanted—complex plots and characterizations. It was a night out, meant for casual entertainment.

Things have changed quite drastically. *Next to Normal,* a musical that won the Pulitzer Prize for Drama in 2009, is about a bipolar heroine struggling against a deepening depression, who sings about her abnormalities when she is not singing duets with the ghost of her dead son. There are no songs that stand apart from their context, as was always the case decades years ago.

Opera buffs who attended the London premiere of a new opera, *The Duchess of Malfi,* based on an early seventeenth century tragedy by John Webster, were required to wear carnival masks while watching some scenes taking place simultaneously and hearing music coming at them from other rooms. The world is constantly changing, and the musical stage is no exception.

The musical stage is one of the oldest of humanities' disciplines. Opera and ballet have long histories; they have achieved high stature in major cultural centers. **Music theater**, which includes musical comedy and that more recent phenomenon known as the musical play, have shorter histories but now rank among the world's favorite theatrical genres.

◀ **Renée Fleming, *The Marriage of Figaro*, 1998**

The Countess in *The Marriage of Figaro* laments the passing of love and youth in the Metropolitan Opera production.

Beatriz Schiller/Time & Life Images/Getty Images

Early History of Musical Theater

Theater and music have always been closely associated. It is hard to say which came first or whether they were inseparable from the start. A good guess is that musical theater history extends back to the rituals and ceremonies of very early cultures, which combined some form of dance and some kind of rhythmic accompaniment.

Perhaps we can imagine such a ritual. A group of people took part in a prescribed series of movements and songs to mark certain important occasions such as the change of seasons; and when people enter into a collective consciousness, focusing on movements, gestures, or some kind of chant, are they not in a sense *acting*? It is tempting to believe that musical theater was among the very earliest forms of human artistic expression.

Cultural anthropologists have dated musical rituals as far back as 30,000 B.C.E. Cave paintings of that long-ago time show human figures engaged in what has come to be known as the "buffalo dance." This was a symbolic reenactment of the hunt for the life-sustaining animal in which "actors" played either the hunters or the hunted. The theory is that, by taking the part of the buffalo, hunters would be assured of the kill. Many thousands of years later, the Blackfoot nation of Montana still performed that particular ritual, which had, of course, become more structured, its musical accompaniment more sophisticated.[1]

Music, song, and dance combined to create the Dionysian festivals in early Greece, and there is much information about these rituals. They were held annually in spring to celebrate the return of Dionysus, the god of fertility, from the underworld (see Chapter 7). A chorus of men, dressed in goat skins and wearing masks, went through a series of elaborate and complex songs and dances accompanied by music of some sort, though we do not know what this music sounded like. In *The Republic* Plato approved of music that aroused national spirit but did not exist solely to stir emotion. We suspect that the dancing in the Dionysian rites not only stirred emotion but perhaps even drove spectators into a frenzy (an ancient version of the rock concert!).

> *"We do not know when music drama began, because we do not know a time when man had no music drama."*
>
> **—John D. Drummond**

The time of Shakespeare—late sixteenth to early seventeenth centuries—represents the Golden Age of English theater. If the bard did not write musical plays, he certainly wrote many plays *with* music. Romeo and Juliet meet at a party in which there is masked dancing to an ensemble of musical instruments. At the beginning of the memorable final scene in *Othello,* Desdemona, the wife Othello suspects of adultery and will soon murder, has a premonition of impending doom while her maid is brushing her hair and expresses it in the haunting and melancholy *Willow Song,* for which both lyrics and music survive. In Verdi's opera version of the play, the scene is highlighted by the magnificent *Ave Maria.* In both scenes music enhances the dramatic impact.

In Shakespeare's comedies, mirth and song as well as dance abound. *Twelfth Night,* in particular, named for the joyous celebration that marked the end of the Christmas season, comes close to being a musical play. The songs have been printed and reprinted thousands of times and are in the repertoire of both folk singers and opera stars. *A Midsummer-Night's Dream* is frequently performed almost like a ballet, enhanced by the incidental music composed for the play by Felix Mendelssohn. Without music in the productions, Shakespeare's theater would be greatly diminished, though the poetry of the plays, when spoken by the best of actors, can be called unaccompanied music.

Audiences must have clamored for the inclusion of more and more music into theater. By the late seventeenth century, *opera* was already being developed in Italy. During the eighteenth century Italian opera became one of the world's premier art forms and composers of other nationalities were forced to compose their operas in the Italian language if they ever hoped to get produced.

An Austrian-born composer, most of whose operas are written in Italian, would carry the genre to a new level, reaching heights that many believe have never been equaled. His name was Wolfgang Amadeus Mozart. Important opera composers paved the way for him.

The word **opera** is the Latin plural of "*opus*" ("work"), a label applied during the Renaissance to what was then a new musical art form combining the work of a playwright (librettist), a composer, an orchestra, singers, and dancers. The growth of opera was an inevitable byproduct of the Renaissance rediscovery of classical literature and art and the desire to create works that were elegant and noble enough to rival their ancient predecessors. Opera fitted nicely into the new striving.

Claudio Monteverdi

Since the Renaissance began in late fourteenth-century Italy as an artistic and political movement, it was inevitable that Italy would create the first operas. The baroque composer Claudio Monteverdi (1567–1643), born three years later than Shakespeare, laid the foundation for the great achievements to follow.

Monteverdi may be considered the true father of opera, having created the continuous musical line which is interrupted by memorable arias. Mozart, influenced by this invention, created the recitative, or sung dialogue.

Renaissance music gloried in the invention of new instruments, making possible new sounds, and in the harmonies of different vocal lines played or sung at the same time. Renaissance music tended to repeat musical themes over and over, possibly because melody, as we know it, was a novelty and listeners did not tire of hearing the same sounds. Moreover, the constant repetition made the melodies easy to remember.

Renaissance composers were acutely aware of the public's hunger for melody, but librettists were supplying them with well-known classical myths that had to be told exactly as they were. Consequently, a problem arose: how to reconcile abundant use of melody with the need to move a dramatic plot forward. Events in a play, unlike melodic lines, are not repeated; and characters change as they are affected by experience. It seemed only logical that the music in these sung dramas should keep changing as well. But wouldn't that distress audiences who, having heard a beautiful melody, longed to hear it again—and yet again?

The problem of melodic repetition versus dramatic change is still with us and may explain why the most popular operas are still those with strong and memorable songs (*arias*) and duets—that is, melodic lines that recur. In Georges Bizet's opera *Carmen*, for example, tragic fate is represented by a particular theme that is heard again and again, always announcing disaster, which tends to elevate the drama.

At any rate, the opera of the seventeenth century found a way to move the story forward while keeping the audience interested in the music. Claudio Monteverdi pioneered in the development of the continuous musical line interrupted at regular intervals by a memorable aria. His breakthrough work was *La Favola d'Orfeo* ("The Fable of Orpheus") in 1607, seven years later than Jacobo Peri's *Eurydice,* based on the same tale and credited with having been the world's first opera.

In the legend, whenever Orpheus played on his lyre, all those who heard him were struck dumb with wonder. Not only humans, but animals, would weep for joy at the sound. Even inanimate objects such as rocks would delight in the music. Orpheus became the very symbol of glorious sounds. How appropriate that his story would become the basis for the first major opera!

Monteverdi's opera gives the myth of Orpheus a happy ending. If it didn't, the opera would be saying that music can die.

Orpheus falls in love with and marries Eurydice, who dies in the flower of youth and is transported down into the underworld. The abandoned lover plays such heartbreaking music on his lyre that Pluto, the god of the underworld, is moved to tears and promises to allow Orpheus to reclaim his wife and return to earth with her—on one condition: Eurydice is to follow behind him, but he must never turn around to see whether she is there. If he does, she will be lost to him forever. Midway through the journey, Orpheus, unable to bear the strain of not knowing, disobeys the order and looks back. True to his word, Pluto takes Eurydice back.

Monteverdi's opera, however, provides a happy ending to the myth. Eurydice is not lost. Apollo descends from heaven in response to his son's grief and promises that husband and wife will eventually be reunited and live forever, for music cannot die.

To solve the problem of repetition versus dramatic line, Monteverdi uses recurrent themes to represent the characters. This form of repetition would be made famous by Richard Wagner (discussed later in the chapter) who called it the **leit-motif** (or "leading theme"). The *leit-motif* gave audiences melodic lines to remember and to recognize with pleasure when they heard them again; but, since the theme was tied to character and character changed with events, the theme could be both recognizable and somewhat altered.

Classical and Baroque Opera

By the eighteenth century, European writers, artists, and composers started turning away from the robustness of the Renaissance and the decorative splendors of the baroque period seen in its church architecture and heard in the complex harmonies and counterpoint of its music. European society settled into a time of polite behavior, elegance of dress, and the belief that excessive displays of emotion were vulgar and uncouth.

The baroque musical style of Monteverdi's *Orfeo* saw the composer developing the drama of his characters while striving to maintain a solid musical structure. Often, however, as in the music of Bach, both Dionysian excitement and Apollonian structure can be heard. Early eighteenth-century opera is, on the whole, marked by greater restraint and can properly be labeled *classical*.

A prime example of this classicism is found in yet another version of the Orpheus myth. In *Orfeo et Euridice* (1762) by German classical composer Christoph Glück (1714–1787), when Eurydice dies and is taken to the underworld, Orpheus is understandably grief-stricken; and what could be more appropriate for an operatic aria than the sorrow of a young man robbed of his only love? His aria beginning "So I mourn her death" contains one of opera's most unforgettable melodies, but it is precise and carefully rhythmic, allowing little room for a tearful rendition. In fact, it could almost be played without words as an aristocratic minuet. Yet the lyrics express the hero's broken heart.

There is still some baroque complexity in the furious rhythms of the ballet danced by a chorus of furies (who were the mythological demons tormenting unworthy residents of the underworld). This is, however, immediately contrasted with the placid "Dance of the Blessed Spirits" and, later, with arias gently titled "These Meadows Are a Place of Blissful Peace" and "What a Clear Sky Decks This Place." The latter two arias represent a musical description that suggests the Christian concept of heaven, suited to the music of classical restraint.

Wolfgang Amadeus Mozart

In the opinion of many, the art of opera was fully developed—and perhaps never surpassed—in the work of Wolfgang Amadeus Mozart (1756–1791), often considered the most naturally gifted composer who ever lived. In his operas, as well as in his many other astonishing achievements, Mozart represents a major transition from the classical to the *romantic* style. In Chapter 6, romantic music was described as being extremely melodic with greatly expanded orchestrations and musical forms lengthened to accommodate the expressions of emotion. Yet Mozart's early training was at the hands of the greatest pure classicist of German music—Franz Josef Haydn (1732–1809); and so we should expect Mozart operas to display a blending of graceful, symmetrical arias and interludes as well as swelling, romantic sounds.

"Mozart gives us permission to live."

—John Updike

By the time this prodigy reached the age of four and his creative drives were already pushing him forward, opera had taken its place among the world's premier arts. The great Italian opera centers—Rome, Florence, Venice, Milan, Bologna—beckoned wealthy tourists and aspiring composers. At the same time, other cities in Western Europe were developing their own singers and orchestras; other composers of opera were eager to be heard, though Italian remained the required language for libretti.

Mozart was born in Salzburg, a city that boasted not only an opera house but a great musical environment in general. His father was an accomplished musician who quickly recognized his son's prodigious talents. By the time he was thirteen, Mozart had become concertmaster for the archbishop of Salzburg and been decorated in Milan by the pope himself. Having been a truly *serious* composer from the age of six, when he wrote five pieces for the piano, he was probably not surprised that he was asked to write an opera for the Milanese audiences at the advanced age of fourteen. He not only composed but directed *Mithridates, King of Pontus,* accomplishing this feat before his sixteenth birthday. For the next nine years, without the patronage of Emperor Franz Josef of Austria, his abandoned country, he struggled for financial security, nevertheless giving the world the most astonishing outpouring of great music ever received from one human being in so brief a time.

"Music hath charms to soothe the savage breast,
To soften rocks or bend a knotted oak."

—William Congreve

Opera intrigued him—the challenge of combining so many elements into one unified work. He mastered the complexities of orchestration and developed a distinctive style, which was at once personal and characteristic of his cultural heritage. His first major opera, *Idomeneo,* with an Italian text, was followed by *The Abduction from the Seraglio,* a delightfully complicated comic opera that has become famous for two reasons aside from its lilting and graceful music.

One reason is that it introduced the truly Mozartean operatic style: melodious arias alternating with dialogue, sometimes spoken but mostly sung—the composer's solution to the problem of telling a dramatic story in song. Sung dialogue is called **recitative**. The combination of recitative and song is called **singspiel**. Broadway composers, including Frank Loesser (*The Most Happy Fella*) and Stephen Sondheim (*Sweeney Todd*), have aspired to bring the musical closer to opera. The two works cited, and others like them, have revived the art of the *singspiel,* not always to the pleasure of musical theater audiences who expect to hear one melodious song after another.

Another reason for the fame of *The Abduction from the Seraglio* is that boldly—and shockingly to opera-goers of the time—the **libretto** was in German rather than in the standard Italian expected by the Viennese audience. Opera in German was revolutionary in 1782.

> "*Opera . . . is one of the strangest inventions of Western man. It could not have been foreseen by any logical process.*"
>
> **—Sir Kenneth Clarke**

In 1786 Mozart met a clergyman named Lorenzo da Ponte, who was also a poet and dramatist. The collaboration resulted in three acknowledged masterpieces—*The Marriage of Figaro* (1786), *Don Giovanni* (1787), and *Cosí fan tutte* ("Thus Are They All," or sometimes translated loosely as "Women Are Like That"; 1790). Together they produced three of the greatest operatic works of all time—in only four years!

The Marriage of Figaro. Of all the Mozart operas, *Figaro* has arguably become the most popular with international audiences. Why then was the work coolly received in Vienna and successful only in Prague? There are several possible explanations.

One is that while the opera was sung in the acceptable Italian, the composer was still Austrian by birth. The official composer on the emperor's court was an Italian, Antonio Salieri. Though legend has it that Salieri was obsessively envious of Mozart and may even have poisoned him, the facts appear to tell a different story. Salieri had no reason to wish Mozart dead. He was far better known in the highest musical circles than was Mozart. Besides, Vienna preferred a real Italian to a local boy "borrowing" the language of opera.

Another reason is that it was probably a mistake to hold the première in Vienna. The story of how two lowly servants outwit the master of the house—a Count—could not have pleased many of the aristocrats in the audience. The composer, an upstart from a little town of no consequence (at the time), already had a reputation for being a nonconformist. And indeed Mozart was just that. Nonetheless, as often happens in the history of the humanities, the future was on Mozart's side.

Listen on **MyHumanitiesKit.com**
Mozart, *The Marriage of Figaro*

The glorious arias in *Figaro* have made it one of the world's favorite operas. In the *recitative* Mozart has idealized human interaction. If Shakespeare's characters can talk to each other in verse, Mozart's characters can talk to each other in music. All theater, whether musical or not, depends upon a contract between performers and audience. "We are going to do this and this," say the performers; and the audience replies, "We will believe you as long as you are consistent." In a Mozart opera, characters sing the dialogue between arias and duets throughout.

For his libretto da Ponte adapted a French farce concerning a Count who has grown tired of his wife and seeks fresh young conquests. According to custom, the Count has *le droit du seigneur* (the privilege of the master to enjoy the sexual favor of a servant on her wedding night—before the groom may do so!). The young bride-to-be is a beautiful girl engaged to marry Figaro, another servant. The Countess, weary of her husband's philandering, helps the unhappy pair outwit the *seigneur,* who denounces his profligate ways in time for a rousing and joyous finale.

Many elements justify the prominence now enjoyed by this opera in the standard repertoire. First, there is the genius of da Ponte himself, who, while retaining a lot of the farcical nonsense from the original, transforms the Countess into a character of depth: a lonely wife facing the sorrow of aging and longing for the love she and her husband had once shared. In the tradition of farce, the wife of a cheating husband was usually a nagging shrew, and the philandering husband, a charming rogue. Da Ponte gives the Countess almost tragic dimensions, and, even though the aristocratic opening-night audience did not shout its approval, there must surely have been among them many women who understood the Countess's sadness.

The libretto with its unprecedented mixture of lively farce (the tricks played on the Count) and its unhappy Countess and its parallel plots of happy young lovers and a troubled middle-aged marriage gave the young Mozart a chance to reach into his amazing musical resources and put together a glorious score. What matter even long stretches of *recitative* when these are always followed by arias that are almost so beautiful that the listener *needs* some breathing space? Many other operas contain perhaps two or three famous arias for which the audience patiently waits. In *Figaro* the magic never stops.

For the Countess, a role to which dramatic sopranos aspire, Mozart wrote two of the greatest arias in the history of opera. In the first, "*Porgi, amor,*" she asks Love itself, which had once filled her life with joy, one final favor: restore her husband's affections or help her to find peace in death. In the second, "*Dove sono*" (so magnificent that critics have placed *the* before the title, an honor accorded to the *Oedipus;* the *David* of Michelangelo, and the *Mona Lisa* of Leonardo), she asks a question that people have been asking for centuries: Where have the golden moments fled? Why are happiness and love and youth gone before we know it? Why can't they last?

The final act of *Figaro* has been hailed as the very summit of opera. The French play on which the libretto is based concludes with a farcical scene involving disguise, mistaken identity, hiding behind bushes, and so on, a scene that da Ponte does indeed copy faithfully. At first, everything seems to be rushed so that the curtain can ring down on happy people in a rousing finale. But then comes a moment when the injured wife forgives her husband. Da Ponte stays true to the spirit of farce but Mozart transcends it with his music. The philandering husband falls to his knees and simply sings "I ask for your pardon," to which the Countess replies "I consent." However contrived this ending may sound, the music makes it thrilling.

Mozart turns the moment into a soaring musical passage, an almost divine act of forgiveness from the soul of a woman who has long suffered neglect but has never lost her love and understanding. The stirring melody is then repeated by full chorus with the voice of the Countess heard above all the others, reaching ever higher and higher. The moment suddenly has attained all the majesty of a solemn requiem sung in an enormous cathedral, filled at last with the joy of redemption.

In the 1981 film version of Peter Shaffer's play *Amadeus,* Salieri, who is obsessed by his jealousy of Mozart, is shown watching the final act of *Figaro*. As he listens to the countess sing her forgiveness, his eyes fill with tears and a voice inside him acknowledges that this music is what it would sound like if God could sing!

> *"We cannot know whether the composer ever predicted the immortality of his opera. Most likely he did not. Listen to the Countess sing sweetly about events that usually provoke anger, and learn to forgive history. Listen to the Countess . . . She drinks "reality"—foul air—and transfigures it."*
>
> **—Wayne Koestenbaum**

Verdi and Romantic Opera

Though portions of Mozart's operas have the grace and balance of the classical style, most of the arias and duets, in keeping with the emerging romantic, spirit allow for a freer expression of emotion. The romantic movement—political, artistic, literary, and musical—protested against restraint: political and social restrictions on human behavior, as well as Apollonian restrictions preventing poets, playwrights, and composers from being carried away emotionally. While French opera tended to be faithful to its classical roots, Italian and German opera embraced the new emotional freedom that Mozart had already shown.

The works of Giuseppe Verdi (1813–1901) offer major examples of the romantic style. They contain an abundance of melodious arias and less sung dialogue. Two of his operas—*Rigoletto* in 1851 and *La Traviata* in 1852—are among the world's favorites. They became international successes almost at once, but they are forever associated with their original home: La Scala in Milan, still one of the world's great opera houses. Many notable singers have sung their first roles there.

> *"Whenever I go to an opera, I leave my sense and reason at the door with my half-guinea, and deliver myself up to my eyes and my ears."*
>
> **—Lord Chesterfield**

A standing ovation at La Scala guarantees stardom, but success there is hard-won. Italian audiences are notorious for their treatment of inadequate performances and judge newcomers by the most severe standards. Many a singer has been booed off the stage at La Scala, often for the failure to sustain a high note for as long as the audience requires. On the other hand, audiences have been known to stand on their chairs screaming approval for fifteen minutes or even longer. It is particularly risky for a singer to debut at La Scala in an opera by Verdi, Italy's national treasure.

Without their music, Verdi's operas would have to be termed melodramas, the plots of which allow for many scenes of heartbreak and self-pity. Yet when these moments are combined with soaringly beautiful melodic lines, audiences are transported into a realm that great art provides.

Rigoletto, like Mozart's *Figaro,* contains so many familiar arias that audiences feel toward it as they would to a dear friend. The plot is typical of nineteenth-century melodrama. A court jester's daughter is seduced by her father's master. The angry father, hungry for revenge, plots to have the man killed. The daughter overhears that someone is to be murdered and deliberately walks into the trap, sacrificing her own life. The opera ends with the grieving father holding his dead daughter and singing one of Verdi's many glorious arias.

Verdi insisted upon plots that would allow free reign to his genius for combining emotion and melody. In *La Traviata* (literally, "the strayed one") he found a perfect vehicle, a work that transcends period melodrama and could stand alone as a tragic play. Add to it the glorious music, and you have Verdi's masterpiece.

Based on a famous French literary success, *La Dame aux Camelias* ("The Lady of the Camelias"), *La Traviata* is the story of a courtesan named Violetta, a woman living in luxury provided by wealthy male companions. Her beauty attracts a handsome young man named Alfredo. Although she struggles against real love and insists on living a free life (expressed in the aria "Sempre Libera"—"Always Free"), the suitor overcomes her objections, and they begin living together in the country.

Alfredo's father visits the courtesan and begs her to renounce his son, whose affair would damage the family's reputation and prevent his daughter from marrying into a respectable family. Violetta tearfully agrees to leave her lover, and then writes a note saying she prefers her previous life in Paris and is leaving him.

In the final scene Alfredo returns to vow his love once more but finds that Violetta is dying of consumption. This turn of events allows Verdi to

AP Images/Mary Altaffer

James Valenti and Angela Gheorghiu, *La Traviata*, 2010

The New York Metropolitan Opera House's production of Verdi's *La Traviata* demonstrates the enduring power of its tragic story.

write some of the most memorable music in all of opera. In true romantic fashion, love has been thwarted by social restrictions. Violetta is another of the great roles for dramatic sopranos because of the demanding score and the complex characterization of the heroine. In a sense Violetta has sacrificed herself for her lover, a melodramatic convention, but in contrast to the daughter's sacrifice in *Rigoletto,* hers is motivated by real passion, an outgrowth of real character.

Richard Wagner

Romanticism also fostered nationalism, especially among countries that had not yet found a prominent place in the world. Germany in the nineteenth century was experiencing its first excitement of world recognition. German music had reached a position of supremacy with Beethoven and many others, including Felix Mendelssohn and Johannes Brahms, who followed in his footsteps.

> *"Whereas the Greek work of art expressed the spirit of a splendid nation, the work of art of the future is intended to express the spirit of a free people irrespective of national boundaries. The national element in it must be no more than an ornament, an added individual charm, and not a confining boundary."*
>
> **—Richard Wagner**

On the opera front the showdown between Germany and Italy was inevitable. Mozart's one great opera with a German libretto, *The Magic Flute,* still did not eclipse the composer's Italian-language works. Several decades later, the growing respect for a truly German opera can be largely attributed to the work of Richard Wagner (1813–1883), who, by coincidence, was born in the same year as Verdi.

Wagner's works are enormous, epic, heroic, often noble and inspiring. Wagner made the German language as powerful on the stage as Italian, and his masterpiece, *The Ring of the Nibelung,* is based on stories from Germanic mythology, which was little known in the rest of the world. *The Ring,* consisting of four huge operas, made Germans proud that the world was now aware of a mythological heritage to rival that of the Greeks and the Romans.

Wagner went one step further than either Homer or Virgil. He added monumental symphonic music demanding full orchestral accompaniment and singers of extraordinary vocal power. To this day the label "Wagnerian singer" carries with it prestige and critical respect. He added powerful dramatic confrontations and scenic effects, justifying his restoration of the label *music-drama.* He made the most memorable use of the *leit-motif,* giving all of the major characters a musical theme heard when they appeared or, in variations, included in their arias or in the symphonic introductions to scenes. The Wagnerian *leit-motives,* running throughout the four operas, lend a unity to what might otherwise have been a sprawling musical narrative.

Lebrecht Music & Arts/Alamy

Lenbach, portrait of Richard Wagner, date unknown

Composer who gave Germany a mythology.

In addition to being a composer, Wagner was a political radical, very much involved with revolutionary ideologies sweeping Germany in the mid-nineteenth century. He took part in rallies and protest marches and translated into music his ideals of liberation. In *The Ring* cycle the all-powerful gods are destroyed in the final act.

He wanted to liberate opera from both its classical restraints and its Italian melodrama. He wanted to create true music-drama that would be critically placed beside the great works of Sophocles and Shakespeare. He wanted characters that were larger than life: characters that were heroic and noble and met tragic destinies with courage and honor. An opera historian writes: "Wagner's essential standpoint was that opera should not be mere entertainment, but (and he drew on Greek tragedy to support this) a fundamentally educative and ennobling experience."[2]

Wagner believed Italian opera had made an aesthetic mistake in subordinating the drama to the music, beautiful as it might be.

He wanted to reverse course and elevate drama to the position of dominance; otherwise, audiences would be there simply for a concert and would be denied the overwhelming emotional experience he knew opera was capable of providing. In order to do this, he realized, the composer must also write the libretto, thus assuring the creation of a solid unity never before seen or heard.

Wagner turned first to the heroic figures of world mythology, to stories he thought worthy of his enormous talent. (Wagner was never modest about his genius.) As he was composing his first major opera, *The Flying Dutchman* (1841), he realized he was facing the same problem that both his classical predecessors and his Italian contemporaries had encountered: how to provide beautiful music and keep the flowing dramatic line from becoming uninteresting. In *Tannhäuser* (1845) and *Lohengrin* (1848) he found his answer. If the dramatic line were to be the dominating factor, the music that sustained it could never be less than glorious. He felt there was no choice but to conceive of an opera as a giant symphony, written for a full orchestra and singers with the vocal power to be heard soaring above the music. Orchestra and singers were to form a unity never before known.

Tannhäuser and *Lohengrin* drew on Christian and Arthurian legends. Now the time had come to base an opera on Teutonic mythology, which bore a close kinship with the old Norse stories of gods and mortal heroes. In Norse tales, the king of the gods is Odin; in German, Wotan. The hero of *The Ring* cycle is Siegfried, who appears in the Norse sagas as Sigurd. Wagner took the old myths and turned them into an epic tale about the downfall of those who struggle for the power that a magic ring bestows upon the wearer. In true romantic fashion, it is love that is ultimately greater than the lust for power.

The Nibelung are a race of elves, or dwarfs, who control a huge store of treasure, including a wondrous lump of gold, which, if made into a ring, would have the power to make the wearer the supreme ruler of the universe—as long as he remains chaste. Wotan, wanting no one to be his superior, steals the ring which has been forged by a dwarf named Alberich, who places a curse on it. As a result, disaster after disaster occurs. Only genuine love will lift the curse. Until such time, which Alberich is confident will never come, people will destroy each other in the struggle for the power the ring holds.

The four-opera cycle reaches a stirring climax when Brunhilde, one of Wotan's daughters, commits suicide by riding her horse into the funeral pyre on which the body of her beloved Siegfried is being burned. The fire is so spectacular that it consumes Valhalla, the palace of the gods, who are also destroyed, after which the Rhine River overflows its banks to quench the flames. The marathon cycle of operas comes to a magnificent close with a lyrical melody that represents the return of love to the world and the end of inhuman power.

The mythology of a magic ring is not limited to Norse and Germanic sagas or to Wagner's telling of the story. The fable of the ring of Gyges was originally found in Plato's *Republic* (see Chapter 11), and *that* ring also bestowed magical powers upon the wearer, who could, in this fable, become invisible at will, causing no end of damage. Readers will certainly think of the modern version of the story, Oxford professor J. R. R. Tolkien's *The Lord of the Rings* trilogy, made into three epic films. In Tolkien, the magic ring is similar to that found by Plato's Gyges in that its power lies in allowing the wearer to become invisible and thus to rise above all human law. In Plato, Wagner, and Tolkien, the message is the same: power corrupts, and only selfless love can save the world.

> *And we have all heard the anecdote of the composer who played his latest piece to his guests, after which they asked him what its meaning was. The composer sat down at the piano again and played the piece through once more.*
>
> **—Jacques Barzun**

Wagner's achievements illustrate an interesting facet of the humanities. The writer Katherine Mansfield once said that a great poet must be a great poem, meaning that there should be no distinction between an artist's work and an artist's life, but in Wagner's case there was considerable disparity. He dwelt on themes of love and redemption, but he himself was a total egotist, subjecting his acquaintances to lengthy readings of an opera newly finished, borrowing money he never paid back, and practicing infidelity. Theoretically liberal in his views, he was also strongly anti-Semitic. He was the center of his own universe, the diametric opposite of a Vincent van Gogh, who constantly reviled his own work. Genius, apparently, is unevenly distributed, but it cannot be ignored.

Modern Operetta and Opera

Like all forms of music, not to mention the other arts, opera in the modern period has its own idioms and purposes. Italian is no longer the required language. Composers choose libretti written in their own tongue. If they do not, like Wagner, create their own libretti, they usually work closely with their authors. Wagner's ideal of opera as a unity of music and drama still applies, though by now the flow of the dramatic line is so completely dominant that audiences often long for outbursts of melody. More and more, the aria is replaced with a musical underscoring of dialogue. Often the question has been raised: "Why is this play set to music at all?"

Opera, among the summit achievements in the humanities, inspires modern composers to try reaching its heights. Similarly, modern playwrights often want to write tragedies that can rival those of the Greeks and Shakespeare. But the passage of time has affected musical styles. Melodious passages are considered dated and hackneyed by many young opera composers. Rarely do we hear a definite aria that stands out from the rest of a scene. To find one, we must often turn to the Broadway musical stage, to Leonard Bernstein's *West Side Story* or Stephen Sondheim's *Sweeney Todd,* which approach grand opera but keep their Broadway roots at the same time.

> *"A musician must make music, an artist must paint, a poet must write, if he is to be ultimately at peace with himself. What a man can be, he must be."*
>
> **—Abraham Maslow**

Showboat

The **operetta** was a nineteenth-century European invention given worldwide fame by Austrian composers such as Johann Strauss (1825–1899). In an operetta, spoken dialogue moves the play forward but is continually interrupted by lengthy and melodious arias that are far more important than the drama itself. For many composers, the form solved the problem of how to keep the audience's attention during the spaces between songs: it shortened the spaces. In an operetta there are so *many* songs that audiences don't have long to wait for the next one. The story line is either silly and complicated but fast-moving or filled with tear-jerking sentimentality that never requires close listening. Characters in operetta tend to be two-dimensional with identifying traits that remain unchanged throughout the proceedings. The songs vaguely grow out of the context of a scene, but nobody complains if the two are not closely related.

Showboat (1927) with Jerome Kern music and Oscar Hammerstein II lyrics is important for both its songs, many of which remain popular to this day ("Ol' Man River," "Only Make-Believe," "Why Do I Love You?", "Can't Help Lovin' That Man," "My Bill," and "You Are Love") and for the fact that it was really the first operetta to aim at a serious unification of music and story. Some historians of the musical stage have called *Showboat* the precursor of the musical play as well as a link between Broadway and opera.

The story is embedded in nineteenth-century sentimental drama. The heroine is Magnolia, a sweet Southern lady who falls madly in love with a Mississippi river-boat gambler improbably named Gaylord Ravenal. A handsome charmer, he sings divinely—and often—but we know that his addiction to gambling bodes no good. They marry, have a child, fight over his gambling, then separate. A reformed Gaylord eventually returns and has a tear-filled scene with his grown daughter, who doesn't know who he is, but that doesn't stop both of them from singing a duet. Ravenal is finally able to persuade Magnolia that he has changed for the better. The curtain falls on the required joyous finale.

Yet *Showboat* has darker undertones. "Ol' Man River," one of the classic songs of the American musical stage, is sung by an African American dockworker with no future except for endless and exhausting toil. His few leisure moments are fraught with danger: "Git a little drunk, and you land in jail." He is "tired of livin', but scared of dyin'." *Showboat* dared to confront racism in America. *Showboat* was a sensational hit, and its racial theme reached huge white audiences.

Porgy and Bess

George Gershwin, already discussed in Chapter 6 for his *Rhapsody in Blue,* shared the desire of many American composers to reach the heights of grand opera and achieve worldwide recognition. And why not? He had already proved that he was capable of writing rich symphonic scores. His brother Ira was a distinguished lyricist. All they needed was a subject that would allow them to keep their American roots and to create opera out of truly American sounds. They found the perfect subject in a novel called *Porgy* by DuBose Heyward, who was willing to write the libretto. So *Porgy and Bess* (1935) was born, a work that met with critical coolness but has since been hailed as a supreme example of true American opera. From its beginnings, disguised as a Broadway musical to lure audiences, it has moved on and been performed at the world's major opera houses. Unfortunately, Gershwin, who died at 38, did not live to see *Porgy and Bess* hailed as a masterwork.

Terrence McCarthy

Laquita Mitchell and Eric Owens, *Porgy and Bess,* 2009

The famous duet "Bess, You Is My Woman Now."

The setting for both the novel and the opera is a rundown section of Charleston called Catfish Row. Porgy, the unlikely hero, is crippled and gets around in a goat cart. He is high-spirited and optimistic despite his poverty. His first aria is the jaunty "I Got Plenty of Nuthin' and Nuthin's Plenty for Me." Bess, the heroine, is stunningly beautiful but shunned by the residents of "the Row" because of her lax morals. She lives with Crown, a violent lawbreaker, who abuses her but whom Bess finds irresistible.

When Crown is forced to flee the law, Bess is abandoned and accepts Porgy's offer of a place to stay. Though at first Bess is just using Porgy until such time as Crown returns, she becomes aware that the man in the goat cart loves her with all his soul. Little by little she responds to his love and affectionate kindness. "Bess, You Is My Woman Now," one of the glorious duets in modern opera, remains a concert favorite for singers and audiences, as does Bess's aria "I Loves You, Porgy" in which she pleads with her newfound love not to allow Crown to force her back.

Crown, however, does return and is killed by Porgy. The Row inhabitants—and the audience—believe the act is justifiable, and we are prepared for a happy ending. However, in the tradition of the greatest love stories, such as *Romeo and Juliet* and *La Traviata,* the curtain must fall on tragedy, this time brought about by Sportin' Life, a gambler, a pimp, and a drug dealer, dressed out in glittery, expensive clothes. Sportin' Life exudes Dionysian charm and almost wins the audience over, but then his true nature is revealed when he exploits Bess's weakness for drugs. He promises her a lifetime supply if she will just go with him to New York. She struggles briefly with the dilemma, but Sportin' Life wins out. Though abandoned, Porgy remains optimistic about finding his lost love. He doesn't know where New York is, except that it's "over that way." The opera ends with Porgy setting off in his goat cart as he and the chorus sing the rousing but ultimately sad "I'm On My Way."

> *"True music must repeat the thought and inspirations of the people and the time. My people are Americans. My time is today."*
>
> **—George Gershwin**

Other Modern Operas of Note

Though their contributions to modern opera have not yet achieved the international fame of *Porgy and Bess,* there are at least four modern composers of opera who should be included in a humanities text; Gian-Carlo Menotti, Leonard Bernstein, Stephen Sondheim, and John Corigliano have already left behind a considerable legacy of works in a number of musical genres, including opera.

Amahl and the Night Visitors. Italian-born Gian-Carlo Menotti (1911–2007) is assured of lasting musical fame, if only as the founder of one of the world's most prestigious music festivals held annually in Spoleto, Italy, with an American version in Charleston, South Carolina. New works are premiered in both places, along with performances of standard repertoire by outstanding musicians and conductors. Menotti has given the world perhaps the most prodigious offerings of the four composers we have singled out for special mention, beginning with his 1951 Christmas opera *Amahl and the Night Visitors,* written for television when that medium was in its infancy and since performed hundreds, perhaps thousands, of times until it has been seen by more viewers than any opera in history.

The one-act opera concerns the night when the three kings following the star of Bethlehem stop at a humble dwelling in which live Amahl, a crippled shepherd boy, and his mother. The kings tell the boy about their mission to follow the star until it leads them to the place where the holy child is about to be born. Amahl, who is very poor, nonetheless gives the kings a humble gift for the child and is miraculously rewarded for so doing. The simplicity of the story and the extremely beautiful music make the work enduringly popular even among those who profess no traditional faith.

Both Bernstein and Sondheim achieved success on the Broadway stage and both composed works that combined Broadway styles with genuine opera elements.

Candide. Leonard Bernstein (1918–1990), who will be discussed later in this chapter as the composer of *West Side Story,* one of the most revolutionary of Broadway musicals, also composed an operatic adaptation of Voltaire's classic *Candide* (1956). Critics have debated whether the work is really an operetta, but labeling it seems beside the point. It has elements of both genres.

With a libretto by Richard Wilbur who based it on the famous eighteenth-century satire on the philosophical idealism current at the time, Candide concerns a naive young man who has been led to believe by his tutor that "everything happens for the best in this best of all possible worlds." In the high comedy of pure satire, everything goes wrong in what turns out to be the worst of all possible worlds. The dialogue, combining the wit and wisdom of Voltaire and the poetic sounds of Wilbur, make the libretto of *Candide* far stronger than that of most operas.

Bernstein's music is every bit as strong and takes the work very close to the realm of opera. The aria "Glitter and Be Gay," sung by the heroine who pretends she is faking enjoyment of her life as a prostitute but secretly loves it, is now in the repertoire of world-famous opera sopranos. The final chorus, "Make Our Garden Grow," is as rousing an ensemble piece as any opera has given us.

Sweeney Todd. Stephen Sondheim (b. 1930) was still in his twenties when he wrote the lyrics for Bernstein's *West Side Story.* With songs such as "Maria," "Tonight," and "Somewhere," which have become classics, Sondheim quickly established a huge reputation for himself as a wordsmith. He became the dominant force in the American musical theater during the last quarter of the twentieth century, ultimately composing *both* music and lyrics and working closely with his librettists to ensure the unity of every component.

Thus far, his masterpiece is a work with little spoken dialogue, which is now being recognized as a genuine opera: *Sweeney Todd, the Demon Barber of Fleet Street* (1979), adapted from a creaky nineteenth-century melodramatic thriller. In the hands of Sondheim and Hugh Wheeler, the librettist, the melodrama disappears, replaced by genuinely tragic dimensions, with a symphonic score of concert-hall importance.

Sweeney Todd returns to his home and business in London after serving a jail term imposed by a judge who lusted for and then raped his wife. In his obsession for revenge against the entire judicial profession, Todd rents rooms upstairs from Mrs. Loveit, a piemaker whose business is faltering because she makes, as a song suggests, "The Worst Pies in London." He opens a barbershop, and, when a customer turns out to be a judge, he slashes the man's throat with a razor, sending the body down a chute to the waiting Mrs. Loveit, who then dismembers and bakes it into a pie. Her business skyrockets, and she becomes famous for serving up the *best* pies in London. Todd, of course, awaits the day when the villainous judge who destroyed his wife will come in for a shave.

Pictorial Press Ltd./Alamy

Johnny Depp, *Sweeney Todd*, 2007

The demon barber of Fleet Street in the film version of *Sweeney Todd.*

The development of Todd from a wronged husband to a cold-blooded killer is carried out with meticulous and chilling precision by Sondheim and Wheeler. The barber's burning desire for revenge is thwarted when the judge escapes his grasp, a turn of fate that drives Todd into total madness and random killings. In the final scene, the work approaches tragic heights when the crazed barber murders a prostitute, only to discover that she is his wife. His blood-curdling cry of "*No!*", accompanied by crashing chords from the orchestra, rivals the cries of despair often heard at the climax of great tragedies.

Though there are memorable songs along the way—notably "Joanna," "Green Finch and Linnet Bird," "Not While I'm Around," and the grimly hilarious "A Little Priest," a duet in which Todd and Mrs. Loveit sing about the various professions to be found in her pies—the emphasis is on the onrushing flow of the drama. Sondheim sacrifices opportunities for hit songs in the interest of the plot. Much of the dialogue is sung in an updated version of the Mozartean *recitative*.

The Ghosts of Versailles. Unlike Bernstein and Sondheim, John Corigliano (b. 1938) has never written a Broadway musical, but he did win the Academy Award for scoring the 1997 dramatic documentary *The Red Violin* about the 300-year-old history of an instrument that affects many lives in many different ways. He is also known for having written several important symphonies and an award-winning opera, *The Ghosts of Versailles* (1991), about what the ravages of the French Revolution did to genteel eighteenth-century French society, of which the Palace of Versailles still stands as a symbol. Like most contemporary works based on historical incidents, however, the opera is really about the recurring human tragedy of war.

The Broadway Musical

If ragtime, blues, and jazz are established American contributions to the humanities, the same holds true for the Broadway musical, still popular after a century and a half, still dominant at the box office, and perhaps more widely performed throughout the world than most other theatrical genres. It has, of course, undergone a number of changes throughout its history.

> *"Those in the free seats are the first to hiss."*
>
> **—Chinese proverb**

The heyday of American **musical comedy** was from World War I to the early 1950s, though the form is far from obsolete, with many of the classic shows enjoying continual revivals. It appealed to a public hungry to forget the devastation of war, and then later, to a public seeking escape from the financial distress of the Great Depression and anxiety over another approaching global catastrophe. Finally, it appealed to a public in the mood to celebrate newly won (if short-lived) world peace.

The typical plot was threadbare, the characters two-dimensional, the dialogue unbelievable; but these elements simply existed for the songs that were for the most part so bouncy that audiences silently moved their feet in accompaniment. Every now and then the pace slowed, and the audience was treated to a ballad with simple, easily remembered lyrics. The sheet music of the show's hits was for sale in the lobby so that the songs could be played in parlors throughout the country. If one could not play well enough, there were piano rolls to be inserted into pianolas (player pianos), which made the keys move as if by magic. The hit songs from the musical comedies were parallel to the romantic opera arias that stood out from their context, and there was never a problem of how to keep the dramatic line going. Nobody really cared.

Of Thee I Sing. An outstanding musical comedy of the period, *Of Thee I Sing*, was the work of the Gershwin brothers. It elevated the stature of the Broadway musical by winning the Pulitzer Prize, up to then reserved for serious nonmusical work. *Of Thee I Sing* was anything but serious. It is a swiftly moving satire on presidential politics that is often revived in election years. So consistently hilarious yet right on target did the show prove to be that some critics compared it to the

> *"Your audience gives you everything you need. They tell you. There is no director who can direct you like an audience."*
>
> **—Fanny Brice**

*Manhattan crowds,
With their turbulent musical chorus!*

—Walt Whitman

comic operas of W. S. Gilbert and Sir Arthur Sullivan, which had taken London by storm during the last quarter of the nineteenth century.

The theme of the show is that candidates will do almost anything to win the presidency—anything, that is, beside having a serious, profoundly considered agenda. The "hero," Wintergreen, is chosen as his party's candidate because of his innocent and appealing nature. That he has little brain power appears not to be a problem. For his running mate, the party corrals a dolt named Throcklebottom, whose name they never can remember. The major problem is that Wintergreen has no wife, so the party conducts a beauty pageant to find "Miss White House."

The winner of the pageant is Diana Deveraux, empty-headed and gorgeous; but our hero has already fallen in love with and proposed marriage to Mary, a young woman who lacks glamour but has common sense (the only character who does!). Not only that, she can bake corn muffins. When the jilted beauty queen sues the candidate, the Supreme Court has the case dismissed on the grounds that the country needs the corn muffins to feed the homeless. A grateful country elects Wintergreen.

The Supreme Court is called back into session to debate the sex of the "first baby," which turns out to be boy/girl twins, showing that the court is not always on top of things. There is an impeachment hearing, prompted by the rival party's efforts to use the jilting of Diana to its own advantage. The problem is resolved when Wintergreen's party bosses force Diana to marry Throcklebottom, who has nothing to do and cannot even find the Capitol. The curtain falls on a joyous finale that has everyone united either in marriage or political unity.

The Musical Play

By the late 1930s Hollywood was luring serious-minded audiences away from live theater by presenting films which confronted major social issues and with characters of increasing depth and complexity. The lightweight Broadway show was starting to show its age. Major Broadway show composers and wordsmiths recognized that the time was right for more serious work if the musical stage were to survive.

Pal Joey. An important transition work of the Broadway theater is *Pal Joey* (1940), with music by Richard Rodgers and lyrics by Lorenz Hart. Still very much in the musical comedy tradition with peppy songs, tap dances, and ear-caressing ballads, *Pal Joey* also deepened the Broadway musical and deserves to be considered a pioneer **musical play**. It cast some dark shadows on the traditionally sunny landscape of the musical stage and provided the audience with a very *un*traditional hero who could sing and dance but was self-centered and not very likeable.

After it is expertly done, can you draw sweet water from a foul well?

—Brooks Atkinson

The authors were already established as major collaborators whose marquee names alone guaranteed the success of any venture, thus minimizing risks to the backers. The libretto was by John O'Hara, a leading author of serious fiction, known for his novels, screenplays, and short stories for the *New Yorker.*

It all happened by chance. O'Hara, tired of the compromises a screenwriter was forced to make in order to satisfy studio executives, was determined to make a living by selling his stories only to the *New Yorker*. Unfortunately, the editor of the magazine rejected the new work, declaring that he would never publish another O'Hara story unless he understood it. Feeling sorry for himself, O'Hara went on a drunken binge; and when he recovered, he began writing a story about a ruthless heel, a master of ceremonies in a seedy nightclub. The character, Joey Evans, suited O'Hara's bleak mood. At first he had no idea where the piece was going, but "the more I wrote about the slob, the more I got to like him."[3]

The story became a whole series of stories. A close friend read them, fell in love with the charming scoundrel, and suggested that O'Hara write a play about him. O'Hara liked the idea but thought it should be a musical because of its nightclub setting and Joey's profession as a showman. Rodgers and Hart, who were looking for more challenging subject matter, became O'Hara's collaborators.

"There is a traditional trick that theatre people have played as long as I can remember. A veteran member of a company will order a gullible newcomer to find the key to the curtain. Naturally the joke is that there is no such thing . . . but all my life I've been searching for that key."

—Richard Rodgers

The work did not erupt overnight into a theatrical masterpiece. The first draft of the libretto was called "disorganized" by George Abbott, hired to direct the show. He also thought Joey might alienate the audience. The final version, however, was reached after numerous rewrites that still did not fit the mold.

Rodgers and Hart insisted on retaining some musical comedy lightheartedness. They decided to exploit the nightclub for all it was worth, introducing a chorus line of broken-down, no-talent singers and dancers who, according to reports, kept the audience in an uproar.

They also wanted to characterize in song the spoiled socialite who ventures into the club, seeking escape from a dull and loveless existence. She meets Joey, and, though she sees through him instantly, she is unable to resist his charm and sexuality. Rodgers and Hart gave her one of their greatest songs—"Bewitched, Bothered, and Bewildered"—which became an anthem for all those obsessed with absolutely the wrong people. Of course, the affair is a disaster. Joey will never change, but she will always love him. O'Hara refused to violate his plot so that the audience could go home happy.

The biggest *coup* of the enterprise was finding just the right person to play Joey. It was Gene Kelly, who later became a Hollywood legend as one of the greatest dancers ever to hit the screen. Not only could he overwhelm audiences with his complex choreography but he had a velvet singing voice and an outgoing personality filled with the charm without which the show could not have succeeded.

Audiences kept filling the theater, and the show's box-office success would encourage others to strive for greater depth in the genre. Despite the efforts of Rodgers, Hart, and Abbott to keep the show within the parameters of musical comedy, the tide of change was irresistible. As William Hyland writes,

> *Although the excellent music . . . was integral to the spirit of the play, for once Rodgers was overshadowed by the character, the lyrics, and the play itself. Because of the harsh and realistic story and the biting lyrics, the show became a landmark . . . a milestone in the liberation of the musical from the stale forms of the 1920s and 1930s.*[4]

Photofest

Gene Kelly, *Pal Joey*, 1940

As Joey, Gene Kelly exuded the audience magnetism that made him a star.

Oklahoma! The resistless tide finally swept up Richard Rodgers himself. He remembered a play he had seen in 1933, which he thought would make a good musical. He suggested the venture to Hart, who read the script and said it wasn't suited to his brand of worldly-wise lyrics. But Oscar Hammerstein II, librettist of *Showboat*, was also seeking more challenging material and found the project to his liking. The libretto and lyrics for *Showboat* had displayed his abilities as a poet and potential as a serious dramatist.

Green Grow the Lilacs was a folk play about the rivalry of two cowboys for a sweet and innocent young woman. One was handsome and honorable, the other villainous, placing the heroine in grave danger. On the face of it, it was a tired old plot, reminiscent of

"*Every once in a while a theatre-goer needs a shot of Rodgers and Hammerstein to make the world seem a better place or allow newbies to gain an appreciation of what musical theatre is all about.*"

—Roy Berko

nineteenth-century melodrama. Yet Rodgers had been charmed by the folksiness and relative simplicity of it.

Not only was *Green Grow the Lilacs* different from anything Broadway had ever seen but the collaborators thought, it might also satisfy audience need for an escape from concerns over the war in that year of 1943. The play was set in the late nineteenth-century Midwest, when tensions could arise over which young man would offer the highest bid for a girl's picnic basket and win the right to be her companion for the festivities.

The first version of the musical was given a tryout in Boston, as was customary in those days. Called *Away We Go!*, it received lukewarm to poor critical notices and the producers feared they couldn't raise enough money to bring the show into New York. They did, however, find someone willing to invest the necessary $50,000 (a sum that eventually grew into millions). The collaborators spent long nights in a Boston hotel reworking every scene while trying to retain the show's down-to-earth honesty and simplicity. They also knew it needed a rousing choral finale, without which a show could not survive, a number that would explode on the stage and send the audience home in high spirits. Since the setting was the Oklahoma Territory just prior to its achieving statehood, the authors realized they needed to give prominence to the huge event. What better way to end the show than singing of the promise that statehood brings, the promise of a better life in a better world?

Rodgers and Hammerstein named both the number and the show *Oklahoma!* and opened it in New York to ecstatic reviews and the largest post-opening box office any show had ever known up to that time. Ticket scalpers were charging up to fifty dollars—at a time when three and a half dollars was the reigning box-office price for an orchestra seat. On a radio sitcom, one character promised his beloved tickets to *Oklahoma!* if she would marry him. Her answer was, "And where would you get them?"

From the moment the curtain rose, audiences were seeing something completely different on the musical stage. Instead of a chorus line of scantily clad beauties, they saw only an elderly farm woman churning butter on her porch and listening to an offstage cowboy singing "Oh, What a Beautiful Mornin.'" The cowboy enters, finishes the song, and talks about his love for the woman's niece, who soon appears and seems annoyed at the cowboy's attentions. He returns her jibes. Instead of the usual love-at-first-sight sentiments, each demands that the other refrain from showing any sign of affection in front of others because "People Will Say We're in Love—."

Everything about the story works to musical stage advantage. The settlers in the territory make up the chorus. The picnic auction allows for folk dancing. The crux of the drama comes when Laurie, the heroine, has to decide between the handsome Curly and the farmhand Judd. The conflict is dramatized in a spectacular dream ballet called "Laurie Makes Up Her Mind," for which choreographer Agnes DeMille cast highly trained dancers, performing against surrealistic backgrounds rich with Freudian symbolism. The ballet started a trend that lasted for decades. Musicals *had* to tell part of their story in ballet form.

Oklahoma!, still given the credit for having taken the musical stage in a startling new direction, was followed by one huge success after another for Rodgers and Hammerstein: *Carousel* (1945), *South Pacific* (1949), *The King and I* (1951), and *The Sound of Music* (1959). The death of Hammerstein in 1960 brought to an end the most productive collaboration in musical theater history.

Oklahoma! *was so poorly reviewed in its Boston tryout that it almost never made it to Broadway.*

West Side Story. Given the increasing number of dance elements in musicals since *Oklahoma!*, the arrival of *West Side Story* in 1958 was inevitable. The show is a musical play dominated by intricate ballets, modern dances, and a symphonic score that has become standard in the repertoire of great orchestras. An updated version of *Romeo and Juliet,* it also relies heavily on the drama of the doomed love affair. Because of the Shakespearean origins, the audience readily accepted the tragic ending.

West Side Story is a product of upscale collaboration. The idea of making Shakespeare's tragedy into a modern tale of two lovers caught in the feud between rival New York street gangs belonged to Jerome Robbins (1918–1998), a choreographer famous in the world of modern dance. Leonard Bernstein, the composer, had been classically trained at Harvard and was destined to become one of the world's leading conductors as well as composers.

Robbins and Bernstein had collaborated in 1944 on a sprightly musical comedy called *On the Town,* which chronicled, largely in dance, the adventures of three sailors on a 24-hour leave in New York City. The new project resulted in what some critics called a "dance opera," but the play itself was never subordinated to the other components because the libretto was written by Arthur Laurents, a recognized playwright not known as a writer of musicals. The work is so rich in every element that it is still performed as both a Broadway musical and as an opera. The dance sequences have been taken out of their dramatic context and performed by international ballet companies. Theater companies have performed love scenes from Shakespeare interspersed with Bernstein songs (or arias); the pairing creates a flowing unity.

AP Images/Rudi Blaha

Marisol Montalvo and Jesper Tyden, *West Side Story*, 2003

The balcony scene in a modern production of *West Side Story*.

The third member of this extraordinary collaboration was a young lyricist named Stephen Sondheim, a protégé of Oscar Hammerstein and, as Broadway later discovered, a composer in his own right. The lyrics here have a simplicity not characteristic of Sondheim's later work but are eminently suited to the tragedy.

In *West Side Story,* Romeo becomes Tony, of Polish descent and a reluctant member of the Jets, who respect his sensitivity and idealism but nonetheless expect him to fight when they say the need arises. The archrivals are the Sharks, young Puerto Ricans battling to own the neighborhood turf and rid the streets of non-Hispanics. The gang members on both sides were all played by seasoned ballet dancers.

Juliet becomes Maria, sister to the leader of the Sharks, and therefore sworn to be an archenemy of the Jets. She and Tony meet at a school dance, even as Romeo and Juliet meet at a masquerade ball. The famous balcony scene of Shakespeare is transformed into the duet "Tonight," sung by Maria on her fire escape and a lovesick Tony in the alley below. Meanwhile, the Sharks invite the Jets to take part in a "rumble," an all-out street fight, with the victors laying claim to the "turf." Tony is reluctant, aware that the Sharks' leader is Maria's brother. But gang loyalty forces him to take part in the rumble, during which Bernardo keeps daring him to strike the first blow. Tony holds back, but when Bernardo draws a knife and kills Riff, the Jets' leader and Tony's best friend, the anguished hero kills Bernardo in revenge, even as Romeo slays Juliet's cousin Tybalt in a sword fight.

In Shakespeare, the tragic climax is brought about by a quarantine that prevents Romeo, in exile, from getting a letter assuring him that Juliet is alive and waiting for him. In the dance opera, Tony is deceived into believing Maria has been killed by her jealous boyfriend. Bereft of all hope, the hero rushes into a darkened street, pleading to be shot. Hearing his voice, Maria goes joyfully to meet him, but the boyfriend shoots him before he can see her. She cradles the dying Tony in her arms as a police siren is heard, too late to prevent the tragedy.

Many of the arias from *West Side Story* have become classics. In addition to "Tonight," they include the jazzy "Jet Song," the haunting ballad "Maria," and the main theme of the dream ballet, "Somewhere," which tells of a happy land where there is "a place for us" with "peace and quiet and open air." Barbra Streisand chose this aria to close her final public concert in 2000.

Spring Awakening. The rock musical and the rock opera have become increasingly ensconced in the Broadway scene. *Rent,* mentioned on p. 272 as a rock adaptation of Puccini's *La Bohème,* inhabited a Broadway theater for more than a dozen years, testifying to the power and versatility of rock to communicate stories of love found and lost and to celebrate the joy of life.

Its source is a dark 1906 German play about middle-class moral rigidity. It adheres to its roots, changing little of the story and not providing an unbelievable happy ending.

Spring Awakening (2007) may be regarded by historians of the musical stage as a consummate achievement in blending serious, even tragic drama with a rock score. Its source is a darkly tragic 1906 German play of nearly the same title by Frank Wedekind (1864–1918), a dramatist and poet who, in this work, exposed middle-class moral rigidity as Ibsen had done in Norway. Unlike *Rent, Spring Awakening* adheres closely to its roots, changing very little of the story and, of special importance, not providing an unbelievable happy ending. This indeed is a tragic musical play. A forced happy ending would have destroyed a work many consider a masterpiece in its own right. Adaptation to the musical stage was risky; adding a rock score even more so. The time period of the play is 1891. So what is rock music doing in a German prep school of more than a century ago?

The music, so completely out of place for the time and setting, is an externalization of the suppressed emotions, especially sexual desires, of teenage students raised with no knowledge of where babies come from and no one to assure them their hormonal awakening is natural and not to be denied. Since, in this society, parents never discuss sex, either pro or con, the children grow up obsessed with the subject and filled with wrong information passed from one student to another in fearful whispers.

Joan Marcus

Lea Michele and Jonathan Groff, *Spring Awakening,* 2007

The teenage lovers in *Spring Awakening,* unaware of what's to come.

Melchior, the hero, is academically gifted and intent on probing the mystery of life, hiding forbidden books under his mattress and reading them late at night. Gradually he achieves an understanding of sexual intimacy as a natural rite of passage, dangerous if suppressed (much as Sigmund Freud theorized, shocking that same society). The result of his awakening is to write an essay explaining the sexual process in minute detail and then distributing it among the student body. He is painfully aware that his close friend, Moritz, had been so obsessed with misunderstood sexual urges that, unable to study, he had failed his exams and committed suicide rather than face his family.

Melchior's girlfriend is the innocent Wendla, who at first resists his protestations of passionate longing for her and his assurance that their sexual coupling would be both natural and beautiful. Wendla, so much a victim of sexual denial and the subconscious need to throw off her moral shackles that she can think of nothing else than being alone with Melchior, finally allows the young man access to her body. They sing one of the show's memorable songs, a slow rock duet called "The Word of Your Body," in a scene tender and beautiful but filled with grim foreboding.

Their joy doesn't last long. The authorities have discovered that Melchior has written the shocking essay. He is sentenced to solitary confinement in a reform school, a sequence dramatized in the symbolic style of early twentieth-century German **expressionism** with Melchior tied to the backstage wall in a crucifixion tableau. Wendla becomes pregnant, though she does not understand what is happening inside her. The desperate parents send her to a doctor who supposedly specializes in handling these delicate matters; he diagnoses the pregnancy as a disease and gives her a fatal overdose of medicine.

Amazingly, the rock score balances the tragic bitterness of the play. The chorus of students can both sing and dance, as they break into rock affirmations of sexual attraction and rebellious denunciations of society's repressiveness. Like many important works in the humanities, this one awakens not only spring, but thought.

Next to Normal. By 2009, the year *Next to Normal* opened on Broadway, a rock score was no longer revolutionary. Rather, it was almost expected. But that did not mean it still could not be put to *un*expected uses. *Next to Normal* took the musical stage into a territory it had never known before: the often chaotic world of mental disorder, in which the complex musical lines and lyrics of rock were an apt—really, the only possible—means of creating a sense of what mental dysfunction was really like. There are fewer songs in the production compared to the show's predecessors. Rather, music and lyrics form a continually flowing line.

The show won the Pulitzer Prize for Drama in 2010, only the eighth musical ever to earn this distinction. The Pulitzer committee oabserved that *Next to Normal* deserved the prize for raising the level of the musical stage in dealing with a hitherto untouchable subject. Certainly, without the music to balance the play's bleakness, it could have proved uncomfortable to watch.

Alice Ripley won the Tony for Best Actress in a musical, but could have received it for drama as well, so profoundly does she plumb the depths of her mental anguish. She plays a bipolar mother whose son died sixteen years earlier and who was so traumatized by his loss that she can no longer remember his name or even that she ever *had* a son. Her husband and a psychiatrist do their best to support her in hopes of restoring her to a relationship with reality, but to no avail.

The work gains an added dimension with the spirit of the dead son watching over his mother at the top of a three-storey set. In one of the show's few songs as such, Gabriel sings to her "I'm Alive," but of course she

Sara Krulwich/The New York Times/Redux Pictures

Aaron Tveit, Alice Ripley and J. Robert Spencer, *Next to Normal*, 2009

The musical play *Next to Normal*, about a bipolar mother who doesn't believe her son is dead, won the Pulitzer Prize in 2010.

cannot hear him. If the opening night audience expected, or at any rate *hoped* for a happy recognition scene, they were in for a disappointment. There is only a slight ray of hope in the closing moments when the mother almost hears Gabriel. But not quite.

Perhaps audiences of today have grown accustomed to sad endings because of *Spring Awakening* and, earlier, *West Side Story.* Just as *Oklahoma!* in 1943 made it impossible for the Broadway musical ever to return to the bouncy whoop-de-do of the '20s and '30s, so too has the evolution of the genre taken a turn that may never be reversed.

Dance

Pianist Leon Fleisher, rank-ordering the elements of music, puts rhythm first, followed by harmony, and then melody. His rationale appears to be that, although music can and indeed does exist without harmony or melody (in the romantic sense of that word), it has to have a rhythmic underpinning or else it becomes random sound. Music historians have indicated that rhythm came first, probably as an accompaniment to rituals of birth, coming of age, planting and harvesting, death, and burial. These rituals thus can be considered early forms of dance, which has been traced back 30,000 years.

Alan Novelli/Alamy

Maypole, Cheshire, England, 2009

Children participating in an annual Maypole dance, probably unaware that it dates back to a forbidden mating ritual.

Early History

The Egyptians are known to have taken part in highly elaborate dance ceremonies in which they imitated the movement of heavenly bodies. Pharaohs required slaves to entertain them with dances that involved unusual gyrations and acrobatic skills. Around the same period, the Hebrew Bible refers to dance as an expression of joy as when Miriam, sister of Moses and Aaron, dances to celebrate the Red Sea escape from Pharaoh's soldiers.

In Greece, beginning around the sixth century B.C.E., the art of the dance became an official form of public entertainment. Dancing became a respected profession, and those with sufficient strength and suppleness of limb were trained from an early age. During the Middle Ages, dancing was banned by the church because it was associated with pagan rituals and religions. Folk dancing, however, was practiced despite the ban, and remnants of it survive to the present time.

The Maypole ritual dance, perhaps originating in ancient Ireland, continues to be practiced on both sides of the Atlantic. Circling a pole decked out in (usually) crepe paper of varied colors and chanting words such as "May party, May party, rah-rah-rah," the dancers, often young children, probably do not realize that their joyful activity dates back to an annual but forbidden spring mating ritual: for young people, a symbolic rite of passage.

During the Plague of 1348 known as the "Black Death," a terrified population of Western Europe released their fears by performing a "dance of death," usually led by a dancer dressed as a skeleton. Children today still do this dance and chant:

Ring around the rosey,
A pocketful of posey.

Ashes! Ashes!
All fall down!

Today's dancers probably may not know the original meaning of "rosey"—a reference to the reddish boils on the skin of those afflicted with buboes (hence "bubonic" plague). Today's young dancers fall on the ground giggling with excitement, unaware they are reenacting a catastrophe.

In the thirteenth century, an Islamic spiritual leader named Mevlana Rumi established a religious sect, the Mevlevi Order, whose members took part in a ritual still practiced today. Known as whirling dervishes, they turned ever faster and faster until they achieved a trancelike state, which they believed liberated their souls from earthly bondage and allowed direct union with Allah.

In the late Middle Ages, as major cities grew in size and sophistication, dance became a highly refined art form for which only the graceful few were suited. Mimes, such as those in Italy's celebrated *commedia dell'arte* (see Chapter 7), studied dance to give their bodies the flexibility to execute their seemingly nonsensical movements, including sudden pratfalls that seemed painful but were in reality skillfully rehearsed movements. Pratfalls are still a mainstay of circus clowns.

In the early eighteenth century, the *kathak* dance was integral to the entertainment of a royal court in northern India. Originating as a stylized method of telling stories and educating viewers about their mythology, it became a highly professional art form with elegantly swirling movements, lightning quick pirouettes, sudden poses, rapid stamping of feet, and subtle gestures capable of expressing a wide range of emotions. Dancing has long been indigenous to Indian culture.

Dancing satisfies a universal human need, whether everyone assembled takes part in it or simply sits and watches. Seated audiences empathize with the motions and rhythms on stage, so that they too are in a sense participants. Dance awakens the Dionysian spirit in all of us, a spirit that longs to be free.

Ballet

Acknowledged as the premier form of dance art, ballet developed from Italian street mimes before it became a court entertainment for aristocrats. Ballet is fundamentally a series of controlled bodily positions and combinations that require years of arduous training to perfect, yet must seem effortless to an audience. Ballet dancers seem to float across the stage, and viewers forget the unnaturalness of the motion. Ballet forces the body to do things the body is not basically equipped to do. In the daily training exercises (even required for the stars!), a basic position is to have the feet turned outward with the heels touching. Most of us could manage that. But the dancers are then required to turn each foot horizontally in opposite directions, heels still touching, Try that one!

Females must stand on their toes for unnaturally long periods. Males must be strong enough to lift and then hold the ballerina with one hand. They must be muscular and lithe at the same time, their bodies resembling classical statues.

To the French and the Russians in the nineteenth century must go the credit for having formalized the art of the ballet, the French having been first in establishing the rigorous training exercises. Ballet positions and movements still bear French labels. A **plié** is a lowering of the torso while keeping the feet turned outward as described above. A **jeté** is a leap, executed so lightly that the landing is almost silent (unless you're in the front row). A **pirouette** is performed by the ballerina standing on the toes of one foot as her body spins around and around, faster and faster. If the

> *"I put my dancing feet before my allegiances to friends and lovers, even husbands: before my home. . . . I gave one hundred percent of myself to my art, and my art has repaid me."*
>
> **—Alexandra Danilova**

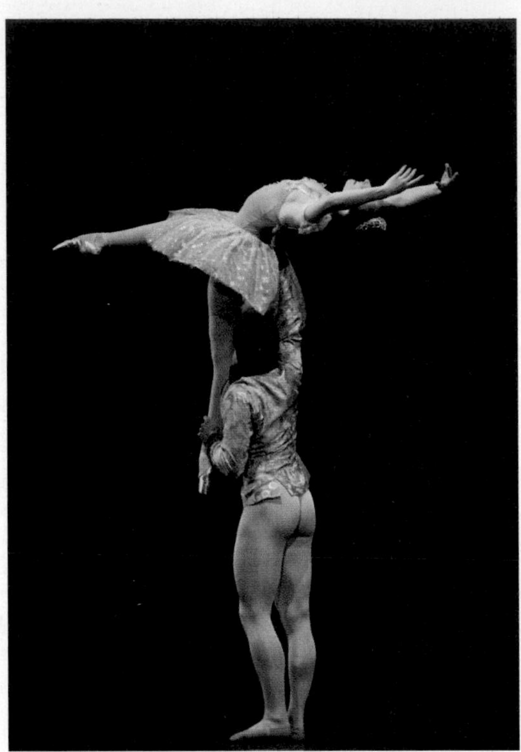

testing/Shutterstock

Czech National Theater ballet troupe, *The Nutcracker*, 2010

The *pas de deux* is a mandatory element of the classical ballet.

movement is observed closely, the viewer will see that the dancer does indeed put her other foot down in order to maintain balance, but the greatest dancers whirl so rapidly that they become almost a blur and the foot rest goes unnoticed.

Classical ballet often tells a story, but it need not, since viewers don't come for the plots. Story or otherwise, classical ballet follows a traditional and expected format. There is an ensemble of males and females as well as a male and female soloist. The ensemble performs intricate combinations, then exits as the ballerina enters on her toes **(en pointe)** performing a complex combination, with complex design, especially if she is a major personality in the ballet world. She whirls offstage, still en pointe, as the male lead leaps onto the stage with many pirouettes, athletic jumps, and body spins high in the air. The great dancers—Nijinsky, Nureyev, and Baryshnikov—are famous for the amazing heights they could reach. Finally, the ballerina returns, holds out an arm to her partner, and the two perform an exquisite **pas de deux** to a slow, melodious accompaniment.

French Ballet: *Giselle*. Since ballet terms are all French, we should expect the art form to have originated in France. By the late seventeenth century, French operas had to include a ballet, whether relevant to the story or not. By the following century, French ballet had become an internationally recognized institution.

By the nineteenth century, the spirit of romanticism, with its less restrained emotionalism, became popular in France, and the blending of classical movement and romantic music gave the ballet world one of its enduringly popular works, *Giselle* (1841), with music by Adolphe Adam (1801–1850). The ballet has an appealing story line, as well as traditional components such as the *pas de deux* and a chorus of beautiful young women executing complex movements *en pointe*.

The story centers on the love of a young maiden for an aristocrat named Albrecht, who has courted her disguised as a suitor on her social level. Eventually betrayed by him, Giselle dies from a broken heart and is destined to join the ranks of the Wilis (*Willies*), the souls of young women jilted before they reached the altar. Their mission is to torment the men responsible. In true romantic fashion, however, Albrecht has a change of heart, and, while mourning at Giselle's grave, is visited by her spirit. Instead of tormenting him, she joins Albrecht in one last *pas de deux*. We leave the theater, knowing their love will last forever.

Russian Ballet: Tchaikovsky and Diaghilev. Russia has proclaimed itself the dominant force in ballet since the nineteenth century for a number of impressive reasons. The first is that Peter Ilich Tchaikovsky, discussed in Chapter 6 as a master of romantic melody, wrote some of the greatest scores in the ballet world: for *Swan Lake* (1875), *Sleeping Beauty* (1890), and *The Nutcracker* (1891).

In the first of these dances, a prince, melancholy at being forced to select a bride from among the eligible young ladies approved by his parents, goes out to hunt swans. As he is about to shoot one of them with his arrow, the Swan Queen intervenes, informing him that she and the other swans are women transformed by an evil sorcerer. He falls in love with her and promises marriage.

During a ball sequence at the palace, the sorcerer enters with his beautiful daughter made to look like the Swan Queen. The prince announces that she is to be his bride, but he catches sight of the real queen outside the window. Rushing to the lake, he arrives just in time to hold her, dying of grief, in his arms. The story, typical of nineteenth century sentimental melodrama, is more than overshadowed by the music and dazzling choreography, always evident in major productions.

Sleeping Beauty is based on the popular fairy tale of a girl who is cursed in revenge by an evil witch, furious at not being invited to her christening, and is fated to die when she is 16. The evil prophecy comes to pass, but because of the girl's beauty, her parents refuse to bury her. When a handsome prince hears of her, he journeys to the castle, falls in love instantly, and kisses her lips. The kiss breaks the spell, and they live happily ever after.

The Nutcracker, performed during the holiday season in hundreds of theaters, often gives children their first exposure to ballet; and adults, perhaps having shared the same experience in *their* childhood, continue to watch it year after year. A little girl is given many expensive holiday gifts, but the one she loves most is a nutcracker doll. Late at night, when she sneaks into the parlor to play with the doll, she is suddenly threatened by an army of aggressive mice. The Nutcracker springs to life and, with the assistance of the toy soldiers, challenges the mice in battle. The Mouse King corners the Nutcracker and is about to slay him when the little girl intervenes and pulls off the mouse's tail. The deed breaks yet another magic spell, and the Nutcracker turns into a handsome prince, who becomes her guide as she watches a variety of dances from around the world before she wakes up with memories of a wondrous dream.

Ron Burton Mirrorpix/Newscom

Dame Margot Fonteyn and Rudolph Nureyev, *Pélleas et Mélisande*, 1969

Two stars of the twentieth-century ballet world, in a famous *pas de deux.*

Having produced these as well as most of the world's most famous ballets, Russian companies became internationally well-known. *Ballets Russes de Monte Carlo,* the most outstanding, was founded in 1909 by Sergei Diaghilev (1872–1929). He was a brilliant choreographer with a multitude of skills and talents, but it was in ballet that he found the most intense challenge, combining as it did dance, drama, visual art, and symphonic music.

Next to being the impresario of the world's leading ballet company, Diaghilev is famous for having fostered the career of a revolutionary dancer, one whose creative imagination and athletic agility have influenced male dancers ever since. In the opinion of many, Vaslav Nijinsky (1889–1950) was the greatest male dancer of all time. In 1913, Nijinsky both choreographed and starred in *The Rite of Spring* (Chapter 6), a work that alternately bewildered and scandalized audiences accustomed to the prettiness of classical dance.

The Nijinsky choreography, with graphic depictions of mating rituals, and the dissonant score by Stravinsky, did in fact change the direction of both music and dance. The transition took a while, however, especially in dance. Males would have to train long years to emulate Nijinsky's high-flying leaps and spins. One who did come close was Rudolph Nureyev (1938–1993), star of Britain's Royal Ballet (shown earlier, with another star, Dame Margot Fonteyn).

The man who brought Russian ballet to the West was George Balanchine (1904–1983). In the late 1900s he founded the New York City Ballet, and in 1934 the School of American Ballet, dedicated to the training of American dancers so that companies on this side of the Atlantic would not have to import their stars from Russia. Balanchine married the great ballerina Maria Tallchief, who had been born on an Oklahoma reservation.

"*I don't want people who want to dance. I want people who have to dance.*"

—George Balanchine

Balanchine in turn took ballet into new directions. He incorporated American jazz into his dances, and even teamed up with Rodgers and Hart for the musical *On Your Toes,* for which he created the ballet *Slaughter on Tenth Avenue* using intricate and highly athletic dance combinations to tell the story of passion and murder in a Manhattan saloon.

Modern Dance

> *Art is the only way to run away without leaving home.*
>
> —**Twyla Tharp**

Modern dance is not so-called just because of its roots in the modern world. It is a recognized style of serious dance that has broken with the classical tradition and is now a required subject in dance schools. It has its own rigorous training methods. Its ancestor was *The Rite of Spring* choreography, which gave dancers freedom of movement and body positions.

Training begins with classical positions and combinations, then adds complex variations: leaping, catching and being caught, falling to the floor, rolling, springing up with seeming effortlessness, and much physical contact with other dancers. A male dancer might lift a ballerina, hold her aloft with one hand, then suddenly release her as the audience gasps and she slides down and around his body, reaching the floor, then touching his neck with a leg extension attained after years of difficult practice.

Males must do weightlifting and other strenuous exercises in order to perform athletic movements in the style of Nijinsky and Nureyev. One of the stars in Balanchine's company was Edward Villella (b. 1936), who started in classical ballet, but then made use of his early life as a boxer by bringing his muscular physique and dazzling footwork to modern dance. In 1988 he founded the Miami City Ballet, which rapidly gained international recognition.

Another dancer, at home in both classical and modern dance, is Mikhail Baryshnikov, born in Latvia in 1948. His athleticism and superconditioning made him a star of the famed Kirov Ballet at a young age. Dissatisfied with being limited to the standard ballet repertoire, Baryshnikov immigrated to the United States, where he created legions of new fans for modern dance. Audiences packed theaters to see his breathtaking leaps which sometimes exceeded those of Nijinsky in height. According to reports, he still holds the record for the longest midair spins, from which he would recover in a graceful leap and go immediately into a pirouette, spinning so fast he almost became invisible.

Martha Graham. A pioneer in modern dance was Martha Graham (1894–1991), who continued creating new works until she was well into her eighties. American-born Graham introduced strenuous movements and extensions into her narrative dances. Whereas in classical ballet the body is held rigid for long periods, Graham trained her dancers to be flexible and loose of limb and able to contract themselves inwardly as well as outwardly. There are much lifting and rolling of shoulders in Graham and much floor work. Her style requires dancers to express emotion with their bodies, and therefore their bodies have to seem as free as possible.

Graham was deeply rooted in America and its cultural traditions. She studied many kinds of folk dancing and used them for her masterwork, *Appalachian Spring* (1947), with its great symphonic score by Aaron Copland (Chapter 6). These stylized folk dances, some in unexpectedly slow tempos, are rhythmically complex. Instead of adhering to customary combinations in which dancers count from one to eight in time to the music, Graham allowed the music and the story to dictate what the count should be. Watching the dance, you would not be aware at times of an underlying rhythm, so completely fused are the dramatic moments, the music, and the movements.

Other Schools of Modern Dance. Graham, along with Agnes De Mille, the choreographer of *Oklahoma!*, greatly influenced the Broadway stage, which now incorporates modern dance as well as ballet elements into many shows. In 1975, a show about dancers, *A Chorus Line,* with choreography by Michael Bennett, focused on a collection of young people auditioning for a Broadway musical. In truth, it was a musical play, without a hero and a heroine. It told the story of each aspiring dancer, and bits and pieces of what would be a rousing production number were rehearsed along the way. The dancers were dressed in rehearsal clothes—mostly shorts, T-shirts, and sweatpants. In the famous finale the entire ensemble reappears in white and gold suits, top hats, and canes, to perform the finished version of what has been in rehearsal. The synchronization of the dancers was (and continues to be) astounding. They move as one (and "One" is the name of their song). The audience comes away having made the acquaintance of each member of the line, and with a better understanding of what it takes for many different personalities to merge into a tight unity.

Far seeing choreographers have kept adding new kinds of movement, making possible more and more complex narratives told through dance. One such choreographer was José Limon (1908–1972), who formulated a new aesthetic rationale based on the dancer's relationship to gravity. Dancers first develop a sense of weight and method for translating weight into energy. Limon also taught techniques of breathing so as to distribute energy throughout the body. His most famous work is *The Moor's Pavanne,* a retelling in dance of Shakespeare's *Othello.*

Also of great importance are the contributions of Alvin Ailey (1931–1989), founder of the dance company that still bears his name and keeps alive his innovations. As a teenager, he became interested in dance, but, although he studied with Lester Horton, a major choreographer, he believed professional opportunities would be limited because he was African American. At the time, most dance companies were not racially mixed. In 1953, however, Ailey's debut performance in Horton's company was a thunderous success; and in 1958, encouraged after Horton's death by further studies with Martha Graham and Doris Humphrey, he founded the Alvin Ailey Dance Theater.

***A Chorus Line,* 1985**

The chorus line, each member of which the audience has come to know as an individual, comes together in the finale and performs as "One."

Ailey introduced dazzling movements new to modern

Ailey's early work benefited greatly from African dance and music traditions introducing dazzling movements that were new to modern dance. At performances of Revelations*, a gospel musical, audiences have been known to dance in the aisles.*

dance as well as realistic glimpses into Southern poverty. But Ailey was also steeped in classical training. Some of his dances included traditional male and female partnering in addition to folk and jazz dancing. One of the favorite works in the company's repertoire is *Revelations.* With gospel and spiritual music the piece depicts Sunday worship, a baptism ritual, a quiet solo of personal union with God, and a rousing finale in which the company joyously celebrates togetherness. Audiences of all ethnicities regularly clap their hands to the music, and some have even been known to dance in the aisles.

In 1963, Ailey integrated the company, incorporating styles and techniques from Japanese and Native American dance traditions. The varied international repertoire led to an invitation from the Soviet Union; the Ailey company was the first American troupe to tour that nation in half a century.

Twyla Tharp (b. 1941) combines classical and modern dance with jazz and pop music. Like Martha Graham's dancers, her loose-limbed dancers exhibit freedom of the body attained after years of disciplined exercises and adapt readily to many kinds of music, especially those once thought unsuitable for the serious world of dance. For example, Tharp has created a piece called *Come Fly with Me* (2010) set to the songs of Frank Sinatra. She carefully chooses the pieces that deal with the struggles between the sexes. She takes the classical *pas de deux* and turns it into a tense tug-of-war between male and female dancers.

Like Alvin Ailey, Tharp emerged from rigorous classical dance training to become unique in her approach combining ballet, modern, jazz, and tap—accompanied by as broad a range of music as the dance world has heard. In 1973, her ballet *Deuce Coupe* juxtaposed classical combinations with a soundtrack by the Beach Boys. *Push Comes to Shove* (1976), created for Baryshnikov, mixed up humor, Mozart, and Joplin rags.

Today, both classical ballet and the varieties of modern dance can be offered by the same company on any given night. Electronic sound technology can substitute for a live orchestra, allowing many regional companies to have a repertoire as large and exciting as those of dance theaters in metropolitan areas. Whether or not you live in or near a big city, chances are that a dance company is not very far away and you can treat yourself to the joy of watching perfection of form and motion.

Folkloric Dance

Folkloric dancing is rooted in time-honored customs and values of given cultures. Sometimes it is vastly different from formal dance, requiring little or no training. Sometimes, as in flamenco, it is a highly disciplined art form, requiring, like the ballet, years of rigorous training and practice.

Native American Traditional Forms. Native American dance varies from one tribal nation to another. Each membe r of a nation grows up learning how to execute dances appropriate to a particular occasion. In Canada and Alaska, for example, the dead are remembered and honored in drum dances involving everyone. Participants wear masks and elaborate costumes. Visitors come from all over to watch the spectacle and are usually given gifts as a show of hospitality.

In the Northwest there is a Native American tradition known as **potlatch**, a coming together of community members to a feast and dance that celebrates a significant occasion, such as a marriage or a new birth. At one point in the dance, younger members take over and create their own steps to show the continuity as well as the evolving nature of the people.

Native Americans have a long unbroken relationship to the earth (see Chapter 15), and their dances often reflect their reliance on and glorification of nature as provider. The Bear Dance, performed by nations of the American Far West, is a reenactment of a very ancient ceremony ritualizing the hunt and the gathering of enough food to sustain the community through the long winter. Recall the Buffalo Dance, mentioned earlier, which dates back 30,000 years.

In the Plains, the tradition of the **powwow** dance is very strong. It is a component of a tribal reunion and offers an example of how a folk dance becomes an art form. Throughout its evolution the powwow has developed codified sequences that are strictly observed. It begins with the pageantry of the Grand Entry, in which young and not-so-young participants perform a rhythmic march to a regular drumbeat. This is followed by the group's singing of the tribe's anthem and then a series of dances celebrating activities such as planting, harvesting, courtship, and marriage. Non-natives who are frequent visitors may be invited to join in the dances, but only if they can be trusted to follow the strict guidelines.

Flamenco. A dance form with roots in the folk traditions of many cultures is the **flamenco**, now identified with Spain, or more specifically, with the province of Andalusia. It emerged, however, from gypsy songs thought to be from India, Hebrew incantations, Moorish (Arab) rhythms, and Andalusian folk music. Of all the folkloric arts, flamenco may be the one characterized by the strictest possible rules. It involves guitar playing, singing, and a dance with powerful foot-stamping rhythm accompanied by hand clapping (which has become an art form in itself and must be rigorously practiced before it can be performed in public).

Its first professional embodiment occurred in 1842 as part of Andalusian café entertainment. Within two decades, flamenco had spread to Madrid and other parts of Spain. A typical performance involved four females and two male dancers, two guitars, and two singers. As a result of the popularity of the dance, the guitar became the leading Spanish instrument. Today flamenco guitar solos can be heard in concert halls all over the world.

Denkon Images/Alamy

Flamenco dancers

Flamenco dancers follow rigid guidelines.

Mexican Folkloric Ballet. Similar to the flamenco, the Ballet Folklórico de México evolved from folk traditions. It has become a world-famous institution, with a number of dance companies performing in many venues. Most of the major Mexican cities have their own Ballet Folklorico, but they all share a style of dancing as well as a common repertoire; individual companies attached to their own locales will add pieces reflecting the region's mythology. All of the dancers are as highly trained as those found in the best professional companies anywhere in the world.

Under the guidance of Amalia Hernández, the Ballet Folklorico originated in Mexico City in 1952, and this company remains the most important and honored of all the companies. The mission of the entire institution is to preserve the traditional culture, which has always been rich in dance, and to educate outsiders about the Mexican heritage. Depending on the financial resources of a given area, the folkloric presentations can have elaborate costumes and stage sets, or be sparsely but no less artistically performed.

Certain set pieces form the basis of every performance, no matter where. The "Stag Dance," for example, is a traditional work in which a male dancer wearing a stag's head is chased by hunters, eluding them cleverly until the very end, when he succumbs to a wound from a huntsman's arrow. Again, we think of the ancient Buffalo Dance. Other set pieces celebrate love, marriage, and the cycle of life. The mood is generally one of joy and pride in an artistic legacy.

The Ballet Folklorico has a well-established dance school in Mexico City and other venues throughout Mexico and the United States. Folkloric training can be found in universities such as Dartmouth and Princeton, and the study of folkloric techniques is part of many high school curricula.

Various companies regularly tour, performing not only in recital halls but in schools as part of the institution's cultural mission, which continues to extend its reach. The Ballet Folklorico de Mexico is a prime example of the humanities as an ambassador of goodwill and cultural enrichment.

Asian Dance. Also dedicated to the preservation of a cultural art are those who perform ancient Buddhist dances of Tibet and Nepal. In the Tibetan city of Karnataka there is a college that offers training to Buddhist monks. The curriculum includes traditional dances performed at religious ceremonies. Every dancer is a monk, and the audience is limited to students. There is no attempt to win wide approval.

In the first dance, the participants wear black metal caps adorned with peacock feathers. The group enters in a solemn line, making graceful gestures with their hands and moving slowly to the accompaniment of deep-throated chants. The movement is intentionally monotonous in order to still the emotions and bring about a serene acceptance of existence without the illusions created by ego. Of all the dance traditions in the world, Buddhist dance is least likely to arouse a state of excitement.

Tibetan Buddhist dance movements are monotonous, suggesting the void that is life.

In the next dance, colorful silk garments are worn, perhaps because of the Tibetan Buddhist belief that color can, if only briefly and occasionally, be experienced. (In Japanese Zen Buddhism [see Chapter 10], black is the preferred color of all human surroundings and garments, because color will only foster the illusion that there is no void, that existence can have a meaning.)

In this chapter we have explored many varieties of dance in the human experience. Movement to rhythmic accompaniment answers a universal need both for the dancers and those who watch. Most dance forms can stir the emotions of the viewer, bringing about the catharsis discussed in Chapter 7 as central to Aristotle's theory of tragedy. Or they can, as in the Buddhist dance styles, serve to calm us into a state of detachment from inner emotional stress. Actually, all dance forms lead to the same destination and are of vital importance to our lives.

LEARNING OBJECTIVES

Having read and carefully studied this chapter, you should be able to:

1. Give three examples of early rituals and ceremonies that may be the ancestors of the musical stage.
2. Discuss the origins of opera.
3. Show the characteristics of classical opera by citing two examples.
4. Show how Mozart solves the problem of sustaining a dramatic line in between arias.
5. Differentiate between operetta and opera.
6. Explain why the French and the Russians are given credit for being the founders of ballet.
7. Differentiate between ballet and modern dance.
8. Single out three distinguished choreographers of modern dance and cite an example of the achievements of each.

KEY TERMS

en pointe ballet term for standing on one's toes.

flamenco style of dance originating in Andalusia, involving precise foot movements and hand clapping, accompanied by guitar.

jeté ballet term for a leap

leit-motif musical theme associated with Wagnerian opera identifying a particular character or a force, such as fate or a curse, repeated throughout the work.

libretto the lyrics and recitatives of an opera, or the book and lyrics of a musical.

music drama name given by Wagner to his works.

musical comedy genre of the musical, prevalent in the 1930s and 1940s, featuring songs that often have little to do with the plot, or what there is of one.

musical play genre dating back to *Pal Joey* in 1940 and *Oklahoma!* in 1943 with strong plots, much dialogue, developed characters, and songs that spring from the situation.

opera the plural of "opus" (Latin for "work"), a genre with all, or most, of the dialogue sung, and often interspersed with melodious arias.

operetta lighter version of opera, featuring melodious arias and duets which often have only a thin relationship to a scene; libretto is usually just an excuse for having the music.

pas de deux French phrase meaning "step of two," a usually slow dance duet set to melodious accompaniment.

pirouette spinning movement executed by the dancer balancing on one foot.

plié French ballet term for a basic position in which the dancer squats down, keeping the feet extended horizontally with heels touching.

potlatch Native American community gathering to celebrate significant occasions such as marriage or birth.

powwow dance performed by Native Americans of the Plains as a means of community unification.

recitative sung dialogue in an opera.

singspiel German term for opera dialogue that is half sung and half spoken.

TOPICS FOR WRITING AND DISCUSSION

1. As early as the seventeenth century, opera composers such as Monteverdi faced a problem with maintaining audience interest in the story during the sections without arias. What was that problem, and how did Monteverdi solve it?
2. Have some fun with opera. Take a familiar fable or fairy tale, updated of course, and write a short opera libretto for it. If you're ambitious, you and some friends could sing it to the class, using, if necessary, familiar tunes.
3. *Of Thee I Sing* rose above the run-of-the-mill musical comedies of its time because of its libretto, a hilarious satire on politics. Outline your own libretto for a contemporary musical satire. You can also include some familiar songs with words that fit your subject.
4. If you are fortunate enough to have a heritage that includes dances for special occasions, share a description of one of these with the class, giving its background and function for the population that uses it. It will be a plus if you can provide a little demonstration.
5. Although *Sweeney Todd, the Demon Barber of Fleet Street* is a musical version of a creaky old melodrama, this update by Stephen Sondheim, in the opinion of many critics, reaches tragic heights. Study the summary of *Sweeney Todd* provided in the chapter and explain why, in your opinion, it does or does not.
6. What is an *antihero*? Illustrate by citing the example of a contemporary character (stage, screen, or television) who should be so identified.
7. When advance publicity for *Spring Awakening* first circulated, some theater-goers may have wondered what a rock score was doing in a tragic musical play set in 1906. Explain what it *is* doing there, and why it has apparently been so successful.
8. The chapter suggests that the rock score for *Next to Normal* was probably not a surprise to the audience, since so many shows today have such scores. From the description of the work provided in the chapter, does the score seem to fit the subject?
9. Though modern dance may well be the dominant style of dance art nowadays, the chapter also suggests that modern dancers need to be classically trained as well. What is the reason for this?
10. Coming from widely different cultural backgrounds, Native American ceremonies, the Ballet Folklórico de México, and the Buddhist monk dances of Tibet and Nepal do have something in common. What is it?

TAKE A CLOSER LOOK: Exploring *La Bohème* and *Rent*

AP Images/Franklin Franklin II

Anna Netrebko and Piotr Beczala, *La Bohème*, 2010

London Entertainment/Splash/Newscom

Vanessa Hudgens and Aaron Tveit, *Rent*, 2010

Madame Butterfly (discussed on page 27) was not Giacomo Puccini's (1858–1924) only work to be totally rewritten in a modern context. One of the most enduringly popular operas is his *La Bohème*. Since its 1896 premiere, it has been performed hundreds of times throughout the world. Audiences seem never to tire of its lush romantic score and its touching, tragic tale of the love between Rodolfo, a poet, and Mimi, a seamstress, living in the shabby bohemian section of Paris along with a number of friends, most of them artists, all of them poor but always hopeful of selling a poem or a painting. The story captures for all time the myth of starving artists living in a garret; and its main characters are, like Romeo and Juliet, doomed to be separated. The final scene in which the fragile Mimi dies from consumption in Rodolfo's bitterly cold attic room has probably brought even the most alienated Apollonian viewer close to tears.

In 1996 what appeared to be a modest, low-budget rock-musical retelling of *La Bohème* called *Rent* opened in a tiny off-Broadway theater. To accommodate the crowds, it moved to a large theater on Broadway and later became a successful film. With an infectious and unrelenting rock beat and its twenty-first-century cast of characters, *Rent* would have bewildered Puccini's original audiences. In the modern version, Rodolfo is transformed into Roger, an HIV-positive rocker determined to write a great song before he dies. Mimi keeps her name, but now she is a drug addict, also HIV-positive. Their friends include a gay couple, a lesbian couple, and a transvestite. Like the bohemians of Puccini's Paris, Jonathan Larson's characters live together in blissful poverty, singing wildly joyous songs pulsating with hope for the future, though the shadow of death is slowly encroaching.

Examine the photographs and the description above to gain a sense of the similarities and differences between *La Bohème* and *Rent*. The following questions will help you explore *La Bohème* and *Rent* as a critical viewer.

1. What aspects of the story and elements of our culture make *La Bohème* translatable to the twenty-first century?
2. In Chapter 2, we explored the modernization of Puccini's *Madame Butterfly* into *Miss Saigon* and in this chapter we explored the modernization of *Spring Awakening*. What do you think are the characteristics necessary to make a work relevant, even from startlingly different historical periods?
3. Imagine that you are buying tickets for the theater for next Saturday night. One of the two theaters in town is performing *La Bohème* and the other *Rent*. Which are you more interested in viewing? Why?
4. Think about the other musicals, operas, or dances explored in this chapter. Do any spring to mind as ripe for a modern reinterpretation? Where and when would you set the work? Why?

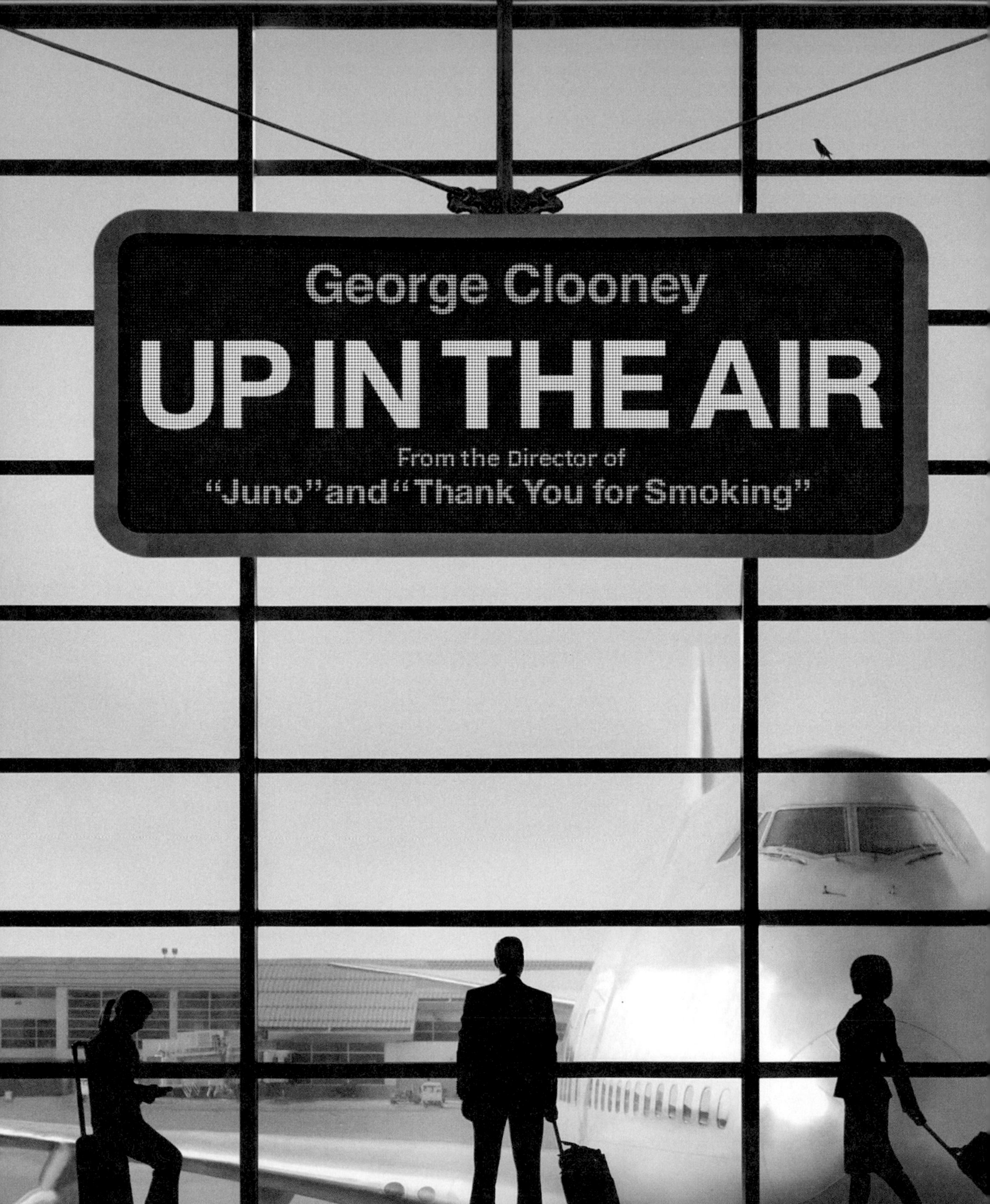
George Clooney
UP IN THE AIR
From the Director of
"Juno" and "Thank You for Smoking"

Chapter 9

Cinema

The motion picture, like other arts, is a vehicle of creative expression, and no study of the humanities is complete without including the medium. It is the most collaborative art form, involving many contributors. (think of those closing credits!)

After each weekend, box office rankings of current films are reported in newspapers and on television; such information is seldom given concerning art gallery openings or the premiere performance of a new musical composition. Further evidence of public attachment to film can be found each year when nominations and awards in the industry are announced. Most of the early part of the Academy Awards telecast is spent honoring editors, sound mixers, composers of background scores, costumers, and others who toil behind the camera and are frequently overlooked. But for at least one night the public is aware that film is indeed the most collaborative of all the arts. When all of the participants somehow blend their talents, the result may be a film classic with a wide following for years to come.

Films on DVD allow viewers to follow scene by scene the choices made by directors in achieving an effect. They are thus able to understand the reasoning behind camera angles, music or its lack, and, for astute critical viewers, even the compromises between the final product as shown on the screen and what the director may have originally intended. Documentaries that often accompany the film itself encourage critical analysis, showing viewers behind-the-scenes activities that contributed to the creative process itself.

This chapter begins with a discussion of the various elements, or conventions, of the cinema; for only by understanding their function can we view a film more critically and, if all goes well, with greater enjoyment. Next come milestones in early film history, followed by an analysis of some popular film genres.

Movie poster for *Up in the Air*, 2009

George Clooney plays a man whose job makes him fly from one place to another and who has no real home except an airport in *Up in the Air*, a memorable portrait of the alienated hero.

Conventions of Film

In film, as on the stage, **conventions** are conditions that audiences agree to accept as real. They include the rules or the grammar of seeing a film. Beginning readers learn the "rules" for print—read left to right, top to bottom; capital letters, periods, etc. Rules for film begin with a darkened theater, a screen, and a projector causing light to appear on the screen.

Sound

Before the introduction of *sound* in 1927 (perhaps the most revolutionary of all the conventions), silent movies had printed cards inserted to indicate necessary dialogue or information. Though the modern viewer may think of silent films as old-fashioned, in reality they developed pantomime to a high art in the work of Buster Keaton, Mack Sennett and Charlie Chaplin. Music underscoring the action was at first played by a pianist in the theater and was later imposed on the film itself, leading the way to "the talkies."

Music continues to be a major convention of film. Like the camera, it is always there, and we are meant to forget that in real life music does not suddenly come out of nowhere. Sometimes pounding music underscores violent action, but imaginative directors may often use music as ironic counterpoint to what is being shown, as in Oliver Stone's 1987 antiwar film *Platoon,* in which the violent destruction of a Vietnamese village by American troops is played against the slow and melodic sounds of Samuel Barber's "Adagio for Strings."

The Camera

The *camera* itself is a major convention, though audiences don't always "see" it there. They are not supposed to; but the critical viewer "disobeys" the rules and is acutely aware at all times of what the camera is up to. Continual developments in camera technology can make critical viewers more and more demanding of innovation, whereas early moviegoers were enthralled while watching a horse galloping or a locomotive hurtling along the track.

Point of view is the way the camera is positioned in any given scene so it is clear which character or which mind is experiencing the action. In a murder mystery, for example, the detective's consciousness may be pivotal, and scenes are shot from his viewpoint. If all of the other characters are suspects, we should not be allowed to see things from their perspective. On the other hand, if the central character is a clever thief whom we really don't want to see caught, the camera keeps us in that *character's* mind.

A story can be told from more than one point of view. In the Japanese film Akira Kurosawa's *Rashomon* (1950), each witness to a crime in the woods describes the events and motivations of the participants in a different way. A film may also begin with confusing dialogue and action which seem to spring from no point of view. The Mexican film *Amores Perros* (2000) begins with a car chase and frantic dialogue by the occupants of one car about the effort to stop the bleeding of a dog. The audience doesn't know the identity of the occupants or why they are being chased. Then there is a crash, and the first of three stories begins, each from a different point of view, showing the varied impact of the crash on the lives of the characters. By the end of the film, the three stories come together, and the importance of the accident is revealed in the line "God laughs at those who make plans." We finally understand why there is no focus on one character throughout the film. The director has become a philosophical observer.

Color

Color—or the lack of it—is an important element in **cinematography**. Before 1936, when the first major technicolor movie appeared (*The Trail of the Lonesome Pine*), all films were shot in black-and-white, a convention that is not necessarily an old-fashioned relic to be patiently endured when you are watching an older movie. Some of the best films ever made, such as *Citizen Kane* in 1941, analyzed later in the chapter, derive much of their power from the contrast between light and shadow that black-and-white film makes possible. Although some contemporary filmmakers might still prefer to film in black-and-white, they rarely do so, because color is demanded by audiences and those purchasing television rights to a film. When a film classic such as *Casablanca* is colorized, however, there is generally an outcry from loyal fans, as if an artist's original had been defaced.

Time

The convention of *time* is as flexible as the director chooses to make it. An action meant to last a minute can be prolonged on screen for several minutes, as the camera focuses on separate objects or people—and returns to them again and again. The introduction of the sophisticated handling of time is found in the work of great pioneers like D. W. Griffiths and Sergei Eisenstein, discussed later.

The objects that appear on the screen appear to be distant or close because the camera can change their size at will. The convention of the **close-up** allows the director to guide the audience to concentrate on a hand gesture, eyes that reveal hidden secrets, or a letter left lying on a desk, signaling that it will prove crucial later on. In the early days of film, when cameras were much less sophisticated than they are now and directors had only one or two cameras to work with, a film was often like a photographed play, lacking in close-ups. This lack was also a convention of its time. Nowadays a director who chooses not to employ close-ups would be considered highly experimental.

> *"To be an artist means never to avert one's eyes."*
>
> **—Akira Kurosawa**

A **dissolve** occurs when one scene fades into another, a technique that replaced the older fading to black to mark the end of a scene. The dissolve often marks a transition in time or place. One scene is fading out as another is superimposed. In one of the cinema masterpieces of the twentieth century, *Casablanca* (discussed later in the chapter), the protagonist Rick sits alone in his café late at night while the room in back of him slowly changes into a scene in Paris, the subject of his thoughts.

Deliberately *slowing down* the film signals a lyrical, dreamlike scene, perhaps a beautiful memory or fantasy. Shutting it down completely results in a series of still photographs or **freeze-frames**, a technique used by François Truffaut at the beginning of *Jules and Jim* (1961) and later by Martin Scorsese in his gangster film *Goodfellas* (1990).

Deliberately *speeding up* the film makes the characters either comical, like Mack Sennett's Keystone Cops of the 1920s, or surreal and mechanical, like the thugs in *A Clockwork Orange* (1971) fighting each other in fast, jerky movements—all to the music of the equally fast Rossini overture to *The Thieving Magpie*. The unnatural speed produces a sense of machines rather than human beings, with no more lasting effects than the violence in an animated cartoon.

Just as time can expand or contract, so too can space. An example of the **tracking shot** is found in the 1939 film *Gone With the Wind,* when Scarlett (Vivien Leigh) rushes wildly into the street to find the family doctor, who is desperately trying to save lives at the train depot. Blundering onto a scene of unburied corpses, and, in her dazed condition unaware at first of where she is, Scarlett slowly perceives she is in the midst of death on a scale she has never dreamed of. As the camera slowly backs away from her horrified face, the scene opens wider and wider to reveal hundreds upon hundreds of bodies. The tracking shot is achieved by placing the camera on rollers or a slowly moving platform so that it can track inward or outward, or even complete a circle around characters, as in the famous kissing scene in the 1959 film *On the Beach,* which also involved the elongation of real time.

Challenging Conventions

No one minds when a character defies gravity by dancing on the wall, as Donald O'Connor does in *Singin' in the Rain* (1952). Asking "How was he able to do that?" would spoil the fun. In what is still considered the greatest film about ballet ever made, *The Red Shoes,* released in 1947 and still popular in its restored form, both realism and artificiality can be found. The ballet of the title, based on a Hans Christian Andersen fairy tale about a dancer who puts on a pair of red ballet shoes that have a life of their own and insist on dancing until she finally dies from exhaustion, is preceded by a realistic panorama of backstage life.

From the moment the heroine (played and danced memorably by Moira Shearer) is attracted by the shoes shining invitingly from a shoemaker's window, realism disappears. As she dances wildly on and on through the night, sets come and go. We don't know whether we are seeing what is supposed to be taking place on the stage or a montage of images in the dancer's imagination. It hardly matters.

With so much technology available to them, directors of the present have continued to build on the "new" traditions. Science fiction, horror, and so-called action films can be shown in 3-D. Many combine advanced computer-driven animation with human characters. James Cameron's spectacular *Avatar* (2009) is a prime example. The highest grossing film in history (up to that time) thrilled audiences both on regular screen and in 3-D. Those who insist that a film have a linear story they can follow would be able to summarize it as being about a mortal who becomes so sympathetic with a group of nonhuman creatures that he abandons his own kind to become one of them. But does telling the story really "tell the story?" Audiences flocked to experience the unprecedented special effects.

Photos 12/Alamy

Computer-generated versions of Zoe Saldana and Sam Worthington, *Avatar*, 2009

James Cameron's amazing *Avatar* combined computerized animation with human actors to give audiences an unprecedented visual experience.

Some Early Milestones

Film historians trace motion pictures as far back as 1824, when Peter Mark Roget, creator of the popular *Thesaurus,* formulated a theory called *The Persistence of Vision with Regard to Moving Objects.* Roget gave some thought to something we all do thousands of times every day: *we blink our eyes.* He realized that when the eyes are covered, vision should be interrupted by intervals of blackness, but vision is continuous. The reason, he determined, is the eye's ability to retain an image for a split second after vision is stopped—that is, during the time it takes for the eyelid to close and reopen. Though the eyes keep blinking, the images retained keep overlapping each other, producing an *illusion* of continuous vision. If the object of vision is in motion, the eye is actually absorbing a series of individual "frames," though it sees fluid movement.

Thomas Edison invented the movie projector, but it was his assistant who made the first movie, which lasted ten seconds.

Soon after the publication of Roget's theory, entertainers developed the trick of showing an audience drawings of a figure in successive states of motion. They were stacked together like an accordion and held firmly so that the pages could be flipped through rapidly. The figure actually appeared to move. During the mid-nineteenth century, the development of photography made people hungry for tricks in which pictures of actual people replaced drawings. Inventors on both sides of the Atlantic began to develop mechanisms to move the pictures faster and create an ever better illusion of motion. One such mechanism was a circular drum with slits through which the eye peered. Inside the drum, still images were fastened, and, when the contraption spun around, the eye saw fluid motion.

The invention of the motion picture camera and projector is attributed to Thomas Edison (1847–1931), who had made the first "peep show," a machine with a slot for the eyes and a crank handle for turning the pictures inside. The peep show led to the building of penny arcades where the public could play with the new technology. But Edison, at first more concerned with reproducing sound, concentrated on the earliest phonograph, and he put aside his work on simulated motion. One day in 1889, his assistant amazed him by putting sound and sight together when he showed his employer a ten-second movie in which an actor (himself) seemed actually to move and speak.

By 1896 projection technology had advanced to a point at which people could go to the movies to watch extremely brief films presenting one action, such as someone swimming, running, or starting to sneeze. These novelties were presented as interludes in the more important entertainment of the time, live singing and dancing on the vaudeville stage. Full-length films appeared soon after the turn of the century.

Early Filmmakers

D. W. Griffith. In 1915, when the elegant and huge Strand Theatre opened on Broadway, D. W. Griffith (1875–1948) gave *The Birth of a Nation*—all three hours of it—to a dazzled public. The film, which dealt with the American Civil War and the Reconstruction period in the South after the war, established movies as a mass medium. Griffith imposed his own point of view on history, one that was sympathetic even to the attacks of the Ku Klux Klan on the carpetbaggers—money-seeking politicians and scam artists from the North who came to the south with false promises of rebuilding shattered homes and cities. The Klan was guilty of torturing and murdering people who wanted to bring a new order to the South, but in Griffith's film, the Klan was justified.

"Griffith has been called the father of film because he consolidated and expanded many of the techniques invented by his predecessors and was the first to go beyond gimmickry into the realm of art."

—**Louis Giannetti**

Many critics praised the marvelous, for its time, cinematography and the film's epic sweep, hailing Griffith as the first genius of the new art form, while others denounced the director as a racist, using movies as propaganda. At any rate, the film had everyone talking, and the more intense the controversy, the longer the lines in front of the theater.

The Birth of a Nation was the first film to exhibit a definite directing style. Griffith's camera moves in for a close-up at a climactic moment, then **cuts** to a scene that moves at a different tempo. His work has been called rhythmic because of the editing which does not simply tell a story but controls the pace at which the story is experienced by the audience.

The film also introduced the **lingering take**, which became Griffith's trademark. During one famous moment, a young Confederate soldier rushing across a battlefield stops at the sight of a corpse lying on the ground. He recognizes that his Union counterpart had been his closest friend before the war. The soldier's grief is short-lived, for he is suddenly pierced by a bullet and falls across his friend's body. Instead of dissolving the scene, Griffith allows the camera to hold the moment silently. There they are, two friends, both dead, two young lives never to realize their human potential. In summing up the contribution of Griffith to the history of movies, critic Gerald Mast wrote, "The film remains solid as human drama and cinematic excitement, flimsy as social theory."[1]

Sergei Eisenstein. A very different, but no less innovative, style was offered in 1925 by the Soviet director Sergei Eisenstein (1898–1948). His film *The Battleship Potemkin,* about an unsuccessful mutiny against the Czarist regime, features a now famous episode that supposedly recreates a horrifying event in which loyal Cossack soldiers, storming to quell the mutiny, massacre hundreds of innocent civilians on the town steps in the city of Odessa. As it turns out, the massacre never happened, but the film has nevertheless been so widely admired for its editing techniques that it is still required viewing in film schools.

Eisenstein's Odessa Steps sequence in Potemkin *revolutionized the art of film editing.*

Explore on **MyHumanitiesKit.com** Eisenstein, *The Battleship Potemkin*

Pictorial Press Ltd./Alamy

***Battleship Potemkin,* 1925**

One of the most famous scenes ever filmed, the Odessa Steps sequence set a new standard for screen editing technique.

In 1905 the Bolshevik attempt to overthrow the czar failed. It was to succeed in 1917, and Vladimir Lenin, the first leader of the Soviet Union, recognized the power of film to instruct the public with a message favorable to the state. When Eisenstein was chosen to commemorate the failed uprising, he depicted the brutality of the Cossacks by inventing the massacre on the steps. Though Eisenstein was a loyal Communist party member and was committed to the Soviet doctrine of art as Communist instruction for the masses, he was also an artist and used film in an innovative way that went beyond mere propaganda.

The film was shot on location, using a flight of steps deemed appropriate for the action. The sequence, six and three-quarter minutes long, depicts a minute or two of real time and required the splicing of 157 shots. The sequence begins with 57 shots that show an assortment of happy and unconcerned townspeople on the steps. Carefully, Eisenstein introduces key figures to whom he will return again and again while the atrocities are being committed. Most significant of all is a young mother wheeling her baby in a carriage.

Then the soldiers on horseback come thundering to the top of the steps, splattering carnage as they ride. A little boy is separated from his mother and crushed to death in the stampede. The mother, having found her son's body, lifts him as an appeal to the soldiers, who respond by gunning her down. Back to the baby carriage sequence, we see the mother being mangled by Cossack sabers. Now a close-up of the abandoned carriage rocking back and forth dangerously on the edge of the steps reveals the mother, bleeding to death, leaning against it for support and pushing it over the brink. The next close-up shows the innocent child inside the careening vehicle, which is hurtling down the steps over and around hundreds of corpses. Another character is an apparently cultured woman wearing fragile reading glasses. Throughout the massacre the director returns to her, and each time she is splattered with blood. Finally we see a Cossack rider slashing at something out of our view, followed by a rapid cut to the woman's face. She has been mortally struck in the eye, but we do not actually see the saber strike her. Eisenstein instead gives us a close-up of the glasses lying on the steps, broken.

We might say that Eisenstein was led to art through some inner urge. Using the cinema of Soviet propaganda, he nevertheless could not ignore the artist within him.

> *"Film is strongest when it makes greatest use of what is peculiarly its own—the ability to record time and space, slice them up into fragments, and glue them together in a new relationship."*
>
> **—John Bigby**

Major Film Genres

The film **genre**—whether a farce or a three-hankie sentimental melodrama—was born almost as soon as film moved beyond short sequences and began to tell stories. By the mid-1920s the tastes and preferences of the moviegoing public controlled what studios could present. Popular were the Western and the gangster film, with mainly predictable stories designed for quick and easy production to take advantage of public hunger for entertainment. But there was also an audience for language-oriented plays about the marriage problems of the affluent. This genre can be called the *filmed play.* Directors used stage-trained diction coaches to turn film stars into replicas of British actors carefully articulating each word and projecting their voices in a manner more suitable for the stage than for screen close-ups.

In this section we analyze screen genres that are still prevalent however much they have changed with the times.

> *"Hollywood's a place where they'll pay you a thousand dollars for a kiss and fifty cents for your soul."*
>
> **—Marilyn Monroe**

Slapstick Comedy: Sennett and Chaplin

Mack Sennett (1884–1960) was the father of movie **slapstick**—rapid and violent farce in which people completely lost their human dignity, got struck in the face with pies, crashed their cars into each other, and wound up getting doused with water. Sennett's world is one of total chaos kept in disorder by a band of idiotic, incompetent, bungling lawmen known as the Keystone Cops.

Today we tend to think that the speeded-up, jerky movements of the Sennett films were unplanned consequences of early technology. Nothing could be further from the truth! Sennett became obsessed with the sight gag and the potentially unlimited resources of film to provide it. After all, a director could control the speed at which motion was viewed on the screen. He photographed action at an average of ten frames per second, but ran the film through the projector at an average of eighteen frames per second—almost twice as fast as it really occurred in the studio. The effect was to dehumanize the characters so that the violent catastrophes—Sennett's stock in trade—could not be taken seriously.

Pictorial Press Ltd./Alamy

Keystone Cops, c. 1910–1930

Sennett used a speeded-up effect to dehumanize the characters so that their disasters could not be taken seriously.

While working for Sennett, an aspiring young comic named Charles Chaplin (1889–1977) happened to put together a funny costume to wear in a crowd scene, probably as a means of getting a little attention. That costume became his signature outfit and would be worn again and again. In baggy trousers and shoes much too big for him, Chaplin became the Little Tramp, the prototype of the social misfit. Chaplin's developing interest in character, not sight gags, as the main source of comedy led him to leave Sennett and strike out on his own. The result: Charlie Chaplin became the first truly big and international star.

Moviestore collection Ltd. Alamy

Charlie Chaplin, c. 1910–1920

The Little Tramp is humanized by his attempt at dignity.

The Little Tramp is an incongruity—always out of place wherever he is—and people can laugh at incongruities. Yet he is not completely ridiculous; what humanizes him is the attempt at dignity implicit in both his costume and characteristic swagger. He is also a survivor. In a cruel world he manages to get by. Even though he is thin and weak-looking, the villains and bullies who threaten him are always naive and able to be outwitted. The ongoing myth in Chaplin films is the eternal triumph of the underdog, a myth with universal appeal.

Chaplin won his reputation during the era of silent films, both short- and feature-length movies. Even after the introduction of sound, his films depended largely on his ability to tell a story through mimed actions. In *The Gold Rush* (1925), the tramp becomes so hungry he cooks his shoes and eats the shoelaces like spaghetti, delicately twirling them on a fork and dabbing at his mouth to wipe away the imaginary gravy. Though far from nutritious, the shoelaces keep him alive. When his tiny Alaskan cabin is blown to the edge of a cliff during a blizzard, he unknowingly exits through the door—nearly to his doom. Teetering and tottering, he always manages to avoid certain disaster.

In what is often considered his masterpiece, *Modern Times* (1936), Chaplin shows his sensitivity to social issues. The film tells the story of a Depression-afflicted society in which thousands have been replaced by machines and those lucky enough to have jobs are treated like animals. In the opening sequence, the screen is filled with sheep all headed in the same direction. The next shot is of a horde of men coming out of the subway, looking like a herd of sheep. In the factory, Charlie works on an assembly line, where his job requires him to tighten the screws on products moving evermore swiftly. In an effort to save time from the workers' lunch break, the boss considers installing an automatic feeding machine so that the employees don't have to stop working. In the most famous scene, Charlie is caught in the gears of a giant machine, becoming part of it. As usual, there is a girl who loves him, as well as an idyllic dream sequence showing how life ought to be, with love and respect for each individual. And as usual, Charlie is ever gallant, courting his girlfriend and swaggering in his ill-fitting but clean clothes.

Farce: The Marx Brothers

The Marx Brothers—Groucho, Chico, and Harpo—dominated the comic scene during the 1930s into the war years of the early '40s. Usually on the wrong side of rules and regulations, they manage never to be caught, thus still delighting those who cheer for the underdog. Whether it's their inability to pay a huge hotel bill or stowing away on ocean liners, they never play it safe, never walk the straight and narrow. Yet audiences always know that the rules they break are somehow unfair, or else codes of behavior that only snooty aristocrats would approve.

Their masterpiece, one of the screen's most memorable comedies, is *A Night at the Opera* (1935). In an early scene, Groucho, always the suave con man, and Chico, always the seemingly dumb but really clever purveyor of his own brand of common sense, are negotiating a legal contract for the services of an unemployed tenor. The scene is a hilarious satire on legalese language. The two tricksters keep tearing out what is incomprehensible until there is nothing left.

One of the most famous scenes takes place in the tiny stateroom in which the three brothers and the tenor, now smuggled on board, are supposed to be living. Into the narrow space pour repairmen as well as maids who are supposed to be making up beds. In addition to the outlandish number of people, there are several huge trunks. Finally, a chambermaid appears and tells Groucho, "I've come to mop up," to which he replies, "You'll have to start on the ceiling." Then someone opens the door from the outside and everyone cascades into the hallway.

The thing about a masterpiece is that when creative inspiration is rolling it becomes unstoppable. The climactic episode of *A Night at the Opera* is the most uproarious in the entire film. At a performance of Verdi's *Il Trovatore,* both the tenor and the soprano he loves have been unfairly excluded according to the brothers, who wreak havoc on the opera with their shenanigans. Harpo (a classic mime, never speaking in any Marx Brothers film) inserts the music of "Take Me Out to the Ball Game" as part of the overture, dutifully played by the orchestra. As detectives and police raid the back of the theater,

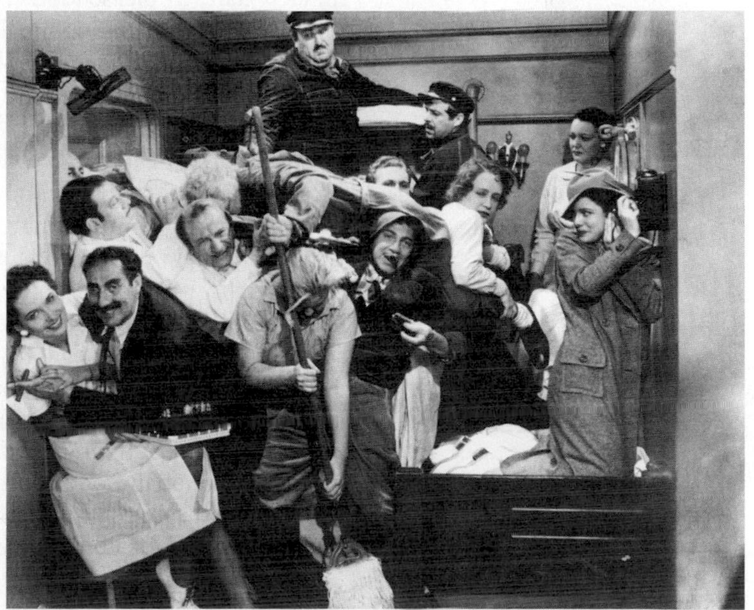

The Everett Collection

The Marx Brothers, *A Night at the Opera*, 1935

An all-time classic scene, the packed stateroom about to explode.

Harpo evades them by climbing up the ropes that change the backdrops. The villainous tenor on stage continues his aria as scenes of New York street vendors and Grand Central Station appear and disappear. After he is knocked unconscious backstage, the sympathetic tenor and soprano are urged to finish the opera, and all ends happily, something that can be depended on to happen in a farce.

Enduring Appeal of the Animated Film

By the early 1930s the movie-going public was treated to a lengthy evening of two films (an A, or feature, movie, preceded by a B, or minor movie) as well as a newsreel, often a short subject, and the required cartoon, with Mickey Mouse and Donald Duck achieving international fame. But what had fans lining up at the box office was the first full-length animated feature: Disney's *Snow White and the Seven Dwarfs* (1936), with color and artwork never before seen and an unforgettable musical score. The film continues to be revived and to enjoy lively DVD sales.

Animation technology has become so sophisticated that the simplicity of *Snow White* makes it appear dated. Its dialogue and songs are never in close sync with the mouth movements of the characters, though the everlasting charm of the story still delights youngsters and allows adults to enjoy a brief excursion back to their youth. The Disney group and others who now employ top-notch artists and computer geniuses have developed the means of populating animated films with both human and animal figures that seem almost three-dimensional. Ever more complex dialogue is spoken in perfect synchronization. The new world of animated film is a virtual universe with its own reality.

The new technology has resulted in works that both children and adults can enjoy on different levels. One such film is Disney's *Ratatouille (2006),* the story of Remy, a gourmet rat who saves the reputation of a fine restaurant by hiding in the chef's hat and instructing him how to cook. His meal wins the approval of an inordinately hard-to-please food critic.

Ratatouille enraptured children with its adorable rodents, but it also pleased adult critical viewers with its theme of what constitutes good taste—rare for any film and heretofore nonexistent in an animated one. Similarly, *Up* (a 2009 Academy Award winner) has exciting balloon sequences that guarantee appeal to children, but there is also a sophisticated story of the main character's courtship and marriage, with complexities only adults can truly understand.

Film Noir

During the 1920s, after Congress passed legislation prohibiting the sale and consumption of alcohol, illegal drinking establishments called speakeasies were supplied by bootleggers with liquor from abroad or else an infamous and potent local concoction referred to as "bathtub gin." The underworld liquor traffic triggered the rise of organized crime and led to the archetype of the film gangster, a cynical antihero who justified his contempt for the law with a belief in a generally corrupt world in which those who followed the rules deserved no mercy.

As appealing as the gangster, the private eye hero was a pay-for-hire investigator, sometimes a former gangster himself, who knew every dark corner of the city and every murderer lurking in the shadows, someone who shot just as straight as the criminals themselves and who, like them, could kill without a moment's reflection. He operated just outside the law, but was forgiven, even admired, by the audience because he never killed for personal reasons. Identifying with him was easy and unambiguous. He was hired to find the bad guys, and did so, even if his methods were straight out of the gangster's handbook.

Like many of his gangster counterparts, the private eye projected a deep-rooted cynicism about the corrupt world; both knew that ruthlessness was necessary for survival. He paved the way for a new film genre called **film noir** by French critics to describe a type of film that is characterized by "its dark, somber tone and cynical, pessimistic mood . . . [The label] was coined to describe those Hollywood films of the 40s and early 50s which portrayed the dark and gloomy underworld of crime and corruption, films whose heroes as well as villains are cynical, disillusioned, and often insecure loners . . . [It] characteristically abounds with night scenes . . . with sets that suggest dingy realism, and with lighting that emphasizes deep shadows and accents the mood of fatalism."[2]

> *Film noir makes use of dark, shadowy camerawork to evoke a menacing hostile universe in which nothing is as it appears.*
>
> **—Geoff Andrew**

The private eye proved an apt hero for film noir. He usually worked alone or with one partner, had no family ties, and was good at his trade because, operating on the fringes of society, he knew the underworld and could easily pass for a gangster. At the head of the class in this genre still stands John Huston's *The Maltese Falcon* (1941), which created the powerful screen **persona** of Humphrey Bogart (1899–1957). In earlier films, Bogart had played a typically ruthless gangster. In *The Maltese Falcon* he was given the opportunity to add a moral streak to his tough-minded realism, and this addition would give depth to his most memorable screen creations.

Here, Bogart plays the role of Sam Spade, who shoots to kill if he has to. He has no illusions about the world and the kind of people who inhabit it. But he has his own principles, his own code of ethics, even if others have none. The death of his partner involves him in a labyrinth of dangerous intrigue, murder, and deceit as he seeks to solve the murder: "When your partner is killed, you're supposed to do something about it."

Throughout the film, Spade is in trouble with both the police and a conspiracy of international crooks, who are among the evil-doers seeking the expensive, jeweled bird of the title. Like a warrior of old, he is equal to any task, despite being threatened, deceived, cheated, and knocked unconscious. But he has something else: vulnerability. He becomes romantically involved with an attractive woman, a client, who may or may not be worthy of his trust. Yet, love notwithstanding, he never allows emotion to override either his reason or his ethics; instead, he remains a principled realist to the end. In a world like this, he seems to say, you cannot afford to be anything else.

> *. . . Rather than amorality . . . [it was] honor among detectives. Find your partner's killer even if it meant breaking your heart. Spade has done the Right Thing and ends up the ultimate cynic.*
>
> **—A. M. Sperber and Eric Lax**

A variation on the film noir is *Double Indemnity* (1944) by writer-director Billy Wilder. This time the protagonist (played by Fred MacMurray) is not a private eye but an insurance investigator persuaded by a beautiful woman (played by Barbara Stanwyck) to assist in the murder of her rich husband and help her collect on a huge policy. The woman pretends to have emotions but is unable to feel either genuine love for the investigator or remorse for the crime they commit. The investigator, recognizing that the woman is not what he had thought, becomes cynical and hard-boiled, the two requirements for a film noir hero. Like the typical persona the protagonist is cynical, having seen human nature, including his own, at its worst, but he too achieves a moral vision, confessing to the crime and admitting his corruption.

Romantic Comedy

A movie theater used to be the perfect place for romance, on screen and off, perfect for a Saturday night date, when couples sitting in the dark could look at other couples on the screen, secure in the knowledge that no matter what has kept them apart for most of the film, they will surely end in each other's arms.

The man and woman on the screen were apt to be better looking, better dressed, and richer than the couple on a date. For Depression-era audiences, looking at the luxury in a film offered welcome, if temporary, escape. The sets were authentic recreations of Art Deco, and the costumes worn by the actresses were products of world-famous designers. The characters—often a man and woman who really do love each other—become enmeshed in a ridiculous disarray of circumstances that very nearly but not quite terminate the relationship. After all, if Boy Meets Girl, and soon Boy Gets Girl, the film would not be feature length. Boy loses girl through misunderstandings, jumping to conclusions, refusing to listen to facts; wisecracks substitute for sentimental admissions of affection; true love is hidden rather than spoken up until the end. Audiences knew the admission was coming, even if it didn't turn out that way in real life. But then, who needed a reminder of what real life was like in those hard times?

Classic Romantic Comedy. Frank Capra's *It Happened One Night* (1934), concerns an extraordinarily wealthy young woman (played by Claudette Colbert) and her attempts to find true love. At the beginning of the film, the audience knows immediately that she is making a mistake in her choice of mates, but the runaway heiress is so determined to marry the fortune-hunting playboy against her father's wishes that she escapes from the family yacht by swimming to shore. She avoids her father's detectives by taking a bus on which, in the destined-for-each-other world of romantic comedy, she meets a charismatic reporter (played by Clark Gable, the reigning matinee idol of the period), who will, of course, become her true love but only after a rocky start.

As a formerly spoiled and protected but now penniless heiress, she lacks survival skills, but these are quickly furnished by the reporter, who intervenes to protect her from a lecherous man in the adjoining seat and offers her the seat next to his. As is customary in the genre, the heroine at first resents the help offered, but will find that she is helpless without it.

After a flash flood forces the bus to stop, the pair must share the one remaining motel room. The hero constructs a clothesline with a blanket thrown over it to separate the twin beds, dubbing the divider "the walls of Jericho." At breakfast he shows her how to dunk a doughnut, a talent her upbringing has never before required. When bus travel is no longer possible, he attempts to explain the technique of hitchhiking, but the novice turns out to be better at it than her more experienced companion.

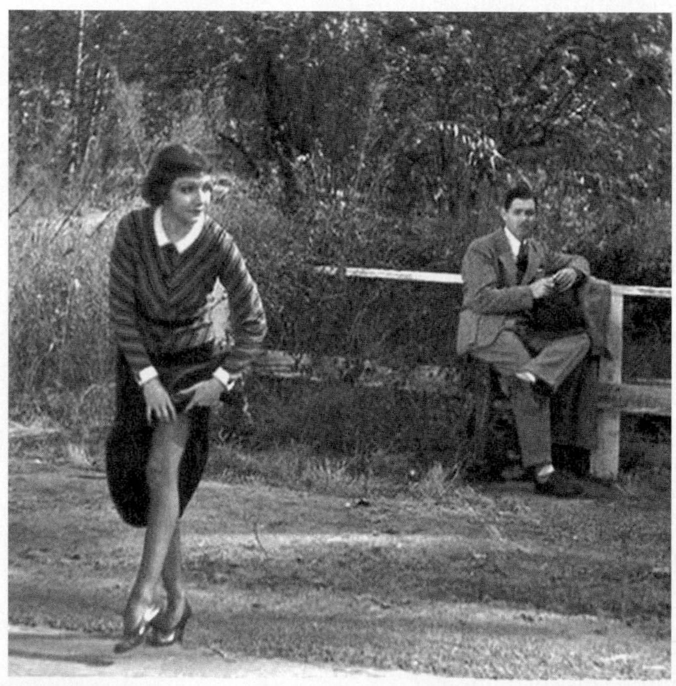

Columbia Pictures/Photofest

Claudette Colbert and Clark Gable, *It Happened One Night*, 1934

In a classic romantic comedy of the 1930s, a sheltered heiress proves to her macho companion that a woman can be an adept hitchhiker.

In the film's most famous scene, her provocatively lifted skirt and revelation of a shapely leg prove more effective than the reporter's confident waving of his thumb. Despite the fact that the heiress seems disorganized in the early portions of the film—and in need of a strong man to guide her—she gradually proves to be the strong man's equal, though he is slow to admit it. The romantic comedy heralded the liberation of film women from earlier stereotyping.

Of course, the story cannot end here. The reporter's salary is a mere 30 dollars a week. In the romantic comedies of the Great Depression, audiences loved to be reminded that money cannot buy happiness. Even though the father of the heiress had given his permission for her to marry the playboy, he decides that the reporter is honest and hardworking, the sort of person he now wants for a son-in-law. He tells his daughter as she is walking up the aisle that she is marrying the wrong man. As the crucial "Do you take this man?" question is asked, the heroine flees the church and dashes to a car conveniently waiting outside—a motif repeated in many films since then.

The finale, naturally, has to be the return of the heiress and her reporter, now bridegroom, to the same motel, but this time the blanket on the clothesline will come down like the biblical Walls of Jericho. The reporter has been so charming, so sincerely in love he has been able to bridge class differences and earn the right to marry the rich man's daughter, to the delight of the audience who may have decided the moral of the film was *love is greater than money.* In point of fact, however, the girl remains an heiress, and her approving father will, of course, always be there.

> *Screen writers had to invent dialogue that was rich and colorful, pungent and amusing, but also stripped of inessentials.*
>
> **—Arthur Knight**

Class differences in the film are swept aside since audiences of the '30s were seldom the social equals of the heiress and would have been disappointed had she actually married the "wrong man." But by the 1950s the unemployed working classes were enjoying the relative prosperity of the postwar boom. A major romantic comedy of the period was William Wyler's *Roman Holiday* (1953) featuring Audrey Hepburn as a princess paying a royal visit to Rome and becoming romantically (and briefly) involved with, again, a reporter (Gregory Peck). On a sudden impulse she decides to break free of her closely guarded life and have a little fun without being recognized.

Similar to Gable's character in *It Happened One Night,* Peck's reporter knows he is out on the town with a princess, pretends he doesn't recognize her but has his sidekick, a photographer, tag along and, unobtrusively, photograph her in a variety of wild actions, intent on delivering a prize story to his paper. The next day Peck and the photographer are in attendance when the princess, hung over from her night out but now artfully concealing it, greets the press and invited guests. In a scene of beautiful restraint, the two newspapermen shake her hand; and, having observed the woman's dignity and royal bearing, the reporter slips her an envelope containing the pictures he has taken. Class will tell, and class is not allowed to be violated. The predictable happy ending of past romantic comedies does not come to pass.

Modern Romantic Comedies. In 1977, Woody Allen, once a stand-up comic who used the persona of a neurotic man to great effect then turned to directing, made *Annie Hall,* critically described as the first modern romantic comedy. It certainly was different from its predecessors in pairing a seemingly ill-matched couple. Alvy Singer is a neurotic (like most of Allen's characters). Annie Hall (played by Diane Keaton) is trying to fit into intellectual circles. She is in awe of Alvy's knowledge and conversational ability. Their differences cause them to separate. When they meet up again, however, Alvy realizes what he has lost. Unlike many romantic comedies, *Annie Hall* does not have a traditional ending.

By the 1980s romantic comedy was beginning to reflect the change in gender roles. In 1934, Claudette Colbert willingly surrendered her independence to masculine Clark Gable. In 1989, Meg Ryan is self-assured and can get along without male guidance.

In Rob Reiner's groundbreaking, for its time (1989), *When Harry Met Sally,* independent woman Sally (Meg Ryan) encounters traditionally disposed man Harry (Billy Crystal), who has offered her a cross-country ride. Sally accepts even though Harry *is* a complete stranger to her, confident that she can take care of herself in any situation. Along the way, casual conversation turns to sharp repartée, a battle of wits between a woman who believes a nonsexual, friendly relationship can exist between two people and a man who argues that sex will always be the main issue, whether talked about or not. She adds that women aren't nearly as interested in sex as he believes but often pretend to be enjoying it. In earlier times, her attitude made audiences anticipate that she would finally relent and agree with the man, but it does not happen here. There is no new version of the fall of Jericho. This new kind of romantic comedy redefines romance as often involving a "draw" in the battle of the sexes, with neither combatant yielding ground.

In the two decades following *When Harry Met Sally* women continued to make strides in society, often occupying positions of authority over male workers. The male, in films and on television, was frequently depicted as hapless and very much in need of female guidance. In a *New Yorker* article, film critic David Denby analyzes the shift from earlier male-female screen relationships. Using the 2007 comedy *Knocked Up* as a contemporary example, he contrasts the squabbling lovers in the old films with their modern-day counterparts and finds that today's are no longer equal partners.

> *There they are, the young man and young woman of the dominant romantic comedy trend of the past several years—the slovenly hipster and the female straight arrow. The movies form a genre of sorts: the slacker-striver romance. . . . For almost a decade, Hollywood has pulled jokes and romance out of the struggle between male infantilism and female ambition.*[3]

A partnership between two Washington power figures is central to Rob Reiner's 1995 *The American President*. As the title indicates, one is the president of the United States, and the woman this time is a strong lobbyist for legislation that will protect the environment. The president (Michael Douglas) is a widower, and the lobbyist (Annette Bening) has caught his eye. When he invites her to spend the night with him, she at first has difficulty getting past his title, to see him as just a man. The morning after, he remarks apologetically that it's been a long time since he has made love. She smiles reassuringly and says, "I'm no expert, but I'd say it was good." There is no longer a question of Jericho walls, but the ending here is far from predictable. Washington politics are too strong.

A conflict erupts between the would-be lovers when he at first refuses to sponsor her environmental protection bill in favor of a crime prevention bill that had been his top priority. When she leaves him, he has a change of heart. Both the woman and the environment win out.

In the aptly titled *As Good As It Gets* (1997), directed by James Brooks, Helen Hunt plays a struggling single mother working as a waitress to earn enough for her and her asthmatic son. A cranky older man (Jack Nicholson) finds himself attracted to her. He is obsessed with order and neatness, and the two make as unlikely a pair of potential lovers as has ever been seen in a romantic comedy. Without giving a hint of the proverbial "heart of gold," Nicholson acquires good medical help for the boy. Her gratitude encourages him to become somewhat romantic toward her to the point at which he suddenly proposes marriage. The heroine's mother reminds her that this may be "as good as it gets," and the embrace in the final scene tells us reality demands that we take what we *can* get.

The trend toward a bittersweet kind of romantic comedy has grown. Witness the 2009 George Clooney film *Up in the Air*. Its world is made up mainly of airplane and airport interiors. Clooney plays Ryan, a man whose career depends on his ability to visit high-salaried employees and fire them for CEOs who don't want to be the ones to break the news—in short, to do their work with skill and subtlety. Ryan has no other function in life, no real home, and, in truth, no identity. All he has is his handsome face, his charming mannerisms, and commitment to the tasks he must undertake day after day.

So where is the romance, or near romance? She appears in the person of Alex (played by Vera Farmiga), a high-powered career woman, who meets up with Ryan every so often for a brief encounter and who, like him, wants no commitment. When, at length, Ryan decides he is ready to settle down with her and to propose marriage, he goes to her home and has a rude awakening. Her single, carefree existence has been a lie. She has long ago made a commitment, and Ryan has been merely a pleasant diversion. What a long, long way from the walls of Jericho!

The Screen Musical

The stories in musical films, hugely popular in the 1930s into the 1950s, were often similar to those in romantic comedies of the period. The couple were kept apart until the final embrace, except when they sang and danced together. This formula was especially true for Fred Astaire and Ginger Rogers, who, despite having different names from one film to the next, always played essentially the same people. Once again the clothing and sets were lavish. Impeccably garbed Fred, with top hat and tails, and sleek and satin-gowned Ginger, with sequins and feathers, dance up and down stairs, on tabletops, and even on miraculously cleared dance floors in intricately choreographed routines (even though the script may indicate they have just met and obviously had no time to rehearse). No matter what minor misunderstanding may have separated them, when the band began to play, the logic of the story, such as it was, disappeared as they tapped, waltzed, swirled, and introduced breathtakingly new dance routines.

Dancing at any moment was a convention of musical film, as was singing that could happen anywhere, not necessarily as part of a nightclub show: on the deck of a ship or in a moonlit garden; anytime the lover wanted to woo with music so he (usually he) could describe his feelings in song. The only requirement of his listener was to look delighted and sometimes to join in a refrain. An often unseen orchestra offered accompaniment, as the singing and dancing that brought them together offered a preview of a future of harmony. Opera had long had sung dialogue and orchestral accompaniment, but musical comedy songs offered more spoken dialogue and songs that could be sung by the untrained voices of a public expected to buy the records.

The major choreographer of Hollywood musicals in the 1930s was Busby Berkeley (1895–1976), who placed beautiful women in designs that would have been impossible on the stage. Audiences loved synchronized dancing, like that of Radio City Music Hall's high kicking, long-legged Rockettes (still packing them in), a tradition carried on by the top-hatted ensemble in the finale of *A Chorus Line* and the Irish step dancers of *Riverdance*. Berkeley arranged his dancers in intricate configurations horizontally, photographed from above, with some of them in the

Everett Collection

Gene Kelly, *Singin' in the Rain*, 1952

In what has been called the greatest movie musical ever made, there are not only joyous singing and dancing but a believable plot.

dark and others in the light as they swirled into kaleidoscopic patterns.

Singin' in the Rain (1952), directed by Stanley Donen and Gene Kelly, is still considered the greatest musical Hollywood has ever made. For a change, the plot is believable and deals not with the usual banter between hero and heroine but with what really happened when movies first acquired sound. Gene Kelly, who also stars in the film, dances in joyous abandon on every kind of surface, including a rain-soaked street. In the famous title number, Kelly sings about the happiness of being in love, as he splashes and dances through puddles, umbrella in hand—a scene which can be separated from the story and viewed with delight as an expression of pure joy. *Singin' in the Rain* proved to be glorious escapist entertainment for the public without sacrificing integrity of plot and characterization.

Films became more special effects–oriented during the 1980s, and a number of screen musicals tried, not always with success, to adapt to the changing fashions by venturing into unexplored territory. *Dirty Dancing*, in 1987, however, kept many of the ingredients that always had audiences lined up at the box office, adding some exciting innovations, such as spectacularly complex dance routines that made plot almost nonexistent (hence the disappearance of by now hackneyed elements). There isn't even any singing in the film; we never hear an orchestra suddenly and mysteriously present as a lead-in to a romantic duet.

In some respects Rob Marshall's 2002 Oscar-winning *Chicago* is like earlier musicals in its lavish, glitzy production numbers, but unlike them in the seriousness of its cynical satire on ambition, crime, tabloid journalism, and public celebrity worship that exceeds all bounds of reason. Though based on the long-running Broadway musical of the same name, *Chicago* is nothing like a photographed stage musical. It is pure cinema, with quick cuts used in ways undreamed of in the past.

A show-stopper is the soft-shoe dance by the attorney (played by Richard Gere) who is defending a clearly guilty murderess (played by Renée Zelwegger) by musically describing how clever lawyers hoodwink and outthink gullible juries. "Give 'em the old razzle-dazzle," he sings. As he goes into his dance, the camera keeps cutting to scenes of an actual court trial, then back to Gere's glittering showmanship.

The Western

"Talk low, talk slow, and don't say too much."

—**John Wayne**

No film genre is more historically associated with Hollywood than the Western tale of good and evil. In one film after another, bad guys menaced the decent folks in a town that was often the same studio back-lot set, complete with horses, a stagecoach, the jail, the general store, the saloon, and a dusty main street, scene of a thousand shootouts.

Fred Zinnemann's *High Noon* (1952) rises to the level of screen art. Will Kane (Gary Cooper), is retiring from the office of marshal. With his replacement due to arrive the following day, Kane plans to leave the town and open a store with his bride Amy (Grace Kelly), whose Quaker religion opposes the use of firearms. But on Kane's last day, the town is facing the reappearance of a deranged killer who will arrive on the noonday train and, with his brothers, seek revenge against the marshal responsible for his prison sentence. The film examines a legitimate moral dilemma. Kane must decide whether to stay and defend both himself and the law-abiding citizens of the town, who will be in danger should the menacing gang triumph, or to accompany his wife away from violence, to a life of peace.

The plot continues to darken in this complex—and, to many, greatest ever—Western. As the clock approaches high noon, Kane seeks help from the other townsfolk. Though the town has seemed united in its moral denunciation of the bad men, no one else is willing to fight. After all, it isn't their problem. Kane's pacifist wife begs him to leave, with an ultimatum threatening their brief marriage, but his integrity and loyalty to his duty as marshal cause him to reject the ultimatum. When a final effort to assemble a posse fails, he is left alone to decide whether to fight against overwhelming odds or to flee, knowing none would blame him.

The film has been called the *Hamlet* of the Western genre. Like Shakespeare's Prince of Denmark, Will Kane continually asks himself why he should be the one to carry out a dreadful task (in Hamlet's case, the murder of his uncle), why he should have to die for a town that has betrayed him.

> *It is easy enough to guess why American presidents like* [High Noon] *so much. The man with the nuclear club who thinks to himself that he often must do the hard thing, the unpopular thing, would also like to think of himself as spiritually resembling Gary Cooper.*
>
> **—Paul Buhle and David Wagner**

In the famous climactic shootout, Kane manages through his superb marksmanship to do away with three of the four villains—all but the deranged killer himself, who appears to be every bit his equal in hitting his target. As the killer is about to blast the unsuspecting Kane, who is now vulnerable in the middle of the abandoned street, his Quaker wife suddenly picks up a gun and sends the killer, who has no idea she is even there, to his death.

Much has been made of the fact that the appearance of *High Noon* coincided with the start of the Korean War. Is this film also saying, as *Destry Rides Again* had in 1939, that pacifism is not always a valid position to hold? That, when necessary, one must fight fire with fire? At the eleventh hour, doesn't the wife recognize that preserving justice at all costs is everyone's obligation? In the tradition of much high art, *High Noon* is content to remain ambiguous, perhaps understanding that it has posed questions for which there are no easy answers.

If nothing else, in the manner of the very best myths, it tells us that, when a hero is needed, a hero will be there, because *somebody has to be there*. It doesn't guarantee that "being there" is necessarily its own reward. In the famous last scene, as the townspeople suddenly reappear to congratulate him, Kane bitterly removes his badge and drops it in the dust.

A popular 1969 Western boasted of two heroes, who, unlike Kane, were on the wrong side of the law. They were a charming pair of bank robbers (played by Paul Newman and Robert Redford) named, like the film itself, *Butch Cassidy and the Sundance Kid*. Throughout George Roy Hill's brand of Western, the rogue protagonists commit one crime after another, always managing to escape—and, in the true tradition of the rogue hero, with audience approval. (It is much easier to identify with a handsome, smart-talking Dionysian duo than with their humorless pursuers.)

Chased to the edge of a very high cliff, Butch urges Sundance to jump with him into the river below, only to learn that his partner can't swim. Hill makes use of the *freeze-frame*, a then-new convention in which the camera stops an action suddenly. The loveable crooks are stranded in midair, bringing unexpected whimsy into a story that is moving toward an inevitable tragic ending. Yet the director's smile never entirely disappears, even when Butch and Sundance are ultimately riddled with bullets by Bolivian police. They die without a shred of remorse or self-pity.

Western mythology was replaced with issues relevant to audiences in Kevin Costner's 1990 *Dances with Wolves,* which reexamines the history of Native Americans. The film treats Native Americans more sympathetically than in previous days when they were shown as stereotyped menaces to white settlers, who killed them one by one as audiences cheered. *Dances with Wolves* views Native Americans as victims of oppression and clearly belongs to the serious tradition of film as something more than popular entertainment. It is also a classic example of revisiting a film genre in a new context.

Social Issues

> *"Beginning with* Mr. Deeds Goes to Town *. . . with Gary Cooper as the small-town man who triumphs over city slickers, Capra's work emphasized the common-sense skills and leadership qualities of little people."*
>
> **—Robert Sklar**

Very early in screen history, some directors recognized the power of film as a medium for social criticism. Such works made a statement about institutions and economic policies that are the root causes of human problems.

In 1909 the one-reel silent movie *A Corner in Wheat* took on the stock market and the tragic results of human greed. Like most early films, it exaggerated its case. The discrepancy between the haves and have-nots could not be missed. In one scene, newly made millionaires lifted champagne glasses in celebration; a quick cut showed miserable-looking crowds on a bread line.

In addition to romantic comedy, Frank Capra created films about bigotry, political corruption, and the abuse of workers' rights featuring attractive, plain-talking heroes. An immigrant himself, the son of a fruit-picker, he had firsthand knowledge of poverty; but he also had profound respect for America, the land of opportunity. The optimism with which he ended his films worked box-office magic, although he has been criticized for providing easy solutions that could never happen in reality.

In *Mr. Deeds Goes to Town* (1936), Gary Cooper plays the ideal Capra down-to-earth hero, in this case one who tries to distribute an inheritance of $20 million to the poor and must fight a legal battle to prove his sanity. Goodness once again prevails, and the Depression is over for a lucky few.

In Capra's most popular film, *It's a Wonderful Life* (1947), a desperate bankrupt hero George Bailey (James Stewart) is saved at the last minute (and, not coincidentally, on Christmas Eve) by the contributions of grateful townspeople whose homes were spared by his bank. He had been contemplating suicide, believing that he was a total failure in life. The film's message—that people's worth is measured by the amount of good they do—has elevated the movie to almost myth status. Alternately condemned as unabashed sentimentality and praised as a welcome addition to the Christmas spirit, *It's a Wonderful Life* is revived every year during the holiday season.

John Ford (1895–1973), who, like Capra, was the son of immigrants, was another director who grew up knowing the underprivileged side of life. The central characters in *The Grapes of Wrath* (1940), adapted from the John Steinbeck novel mentioned in Chapter 4, are the poor Joad family forced to leave their farm after a bank foreclosure.

The land, unable to sustain them, has become part of the Dust Bowl, and the only opportunity appears to be in California, where, they have heard, fruit pickers are desperately needed. Ma Joad (Jane Darwell in an Oscar-winning performance) is a source of quiet wisdom. Her son Tom (Henry Fonda, who brought naturalistic acting to a new level) is an impatient rebel. When they manage to drive their rickety old car to California, they learn that the rule of supply and demand is in full force. So many would-be farm workers have arrived that the advertised wages have been slashed. Tom Joad sees that the struggle for justice must transcend his own family and his own self-interest. He will dedicate his life to the cause of saving all of humanity.

Spike Lee (b. 1957) is in the tradition of those who, like Ford, use the medium of film to confront real social problems. Rejecting the opportunity to go to private schools with students who were wealthy and white, he was educated in public schools attended by other African Americans. Early on, he decided he would devote his life to making films about oppressed minorities and enrolled at NYU.

One of Lee's first assignments was to make a short film. His was short enough—ten minutes—but its subject matter was radically different from what his teachers expected. Lee ridiculed the stereotypes of African Americans found in films like *The Birth of a Nation,* substituting *white* stereotypes.

Lee survived criticism of his school exercise, but the desire to shock by shaking up cherished beliefs has not left him. In his professional career he has remained socially oriented, tackling such themes as racism, interracial romance, and prejudiced police. The biography of *Malcolm X* (1992) is considered by many critics to be his finest film so far. In making *Malcolm X,* Lee battled against a studio decision to allow a white director to make a film about the hero, and, when he was finally given the job, he refused to be constrained by what he regarded as an inadequate budget. Instead he went out and raised private funds.

In *Do the Right Thing* he won critical acclaim for his use of an unusual film convention—a revival of the Greek Chorus—in this case a group of men sitting on the front steps of a house and commenting on what is happening in the neighborhood.

Lee's films continue to stimulate debate about whether he exaggerates or is delivering a needed message; whether audiences will imitate violence seen on the screen; and whether he himself is using damaging stereotypes. If Lee ever does make a film totally uncharacteristic of him—some sort of mindless entertainment, for instance—viewers will be so astonished they will no doubt insist on his doing what has brought him to the forefront of today's filmmakers: tough-minded social criticism.

Documentaries

Nonfiction factual films, or **documentaries**, are often respected for their efforts to tell the truth. At the same time films claiming to be documentaries have aroused opposition because of the possibility that truth has been doctored in order to make a case.

> *"A film is a petrified fountain of thought."*
>
> **—Jean Cocteau**

One of the outstanding and influential exponents of this genre is Frederick Wiseman (b. 1938), who specializes in showing familiar institutions in unique ways. Over the years he has made films whose titles hint at their content: *Hospital, Welfare, Racetrack, The Store, High School, Meat.* Unlike some documentary makers who add biting social and political commentaries to their work, Wiseman refrains from making comments or using interviews. He allows what is being filmed to speak for itself.

His best-known work, *Titicut Follies* (1967), exposes the brutal treatment of inmates in a Massachusetts hospital for people labeled criminally insane. The work was banned in that state until just recently. *High School* (1968) uncovers what really happens on a typical day: the bells, the regimentation, the strict enforcement of institutional rules. "Where's your pass?" snaps a hall monitor to a student. A dean is overheard telling another student, "We are out to establish that you are a man and that you can take orders."

"Humanity is sitting on a time bomb."

—**Al Gore**

The documentaries of Michael Moore (b. 1954) leave no doubt about his sympathies. His *Roger and Me* (1989) attacked the closing of Flint, Michigan's main industry when General Motors moved factories out of the country. The "Roger" of the title was the CEO Moore pursued throughout the film in an effort to get answers about the corporate decision. *Bowling for Columbine* (2002), about the two Colorado high school students on a murderous rampage in 1994, made a plea for tough gun control laws. *Farenheit 9/11* (2004), which was selected as the best film shown at the Cannes Film Festival in that year, gathered an enormous amount of footage to demonstrate what Moore considered the government's lax handling of the World Trade Center attacks as well as the wars in Afghanistan and Iraq. Moore's narrative voice guides the way audiences are meant to view the film.

Sicko (2007) investigated medical problems in the United States, especially the managed health care and pharmaceutical industries. So powerful has this filmmaker become that several major pharmaceutical companies refused to allow their employees to grant him interviews. His critics—and there are many—contend that while documentaries are meant to look as authentic as possible they still represent a director's selectivity. Still, what powerful voices in the humanities have not incited controversies?

Historical accuracy has seldom been the goal of the fictionalized biography. If the subject's life is not as interesting or dramatic as filmmakers would like, they go ahead and change it.

The Suffering Artist

Films depicting the lives of geniuses pose the problem of how to make their work as interesting as the drama of their tormented lives. To the credit of writers and directors of the past, some, but not all, of the films about visual artists have actually left audiences with memories of the art as well as temper tantrums and mental illness.

Michelangelo, Vincent van Gogh, and Paul Gauguin have all become known to a wider public because of film biographies. In *The Agony and the Ecstasy* (1965) audiences saw Michelangelo cramped and strained as he heroically paints the ceiling of the Sistine Chapel (when, in fact, the artist had a number of assistants who did their share of the work). They also saw fictionalized bitter and tension-filled confrontations between Michelangelo and Pope Julius II. In *Lust for Life* (1956) they saw van Gogh and Gauguin arguing violently in the tiny house they shared, so violently that, on one occasion, van Gogh is shown rushing upstairs to cut off part of his ear (an event that took place elsewhere). All the while they are fighting, the two men continue to generate great paintings. Despite the overacting in the scenes depicting the madness that led van Gogh to suicide, however, the final moments of the film are impressive indeed as the camera slowly **pans** along a wall on which hang the artist's greatest works. For many, this art show may have been an extraordinary introduction to the genius of a tragic artist—and more than enough justification for the filmography genre.

Composers have suffered their share of inaccuracies. The Mozart in both the play and film version of Peter Shaffer's *Amadeus* (1984) was flamboyantly portrayed as a giggling, childlike man given to bawdy jokes, uncouth gestures, and continual flirtations. How he found time to compose forty-one symphonies, a score of operas, as well as innumerable chamber and piano works was a mystery. Both versions also dramatized the totally unfounded legend that Mozart was poisoned by his archenemy, Antonio Salieri, a celebrated (at the time) court composer who is supposed to have been obsessed with jealousy. According to the script, Salieri paid Mozart to compose a requiem mass he intended to pass off as his own work after the poison took effect. In point of fact, someone else commissioned Mozart to write the requiem, and the composer died from causes still under investigation, possibly typhoid fever, before completing it. Less dramatic than attempting to appropriate another man's work after poisoning him is the question of the real-life Salieri's relations with Mozart. The film shows him burning with hatred of his rival. History shows him as an admired musician willing to help the younger man.

Lovers of Edith Piaf's songs have no doubt been delighted to see *La Vie en Rose* (2006), the film based on her life of both success and inner pain. The soundtrack features old favorites such as the title song, as well as the passionate and highly personal "Non, Je Ne Regrette Rien" ("No, I Regret Nothing"). The actress Marion Cotillard, who portrays the singer, is convincingly tormented. Yet those who thrilled to the music may still be wondering whether Piaf was really abandoned by a parent or lived on the street or had a child out of wedlock. Those who head for the library for her accurate biography can still have the wonderful music to remember.

Loosely Based on the Original

A film made from a popular literary work is under no obligation to follow the book closely, as long as it is now in the public domain or the still-living author cannot resist a vast sum offered by the studio. Early on, Hollywood snapped up the work of important writers, promising more money than they hoped to earn from publishing alone. Ernest Hemingway (Chapter 4) saw his masterworks turned into films that usually bore little or no relationship to the original.

The great short story "The Killers," hailed by some literary critics as a nearly perfect example of the genre, became a two-hour routine 1946 gangster movie. The original was about the sudden appearance of two stereotyped hit men in a sleepy middle American town that has been remote from any real contact with evil. Their mission is to kill a fighter who did not throw a championship match. Hemingway knew that for most ordinary folk direct confrontation with genuine evil is unthinkable. Nick Adams, the coming-of-age hero, has never experienced such a confrontation. When he does, all he can say is "It's awful." The older and wiser man who owns the diner in which Nick works responds in typically laconic Hemingway fashion: "Well, you'd better not think about it." We are never told whether the fighter is eventually killed. It doesn't matter. What does matter is that most of us are powerless to do much about evil in the world. Whether not thinking about it is the best course to take is, of course, open to question, but great literature does nothing if not make us ask questions.

In the film Nick Adams is relegated to a minor role. The movie focuses on the prize fighter and his impressive biceps, displayed prominently enough to make a star of Burt Lancaster. Hemingway's story is all about Nick's coming of age.

Even when some fidelity to the original is attempted, Hollywood has often tacked on an ending totally at odds with the author's obvious intention. In Thomas Hardy's novel *Tess of the D'Urbervilles,* the heroine, having killed the man who seduced and deserted her, is sent to the gallows without mercy, an ending consistent with the author's generally pessimistic view of life. The filmmakers, believing the public needed a happy ending, twisted the plot so that Tess could be rescued. Hardy, outraged at what Hollywood had done to his work, sadly observed, "I am an old man and have no defense against this sort of thing."

Two American Film Classics

On almost everyone's list of classic American films are two masterpieces that appeared within a year of each other: *Citizen Kane* (1941) and *Casablanca* (1942). The timing may not be a coincidence. The history of the humanities is filled with such chronologies. Masterpieces, as well as the artists who produced them, have a way of appearing close together. Perhaps creativity is highly contagious. Remember that three of the greatest artists of all time—Leonardo, Michelangelo, and Raphael—all lived and worked at the same time in Florence.

Citizen Kane

Its techniques were too unfamiliar at the time, but its reputation as the best film ever made has grown steadily with each passing decade.

Here was a relatively low-budget film, consigned to an amazing 26-year-old named Orson Welles. Several years before, he had done the radio adaptation of H. G. Wells's *The War of the Worlds* that created panic throughout the United States. After the furor and subsequent notoriety for Welles, Hollywood gave him free rein within the confines of a modest budget. The resulting film, *Citizen Kane*, was far from a box-office sensation. Its techniques were too unfamiliar at the time, but its reputation as the best film ever made has grown steadily with each passing decade. Like many another artist, Welles died without ever quite knowing the full extent of his achievements. During his lifetime he was admired for his courage to do what his taste compelled him to do, but feared as one who could be counted on to lose money for a studio.

To be acclaimed "the best" is to challenge other aspirants to the title. Why *Kane*? Why not any one of the other films which have lasted long enough to deserve to be called classics? Is it one of the film's major themes—the question of whether money can buy happiness? Then again, other films have dealt with that theme. We don't really attend movies in order to learn lessons about happiness, or pride, or whether crime pays. It must be something else—something bigger. In its exposure of the hollowness of the American Dream, it has been compared to Fitzgerald's masterpiece *The Great Gatsby* (Chapter 4).

Welles's title character embodies the dream in this rags-to-riches story of a supremely ambitious and energetic man who makes a great fortune as the head of a newspaper empire, influences public opinion, collects great treasures, and dies—fulfilled? His fame is so great that newspaper reporters seek the answer to the mystery of his dying word: "Rosebud."

The plot, which centers on one reporter's attempt to unravel that mystery, unfolds in a technique innovative for its time and part of the reason for the film's acclaim. The story is told from several points of view. One is the director's objective presentation of the facts, such as the opening: Charles Foster Kane, a man who has interested the public for decades, is on his deathbed in his legendary mansion Xanadu. We hear the unseen protagonist whisper his final word; then we see his hand drop to the side of the bed.

Citizen Kane was not a box-office sensation when it opened; its techniques were too unfamiliar for too many viewers.

The retrospective of Kane's life begins as a voice-over narration by the reporter who is investigating the meaning of the word. Knowing that the camera cannot photograph what is inside a human being and that the audience can only guess at what lies hidden, Welles makes the investigating reporter the central character. The camera becomes his (and our) eyes.

Testimony comes from several sources, as the reporter interviews everyone who knew Kane. In the shadowy catacombs of the public library, he studies old newspapers in an attempt to recreate every incident in the life of a famous and

Moviestore collection Ltd/Alamy

Orson Welles, *Citizen Kane*, 1941

Citizen Kane reveals the hollowness of the American Dream, much like *The Great Gatsby*, with which it has been compared.

incredibly wealthy man who started out as a carefree little boy, a boy who inherits a great deal of money and must leave home to collect his fortune.

The investigation centers on documents and eyewitness accounts that can assist the search. One sequence is told from the point of view of the man who knew Kane as a boy; one from a longtime associate in the newspaper business; another from his best friend who became disillusioned by Kane's unethical behavior; and the last by the woman who became Kane's mistress and then his second wife. Some incidents appear more than once, but they are told in different versions.

As the reporter pieces together the fragments, we follow the success of Kane's first newspaper venture, the opening of his vast chain, his increasingly gaudy lifestyle, his developing megalomania—the total self-absorption of someone who has everything but is never satisfied. Kane wants to be governor, then perhaps president, but with enough money and power one can become almost *royal*. His political progress is stopped by scandal, when, as a married man, he is shown to be having an affair with a young woman. He then employs his great wealth and influence in an unsuccessful attempt to make his mistress into a star of grand opera. Eventually, he and the woman retreat to a mansion surrounded by statues and other art objects Kane has imported. The woman, bored, does jigsaw puzzles, complains, and abandons him. Kane dies, alone.

In Citizen Kane Orson Welles did not romanticize the American Dream. His film ultimately reveals the hollowness behind the dream and the tragedy of those whose only concerns are money and power.

Individual scenes are as compelling as the innovative structure. In one, the disintegration of Kane's first marriage is indicated in a rapid montage of the couple at the breakfast table, at first sitting next to each other, then sitting farther and farther apart until, in a few seconds of screen time, the wife is shown at the opposite end of a very long table reading a newspaper published by Kane's rival.

In another scene, Kane's second wife, Susan, the would-be opera star, is shown on the stage, shrieking an aria for the small audience of Kane's friends and employees. As the lady trills on and on in uninspired cadences, the camera slowly ascends from stage level, up through the massive riggings that raise and lower the backdrops, finally coming to rest on a gridwalk hundreds of feet above the appalling desecration below. As one stagehand looks on in amusement, the other pinches his nose with two fingers to signify his critique of the performance.

The final scene of Citizen Kane *reverses the famous tracking shot of the train station in* Gone with the Wind. *The camera starts wide, without focus, then finally comes to rest on a trivial object: Rosebud.*

Another shot illustrates an innovative technique known as *depth focus*, made possible by the wizardry of Welles's cinematographer Greg Toland, who subsequently became a star in his own field. In the scene, Kane's friend Jed, the music critic for Kane's paper, is sitting at his typewriter finishing a scathing review of Susan's "performance." He is shown in the foreground, as Kane enters the large room and stands in the background. An obvious rift is implied by the relationship of the figures. Kane is kept in the background so that we can only guess at what he is thinking.

Kane has tried but failed to manipulate a successful career for the untalented Susan. Since he cannot claim ownership of a world-famous diva, he continues to purchase more treasures to fill the vast salons of the mansion, ultimately not able to find room for any more.

He has become a lonely, lost old man, dying with no one by his side. And the mystery of "Rosebud" is finally understood by the audience in the famous final close-up that reveals a seemingly worthless remnant of his lost childhood in snowy Colorado. Even so, neither we nor the reporter ever learns the complete truth about the man. The film captures the ambiguities in human nature and offers as profound an analysis of power seeking as Hollywood has ever achieved.

Citizen Kane was widely believed to be based on the career of the real-life William Randolph Hearst, a newspaper publisher famous for manipulating the news and sensationalizing events that might otherwise have gone unnoticed. Hearst even tried to prevent the studio from advertising and distributing the work. The character of Susan was said to be based on Hearst's long affair with movie actress Marion Davies. Yet Hearst's California mansion San Simeon, although filled with treasures like Kane's Xanadu, was peopled by interesting guests who reported that Hearst's hospitality was genuine and bountiful. Unlike Susan, Marion Davies remained faithful to the end and seems not to have depended on jigsaw puzzles to pass the time. Reality, however, would have suited Orson Welles much less than the opportunity to create a film of vast, shadowy complexity that continues to fascinate. What he created was not at all the same as a deliberate distortion of historical fact, nor a Hollywoodized decimation of a great literary work. It is a great work of cinema standing entirely on its own.

Casablanca

Casablanca (1942) became immortal almost in spite of itself. Each day the scriptwriters would give revised scenes to the cast, who would make fun of the whole venture when the day's shooting was over. None of them knew how the film would end, and almost everyone thought it would be a disastrous failure. The United States had just entered World War II, the outcome of which was by no means certain. War movies abounded in Hollywood, most of them filled with multiple scenes of artillery fire, bombings, and mine explosions. Audiences were given Allied successes on the battlefield and reason to cheer. Yet *Casablanca*, despite its wartime background, lacked the expected kind of action scenes. Somehow, through revision after revision, it became a powerful story about one man's ethical dilemma and his conflicting moral values.

Chances are the continuing appeal of *Casablanca* springs from its film noir hero, the hard-boiled but idealistic Rick Blaine, a character who transcends the stereotype, becoming instead a three-dimensional, fully realized human being who learns to conceal a broken heart with a facade of toughness that ensures he will never be hurt again. Bogart's portrait has been reproduced on countless posters, showing him in a white jacket, with a drink and a cigarette, remembering the lover who left him without warning after a few glorious days in Paris. The song from the film, "As Time Goes By," has become a classic in its own right, as has the image of Sam, sitting at the piano and being asked to "Play it."

One of the memorable lines in screen history became Bogart's trademark: "Here's looking at you, kid"—a line that seems to express love quite as much as Romeo's great speeches do. If Juliet is the "sun," Rick's lost love is the "kid."

Because the Hollywood studio system of the 1930s and 1940s tied up big-name, "bankable" stars to long-term contracts, studio executives had to commission screenplays tailor-made for a star's identifiable screen personality. Bogart became such a bankable star after *The Maltese Falcon* and was now perceived as specializing in the film noir hero: a tough, unflinching man of steel with a susceptible heart and an uncanny ability to survive both danger and personal tragedy.

The film, directed by Michael Curtiz, whose fame up to then rested on his action-adventure work, was, as we have said, supposed to be nothing more than that. Despite the fact that Bogart's screen persona had become not only tough but ethical, Bogart was still viewed as an action hero, someone who could shoot when he had to and never miss.

The studio thought it had found just what it was looking for in the story of an expatriate American who operates an illegal gambling casino in the capital of French Morocco, supposedly a neutral territory during World War II. Yet French and German police prowled the streets on the lookout for people trying to buy exit visas, which would allow them to escape. The basically tenderhearted Rick Blaine helped them—by letting them gamble for the money. Yet there was always a gun in his pocket, just in case his business was threatened. The ingredients for melodrama were all there. They had to be, or the film would never have been made.

As the rewriting continued, Bogart's character apparently took center stage. He is shown as an unemotional realist: at heart concerned about the refugees but unwilling to become involved in their lives. He cannot afford to. With the apparent blessing of Louis, the police chief who would like nothing better than to crack his veneer, Rick maintains a well-run establishment in the well-ordered world he has created for himself.

Basic to his philosophy of uninvolvement (his defense against the hurt he experienced in Paris) is a refusal to take sides in the war, despite the fact that his country is fighting against the Nazis. He shares nothing with anyone about his private life. When the police chief attempts coyly to find out what he is doing in Casablanca, Rick answers in his typical deadpan that he came for the waters. Reminded that they are in a desert and there are no waters in Casablanca, he replies calmly, "I was misinformed."

In one early scene his tough exterior softens just a bit when he counsels a desperate young wife who has come to him for advice. The police chief has offered her a substantial amount of money—enough for a letter of transit—if she agrees to sleep with him. She doesn't want to be disloyal to her husband, but does Rick think she would be wrong to accept the offer? He advises her, instead, to gamble at the roulette wheel and covertly directs the croupier to let her win. The police chief knows what has happened and smilingly accuses Rick of being "a sentimentalist"

> *"The world's favorite Hollywood love story is all the more romantic because it doesn't exalt romantic love above all."*
>
> **—Stephen D. Greydanes**

at heart. But Rick is careful never to show this side of himself. He is a loner, just supervising the club, refusing to drink or make friends with the patrons.

Inevitably his armor is pierced. The lost love, Ilsa (Ingrid Bergman), walks in one night with her husband, Victor Laszlo (Paul Henreid), the number one Resistance fighter against the Nazis and, for them, the top of the Most Wanted list. Later, after everyone else has left, Rick sits at a table with a drink and a cigarette. The shape of the doorway in back of the room dissolves into a similar shape, that of the Arc de Triomphe in Paris, as the flashback shows him remembering the joy of his passionate love affair with Ilsa and their mutual determination to escape the approaching German troops. Ilsa has agreed to leave with him on the last train, but he waits at the railway station in vain. Only when she reenters his life does he learn that she was married all the time they were together in Paris but believed she was a widow. When she discovered at the last minute that her husband was alive, she decided to return to him rather than leave with Rick.

Back at the café, in present time, Rick, still hurt and angry, is nevertheless forced to abandon his neutral stand. When Ilsa's husband asks the café orchestra to play the French national anthem to drown out the singing of Nazi soldiers at a nearby table, the orchestra leader looks to Rick for permission. He nods. The refugees stand, joining the café entertainer in an emotional singing of *La Marseillaise*. Rick makes no effort to stop them, and from that point on, it will be difficult for him to remain uninvolved.

After Rick kills the Nazi commander, the French captain shields him by ordering his men to "round up the usual suspects."

The Nazi major seems ready to capture Laszlo, who knows he and Ilsa must find a way to escape from Casablanca. Ilsa confronts Rick with a gun to get the exit visas she knows he has. He tells her the flame of passion has reignited, and he will give the visas to Laszlo if she will stay behind with him. Unable to resist for a second time, she agrees. A plane to freedom awaits at the airport, a plane that Victor and Ilsa are supposed to board. Victor does not know that Ilsa will go with Rick, not him. Legend has it that the scriptwriters did not know what they were going to do with the scene. Through the mysterious, often chaotic labyrinth known as the creative process, their dilemma suddenly turned into Rick's famous moral choice.

That choice (which should be obvious from what we have told you about Rick) in that scene, a scene that was not written until the final day of shooting, has made film history.

Citizen Kane and *Casablanca* have much in common. Both begin with exposition provided by a news broadcast. Both films employ dialogue sparingly. Neither central character reveals himself through what he says. Both use the screen medium to create a complex reality that we must interpret because neither makes a direct, easily phrased statement about people or existence. Yet the two films are different in that *Citizen Kane* was consciously designed to be a quality film made by an independent young director with no ties to Hollywood. *Casablanca* was the product of a studio paying high prices to its stars and directed by a man who specialized in action-adventure movies rather than artistic masterpieces. Two opposite roads led to the same destination: a secure niche in the history of classic films.

AF Archive/Alamy

Humphrey Bogart and Ingrid Bergman, *Casablanca*, 1942

One of the most famous decisions in the history of film: "Here's looking at you, kid."

The Film Auteur

The French word **auteur**, or "author," has been applied to the most significant directors, those whose special style and themes are so evident that their work is instantly recognizable. "A film by . . . " usually means the director rather than the scriptwriter (unless they are the same person). The work of the auteur bears signs of individual technique—like an author's unique use of language or an artist's unique brushstrokes. It can be recognized in camera angles, overlapping dialogue, swift transitions, and a personal view of reality.

> *Write what you feel, not what you think the audience wants.*
>
> **—Stephen Sondheim**

Ingmar Bergman

Swedish director Ingmar Bergman (1918–2007) did not come to film because of its glamour and the promise of quick wealth. He was a serious theater director intent on creating art, and he saw in film a challenging medium offering him great freedom to explore his subjects. For a decade he studied the techniques of cinema, and then by the mid-50s he had made Sweden very nearly the art film capital of the world.

The Seventh Seal (1957), one of his major works, is a medieval fable about a knight who has survived the Crusades, then ironically finds Death waiting for him when he returns home. He challenges the Grim Reaper to a game of chess, the contract being that he can stay alive until Death reaches checkmate. The knight is determined to delay the inevitable until he discovers the meaning of his life. While the fantasy game proceeds, the knight is also journeying about the countryside in search of something—a person, a cause, a religion—that will convince him existence is not an absurd waste of time. The knight's quest very likely paralleled Bergman's own philosophical journey.

In the great tradition of the mythic journey (Chapter 3), the knight has many adventures and interacts with many people along the way, including his former teacher, a brutal hypocrite who had urged him to join the Crusades, and a young woman being tortured and finally burned at the stake as a witch. Various penitents thrash each other and themselves as signs of penance for sin and as a means of getting rid of a virulent plague. Organized religion, he finds, does not make existence seem valuable. He discovers the fullness of life only when he meets a young married couple named Joseph and Mary who have one child. In the loving warmth of the family circle, where members support and nurture each other, life begins to make sense. Contrasted with one dark scene after another is the scene in which he and the family share strawberries and fresh milk in the sunlight. Not to have known love and joy is, he realizes, not to have lived. And now Death reaches checkmate.

Topham/The Image Works

Max von Sydow and Bengt Ekerot, *The Seventh Seal*, 1957

In Bergman's great film *The Seventh Seal*, a knight challenges Death to a game of chess in order to gain enough time to seek the meaning of life.

Bergman's message is simple but not simplistic. The Knight finds the answer to life only after struggling with utter nihilism (the belief that all comes to nothing in the end). With the

The knight, challenging Death to a chess match in The Seventh Seal, *learns that death is nothing to fear if one has found meaning in life.*

knight's help, the young family escapes Death. Though he himself will die, his final vision is a joyous one; and the film ends with the happy family standing by the sea as the knight joins a joyful procession silhouetted against the sky and led by the figure of Death. There is nothing mournful here. Death is not to be feared if one has lived for something.

The title *The Seventh Seal* is taken from the Book of Revelations, according to which the end of the world will be preceded by the opening of seven sealed scrolls, the first six containing a multitude of catastrophes such as war, famine, and plague. The seventh calls forth in turn seven trumpet blasts, the final one signaling the arrival of Christ and the final judgment. Though death is the final destination for everyone, those who have led an exemplary life will know eternal peace. Hence the knight's chess defeat is not a death at all, but the triumphant end of a meaningful life.

Federico Fellini

"There was in Fellini a joy in images, a sad flavor of life, a something of Cervantes and Rabelais that somehow makes us finally shout "Yes but" to all criticism."

—Donald Lyons

The young Federico Fellini (1920–1993) learned his craft from the Italian neorealistic directors who, in the aftermath of World War II, had little money to work with and often used untrained actors to tell stories of ordinary people amid the streets and buildings bombed out during that war. Fellini, however, dissatisfied with the limitations of using the camera to photograph only external reality as it unfolded, saw other possibilities. He wanted to be a true artist, using the camera for the haunting imagery it could film. He sought to combine realism with poetry. To retain control of his vision, he became his own screenwriter and, eventually, won international fame as a film *auteur.*

In *La Strada* (1954) Fellini tells the story of Gelsomina, a simple-minded young woman (Giulietta Massina) working in a traveling carnival as assistant to Zampano (Anthony Quinn), billed as the world's strongest man. Secretly in love with him, she becomes his virtual slave. Zampano's enormous ego doesn't allow him to treat her like a fellow human being. He rebukes her for every little mistake and eventually deserts her altogether, leaving her penniless in a world she can never hope to comprehend. The only tenderness she is ever shown comes from a musician, also a victim of Zampano's brutality, who teaches her to play a simple tune on a trumpet. In the final scene, as Zampano sits on the sand near the water and recognizes that for all his strength he is nothing, he begins to recall Gelsomina's devoted smile and the sound of her music. He weeps.

Moviestore collection Ltd/Alamy

Giulietta Massina, *La Strada*, 1954

In Fellini's *La Strada*, a simple-minded girl falls in love with a carnival strongman, who uses, then deserts her, only to realize at the end that he is alone in the world.

La Strada leaves an ambiguous message: is love the answer? To what question? The girl's love for Zampano bore no fruit, and the strongman is left with no one to love him. Is love just another myth, sweet and poetic but, sadly, nonexistent?

As he continued to experiment, Fellini became more and more complex. He turned inward upon himself and concentrated on the often tragic waning of the artist's creativity (fearing that it was happening to him?). In what many consider

Fellini's masterpiece, *8 1/2* (1963), the protagonist is himself a film director who, like Fellini, has made eight films and is now seeking to finish his ninth, except that he never quite gets there. Early commercial success, fame, a restless sexual appetite, and the continual pressures exerted by Hollywood-influenced studio executives all conspire to keep him from focusing sharply on his goal.

The opening shot is memorable. The hero is inside an automobile on a ferry, windows shut tightly so that sounds of reveling passengers cannot be heard. It is the artist alienated within his environment. Yet there is no comfort in that inner space, only more confusion. Fellini in a few breathtaking seconds has summed up the plight of the artist in an indifferent world. The fantastic final scene, in which various kinds of artists are shown dancing in a ring, gives hope that somehow the creative imagination will survive, but it might also mean that true art is simply going in circles within itself and can never reach an audience.

Alfred Hitchcock

Unlike Orson Welles, who came to Hollywood determined to create film art, British-born Alfred Hitchcock (1899–1980) was imported to make scary melodramas and only gradually acquired the critical reputation his work continues to merit. Known first as a man who made thrillers about spies and murders among highly civilized people, he was dubbed the "master of suspense" in the late 1930s. The plots in his films were filled with unexpected twists, and always there was a breathtaking and surprising finale with an always new and ingenious kind of danger.

Hitchcock, however, soon tired of exploiting in obvious ways the audience's love of terror. His work acquired greater subtlety. His evildoers were generally suave, sophisticated beings on the surface, but underneath were inhuman, disordered, and dangerously antisocial. Evil enters the lives of ordinary, decent people, whom we get to know and like, and only then does Hitchcock, the master craftsman, put them in danger, causing the viewer's heart to pound a little faster.

> *"Drama is life with the dull bits cut out."*
>
> **—Alfred Hitchcock**

The director believed implicitly that we live in a fundamentally amoral universe in which good triumphs only by accident, in which, despite the civilized facade we erect, chaos is the law of nature. In *The Birds* (1963) that chaos comes frighteningly to life in a formerly peaceful northern California village. Without warning and without any known motives, the birds gang up on the town's inhabitants, killing some, injuring others.

The most memorable scene is typical Hitchcock: the juxtaposition of danger and normal activity. A woman waits outside an elementary school, totally unmindful of a grim scene taking place behind her, where hundreds of blackbirds are massing in the schoolyard. From inside the schoolhouse comes the joyful sound of innocent young voices singing. Suddenly the calm erupts into a scene reminiscent of the **elongated moment** in Eisenstein's Odessa steps sequence in *The Battleship Potemkin*. The woman, the children, and the teacher are running down a steep hill, holding up their arms to shield themselves from the shrieking onslaught. Hitchcock cuts from one fleeing person to another in a montage so rapid that we actually *see* very little of the devastation but *think* we see it all.

Hitchcock had already used this technique in *Psycho* (1960), considered by many critics to be his masterwork. The film, which remains popular, may well be the scariest movie of all time. Here evil assumes the form of an apparently sweet, shy, and lonely young man who so yearns to be reunited with his dead mother that he sometimes wears her clothes and assumes her identity. In this guise he is capable of committing brutal acts without knowing what he is doing.

In the shower scene of Psycho *we think we are seeing every moment of gruesome horror, but in fact the scene moves so quickly that we actually see only a collage of camera shots. We have not witnessed the actual stabbing.*

In *Psycho*, the Hitchcock vision of the world is fully realized. His philosophy of evil provides him with a signature technique for terrifying the audience. As usual, he places a twisted individual next to people who are unaware they are living in a dangerous world. An attractive young woman who has calmly and methodically embezzled a huge sum of money is driving away from the scene of her crime but finds herself caught in a blinding rainstorm. Seeking shelter for the night in a motel where she is the only guest, she is relieved to be the recipient of warm hospitality by the handsome young owner. As the woman prepares for bed, feeling snug and cozy and happy that she has evaded pursuit, she steps into an invitingly hot shower, apparently safe.

The shower scene is one of the most admired ever filmed. We do not expect terrible things to happen in the safe confines of a bathroom. What surroundings could be more conventional and uncharacteristic of a horror film? As the woman lathers herself generously, washing away her guilt, enjoying the warm stream of water gently caressing her face, suddenly there appears a silhouette of someone who seems to be holding a knife. Against a score of violins imitating the sounds of a scream, the woman is repeatedly stabbed. We think we are seeing every moment of her agony, but in fact the scene moves so quickly that we are actually watching only a collage of camera shots: the water, the shower head, the woman's hands to her face, blood swirling into the drain; finally there is only an ominous silence as we are shown a closeup of a dead face, eyes still open in horror. We have not seen the murderer, nor have we seen any actual stabbing. The scene, which lasts only 45 seconds, was composed of 78 distinct shots, edited to move so rapidly through the projector that the effect is one of subliminal horror.

Akira Kurosawa

"Kurosawa is a man of all genres, all periods, bridging in his work the traditional and the modern, the old and the new, the cultures of the East and the West."

—Ephraim Katz

We have already mentioned the Japanese film *Rashomon* as an example of how cinema is able to show the same scene from different points of view. That film catapulted its director, Akira Kurosawa (1910–1998), into the forefront of internationally recognized filmmakers and brought new audiences to an appreciation of the non-Western cinema.

Though he had studied Western techniques very carefully, learning the wizardry of the camera, Kurosawa was also dedicated to recreating his country's past and bringing it to the attention of a worldwide audience. His masterpiece *Seven Samurai* (1954) introduced that audience to the code of feudal Japan's warrior class, their nobility, their sense of honor and decency, as well as their super-swordsmanship, which they were always prepared to demonstrate in a good cause. In some sense, the *samurai* were the equivalents of King Arthur's Round Table knights.

The Seven Samurai strengthened Kurosawa's already growing reputation and caught the attention of Hollywood, always eager to jump on a new bandwagon. In 1960 director John Sturges brought forth *The Magnificent Seven*, an unabashed Westernization of feudal Japan, in which a band of roaming gunfighters with no allegiances finds itself fighting against an army of bandits terrorizing the innocent inhabitants of a Mexican village. The blazing and dangerous shootout turns the previously lawless bunch into righteous crusaders. The film, which owes everything to Kurosawa, was hailed by critics as an ethical Western with a solid sense of values.

Kurosawa is also noted for his meticulous approach to filmmaking; he often held up production if something about the set was not quite right. On one occasion, during the filming of *The Seven Samurai*, he insisted that the painstakingly

The Everett Collection

***The Seven Samurai*, 1954**

Kurosawa's masterpiece *The Seven Samurai* introduced Western audiences to Japan's noble warrior class.

constructed sixteenth-century fortress—a set costing over a million dollars—be completely torn down and rebuilt because the carpenters had used steel nails, which, of course, didn't exist at the time. When someone objected with "Who'll know there are steel nails holding up the set?" he answered, "I will."

Stanley Kubrick

An American director whose films were sometimes funny, even when his themes were death and the destruction of the planet and the cosmos, Stanley Kubrick (1928–1999), in the best tradition of satire, lashed out at self-deception and hypocrisy. He always did the unexpected, refusing to turn out formula work designed for the "blockbuster" market. He used a lot of music in his films, but never as an obvious parallel to emotion. He took many chances in an industry where risk-taking has become increasingly expensive. Very much in the tradition of Orson Welles, the earlier bad boy of Hollywood, Kubrick attained worldwide recognition as a true auteur.

> *"I think clearly that there's a basic problem with people who are not paying attention with their eyes. They're listening. And they don't get much from listening . . ."*
>
> **—Stanley Kubrick**

Paths of Glory (1957) is an early, straightforward narrative film based on an incident that struck Kubrick as too bitter for satire. It denounces officials who save themselves at the expense of innocent men serving under them. In World War I an ethical young French officer (played in the film by Kirk Douglas) finds himself at odds with some generals who he believes are attempting to conceal their responsibility for a mistaken strategy that has resulted in unnecessary bloodshed. In an effort to prevent the remaining soldiers from resisting their next order, the generals have decided to make an example of three soldiers chosen at random and convicted of cowardice. They are to be given a speedy trial with a foregone conclusion—conviction and death by firing squad.

The officer is assigned to defend them but refuses to go through the motions and play the military game. Instead, he investigates, learns the truth, including the fact that a lieutenant chose one of the men for death not randomly, but for personal reasons.

Despite the eloquence of the hero, the men, as expected, are condemned to die. On the night before the execution, they face the prospect in different ways. One becomes so hysterical he needs to be drugged into insensibility. When another points out that a cockroach in the cell will continue to live after they have died, the third man matter-of-factly steps on it and remarks, "Now he won't." The third condemned man has suffered so many injuries during the fighting that he cannot walk. Nevertheless, at dawn he is carried outside on a stretcher that is placed upright in range of the firing squad.

After the execution is duly carried out, the defending officer is congratulated for dispatching his assignment so well. He knows that if he remains silent about the costly errors of the generals he is sure to earn a promotion. To their astonishment, he insists on telling the truth, then walks out of the meeting after hearing that the next morning the troops will once again be commanded to suffer more bloodshed in a hopeless cause. In a moving final scene, he passes a tavern where a captured German girl is singing a plaintive song for the entertainment of happily drunken soldiers. He decides to delay telling them the grim news about what awaits them the next day.

Dr. Strangelove, Or How I Learned to Stop Worrying and Love the Bomb (1963) continued Kubrick's interest in antiwar, antihypocrisy themes, but this time in a blatantly satiric style. The film concerns the effort of a general named Jack D. Ripper to start a war by ordering American pilots to drop a nuclear bomb on the Soviet Union. When word reaches the Pentagon, the president and his staff are able to rescind the order, but one bomber crew continues flying. Kubrick parodies World War II movies by making the bomber crew the customary cross-section of geographic and ethnic backgrounds. The music accompanying the bomber as it flies over Soviet territory is the Civil War song "When Johnny Comes Marching Home Again." The pilot, wearing a ten-gallon hat, discovers that the bomb bay door will not open; but, undaunted, climbs on the bomb himself and, uttering a triumphant "Yee-haw," rides it gleefully to the destruction of both himself and thousands of civilians below.

The president of the United States puts in a call to the leader of the Soviet Union. In an effort to be fair, he suggests that, since an American plane has bombed Soviet territory, perhaps the Soviet leader would like to retaliate by bombing only one place in America. But that solution would not work. He learns that a Doomsday Machine designed by the Soviets to rid the planet of all life for the next ninety-nine years has started its countdown. Nothing can stop it. As politicians and military strategists on both sides prepare to take shelter deep underground (accompanied by lovely young women who will breed future generations), they look forward to a time when their descendants will be able to continue the hostilities, once the earth has breathable air again. The final scene shows an airplane being refueled by another plane in mid-air to the tune of "We'll Meet Again."

Francis Ford Coppola

In the *Godfather* trilogy Francis Ford Coppola (b. 1939) took the popular theme of rival Mafia families and, especially in the first two films, transcended Hollywood formula to achieve works of Greek-like tragic dimensions, the dream of many an artist working in both theater and film.

In Mario Puzo's powerful novel of a Mafia empire and its ruling patriarch, gunned down in a bloody assassination, Coppola saw the stuff of which great tragedy is made: a proud family dynasty in which the sins of the father condemn the next generations to repeat the same crimes of extortion and brutal murder and to suffer the vengeance of their enemies. The protagonist of the saga is the son (Al Pacino) of the murdered patriarch or "godfather," a young man of basic moral decency, who, like Hamlet, is forced into upholding his father's honor though he lacks the tough-mindedness for the job.

> *A belief in a supernatural source of evil is not necessary; man alone is quite capable of every wickedness.*
>
> **—Joseph Conrad**

Copolla brought other riches to the project besides coauthorship of the screenplay and a director's keen sense of rhythm. He possessed the stage director's ability to extract performances of sustained psychological realism and subtlety and the film director's ability to tell a story in image, sound, and quick cuts, always in control of a pace that kept audiences on the edge of their seats. In one memorable and representative scene, the idyll of a Sicilian wedding filmed against a glorious background of mountains, olive trees, and azure sky, with a lilting Italian melody playing off in the distance, is abruptly interrupted by a car bombing. *The Godfather* renders themes of family tragedy, violence, and betrayal with a haunting visual lyricism never before achieved in a gangster film.

> *Let me put it this way: I'm always questioning . . . You save a man on one corner and on the next corner a man dies . . . It begs the question, the constant question of what our existence is, the "Who-are-we? Why are we here?" kind of thing.*
>
> **—Martin Scorsese**

A Word on Critical Viewing

Throughout this book so far we have stressed the primacy of critical thinking in your life and the role played by the humanities in helping you to develop the skill. The critical viewing of films is a way to bring the pleasure of movie-going to a new and higher level. Recognizing the choices made by filmmakers is akin to learning more about the craft of a poem or a painting. Films come in a variety of themes and styles. Here are some criteria that will help you determine the merit of a film:

Use of a Style Unique to Cinema. No other medium can so skillfully show quick cuts, overlapping dialogue (in contrast to the long speeches of many stage plays), and powerful imagery that needs no words. (In Luis Buñuel's *Viridiana,* an imperious employer reaches out to seduce a frightened servant. Instead of showing the human attack, the camera shifts to a cat pouncing on a mouse.)

Characters with Complex Inner Lives. The best films, like the best novels and plays, reward close attention of viewers willing to listen carefully and concentrate. For example, Rick Blaine in *Casablanca* is both the hard-boiled realist of film noir and a tender-hearted romantic who would like the world to be a better place.

Relevance to the Times. Both documentary and fictional films are sometimes responses to social conditions in need of reform. Ford's *The Grapes of Wrath,* which dealt with displaced farmers forced to become ill-paid migrant workers and Chaplin's *Modern Times,* which showed the dehumanization of the working class during the Depression, are good examples.

Integrity. Films that present serious problems should respect their audiences enough not to hand them unbelievable solutions. The unsentimental woman in the 1998 Brazilian film *Central Station* helps a young boy find his father but does not become unbelievably transformed as a result. The hero of Coppola's first *Godfather* film would rather not become a ruthless killer expected to vindicate the family honor. Coppola might have distorted Mario Puzo's novel by having the hero's moral sense triumph, but he did not. He remained faithful to the novel's recognition that, in Mafia culture, family honor supersedes all else.

Gravity of Theme. A film's dealing with a timeless subject is usually a sign that the writer or director is reaching for art. *Citizen Kane* concerns the moral decline of a man who values wealth and fame above all else. Bergman's *The Seventh Seal* is concerned with the search for the meaning and purpose of life. But a big theme does not always guarantee an artistic result. Two-dimensional characters and stilted dialogue can doom even the most high-minded film.

No Violations of Probability. Distortion of the events in the biography of a public figure is inexcusable, as are tacked-on happy endings not justified by the events leading up to them. Cinema announced early in its history that anything could be fair game when pleasing an audience was at stake. The film version of Thomas Hardy's *Tess of the D'Urbervilles* had the heroine sentenced to die saved by a last-minute, improbable reprieve. Hollywood has always been cynical about audience willingness to face reality.

In 1940, the play *Our Town* (Chapter 7) became so popular that Hollywood immediately secured the film rights. On the stage the heroine dies in childbirth, and the statement made is that birth and death are natural to the life cycle; people have to live with that. It would have been dishonest for the playwright, Thornton Wilder, to ignore death, nor should death have come only to old people. Wilder knows that life does not follow an expected scenario. In the screen version, however, the heroine is brought back from near death, apparently through the strength of love. The film distorted the author's intention. It lied about life. To lie when a film promises to be true to life is to cheat those in the audience who appreciate screen art and do not require a sugar-coated fantasy.

Realistic Depiction of Gender. Except in films of social realism, the stereotypical woman has been a decorative "handmaiden" whose happiness depends on victory in the mating game. Typically she is well-groomed and well-dressed (though never seen at an ironing board) and has the goal of finding a powerful man. As we have seen in the depiction of independent heroines, gender on screen has now broken the mold, but Hollywood is still turning out stories, particularly in horror and suspense films, with old-fashioned helpless heroines who must be rescued by strong males. Films from abroad, especially countries with serious problems of gender inequality, are giving audiences realistic, often painful, insights into the unfair treatment of women.

This chapter has discussed many films. If you have viewed the ones we singled out for praise, you may disagree with our assessments. Nothing could be more harmonious with the spirit of the humanities than disputes among critical thinkers giving serious consideration to a work that aspires to be art. Often the dispute itself is more important than the work.

LEARNING OBJECTIVES

After having carefully studied the chapter, you should be able to

1. Explain the conventions of film.
2. Summarize film milestones.
3. Summarize in detail the major genres of film.
4. Indicate reasons that *Citizen Kane* and *Casablanca* are regarded as classics.
5. Explain the meaning of *film auteur* and present an example.
6. Summarize what the critical film viewer looks for.

KEY TERMS

auteur French term for author, used by film historians in reference to certain directors who develop a reputation as serious artists whose imprint is found in almost every film they make because of recognizable camera styles, rhythms, themes, and symbols.

cinematography the way the camera tells a story.

close-up in film, when the camera moves in to enlarge the image of one character on the screen.

conventions elements of filmmaking often unnoticed by audiences, e.g. the presence of the camera and its variety of shots.

cut a director's command that the shooting of a scene must stop; also, when the camera moves from one character to another or from one scene to another.

dissolve when one scene fades out to be replaced by another; or when the camera, instead of cutting from one scene to another, superimposes the next scene on the present one, then gradually fades out.

documentary nonfiction film that usually has a narrator but not a structured storyline.

elongated moment technique associated with Eisenstein in which an action that may be brief in real time is broken into component details and thus lasts longer in screen time.

film noir French term for a genre of film known for dark settings, cynicism, and emphasis on the seamy side of human nature; the story usually centers on crime in the city investigated by an alienated tough-guy hero.

freeze-frame when the camera suddenly stops in mid-scene and the image becomes a photograph.

genre a category of film, such as romantic comedy, Western, or film noir; recognizing genre helps filmgoers know what to expect about style and content.

lingering take technique associated with Griffith in which the camera lingers on a face or an object to underscore a dramatic effect or a significant moment.

pan when the camera travels from one character to another, from one object in a room to another, and so on without pausing on anyone or anything.

persona a characterization identified with a certain actor, such as Humphrey Bogart, often to the point where the public comes to believe the actor and the character are the same person.

point of view the vantage from which the camera is filming a scene so the audience knows whether it is supposed to be inside a character's consciousness or sharing the director's objectivity.

slapstick an enduring comic style in which characters are totally dehumanized, fall down, get hit repeatedly or flattened against a wall when a door violently opens; the term comes from the sound made by two sticks being slapped together, a sound often used in old films and plays to make a slap or a punch in the nose seem more violent.

tracking shot the camera on rollers or rails moving in for a close-up or moving outward to display a wider area, such as the gradual revelation of the hundreds of dead or dying soldiers in the railway depot scene from *Gone with the Wind.*

TOPICS FOR WRITING AND DISCUSSION

1. Some of the films mentioned in the chapter—*Citizen Kane,* for example—did not fare well at the box office though they were critically acclaimed. Others were poorly reviewed yet showed soaring box-office receipts. Some critics look with disfavor on the blockbuster, implying that a broad segment of the public is lacking in taste and patronizes bad films. Identify a film you have seen recently that did well at the box office but not with critics and that you consider cinema art. OR identify a film you have seen recently that did not fare well at the box office but that you consider a work of art. Explain why in either case.
2. Write a short paper on a director not mentioned in the chapter whom you consider a film auteur or who might one day achieve such stature.
3. Chaplin and Bogart were discussed in the chapter as having screen personas. They, of course, belong to the history of films. The screen persona seems to have all but vanished as well. Why do you think this is the case?
4. Does it make any difference that the famous Odessa steps sequence in Eisenstein's *Battleship Potemkin* never happened? In other words, if a film pretends to be history, is it able to stray from the facts? Does historical accuracy add to a film's value as entertainment?
5. Women and minorities did not fare well in many earlier films. Has the situation improved? Does more need to be done? If so, suggest some remedies.
6. Almost every film of today is shot in color. Earlier masterpieces such as *Citizen Kane* and *Casablanca* are in black and white. In the case of both of these films, color was available but not chosen. Recent reissues have tried "colorizing" classic black and white films, but they have been uniformly rejected by fans. What reasons can you think of for their rejection?
7. Reread the section on Alfred Hitchcock's techniques for creating horror scenes. (Or better still, rent *Psycho*.) Compare these techniques with those found in a contemporary horror film. If you have actually watched a Hitchcock film, which do you prefer—the old or the new? Why?
8. Special effects, such as those in mega-hits like *Avatar, Clash of the Titans,* or the *Iron Man* films, are hugely popular with audiences. What is *your* opinion? Do you prefer a lot of special effects rather than a straightforward story with no special effects?
9. Many critics decry what they consider to be the decay of genuine screen art. On what do you think they base such an opinion? Does it seem fair? Explain your answer.
10. Discuss a film genre that has been overhauled, restyled to fit contemporary tastes. Cite an example of a recent film in the genre and compare it with one you learned about in the chapter.

Study and **Review** on **MyHumanitiesKit.com**

TAKE A CLOSER LOOK: The D-Day Scene in *Saving Private Ryan*

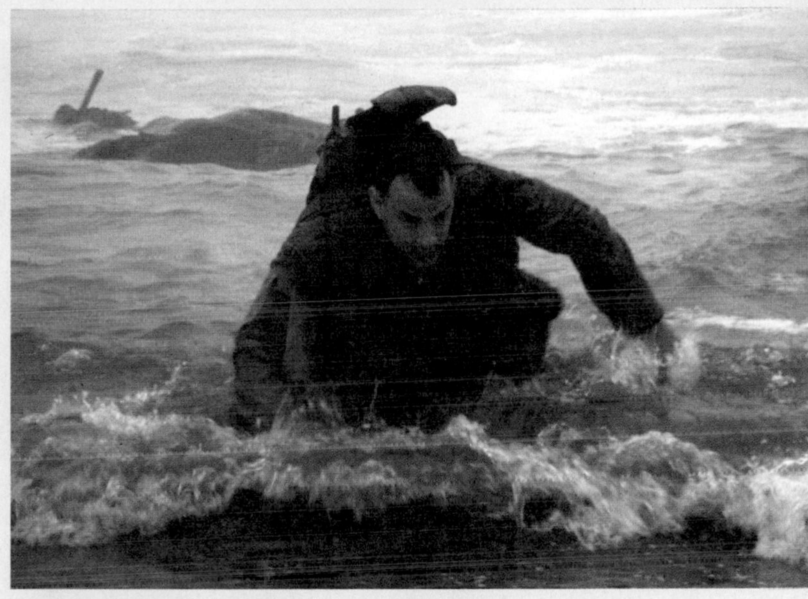

Moviestore collection Ltd//Alamy

Tom Hanks, *Saving Private Ryan*, 1998

A major turning point in the European theater of World War II, the invasion of Normandy (popularly known as D-Day) on June 6, 1944 was intimately familiar to American audiences through their history classes and countless depictions in World War II epics. Yet the first 27 minutes of Steven Spielberg's 1998 film *Saving Private Ryan* shocked audiences with an intense depiction of the invasion of Omaha Beach as they had never seen it before.

After a brief scene featuring an elderly gentleman visiting the battlefield memorial, the camera focuses in on his eye and then out to reveal a man with shaking hands on a boat approaching Omaha Beach. From the first shot, viewers are placed firmly in the heat of the battle. We are with the soldiers as they disembark the assault ships, wade to shore, and charge up the beach. All around us, soldiers are dying graphic, bloody deaths. For 27 minutes, we hear a nonstop cacophony of cries of fear and pain, explosions, gunfire, and shouted orders. As the battle ends, we witness the merciless killing of surrendering enemy soldiers. The violence and intensity of the scene has been described as overwhelming and gruesome, yet it has also been noted for its dedication to realism.

The filming of the scene involved fifteen hundred extras and cost $12 million to produce. Spielberg used actual landing craft from the D-Day invasion, incorporated underwater camerawork to capture bullets and soldiers racing through the water, and hired amputees to play maimed soldiers. About the scene, Spielberg says, "I didn't want to shoot the picture in a way that would seem like a Hollywood production coming to Omaha Beach and making a gung-ho extravaganza. This is really trying to approximate the look and the smells of what battle and combat is really like." To produce the battle accurately, Spielberg consulted with noted historians and military experts. And while the scene features some historical inaccuracies, it has been described by many veterans of that day as the most realistic depiction that they have seen in film.

Overall, the film grossed $481 million at the box office, was nominated for eleven Academy Awards, and won Spielberg his second Academy Award for best director. After the noted battle scene, the film follows a small group of soldiers (led by Tom Hanks) on a public relations mission to find and rescue Private Ryan (Matt Damon), the only remaining brother of four—all recently killed in action. In many ways, the film fits the conventions of a World War II drama: a war-weary, multicultural group of soldiers sets out on a mission climaxing in another dramatic battle scene. *Saving Private Ryan,* however, also allows its characters to question their mission: why should eight men risk their lives for one? Despite the other merits of the film, however, it is the D-Day invasion scene that has earned *Saving Private Ryan*'s place in film history.

AF Archive/Alamy

***Saving Private Ryan*, 1998**

Examine the stills to gain a sense of the intensity of the scene. The following questions will help you explore *Saving Private Ryan* as a critical viewer.

1. Comment on Spielberg's dedication to realism in the D-Day scene of *Saving Private Ryan*. How does filming on location at Omaha Beach with many of the original vehicles affect the realism?
2. What's the value of realistic combat violence? Compare Spielberg's dedication to realistic combat violence to the strategies used to depict violence employed by Eisenstein in *Battleship Potemkin* and Hitchcock in *Psycho* and *The Birds* (described earlier in this chapter).
3. Spielberg's use of realistic combat violence in *Saving Private Ryan* has profoundly influenced the war movie genre. Describe and analyze two war movies that you are familiar with and their portrayal of the violence of war.
4. How does seeing the D-Day invasion portrayed in *Saving Private Ryan* affect your understanding of the event? Does the depiction correspond with how you imagined World War II? Does the depiction correspond with how you have seen World War II portrayed in other films?
5. Describe Spielberg's use of color. How do you think the color affects the realism of the scene?
6. What other Spielberg films are you familiar with? (*Jaws, E.T., Jurassic Park,* and *Schindler's List* are prominent examples.) In your opinion, is Spielberg an auteur? Why or why not?

If you wish to explore further, *Saving Private Ryan* is readily available on DVD and selections can be found online (caution: the scene is extremely violent and graphic). The movie also plays frequently on television in an edited (but still intense) version.

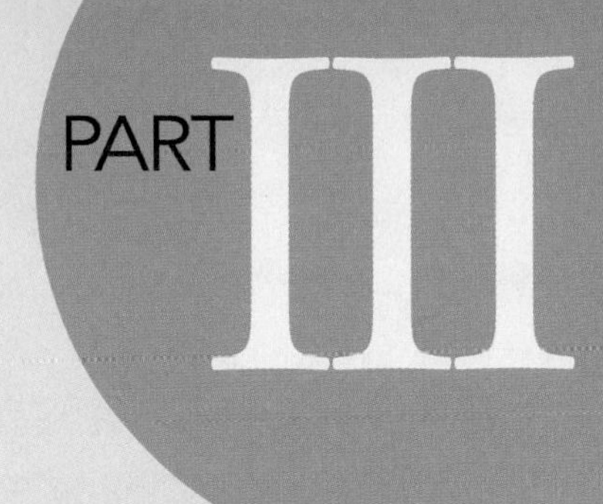

Themes of the Humanities

"If only we could order self-sacrifice from the Sharper Image catalogue . . . we yearn for the old verities—heroism, duty, honor, loyalty"

—Maureen Dowd

Chapter 10

Religion

Religion is integral to daily life for billions of people around the world. They read books, wear sacred symbols, eat or don't eat certain foods in holiday observances, and are born, married, and laid to rest in accordance with the requirements of a given faith. Because religion is so prevalent and because religious themes appear so frequently in the arts, philosophy, and literature, recognition of the enormous influence of this powerful force is indispensable to a study of the humanities.

Among the sacred books of the world are the Hebrew and Christian Bibles, the Qur'an (Koran) of Islam, the Vedas of India, the Buddhist scriptures, and the *Tao Te Ching* (*The Way of Life*) of China, books that offer information about the past and guidelines for living in the present.

Artists and sculptors have for thousands of years depicted the appearance of God, the gods, the afterworld, and innumerable supernatural beings, both demonic and angelic. Religion and religious questions underlie some of the great works of literature such as Dante's *Divine Comedy,* with its descriptions of Hell, Purgatory, and Heaven, and Milton's *Paradise Lost,* with its interpretation of the Adam and Eve story from Genesis and its solution to the age-old dilemma of how to account for evil in a world created by a benevolent God.

Questioning of traditional belief is found in works such as the novels of Fyodor Dostoevski (1821–1888), who eventually decided, after much soul-searching, that Christianity is the answer to the world's troubles. The final sentence of *Tess of the D'Urbervilles* by Thomas Hardy (1840–1928) clearly makes a negative statement about religion, when, after the execution of the heroine for having murdered her seducer, the narrator comments: "The President of the Immortals had ended his sport with Tess."

Debates over religious doctrines have been widespread in Western humanities for many centuries, but far less among Eastern writers. Western minds have long been accustomed to inquiry and analysis. Even as far back as Augustine, as we shall see later in this chapter, a profound questioning of belief preceded acceptance of it.

Religion has aroused a great deal of discussion and has even led to devastating wars. It continues to spur heated debates between those who believe in the literal interpretation of a sacred text and those who view the writings as allegorical and metaphoric and therefore not literally true, between those who believe the religion they follow is fixed for all time and those who are flexible, willing to explore and discuss. Others find themselves somewhere in the middle, or else they ignore religion altogether—until it is the center of an issue such as tax support for sectarian schools, public prayer, or a family member's unexpected choice of marriage partner.

In this chapter we shall consider some of the many ways in which religion affects us and the humanities. Religion is presented here as a phenomenon found in all cultures and all periods of time, as a recognition of

◀ **William Blake, *Job Rebuked by His Friends*, 1826**

The Book of Job confronts one of the most challenging questions for religious writers: Why do disasters befall the innocent?

The Pierpont Morgan Library/Art Resource, NY

the need to believe in a higher order, and as an investigation into various pathways to divinity.

We have divided the chapter into studies of religions that believe in more than one god; those that see deity as a universal, spiritual order, but not a person; and those that believe in one god only. We conclude with a sampling of religious themes in the humanities.

The Belief in Many Gods

Early religions practiced **polytheism**, with ceremonial rituals honoring different gods. The concept of **monotheism**, the worship of a single deity responsible for the creation and governance of the universe, dates back only a few thousand years to the time of the Egyptian pharaoh Amenhotep IV (c. 1410–1375 B.C.E.). Monotheism, highly controversial at the time in Egypt, replaced traditional polytheism for just a short time.

A considerable body of mythology was created around the many gods of early religions. Some gods, like Thor, the iron-fisted ruler of the Norse otherworld, were fierce and terrifying, wielding enormous power over the human race. The Greek goddess Aphrodite, on the other hand, brought love to the world and the Greek god Apollo brought enlightenment.

Egypt

Beginning at least seven thousand years ago, religion and daily life were inseparable in Egypt. Kings were to be worshiped as gods, and for them great cities and monuments were built. Ordinary people were surrounded by reminders of their god-rulers. This secular religion thus fostered an extraordinary early civilization. Giant statues, stone busts, heads made of precious metals, temples adorned with elaborate stone carvings, and, of course, the pyramids and tombs built to provide a luxurious afterlife for the pharaohs all came into existence because the principle of the king as god demanded it. Little remains of the cities, but because the great tombs, containing so much artwork and so many artifacts, have stood supremely independent of time, we can piece together an understanding of what ancient Egypt was like.

The walls of the tombs are inscribed with hieroglyphics—carved pictures and symbols representing words and ideas, functioning, as far as we know, as the Egyptian alphabet; and from deciphering them, we have learned that Egyptians thought of life as a continuous, orderly process governed by a succession of king-gods who passed their divinity to the next generations. The period of time in which a given family held power is known as a *dynasty*.

The history of Egyptian art is divided into dynasties. Each has its particular art style, though for thousands of years pharaohs were depicted in similar ways as idealized versions of human beings, always noble-looking. Traditional Egyptian art probably influenced the techniques used by Greek and Roman artists to create visual images of their own gods. Since the pharaohs were deities who would live forever in their tombs, there could be nothing "simply" human about the way they looked in stone or metal.

In the late fourteenth century B.C.E. a change took place. Amenhotep IV declared that the universe was ruled by one supreme god, Aton, whose visible appearance was the sun's disk; and the king changed his name from Amenhotep to Akhenaton, or son of Aton. He said that pharaohs were the earthly representatives of this god and commanded adoration and worship though they were no longer to be regarded as gods. After their deaths, kings would enjoy the pleasure of eternal existence. Their tombs were to be built and decorated as before.

The style of Egyptian art, however, was altered during the reign of Akhenaton, as the photograph of this **bas relief** (a stone wall carving) clearly shows. The profile is far from idealized. The features are coarse and the jaw so prominent that it could almost be a caricature.

Akhenaton was succeeded by his son-in-law, Tutenkhamen (exact dates unknown), who died at eighteen but still managed to overturn the monotheism of his predecessor. Presumably, as king, he considered himself a god. Preparations for his departure from the world must have begun as soon as he came to the throne because his tomb, discovered in 1922, is filled with some of the world's greatest art treasures. The pharaoh has become immortalized as "King Tut," a name sometimes used to mean an incredibly wealthy man who flaunts his ownership of every possible material possession.

Bildarchiv Preussischer Kulturbesitz/Art Resource, NY

Relief sketch of Akhenaton, c. 1350 B.C.E.

This image of Akhenaton shows a movement away from the traditionally idealized depiction of kings as god in Egyptian art.

An exhibition of the tomb's contents has attracted thousands of people crowded into major museums marveling at the magnificent pottery, the still intact carvings, and, above all, at the solid gold casket with its reclining statue of Tutenkhamen, arms crossed, each hand holding a scepter of kingly power.

The wonders of Egyptian art arose from the need of powerful men to be enshrined and adored, and this need in turn arose from a religion that conferred godhead over and over to a continuous line of god-rulers.

Hinduism

During the third millennium B.C.E. the land of India was invaded and occupied by numerous armies and cultures, all bringing their own gods, rituals, and practices. Scholars have assigned the date of 1500 B.C.E. as the beginning of the long Hindu tradition because it was around this time that the *Aryans* (the word means "noble") took over, brought the Sanskrit alphabet, and established a national religion.

Diyaus Pita was the Aryan equivalent of Zeus, the main god in Greek polytheism (Roman name, Jupiter). Prithivi was the earth mother; Indra, the god of storms and war; and Varuna, the god of the sky, responsible for the order in the universe. One of the principal rituals was that of sacrifice (probably human in its earliest phases), for the belief was that the gods would come to earth to help those who had performed the sacrifice. In almost every early religion the gods had to be appeased continually; otherwise, mortals would suffer terrible consequences.

> *He who hath no understanding, whose mind is always unrestrained, his senses are out of control, as wicked horses are for a charioteer.*
>
> **—Katha Upanishad**

The sacred documents are the *Vedas,* of which the *Rig-Veda* is considered the most important. It contains poems and hymns used in rituals as well as the names of the various gods to whom the rituals were directed. The Vedas are the sacred words revealed to mortals. In this respect they are similar to the Hebrew Bible and the Islamic Qur'an. Closely related to them are *The Upanishads*—not revealed religious truths but rather philosophical dialogues between holy men and their students. They contain strict guidelines for living and are therefore also considered sacred. One of the most beloved texts is *The Bhagavad-Gita* ("Song of the Lord"), a still widely read epic poem, which, like *The Upanishads,* offers philosophical views

Photos.com/Thinkstock

Bronze artifact of Shiva, c. 16th century

Shiva, second in the Hindu trinity, shown here as Lord of the Dance, responsible for continual change.

on both human and divine existence. In addition to these writings are literary works that depict the heroic deeds of ancestors as well as more philosophical arguments about the meaning of life and the responsibilities of human beings toward the gods.

The earliest of these texts is *The Mahabharata* (*"The Epic of the Bharata War"*). The Bharata was one of the Aryan tribes, and the epic—the longest poem in the history of the world, running to more than 100,000 stanzas—provided descendants with a proud history, much as did the Roman epic *the Aeneid* of Virgil, discussed in Chapter 4. The hero is Krishna, a god who could also become mortal and assist in a just cause.

Not as long but equally cherished is *The Ramayana,* which describes the heroic exploits of Rama, another mortal who is also a deity—in this case the god Vishnu. In addition to the heroic acts, the poem contains passages of advice to mortal beings on how to lead a happy life despite the pain and suffering that abound in the world. The work continues to be held in the highest esteem, and its teachings are still followed by the devout Hindu.

As time passed and cultural strains crisscrossed, the religious tradition of India underwent many changes. Coming to the fore was the threesome of deities: **Brahma**, the Creator of all that exists in the visible universe; **Shiva**, the Destroyer, who makes sure everything eventually passes out of existence, making way for the new; and **Vishnu**, the Preserver, who balances the two forces of creation and destruction so that the continuity of existence is assured. As time passed, Shiva and Vishnu assumed greater and greater prominence in the pantheon of gods.

Vishnu is especially important as the bringer of stability. In the Hindu view of life, the individual, on a day-by-day basis, is aware of continual change, but change is only an illusion. The failure to see the eternal nature of existence is the cause of human suffering.

Shiva is the god of change. He is often shown in Hindu statues and paintings doing an elaborate dance with his multiple arms and legs. The dance represents the continual movement and changing nature of the visible world, and learning to accept it without being overwhelmed is one of the fundamental goals of Hindu thought.

Beyond the constant dance of life, with its comings and goings, and daily commerce; beyond wealth, poverty, hard work, love won and lost; beyond pain and death . . . beyond all these is a universal, unchanging soul, **Brahman**, of which everything and everyone are parts. The three gods Brahma, Vishnu, and Shiva are godlike embodiments of this universal, unchanging soul, defining its workings: creation, destruction, stability. Brahman transcends the separate gods, but it can be known only through them.

Hindu Philosophy in the Western World. Western philosophers and artists have been influenced by the Hindu concept of a unifying spirit behind the universe and have given it various names. The German poet Johann Wolfgang von Goethe (1749–1832) called it the "world-soul." The American philosopher Ralph Waldo Emerson called it the "over-soul" and wrote a famous essay by that title. In John Steinbeck's *The Grapes of Wrath,* a novel discussed in Chapter 4, the hero, Tom Joad, explains to his mother that he cannot remain with the family working only for their survival when so many others are hungry and homeless. He believes all people are part of "one big soul," and, now that he has realized this truth, he has no choice but to work for others, even if it means sacrificing his own safety and the possibility of a happier future.

Walt Whitman. Walt Whitman, an American poet also greatly influenced by the religious thought of India, entitled his most famous work *Leaves of Grass*. Grass, like Brahman, is a totality that exists only through its individual leaves. If you have just one leaf, you have grass. If you have one drop of water, you have water. If only one person is left on earth, humanity has survived. Any individual is as important as all others, and no one individual is more important than the rest. Whitman's famous opening lines should not be interpreted as egotism.

> *I celebrate myself, and sing myself,*
> *And what I assume you shall assume,*
> *For every atom belonging to me as good belongs to you.*[1]

On the other hand, one solitary leaf would be lost in the universe, and so would one lone individual isolated from the human family. Whitman's idea of democracy and the relationship between the private citizen and the whole population is a political extension of an ancient religious philosophy.

> *The smallest sprout shows there is really no death,*
> *And if ever there was it led forward life, and does not wait at the end to arrest it,*
> *And ceas'd the moment life appeared.*
>
> **—Walt Whitman**

Whitman, a proponent of human rights, was against all totalitarian governments and against bureaucracy in his own country. Indian religion was necessarily egalitarian, at least in principle. As Brahman was the big soul, so too in each of us was the individual soul called *Atman*. One was the equal of the other. Religious scholar John A. Hutchinson tells us that in the Hindu mind

> *. . . there is a complete identity between the absolute or universal reality underlying the objective world and that which every man may find at the foundation of his subjecthood. These are two paths to the same Supreme Reality. Of this Reality each human soul is a broken fragment. Hence man's highest destiny is to realize this fact and so to realize the great identity or unity which is fulfillment, salvation, and blessedness.*[2]

Native American Religions

Native American culture and the various religions practiced within it are as diversified as any in the world. People who live near reservations and areas dominated by a particular native population may be accustomed to attending exhibitions of arts and crafts as well as ceremonies and rituals that are open to the public. Yet confining one's knowledge of Native Americans to often necessary profit-making events is to deny oneself a deeper understanding of an extraordinarily complex civilization that may be much older than those of the West, which are too often regarded as the very beginning of significant human achievement.

> *The culture, values and traditions of native people amount to more than crafts and carvings. Their respect for the wisdom of their elders, their concept of family responsibilities extending beyond the nuclear family to embrace a whole village, their respect for the environment, their willingness to share—all of these values persist within their own culture even though they have been under unremitting pressure to abandon them.*[3]

"Mi taku oyasin.
We are all related."
—Lakota pipe-smoking ceremony

Some anthropologists believe that various North American groups can be traced back to migrations from northern Asia over ten thousand years ago, when it would have been posssible to walk from Siberia to Alaska. But some Native American tribes maintain that their culture has always existed in the Americas, having originally emerged from beneath the earth.

Whatever their beginnings, Native Americans long ago divided into groups migrating throughout both American continents, establishing early civilizations wherever they settled, developing their own languages, and practicing their own religions. Cultural anthropologists who have made a careful study of the many groups found certain common beliefs and values as well as many differences.

An overarching common belief is a polytheistic one. However, like the Greeks and Romans who were to come, the various groups tended to think of the gods and their world as an extension of this world. Just as some mortals were better hunters than others, so too were there gods and goddesses who controlled the hunt, rewarding those who led exemplary lives, which included performing charitable acts such as sharing of food, and punishing those who didn't by making game scarce for them.

The Inuits of Alaska, who depended on the sea for their bounty, worshiped a goddess named Sedna, who was part human and part fish and lived underwater. She kept a watchful eye on the daily lives of her people, allowing the good to haul in as many fish as they needed. Other gods and goddesses were connected to agriculture by those who depended on the land for survival.

The arrival of Christianity in or about the sixteenth century created massive changes in belief, lifestyle, and religious practice. In many cases, there was a blending of the old and the new. The Christian God sometimes became the Great Spirit who controlled the entire world, but with many helpers who oversaw the hunt, the planting, and the harvest; and so religious worship became divided into a number of rituals performed in honor of both the Great Spirit and the other gods and goddesses.

Transitions did not come easily. Often there were terrible clashes between Christian settlers and Native Americans, who were looked upon as savages, children of the devil. There were frequent massacres, thus intensifying their reputations as uncontrolled warriors who needed to be slaughtered or converted for their own good. Eventually reservations were established, and many still remain. Assimilation into mainstream culture has taken place, but great numbers of Native Americans continue to cherish and practice their traditional customs and modes of worship.

There is a prevalent opinion among some natives that no such thing as "Native American religion" exists at all, that what some have considered religious practice is in reality the daily mode of existence among a people with close ties to the earth, the sea, and the sky. The contention is that, unlike people in other cultures with religious observances limited to certain days of the week or certain hours of the day, Native Americans are continually aware of the forces that govern them.

For some Native Americans the Great Spirit is a personal god in human form. The native version of the Twenty-third Psalm describes the next world as a tepee in which sits a council of wise men, presided over by a supreme chieftain. Many others, however, view the Great Spirit as the force behind nature on which the survival of humanity depends.

Belief in an Impersonal Divinity

Hinduism, with its principle of the universal soul, does not include a belief in a personal God promising freedom from pain. True, it gives a name to the universal soul, but Brahman is not a conscious being. Brahman is universal order. Brahman is what believers mean by "it" in the sentence "It is raining." Rain is in the nature of things, and Brahman *is* the nature of things.

Are suffering and pain also part of that nature? Or are they, too, like change, an illusion? The devout in India believe that suffering, if not intentional on the part of some god, must be part of the universal order. Somehow there must be a reason for it, or at least the hope of tolerating it. *The Upanishads* ask the question of whether life is worth living. The answer is in the affirmative, and this fact means that eventually there will be emancipation from pain.

This condition was at first called **moksha**, and later, in Buddhism, **nirvana**, a state of bliss that is freedom from the pain and stress of life. Without pain there could be no such thing as bliss. How could anyone recognize bliss if it were attained without a struggle?

> *"We live very close together. So our prime purpose in this life is to help others. And if you can't help them, at least do them no harm."*
>
> **—The Dalai Lama**

Reaching moksha is extremely difficult for the average person. Pain must be the result of unfulfilled desire; so, clearly, desires are bad. Transcending desire must therefore be the primary human goal, even if one is poor and desires a better life. But freedom from desire cannot be accomplished overnight. For some, it can take centuries. But how is that possible?

Feeling constant anger over life's tribulations can easily lead to wrongful deeds, such as robbing another to satisfy one's own needs; lying and cheating; even killing. Wrongful deeds result in further misfortune for the individual because punishment for immoral behavior is also in the nature of things. **Karma** is the name given to the cumulative moral consequences of actions. *Good* karma means an accumulation of good deeds; *bad* karma, the accumulation of sins. At the end of one's life comes the summing up. A preponderance of bad karma results in having to be reborn into a lower social class and attempting once again to lead a virtuous life regardless of suffering. Good karma results in reincarnation in a higher social class with better living conditions and less suffering.

Still, the temptations of this world are great, and so the cycle of death and rebirth can be expected to continue for a very long time. Eventually, however, perhaps after many thousands of years, one might attain moksha, the reward of eternal release from pain—not heaven, just peace at last. Within such a state, it was promised, the rightful order of the universe would be understood. One would achieve **enlightenment**, the total union of Atman and Brahman, and the cycle would end.

The sacred books, however, said that rarely a person would lead a perfect life and achieve enlightenment without ever having to be reborn. This person was called a **buddha** (meaning "enlightened one"). The coming of a buddha occurs perhaps every 25,000 years.

But that belief changed for a small group of people more than 2,000 years ago who would become the ancestors of what is now one of the major religions of the world. Someone came and declared that it was possible for a human being to reach enlightenment in a single lifetime. After undergoing much pain and suffering to reach enlightenment, this person was hailed as the promised Buddha; and, inadvertently, become founder of a new religion, one that at first held an impersonal view of divinity—until that person himself came to be looked upon as a god.

Sherab/Alamy

Painting from a temple in Bodh Gaya, Bihar, India, date unknown

Unlike many representations of a fat Buddha, this one appears to illustrate the legend more accurately.

Buddhism

The one who was called the Buddha has become, for millions of Buddhists ever after, a godlike figure, though he would not have thought of himself in that fashion. Nonetheless, hailed by his followers as Jesus would be hailed by his, he was originally an unlikely candidate for the honor. Siddhartha Gautama (564?–483 B.C.E.?) was born a prince in India, surrounded by luxuries beyond imagining. He married a beautiful woman, who bore him a handsome son. The family lived in the gorgeous palace he inherited from his father. He was the envy of all who knew him. Yet he became restless and unhappy. Something kept telling him he did not belong where he was, leading a life that was filled with sensual pleasure but was essentially meaningless. He would grow old and die, leaving behind mementos of a wasted life.

One day, according to legend, Siddhartha went for a walk through his village and he encountered three things that were new to him. The first was *poverty*. Everywhere he looked he saw beggars reaching out their bony hands for alms. The second was *sickness*. He saw people who could no longer sit up and beg but could only lie there, wasting away from malnutrition and disease. Finally, he saw *death*. A man in the prime of life had just died, and his relatives were preparing the body for cremation right there on the street. Siddhartha was appalled by the fact that for the poor people outside the privileged confines of his palace, life amounted to nothing more than a desperate attempt to survive, and the "reward" for the struggle was death and rebirth into perhaps an even more wretched existence.

Siddhartha is reputed to have experienced a sudden conversion, like Paul of Tarsus, the Emperor Constantine, and Mohammed after him. Legend has it that on that very day he went home, threw off his royal apparel, dressed himself in cast-off garments and rags, bade farewell to his wife and son, and, abandoning the comforts of the palace forever, set out on a quest for another way to live.

Like the beggars he had seen, he sank into abject poverty. One story is that he denied himself food, except for one sesame seed a day, until he grew so weak that he knew he would die before he discovered the secret of a truly meaningful and virtuous life. He was so obsessed with the search for the exact opposite of his former life that he was killing himself in the process. One day he said: "If the string is too tight, it will snap."

Finally, in a state of near total exhaustion, he found a large *bodhi,* or rose apple, tree and flung himself down under it. He sat there in a cross-legged position, not resting against the trunk, because he found that, by sitting perfectly upright, with his back straight, he was wide-awake, and, in that state, he suddenly began to see everything and everyone around him with a clarity he had never known. No doubt in the beginning his inner thoughts collided with his observations of the outside world, but as time went by he must have become less and less aware of his inner life, of being an isolated self and more and more a part of what he was observing. Putting his ego to rest, Siddhartha engaged in the first recorded instance of the **meditation** practice that Buddhists called simply sitting.

Buddhist scripture tells us that there were howling storms, even floods, during the long sitting, which was said to have lasted for forty days and forty nights. Those who gathered around were amazed that Siddhartha never moved or reacted in any way to the pounding of the elements. The scripture also reports that evil demons attempted to distract him, sometimes disguised as beautiful women holding out large baskets of food, but Siddhartha was not to be swayed. At length the storms and demons went away, and there was peace, not only there but all over the world.

> *Mandarava flowers and lotus blossoms, and also water lilies made of gold and beryl, fell from the sky onto the ground near the Shakya sage . . . so that it looked like a place in the world of the gods. At that moment no one anywhere was angry, ill, or sad; no one was evil; none was proud; the world became quite quiet, as though it had reached full perfection.*[4]

Siddhartha had attained enlightenment, an important step on the way to nirvana. In the West, enlightenment means cognitive understanding. In **Buddhism**, an enlightened person loses all consciousness of ego and, utterly detached from participation in the stream of life, sees everything as it is, and, gaining total objectivity, begins to understand everyone's thoughts, motives, joys, and sorrows. Since it is freedom from the emotional strain of living within one's ego, enlightenment in Buddhism is the gateway to achieving total peace—nirvana, which is not death but peace without end. In nirvana, Atman, the individual soul, is reunited with Brahman, the universal soul.

Listen on **MyHumanitiesKit.com** from The Dhammapada

After forty days, according to legend, Siddhartha finally rose from his meditation and decided that he had a greater mission than to remain in the blissful state of enlightenment. He would first advise those who would listen that they must find a middle way between the extremes of total self-denial (as when he had denied himself food and money) and a total mystical withdrawal from life. One should conduct oneself like a string that is neither too tight nor too loose. In many statues of Buddha the fingertips are lightly touching, perhaps suggesting the analogy with the string.

As he walked through the villages of India, Siddhartha would pause to speak to anyone who would listen. Gradually he attracted followers who trudged beside him, and from time to time he would stop to share with them the insights that kept flooding his mind. The long meditation had sharpened his rationality. He arrived at what were to him the four basic truths of life. He called them the Four Noble Truths.

Life is filled with pain.
Pain is caused by unfulfilled desires.
There is a way out of pain.
The way is to follow the Eightfold Path.

The Eightfold Path has become the Buddhist guide to a life of peace and harmony, a life in tune with the Way, and a life that can, as death nears, be recalled happily, in the knowledge that one has brought goodness into the world. The Path consists of:

- Right views
- Right intentions
- Right speech
- Right conduct

- Right livelihood
- Right effort
- Right mindfulness
- Right concentration

Right means acting, reacting, and thinking relative to things as they are, not as we would like them to be or as we pretend to ourselves that they are. It means walking in a constant state of wakefulness so that all actions are appropriate and not based on narrow self-interest.

- Right views are opinions based on a knowledge of things as they are.
- Right intentions are decisions to act on such views.
- Right speech is saying what is appropriate, guarding one's statements so that they do not provoke anger and defensive behavior in others; but it does not mean saying what is known to be false in order to avoid giving offense.
- Right conduct is behaving toward and interacting with others in accordance with things as they are, not as you want them to be.
- Right livelihood is earning what is needed to survive and help others to survive, but never earning for its own sake and for unnecessary possessions earning makes possible.
- Right effort is striving to do what needs to be done, not to advance one's own cause or prestige.
- Right mindfulness is maintaining the sitting or meditative attitude anywhere, whether in solitude or in society.
- Right concentration is focusing unwaveringly on reality without the intrusion of ego and the idle chatter that floods the mind.

> *"It is this fear of exposure, this denial of impermanence that imprisons us. It is only by acknowledging impermanence that there is a chance to die and the space to be reborn and the possibility of appreciating life as a creative process."*
>
> **—Chögyam Trungpa**

The Buddhism of Siddhartha was never intended to be a religion as such. Its practice was intensely personal. Instead of commandments, it offered advice for leading a life of goodness. As the centuries passed and followers numbered in the millions, Buddhism acquired many different aspects.

Hinduism, continuing to evolve, had followers who incorporated many of Siddhartha's teachings as well as features of the ancient Vedic religion of Brahma, Shiva, and Vishnu and the wisdom of the sacred texts into their belief systems. Statues of the Buddha can be found in India, where he is sometimes referred to as Lord Buddha.

The meeting of Hinduism and Buddhism was not, however, always a peaceful one. Onc Hindu sect developed the legend that Krishna, the god-hero of *The Mahabharata,* came to earth in the guise of the Buddha for the purpose of leading bad people away from the Hindu faith, thus guaranteeing that they would be damned forever.

A major difference between Hinduism and the Buddhism of Siddhartha is the matter of attaining nirvana (or moksha) in one lifetime. Hinduism retains the belief that only the rare individual escapes having to be reborn. The concepts of karma and reincarnation continue to underlie the caste system.

Historically, caste was not a social class defined by economic resources and the hopeless lifestyle these made possible. The caste system rigidly confined the people born into it because it was tied to religion. Those born into dire poverty on the lowest rung of society were assumed to have had bad karma. The hapless beggars doomed to this miserable existence were called the *untouchables.* The polar opposite was known as the *Brahmin,* or priestly, caste. Its members were affluent and deserving of the respect of their inferiors, for it was believed that they had lived over and over, gradually perfecting their lives so that, when they died, they would not have to come back. Though Indian society has become more flexible, some rigidity in social strata related to religious tradition still exists.

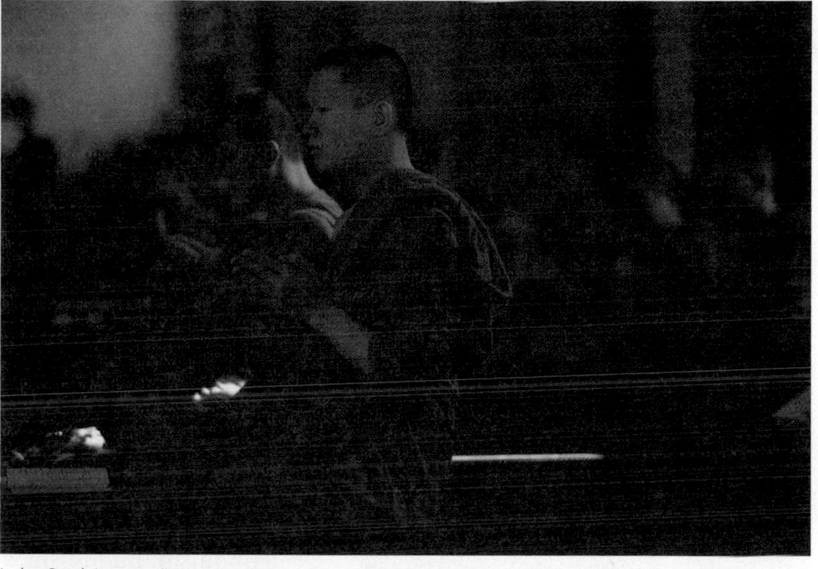

Index Stock Imagery/Newscom

Phitsanulok, Thailand, 2005

Monks meditating in zendo. Zen meditation requires long hours of sitting under the watchful supervision of a stern Zen master.

Zen Buddhism. *Zen Buddhism* is that strain of the parent philosophy and practice that came to be closely associated with Japan. It was carried from India to China, however, before reaching Japan. The word **Zen** is a Japanese version of the Chinese word for meditation: *ch'an.* It is an austere, monastic form of Buddhism requiring many years of practicing detachment and a continuing regimen of lengthy meditation sessions.

The Zen tradition is traced to a Hindu monk named Bodhidharma. A thousand years after Siddhartha's enlightenment, he traveled to China with missionary zeal to win converts to Buddhist teachings. According to legend, this pious individual sat in cross-legged meditation on a mountaintop for nine years until his legs fell off.

Zen is now practiced not only in Japan but in all Western countries. Zen novices enter a monastic facility called a *zendo* and are instructed in meditation technique by Zen masters, who are traditionally severe with their charges. They keep hawklike eyes on them during the meditation sessions and have been known to discourage sleeping by striking offenders between the shoulders with a thick wooden board.

Zen masters and their students engage in dialogues in which questions are asked that cannot be answered through logical reflection. Confused at first, the student gradually becomes adept at answering intuitively with what is called the *non-mind.* A typical exchange might be the following:

MASTER: How great is the merit due to me?
STUDENT: No merit at all.
MASTER: What is the Noble Truth in its highest sense?
STUDENT: It is empty, no nobility whatever.
MASTER: Who is it then that is facing me?
STUDENT: I do not know.

The most famous Zen question—*What is the sound of one hand clapping?*—has been traced to the teachings of an eighteenth-century Zen monk named Hakuin Ekaku (1686–1769), who was also an artist. The aim of this question and response training is to clear the mind of the traditional reasoning process, which separates the individual from reality. In Zen Buddhism, reality has no words and thus cannot be understood rationally. The aim of meditation is to confront the void that is reality, thus losing ego and its fantasies.

"Zen is a way of liberation, concerned not with the discovery of what is good or bad or advantageous, but what is."

—Alan Watts

Robert Harding Picture Library/Alamy

Bodhidharma, date unknown

This portrait captures the aggressive wakefulness of Zen's founder.

Zen art has many facets, ranging from quick pen-and-ink drawings produced rapidly after a lengthy period of meditation, to sophisticated portraiture, such as this depiction of Bodhidharma. The wide-open eyes suggest a state of total wakefulness, which is the goal of Zen; and the absence of eyelids is derived from the legend that Bodhidharma pulled them off in order to remain awake.

Modern Buddhism has monasteries in which Buddhist monks and nuns spend long hours in silent meditation. Interaction with the outside world is limited to purchasing necessities or tending to the poor and the sick. But many Buddhists paint or write poetry, stories, and music in their spare time. Or they record philosophical insights in journals they carry with them.

Though the schools of Buddhism are varied, the common thread is to trust the workings of the universe. Just as "it" knows when to rain, when to grow and yield the harvest, people must learn to walk in step with "it." If they do, they will behave righteously toward others, they will be treated righteously by others, and they will be at peace.

Hinduism, Buddhism, and Taoism, a religious philosophy developed in China, share a belief in an intelligent spirit that controls the operations of nature, which is its outer garment. If left alone, its workings ensure peace and harmony to all living creatures. Unfortunately, some of these creatures seek to control it for their personal gain, thus destroying peace and harmony.

This intelligence is **Brahman** in Hinduism, **dharma** in Buddhism, and the **Tao** (Dow) in Taoism. A common definition is "the Way." Morally right actions are aligned with the Way. The individual who follows the Way lives in harmony within society and the environment, and both of these live in harmony with the individual.

Taoism

Of Chinese origin, Taoism can be traced to the writings of Lao-tzu, who is believed to have lived some time during the sixth century B.C.E., but about whom little else is known. The name Lao-tzu, simply meaning "the old one," may have been shared by a number of writers who contributed to the little book called *Tao Te Ching* (*The Way of Life*). Reprinted continually, it is a slender volume of short poems, often cryptic, seemingly simple, but at the same time extremely profound, containing the view that The Way is an impersonal divine order that rules the universe. Taoism is a religion only in the sense that its followers are obligated to live their lives in accordance with this order. It is expressed through the health of the body's system, the mind's harmonious processes, ethical dealings in all human interaction, respect for elders, and hospitality toward strangers.

The philosophy grew out of a Chinese civilization that was rapidly advancing and was proud of its urban culture. In India at approximately the same time, the era of Siddhartha, there was a great disparity between the poor and the affluent. Siddhartha, a prince, saw no reason to be proud of luxury and left his place in society. Taoism, on the other hand, tells us we are all part of that society, with all of its prejudices and double-dealing, and teaches us to conduct ourselves honorably and ethically within it.

Fundamental to Taoism is the belief that the Tao operates through the continual interactions of opposites: joy and pain; birth and death; male and female; day and night; cold and heat; success and failure, and so on. We cannot embrace life without being prepared for death. The fear of death—or for that matter, of anything opposite to what we hold dear—leads to suffering. If youth, vigor, and unwrinkled good looks are all-important, we must know they cannot last and we must therefore feel no anguish with the onset of age. Success and failure are implicit in the way the world goes. Today's failure might be tomorrow's brilliant achiever.

The universe was created by the entwinement of the fundamental opposites: **yin,** the passive element, and **yang,** the active energy. In Chinese art, yin and yang are visually represented as a circle with a white crescent and a black crescent, each side containing a smaller circle of the other's color. The white crescent, yang, is the sun, the source of all life, and is traditionally known as the masculine principle. The black crescent, yin, is the moon, the passive and traditionally feminine principle. The passive yin requires the driving force of the active yang to bring forth the variety of things that go to make up the world.

iStockphoto/Thinkstock

Ying/Yang symbol

The cosmic opposites in Taoism: yin, the passive element; yang, active energy. Though they are opposites, each is depicted as containing part of the other.

Wu Wei. Central to Taoist teachings is the concept of **wu wei**, which is difficult to translate exactly into English. Perhaps the closest definition is *to do without doing*. Exponents of Taoism experience difficulty explaining to the Western mind what they mean by *doing*. One possibility is that *doing* in this sense is *attempting to manipulate the reality in which we find ourselves*—to alter it in accordance with the way we want it to be. This altering involves manipulating the thought and behavior of the people with whom we have to deal, even to lie and cheat to do so. On the other hand, if we allow the Tao to work freely, then we are not *doing*.

If you do without doing, you are following your true nature, and you will be successful no matter how insignificant your accomplishments may seem to others. Every true person contributes to the richness of the Tao, and the Tao enfolds that person in its protective arms.

Does *wu wei* mean that we should remain passive while others manipulate us? Does it mean that our goal is to sit back while others suffer pain or injustice? Not at all. Lao-tzu also says: "*The Tao does not do, but nothing is not done.*" Taoism teaches that we must take appropriate action whenever necessary and possible. The Tao is ethical in all things, and your true nature is ethical as well. If you become aware that a close friend is guilty of wrongdoing, it is your obligation not to turn away or say "I really don't want to become involved." You must act to prevent the wrong from happening, or, if it has already happened, to see that the action does not go unreported. Putting friendship before ethical responsibility may be deeply rooted in our natures, but these natures are distortions of the Tao, acquired from a long history of living within complex society and adopting its values.

Taoism has readily found its way into the rest of the world. It has been warmly greeted, especially in the West, where the *Tao Te Ching* of Lao-tzu can be found in bookstores and libraries. It appeals to those who are tired of the ceaseless quest for money and fame, but also the need to comprehend and then alter the way the universe works. "Leave it alone!" is the motto of Western Taoists. "Leave it alone, and it will run as it should." They want forests, for example, to be left as nature intended. They may even say that wolves should be allowed to eat sheep because

"All religions are the therapies for the sorrows and disorders of the soul."

—Carl Jung

that's what wolves do. But they may also recommend cutting undergrowth to diminish the danger of wild fires, though they realize some fires can be nature's way of cleansing itself. Echoing Taoist sentiments, environmentalists believe in working in close cooperation with nature. Opponents believe that human reason can and should bend nature to its will.

Some Western scientists find Taoist philosophy profoundly meaningful and hardly limited to Chinese culture. In 1976, for example, Fritjof Capra published *The Tao of Physics,* in which he shows parallels between the Taoist concept of yin and yang and the basic forces in nature that involve the interaction of opposites, as in the magnetic force that binds protons and electrons to form the nucleus of the atom.

Winnie-the-Pooh as Taoist Literature. Taoism has found its way into Western literature in the not-only-for-children books of British author A. A. Milne (1882–1956) about the little bear Winnie-the-Pooh and his friends. In *The Tao of Pooh* (1982) Benjamin Hoff gives us an imaginative introduction to Taoist philosophy, using characters and incidents from the Milne stories. The innocent and childlike Pooh seems a perfect spokesperson for Lao-tzu. Pooh is open to experience; he is close to every moment as it passes. He is never confused by the need to make sense of things, nor is he ever driven by self-interest. Unlike his friend Piglet, Pooh has no sense of self.

In the first book of the series, the 1926 *Winnie-the-Pooh,* all the animals are excited because Eeyore the donkey is about to have a birthday. Each of them wants to give Eeyore a present, but Piglet, seeking the gratification that Eeyore's effusive thank-you will bring, wants to be the first to present a gift. But the Tao takes care of him!

> *. . . Piglet had gone back to his own house to get Eeyore's balloon. He held it very tightly against himself, so that it shouldn't blow away, and he ran as fast as he could so as to get to Eeyore before Pooh did; for he thought that he would be the first one to give a present, just as if he had thought of it without being told by anybody. And running along, and thinking how pleased Eeyore would be, he didn't look where he ws going . . . and suddenly he put his foot in a rabbit hole, and fell down flat on his face.*[5]

Does Piglet learn from this experience? No. He interprets it in a way that shows his continuing preoccupation with self.

> *Piglet lay there, wondering what had happened. At first he thought that the whole world had blown up; and then he thought that perhaps only the Forest part of it had; and then he thought that perhaps only* he *had, and he was now alone in the moon or somewhere, and would never see Christopher Robin or Pooh or Eeyore again.*[6]

Hoff's study of Taoism in the Pooh stories does not necessarily mean that Milne was consciously imbuing his work with ancient Chinese wisdom. Minds widely separated in time and place can, after all, arrive at the same ideas, testifying to their strength and durability. In any case, Milne made a sizable contribution to the humanities. His books are very wise indeed, proving that sometimes the most complicated things are best explained in simple, not complex intellectual, terms. Certainly *wu wei* can defeat the efforts of learned philosophers, but can be intuitively accepted with the innocence of a small bear "without a large brain," whose only bout with self-interest revolves around his pot of honey, which he, quite naturally, hides because that is what bears are supposed to eat according to their true nature.

There are some actual references to Chinese philosophy in the Pooh stories, not to the Taoists directly but to the followers of Confucius (557?–479 B.C.E.), a Chinese master whose wisdom is preserved in a work called *The Analects* (*Sayings*). Confucius negated Taoism, telling his followers that Taoists were out of touch with reality. He did not believe that ethical actions came naturally to us. They had to be taught, and to this end he opened a school dedicated to the teaching of ethics in government, in the family circle, and in all social dealings. But Pooh calls the followers "Confusionists," perhaps thinking of the legend that Confucius died at 72, unhappy because he could not establish his ideal society.

Socrates and Plato

The great Athenian civilization of the fifth century B.C.E. witnessed a surge of philosophy, including that of Socrates and Plato, that did not further the cause of polytheism in Greece. Socrates (469–399 B.C.E.) specialized in the **dialectic**, an analytical method of thinking. Instead of merely presenting an idea, he arrived at it by revealing the flaws of its opposite. Though his contributions to human thought are recorded in no writings of his own, his esteemed follower, Plato (427–347 B.C.E.), did leave behind some of the greatest works of the humanities, most of them written as dialogues in which Socrates debates with his students on philosophical matters. One of these is *The Republic,* which offers a profound vision of the ideal society.

Socrates was arrested on charges of preaching atheism and corrupting the youth of Athens. Historians of philosophy, however, believe that the true "crime" that condemned him to imprisonment and execution was that he taught his young followers to think for themselves, a goal that makes many governments uneasy. Socrates even referred to himself as "gadfly to the state," and he said it with pride.

According to Plato, Socrates refers both to "gods" and "a god," and it is not clear whether he is making metaphoric use of the terms. In his famous speech to the assembly of citizens who have just condemned him to death, a speech Plato records in *The Apology of Socrates,* he tells them that he harbors no ill will toward them and that they are not to pity him. Rather, they should

> *be of good cheer about death, and know of a certainty that no evil can befall a good man, either in life or after death. He and his are not neglected by the gods; nor has his own approaching end happened by mere chance.*[7]

The polytheistic reference does not extend to the considerable body of Socratic thought written down by Plato and may simply have been intended to show the citizens that he was in the good hands of a higher authority; that they had not in fact won a victory over him. That authority was probably his own virtuous existence guided by the principle of reason.

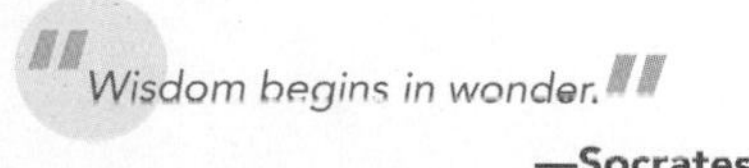
"Wisdom begins in wonder."

—Socrates

> *He concludes the speech by saying that the hour of departure has arrived, and we go our ways—I to die, and you to live. Which is better God only knows.*[8]

The singular "God" here should not be taken as a sign of an emerging monotheism. Nothing about the thought of Socrates and Plato suggests faith in any force except the inherent rationality of the universe and in the individual willing to think. Rationality was divinity to them. In *The Republic* they created a vision of the ideal state, governed by a philosopher-king, not a god-king like that of the Egyptians.

Aristotle's Unmoved Mover

Plato opened the first official university in the West, the *Academy* (named after the public groves of Academe, in which Socrates walked with his followers), and there he influenced his star pupil, Aristotle (384–322 B.C.E.), who would later open his own school, the *Lyceum*. Aristotle formalized logic as a method of thinking. In his metaphysics, he pondered the problem of how the universe got started. His conclusions came close to the monotheism of Judaism, and Christianity later embraced him as the pagan who anticipated Christian doctrine.

Aristotle believed that the universe, an orderly system of sun and planets, always existed, but in the beginning it was cold, lifeless, and without motion. Motion by definition always has a cause. Logic impelled him to conclude that the whole system must have been *set* in motion, far back in the past, by something that was not in motion itself. If it were, we would then have to determine the cause of *its* motion, and so on into infinity.

The result was the principle of the **Unmoved Mover**, to be thought of as a cause that led to the first effect, which was motion, but not as a causer. This distinction is all-important. Causers can become personalized, and that is precisely what happened later. For Aristotle, the cold and lifeless universe was not created. It just *was*. But his system required a mover, one that was a principle of motion—a *potentiality* for motion that was always there. He could not fathom how what existed, including the principle of motion, could ever have been nonexistent.

> *For if it had ever come into existence, we should have to suppose an original constitutive element "already there" for it to come out of. But this character of being "a subject already there as a basis of change" is precisely the thing we have just been inquiring about; hence, if the matter of what changes were itself to change, it would have to exist before its own coming into existence.*[9]

The three religions that were to dominate the Western and Middle Eastern worlds would make a separation between what creates (God) and what is created (the universe). Lacking a theory of God the Creator, Aristotle had to explain just what the Unmoved Mover was and where it was found.

He envisioned the universe as a sphere, the outer two rims of which were the circle of the sun and the planets and the circle he called the Prime Mover. Beyond this sphere was the *Empyrean*, the abode of the Unmoved Mover. Whether he knew it or not, Aristotle was getting close to monotheism, or, at least, a philosophical foundation that would support monotheism.

The Belief in One God

Monotheism is a powerful religious concept central to three major religions in the world today: Judaism, Christianity, and Islam. It can be traced back over 3,000 years to the short reign of the pharaoh Akhenaton, but his idea of one god did little to eclipse the overwhelming polytheism of early cultures. The monotheism that would eventually dominate Western religious thought had many obstacles to overcome.

Judaism

Judaism, the religion of early Semitic tribes who traced their ancestry to the patriarch Abraham, introduced the first powerful vision of one almighty deity, a vision later shared by Christianity and Islam.

The earliest of the three major monotheistic religions of the world, *Judaism* derives its name from Judah, a son of Jacob. Of the original twelve Hebrew tribes, the one descended from Judah became dominant. Its monotheistic religion may have existed in many forms before the time of Siddhartha, Lao-tzu, and Confucius.

The Hebrew Bible. The Hebrew Bible is presumed to have been collaboratively written over a period of many centuries some time after the exodus of Hebrew slaves from Egypt in the thirteenth century B.C.E. Much later, it is believed, Hebrew scholars, desiring to gather together the history and literature of their people, organized and wrote an early version of Judaism's sacred book.

> *From listening comes wisdom and from speaking, repentance.*
>
> **—Jewish proverb**

The Hebrew Bible was and remains the foundation of Judaism. Because the text has been subjected to so much scrutiny and so many interpretations, almost any statement about evidence or meaning can be open to debate. There is disagreement about the origin of the book, whether the writers were putting down the literal word of God; about how certain words should be translated; and whether the book is to be read as history, legend, or literature. At one extreme are fundamentalists who continue to seek evidence of biblical truth, such as a piece of wood from Noah's Ark. Others, concerned with how biblical stories and characters can be applied to today's world, concentrate on a psychological approach. Still others prefer an anthropological investigation into what the development of the Bible tells us about the changing nature of divinity. For some people, regardless of their beliefs about the ultimate, the Hebrew Bible is a source of solace and wisdom.

The first five books of this Bible, traditionally attributed to Moses, are known as the **Torah** or Pentateuch. The Torah begins with Genesis, one of the most remarkable documents in the history of the humanities, tracing, in compact prose, the early history of the Hebrews and containing stories and characters familiar throughout the world. It begins with an account of how the universe was created and how Adam and Eve, the first human beings, were expelled from Eden for disobedience. It tells of the covenant (or pact) between God and Abraham and the Promised Land given as a reward for obedience. It can stand on its own as an epic, rivaling the *Iliad* and the *Aeneid.*

Episodes recounted in Genesis have inspired poets and artists down through the centuries. Rembrandt's famous painting *Joseph Accused by Potiphar's Wife* is one of many thousands of works biblically inspired.

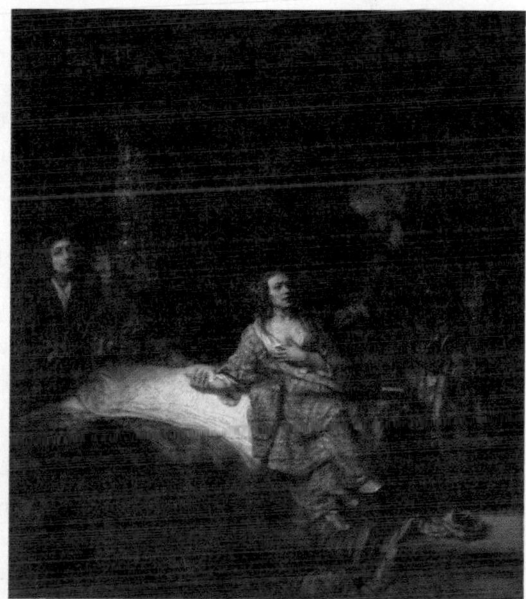

Bildarchiv Preussischer Kulturbesitz/Art Resource, NY

Rembrandt, *Joseph Accused by Potiphar's Wife*, 1655
One of the many works of art inspired by the Hebrew Bible.

Joseph, a son of Jacob, hence grandson of Abraham, the first of the Hebrew patriarchs, was his father's favorite. After Jacob gave Joseph a present of a many-colored coat, his brothers became jealous. They cast him into a pit without water, assuming he would die and they would not be blamed. But Joseph was rescued by some traders, who took him into Egypt, where he became a trusted servant of Potiphar, the pharaoh's brother. Potiphar's wife, attracted to the young man, pleads with him, "Lie with me." Joseph refuses, saying he could not betray his master nor give offense to God. Furious, Potiphar's wife accuses him of making improper advances, whereupon Potiphar has him thrown into prison. But God intervenes, and Joseph soon wins the protection of the pharaoh because of his ability to interpret dreams.

The second book of the Torah, Exodus, tells the story of the liberation of Hebrew slaves and their flight from Egypt into the desert under the leadership of Moses, who receives the Ten Commandments on Mount Sinai. The last three books are Leviticus, Numbers, and Deuteronomy. Leviticus contains priestly laws about temple rituals. Numbers contains a census of the Hebrew population and the story of an attempted rebellion against Moses. Deuteronomy recounts the farewell speech of Moses, who dies before reaching the Promised Land.

Other books of the Hebrew Bible tell stories of kings, generals, judges, and prophets, of war and treachery, family betrayals, and reconciliations. The central figures are human rather than idealized as they struggle to learn about God and to maintain their communities.

In biblical texts beginning in the tenth century B.C.E., there are indications of changing attitudes about the nature of God, who is perceived not only as the supreme ruler but as a father and comforter. The Psalms, lyrical poems attributed to David, the second king of Israel, who succeeded Saul around 1000 B.C.E., contain contrasting views of divinity. Some are pleas for God to strike down an enemy, and some reflect a gentle, loving God, who cares for his people—or his "flock," as in the well-known Twenty-third Psalm.

During the sixth or seventh century B.C.E., the age of the Hebrew prophets began and the books of the prophets were added to the Bible as works by definite writers. Some of these works corresponded to actual events, such as the fall of Jerusalem; others were tales with a philosophical and moral purpose. Judaism underwent a profound change, becoming more complex, more concerned with justice for the widowed, the poor, and the helpless. This emphasis on social action remains an important tenet of modern Judaism. But later works also question the wisdom of the Hebrew laws as set forth in earlier books.

What we find in the later biblical period is a God who can be both awesome and wrathful. He has set down absolute laws for human conduct and severely punishes those who violate them. He is a shepherd who restores the soul, but who also controls all the forces of nature, which he can unleash upon humanity. This dual nature of the deity led to the famous question with which theologians and the devout of many faiths and sects have asked and still ask: "*If God is good, why is there so much evil in the world?*" The answer that evil is punishment does not satisfy everyone.

The Book of Job. The agonizing puzzle of God's true nature is examined in the book of Job, considered by many to be the masterpiece of the later period. The work of a profound and gifted writer, the book not only tackles perhaps the most important question raised by monotheism but supplies an answer that has resonated through the ages.

The book rivals the greatest works in the Greek tragic theater, particularly the *Oedipus at Colonus* of Sophocles, in which the protagonist, having exiled himself to a life of blindness and wandering in the desert as a penance for his sins of pride and incest, sees a blinding light as death nears. He walks toward it, his face at last radiant with an understanding of the complex ways of the gods. The burning philosophical question raised by the *Oedipus* play is: Why did Oedipus have to do penance for a sin decreed by fate? Though that fate was the working out of a curse on the descendants of Cadmus, a man who tried to be the equal of the gods, the question remained of why the innocent descendants had to suffer.

> *In Oedipus at Colonus the aged king is still in exile... But his destiny has taken him beyond tragedy, and his death is a holy mystery. Our questions of divine justice are not answered, but they are silenced . . . before the absolute, pride and power and virtue are equally helpless.*
>
> **—Peter Arnott**

The Book of Job, thought to have been written around the time of Sophocles, also faces the challenging question of why disasters befall an innocent man. What Job does not know is that those disasters—the death of his sons, his servants, and his sheep, as well as physical disfiguration—were the result of a challenge given to God by Satan. God has singled out Job as the very model of a good and pious man, but Satan argues that Job's piety comes from the fact that God has never allowed anything bad to happen to him.

But put forth thy hand now, and touch all that he hath,
and he will curse thee to thy face.

Job 1:11

At first Job is resolute in his faith. He "sinned not, nor charged God foolishly." After God allows Satan to cover Job with painful boils, Job's wife chides him for retaining his integrity, urging him to curse God. The afflicted man will not curse God, but he does curse the day he was ever born. He grieves over his lost sons and wonders why he was created with intelligence, only to be torn apart by questions he cannot answer.

Why is light given to a man whose way is hid, and whom
God hath hedged in?

Job 3:23

A famous debate follows between Job and his friends, reminiscent of dialogues between Socrates and his followers. They question everything, and Job refuses to yield up his faith, though holding onto it has become increasingly difficult: "Touching the Almighty, we cannot find him out . . ." Whereupon a mighty whirlwind comes upon them, and God speaks to Job, reminding him of the fact that, since he did not create the universe, he must accept God's justice in all things.

Where wast thou when I laid the foundations of the earth?
declare, if thou hast understanding.

Job 38: 4

As a reward for his patience, piety, and refusal to curse his fate, Job receives, in addition to herds of livestock, a new family of "seven sons and three daughters," and lives long enough (140 years) to enjoy great age and prosperity.

Listen on **MyHumanitiesKit.com**
The Book of Job

Still, both the wager with Satan and Job's "compensation" of a new family seem naive to some scholars, unlike the main body of the story. Rabbi Joseph Telushkin comments:

> *The angel Satan makes his only appearance in the Hebrew Bible, and God is cast in the morally dubious role of wreaking havoc on Job's life just to show off to Satan.*

But, he adds, the ending of the story does not overshadow the stature of the work as a great allegory "about the problem of God and evil."[10]

> "Who is truly repentant? The one who, when temptation to sin is repeated, refrains from sinning."
>
> —The Talmud

The books that follow Job contain prophecies, philosophy, and lament for the destruction of the Temple and for the exile that followed. The major work of the post-biblical period is the **Talmud**, a word that means "learning." The document continues to be studied as an interpretation of the Torah and includes minute discussions of biblical laws, such as rules for payment of laborers, care for orphans, and ways of establishing ownership. The new writings had to take into account conditions of living in foreign lands and responding to the treatment given to Hebrews by the host countries, at times as welcoming as Spain under the Muslims during the tenth to the twelfth centuries, and at other times as intolerant as much of Europe during crusades and pogroms. The religion of Judaism continues to evolve, with the examination and modification of the old texts and the development of new texts about a God thought to be involved in the lives of human beings.

The Hebrew Bible's Influence. Perhaps no other single work in history has had as much influence on art, literature, thought, drama, and especially, popular idiom as the Hebrew Bible. Here are a few examples.

- *"Am I my brother's keeper?"* from the story of Cain and Abel in the book of Genesis, asks a fundamental question about how much responsibility one person has for another.
- *"Spare the rod and spoil the child"* is one of many proverbs offering advice on the best way to raise children.
- *"A coat of many colors,"* from the story of Joseph and his brothers, has become part of the popular idiom as a way of describing privilege and favor. The story is the basis of the enduringly popular Andrew Lloyd Webber musical *Joseph and the Amazing Technicolor Dreamcoat.*
- *"To everything there is a season."* The modern folk song "Turn, Turn, Turn" enlarges on the famous passage from Ecclesiastes beginning "To everything, there is a season." The passage recounts the cycle of life and death, telling us that everything happens at its proper time, "a time to every purpose under heaven." The song, composed by folksinger and political activist Pete Seeger, delivers a strong antiwar message using Ecclesiastes as a comforting reminder that, if there is war, there will also be peace.
- *The Golden Calf,* fashioned by impatient followers of Moses while he was receiving the Ten Commandments on Mount Sinai, has become a synonym for excessive materialism.
- *The Ten Commandments* have formed the basis for civil and criminal laws, including those forbidding theft, murder, and perjury.

Many titles have been derived from biblical sources: for example, *Paradise Lost, The Grapes of Wrath, Earth Abides, Adam's Rib,* and *East of Eden.* Biblical names for children, including David, Sarah, Samuel, and Joshua, though at times considered old-fashioned, have nonetheless managed to retain their popularity through the years. For art lovers, no matter what their religious affiliation, a knowledge of biblical persons and events adds to the enjoyment of a Rembrandt painting or a Michelangelo sculpture, as well as countless other masterpieces.

Composers of past and present have been inspired by biblical themes. Mendelssohn's nineteenth-century *Elijah* is one notable example, as is Leonard Bernstein's twentieth-century *Lamentations of Jeremiah,* based on the book that reflects deep despair over the fall of Jerusalem to an invading army, a fall permitted by the Lord because "Jerusalem hath grievously sinned." Here God is regarded as the supreme ruler of the universe, the creator of that universe, the administrator of punishment to those who break his commandments.

> *The Lord hath done that which he had devised; he hath*
> *fulfilled his word that he had commanded in the days of*
> *old: he hath thrown down, and hath not pitied . . .*
>
> Lamentations 2:17

The stories and characters in the Hebrew Bible have provided poets, philosophers, and artists with subject matter, plots, and profound questions for thousands of years; and, as we can see from the examples above, its influence strongly continues.

Christianity

Even as the followers of Siddhartha believed he was the promised Buddha of the scriptures, so too did the followers of Jesus believe that he was the Messiah foretold in the Hebrew Bible by the prophet Isaiah.

> *"The cosmic religious experience is the strongest force and the noblest driving force behind scientific research."*
>
> **—Albert Einstein**

> *Therefore the Lord himself shall give you a sign;*
> *Behold, a virgin shall conceive, and bear a son,*
> *and shall call his name Immanuel.*
>
> Isaiah 6:14

The prophecy is followed by predictions of dire catastrophes to be suffered by Isaiah's people until they are saved by the birth of this child.

> *For unto us a child is born, unto us a son is given: and*
> *the government shall be upon his shoulder: and his name*
> *shall be called Wonderful, Counsellor, The Mighty God,*
> *The Everlasting Father, The Prince of Peace.*
>
> Isaiah 9:6

The historical Jesus, walking among the Hebrews at a time when they were occupied by the Roman Empire, was a source of controversy. Some hailed him as the Messiah, the Promised One of the prophecy, the bringer of a philosophy that would end oppression and bring peace to the world. Others refused to accept him as the Messiah. That difference caused the separation of Judaism and what became Christianity, a religion founded by Paul of Tarsus, based on the teachings of Jesus and the belief that he was sent by God to save the world. Hebrews who did not accept his divinity and Romans who saw him as a fanatic, a troublemaker both protested against him. After a trial officiated by Pontius Pilate, the Roman proconsul of Judea, he was crucified, and, according to Christian belief, rose from the dead and eventually ascended into heaven.

The Christian Trinity. Most knowledge about Jesus is derived from the Four Gospels at the beginning of the Christian Bible. The Gospels are attributed to four of the disciples: Matthew, Mark, Luke, and John. Biblical scholars have long discussed the so-called "*synoptic problem,*" noting that the four accounts offer different views of Jesus and report different acts and events. For example, the well-known nativity story is found in Luke but not the others. The Sermon on the Mount is told in Matthew only. This discrepancy suggests that the Gospels were not eye-witness accounts; however, their influence cannot be minimized.

The Sermon on the Mount is a major source of the split between Christianity and Judaism. Jesus reviews the Ten Commandments approvingly but adds that they don't go far enough. They condemn wrongful action, but not wrongful intent. In Chapter 11, you will find a further discussion of differences between the commandments and the sermon.

The Gospels all agree, however, that Jesus was the son of God. Christians point to the word "son" in the prophecy. But the son is also referred to as the "everlasting Father." Ultimately the Christian church adopted the belief that Jesus was both Father and Son, as well as a spiritual being they called the Holy Ghost. The Trinity—the idea that the one God existed as three divine persons—became mandatory for Christians to accept after a meeting of the Council of Nicaea in 325 C.E.

Christianity, which swept over the Western world after the fall of the Roman Empire in the fifth century C.E., demanded absolute acceptance of its beliefs as the church began to impose severe penalties on those who questioned. In the early stages of the religion, however, Christian philosophers struggled to reconcile Christian mysticism with human logic.

For example, the idea of how the world was created, clearly stated in the book of Genesis and adopted by Christianity, troubled some minds.

> *In the beginning God created the heaven and the earth*
> *And the earth was without form, and void; and darkness*
> *was upon the face of the deep. And the Spirit of God*
> *moved upon the face of the waters.*
> *And God said, Let there be light: and there was light.*
>
> Genesis 1:1-3

This passage implied that God existed before there was a world and created that world out of nothing. In Christian philosophy the concept became known by the Latin phrase ***creatio ex nihilo***.

Plato had taught that knowledge preexisted, and Aristotle that the Unmoved Mover must have preexisted in order to set everything else in motion. The concept of nothingness made classical thinkers uneasy. The Greeks, for example, did not recognize zero as a number. Yet now the idea of *creatio ex nihilo* seemed obligatory, if the one and only God had created everything else. Aristotle's Mover only supplied motion, but everything that had to move was already there.

The *creatio* would not be the last monotheistic idea to cause consternation, and, like others, it had to be taken on *faith* rather than by *reason*. But it was difficult for Christian philosophers to abandon the right to question, especially in the centuries before official doctrine came into being. Here are some of the many problems they encountered.

- *Can this world have been the extent of God's creation?* If the ability to create matter out of nothing is intrinsic to God, then did creation stop with this one achievement?

- *Could God have had any purpose in creating the world?* How could an all-powerful God be so limited as to have had a purpose? Purpose implies need. What could God need?
- *Does God think?* This question was debated for centuries. If it is assumed that human beings engage in thought in order to know something that was not known before, what could a perfect God not know?
- *Does God feel?* Both Judaism and Christianity insisted that human sinfulness offends God. The Hebrew Bible's stories of God's wrath against humanity, such as those of Noah and the terrible flood or the destruction of Sodom and Gomorrhah, implied emotion. But, it was argued, emotion is a response to what is beyond control. Were there things God could not control?
- *If God does not think or feel, how can he respond to human need?* What was the use of praying to a God who neither thinks nor feels and therefore must be oblivious to us? Was it not futile to believe that God would intervene in human affairs?

As the centuries rolled on, questions increased. It did not take much for anyone to realize that the world was filled with corruption, depravity, and cruelty. If God knew in advance that these would come about, why did he not prevent them? Why did he not prevent maritime disasters or volcanic eruptions? Why did the good have to suffer? (This ominous question had already been posed in the Book of Job.) If God knew about catastrophes *before* they happened, did failure to prevent them indicate indifference? callousness?

> *"It is easy enough to be friendly to one's friends. But to befriend the one who regards himself as your enemy is the quintessence of true religion. The other is mere business."*
>
> **—Mahatma Gandhi**

Augustine. The major Christian philosopher of the early Middle Ages, Augustine (354–430), would ultimately conclude that philosophical questioning and analysis could not take Christians where they needed to go. Analysis could lead only to a weakening of belief and even to atheism, a destination unthinkable for Christians. But before he found an answer that satisfied him, he had to wrestle with his own doubts.

Like Paul, who preceded him by several centuries, Augustine became a convert during his adulthood. As a young man without any religion, he lived for pleasure. His Christian mother despaired over her son's wanton ways and kept urging him to reform and find God. Though Augustine eventually renounced his life of sin and entered the Christian fold, he did not do so easily.

Augustine's *Confessions,* one of the most personal and candid works ever written by a philosopher, deals with the intellectual difficulties facing him upon his conversion. One of his first concerns was reason itself. Why was it given to us by God when it was of no use in trying to comprehend God or the universe? The doctrine of *creatio ex nihilo* puzzled him. In this passage he speaks directly to God:

> *Nor in the whole world didst Thou make the whole world; because there was no place to make it before it was made, that it might be. Nor didst Thou hold anything in Thy hand, whereof to make heaven and earth. For whence shouldest Thou have this, which Thou hadst not made, thereof to make anything? For what is, but because Thou art? Therefore Thou spakest, and they were made, and in Thy Word Thou madest them. But how didst Thou speak?*[11]

The Concept of Faith. Philosophy, ancient and modern, has had as a major concern the nature of the good. The hedonists of ancient Greece defined the good as a life filled with all possible pleasures (Chapter 12). Socrates and Plato use *good*

John Ferro Sims/Alamy

Local muralist, British Virgin Islands, date unknown

An artist imagines the Garden of Eden in the style and mythology of his heritage. Countless other artists of various ethnicities have done the same.

in an ethical sense, referring to actions that are performed not for the sake of personal enjoyment or gain but for the sake of what reason decrees is right and just. *Evil* in ancient thought is the pain and suffering that are part of life, often rained down upon human beings by the gods or by the whimsies of fate. Socrates is famous for having said, "No evil can befall a good man." The statement was made in his speech, already mentioned in this chapter, to the assembled citizens of Athens who were to judge him guilty or innocent of corrupting their youth. What he meant by "evil" was the pain of death should the jury of citizens reach a guilty verdict. In other words, evil was a synonym for disaster, or what most people would consider disaster. It did not imply malicious intent.

The myth of Pandora, mentioned in Chapter 3, was one explanation for how evil came about. Locked in the box that Pandora was not supposed to open were war, plagues, and all natural disasters like fire and floods. In this myth there is no implication that people are *born* evil. Evil is something that *happens* to them. Even the brutal killing of Hector by Achilles, as recounted in the *Iliad,* is less the action of a truly evil person than it is the fulfillment of a warrior's obligation to show his superiority in battle.

The Hebrew Bible gives a clear explanation of both good and evil. In Genesis, God creates Eve from Adam's rib and is satisfied that he has created two innocent human beings, whom he places in the Garden of Eden to be fruitful, to multiply, and to act as custodians of the earth. He also warns them about the Tree of Knowledge, the fruit of which they may not eat; if they do, they will learn the difference between good and evil, but it will be too late. They will be punished for disobeying God.

Adam and Eve are thus not born evil. They are born good—that is, without sin, the tendency to disobey God's commands. What changes them? A talking serpent that entices them to eat the forbidden fruit. At first they are afraid because God has told them that if they disobey him they will surely die. The serpent tells them this is a lie. He gives this as the real reason for the command:

> *For God doth know that in the day ye eat thereof, then your eyes shall be opened, and ye shall be as gods, knowing good and evil.*
>
> Genesis 3:5

Early Christianity accepted the Hebrew Bible as an accurate account of the beginnings of humankind, though it modified and expanded the range of the Ten Commandments. Christianity also transformed the serpent into the Devil, an embodiment of pure evil and one of the most influential of all archetypes. Pitting God against the Devil, Christianity thus created the concept of the eternal conflict between absolute good and absolute evil, a concept leading in turn to the agonizing question asked by early Christian philosophers and by Augustine: *If God is good and all-powerful, why does evil exist?*

In Genesis, the attitude of an angry God toward the sin of Adam and Eve is accepted as being appropriate for a supreme being. God curses the ground on which they walk and invents death for them but only after Eve brings forth progeny in utmost pain. Things only get worse. By the time of Noah, God is so disgusted with the race he has created that he sends down a flood to destroy it—all except Noah, the one good man, who pleases God with his piety and his burnt offerings:

> *And the LORD smelled a sweet savour; and the LORD said in his heart, I will not again curse the ground any more for man's sake; for the imagination of man's heart is evil from his youth; neither will I again smite any more every living thing, as I have done.*
>
> Genesis 8:21

Thus God became a supreme being and an angry father who was quickly offended by human sinfulness but pleased by piety and goodness.

Yet by the time of the early Christian philosophers, it was becoming difficult for those who questioned things to be content with the conflicting ideas that evil was inherent in humankind but that the choice of being good was always there, the choice of not being tempted to disobey. Did not God create the serpent? Had he done so deliberately to throw temptation into his children's path? Why would God do such a thing? Why not create a perfect race to begin with—without serpents?

By the time of Augustine, the problem of evil was well-known and widely discussed. To the philosopher, it proved just as puzzling as that of creation. To a thinking person it seemed evident that evil happened *despite* God. Traditional Christian belief was that the universe was divided into two distinct substances: one, material; the other, immaterial. It was unthinkable to Augustine that evil should exist in the immaterial world. But God was also the creator of the material world, was he not? And the material world was the abode of evil. If one denied that God was responsible for evil but *was* responsible for the material world, then it followed that evil was neither material nor immaterial. Evil, then, could not exist!

Augustine reasoned that what we call evil must be *the absence of good* in the same way that disease is the absence of health. Evil was, then, moral disease. When a person sins, moral perfection departs. The world, like the human body, was perfect when created and returns to perfection when the disease is gone.

Yet why do people sin? If they were created perfect, where did moral disease come from? Here Augustine developed an idea that remains with us—not just in religion, but in philosophy and psychology as well. This idea was *freedom of the will,* and we shall be talking further about it in Chapter 16, *Freedom*. Augustine concluded that people sin because God allows them to choose between good and bad actions. He knew this had to be the case, because God exacted penance from sinners and doled out punishment to the unrepentant. The Tree of Knowledge was put there in the Garden as a test, and so freedom of choice made perfect sense.

Or did it? The matter of God's nature crossed Augustine's mind. An all-knowing God must be aware in advance of what our choices will be. Before we are tempted to appropriate the money carelessly left on a table by a departing guest, must not God know that we will or will not take it? In God's eyes, the deed has already taken place. Where then is the element of choice? And without choice, how can there be responsibility?

Augustine advanced the idea of **predestination**, which states that, before birth, the course of a human life is already determined. The philosopher believed that the concept of an all-powerful, all-knowing God made predestination mandatory for mortals to accept. There could be no argument about God's foreknowledge of human choice; at the same time humanity could not be absolved of responsibility for sin. It was unthinkable that God should be blamed for human evil. Otherwise, what incentive was there to be good and to win God's approval?

Free will offered a way to make the two beliefs compatible. An all-powerful God could choose to bestow on humanity the *gift* of freedom. An all-knowing God could tell what our choices would be *without having willed those choices.* Thus freedom was real on the human level; predestination was real on the divine level.

If reason was too weak to reach these conclusions, then faith must be stronger than reason. How could humanity expect to understand God? Reason could take us to a certain point at which the paradox of fate and free will must be accepted. Faith, which was the answer in the Book of Job, stepped in to make acceptance possible. But again the matter did not end there. Some religious thinkers, in Judaism as well as Christianity, would not be satisfied with Augustine's conclusion that faith was all. Why did we have reason if we weren't supposed to use it? They would eventually say that reason *can* lead to an understanding of God, though critics of religious logic often point out that it only shows why a God must exist, not what *kind* of God.

Proving God's Existence. As we have seen, early Christian philosophers had many concerns about the doctrines they were being asked to accept, but Judaism also had its questions. In the Book of Job, the central character is told by the voice from the whirlwind that the running of the universe is not humanity's business. Faith in God has to convince us that God has his reasons for everything. In the twelfth century C.E. there emerged a rabbi who was also a profound philosopher and scholar, and he would show how logic and faith were not incompatible.

"Do not imagine that character is determined at birth. We have been given free will . . . We ourselves decide whether to make ourselves learned or ignorant, compassionate or cruel, generous or miserly."

—Moses Maimonides

Moses Maimonides (1135–1204) was born in Spain of Hebrew ancestry. Threatened with persecution, he moved to Egypt, where he became physician to the Muslim ruler Saladin. Trained in medicine, he decided that philosophy and theology were as important as healing the body. Besides, in the world of both Hebrew and Muslim scholars, if a man wished to be considered learned, he was expected to demonstrate knowledge in many areas.

At first Maimonides was appalled at the Muslim philosophical acceptance of the philosophy of **materialism** that had been advanced centuries before Socrates and Plato, maintaining that only matter existed and so-called spiritual experiences were solely in the mind. A devout Jew himself, he maintained that the material world was created by God out of nothing, but he was enough of an Aristotelian to realize that he would have to use logic to defend his belief. Although many of his Hebrew contemporaries were content to accept the Bible as mystic revelation, Maimonides was also a scientist living among Muslims who had inherited and further developed the logical and mathematical theories of the classical world. They were fully acquainted with Aristotle, Euclid, and the work of mathematicians in India. His mission was to show his contemporaries that a belief in God was not only desirable but logically, not just mystically, inevitable.

Since he was familiar with Aristotle's theory of the Unmoved Mover, it made sense to him that nothing can be in motion uncaused by something else, but cause and effect cannot be traced back into infinity. Sooner or later there has to be a causer that is not in motion itself. What Maimonides did was to give the name of God to the Unmoved Mover. The perfection of God made the Unmoved Mover plausible. God was thus defined as *that which cannot be caused.* Depending for his existence on a prior cause would make God imperfect. A perfect being cannot be dependent. If there *were* a prior cause which created God, then that cause would be God. No matter how far back you went, you would always find God waiting.

Some Hebrew scholars and theologians denounced the writings of Maimonides on the grounds that his so-called logic was founded on a strong belief in God to begin with and consequently was unnecessary—not only unnecessary, but an affront to the traditions of their forefathers for whom revelation was sufficient. Hadn't God told Job that it was not the place of humanity either to understand or to question the nature and ways of God? If, in fact, you needed proof, you were not truly religious.

The world of Christian thought was also influenced by mathematics, stirrings in science, and the work of Aristotle. Thomas Aquinas (1225–1274) never doubted his own faith, but he was imbued with the spirit of inquiry that became widespread during the later Middle Ages. Educated by Benedictine monks and having become a Dominican, he moved to Paris, which was already an intellectual center, a place where bright young students met exciting teachers and where even the clergy were not afraid to question established beliefs.

Here Aquinas came into contact with Aristotelian logic and was responsible for creating a system of thought designed to persuade nonbelievers that God must exist. Once introduced, his theories gradually found their way into Christian tradition. Even today, students in Catholic seminaries are thoroughly trained in *Thomism,* the name given to the philosopher's logical methods of proving God's existence.

Aquinas gave five proofs of God's existence, all based, as were the theories of Maimonides, on Aristotle's Unmoved Mover. The first, *Argument from Motion,* is a restatement of that theory, as is the second, *Argument from Causation.* The third, *Argument from Being,* is cited by many philosophers as the strongest. Here is a paraphrased summary of that argument:

> *Though we have only to look around to see that things* are, *it is indeed possible to imagine that they should not be. On the other hand, though it is conceivable that nothing should be, it is clear that this is not the case. Hence there must be a principle of necessary being which cannot be imagined as not existing. Only God can be so imagined.*

The fourth, *Argument from Gradation,* asserts that wherever we look we see greater or lesser amounts and qualities. We cannot conceive of "better," for example, unless we can also conceive of "best," for it stands to reason that we cannot go on into infinity finding "better" things. Eventually there has to be a "best" beyond which the mind cannot go. God is therefore the fullest realization of "best."

> "Absence of evidence is not evidence of absence."
>
> —**Carl Sagan**

The fifth, *Argument from Design*, is probably at once the most famous and the most hotly debated. It asserts that since there is clear evidence of order in the operation of the universe, it cannot have been put there by accident. If there is a design, it follows that there was a designer. Countless millions continue to use this argument. Others say that a universe governed by laws that have been experimentally verified is not equivalent to design. There is no universal agreement.

Islam

The third of the great monotheistic religions, Islam, was founded by the prophet Mohammed (571–632), an Arab who was a well-respected leader, a husband, and a father, successful in all aspects. While stopping in the city of Mecca, in what is now Saudi Arabia, he was visited by the angel Gabriel, sent by Allah (the word means "the one God"), and commanded to deliver God's word and his laws to the world, even as Moses was told to deliver the Ten Commandments he received on Mount Sinai.

Mohammed. Mohammed listened, but thought he must be going mad. He told his wife, who suggested he visit a wise relative and ask his opinion. This man assured Mohammed that he was blessed among all men and had been clearly chosen to restate the laws of God. The hearing of a divine voice convinced Mohammed that his relative had been right. The voice told him he must devote his life to teaching. Those who listened to his sermons wrote down what he said, and thus the Qur'an (Koran) came into existence. It is the sacred book of Islam, the central component of the religion.

Islam means "submission," and Muslim means "one who submits." Islam's followers are believed to be descendants of Ishmael, the son of Abraham, who conceived him with Hagar after Abraham's wife Sarah was found to be infertile. At first honored and groomed to succeed his father as patriarch of the Hebrew tribes, Ishmael lost this favored position when Sarah did in fact conceive a child, Isaac. Ishmael was cast out and became a wanderer in the desert, until, according to Islamic belief, he came to the city of Mecca, where Mohammed later founded the religion.

As Mohammed grew older, he wanted to do more than preach the word of God. He wanted to help fashion a society of brotherhood, peace, and ethical dealings—all based on Allah's laws. He became a political consultant and an agent for social reform, unlike Siddhartha, who taught the Eightfold Path and believed reform would come about by itself as more and more followers heeded his message and incorporated it into their daily lives. Mohammed's vision of the ideal world is still the basis of government in Islamic nations; that is, the function of government is to implement the laws of God. There have, historically, been disagreements over how those laws should be interpreted.

As in all religions, Islam has its fundamentalists—believers in the very letter of the law—as well as those who support greater flexibility. The separation has grown stronger over the centuries. In the beginning, Mohammed as spiritual leader allowed Christians and Jews living in Islamic communities to practice their own faith openly and commanded his followers not to persecute or try to convert them. He told the people that Arabs, Jews, and Christians all prayed to the one God and that they were entitled to heed the word as passed down in their own sacred books.

> *"Who so has done an atom's weight of good shall see it; and who so has done an atom's weight of evil shall see it."*
>
> **—The Qur'an**

The Qur'an bears striking similarities to those books. The commandments given to Mohammed by Allah are very much like those given to Moses and accepted, with modifications, by Jesus. In fact, Moses and Jesus were accorded much honor by Mohammed, who declared that they were pious and honorable men, much beloved by God, who had also spoken to them.

There are, however, significant differences among the three religions. Judaism, at least a thousand years old by the time of Mohammed, saw in Jesus a latter-day prophet but not the son of God, not the promised Messiah. Islam, recognizing the historical importance of Moses and Jesus, nonetheless saw in Mohammed the one true prophet. If he were not, why should God have felt the need to have his commandments restated?

Like Christianity, Islam believes there will be an inevitable ending of the world, followed by a Judgment Day, in which the good will be rewarded with eternal life in heaven, and the bad will suffer the torments of hell. Heaven and hell are vividly described in the Qur'an.

Devout Muslims, firm believers in a blissful eternity beyond this life, follow a rigid pattern of worship. The Qur'an demands the observance of five activities: *confession, prayer* (at least five times a day), *fasting, charity, and pilgrimage.*

Confession is not made to a priest, as in the Catholic faith, but directly to God. Worshipers speak their daily prayers sometimes alone but, as often as possible in groups, reflecting Mohammed's insistence on community. Fasting, taught Mohammed, builds discipline, necessary if one is to resist the temptations of the world. During the sacred month of Ramadam, Muslims are required to fast each day and to refrain from all sexual activity from sunrise to sunset. Ramadam commenorates the communication of the Qur'an to Mohammed. It occurs during the ninth month of the Muslim calendar, which is based on the revolution of the moon, and advances ten days each year according to the Western calendar.

Strict Islamic law forbids gambling and drinking alcohol at all times. Instead of stressing redemption, the forgiveness of sin, Islam seeks to make its followers morally perfect. Redemption is thus unnecessary.

Martin Lehmann/Shutterstock

The Blue Mosque, Istanbul, 17th century

Islamic architecture has done much to beautify the world. Mosques such as this are among the finest examples of architectural art.

God and Science in the Islamic World. Like Judaism and Christianity, Islam produced its questioners. One in particular, Al-Ghazzali (1058–1111), was trained in both law and theology. He taught at the University of Baghdad and was eventually caught between worldly matters and the austere discipline of the Muslim faith. He had problems with both extremes.

The Arab world was becoming a center of culture and erudition, rivaling those of the great Western cities such as Paris and Bologna. There were many temptations that could easily lead one to forego, for example, the daily prayers or the fasting. Al-Ghazzali realized he had to make a choice: either total immersion in the pursuits of the material world or total submission to the will of Allah.

He also found Islamic tradition too demanding for its followers, with its emphasis on discipline, and too remote from God. Wherever he looked, he could see people disobeying the laws set forth in the Qur'an. He realized that, if he were to practice total submission, he could not do so and lead a secular existence as well.

Then he discovered the *Sufi,* Islamic mystics who practiced meditation in their efforts to achieve total unity with God. In this they resembled some of the monastic orders of Christianity and the Hasidic branch of Judaism, whose members gave free rein to song and dance as a means of transcending cold reason. After his conversion to Sufism, he again took up his teaching duties, but this time he taught his students that God must be an active force in their lives, not a distant figure in whose name they went without emotion through their daily practices.

After the death of Mohammed, there was considerable disruption in Islam, a profound division between those who believed Muslim leadership belonged to Mohammed's father-in-law Abu Bakr and those who wanted Mohammed's cousin and son-in-law Ali. Abu Bakr emerged victorious after a long struggle between the two parties, but followers of Ali insisted that the command had been wrongfully taken from him. At length, those loyal to Abu Bakr became the Sunni Muslims, while those loyal to Ali became the Shiites. Both parties, living in Iraq, Iran, India, and Pakistan, continue to believe that control of the Islamic faith is rightfully theirs.

Both Islam and Christianity believe in an afterlife, though they are differently visualized. Lately there has emerged a worldwide interest in this phenomenon, independent of any religious affiliation.

Recently a science-based study of "near-death" experiences has appeared. The stories of more than 1,300 people who came so near death that in many cases they were pronounced dead until their surprising revivals are recorded in *Evidence of the Afterlife* by Jeffrey Long with Paul Perry (2010). The author found amazing similarities in these accounts.

> *Because NDEs happen to people all over the world, they are a spiritual thread that binds us together. . . .*

Many have reported heightened senses, generally positive emotional feelings, passing through a tunnel, encountering a brilliant light, and encountering other beings, such as deceased relatives or friends.[12] Though the author refers to a "spiritual thread," there is no religious connotation intended.

The Protestant Reformation

As Christianity spread and gained millions of converts during the Middle Ages, it became Catholicism, meaning "the one, true religion." It was a powerful empire in itself and would command the faithful to refrain from sin or face the fires of hell. Among the greatest of sins was that of **heresy**, words or deeds interpreted as being anti-Christian. During the late Middle Ages, a tribunal of church officials conducted the **Inquisition**, a high religious court in which heretics were tried and, if found guilty, imprisoned or even burnt at the stake.

There were rumblings of discontent. Dissidents in private complained about the growing wealth of the church as well as the continuing poverty of most worshipers. They also took exception to the church doctrine that salvation was impossible without the intervention of priests. They believed that God listened to each of his children, who could communicate with him privately. They called this principle "the priesthood of the true believer." They also condemned the church for its giant, expensive cathedrals (such as Notre Dame in Paris), with their artifacts of gold and silver, their expensive frescoes and statues. Such extravagant displays in the name of religion amounted to idolatry, which horrified them.

Ultimately the quiet questioning flared into an open rebellion led by Martin Luther (1483–1546), who made a list of 95 proposals for religious reform and nailed it to the door of the church at the University of Wittenberg. He hoped thereby to encourage open forums in which those who were protesting (Protestants) could confront church officials. The result was the great division in Christianity between the Protestants, who wanted to simplify religious worship and divest it of its bureaucracies and worldly power, and Catholics, who held tenaciously to the belief that the pope was the one true representative of God on earth and priests were chosen to carry the word of God to the people and carry to God the prayers of the people. Lutheranism was thus the first Protestant sect. But Protestantism would eventually give rise to further disputes and the formulation of other sects.

> *The church must be reminded that it is not the master or the servant of the state, but rather the conscience of the state.*
>
> **—Martin Luther King Jr.**

All of the religions discussed in this chapter are still very much with us. Some have strict rules that are binding on their followers, while others encourage the faithful to seek their own path to God, arguing that what matters in the long run is the development of a moral human being.

Doubt

Non-believers and those who dared to dispute the mandates of an organized religion have been imprisoned, tortured, or executed. There are still places in the world where the harshest penalties are imposed upon those persons whose lifestyle and mode of dress deviate from prevailing religious requirements. The strict enforcement of religious law runs counter to widespread philosophical positions that question or openly deny the existence of God. As philosophy has been and continues to be an instrument for the logical proof of God, so too can it be used for the opposite purpose.

Agnosticism

An **agnostic** (from a Greek word meaning "unknown" or "unknowable") is a person who does not patently disbelieve in God but who asserts that nothing about God, including his existence, can be known for certain. Agnostics are sometimes accused by the faithful of being too lazy to bother with religion. They are challenged to prove that God cannot be proven.

Yet agnosticism is a valid philosophical stance, often arrived at after much soul-searching. William James, a late nineteenth-century philosopher who will be discussed in the final chapter of this book, was an agnostic with compassion for those who relied upon religion to see them through difficult times. Sometimes called the father of modern psychology, James counseled innumerable people who were trying to make sense out of life, who had suffered grievous losses and were desperately seeking reasons. His advice was that if religion is essential to happiness, who is to deny someone the right to believe? Carl Sagan, a widely read popularizer of modern science, once remarked, "Absence of evidence is not evidence of absence."

In the arts one finds many who are "God-obsessed." They are angry because reason prevents them from believing in God yet offers nothing to take God's

"I have a conscience. It does not depend on religion."
—Isaac Asimov

place. The American poet Edwin Arlington Robinson (1869–1935) concludes his great work "The Man Against the Sky" with these lines that attack the rational denial of faith.

If after all that we have lived and thought,
All comes to Nought,—
If there be nothing after Now,
And we be nothing anyhow,
And we know that,—why live?
'Twere sure but weaklings' vain distress
To suffer dungeons where so many doors
Will open on the cold eternal shores
That look sheer down
To the dark tideless floods of Nothingness
Where all who know may drown.[13]

For the confirmed agnostic, it makes sense not to burn bridges or to risk drowning in Robinson's "floods of Nothingness."

Atheism

Unlike the agnostic, the **atheist** takes a bold negative stand. Instead of shaking their heads and saying, "I don't know," atheists challenge believers, especially those who use logic to prove God's existence. They sometimes take that very logic and use it to prove that the nonexistence of God is logically necessary, but sometimes people who call themselves atheists do not do so on logical grounds.

One method, which can be called "*informal*" logic, is to point out that the very question "Does God exist?" is meaningless since its subject has not been shown to have a valid identity. Consequently, all answers to that question have to be disregarded. Atheists are fond of the poem by Lewis Carroll (of *Alice in Wonderland* fame) called "The Hunting of the Snark," which concerns a dangerous sea voyage in search of the Snark, a creature no one has ever seen. The voyagers have been warned to be careful because there are rumors that the snark may really be a boojum. At length, in a hilarious conclusion, which could be a parody of *Moby-Dick*, the Snark, finally encountered, destroys the ship, and we are left with the mournful final line: "The Snark was a Boojum after all."

A foremost American proponent of atheism was Charles Sanders Peirce (pronounced "purse," 1839–1914), who was deeply involved in a philosophical movement known as **pragmatism**. According to pragmatism, no philosophical question is important if it makes no difference to the actual conduct of life. Like William James, Peirce realized that religion did indeed make a great deal of difference to a good many people. In a pivotal essay called "How to Make Our Ideas Clear," he turns the notion of belief inside out. He analyzes it in terms of three properties:

> *First, it is something we are aware of; second, it appeases the irritation of doubt; and third, it involves the establishment in our nature of a rule of action, or say, for short, a* habit.[14]

One difficulty with belief, Peirce argues, is that we are likely to seize on any sort that will appease the "irritation of doubt." We cannot stand not to know or be able to explain, and for the majority of us, it is important that a belief be *good* rather than necessarily true. In his opinion, religious beliefs are notoriously successful in appeasing the irritation of doubt. Indeed they are held more often for this reason than for any other, no matter what claims for their logical necessity may be made. They are particularly difficult to dislodge from people's lives (or habits) because, if they cannot readily be proved, the believer is confident they cannot be disproved.

> *Thus if it be true that death is annihilation, then the man who believes that he will certainly go straight to heaven when he dies, provided he has fulfilled certain simple observations in this life, has a cheap pleasure which will not be followed by the least disappointment.*[15]

> *If the premises are in fact not doubted at all, they cannot be more satisfactory than they are.*
>
> **—Charles Sanders Peirce**

The passage has become famous, not least because of its wit. Peirce is throwing down the gauntlet. He is saying: *If you don't believe me, prove that there's an afterlife.* Such reasoning employs the philosophical technique of *reductio ad absurdum,* by which you prove your point by postulating that its opposite is an absurdity. Take as example the statement *There can be no afterlife.* To say that *there is* such a thing is pointless and meaningless. The opposite of *There is no afterlife* is *There is an afterlife*; but the latter statement cannot possibly have any validity since no one has ever visited an afterlife and returned to tell of it. All one can say is "I believe there is an afterlife," but this automatically rules out logic.

The philosophy of Peirce is staunchly rooted in science. Nothing is true that cannot be observed or experimentally verified. In another famous passage he attacks the Catholic belief in *transubstantiation,* which holds that, through the mystical powers invested in the priest celebrating the mass, the communion wafer actually becomes the body of Jesus and the communion wine the blood of Jesus. Peirce noted:

> *. . . we can consequently mean nothing by wine but what has certain effects . . . upon our senses; and to talk of something as having all the sensible characters of wine, yet being in reality blood, is senseless jargon.*[16]

Whether to accept this argument as a logical one is a personal decision, but, if nothing else, it makes clear the fact that the scientific and religious outlooks are on different wavelengths. The atheist is much closer to science, while the devout believer must be willing to accept even the miraculous on faith. Another American atheist, H. L. Mencken, defined faith as "an illogical belief in the occurrence of the improbable."

A number of other atheistic philosophies have become prominent. Friedrich Nietzsche, discussed in Chapter 1 in relation to Apollo and Dionysus, made the famous statement "God is dead"—that is, the very question of whether God exists or not is a dead issue. The implication is that religion had its day, but by the late nineteenth century, the time of Nietzsche, that day was over.

In the same time period, a number of writers and poets expressed disillusionment over what they considered to be the unfounded optimism of the late Victorian

> *Religion alters the mind.*
>
> —**Tony Follari**

age, particularly the use of religion to justify the unstoppable accumulation of wealth and property. John D. Rockefeller, one of the world's richest men, wrote in his autobiography that his wealth showed he was favored by God.

Author Stephen Crane (1871–1900), who wrote *The Red Badge of Courage*, a biting antiwar novel, was also a poet whose moods swing from stark pessimism about a world from which God was notably absent to a belief that humanity would somehow pull itself up from the dark pit of chaos. (His poem "I Saw a Man Pursuing the Horizon" closes this book.) In the following poem Crane's pessimistic side turns grimly humorous.

God fashioned the ship of the world carefully,
With the infinite skill of an All-Master
Made He the hull and the sails,
Held He the rudder
Ready for adjustment.
Erect stood He, scanning His work proudly,
Then—at fateful time—a wrong called,
And God turned, heeding.
Lo, the ship, at this opportunity, slipped slyly,
Making cunning noiseless travel down the ways.
So that, forever rudderless, it went upon the seas
Going ridiculous voyages,
Making quaint progress,
Turning as with serious purpose
Before stupid winds.
And there were many in the sky
Who laughed at this thing.

Religion and the Arts

The question of whether the world is ruled by one or more divine beings has always been of great interest to philosophers. Yet philosophy is only one discipline of the humanities. We must not forget that literature, the visual arts, music, theater, and cinema have been influenced by religion in so many ways that it would take a number of volumes this size to do justice to the subject. We cannot, however, close our discussion of religion without reference to how this huge component of human experience has been affected by those who believe, or at least explore the idea that there is more to reality than the things in our immediate consciousness. The arts have been instrumental in bringing visions of higher realities to that consciousness.

Without religion, the visual arts would have a shorter history. Art and religion have maintained close relations since the beginning. The Egyptians saw painting and statuary as a means to immortality. Polytheism led the Greeks and Romans to erect masterpieces of art and architecture. In addition to the moral laws on which most societies, regardless of their religious orientation, are based, Judaism has given the world masterpieces of literature, poetry, and philosophers. The medieval church brought into the world countless paintings, statues, and frescoes in which heavenly beings and biblical incidents were visualized. The theater of the Western world had its beginnings in the medieval mass.

Islam frowned upon the production of artificial images, but, as we have seen, many of its buildings remain as very models of architectural grandeur.

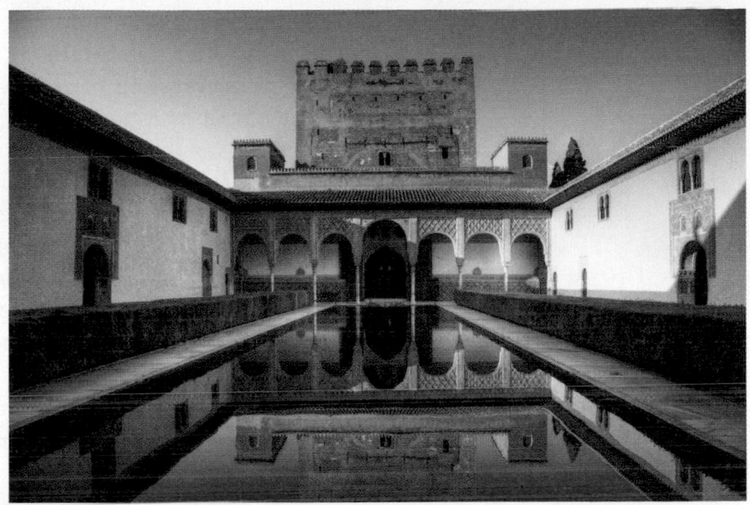

Dmitry Kutlayev/Dreamstime

Alhambra, Granada, 1338-1390

Detail from a Moorish palace. The Moors, an Islamic people, ruled Spain during this period.

Islam's influence on the art of Western civilization has been strong, largely because of the artistic bent of the Moors, a Muslim sect living in northwestern Africa that invaded Spain during the eighth century C.E. In occupying much of Spain for a number of centuries, they were responsible for a good deal of Spanish architectural design, such as that of the Alhambra, pictured here, built as a palace for Moorish kings during the thirteenth and fourteenth centuries and located outside the city of Granada. It is considered the epitome of Moorish art, with slender columns miraculously supporting complex arches and a colorful interior of stucco and mosaic tiles in an infinite variety of patterns and designs. Visitors to the palace may feel as though they have been transported into an *Arabian Nights* fantasy. Though the building is a secular one, its architecture is an outgrowth of the richly designed and decorated mosques, which, like Christian cathedrals, are meant to bring the worshiper into closer touch with the next world.

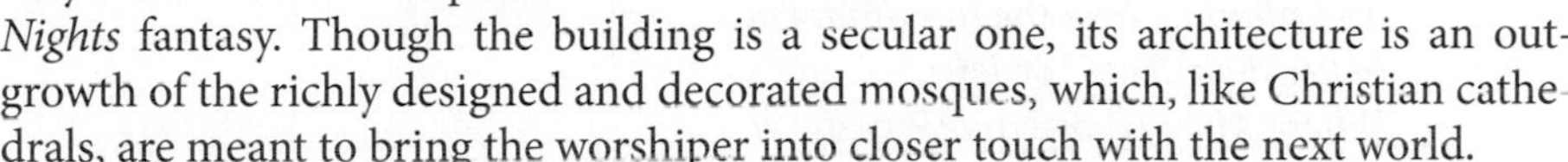

The great artistic works of the Vatican, including Saint Peter's Cathedral and the Sistine Chapel, were deliberately monumental, designed to overshadow and replace the polytheistic art that at one time had been pervasive throughout Rome. The art of Leonardo, Michelangelo, Raphael, and many others gave a vivid and visual reality to religious stories familiar to the public: Adam and Eve, Joseph and the wife of Potiphar, Moses, David, the Prodigal Son, the Virgin and Child, the Annunciation, the Crucifixion, the Resurrection, Judgment Day—the list is almost endless.

During the Protestant Reformation, beginning in the late fifteenth century, church architecture became simplified; but this change led indirectly to the flowering of the baroque art and architecture of the seventeenth century. Baroque churches, as we saw in Chapter 6, were elaborately decorated in what may have been a strong effort to win back worshipers who felt that religion had lost its inspiring grandeur. The complex counterpoint of Bach was another great gift from the baroque period.

Some of the great works of Western literature are reaffirmations of religious teachings, such as Dante's *Divine Comedy* and Milton's *Paradise Lost* (1662), written to "justify the ways of God to man." Both works greatly influenced the way artists, other writers, and millions of worshipers think about God and the spiritual world beyond.

But writers and artists often have their own relationship to religion and give us unorthodox but no less uplifting visions. "Batter my heart," the sonnet by John Donne, analyzed in Chapter 4, speaks of religious ecstasy in highly sexual terms but strongly communicates the idea of submission to God's will in an unforgettable way.

During the Romantic movement in the last part of the eighteenth century and the first half of the nineteenth, Western artists and writers encountered a new kind of religious vision founded on nature and the natural rights of all people. In this poem, "The Divine Image," William Blake speaks of religion as a universal gift that unites everyone. Here Blake transcends all sectarian viewpoints, finding God in the human world.

To Mercy, Pity, Peace, and Love
All pray in their distress;
And to these virtues of delight
Return their thankfulness.
For Mercy, Pity, Peace, and Love
Is God, our father dear,
And Mercy, Pity, Peace, and Love
Is man, his child and care.
For Mercy has a human heart,
Pity a human face,
And Love, the human form divine,
And Peace, the human dress.
Then every man, of every clime,
That prays to his distress,
Prays to the human form divine,
Love, Mercy, Pity, Peace.
And all must love the human form,
In heathen, Turk, or Jew;
Where Mercy, Love and Pity dwell,
There God is dwelling too.

> *"Every religion is true one way or another. It is true when understood metaphorically. But when it gets stuck in its own metaphors, interpreting them as facts, then you are in trouble."*
>
> **—Joseph Campbell**

In Blake's poem, God is a force—imagination, creativity, and, of course, the four cardinal gifts singled out by the poet, whose romanticism, not confined within the walls of a church, also finds divinity outside as he rejoices in the wonder of it all.

A major voice in romanticism is that of William Wordsworth (1770–1850), one of whose masterpieces is "Lines Composed a Few Miles Above Tintern Abbey on the Banks of the Wye." Here are two famous passages from the poem. It is indeed religious, but not in a traditional sense. For Wordsworth, God is the soul of nature, a belief that brings him close to Hinduism.

And I have felt
A presence that disturbs me with the joy
Of elevated thoughts; a sense sublime
Of something far more deeply interfused,
Whose dwelling is the light of setting suns,
And the round ocean and the living air,
And the blue sky, and in the mind of man;
A motion and a spirit, that impels
All thinking things, all objects of all thought,
And rolls through all things.

Religion cannot possibly be exhaustively treated in only one chapter of one text. We have presented an introductory outline of the major religions of the world, as well as major philosophical opposition to religion. We have given some consideration to the role played by religion in the humanities. As always, the purpose has been to stimulate your thoughts and encourage you to think about your own position relative to these matters.

Many people become uncomfortable when religion is analyzed as a human phenomenon, as if discussing it threatens sincerely held beliefs. Discussion should not have this effect. If engaged in intelligently and with an open mind, religious discussion can strengthen your beliefs. Knowing the *why* of belief is far better than expressing allegiance to it without understanding. All important is full awareness of your commitment and your responsibilities after having *made* the commitment.

LEARNING OBJECTIVES

Having read and carefully studied this chapter, you should be able to:

1. Name the sacred books of the major world religions.
2. Define and give two examples of *polytheism.*
3. Indicate with two examples how Hindu philosophy has influenced Western writers.
4. Provide two examples of Native American religions.
5. Describe the Four Noble Truths and the Eightfold Path of Buddhism.
6. Distinguish between Buddhism and Zen Buddhism.
7. Using the yin and the yang, explain the philosophy of Taoism.
8. Describe Aristotle's Unmoved Mover and show how the idea influenced Maimonides and Aquinas.
9. Tell why the statement "The Bible says . . ." does not begin to indicate the varieties of material to be found on religion.
10. Summarize the five problems that early Christian philosophers had with Christian doctrine.
11. Explain Augustine's concept of faith and the problems that led him to it.
12. Indicate similarities and differences between traditional Christianity and Islam.
13. Contrast agnosticism and atheism.

KEY TERMS

agnosticism belief that one cannot possibly know for sure whether God exists.

atheism belief that God cannot logically exist.

bas relief stone wall carving, found in many ancient tombs.

Brahma in Hinduism, a godlike personification of the creative principle in the universe.

Brahman in Hinduism, the name given to the spiritual force that governs the universe; the universal soul.

Buddha Sanskrit term for "the awakened one"; used in Hindu prophecies as a reference to a special being who comes along once in 25,000 years and attains enlightenment without having to be reborn; as the Buddha, a reference to Siddhartha Gautama, who taught that anyone is potentially able to reach enlightenment.

Buddhism lifestyle, meditation practice, and religion based on the teachings of Gautama.

creatio ex nihilo Latin phrase meaning "creation out of nothing"; used in Judaism, Christianity, and Islam to describe the universe that God made.

dharma in Hinduism, the moral structure underlying existence; in Buddhism, the equivalent of Brahman, the universal soul; Chinese equivalent, Tao.

dialectic the philosophical method used by Socrates involving question and answer.

enlightenment in Buddhism, the state achieved by Gautama of total detachment devoid of ego, in which one sees things as they really are.

heresy here, belief held or statement made that challenged medieval Christian teachings.

Hinduism generic term for religion of India dating back to c. 1500 B.C.E., based on the honoring of numerous deities and a belief in reincarnation.

Inquisition high Christian court assembled beginning in the thirteenth century for the trial and sentencing of those convicted of heresy.

karma in Hinduism, a moral summing up of one's deeds that determines where one will be in the next lifetime.

materialism a philosophy that says only matter is real.

meditation in Buddhism, the practice of sitting until one achieves a state of detachment from ego.

moksha in Hinduism, Sanskrit term given to the state of eternal bliss achieved after having successfully gone through many rebirths.

monotheism religion based on one supreme god.

nirvana in Buddhism, a state of bliss attainable to those who devote their lives to meditation and a transcendence of ego; adapted into English to mean a totally stress-free condition.

polytheism religion based on more than one god.

pragmatism philosophy developed in America which holds that the truth of an idea is measurable by experiment and practical outcome.

predestination the belief stated by Augustine that one's entire life, including moral and immoral choices, is already determined before birth; in Calvinism, the belief that one is born either for salvation or damnation.

Ramadan the ninth month of the Muslim calendar, determined by the phases of the moon; held sacred because of the belief that this was the month in which Mohammed received the Qur'an from Allah in the city of Mecca.

Shiva in Hinduism, a personification of the principle of change, of destroying what Brahma has created in order to make way for the new; the second god in the Hindu trinity.

Talmud a collection of writings that interpret the Torah and provide a clarification of biblical laws.

Tao Chinese name, adopted into English, for the moral order that rules the universe.

Torah the first five books of the Hebrew Bible: Genesis, Exodus, Leviticus, Numbers, and Deuteronomy; attributed to Moses.

Unmoved Mover what Aristotle called the force that always existed and was responsible for setting the entire universe in motion but was not in itself set in motion by anything preceding it.

Vishnu in Hinduism, a personification of the force balancing creation and destruction.

wu wei phrase used in Taoism that translates as "to do without doing"; means that people who live their lives in tune with the moral order of the universe will always do the right thing.

yang in Taoism, the active component of existence, symbolized in art as the white crescent of a circle which also contains a small black circle. Both of the small circles symbolize the necessary working together of active and passive elements.

yin in Taoism, the passive component of existence, symbolized in art as the black crescent of a circle which also contains a small white circle.

Zen austere and monastic form of Buddhism centering on the highly disciplined practice of meditating for very long periods of time; from the Chinese *ch 'an,* meaning "meditation."

TOPICS FOR WRITING AND DISCUSSION

1. Scholars of the humanities have told us there are *four* pathways to religion. One is *tradition*—belief because it is part of your culture and background; the second is *history*—belief because it is based on events that can be documented; the third is *philosophy*—belief through rational analysis. What do you think the fourth is? Explain your answer.
2. The Hebrew and Christian Bibles and the Islamic Qur'an all present the commandments of God. They are strikingly similar. Presumably all three religions pray to the same God. Briefly explain some of the disputes they have with each other.
3. At the beginning of Whitman's *Leaves of Grass* is the line "For every atom belonging to me as good belongs to you." While this would at first appear not to have anything to do with religion, the text points out that in fact Whitman was strongly influenced by a certain religion. What was it? What was the influence?
4. Augustine maintained that human beings were given free will by God and thus are responsible for their sins. At the same time, he said that God, being all-knowing, must see in advance everything that we are going to do. How did he reconcile these two apparently opposing ideas? Do *you* think he succeeded?

5. One atheistic argument is based on a principle known as *reductio ad absurdum,* which means that you prove something by showing that its opposite is absurd. For example, the opposite of "God does not exist" is "God exists," which is absurd because it cannot be proved. Its opposite does not have to be proved because it asserts nothing. Do you accept this argument? If not, what are your objections?

6. Non-believers find Augustine's concept of faith unacceptable. Still, are not many things about living taken on faith? Suggest two.

7. Would the discovery of life on other planets strengthen or diminish the role of religion in modern society?

8. In 1927, John Scopes, a high school biology teacher, was tried and convicted for teaching the theory of evolution. What, in your opinion, was the issue at the core of the trial? Has the issue been resolved once and for all? Explain your answer.

9. Can you have God without religion, or religion without God?

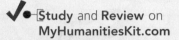

Study and **Review** on **MyHumanitiesKit.com**

Chapter 11

Morality

Because **moral** problems arise every day of our lives and because artists and philosophers are so often concerned with questions of right and wrong, morality is a major theme in the arts. It is, of course, central to religious thought, philosophy, and law.

Morality can be defined as the basis for a choice among *significant options*. A popular definition is: *Morality is what others do wrong*. This definition eliminates considerations of all sides of an issue. This chapter is about moral problems that have concerned and still concern thoughtful people.

Two of the first words most babies learn are "good" and "bad." Whether the words are used with a smile or a shaking finger, they are soon integral to early understanding of the world. As a child grows, the terms become the basis of approving others' behavior. Sometimes the words generate serious consequences—and even death.

Those two words—good and bad—are with us for life, though applied in many different ways. We often use them when celebrities appear to misbehave. We imply our own norms when we remark, "After all, he promised . . ." or "Just think—at *her* age!"

Samuel Butler, a nineteenth-century novelist, defined morality as "the custom of one's country, and the current feeling of one's peers." But which custom? Which country, and which section of that country? Which peers? In times of heated controversy, morality remains divided among groups and smaller subgroups.

In centuries past, for example, if one person killed another in a duel fought according to agreed-upon norms of behavior, nobody called it murder, though it would be today. If a young woman of social stature and marriageable age spent unsupervised time alone with a man, her reputation was probably ruined. Not so anymore. Hundreds, even thousands of people, were owned by families of wealth and property. Children of those families were expected to carry on the family work and marry within the same (or higher) social station. Moral questions were decided by those in authority (usually men) and accepted without question.

Today, violations of marriage vows by a celebrity or a candidate for political office are condemned as "immoral." Loyalties to athletic teams and nationalistic pride encourage the "Us versus Them" attitude. "Partner" and "companion" have become acceptable ways to describe an individual in either a different- or same-sex relationship. Family traditions, education, and agreed-upon social norms are all influential, as are fairy tales, literature, plays, movies, and television.

◀ **Sixteenth-century statue of Lady Justice in St. Veil, Carinthia, Austria**

Is justice always blind? What is the purpose of the blindfold?

Fiore/Topfoto/The Image Works

Morality and the Arts

The arts have played a prominent part in influencing moral attitudes, past and present. The belief that art ought to be sincere and "infectious" to encourage morality was held by Count Leo Tolstoy, who opposed art as mere entertainment. He wrote:

> *Formerly people feared lest among the works of art there might chance to be some causing corruption, and they prohibited art altogether. Now they only fear lest they should be deprived of any enjoyment art can afford, and patronize any art. And I think the last error is much grosser than the first and that its consequences are more harmful.*

There are still those who would urge censorship "for the good of society."

One of the works deemed scandalous and *not* for the good of society was Édouard Manet's *Olympia*, which depicts a reclining nude woman. Not only was she obviously a courtesan, but her bold gaze was accused of staring shamelessly at the viewer. Exhibited at the Paris Salon of 1868, *Olympia* provoked one critic into writing that Manet had sunk to an incredibly low level and that his ugly portrait of a disgusting whore was brazen and offensive to all decent-minded people.

Published earlier in the century, Nathaniel Hawthorne's novel *The Scarlet Letter* (1850) suggests that the individual citizen does not have to be bound by a community's moral rules. Hester Prynne, the heroine, who lives in an austere community of rigid religious conservatives, finds herself trapped in a loveless marriage. While her husband, aptly named Chillingworth, is away, she succumbs to her passion for a handsome young man, who cares for her in a tender way she has never known. When a child is born and Hester refuses to name the father, the outraged

Explore on **MyHumanitiesKit.com** Manet, *Olympia*

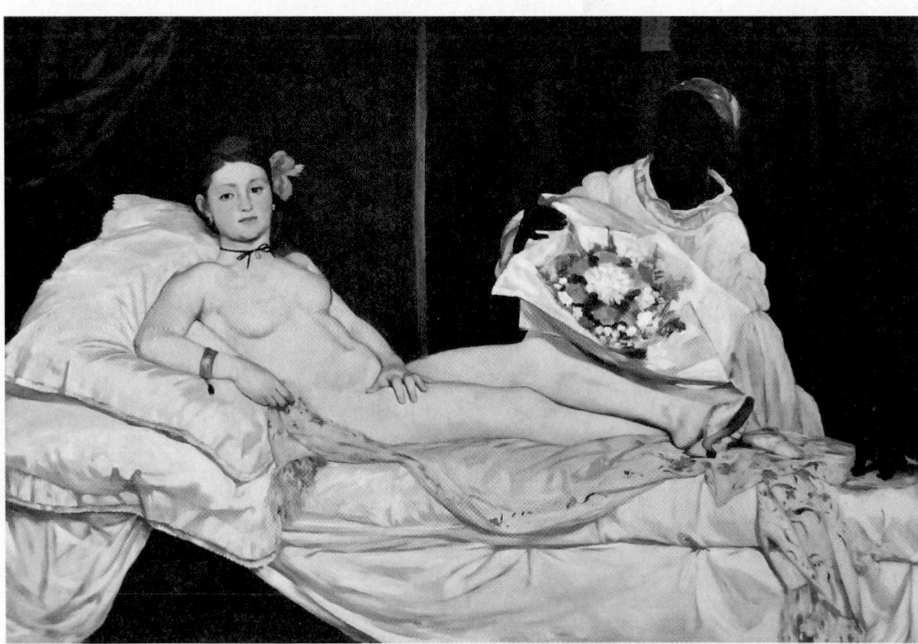

CuboImages srl/Alamy

Édouard Manet, *Olympia*, 1863

Manet's painting, now priceless, was condemned by a prominent art critic as a brazen attempt to replace traditional values.

community, led by the elders of the church, force her to wear a scarlet *A* (for adulteress) and to endure the scorn of the citizens. Though Hawthorne himself was brought up as a strict Puritan, the growing liberal side of him came to believe that an inflexible moral code was more sinful than the adulterous relationship, which had, after all, grown out of sincere love. Even though *The Scarlet Letter* was written more than a century and a half ago, the question of whether genuine love supersedes a community's moral values is still with us, especially if the transgression is in the neighborhood.

North Wind Picture Archives/Alamy

Handcolored woodcut, 19th century

Hawthorne came to believe that an inflexible moral code was more sinful than Hester's adultery.

The Banning of *Ulysses*. Irish novelist James Joyce (1882–1941) faced much disapproval for his pioneer effort to create fiction that truthfully mirrors the workings of the human mind, including its forays into forbidden sexuality. *Ulysses* (1922), eventually cited by a panel of literary critics as the greatest novel of the twentieth century, was initially banned in Britain (for fourteen years) and the United States (for eleven years). It also became the subject of a famous court case. In 1933, an American judge named John M. Woolsey was asked by booksellers to decide whether the sexually explicit language of the book was so morally offensive that the public should not be allowed to read it.

After two careful readings, the judge stated that the book was difficult but not pornographic; rather, the author had made one of the most objectionable characters express feelings that would have been appropriate for a woman of her station in the time frame of the story. The character in question was Molly Bloom, Joyce's modernized version of Penelope, the wife of Ulysses in Homer's *The Odyssey,* who, like a modern Penelope of Homer's *The Odyssey*, was also waiting for her husband to return home from *his* wanderings. Joyce revolutionized fiction by taking the reader inside Molly's mind to show what was really going on. In doing so, he shocked many readers as well as many more who joined in the moral crusade against the novel without having read it.

Embedded in the final stream-of-consciousness passage, which runs forty pages without punctuation, are language and images many found highly improper for an author to put into the mind of a woman. Nobody said Joyce was being untrue to human nature—only that such truths had no place in fiction. In lifting the federal ban, Judge Woolsey struck a blow against those who believe the purpose of art is solely to improve society. The struggle is far from over.

Listen on **MyHumanitiesKit.com** Joyce, Molly Bloom's Soliloquy

Outrage over Moral Wrongs. Picasso's *Guernica* (see Chapter 5) remains one of the most potent statements ever made about the horrors of attacking an enemy city and killing hundreds of innocent civilians, including women and children, an outrage echoed more recently by opponents of the wars in Iraq and Afghanistan, in both Christian and Muslim communities. Oliver Stone's 1978 film *Platoon* showed the burning of a Vietnamese village, with Samuel Barber's mournful *Adagio for Strings* as background music, while the action was deliberately slowed in order to make the same point Picasso had made in *Guernica.* Supporters of these conflicts often argue that a just cause can result in terrible disasters, but nonsupporters ask whether even a just cause can excuse acts of inhumanity.

Beethoven's gigantic later works are in part fist-shaking denunciations of what he saw as the cosmic injustice that turned him totally deaf—he of all people, whose life was devoted to creating wondrous sounds. He expressed his rage in the *Heiligenstadt Testament* of 1802, in which he says, "What a humiliation for me to

Explore on **MyHumanitiesKit.com** Picasso, *Guernica*

Sylvia Beach Library. Manuscripts Division. Department of Rare Books and Special Collections. Princeton University Library.

James Joyce and Sylvia Beach, c. 1922

Joyce and a friend calling attention to the novel that shocked so many, was banned for years, but was eventually to be voted the greatest novel of the twentieth century.

be standing next to someone who . . . heard a shepherd singing . . . and I heard nothing." All of his life he had been a champion of individual rights. In his Symphony No. 9, created from the depths of his despair, Beethoven nonetheless achieves a glorious affirmation of the joy of creativity, the joy of living, probably because the act of venting his feelings caused him to hear sounds no one ever heard before. The fourth movement, utilizing a huge chorus in a musical setting of the poem "Ode to Joy" by Friedrich von Schiller, is a statement, by implication, that all people must be free to experience this joy

The symphonic work *La Valse* by Maurice Ravel (1875–1937), written in 1918–1919, has been interpreted as a musical vision of the chaos of Europe after the devastation of World War I. Beginning as a disciplined, politely played waltz, then gradually reflecting increasing chaos with crashing dissonance and electrifying rhythmic effects, the work may be heard as the product of an artist mourning the passing of an age in which moral values were clear and straightforward—and musical compositions followed strict guidelines.

Moral issues can also be treated humorously. A *New Yorker* cartoon (July 18, 1988; Bernard Schoenbaum) shows a prisoner explaining to his cellmate: "All along I thought our corruption fell within community standards." But don't many business tycoons found guilty nowadays often believe they are violating no moral principles?

Listen on **MyHumanitiesKit.com**
Beethoven, Symphony No. 9

Fables for Our Time by humorist James Thurber (1894–1961) looks at Benjamin Franklin's oft-quoted "Early to bed, early to rise, makes a man healthy, wealthy, and wise." Thurber took much pleasure in blasting moral clichés. He tells of a good clean-living citizen whose life is one of strict moral and physical discipline, so predictable that his bored wife knows she can take advantage of his clockwork bedtime habits by sneaking out to meet her lover. At length the pair decide to do away with the husband. Waiting until the appointed hour when the husband always falls asleep, the lovers steal into his bedroom and strangle him. The moral Thurber draws is: *Early to rise, early to bed, makes a man healthy, wealthy, and dead.*

Morality and Philosophy

"Elevation of morality over other goods in human life has been honored, wherever it has been achieved, as a tempering of the otherwise unquenchable human appetite for power, wealth, pleasure, and the rest."

—Jack Miles

As we said earlier in the chapter, morality can be defined as the basis for a choice among significant options. Through the ages philosophers have been faced with such options. Here are some of the major ones in the form of Five Moral Questions in Philosophy.

1. *Does the end ever justify the means?* Put another way: If the overall goal is considered beneficial, is it morally right to do *anything* to get there—including certain acts that on their own would be regarded as wrong, criminal, or even evil? Machiavelli, a Renaissance philosopher discussed

later in this chapter, says yes. Others maintain that any moral transgression, even telling a lie, is wrong under every circumstance.

2. *Are punishment and the fear of punishment the only things that keep us from doing wrong?* The question of whether to obey the law when we can get away with breaking it is at the heart of a famous debate between Glaucon and Socrates in Plato's *Republic,* also discussed later in the chapter.
3. *Do the needs of society outweigh the needs of the individual?* Some philosophers agree that the individual always comes first when it's a question of which takes precedent, society or one person. Altruism, discussed later in the chapter, maintains that you should be more concerned for others than for yourself. Opponents of altruism insist it's an unnatural position to take.
4. *Should all economic resources be controlled by individuals or communities?* Some political and economic leaders defend the free market, as defined by Adam Smith, while others insist the free market system does not work in quite the way Smith described. Others say the perception of totally free enterprise as moral or not depends on one's economic status.
5. *Are results all that matter, or do intentions also count?* Jeremy Bentham says that moral decisions depend on outcome rather than motives.

> *"Morals are an acquirement—like music, like a foreign language, like poetry, poker, piety, paralysis—no one is born with them."*
>
> **—Mark Twain**

Moral Systems

A network of related values on which moral choices are based is called a **moral system**. Most religions share the belief that a divinity has set down certain rules that must be followed whether or not they interfere with an individual's personal desires. Often those rules are found in a sacred book. Accepting these rules thus involves faith in the existence of the divinity and faith that the sacred book was written by people in a position to record accurately the words of that divinity.

Alternate moral systems are based on reason, not faith. One does what is right because reason determines that it is right and therefore doing wrong is irrational. It can, however, be argued that this view really depends on faith that reason is the ultimate decision-maker in all matters.

People who have a hard time making up their minds when faced with a difficult choice may wish to consult a moral authority, such as a well-known and trusted philosopher, a spokesperson for religion, or even a close friend with a reputation for making intelligent decisions. Yet here's a question that inevitably arises: *In the event that two sources offer sharply divergent opinions, which one do we follow?* Will we follow our intuition? Will our decision in the end come down to self-interest? Or will we lack confidence in our own reasoning and find it easier to follow a moral authority, provided we don't find ourselves torn between two opposing views? And if we *do* settle on one or the other, how will we ever know that we made the right choice? As you can see, the ever-present problem of right versus wrong can lead us into a vortex of questions that never seem to stop.

> *"Conscience is the inner voice that tells us someone may be looking."*
>
> **—H.L. Mencken**

The terms *should* and *should not* are constantly cropping up, especially in commentaries by religious moral authorities. The words also abound in rules of the military, the family, schools, sports, and games.

People who feel uncomfortable with an absolute *should* are apt to reject the word in favor of *moral relativism*: "Who's to say what's right?" "People are different. What's good for one may not be good for another." "Times have changed; there are no more universals." A popular maxim has been "As long as you don't hurt anybody and it makes you happy, do it!"

Life pushes us into so many quandaries that doing the right thing in every instance is exceedingly difficult. That is why the humanities are sensitive to the pain that can be caused by moral dilemmas and the often tragic results of what we thought were the right choices.

The Morality of Self-Interest

When young siblings angrily dispute who owns what, a parent will remind them not to fight. Instead, they are urged to share. In school, children are taught to obey rules, not to be selfish, and to cooperate with others. Public praise for philanthropy reminds us that charity is good, that acting out of self-interest is wrong (except when it was the way the donor's fortune was amassed). Yet free societies are also based on the principle that free enterprise, which benefits the entrepreneur first, also helps employees and their families. Getting ahead is a recognized goal, with its implied corollary that some must win while others have to lose.

Is acting out of self-interest such a bad thing? Is selflessness necessarily good? If everyone acts out of self-interest, does it breed a self-reliance that is better for society as a whole? During the nineteenth century, self-interest came to the fore as the most desirable characteristic of a human being. Even before that, the term was often preceded by the adjective *enlightened*, conveying the belief that self-reliant people, realizing their full potential as human beings, would enrich, not damage, society. Other theories, however, tell us that, in a choice between self-interest and the general good, self-interest must always prevail. That is the position taken by Glaucon in his classic debate with Socrates, detailed in what follows.

Glaucon versus Socrates

Early in Plato's *Republic,* a series of philosophical dialogues between Socrates and his students as chronicled by Plato, a confrontation occurs between Socrates, who is always on the side of reason, and Glaucon, a student described by Plato as "that most pugnacious of men," who is a firm believer that everyone does the right thing out of motives that have nothing to do with reason or innate goodness. To strengthen his case, Glaucon tells the story of a shepherd named Gyges, who discovers that the ring he has removed from a corpse has the power to make him invisible. Taking full advantage of his newfound power

> *he contrived to be one of the messengers who were sent to the court, where, as soon as he arrived he seduced the queen, and with her help conspired against the king and slew him, and took the kingdom.*

An argument then ensues in the class over whether a basically honorable and just man would have done the same thing. Glaucon continues:

> *Suppose now that there were two such magic rings, and the just [man] put on one of them and the unjust the other; no man can be imagined to be of such an iron nature that he would stand fast in justice. No man could keep his hands off what was not his own when he could safely take what he liked out of the market, or go*

"Though no one has identified genes for morality, there is circumstantial evidence they exist."

—**Steven Pinker**

> *into houses and lie with anyone at his pleasure, or kill or release from prison whom he would and in all respects be like a God among men.*[1]

Socrates replies that if the just man decided not to take advantage of the magic ring, he would die in peace, content that his had been a good life. Glaucon quickly counters by asking the group to suppose that somehow the just man had developed a reputation for being unjust, while the unjust man enjoyed the opposite reputation. Would the just man not decide he would be a fool not to use the power of the ring? What would be the satisfaction in doing the right thing if nobody knew it? Furthermore, what if he was made to suffer excruciating torture because of his supposed lack of goodness? (Socrates was, of course, famous for teaching that nothing bad can happen to good people.) It would not be long, concludes Glaucon, before the just man realized that the *appearance* of goodness is all that matters. Doing the good, if nobody knows it, is futile.

Having a reputation for being truthful, hence trustworthy, the unjust man, according to Glaucon, goes on to enjoy all the benefits that come with social approval.

> *With his reputation for virtue, he will hold offices of state, ally himself by marriage to any family he may choose, become a partner in any business, and having no scruples about being dishonest, turn all these disadvantages to profit.*[2]

Society, so goes Glaucon's argument, expects virtue to be only an appearance, the result of pressures brought to bear on each of us, not of the human capacity to determine through reason what is right and what is wrong.

Yet reason is precisely what Socrates relies on, and his counterargument stirs up as much controversy as his opponent's; he maintains that the virtuous act is *done for its own sake.* Rational humans live according to the law, even if the law is harmful to them. Periclean democracy, or the direct rule of citizens, was still new, and many expressed doubts that the ordinary citizen would have enough sense not to take advantage of so much freedom. Socrates firmly believed that the rationality of citizens would give rise to laws that were fair, just, and moral. Plato attributes to Socrates one of the most ringing (and still controversial) declarations in all of philosophy: *To know the good is to do the good.*

> "Truth has no special time of its own. Its hour is now—always."
>
> —**Albert Schweitzer**

Socrates's meaning, which may at first seem naive, is actually awesome in its simplicity and ultimately hard to refute. What he says is that people cannot claim to be deliberately choosing the wrong action despite knowing the right one. If you do the wrong thing, then that is what you know. Acting is part of knowing. In other words, anyone can pretend to know something, but the only proof of that knowledge is action. If your deeds are bad, then there is no evidence that you knew what was right. We may disagree, but the force of the argument is powerful.

Socrates paid with his life for his trust in reason. After being found guilty of trumped-up charges—corrupting the minds of young Athenians and teaching atheism—he was jailed and executed. He refused to bargain for a lighter sentence by agreeing never to teach again. Doing that would have meant no longer seeking the truth, and without possessing the truth, he would be no better than Glaucon's shepherd.

He does observe that the opinions of others is important, but the opinions of knowledgeable good people *only*. Why should one care what ignorant bad people think? If one lives so as to win the respect of the good, then obviously one is leading a good life. Then he gives one of his final lessons before drinking the hemlock that will end his days: "Not life, but a good life, is to be chiefly valued."

Fortunately, on a daily basis, most of us make much smaller choices than the ones debated by Glaucon and Socrates—and we don't face a cup of hemlock for making what we think is the right choice. Still, even without the ring of Gyges, we are often invisible. Consider the opportunities you have to test the theory to do what you know is right. When, driving late at night, without a policeman anywhere around, do you automatically stop the car at a traffic light? At a gym, do you obey the posted rules to wipe down your machine and take a shower before entering the pool? But what if nobody else is around? How many customers call attention to a billing mistake in their favor which they notice once they leave the store? As "invisible" citizens, all of us can rationalize failure to do what we would do if others were around to observe us. One can rationalize by telling oneself that a minor mistake in one's favor by a cashier or a mechanic will compensate for previous visits when a product or service was faulty. Students who work at two jobs can claim that they need to get advance copies of a test (by whatever means) in order to compete with classmates who have more time to study. The choice in each instance is not between two momentous options; but the ring of Gyges is still around.

Nowadays it is not hard to find billionaire tycoons who succeed even without that ring. Their success is equivalent to Glaucon's idea of a good reputation. Also in the Glaucon camp are those who quote with admiration the cynical adage of baseball manager Leo Durocher: *Nice guys finish last.*

> "*They deem him their worst enemy who tells them the truth.*"
>
> **—Plato**

What guided the Athenians who voted for the death sentence? Socrates was convicted not by a jury as we know it today, but rather by an assembly of every male citizen who wanted to participate. Reason may not, after all, have been *their* guiding principle. Political factors appear to have been involved. Socrates was known to have been friendly to someone considered an enemy of the state, and the philosopher's teachings often challenged the state. Did the self-interest of the state, in the care of the male citizenry (which comprised only five percent of the entire population), finally triumph? Can a governing body ever be expected to survive in the name of reason alone?

The Philosopher King

Later in *The Republic,* Plato admits that the majority of people—both the governing and the governed—will generally be driven by self-interest unless held in check by one supreme ruler, a man like Socrates, motivated solely by what reason advises in every instance: a man not out for himself, but rather who rules because he has a clear vision of a state in which justice prevails. He called this ruler the *philosopher king*. Whether such a being has ever existed or could ever exist is a matter of long debate. A number of rulers have made claims about their wisdom, and no doubt have earnestly believed they and their methods were best for their state. But history has not confirmed their claims.

Plato's plan has many problems. For example, who would decide on the credentials of someone who applied for the job? Reason says only the wisest person is qualified to make the decision. Because there can, by definition, be only one "wisest person" in a society, choosing him (Plato doesn't say *her*) would seem to be impossible. Only the wisest person can do that, and we're right back where we started. Glaucon would probably say the struggle for the power of this ruler would result in all manner of underhanded magic-ring ploys on the part of ambitious people who would cheat, even kill, to win the job.

Government and Self-Interest

Henry David Thoreau (1817–1861) begins his famous essay "Civil Disobedience" with this declaration:

> *I heartily accept the motto—"That government is best which governs least," and I should like to see it acted up to more rapidly and systematically. Carried out, it finally amounts to this, which I also believe,—"That government is best which governs not at all . . ."*

He implemented this belief by refusing to pay a tax levied for the privilege of voting, announced he was seceding from the Union, and moved to a woodland hut, where the earth provided all the necessities of life for him. In *Walden, or Life in the Woods* (1854), an account of his life in the hut, Thoreau says his one room was furnished with three chairs: one for solitude, two for friendship, and three for society. He refused to go beyond three.

His friend Ralph Waldo Emerson (1803–1883) had inspired Thoreau's uncompromising individualism as Emerson has similarly inspired countless readers for generations. In his essay "Self-Reliance," Emerson delivers the manifesto of individualism. He advises us to be ourselves, never to imitate others, never to conform if doing so is in conflict with our own will ("Who so would be a man, must be a nonconformist"), and never to be fearful of behaving unpredictably ("A foolish consistency is the hobgoblin of little minds, adored by little statesmen and philosophers and divines"). Among his most dramatic utterances is this: "[I]f I am the Devil's child, I will live then from the Devil."

Except for Thoreau's refusal to pay the poll tax, which supported the war against Mexico, neither man committed acts against government. Their strong individualism was confined to their explosive writings. In these they showed themselves to be part of a sweeping nineteenth-century movement in which self-interest would come to the fore as the most desirable characteristic of a human being. There is no evidence that either man championed the cause of aggressive greed and the destruction of others in a single-minded quest for a secure foothold in this world.

Rebellions against Self-Interest

In his short story "The Idealist," Frank O'Connor (1903–1966) describes a Protestant student in a mainly Catholic public school who has been profoundly influenced by inspirational books about boys for whom honor and tradition are all-important. The student notes that whenever Catholic classmates are late for school, they lie to the headmaster, saying they have been to mass, and thus escape punishment. The young hero, however, is conditioned by his reading to believe in telling the truth at all costs, and he is severely beaten every time he is late without offering an excuse. At length, broken in spirit (and nearly in body) he lies like all the others. The story ends with the headmaster smiling to himself in triumph. The last holdout has finally been tamed.

Frank O'Connor's short story "The Idealist" shows the terrible things that happen to a schoolboy who always believes in telling the truth.

In Robert Bolt's 1960 Pulitzer Prize–winning play *A Man for All Seasons*, the issue is integrity versus self-preservation. Based on historical events, the play concerns a dilemma and subsequent martyrdom faced by the writer and Catholic philosopher Sir Thomas More. Widely admired in his native England and often honored by his close friend King Henry VIII, More was eventually placed in a position of having to approve the king's pending divorce or risk execution by upholding church doctrine. More was a devout Catholic and believed so implicitly in the laws of the church that he could not do as the king demanded, not even to save his life. In Socratic terms and in the context of Catholicism, More's approval would have been a betrayal of reason. In the play, although the king privately pleads with his friend not to die for his belief, More's obstinate refusal to support the divorce leaves the king no choice. In the context of *his* belief system, the execution was a necessary act of reason. In the final, powerful scene, More is beheaded. (He was subsequently canonized by the Catholic Church.)

Satirical Praise for Self-Interest

Not surprisingly, the clergy of various faiths warn their congregations against excessive emphasis on self. One clergyman, Jonathan Swift (1667–1745), was dean of St. Patrick's, an Anglican cathedral in Dublin, and also a satirist who could be bitterly cynical behind his facade of humor. In his famous 1729 treatise on the brutalities of self-interest, "A Modest Proposal," he assumes the persona of a well-bred—and well-fed—English gentleman, who appears to have a perfect solution to the problem of Irish poverty, especially the fact that poor Irish children are forced to subsist on a near starvation diet. His solution? Dispose of the children by having them served up as delicious meals for the rich, and by so doing, raise the economic level of the parents.

George Grosz, *Pillars of Society*, 1926

A modern German artist does his take on greed.

> *I have been assured by a very knowing American of my acquaintance in London, that a young healthy child well nursed is at a year old a most delicious, nourishing and wholesome food whether stewed, roasted, baked or boiled, and I make no doubt that it will equally serve in a fricasse, or ragout.*

The narrator, in a passage that is prophetic of what Utilitarian philosopher Jeremy Bentham would propound seriously some years later, calmly computes the mathematic of the enterprise: 20,000 would be spared for breeding; of these only one-fourth need be males, "more than is usual for livestock." A child of one "will make two dishes as an entertainment for friends, and when the family dines alone, the fore or hind quarter will make a reasonable dish . . . seasoned with a little pepper or salt."

He goes on to itemize the consequences, including the value to the breeders of getting rid of needless expenses. Taverns would have a new dish, and "a skillful cook who understands how to please his guests will contrive to make it as expensive as they please." Marriages would increase, and mothers would be treated more tenderly as they fattened up their children. His proposal, he adds, is not based on any desire on his part for profit: "I have no children by which I can propose to get a single penny, the youngest being nine years old, and my wife past child-bearing."

As can be imagined, "A Modest Proposal" has aroused indignation among those who don't catch on to Swift's humane purpose. Some literalists took him at his word and denounced what they called his "savagery," not recognizing that he was really attacking smug self-interest as the only goal in life.

"Enlightened" Self-Interest: Niccoló Machiavelli

While humanism has historically been against self-interest as a way of life, some philosophers who would consider themselves to be humanists have espoused the theory that self-interest alone is rational and in the best interest of society. *The Prince* is the great work by Niccoló Machiavelli (1469–1527), a prominent Florentine Renaissance philosopher who dedicated the book to Lorenzo de Medici, head of a famous family, a man of extreme wealth and power, patron of many artists, and both loved and feared by hundreds. Lorenzo, as we might expect, had many enemies and critics. Persons with his kind of power and influence usually do.

> "The end may justify the means as long as there's something that justifies the end."
>
> —Leon Trotsky

Machiavelli, however, swore staunch allegiance to Lorenzo. To defend his patron, he composed *The Prince,* which contains advice to all aspiring rulers. Effective leaders, he claims, must never assume their followers would seek a justice inconvenient to themselves. He therefore concludes that the wisest course for a true leader is to curb the self-interest of the population by inspiring in them a sense of awe. Leaders must present an intimidating appearance, both in extravagant dress and in imperial behavior, to let the populace know that someone regal is in charge. They should exhibit signs of their power, such as by riding in magnificent carriages followed by a large retinue of influential friends, security personnel, and important local politicians. This advice has been followed by modern heads of state who fly from country to country in gigantic official planes and arrive at their destinations in police-escorted stretch limousines, long motorcades, and with a parade of bodyguards.

Machiavelli's political philosophy is a continuation of earlier beliefs, such as those held by Plato and Aristotle, who did not trust ordinary citizens to be rational enough to make intelligent decisions. They advocated strong rule from the top in order to guarantee stability and justice. Plato had his philosopher king, while Aristotle believed the ideal government had three major components: the king, the aristocrats, and groups of outstanding citizens known for their wisdom and fair dealings.

All three philosophers—Machiavelli, Plato, and Aristotle—were against ruthless self-interested dictatorships and the whimsical rule by people whose wealth enabled them to buy their way to power. All three were concerned for the welfare of the total society, but they could not recommend direct rule of the populace. Instead, they believed wise rulers best served both their own and their country's interest by imposing rules based on a carefully considered political philosophy of **enlightened self-interest:** serving the self in order to make an effective government that provides for people better than they could provide for themselves.

The term **Machiavellian** has unfortunately become a reference to cynical individuals who scorn the masses, considering themselves superior to all others and therefore entitled to exert power over them. Literature offers a gallery of characters that critics have labeled—and always negatively—*Machiavellian.* These characters are usually villains who prey on unsuspecting goodness.

> Machiavelli believed that by acting in his own self-interest the wise ruler was better for the state than one who was permissive.

Machiavellianism, as understood by the founder of the philosophy, emerged from the Renaissance focus on individualism. In a sense, Machiavelli's ideal ruler typified the new age, for such a ruler was not encumbered by the restraints of the Christlike existence demanded of (but not necessarily realized by) rulers in the Middle Ages.

"Enlightened" Self-Interest: Thomas Hobbes. Thomas Hobbes (1588–1679) was a political philosopher who believed that tight autocratic control was necessary because the masses of people were innately evil and solely out for themselves. He believed egoism was the natural condition of humanity. He described human beings as basically "nasty" and "brutish" and denied that such a thing as a noble purpose could exist. With this pessimistic view of the individual, Hobbes wrote his most famous work, *Leviathan* (1651), recommending a political system based on absolute monarchy. He employed the term *commonwealth* to describe the ideal state, one in which each subject must willingly turn over his rights to the sovereign for the mutual protection of all people from each other. He advises that

> *every man should say to every man, I authorize and give up my right of governing myself, to this man [i.e. the Leader], or to this assembly of men, on this condition, that thou give up thy right to him, and authorize all his action in like manner.*

Although this may sound like a democratic social contract whereby each citizen willingly gives up individual rights for the good of all, Hobbes makes no pretense of democracy, reasoning that power invested in the monarch could not, by definition, be challenged by the people. If it were, the monarch would not be feared, and if he were not feared, order would disintegrate. The monarch, backed by an invincible army, would protect his subjects from each other as well as from attacks by other nations. Hence the term *Leviathan*, which for Hobbes meant "*mortal god,* to which we owe under the *immortal God,* our peace and defense." The commonwealth would then flourish peacefully—an impossibility if each citizen were allowed to think and act for himself. Without the Leviathan, every person would distrust every other person, with the result that no person or property would be safe. Hobbes states in *The Leviathan* that, without the absolute strength of the leader, "every man has a right to every thing, even to one another's body. And therefore, as long as the natural right of every man endureth, there can be no security to any man."

We can see that Machiavelli and Hobbes both favor nondemocratic government as the only way to prevent self-interest from destroying society. Hobbes, further influenced by the rise of rational philosophy during the seventeenth century in reaction to the otherworldliness of the Middle Ages, maintained that reason alone, not a sentimental faith in the inherent goodness of human nature, could allow humanity to live in peace and harmony. Tough-minded as his political philosophy was, Hobbes insisted that it represented the only rational course if the human race were to survive its cutthroat instincts.

Economics and Self-Interest: Adam Smith

> *"Adam Smith correctly observed that it is from the self-interest of the butcher, the baker and brewer that we expect our dinner, not from their benevolence."*
>
> **—Donald Livingston**

The economic philosopher Adam Smith (1721–1790), in contrast, believed the perfect society was one in which all people were free to pursue self-interest. Like Karl Marx, who would come later, Smith observed that economic well-being was the guiding force in human life. People were interested in making money, in getting ahead, in providing the most comfortable standard of living for themselves and their families. Greed itself was not necessarily a bad thing, as long as one did not break the law or harm others in the process of accumulating wealth. Far from being immoral, greed was the natural condition of humanity.

Smith's theory that people should have the freedom to pursue wealth became the basis for the capitalist system of today. To those who argued that unlimited freedom of economic activity would yield a society of constant conflict and dangerous competition, Smith's answer was that *without* such freedom only those in power would enjoy the pleasures that rightfully belong to everyone.

His policy is called **laissez-faire** (literally, "allow to do") and is based on the principle that businesses should be free to charge whatever they want for their goods and services. The public's response, not government controls, should regulate the process. Smith's ideal society has a built-in system of checks and balances that prevent the accumulation of wealth in just a few corporations.

Manufacturers, or *entrepreneurs,* perform a service for the public by seeking to make a profit for themselves. Salaries paid to employees increase the money supply, which keeps circulating throughout the economy, guaranteeing more employment for everyone. Without their being aware of it, says Smith, all people who live in a free-market system are joined together "as by an invisible hand."

It is in the best interest of the entrepreneur to manufacture a product that people actually need. Continuing to produce an unneeded product would result in bankruptcy. (Once the automobile displaced the horse and carriage as the primary means of transportation, who wanted to buy buggy whips?)

Problems develop when entrepreneurs become too greedy (though greed is still what drives the free-market economy). If a product is successful and large numbers of people buy it, the supply dwindles and prices go up. If the price is too high, people stop buying. Companies are forced to lower the cost. The laws of supply and demand always apply and regulate the economy. When the product is cheap enough, people start buying again, and the price goes up, again. The cycle would seem to be infinite. But is it? Economists tell us that while our wants are insatiable, resources are limited. Crude oil, for example, is nonrenewable. The Gulf oil spill of 2010, which squandered millions of gallons, made that much abundantly clear. The most pessimistic predictions are that eventually no oil will be left anywhere.

Smith could not have predicted today's global economy in which nations do not fend for themselves but rather participate in a network of mutual dependence. A bank collapse or a credit crunch in a once powerful nation that had attracted much foreign investment can create chaos all over the world. Economists agree that there is no such thing as an ideally self-regulating market, and therefore Smith's theory that self-interest is in the best interest of humanity is now hotly debated. Recent world problems have only added to the controversy.

Still, those of us in a free society continue to depend on a (more or less) free market and believe (more or less) in Smith's theory. We must admit, however, that it poses problems that may never be resolved.

Ayn Rand. For novelist Ayn Rand (1904–1982), **capitalism** was close to divine. She preached complete reliance on a free market, which she believed encouraged the strong and self-reliant to make the most of their talents without spending a lifetime helping others, who only grow weaker and lose the incentive to help themselves. Born in prerevolutionary Russia, Rand as a teenager witnessed the sweeping changes and promises of a glorious future in a classless society. She resisted indoctrination after thoroughly examining communist ideology, rejecting Karl Marx's claims about the benefits society would receive once the bourgeoisie (middle class) was eliminated.

> *"People create their own questions because they're afraid to look straight. All you have to do is look straight and see the road, and when you see it, don't sit looking at it—walk."*
>
> **—Ayn Rand**

Rand inevitably detected to the West, where she started to write. In one of her famous essays, *The Virtue of Selfishness,* Rand says people of vision should have unlimited opportunities to follow their own laws. In her philosophy, the strident loner does help others, but not out of the belief that it is moral and honorable to make sacrifices for them. The rest of us profit because a strident loner like Howard Roark, the hero of *The Fountainhead* (1943), can use his genius to build great cities and make the world a better place. There isn't an ounce of sentiment in him. He proudly asserts, "No man is worth five minutes of my time." But his arrogance and self-assuredness, Rand believes, only increase his value to the rest of us.

Transcending Self-Interest: Altruism

> *When a blind man carries a lame man, both go forward.*
>
> **—Swedish proverb**

It is hard to deny that self-interest is sometimes necessary. Can there be a place for **altruism**, or a greater concern for the welfare of others than for oneself? Some say no, arguing that even if reason in the Socratic sense requires us to place others before ourselves, what *appears* to be an altruistic or selfless act really springs from secretly selfish motives.

To be sure, many examples of altruistic deeds require no questioning of motives, as when a firefighter loses his life in a daring rescue attempt, or in a case involving a random shooting at an elementary school when a teacher shields the body of a child and receives a fatal bullet. In such instances, the cynics are quiet, later observing that the number of people willing to die for others is trivially small. The deaths of three hundred firefighters in the disaster of September 11, 2001, may have changed the attitude of many such cynics. Nor can we ever know how many of the thousands who perished did so because they stayed to help others.

In the everyday world, altruism does exist: donating an organ to save a stranger's life, or diving into the sea to try to save someone in distress. During the insurgencies in the Sudan, when millions of innocent women, men, and children were slaughtered in acts of "ethnic cleansing," Doctors Without Borders, humanitarian medical personnel, worked tirelessly to save as many lives as they could, even though they faced being shot for their efforts or becoming infected with disease themselves.

> *People are naturally suspicious when they hear that someone has committed a purely altruistic act. Often they will seek out hidden motives of self-interest.*

In the corporate world of today, where workers may become aware of defective auto parts, unsanitary food preparation, or the advertising of products they know carry a health risk, cases of altruistic whistle-blowing exist. There are no easy moral victories here. If nothing else, we learn from them that doing the right thing takes not only courage but the willingness to stand quite alone.

The word "altruism," the extreme opposite of self-interest, comes from the Latin *alter*, meaning "other." While the word does not often occur in ordinary conversation, it has long been viewed as a noble ideal almost impossible to reach The ideal notes that human beings are all connected—and by more than DNA. The stirring words of John Donne (see Chapter 4) are emblazoned in the history of idealism:

> *No man is an island entire of itself; every man is a piece of the continent, a part of the main. If a clod be washed away by the sea, Europe is the less, as well as if a promontory were . . . Any man's death diminishes me, because I am involved in mankind. And therefore never send to know for whom the bell tolls; it tolls for thee.*

The passage inspired Ernest Hemingway to name his 1940 novel *For Whom the Bell Tolls.* The central character, Robert Jordan, is an American who works in causes of liberty, even if they are not his own. In this case the cause is the struggle of guerillas fighting for independence during the Spanish Civil War. Once a loner, Jordan gives up his life to save theirs.

> *To the good I would be good; to the not good I would also be good in order to make them good.*
>
> **—Lao-tzu**

We are accustomed to stories of executives experiencing scandal, indictment, conviction, and imprisonment for dubious accounting practices, insider trading, and generous bonuses unconnected to prudent business strategies. The injured include stockholders, employees, and the occasional whistle-blower who notifies authorities about alleged crimes. Three altruists were at least honored on a magazine cover, but many fade into obscurity. Being known as the guardian of moral behavior does not enhance the job-seeker's resumé.

Finding a job is even harder in these days of practices such as outsourcing, said to benefit the disadvantaged in countries with a lower standard of living than others. Calling to reserve a hotel room or get help for a computer problem often requires speaking to an employee in a far distant location who is paid far less than employers would have to give a U.S. counterpart for the same job. One may wear a dress or a shirt manufactured in a factory thousands of miles away, in which workers toil for long hours and low pay under poor conditions. Charity toward the underprivileged or a new means of amassing huge profits? How many would step forward and refuse to work for an outsourcing company on the grounds that it exploits the downtrodden?

A Philosophical Defense of Altruism. American philosopher John Rawls (1921–2002), having thought deeply about whether altruism truly exists, agrees with Socrates that reason does not support self-interest. He proposes that each of us pretend to be wearing a "Veil of Ignorance" that wipes out all awareness of who we are and where we come from. Starting from Square Zero, so to speak, we then list the requirements for an ideal society. That is, if you didn't *know* you were rich or would be some day, or you didn't know you came from a poor background, what would be on your list? Rawls suggests two major requirements he thinks everyone would cite:

1. Equal and maximum liberty (political, intellectual, and religious) for each person consistent with equal liberty for others.
2. Wealth and power to be distributed equally except where inequalities would work to the advantage of all and where there would be equal opportunity to achieve advantageous positions of equality.[3]

As we can see from this ingenious argument, the Veil of Ignorance puts everyone on an equal plane, which should lead to general agreement about the nature of a just and fair society. What if you put "equal distribution of wealth" on your list and then found out you were going to inherit a fortune one day? You might well reconstruct your list. However, if you were truly honest, you would recognize that self-interest was getting in the way of reason. You would say, "I believe in unequal distribution of wealth because I'm going to be rich." Similarly, if you discovered you were poor and would always be so, you might change "equal distribution of wealth" to "tax the rich and give to the poor." Rawls is not saying that the reconstructed concepts are wrong. He is merely pointing out that self-interest often colors our attitude toward what is right and fair. Yet we are all altruists as long as we wear the Veil of Ignorance! Since this is so, who can deny that altruism does in fact exist? Nobody said it would be followed.

Utilitarianism: Bentham and Mill

Jeremy Bentham (1748–1832) was unwilling to say that self-interest was wrong, though its pursuit was contrary to the rigid morality taught him as a child. Why were moral laws so unreflective of true human nature? Accordingly, he became a philosopher and formulated the theory that since self-serving pleasure is the natural goal sought by everyone, all people ought to have an equal chance of attaining it. He rebelled against the moral codes set forth by religion and traditional philosophy, as well as those that became laws binding on an entire population. What, he asked, gave anyone the right to tell anyone else which pleasures to enjoy and which

> "The greatest happiness of the greatest number is the foundation of morals and legislation."
>
> —Jeremy Bentham

to avoid? But must there not be guidelines? Surely everyone could not wantonly pursue pleasure if this meant interfering with the right of others to do the same. *Unrestricted* self-interest made no sense to him.

As a philosopher, he was attracted to science and mathematics, for those fields offered methods of achieving certainty. Accordingly, mathematics became the basis for a moral system that allowed self-interest to be both defended and restricted. He called it **utilitarianism**.

Bentham's Moral Mathematics

Bentham declared that numbers were the key to moral certainty: a formula would decide the right course of action in every instance. For him, the goal was a society in which the maximum number of people achieved the maximum amount of pleasure *without* impinging on the rights of others. He denied the validity of *moral absolutism* and formulated his famous definition of a moral action as one that provides *the greatest good for the greatest number*.

In Bentham's system, before you choose an action with consequences that will affect others, you assign a plus or minus numerical value to the degree of pleasure or pain the action might cause for the most people. Let us say that, in a modern example, the question is whether to allow a giant resort complex to be built along a lakefront. So many plus points go to the contractors, builders, construction workers, and service personnel, all who stand to profit from the enterprise. For all of them, the construction offers positive pleasure. Additional plus points are awarded to vacationers, who will benefit from having a place in which to relax and relieve stress. Points are subtracted by environmentalists concerned about the inevitable pollution and the extermination of fish and waterfowl, and by residents who see the resort as destroying the neighborhood, thus bringing down the resale value of their property. The calculator (an invention Bentham would have loved) tells the story. Plus points for those who benefit, minus points for those who don't. Assign your own points, do the simple arithmetic, and get the moral answer.

Bentham's **moral mathematics** also adds or subtracts points based on "intensity" and "duration." In the example of the resort, we must consider the annoying sounds and air pollution of road expansion, not to mention the fact that, once the resort is in place against the wishes of many who gave it minus points, it isn't there for a short stay. May points be determined strictly by the number of individuals involved? If so, the displeased residents might outnumber the owners and the contractors. But what if the builders insist that the number of possible vacationers is almost infinite, and so might be the terrific boost to the economy of the region?

Motives and Results. For Bentham, the measurable results tell all regardless of motives. Few would imagine that the owners of the resort complex are concerned only for the economic welfare of the residents. Nonetheless, if they "win" the numbers game, the resort is morally right. But critics of Bentham's morality see many problems.

Suppose the builder of the proposed resort had a longstanding feud with the head of the Environmental Committee, a feud that had nothing to do with business or pollution. What if anger and revenge are his true motives? He has proposed the entire scheme just to embarrass the environmentalist in front of his supporters. Bentham's calculation yields only external results and pays no attention to motives *unless* there is a chance that a motive, once discovered, might cause pain to a lot of people—unlikely to happen in this hypothetical case.

Another example of a numerical question that sidesteps motives is: Is it better to give $10 to a cause you vehemently believe in or $10,000 to the same cause because you want to see your picture in the paper along with a caption praising your philanthropy? For Bentham (and probably for the fundraisers), the larger amount would be preferable and its moral virtue assured.

What might be Bentham's mathematical calculation for a decision on abortion? Or homosexuality? Abortion might be considered right or wrong depending on whether an underpopulated country needed more pregnancies carried to completion. As for homosexuality, the question would be whether the practice of it harms the general population. Would there be fewer marriages, fewer babies born in a society that otherwise believed homosexuals had the right to practice their activities? Even though Bentham was essentially a political radical, to be consistent with himself, he would have to approve of a ban on homosexuality if the greatest number in a given society decided the practice would lessen the population, depriving the future of artists, philanthropists, scientists, dedicated physicians, and so on. In such a society, homosexuality would be mathematically immoral, yet moral in another society that placed the highest priority on human rights.

Bentham believed in various definitions of the good, depending on particular circumstances. The lakeside resort, for example, might bring wealth to its town, but also draw tourists away from another resort twenty miles distant. And what happens when calculations do not agree (which is frequent)? My pleasure, in other words, is your pain—and vice versa.

Bentham proposed that the government would have to step in and be responsible for providing the greatest good for the greatest number. He even organized a political party called the Philosophical Radicals in order to campaign for moral reform based on his mathematical system. The name was eventually changed to the Utilitarian Party, suggesting a practical approach to moral philosophy, basically democratic in that it recognized the equality of all individuals in the matter of decision making, with majority rule holding sway. A countryman who also wanted moral reform was not, however, as generous as Bentham.

Utilitarianism Modified: John Stuart Mill

Also a utilitarian philosopher, John Stuart Mill (1806–1873) came along a half century after Bentham. His father, James Mill, had assisted that philosopher in the development of his political party. James Mill was also an elitist when it came to the education of his son. The boy was allowed to associate only with friends of whose intellectual capabilities the father approved. But he was also taught a Socratic brand of rational liberalism—that is, almost unlimited freedom for those responsible enough to use it for purposes other than the gratification of sexual desires.

As Mill matured, becoming a writer and philosopher, he expressed approval of Bentham's views on government's responsibility to guard the rights of the private citizen, but he disagreed that majority rule is always the proper course. Bentham's mathematics implied that decisions were numerically variable, but what about matters of taste? Followers of Mill continue to question the wisdom of the majority in all decisions. What if, for example, a proposal to erect a new museum or an opera house were put to a popular vote and it had to compete with a new sports stadium? The greatest number might well opt for the stadium, thus depriving those with educated tastes of the pleasures they sought. Imposing "low art" on everyone regardless of preference was, for Mill, as immoral as imposing absolute standards. Yet would not the rule of the majority (an absolute in itself) deprive the opera lovers of *their* moral rights?

> *"We can never be sure that the opinion we are endeavoring to stifle is a false opinion, and if we were sure, stifling it would be an evil still."*
>
> **—John Stuart Mill**

"What is morality in any given time or place? It is what the majority then and there happen to like, and immorality is what they dislike."

—Alfred North Whitehead

Our present-day society's preoccupation with winners—blockbuster movies, sports rankings, bestsellers, awards, and scorekeeping of every kind—causes regret in critics concerned that numbers can overlook quality. The negative accusation of elitism always lurks in the background for those urging criteria other than popularity.

Consider a debate between two men who agree that opera is worthwhile. Both love the art but are divided on the question of whether the public should be asked to support it. Mitchell Cohen, a commentator for *Dissent* magazine, is concerned about the availability of art to the general public. If opera is not subsidized, will only the rich be able to enjoy it?

> *One consideration should surely be inequality in cultural opportunities . . . no important domain of culture should be accessible chiefly to social elites. So I offer a social democratic precept: in access to culture, no citizen should be more equal than others. Public funding for arts (opera among them) ought to help make varied forms of culture available in a fair manner to all citizens.*[4]

Bruce Ackerman, on the other hand, argues that if society is neutral and fair, without preference for one form of art over another, and if we truly respect one another, we would recognize that

> *. . . the Met merely provides another form of entertainment no different from skateboarding or hula-hooping. I myself do not hold this view—but for those who do, the case for selective subsidy vanishes immediately: why subsidize opera, and not skateboarding, if they are simply rival entertainments struggling for the consumer dollar?*[5]

Mary Evans Picture Library/The Image Works

William Hogarth, *The Enraged Musician*, 1741

Hogarth was probably the leading satiric artist of the eighteenth century in England. He poked fun at all levels of English society. The question here is: What is Hogarth laughing at?

Mill recognized that government was needed to balance irresponsibility on the part of the general population. This fact, however, did not give government the right to legislate morality for the responsible few. If Mill were considering the matter of the opera house, the equitable course would be for a committee of acknowledged patrons of the arts to decide that the aesthetic needs of society were more important than a sports stadium, and this committee would have the backing of the local government. In defending the rights of enlightened citizens, Mill proved to be more radical than Bentham.

One of Mill's famous essays, "The Tyranny of the Majority," in his book *On Liberty* (1859) maintains that letting the majority rule in all decisions is just as bad as the autocratic rule of monarchs in previous centuries. Mill writes that his objective

> *. . . is to assert one very simple principle, as entitled to govern absolutely the dealings of society with the individual in the way of compulsion*

> *and control, whether the means used be physical force in the form of legal penalties, or the moral coercion of public opinion. That principle is that the sole end for which mankind are warranted individually or collectively, in interfering with liberty of action of any of their number, is self-protection. That is, the only purpose for which power can be rightfully exercised over any member of a civilized community, against his will, is to prevent harm to others. His own good, either physical or moral, is not a sufficient warrant.*

The English artist William Hogarth (1697–1764), famous for paintings and engravings that poke fun at all levels of English society, gave us *The Enraged Musician* (opposite page), displaying both sides of a conflict. The musician in question sits by his open window, his work interrupted by an extremely noisy crowd. We ask ourselves: What if the musician were to call the police on the grounds that his right to work in privacy had been violated? What if the case ended up in court? Would the judge rule that the crowd has a right to cavort as it pleases as long as no one is physically harmed? Or that the musician is right in objecting to the crowd on the grounds that his artistic work is more important than their fun? What do you think Mill would say?

The Categorical Imperative of Immanuel Kant

Born in East Prussia and a resident there for most of his life, the German philosopher Immanuel Kant (1724–1804) was, like Bentham, impressed with the certainties that science was able to achieve. As a university of Königsberg faculty member, he read insatiably in a number of fields, becoming so adept he was given courses to teach in mathematics, physics, anthropology, logic, metaphysics, and ethics. This impressive background made Kant feel comfortable with both science and philosophy, and he would merge the two into one of the most influential systems of thought ever devised.

The various branches of Kant's philosophy are like the spokes of a wheel radiating from a central belief, adopted from science, that truth is arrived at through experience. He differed, however, from kindred philosophers who took the extreme position that experience is strictly what our senses tell us.

Kant's view was that the input of the senses does not constitute experience until it is interpreted by our inborn rational capacity. He believed that we are born with mental **categories**, into which sensory data are filed—much as a postal worker takes an armful of random mail and flips each letter into an appropriate box. We know, for example, that the chair is next to the table because we categorically understand "nextness." If we did not, the spatial relationship would be meaningless: if someone asked us to go fetch the chair next to the table, we would return a blank stare.

> *"Morality is not properly the doctrine of how we make ourselves happy, but how we make ourselves worthy of happiness."*
>
> **—Immanuel Kant**

Kant also turned his attention to moral concerns. His theory stated that the sense of right and wrong was also inborn. True, we hear "yes" and "no" from our parents, but no learning can take place unless we are able to attach approval and disapproval—first to specific actions, then to the abstract concepts of rightness and wrongness. For Kant, the average person has no trouble reaching those abstractions because the inborn moral sense gradually unfolds in the same way that a bud gradually opens into a flower. He labels this inborn faculty the **Categorical Imperative** or sense of ought: an intuitive classification of actions and choices as morally acceptable or unacceptable. Experience teaches us which specific actions are right, but first we must know rightness or wrongness, and they cannot be taught.

Kant was a dedicated opponent of slavery. He argued that regardless of the number of people who held slaves and justified their actions for a variety of reasons, including religious ones, the fact remained that slavery was morally (hence universally) wrong. That slaveholders had to search for justification clearly indicated a secret knowledge that what they were doing was reprehensible. Socrates said, "To know the good is to do the good." Kant did not believe this was true. Each of us is born with a knowledge of the good, but some disregard it later if it proves inconvenient. He admitted that self-interest all too often suppressed the moral imperative.

Take, for example, the principle of honesty. Without a universal recognition of what it means, we could never ask, "What time is it?" We rely on the honesty of the answer, or we would not have asked the question. People depend on someone's promise to keep an appointment or return borrowed money. If the promise is not kept, we say, "That person has not been honest."

Kant's ethical philosophy is a powerful way of knowing in advance whether a proposed action is morally right. It does not depend on consequences, and it is not relative to varying circumstances. It is a simple procedure. All it requires is that we hesitate before we act and ask ourselves one vital question: *Would it be okay for everyone else to do this?*

A person temporarily down on his luck sees a drunken man weaving his way down the street. A wallet falls out of the man's pocket without his noticing; he continues on his way. The first man immediately picks it up and sees that it contains a considerable amount of money. The drunken man cannot, however, walk very fast, so it would be a simple matter to catch up with him and return the wallet.

The finder of the wallet is now like Glaucon's shepherd. He is invisible as far as the owner of the wallet is concerned. The temptation is strong to wait until the owner is well out of sight and then to disappear with the money. Why not? Who would return the money under those circumstances? Suppose now the finder of the wallet convinces himself he has been unjustly treated by society and deserves whatever he can get. It's a dog-eat-dog world, is it not?

If faced with this example, Kant would surely not assume that the finder of the wallet, knowing deep down inside that keeping it is wrong, would shout for the owner to stop so he could return it. If he keeps the wallet, he is in fact making a definite choice between two options; he is deliberately choosing the immoral one.

But, you ask, how can we be certain that it *is* immoral? Just because the man has been taught by his family and church that keeping what does not belong to him is stealing? Suppose he does not accept this view. He has already convinced himself the world is amoral and anything goes. And so the wallet is not returned, and no one is the wiser for it.

The story, however, does not end there. Having decided to spend some of the money for a sumptuous dinner and a comfortable hotel room, the man is walking down a deserted street and is accosted by a thief who, brandishing a weapon, demands his wallet. The man complies, the thief disappears, leaving him once more homeless and hungry. Would he be bitter? Would he denounce the thief? Or would he say to himself, "It serves you right"?

In Kantian terms, the latter response is indeed possible, but not probable. The chances are good that the finder of the wallet would be furious about the theft.

Translating his anger into philosophical terms, he would, in effect, be saying to himself: *It was all right for me to keep the wallet, but wrong for the thief to steal it from me. I am special.* If we agree that keeping the wallet is stealing, then what is the difference between the first and second thefts? The answer: none. The first thief's reasoning strikes us as absurd. Kant tells us that before we commit an act we need to ask ourselves whether it would be universally acceptable for everyone to do so. If we regard ourselves as the only exception to a moral law that applies to everyone except us, we are swept away in a vortex of nonlogic.

Kant's theory is ingenious, we must admit. In all probability none of us leads a morally perfect life, but that does not excuse us from willing that everything we do is universally acceptable. And this is a tough act to carry off.

Religion and Morality

Kant's parents were deeply religious, teaching that moral laws were set forth by God and could not be altered. As Kant grew older and learned about new theories in science and philosophy, he used reason rather than religion to justify moral principles. For many, however, religion remains a strong moral force. Though some of us may have subsequently entertained moral alternatives, we probably hear the whispers of those early teachings whenever we are faced with a moral evaluation of an act.

> *"Good laws lead to the making of better ones; bad ones bring about worse."*
>
> **—Jean-Jacques Rousseau**

The major world religions—Hinduism, Judaism, Christianity, and Islam—provide moral orientation for most of the world's population. They differ in many respects; all of them, however, share moral precepts. Their followers believe that the world was not created for human beings to do with as they please. Their followers believe that human beings owe an obligation to either a personal God or to the moral order governing the universe. Their followers believe none are free to behave irresponsibly toward themselves (since they did not create themselves), toward others, and toward the earth (which they did not create either).

Basic moral codes for Western societies derive, wholly or partly, from the Ten Commandments, recorded in the Hebrew Bible as delivered by God to Moses as he led his people out of slavery in Egypt. The Commandments

1. require people to recognize only one God
2. forbid the making and worshiping of any graven image
3. forbid the taking of the Lord's name in vain
4. require that the Sabbath be kept holy
5. require that people honor their parents
6. forbid killing
7. forbid adultery
8. forbid stealing
9. forbid the bearing of false witness against another
10. forbid the coveting of another's wife and of another's goods

Most of the commandments have parallels all over the world. Rules against adultery are often legally enforced—sometimes with the death penalty. Rules against killing and stealing are part of a universal criminal code. It is taken for granted that everyone lies for one reason or another, but it is hard to imagine any society in which lying itself is not condemned.

The first four commandments are not found in law books, although some U.S. communities still have so-called blue laws requiring businesses to be closed on

Sunday or at least preventing the sale of beer and liquor in the morning, when people are expected to worship. Nor are there universal rules for how to honor one's parents.

From its beginning, Hebrew moral law served to remind the powerful that they were not exempt from obeying God's commands. Biblical prophets were not afraid to confront sinners no matter how exalted their rank, as when Nathan denounced King David for doing away with the husband of Bathsheba, whom David wished to marry. Biblical scholar Huston Smith describes the democratizing effect of the Commandments:

> *Social as well as individual transgressions were denounced by the prophets. The prerequisite of political stability is social justice. . . . Stated theologically the point reads: God has high standards. Divinity will not put up forever with exploitation, corruption, and mediocrity. . . . One thing is common to all [the prophets]: the conviction that every human being, simply by virtue of his or her humanity, is a child of God and therefore in possession of rights that even kings must respect.*[6]

Hebrew moral law is concerned primarily with actions based on principles. It places limitations, for example, on what an injured party may demand for revenge. "An eye for an eye and a tooth for a tooth" prevents restitution from being more than what was lost in the original crime. Christianity accepted Hebrew laws and added restrictions against evil intents, not just acts, and harboring ill will toward others. The Sermon on the Mount tells us: "Ye have heard that it hath been said, an eye for an eye and a tooth for a tooth. But I say unto you, That ye resist not evil, but whosoever shall smite thee on the right cheek, turn to him the other also" (Matthew 5:38–39).

The commandment to turn the other cheek was already foreshadowed in the Buddhist moral treatise *Dhammapada*: "'He abused me, he beat me, he defeated me, he robbed me'—in those who harbor such thoughts hatred will never cease. For hatred does not cease to be hatred at any time; hatred ceases by love—that is an old rule."[7]

In general, Islam requires its followers to observe the biblical laws, for Mohammed declared that both Moses and Jesus were true prophets (see Chapter 10). He stressed especially the doctrine of brotherhood and placing the interests of others before one's own. He also warned enemies of God not to attack or persecute the devout.

Punishment for disobedience to scriptural laws varies from religion to religion, as do promised rewards for leading a virtuous existence. Hebrew morality focuses on family and community. Disobedience can result in ostracism; leading an exemplary life brings inner peace as well as good repute in the community. After death the good person lives on in the happy memories of friends and family or, for some believers, in the world to come.

Islam fosters the belief that after death the virtuous children of Allah will be with him in paradise, a sentiment echoed in Christianity. Christian concepts of heaven for the blessed and hell for the damned evolved slowly. The Christian Bible's Gospel of Luke reports the dialogue between Jesus and one of the thieves who were also being crucified. The thief refers to the "kingdom" to which Jesus will go after death: "And he said unto Jesus, 'Lord, remember me when thou comest into thy kingdom.' And Jesus said unto him, 'Verily I say unto thee, Today shalt thou be with me in paradise'" (Luke 23:42–43).

"Paradise" is variously interpreted. Does it mean a state of freedom from pain, similar to the Hindu moksha and the Buddhist *nirvana*? The promise that the thief would be "with" Jesus, however, may indicate that the reference is to continuing life in a definite place.

The Influence of Dante and Milton on Western Morality

As Christianity developed and spread, the promise of joy for the virtuous in heaven and eternal torment in hell for the damned became increasingly ingrained in Western religious minds. Vivid images of heaven and hell in *The Divine Comedy* by Dante Alighieri (1265–1321) strongly influenced how many people thought—and still think—of rewards and punishments for sin. (The term "comedy" is used in the sense of "not tragic"; the work ends on a note of joy when the poet-narrator finally sees God.)

The vivid images of heaven and hell in Dante's Divine Comedy *have strongly influenced how many think of rewards and punishments after death.*

Dante pictures hell, or the Inferno, as a deep pit in which the souls of sinners endure degrees of endless pain, depending on the gravity of their offense. Punishment takes place on seven separate circles, not all of which are fiery. Though in the popular mind hell is associated with flames, in actuality the lowest circle in Dante's hell, home of Satan—the worst offender of all—is described by the poet as a lake of thick ice representing a total lack of feeling and a total absence of love.

Purgatory is a mountain on which live those guilty of less grievous sins, those who will eventually ascend to Paradise, the abode of God, the angels, and the souls of the righteous. Paradise consists of nine circles of heaven arranged in a hierarchy of blessedness—from ordinary good people to martyrs and saints. The abode of God is the tenth heaven (ten being considered a perfect number), only glimpsed by the poet, who is unable to describe in detail his mystic vision.

Naturally enough, this drama of sin, punishment, and redemption has inspired writers, artists, and philosophers for centuries. The thought of hell's torments incites as much anger as fear and perennially gives rise to the age old question of why humankind must be punished for sins that were predestined. In addition, the sinner has proved a more durable figure for writers than the virtuous person, even as in popular entertainment the bad guys tend to be more interesting than the good guys.

The classic example of moral ambiguity is the treatment of Satan, called Lucifer in John Milton's epic poem *Paradise Lost* (1667). Milton (1608–1674) declares at the outset that his purpose in writing the poem is to "justify the ways of God to men." Like Hawthorne after him, he was raised in the strict Puritan faith, which painted a portrait of a God perpetually angry at his sinful children yet required a belief that their sins were predestined. The three main characters are Adam, Eve, and Lucifer. We learn that before creation Lucifer had been one of the angels in closest attendance to God, that he became jealous of God's power and organized an unsuccessful rebellion. He and his cohorts were banished from heaven and allowed to live in a dark palace called Pandemonium. There Lucifer becomes a powerful ruler, exulting in his authority and embodying many admirable traits of the defiant individualist. Shaking his fist toward heaven, he cries out that he "would rather reign in Hell than serve in Heaven." Scholars and historians of the humanities continue to debate whether Lucifer is really the hero of the poem.

Huntington Library/SuperStock

William Blake, *Satan Watching the Endearments of Adam and Eve*, c. 1816–25

In this famous picture from William Blake's illustrations for *Paradise Lost*, Lucifer (or Satan) watches the innocent affection between Adam and Eve before the temptation.

The argument that Milton intended Lucifer to be despicable does not convince everyone, even though as the serpent in the garden he eventually loses his heroic qualities. Nor is everyone convinced that the poet entirely makes his point when he tells us that God gave Lucifer free access to human beings in order to tempt them into sin. Milton's God said he wanted no more rebellion in Heaven and so created the race of mortals capable of either sinning or choosing virtue. In this way, only the good would live eternally with God. Milton described the fall of humankind as "fortunate," for the disobeying of divine law required the sacrifice of Jesus. Without original sin, in other words, the path to redemption would never have been revealed.

The morality set forth by religion is exceedingly complex and ever open for discussion and debate, but nevertheless remains a powerful force that helps many understand the agonizing questions in the world today.

The Morality of Work

In the Western world, most of us are taught religious moral codes; in addition, when we go to work for a living, we come under the influence of other kinds of rules. Even before we leave school, we have learned the importance of work. Relatives ask, "What are you going to be when you grow up?" Before we know it, we *have* grown up to face the second question asked at introductions, "What do you do?" With rare exceptions, we are defined according to the answer. Good and bad acquire the connotation of important versus unimportant jobs.

> *"A work life that denies our individuality, our creativity, our moral and aesthetic sensibility is one that denies our dignity as human beings."*
>
> **—Jerome M. Egal**

Studs Terkel on Work

The workplace is for many people, increasingly so nowadays, the means to the good life. As they describe their work, Studs Terkel found, people reveal cherished values, which are also the basis for making decisions. In his 1974 book *Working,* Terkel (1912–2008) records interviews with a variety of workers. One man, the driver of a city garbage truck, speaks with approval of people who take care of their property and disapproval of those who throw garbage out the window. Nor does he approve of the spotters who enforce the rules, the ones who "turn you in for stopping for coffee. . . . But if you're watched continually, you're gonna lay down. . . ." He is concerned with public disregard for his job, with jokes like "How's business picking up?" He knows his kids "would just love to see me doing something else." He tells them there's nothing to be ashamed of. It's a good job. They're not stealing money, are they? "You have everything you need."

A professional hockey player described for Terkel the thrill of being on the ice when an audience of 20,000 gave the team an ovation—and the disappointment of being fired at age 22. He described how his teammates respond to violence.

> *If you get hurt, the other players switch off. Nobody's sympathetic. When you get hurt, they don't look at you, even players on your own team. . . . You don't want to think too much about it.*[8]

He knows that, to the team owner, he's "a piece of property," and cynically observes that the team doctor says he is ready to play even though his shoulder is not yet healed. If the shoulder rips during the game, the player knows the owners are not acting immorally. They are following the rules of a particular workplace, and the players have to accept them.

In an altruistic world, the sanitation truck driver would be credited with good judgment about when to stop for a break, and hockey club owners would express genuine sympathy for an injured player.

Firm believers in the morality of self-interest argue that economics is at the heart of all speculation about work. When unemployment is low, people are needed and are treated better because the laws of supply and demand rule here as they do everywhere else. Others who look beyond self-interest claim that respect, creativity, and idealism are not isolated phenomena but can be found in places never dreamed of by the realists—even in the workplace. Those who believe in altruism insist there are workers taking pride in doing the best possible job for the sake of doing it and want to help fellow workers do *their* best.

Unemployment statistics are reported daily along with gains and losses in the stock market. For job seekers, times of prosperity have offered the opportunity to search for a career that matches their talents and desires. Not finding one has tarnished their sense of self-worth. When the economy takes a downturn, "liking" a job can seem a luxury. *Having* one—almost *any* one—becomes the goal. With job scarcity, too, comes a moral dilemma for workers who know when safety is imperiled (as on an oil rig) and that false claims are all too often made for consumer products. What had seemed "right" can be trumped by an understood need for profit and also by the realization that keeping silent is often the only way to survive.

Moral Relativism

If the opposite of *relative* is *absolute,* it is easy to understand the appeal of the former, a term that promises flexibility and tolerance, versus the latter, which connotes rigid certainty and judgment against nonbelievers. Moral relativists point out that prison, torture, and even genocide have been inflicted by those who are sure there is only one truth and they know what it is. The temptation is great to reject theories that place unwavering restrictions on us. According to moral relativists, beliefs about right and wrong have no universal meaning. It is therefore possible to make (and hear) remarks such as these:

> *"Morality consists of suspecting other people of not being legally married."*
>
> **—George Bernard Shaw**

> "Well, who has the right to tell another what to do? A lot of trouble has been caused by people who were sure they *had* this right."
>
> "It all depends on the situation, the culture, and the times in which a choice is made."

Many of the moral philosophers we have studied helped build a case for absolutism. After all, Socrates believed right and wrong were the same for everyone. Kant believed in an inborn moral imperative. Even Bentham's moral mathematics are not relative to the wishes of the minority who don't belong to the "greatest number" in an important decision. Moral relativists, on the other hand, maintain that right and wrong must be defined within a given context that may or may not include the greatest number.

That context could be the workplace, the community, the family, the educational establishment, or a person's religion or community. Each of these areas governing human behavior may impose absolute standards, but the standards are not always harmonious with each other. Bitter clashes result when two absolutes refuse to give ground: religious laws and those of the community at large, for example.

The Global View

A major factor in the rise of **moral relativism** is the globalized concept of society. New communication technologies continue to shrink the size of the world, and exposure to the customs and values of cultures different from our own inevitably widens the issue of morality. Many cultural observers now argue that the appeal to absolute reason by Socrates and Kant, among others, was narrowly Western. It isn't that other cultures are thought of as not being rational; rather, it is the recognition that, while reason itself may be universally shared, ideas and values arrived at rationally are also influenced by culture, traditions, and circumstances.

Still, some people argue that aboriginal natives, for example, would be better off learning to succeed in the dominant culture, learning its ways and following its rules of behavior. The relativist, on the other hand, points out that the imposition of dominant-culture values causes breakdowns in both individuals and families. In 1959, American novelist James Michener wrote *Hawaii*, a fictionalized account of what actually happened when missionaries from the United States told native Polynesians their sexual morality was unacceptable to civilized people. They condemned immodest clothing, premarital sex, and incest, assuring the "guilty" that they were damned forever. (One "guilty" man felt such shame that he ended his life.)

> "Everybody always did our thinking for us."
>
> —**Winifred Jourdain**

In an example from another part of the world, "The schools took us from our parents and taught us that the ways of our people were shameful and wrong," claims a Cree Indian in a lawsuit alleging cultural abuse in a church-run boarding school supported by the Canadian government. She argued that efforts to make natives assimilate into "white" Canada were wrong, that being forced to learn English, adopt Christianity, and acquire "suitable" job skills led to heavy drinking and domestic disharmony and to the loss of her native tongue and traditions.

The problem offers no easy solutions. Some principles taught in early childhood are so deeply ingrained that they motivate actions throughout life and conflict with those in a different society. An American living in Japan once held a birthday party for her five-year-old son; many of the invited children were Japanese. During a game of musical chairs, the American father noticed that when the music stopped a little Japanese girl stood next to an empty chair but did not sit down.

> *So Gregory scrambled into her seat, and Chitose-chan beamed proudly at her own good manners. Then I walked over and told her that she had just lost the game and would have to sit out. She gazed up at me, her luminous eyes full of shocked disbelief, looking like Bambi might after a discussion of venison burgers. "You mean I lost because I'm polite?" Chitose-chan's eyes asked. "You mean the point of the game is to be rude?" Well now that I think of it, I guess that is the point. American kids are taught to be winners, to seize their opportunities and maybe the next kid's as well. Japanese children are taught to be good citizens, to be team players, to obey rules, to be a mosaic tile in some larger design.*[9]

In a real-life incident involving the moral gulf between cultures, the mother of an Asian visual arts student in an American school refused to give permission for her sixteen-year-old son to attend a life-drawing class in which nude female models posed. The department head later reported attempting to "reason" with the woman, who obstinately held her ground, insisting that her son was being unfairly forced to violate a strict moral principle. Given the ultimatum that the child take the required course or leave the school, she withdrew the boy and enrolled him the next day in a neighborhood school that offered no arts courses. A moral relativist might have wondered whether the art world had been thus deprived of a potentially major talent.

Another source of dispute is a school ban on students wearing head coverings indicating religious affiliations. In order to have a cohesive student body, school officials in some European countries forbid the distinctive Islamic scarf but are often inconsistent about other religious symbols such as those worn as jewelry. Immigrant students who abandon public school secularism for religious school may be encouraged to accept further separation from the dominant culture of the host country through a different set of heroes, villains, and explanations for historical events. In many cases, objectivity is indeed an elusive goal.

Cultural traditions and generational differences exist uneasily side by side: an "assimilated" child impatient with a grandparent's old-world cooking; young people unwilling to accept traditional matchmaking; a religious teenager clashing with agnostic parents. Can the relativist position solve all conflicts by claiming that universal right and wrong are outmoded concepts? Are some moral issues simply a matter of taste, like one's preference for chocolate ice cream?

Moral relativism is attractive to those who believe in tolerance and avoidance of authoritarian excesses, which can take the form of judging foreign customs and religions according to one's own standards. Almost every part of the world is now available to travelers and Internet users, and this increased contact with other cultures may lead to the rejection of a belief that indisputable morality is the exclusive property of one group. Tolerance for the customs of the Cree, for example, would have prevented the conflicts described earlier.

An offshoot of cultural relativism is that what used to be respect for the values of others can turn into the belief that there are *no* absolute values, that no truth can be accepted the world over. In our personal lives, we can see how we view events differently as we mature and age. What frightens children seems benign to adults, just as some of the scandals of one age seem harmless in later times. If a good many moral viewpoints inevitably change, do we then abandon the idea of universal values altogether? What happens to those who stand firm in their belief that they have found the one, the only, the unchanging truth? For them, the suggestion that they respect competing beliefs is heresy! Or does "democratic society" mean places must be found for diametrically opposed beliefs?

Travelers may be delighted to observe cultures different from those in their home country—otherwise why travel at all? If nothing else, the strange customs provide one more story for travelers to tell when they return home. One may be charmed by unexpected hospitality or a gift offered by a merchant at a bazaar, or intrigued by meeting a man accompanied by more than one wife. One is less charmed by seeing brutality and abuse, no matter how traditional the custom is said to be. Child prostitution, genital mutilation, and abandonment of unwanted family members (including those who have lived beyond an age considered reasonable by a given community) are among the practices that horrify observers suddenly unwilling to be moral relativists.

A prime example of moral relativism in action is found in a prize-winning film from Iceland, *The Seagull's Laughter* (2003). The central character is Agga, a teenage girl and amateur sleuth, who suspects that an abused wife has murdered her brutal husband, assisted in the crime by family members. She goes to the police and tells them about all of the clues she has gathered to confirm her suspicions. The police agree to investigate. Agga then has a change of heart, realizing what will happen after the arrest: money would be lost, and a disabled family member would have to be institutionalized. She returns to the police station, announcing she has made up the stories. In her case, the end—peace and prosperity in a poor household—justified the means: allowing the murderer to get away with her crime. The absolutist position is that justice must be served by punishment of all murderers regardless of extenuating circumstances.

Moral relativism, of course, has a few absolutes of its own. The whole institution of the defense attorney in our society rests on the assumption that everyone deserves a fair trial. The attorney's personal opinion about the guilt or innocence of his client is immaterial. Presumably, a person does not take on such a role without believing in the relativity of right and wrong. This, for the attorney, is an acceptable absolute.

Moral relativism of a different sort has arisen during the past four decades from philosophers and cultural historians all over the world who point out that cultural, religious, and literary traditions—whether expressing absolutist or relativistic values—have been dominated by the male viewpoint. In some cases, this coincides with the female viewpoint, but all too often it does not. The discrepancy, they say, is especially obvious in the low esteem accorded to women in many areas of the globe. Restrictions on dress, education, travel, and even expressions of personal feelings continue to exist, though old rules are gradually eroding in many cultures.

> *"I have yet to hear a man ask for advice on how to combine marriage and a career."*
>
> **—Gloria Steinem**

We have said from the outset that being human is an art, and nowhere is that assumption more crucial than in moral matters. You can decide that you are a fully realized human being if you get everything you can from life regardless of how others are affected. You can also decide that moral integrity—doing what you know is right regardless of how you do or don't profit—is the mark of a fully realized human being. There are risks involved, to be sure. The risk of running afoul of someone else's moral code, enforced by bully tactics, is and has always been there. But a ringing declaration in the humanities is that moral integrity is worth the risk. Gambling on integrity may be basic to the human condition in its finest hour.

LEARNING OBJECTIVES

Having read and carefully studied this chapter, you should be able to:

1. Distinguish between the definition of morality recommended by the text and a popular, not recommended definition.
2. List five major questions often asked in moral philosophy and indicate which is most important to you.
3. Briefly summarize the moral argument between Glaucon and Socrates.
4. Relate Swift's "A Modest Proposal" to self-interest as a moral philosophy.
5. Compare and/or contrast Machiavelli and Hobbes relative to enlightened self-interest.
6. Summarize Adam Smith's concept of *laissez-faire* and indicate whether it remains relevant.
7. Explain what John Rawls means by the "Veil of Ignorance" relative to altruism.
8. Distinguish between the utilitarianism of Bentham and Mill.
9. Explain and present an example of Kant's "Categorical Imperative."
10. Explain and present an example of a moral gulf between cultures.

KEY TERMS

altruism the quality of acting out of concern for the welfare of others rather than one's own.

capitalism economic system based on Adam Smith's philosophy that if people are allowed to make as much money as they can, others will profit also.

categories according to Immanuel Kant, mental "compartments" that we are born with which allow us to interpret data from the senses; an inborn sense of reason makes it possible to understand spatial relationships (nextness) as well as the morality or immorality of actions.

Categorical Imperative in Kantian philosophy, the inborn capacity to understand right and wrong when faced with moral decisions; one of the categories, or mental "compartments."

enlightened self-interest condition in which rulers (or other persons who have power) impose their own moral values out of a belief that people under them are better off than if they were free to make their own choices.

laissez-faire French phrase meaning "allow to do"; an economic policy fundamental to Adam Smith's philosophy that allows businesses to operate with little or no government control.

Machiavellian now a negative term, pertaining to the manipulation of others through duplicity; derived from Machiavelli's theory of government that, to ensure order in society, advocates a leader with almost unlimited power.

moral an adjective indicating a choice between significant options, based on principles derived from reading, family teachings, education, religion, or law.

moral mathematics a scientific system of moral choice, advocated by Jeremy Bentham, based on projected quantifiable positive or negative results.

moral relativism the belief that moral standards are not universal, but rather depend on time, culture, and situation.

moral system a network of beliefs that can form the basis on which a moral choice is made, e.g. religion, laws, or Socratic reasoning.

morality the system by which significant choices are made; in popular usage, the user's sense of right conduct, so that a given person is said to be or not be "moral."

utilitarianism moral philosophy that can revolve around the greatest good for the greatest number or what makes the most sense to rational people, regardless of whether or not they constitute a majority.

TOPICS FOR WRITING AND DISCUSSION

1. If, as has been said, morality begins in the home, what happens to someone who has been given a strong moral upbringing only to go out into the world and discover that it is the clever, not the good, people who generally succeed?
2. Strong family opposition to a son's or daughter's choice of a marriage partner can result (and has resulted) in exclusion or even an "honor" killing. These are extreme cases, but what can be said for or against tradition (family, religious, or social) as major factors in individual choices?
3. A dramatic example of the conflict between the law and differing moral systems is the issue of the death penalty. Write a short paper in which you:
   a. summarize the rationale behind the death penalty as held by its proponents;
   b. summarize a major argument that has been advanced in opposition to it; and
   c. present and defend your own view.
4. After Socrates was sentenced to death, his followers urged him to escape and flee Athens. He was being held in a minimum security prison that would have made escape relatively easy. He refused. Pretend instead that he agonized over the choice and asked first Bentham, then Kant, for advice. Indicate what each philosopher would have recommended. Then present and defend your own view.
5. The arts were discussed as a source of moral values. Cite a play, movie, or television show you have seen recently that you believe suggests a recommended moral choice. How convincing do you think it was?
6. You are the mayor of a local government that has commissioners split evenly on the question of how a tax revenue surplus should be spent. You listen to the arguments of citizens who urge you to decide in favor of a new arts center with spaces for rehearsals and performances of dance, theater, and music. Other citizens point to a survey which shows that the majority prefers a new sports arena. You have studied and been impressed by Mill's ideas. The commissioners are tied; you have the tie-breaking vote.
7. Look again at Hogarth's picture of *The Enraged Musician.* Whose side do you think Hogarth is on: the noisy crowd or the musician's? Whose side would Bentham be on? John Stuart Mill?
8. You go to a supermarket with friends, who begin to remove the price labels fastened to the shelf under some items, replacing them with lower price labels taken from underneath other items. They intend to tell the cashier that the computer must have made a mistake and they will only pay the price on the shelf. You are torn between group loyalty and the conviction that what they are doing is morally wrong. Still, you consider the store's pricing structure sometimes unreasonably excessive and it deserves this sleight of hand. But fortunately, you have read this chapter and know something about options offered by major philosophers. What would Socrates do? Glaucon? What might a feminist philosopher suggest?
9. Imagine that a close friend who works part-time in a drugstore tells you she knows for a fact that the manager is charging affluent customers far more than other places do. But she is afraid that if she tells anyone and that person complains to the manager, she would lose her job. What would you advise?

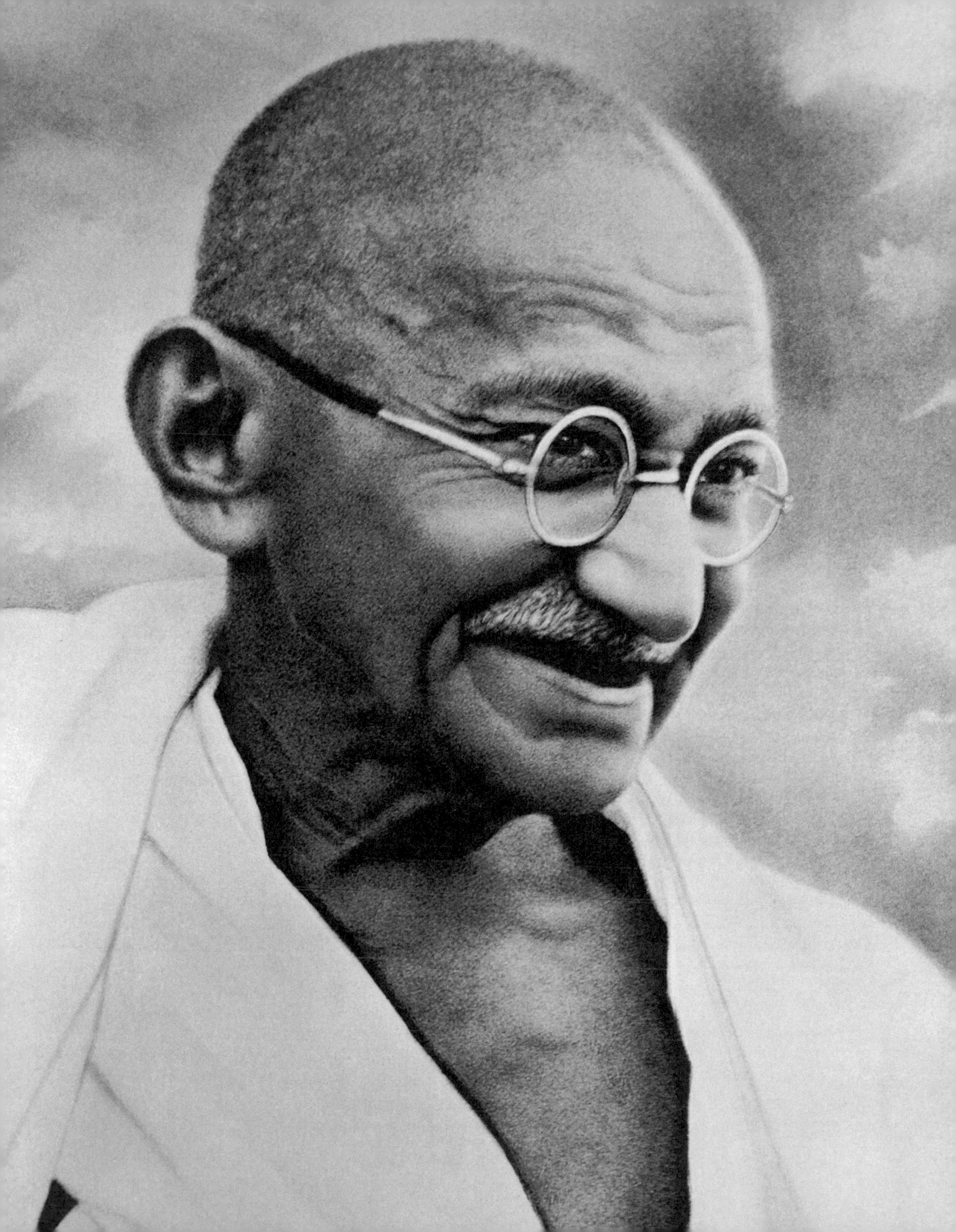

Chapter 12

Happiness

The search for happiness is high on the list of themes in the humanities. There aren't many works about people richly satisfied with their lives. The majority of literary, dramatic, and cinematic works deal with unhappy people and either end sadly, all happiness denied, or conclude with a manipulated happy ending so that viewers or readers may see the world as it should be, not as they know it is. Some of the most memorable characters have been rich people; and even if they are left with their fortunes, they may be regretting the loss of something or someone they hadn't realized was so important to them.

The 2010 widely acclaimed film *The Social Network* is based on the career of Mark Zuckerberg, billionaire creator and owner of Facebook. For most viewers he invites pity for his apparent lack of ability to form lasting friendships. A fictional predecessor is *Citizen Kane* (see Chapter 9), who dies still longing for the simplicity of his childhood.

Moral philosophy, in addition to its concern for defining good and bad actions, also engages in exhaustive analysis of what makes life good and therefore happy. For most of us, analysis seems beside the point. Doesn't everyone want to be happy? Yet how easy is it to attain? Would we know it if it came our way? What is it anyway?

The word "happy" dates back to our earliest memories. It is written in cake frosting, shouted at midnight on New Year's Eve, and invoked during wedding receptions. Are we using the right word when we claim to be happy for a friend's decision to cancel a wedding or leave school? We say, "Oh well, as long as they're happy," as though that's all there is to it.

Is pleasure what makes life good, therefore happy? Or is it based on the observance of strict moral principles, obeyed even if it means a loss of pleasure? Is life happiest when we are praised by others? Or when someone we envy suddenly falls from the pedestal? Is joy equivalent to happiness? Can we be happy *without* joy? The humanities offer many possibilities.

◀ **Mahatma Gandhi, c. 1940s**

Even under persistent adversity, Mahatma Gandhi exemplified what Aristotle would have considered a happy life.

Bettmann/Corbis

Hedonism: Happiness as Pleasure

> *O happiness! Our being's end and aim!*
> *Good, pleasure, ease, content!*
> *Whate'er thy name:*
> *That something still which prompts the eternal sigh,*
> *For which we bear to live or dare to die.*
>
> **—Alexander Pope**

The Greek philosopher Aristippus (435–356 B.C.E.) declared happiness to be the *sum total of pleasures experienced during one's lifetime.* He thought of pleasure in purely physical terms: taste, sexual excitement, touch, and so on. He admitted that a certain amount of satisfaction comes with the knowledge, for example, that one's country is faring well, but nothing mental compares with physical comfort. Bodily pain is far worse than mental pain, and therefore bodily pleasure is better than mental pleasure. People, he said, are by nature selfish animals, concerned solely with their own comfort. He asked the question that has been around for centuries: *Is anything greater than being happy?* He said no, and added that if it were not pleasure, saying you were happy would mean nothing.

The writings of Aristippus have not survived, but a historian named Diogenes Laertius, living in the third century C.E., has provided a detailed summary of his philosophy of pleasure. He pointed out that Aristippus proved his argument by noting that from the time they were capable of making choices between available options people always selected the one that provided the most pleasure and the least amount of pain. Home and society might try to teach less selfish values, but instinct prevailed in the end.

Thus, if Aristippus is right, people prefer not to work, but do so only because what they earn can provide them with pleasure. There is no satisfaction in work for its own sake. As a matter of fact, Aristippus believed there was no satisfaction in even the memory or anticipation of pleasure. Nothing counted except what could be experienced at the moment.

Hedonism (from the Greek for "delight") is the name given to the philosophy that happiness is equivalent to physical pleasure and to the possession of things that provide us with pleasure. Hedonism has survived for thousands of years, substantially unchanged from its inception.

> *Regardless of time and place human beings cherish a common desire for happiness and a wish to avert suffering.*
>
> **—The Dalai Lama**

The artist Diego Velázquez (1599–1660) has given us one of the best visual representations of hedonism in *Los Borrachos* (The Drunkards). The laughing figure on the left is Bacchus, the god of wine, whose associate is bestowing a garland of grape leaves on the kneeling figure. The work seems to make comic reference to the traditional honoring of a hero with a laurel wreath. Even so, the painting allows viewers to place their own interpretation on the scene. To the dedicated hedonist, the pleasure obviously being experienced by the men may be all that is necessary for achieving the highest state of happiness.

Interfoto/Alamy

Diego Velázquez, *Los Borrachos*, 1629

To the dedicated hedonist, the pleasure experienced by these fun-loving men is all that is necessary for pure happiness.

The Greek society in which Aristippus lived may have produced Socrates, Plato, and Aristotle, who spent their lives in thought, but it was also highly receptive to the idea that hedonism was based on human nature. In fact, both Plato and Aristotle addressed the subject, disagreeing with the views of Aristippus but acknowledging the popular appeal of his ideas. In his famous analysis of love Plato does not discredit the pleasures of sex but elevates nonphysical love to a position of greater importance. While Aristippus excludes intellectual pleasure, Plato and Aristotle believe it is one of the defining graces of a fully realized life. Aristotle developed a philosophy of happiness vastly different from that of Aristippus, as we shall see later in this chapter.

Literary Hedonism

Between the austere Middle Ages and the time of the militantly rigid Puritans—both periods of strict moral codes—poets, including Shakespeare, celebrated the "eat, drink, and be merry" life of the hedonist. One of the most famous declarations is this widely welcomed piece of poetic advice from Robert Herrick (1591–1674):

Gather ye rose-buds while ye may,
Old time is still a-flying
And this same flower that smiles today
Tomorrow may be dying.

Another name given to the hedonist view is **carpe diem** (from the Latin for "seize the day"). While the advice is rooted in Aristippus, it has had numerous applications through the ages. For some, it means doing the most with their potential; it means reaching for the stars. For others, such as Omar Khayyam in *The Rubáiyát*, it means, as it does in Herrick, have all you can during your brief lifetime.

((● **Listen** on **MyHumanitiesKit.com**
Khayyam, *The Rubáiyát*

A contemporary of Herrick, Andrew Marvell (1621–1678), makes a plea to a special person he is intent on seducing in a poem called "To His Coy Mistress."

Had we but world enough, and time,
This coyness, lady, were no crime.
We would sit down and think which way
To walk and pass our long love's day.

If he had forever to woo her, the poet adds, he would spend a hundred years praising her eyes, two hundred for each breast, and "thirty thousand to the rest."

But at my back I always hear
Time's wingèd chariot hurrying near.
And yonder all before us lie
Deserts of vast eternity.
Thy beauty shall no more be found,
Nor, in thy marble vault, shall sound
My echoing song: then worms shall try
That long preserv'd virginity:
And your quaint honour turn to dust,
And into ashes all my lust.
The grave's a fine and private place,
But none I think do there embrace.

Many people are proud to call themselves hedonists, boasting of their income and their possessions. They assert that with only one chance to live, they should deny themselves nothing and try to have it all. A bumper sticker proclaims: "He who dies with the most toys wins." Another boasts: "We're spending

"*Can it be that there was only one summer when I was ten?*"

—May Swenson

our grandchildren's inheritance." A current restatement of *carpe diem* is "Life is not a rehearsal. This is it!"

Hedonist Assumptions

For a hedonist, there never seems to be enough pleasurable moments in life. There seems to be so much undeserved pain. "Why me?" is a frequent question both openly and silently asked. "When am I going to get *my* chance to be happy?"

So the first hedonist assumption is that *everyone deserves as much pleasure as possible.* A variant of this assumption is that people *never really get as much pleasure as they deserve.* Other people always appear to have more. Those believed to have more may communicate—even exaggerate—their pleasures, especially unexpected raises, which point out how truly deserving they really are. Those without raises perpetuate the myth that the undeserving are getting more from life.

A second assumption, vitally related to the first, is that *pleasure is automatically good.* In unprosperous times, when some are barely eating enough to get by, those who can eat anything they want are undoubtedly envied. No one feels sorry for the affluent people who might overeat and overdrink!

> *"I fear not the uncleanness of meat but the uncleanness of desire."*
>
> **—Augustine**

Hedonists recognize that people cannot have pleasure every moment of their lives, but still they think they should. A third assumption, therefore, is that *no amount of pleasure is ever too much.* There may be a submerged feeling of guilt about gorging oneself in an "All U Can Eat" restaurant or downing one drink after another at somebody's open house, but the typical hedonist response is, "There will be time enough to cut down; don't bother me now." Besides, overindulgence in moments of plenty supposedly makes up for past disappointments.

A fourth hedonist assumption is that *the absence of pleasure is a misfortune for which compensation is due.* Many who attempt robbery believe they are only getting even with society. Those who carry the hedonist viewpoint through life find themselves plotting continually. "Just wait until *I* have the upper hand!" Since moments without definite feelings of pleasure are an abomination, they entertain themselves by thinking of the tine when they will finally gain "rightful" pleasure.

This particular mindset stems from the **big earnings theory**. An "earning" is considered the pleasure owed to a deserving person for services rendered or unpleasant chores completed. In the ledger that many hedonists carry inside themselves, there is a strict accounting of pleasures owed them; eventually a vast number may accumulate. Unless something happens to change their philosophy of happiness, these hedonists may become obsessed with thinking about pleasures due. If they are paid off, life is good; if not, life is bad. Life is evaluated strictly in terms of total payments received. An excellent life is one in which no big earning is left unrewarded.

Hedonism Reconsidered

> *"Too much of a good thing can be wonderful."*
>
> **—Mae West**

Hedonism has been subjected to ongoing critical appraisal by philosophers and cultural historians alike. The crux of their argument is whether the hedonist definition of pleasure is too limited. Fundamental hedonism is clear: pleasure is experienced through the five senses. People who spend time in thought are denying themselves that much pleasure and, therefore, that much happiness. People who devote their lives to working in a clinic a thousand miles from civilization, who expose themselves daily to the risk of disease without even the reward of outside recognition, are supposedly doing without pleasure. But how can we assume that such people are deliberately perverting their own natures to follow a calling that requires them to labor in the interest of others? Are those whose happiness is not derived from hedonism wasting their time or being cheated of the pleasure they secretly desire?

In describing a conversation with noted author Joseph Heller, the late novelist Kurt Vonnegut (1922–2007) reconsidered hedonism powerfully.

> *True story, Word of Honor.*
>
> *Joseph Heller, an important and funny writer now dead, and I were at a party given by a billionaire on Shelter Island. I said, "Joe, how does it make you feel to know that our host only yesterday may have made more money than your novel* Catch 22 *has earned in its entire history?"*
>
> *And Joe said, "I've got something he can never have."*
>
> *And I said, "What on earth could that be, Joe?"*
>
> *And Joe said, "The knowledge that I've got enough."*[1]

Mystics and members of religious orders who spend hours in prayer or silent meditation lose contact with the self in ways that the hedonist could never understand. Are they robbing themselves of the pleasure that their natures crave? Is it accurate to say that celibacy is necessarily a sublimation of normal sexual passion, as many contend? Or is human nature such that it cannot be narrowly defined? May sensory pleasure be all-sufficing for some and less fulfilling for others?

If, as existentialists (discussed in Chapter 16) maintain, no such thing as human nature exists at all and humanity is indeed a self-defining, self-determining species, then there is ample room for alternate ways of defining pleasure. Those who choose to do so are free to relegate pleasure to a low priority, in fact, without being "unnatural."

Epicureanism: Happiness Is Avoiding Pain

In a musical comedy some years back, the heroine, trying to explain to the audience in song why she adores the hero, compares her love to a number of familiar pleasures, including the smell of bread baking and the feeling she has when a tooth stops aching. In the first instance, she is a hedonist, directly sensual in her values. In the second, however, she turns to a different philosophy of happiness: **epicureanism**. The sudden cessation of a toothache brings happiness, according to this philosophy—*the happiness of not being in pain.*

Epicureanism is named for the Greek thinker Epicurus (c. 341–270 B.C.E.), who first formulated its precepts. Aware of Aristippus and his beliefs, Epicurus was highly critical of a philosophy he believed weak in logic and, more than that, impossible to follow.

Epicurean Assumptions

Epicurus accepted the initial premise of hedonism, that pleasure is a great good, but he added that it was not the only good. He refused to say with the hedonists that the more pleasure we have, the happier we are. "And since pleasure is the first good and natural to us, for this very reason we do not choose every pleasure, but sometimes we pass over many pleasures, when greater discomfort accrues to us as a result of them."[2]

Epicurus was particularly critical of those who recommended pleasures in excess, for these, he knew, would always be followed by both physical and moral pain. "For from prudence are sprung all the other virtues, and it teaches us that it is not possible to live pleasantly without living prudently and honourably and justly."[3]

> *Behind every cloud is another cloud.*
>
> **—Judy Garland**

For Epicurus, hedonism was a time-conscious, death-ridden philosophy. If happiness increases with the quantity of physical pleasure, then logically no life could ever be long enough. We are here for an uncertain amount of time, true, but all of us are subject to the infirmities that come with age—if indeed we do not burn ourselves out before age ever becomes a problem. Therefore hedonists are fundamentally insecure and unhappy, unable to escape the inevitability of age and death, always worrying about the loss of pleasure. Thus the major assumption of epicureanism is that nothing lasts forever and we must accept that fact cheerfully. If we are to define the good life, it is the wiser course of action not to believe that it consists only of pleasure.

Archibald MacLeish, whose poem "Ars Poetica" we studied in Chapter 4, accuses the hedonist Andrew Marvell of being so obsessed with the brevity of life and the thought of death that he could not enjoy life while he had it. MacLeish's "You, Andrew Marvell," begins with these lines

And here face down beneath the sun
And here upon earth's noonward height
To feel the always coming on
The always rising of the night.[4]

Another epicurean assumption is that no one can sustain pleasure over prolonged periods of time. We cannot indefinitely gorge ourselves on delicious food, indulge in sex, stay drunk. Why saddle ourselves then with a philosophy of life that is so limited from the very outset? Unable to satisfy our pleasure-seeking instincts perpetually, we do the next best thing: seek material possessions or fame, both of which symbolize happiness without *bringing* happiness. Money and fame are constantly in the hedonist's thoughts. They are the compensations of having to die. They are the only possible tangible embodiments of a successful life. When age makes physical pleasure less attainable, people turn to the accumulation of wealth. But Epicurus also recognized that the pursuit of wealth was self-defeating, futile. The same is true of insisting on fame: the wealthy or famous person feels insecure and distrustful of others, certain that others are envious and scheming.

Why, asked Epicurus, burden ourselves with a philosophy of built-in frustrations, disappointments, and inevitable pain? Why not rather change the requirements for the good life? He assumed people of reason had free will and could control their desire for pleasure, and therefore they could reduce the amount of pain that always follows pleasure. Complete happiness is a moderate amount of pleasure with freedom from pain—an unlikely scenario for most people, but one that can be more nearly realized as we exert our will not to suffer. To those who would ask, "Why may I not agree to the suffering as long as I have the pleasure?", the epicurean answers, "The anticipation of pain, if it is intense, detracts from the pleasure."

> *A real obstacle to happiness is to expect too much happiness.*
>
> **—Fontenelle**

Insofar as it recognizes the importance of pleasure in our lives, epicureanism is not so much an all-out attack on hedonism as a modification of it. Unpleasantness is part of life, the epicurean admits and therefore plans strategies to ward it off as much as possible rather than march forward in the blind hope that things are going to be fine. The worst that can happen when you anticipate pain is that you will not be disappointed. But clearly, you have a good chance of doing something about life's pain before it occurs *if* you apply yourself conscientiously to the task.

Exerting control and enjoying pleasure in moderation, epicureans share with hedonists delight in the taste of exquisite food—but epicureans, anticipating the pain of overindulgence, stop themselves before reaching their limit. They will drink, but never to the point of drunkenness, and not at all if they are certain their health will suffer.

A character in Ernest Hemingway's story "In Another Country" fully illustrates the epicurean outlook. Before going off to war, a major in the Italian army marries a beautiful woman considerably younger than he. He discovers she was unfaithful while he was fighting. Now, injured and confined to a hospital, he learns his wife has died of pneumonia. "She had been sick only a few days. No one expected her to die." The lesson he gleans from the tragedy is a lesson about how best to live. A man, he explains, should not marry.

> *"He cannot marry. He cannot marry," he said angrily. "If he is to lose everything, he should not place himself in a position to lose that. He should not place himself in a position to lose. He should find things he cannot lose."*[5]

> *"He should not place himself in a position to lose. He should find things he cannot lose."*
> **—Ernest Hemingway**

Confirmed epicureans avoid excess, seeking out many nonphysical pleasures. They are lovers of art, theater, books, and music, perhaps realizing the humanities represent treasures one "cannot lose." After all, intellectual and aesthetic pleasures do not lead to pain. Epicureans are typically lean and trim, exercising their bodies to keep in the best possible shape. They are mentally agile and aware of the latest development in many fields. They are good workers, and the one who finds a marital partner with a similar outlook is likely to build a reasonably happy relationship.

Epicureans are typically lean and trim, exercising their bodies to keep in the best possible shape. They are mentally agile and aware of the latest developments in many fields.

Pure hedonists, however, warn epicureans that they sell themselves too short and may often settle for less than they have a right to expect from life. The hedonist maintains that unless you work aggressively at being happy, you will give up too easily, spending too much time running away from pain that might not be there. Why not go for all you can and take your chances? The pure epicurean, however, might well answer with an old French song that says "the joys of love are but a moment long; the pain of love endures forever."

Epicureanism Reconsidered

One objection that can be raised to epicureanism is that it is as firmly rooted in self-interest as the philosophy from which it departs. It has been accused of being hedonism in a disguised form. In seeking to avoid pain, it may be saying indirectly that pleasure is really the goal. Does it merely redefine pleasure? In addition to the good feeling one gets from the absence of pain, are not the pleasures of reading and spending one's life with the arts ultimately selfish?

Thus another objection is that epicureans are more interested in their own peace of mind than in causes that help others. If not wishing to lose means detaching oneself from life as much as possible, any form of activism is off limits. Concern for one's neighbors, stressed in all of the world's major religions, is generally absent from the traditional epicurean outlook. To be sure, Aristippus and Epicurus belonged to the classical world, and most classical theories of happiness focus on the individual, as though happiness by *definition* were a matter of how one's own life is faring.

> *"Wisdom consists of the anticipation of consequences."*
>
> **—Norman Cousins**

We cannot rule out the possibility that happiness can be achieved only by working to combat pain wherever it is found, and sometimes the battle incurs personal suffering, which is accepted as the high price of success. After all, there are people, seldom mentioned in history books, who have voluntarily devoted their lives to nursing the sick in parts of the world ravaged by plagues and earthquakes, such as the one that ravaged Haiti in 2010. Maybe the new epicureanism seeks not only to avoid pain oneself but to do everything possible to help *others* avoid pain.

The cataclysmic events that befell New York and Washington, DC on September 11, 2001, and took almost 3,000 lives, had an effect quite different from the total chaos the terrorists may have planned. Instead of scattering to save themselves, hundreds of police and firefighters gave up their own lives in an attempt to rescue as many victims as they could. It is now apparent from cell phone calls made to loved ones before the collapse of the towers that a number of those who might have escaped stayed to help others, forfeiting their lives to do so. There are further indications that some of the passengers aboard Flight 93, which crashed in a Pennsylvania meadow, overpowered the hijackers and gave up their own lives in order to save perhaps thousands who might have died had the deadly mission been completed. Who is to say that dedicated epicureans would not, in moments of extreme crisis, forego all thoughts of self-interest? If someone survived by not trying to save another, would that individual lead a peaceful and contented life from that day on?

The cynic might say that social consciousness is only an extension of a principle stated by Epicurus: "The just man is most free from trouble." That is, happiness consists of an undisturbed conscience; if you want tranquility, you must sometimes labor in the interest of others.

Stoicism: Happiness as a Strategy for Survival

> *"The art of life is more like the wrestler's art than the dancer's. It should stand ready and firm to meet onsets which are sudden and unexpected."*
>
> **—Marcus Aurelius**

A famous poster shows a cat holding tightly to the knotted end of a rope and just hanging there in empty space. The caption reads: *When you come to the end of your rope, tie a knot and hang on.* This, in capsule form, is the philosophy of *stoicism*. It operates under even fewer illusions about life than does epicureanism. It tells us neither to plan ahead for a life of unlimited pleasure nor to expect to avoid pain through discipline and moderation. Stoicism asserts pain is intrinsic to living. The best possible course is to prepare for the worst and develop a technique for dealing with it. *Epicureans avoid pain; stoics cope.*

Stoic Assumptions

Stoicism sees the will as the means through which each of us can control our response to external events. Despite the disasters that may befall them, stoics believe in human reason. They believe it is reasonable to know that disasters—natural, social, personal—inevitably happen. Life just occurs. We make plans, but we cannot include happiness in those plans. As one philosopher put it: "Life is what happens while we are making other plans." Nor should we believe that all is chaos in the universe. If there is order in the human mind, there may be order in the universe as well, and the unpredictable things that happen may be *part* of that order. Recognizing this, we can see to it that the will is in tune with events as they occur. The sometimes despairing question "How can terrible things be part of any order?" may be irrelevant. Stoics contend disasters are possible to accept without emotion.

Stoicism was born over 2,000 years ago. Like hedonism and its modified offspring epicureanism, it is the product of Greek intellect; it lays heavy stress on human reason and the belief that humankind is the superior form of animal life. The philosophy of Zeno (335–264 B.C.E.), its first major advocate, is close in spirit to that of Plato and Aristotle.

The school founded by Zeno was located in a columned portico called a *stoa*—hence the name of the philosophy. Central to stoicism is the belief that true happiness is not a matter of circumstance, or good fortune, or of what happens to us, but rather a matter of *how we respond to what happens.* Happiness, like sorrow, is an idea, an attitude, not an object or an event. If no one welcomes the first day of spring, how can it be said that spring is a time of hope and joy? If in some remote civilization with unusual customs and mores the birth of a child were considered a dreadful curse, then the inability to produce offspring might be regarded as a happy stroke of luck.

To find the roots of unhappiness, we must look inward. Nothing is under our control except the way we think about things. Natural disasters, social upheavals, wars, revolutions, outbreaks of disease, rising crime rates—all happen as a result of either accidental or highly complicated causes. Our happiness should not depend on their *not* taking place. We cannot alter external circumstances, but we can decide not to feel negatively about them.

> *True instruction is this: to learn to wish that each thing should come to pass as it does.*
>
> **—Epictetus**

One of the best known stoic teachers was a Greek named Epictetus (50–130 C.E.), who was captured and enslaved by the Romans. His brilliance was eventually recognized and he was allowed to conduct classes. But prior to that, Epictetus was tortured and oppressed in his captivity. On one occasion his leg was broken on his master's whim. During this period of extreme suffering, Epictetus was faced with the choice of surrendering to despair or finding some means of enduring. He chose the latter course, recognizing that nothing, not even torture, was unbearable unless one wished to find it so. After his liberation, he dedicated his life to spreading the stoic creed, which had kept his spirit intact for so many years.

Stoicism later found ready acceptance among the Romans and became a sort of unofficial state philosophy. Its emphasis on reason and the control of negative emotions accorded well with the Roman ideal of the perfect human being. Rome was an empire-building civilization requiring a superbly disciplined military machine to carry out its conquests. It therefore found a meaningful application of stoic teachings: the rigors of military training as well as the hardships of war itself must never depress the human spirit. Good soldiers, with feelings well under control, must become indifferent to their own suffering.

When Christianity began to spread throughout the Roman Empire, many of the converts had already been exposed to stoic beliefs. The by-then ancient and honorable philosophy meshed with the outlook and needs of Christians, who had to face untold suffering including ongoing persecution, flight, starvation, and separation from loved ones. The stoic doctrine of inner control blended perfectly with the Christian belief that only the soul, not the body, mattered. One could endure all manner of pain and still be serene.

> *"Success is getting what you want; happiness is wanting what you get."*
>
> **—Anonymous**

Christian martyrdom was deeply rooted in stoic principles, especially the directives to love one's enemies and to turn the other cheek. A famous martyrdom is that of Thomas à Becket (1118–1170), the Archbishop of Canterbury and, as such, the pope's representative in England, sworn to carry out papal decrees and uphold Christian dogma. By the twelfth century, however, England was becoming a major world power, and the English monarchy assumed more and more authority, even in matters of religion. King Henry II, once Becket's friend, passed laws in direct violation of church canon. The pope was displeased and Becket, of course, sided with him, causing a dangerous rift between monarch and prelate. Late in 1170, Becket urged the pope to dismiss several bishops known to be on the king's side. The king then sent four knights to Canterbury with the king's command to restore the deposed bishops, but Becket refused. Knowing that he had probably signed his own death warrant, the archbishop went into the cathedral to pray.

While he was there, the knights returned, this time with an armed band. Becket's attendants saw them coming, shut the heavy doors and were about to lock them when the archbishop cried out, "God's house must be closed against no man." The assassins, thus given unchallenged entry, rushed to the altar, whereupon Becket made a ringing stoic declaration: "For the name of Jesus and for the defense of the Church, I am ready to embrace death." They fell upon him with their swords, and he was murdered on the altar. The scene was memorably recorded in the verse play *Murder in the Cathedral* (1935) by the American poet T. S. Eliot and later in the film *Becket* (1964).

Whether religiously oriented or not, **stoicism** remains as pervasive as ever and offers to many a genuine alternative to hedonism. In a period of ever accelerating change, of being wary of violence as a condition of life, of the realization that prosperity does not last forever, small wonder that many are asking less for pleasure than for inner peace. Although weekly pilgrimages to analysts continue, some principles of stoicism may be at work here also. After all, self-knowledge is vital to psychoanalysis. Analysts contend that people will be able to transcend negative feelings once they understand what is making them unhappy or ineffective. This may be the same thing as saying that happiness is really within our power to create and preserve. Not everyone agrees.

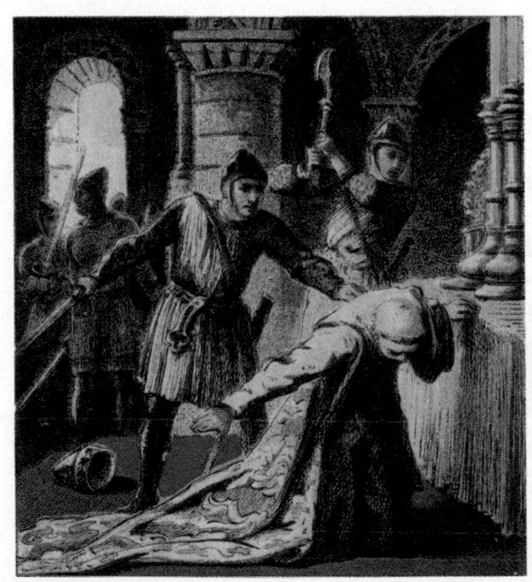

Mary Evans Picture Library/Alamy

Illustration of Becket's martyrdom, date unknown

Thomas à Becket stoically accepts his death rather than closing the doors of his church.

Stoicism Reconsidered

Stoicism in modern dress is, for its advocates, still a viable theory of happiness. Its basic assumption remains much the same as always: tranquility is worth any price. Stoicism has something to offer the chronically poor or the dispossessed, and those who suffer from low self-esteem and cannot see that they deserve any better fate. Even the most zealous social worker might agree that in some cases a stoic attitude is better than false hope for a better tomorrow.

Yet a negative aspect of stoicism is its convenience. If you're down and out, abandoned by family and friends, with no prospects that things will turn around for you, why not become a stoic? Surely the distance is short from "Things are pretty bleak" to "There is no reason to believe things should be otherwise." Does this view mean simply coping but *doing* nothing?

Suppose, however, that the ad hoc stoic—the person who adopts the philosophy out of sheer desperation—suddenly experiences an unexpected reversal of fortune, say, winning five million in the state lottery or, more modestly, finding a good-paying job. Or suppose, as actually happened in the wake of a TV newscaster's human-interest documentary about the homeless in New York, a couple randomly singled out for an interview found themselves swamped with offers of money, jobs, shelter, even a film contract! What happens to stoic doctrines then? Can one embrace stoicism one day and abandon it the next?

> *The stoical scheme of supplying our wants by topping off our desires is like cutting off our feet when we want shoes.*
>
> **—Jonathan Swift**

Some might respond "Why not?" If adversity can be endured because the rational control of emotion makes endurance possible, dropping stoicism when it is no longer working is not necessarily *un*reasonable. Others could object to this line of thought, claiming that reason, which justified the initial adoption of the stoic philosophy during bad times, also requires us to believe that good fortune may not be permanent.

There is an old fable about a tyrannical king who, finding himself plagued by bad fortune, kept asking various wise men to give him grounds for hope. If they could not, their heads were chopped off. Finally, one clever sage gave him a plaque to hang on his bedroom wall: *These Things Shall Pass.* The king, deriving much comfort from the plaque, rewarded the sage handsomely until the king's fortunes took a turn for the better. The maxim, which had once buoyed up his spirits, now angered him, and he ordered the once-favored philosopher to be beheaded.

A frequently raised objection to stoicism is that its advocates secretly want everyone else to be as miserable as they are, yet they don't realize it. Is adversity more bearable when no one around you is having a run of good luck? Loving the company of the miserable may be a fundamental human trait. Enjoying nothing so much as the sad tales of others may be as universal as secretly resenting a friend's prosperity. The German word *schadenfreude* describes the pleasures derived from the misfortunes of others. Radio and television programmers assume there's a smaller audience for good news than for accounts of grisly murders and natural disasters happening to other people.

Yet another objection is that what passes for reason in stoicism should really be called rationalizing, a process by which we find satisfying rather than logical reasons for believing something. The possibility exists that control for the stoic actually means manipulating thoughts so that reality becomes tolerable. When loved ones stop calling, do we endure their absence by entertaining the possibility that they have transferred their affections or have ceased to be interested in us for this or that reason? Or are we more likely to believe whatever makes us feel good? We pick and choose among comfortable versions of reality. In this way, say the detractors, what masquerades as stoic acceptance is a false sense that reality is being fearlessly confronted. We accept what we *want* to accept, rejecting everything else. The trouble, they warn, is that rejected reality can strike back at any time, delivering a crushing blow.

Classical stoicism emerged from two cultures, the Greek and the Roman, with their strong belief in fate. The universe was run by all-powerful deities who intervened in human affairs whenever they chose. The gods and goddesses were capricious and unpredictable, but human reason could counteract heavenly whimsy by expecting ill times before they occurred. In other words: the universe was predictably full of disaster. (This may explain why the Romans were strong on building a well-ordered state.) Critics of stoicism have said the universe does not make even that much sense. Perhaps disasters are no less certain than continuing success. They argue that the uncertainty invites debilitating passivity. Expecting to fail has kept many a potential winner from even getting started.

> *One is happy as a result of one's own efforts; once one knows the necessary ingredients of happiness—simple tastes, a certain degree of courage, self-denial to a point, love of work, and, above all, a clear conscience.*
>
> **—George Sand**

There is also the passivity of the fortunate, especially when it comes to turning away from the fact that people the world over are suffering and that they are in a position to help. "I'm a stoic and believe those who are suffering poverty or the ravages of war would be happier if they would only follow my example" can be an excuse for enjoying a comfortable existence without the nagging of conscience.

Harriet Beecher Stowe's novel *Uncle Tom's Cabin* (1852) opened the eyes of many who were unaware of the wretched poverty in which slaves were forced to live without any hope of liberation. The title character, however, adopts a stoic acceptance of his lot and has since lent his name as the very icon of nonresistance. Looking at the novel from over a century and a half removed, one might become infuriated by conditions that forced those without hope to embrace stoicism. In contrast, one character, Eliza, also a slave, is indeed desperate enough to endanger her life in a flight from the plantation. Modern readers sometimes criticize the passivity of Tom and praise the courage of Eliza.

Aristotle on Happiness

For Aristotle, Plato's star pupil and founder of the Lyceum, an early version of the liberal arts college, happiness is the purpose for which we live. In analyzing this most complex of phenomena, Aristotle concludes that happiness is not a moment-to-moment experiencing of pleasurable things but a way of characterizing how one's life is being conducted. Happiness is living and having lived a good life. It is not measured in momentary eruptions of joy. *Complete* happiness is the final summing up of one's life. If we are leading a good life along the way, we know we are on the right path. Then the philosopher goes on to tell us what makes life good along the way.

> "When a small child . . . I thought success spelled happiness. I was wrong, happiness is like a butterfly which appears and delights us for one brief moment, but soon flies away."
>
> **—Anna Pavlova**

In his great work on the conduct of living, *The Nicomachean Ethics* (named for his son Nicomachus), Aristotle lists the things that make life good, including the *highest possible good,* the one that is valued for its own sake, the one that, when (or if) it is reached, leaves nothing else to be desired.

If you asked passersby what makes them happy, you would probably hear "money," "health," "love," "a good job, "a beautiful home," and so on. No one can deny these are to be counted as among the goods that life can offer. As each one is named, you could continue, "Yes. And is that all?" Chances are that many others would come to the speaker's mind. That is, is money enough? Well, not if my health is bad. Is health then enough? Well, not if I hate my job. Then a good job is enough? Well, not if I'm still looking for someone to share my life.

If someone were to ask you whether it would be enough if you were completely happy, you'd have to think a minute, wouldn't you? You couldn't say, "Not if I didn't have enough money," because, logically, if money were important to your happiness and you didn't have enough, you couldn't say you were completely happy then.

Aristotle concludes that the reason we want money, health, love, and everything else worth striving for is that they *provide* happiness. Therefore none of them by itself can *be happiness.* The person who delivers your mail is not the mail. Individual goods, in other words, are means to the end, but none can be the end in itself, though some people often make the mistake of believing that is possible. For example, a poor person might dream of someday inheriting great wealth from a distant relative. "If I had all that money, I would ask for nothing more." Want to bet? In identifying happiness with any particular state or possession, we could always think of something else that would be even better and therefore our life could be *more* happy at that moment. Just as Einstein told the world that at the speed of light time stops, so too can it be said that in a state of complete happiness, desire and need stop. But only then.

Aristotle therefore defines happiness as the highest, or final, good. Since all of us continually strive for greater goods than we have at any particular time, it follows that reaching the final good is the goal of life. It also follows that what affords us pleasure or joy at any given moment cannot be the same thing as happiness because it is always possible at any given moment to think of something that would be better. Winning gold medals in the Olympics leaves athletes in a state of extreme joy, yet two medals are better than one, and three even better than that. Michael Phelps, who may possibly be the greatest swimmer ever to compete in the Olympics, would never have been satisfied with only one or two medals.

Aristotle believed happiness was not the same as goods we desire in hopes they will make us happy. It was a state, a condition, the satisfaction of knowing that one has lived a good life dominated by reason and virtue.

Reason and Virtue

Aristotle's theory has enormous implications for how we can best live. It assures us that life can be good without our having everything we thought we wanted. Every so often we can stop and take inventory and then decide how our life is going and what the final summing up is likely to be. Is it headed in a direction that can be summed up as "Yes, this is a good life—so far"?

Further, do we want things that make happiness more difficult to attain than need be? The answer, according to Aristotle, is staring us in the face. If happiness is the same as the good life, why not simply *live* the good life and make sure the final summing up will be a positive one? He believed there was one good which stood out above all, one good which was better than all the others that promote happiness, and that was *reason.* If we allow reason to be our guide in making all decisions, we will always do the right thing. By doing the right thing in every circumstance—not the most profitable or immediately pleasurable—one can be sure the summing up will be on the side of the good life.

Aristotle equated reason with virtue. The virtuous course is also the perfection of a particular action. To act out of self-interest, ignoring others, can never be excellence. Too many others can be hurt by the action, and pardoning oneself to avoid guilt means lying. Of what action is lying the perfection? Do we judge a lie to be a perfect action if nobody finds out? Or do we persuade ourselves that no one has been hurt? How can we know? And even if we could be assured that the lie is a harmless one, might we not be encouraged to choose lying over the truth in another, or perhaps even *every,* case? A life built on lies is bound to crumble like a house of cards.

"Happiness arises from awareness of being."

—Trich Nhat Hahn

Aristotle believed the path to happiness was a life lived in accordance with reason and virtue. This cannot be said for a life that achieves only *some* of the goods that are possible: recognition without love, for example, or money without health, or health without fulfilling any other purpose. A life that has displayed reason and virtue in all actions and decisions can be one that is free of care, free of guilt, free from wishing that much more could have been done. In today's topsy-turvy world, however, such freedom could be construed as overpassivity.

A person who lives a totally virtuous life may in the end regret that all goals have not been reached: the pay hike never received, the novel never written, a reconciliation never reached. But—and this is crucial—such regret is not a sign that the life has not been a happy one. In other words, according to Aristotle's theory, life can be good, hence happy, even though you are not always aware of it, by asking every so often *"What am I doing that makes my life good?"* Not *"What is missing in my life?"* If the missing is also the attainable, then you have willfully blocked the road to happiness. Are there people who need your help? Are you in a position to help? Even if *present* conditions depress you, this does not mean you are not on your way to a final, positive summing up of your life.

Happiness: a Government's Responsibility

Aristotle proposed that the purpose of government was to see to it that citizens were happy. Having deduced that the purpose for living is the attainment of the happy life, the philosopher believed nothing should be allowed to hinder the quest. The institutions of society exist to promote the happiness of all and therefore the means to that end.

Law and order in the well-regulated state are necessary; otherwise the happiness of all cannot be guaranteed. People must be protected against their own baser natures, as well as against those who wish them harm. For many critics of this theory, questions remain: How much power should the state be given before it contradicts its avowed purpose, which is to promote the happiness of all? May not some harm be done to the innocent? In this age of DNA testing, some of those executed have later been found to have been not guilty. The justification "Yes, but how many killers has the death penalty kept off the streets?" does not satisfy those who would support the view that the happiness—and therefore the rights—of all must come first. How, they ask, can happiness be guaranteed when freedom is denied?

Aristotle believed the function of government was to provide for the happiness of each citizen.

Aristotle held fast to the belief that the road to happiness was through the exercise of reason and virtue and government must not stand in the way of reason. Government itself should be the very model of rationality. (Alas! Can this ever be the case?) Therein lies the great dilemma. How can government *reasonably* protect the state if it sometimes uses *unreasonable* methods?

There is a further dilemma. What happens when the government's supposedly rational view of happiness differs from the majority's? In *The Republic* Plato reports a famous debate over whether the best interests of the government can coincide with the best interests of the governed. Socrates believed there was only one rational course in every decision that had to be made and that if the government truly followed reason, then it would automatically serve the interests of the people. That belief was the foundation of his decision not to escape from prison, though he questioned the "justice" that brought him there. What he did not question was the logic of having law itself. He was found guilty, however unjustly, and therefore the law required the extreme penalty, death by drinking hemlock. He argued it was unreasonable to assume anyone had the right to escape who thought he had been unjustly imprisoned. Aristotle had a very limited faith in the ability of the average citizen to be rational, but this only made him insist that those who governed *must* be reasonable at all times. Whether this has ever or will ever happen is open to endless debate.

Aristotle Reconsidered

There are always going to be limitations on happiness. Many millions have no choice but to wait and hope for a miraculous change of fortune: people who live under oppressive governments or in places where drought and other natural disasters create famine and the spread of fatal disease, people who have never had or maybe never will have anything that can be called a good. It is almost impossible to tell them their lives are happy without their knowing it. Aristotle would probably not have even tried. Recognizing when one is fortunate in comparison to many others can be a severe limitation on one's own progress toward a happy life. And helping those in need may be the only way to find the path again. Until one does find it and until no further help is necessary (an unimaginable condition), complete happiness is unreachable.

The economic disaster of the Great Depression was addressed by the administration of Franklin D. Roosevelt, which began in 1933 promising what it called the "New Deal." Based on the economic theories of John Maynard Keynes, an English economist, the New Deal was intended to stimulate economic growth. Financed by the government, the Works Project Administration (WPA) and the Civilian Conservation Corps (CCC) put the unemployed to work building and rebuilding infrastructures. The New Deal proclaimed that the government's responsibility was to look out for the welfare of all citizens. In theory at least, everyone capable of working would have a job. Making a fair wage and putting food on the table equated with happiness.

Aristotle assumed that a society with citizens' welfare as the sole concern of government would be on its way to happiness. Since his time, it is clear that all societies have become much more complex and government actions tangled in webs of red tape. Can anyone in any society rely solely on government to provide happiness? Is happiness attainable under a *repressive* government? Is happiness really possible in the strict Aristotelian sense?

The Humanities and Unhappiness

Any theory of happiness is just that: a theory. People whose circumstances are deplorable, who live in fear, hunger, and ill health, whose lifespan is often considerably shorter than it could be, who can rightfully say they never did harm to anyone yet they suffer, cannot be blamed for feeling they deserve a better fate. Misfortune is, unfortunately, inherent in this business of living. The amount of suffering in the world is for many a permanent roadblock to a happy life.

The humanities have not turned a deaf ear to human misery. The sometimes futile attempt to escape from poverty is the subject of much great art and literature. For example, Victor Hugo's *Les Miserables* (1862) called powerful attention to the plight of the poor in France. The hero, Jean Valjean, steals a loaf of bread for his hungry family, is sent to prison, and after his release, gets into trouble again. He is pursued relentlessly by Javert, a police inspector obsessed with punishing anyone who breaks a law, regardless of circumstances. The pursuit continues for hundreds of pages, resulting finally in Javert's suicide because he cannot capture Valjean, who is reunited with his family now as an old man near death—and all because of a loaf of bread!

Conditions in the modern world have not conspired to bring about rosier views in the literary and artistic depiction of life. A popular Egyptian novel in recent years, Alaa Al Aswany's *The Yacoubian Building* (2003), revolves around the tenants of an apartment house in Cairo. To one extent or another, all of them long for prosperity. The central character is Taha, son of the building's janitor, who aspires to become a policeman and then marry the woman he loves. When he is turned away from the police academy even after scoring high on the entrance examination, he enrolls in college, where he is snubbed by the wealthier, better-dressed students but welcomed by those as poor as he. They introduce Taha to a charismatic leader promising change and declaring the way to bring it about is to

> *"Every happy man should have someone with a little hammer at his door to knock and remind him that there are unhappy people and that, however happy he may be, life will sooner or later show its claws."*
>
> **—Anton Chekov**

disrupt the status quo through well-placed bombs. What stands out in the novel is the fact that his solution is not described as a misfortune, but simply a sad commentary on the modern world.

One might ask how it is possible to be truly happy in a world where we are continually facing the suffering of the less fortunate. But now, let us look at a few inspiring examples of people whose lives—and, unfortunately, deaths— exemplify how life *can* be good even under the most trying of circumstances.

Models of the Happy Life

History is filled with remarkable examples of how good lives managed to overcome horrible barriers. Consider this remarkable passage by Austrian psychiatrist Viktor Frankl, who was a prisoner in a Nazi concentration camp. It illustrates how life can be good even in the shadow of death.

> *The size of human suffering is absolutely relative . . . It also follows that a very trifling thing can cause the greatest of joys. Take as an example something that happened on our journey from Auschwitz to the camp affiliated with Dachau. We had all been afraid that our transport was heading for the Mauthausen camp. We became more and more tense as we approached a certain bridge over the Danube which the trains would have to cross in order to reach Mauthausen. . . . Those who have never seen anything similar cannot possibly image the dance of joy performed in the carriage by the prisoners when they saw that our transport was not crossing the bridge and was instead heading "only" for Dachau.*[6]

Reuters/Corbis

Anne Frank, c. 1942

Anne Frank never knew she would become a legendary figure, an icon who continues to teach us the way to be happy even under the most appalling circumstances.

The Aristotelian moral of this story is that the rational course was for the prisoners to put themselves into the hands of a two-pronged fate: Mauthausen or Dachau—certain death or a chance to live, even if imprisoned. Knowing the two possibilities in advance, it was rational to be prepared for either eventuality, not to wish for luck. Had liberation been the only possible good that would have satisfied them, the fact that the transport did not cross the Danube would not have been enough to fill them with optimism. Instead, they made their own "luck."

Anne Frank

Another inspiring example of Aristotelian happiness is that of Anne Frank (1929–1945), a Jewish girl who, with her parents and others, was hidden in the attic of an Amsterdam office building during the Nazi occupation. To occupy her time, and possibly leave something of value behind, she began writing a diary of her thoughts and feelings, a work that was subsequently found, published, and read by millions.

Not the dewy-eyed idealist portrayed on stage, film, and television, Anne Frank was a girl with an adult mind that knew what it was doing at each moment. In 1944: "I have made up my mind now to lead a different life from other girls and, later on, different from ordinary housewives." The "different life" was that of the calm, reflective writer. "I can shake off everything if I write, my sorrows disappear, my courage is reborn." After the war she hoped to write a work of great significance, but if this goal were denied, "my diary will be a great help."[7]

Remarkably able to transcend what would have been an understandable fear for her own safety and that of her family and friends, Anne takes the larger view, thinking sadly of those who have already been captured and sent to camps. "If it is as bad as this in Holland, what ever will it be like in the distant and barbarous regions they are sent to? We assume that most of them are murdered. The English radio speaks of their being gassed; perhaps that is the quickest way to die." [8]

> *Whosoever is happy will make others happy too.*
>
> **—Anne Frank**

Anne's strength may have come from the fact that she knew herself to be innocent of any wrongdoing, and also from an acceptance of the conditions under which she and the others hiding in the attic had to live. She became the mainstay of the entire group. On the occasion of Hanukkah, she made presents for everyone out of old materials she found in the attic.

Her writing consistently reveals a person of resolve, one who has her emotions generally under control, and, like the stoics, one whose spirit refuses to be broken. She admits to being afraid of death, but can that be called irrational? At the same time, she is not obsessed with fear. "When I sat in front of the window this morning I suddenly realized that we have had a great, great many compensations. I mean inward compensation."[9]

She proudly admits to believing nobody is all bad, despite the suffering she and her family have been forced to bear and the possibility of even more dreadful consequences to come. In the context of her brief but intensely rational life, her forgiving attitude seems more the triumph of the happy person (in Aristotle's sense) than the sentimentality of a young romantic. Observations like hers are not the result of a momentary, on-the-spot impulse, a sudden flurry of passing joy unjustified by the circumstances; rather they persist in one form or another throughout the diary, evidence of a mature mind that knows what Aristotle reasoned a thousand years ago: *life is good for one who is good.* Though Anne Frank was eventually captured and died in a concentration camp, we can say, in Aristotelian terms, that hers was a happy life tragically foreshortened.

Martin Luther King Jr.

Martin Luther King Jr. (1929–1968), winner of the Nobel Peace Prize in 1964, devoted his own foreshortened life to nonviolent protest against racism and the denial of civil rights to African Americans and all others so deprived. An ordained Baptist minister, King was often in the midst of police brutality, urging victims to stay calm and not reciprocate in kind when force was used. Considered by many as the greatest American orator since Abraham Lincoln, he gave hope with his stirring rhetoric to millions of the poor and oppressed. He made numerous memorable speeches, but the most memorable of all was his "I Have a Dream" oration, delivered before thousands on the Washington Mall, August 28, 1963.

> *No, no, we are not satisfied, and we will not be satisfied until justice rolls down like waters and righteousness like a mighty stream.*
>
> **—Martin Luther King Jr.**

In this oration, which can be found in U.S. Constitution Online, King confronted the bitter truths of injustice, discrimination, school and housing segregation, and widespread joblessness. Without giving hollow protestations of hope, he gave what he surely must have considered rational reasons for hope, but always stressing nonviolence.

> *Let us not seek to satisfy our thirst for freedom by drinking from the cup of bitterness and hatred. We must ever conduct our struggle on the high plane of dignity and discipline. We must not allow our*

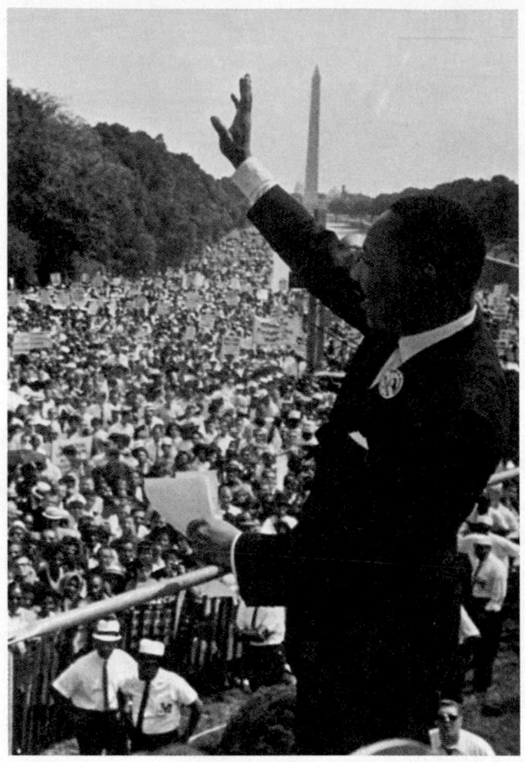

AP Photo

Martin Luther King Jr., 1963

A happy life by Aristotle's criteria: an unwillingness to abandon reason and virtue even if it meant death.

creative protest to degenerate into physical violence. Again and again we must rise to the majestic heights of meeting physical force with soul force.

Later in the speech, King introduced the now famous motif.

I have a dream that my four little children will one day live in a nation where they will not be judged by the color of their skin but by the content of their character.

It is impossible to think that Dr. King was unaware of how dangerous it was to stand by his uncompromising principles and to take his powers of oratory into the most segregated parts of the country, knowing full well how many enemies were lying in wait. Five years after giving this speech that now belongs in the history of the humanities, he was assassinated by a man who spent the remainder of his life in prison, never admitting guilt or showing remorse.

Gandhi

A sterling example of the Hindu path to bliss, or *moksha,* is provided by the life and death of Mohandas Gandhi (1869–1948), who also devoted his life to promoting the cause of nonviolence. He attained a huge following, who anointed him with the title **Mahatma**, meaning "one who is wise and good."

Like Siddhartha, Gandhi wanted to do more than simply save himself by becoming detached from all participation in the world. He wanted to save the world by persuading all those who would listen that a serene and happy existence could come about only through nonviolence and love.

Hindu doctrine teaches that the divine spirit dwells inside each person, that the soul of each person is part of Brahman, the great soul, and therefore is fundamentally good. Unfortunately, the world is filled with luxuries, in plentiful supply to the rich, and with handsome and beautiful human beings who arouse sexual longings that must be fulfilled. The desire to possess both objects (including land) and other people leads to frustration and despair, because, as epicureans well know, there can never be enough pleasure if pleasure is the only goal. The thwarting of burning desire causes people to become violent, to seize what they want by any means.

Gandhi realized that when frustration was multiplied by the entire population of an oppressed land or by an ethnic group subjugated by a stronger power, revolutionary uprisings were inevitable. The endless cycle of violence, war, and death (often of the most innocent) made life bitter. He knew that, for many, the only way to reach serenity was to back off and do nothing. But for himself, there could be no bliss, no serenity in a world ruled by hate. Thus he became, as King would become, an activist determined to make nonviolence a potent counterforce.

> *"Learn to be calm and you will always be happy."*
>
> **—Paramhansa Yogananda**

As a native of India, Gandhi lived under British colonial rule and suffered the pain of discrimination. Speaking out against British imperialism, he acquired considerable notoriety and was frequently denounced in churches and meeting halls. He carried his message to South Africa, where he found the same sort of prejudice and resistance to change. Exhausted and frequently ill from hunger strikes, he persisted, obsessed with the need to convince those who gathered to hear his speeches that there was only one way for people to live a good life: to lay down all weapons and talk to each other. He was convinced that through dialogue everyone would discover the basic oneness of all humanity. How could you hate someone who was really *you*?

Gandhi was painfully aware that the greatest threat to peace in India, even more than British sovereignty, was the irreconcilable divide between Hindus and Muslims—each practicing a different religion: Hindus with their Brahman, the soul of the world but not a personal god, and Muslims with their father-god Allah. To Muslims, Hindus were godless infidels. But often Hindus held the upper hand.

Gandhi stepped into the bitter conflict, seeking to convince each side they could live in peace, tolerate their differences, and respect each other's right to believe as they wished and practice religion as they saw fit. In 1947 India became an independent nation with self-rule, a tremendous step forward for which Gandhi was partly responsible. Yet he was not satisfied. The internal conflicts had to be resolved.

Gandhi's dream, like that of Martin Luther King Jr. decades later, would remain unrealized. On January 30, 1948, as he was about to enter a temple for a period of meditation, he was shot and killed by a Hindu fundamentalist, who apparently hated Muslims and could not tolerate the idea of peaceful coexistence.

Once again we have evidence that if perfect happiness is to be anything more than momentary joy, it has to be recognized as a distant goal that can probably never be reached but can be approached through unceasing effort. One may conclude that Gandhi was a really happy person, who may not have taken the time to think about the matter. If Aristotle's spirit had followed him about like a guardian angel, he might have decided Gandhi was a shining example of the happy life. He did not have health or wealth, two components, but not the equivalents of Aristotelian happiness, though he surely possessed reason and virtue.

Buddhist Paths to Happiness

For Buddhists, bliss, or nirvana, has a twofold nature. Historians of Buddhism explain that over the centuries the practice divided into two schools, both leading to nirvana. One is **Hinayana**, which means "little ferryboat." It developed first and its purpose was to formulate the teachings of Siddhartha into a systematic practice of the Four Noble Truths, which are

1. *life is filled with pain*
2. *the cause of pain is frustrated desire*
3. *there is a way out of pain*
4. *the way out is the Eightfold Path*

The last has to do with how we think, speak, behave toward others, and above all how we find peace through meditation (see Chapter 10).

While Hinayana Buddhism involves moral conduct, which is automatic if we follow all of the recommended steps, its practice was seen by those who came after Siddhartha as too narrow, too limited. It was a wonderful means of self-help, of lifting the spirits of the depressed, but not a way to help others who may have lost their way.

> *"We have no more right to consume happiness without producing it than to consume wealth without producing it."*
>
> **—George Bernard Shaw**

Gradually the school known as **Mahayana**, "big ferryboat," developed by adding a larger perspective and a more expansive concept of bliss. Tibetan Buddhism is Mahayana in scope, continuing the legacy of Siddhartha and teaching that nirvana is attainable in one lifetime by the fully enlightened person, who then becomes a buddha renouncing bondage to the pleasures of this world and doing whatever is necessary, wherever it may be. It can mean something as simple as collecting clothes, food, and other supplies for victims of a devastating fire, storm, or earthquake, or joining a group of volunteers and helping to rebuild damaged homes. Or it can mean becoming a world-renowned person, carrying a message of peace and tolerance to millions. In Buddhism, both meanings have equal importance.

There is nothing self-congratulatory about the Mahayana path. One does not pat oneself on the back and bask in the glow of satisfaction that comes with knowing one has done a good deed or made a tremendous sacrifice. Mahayana Buddhists say it is the logical next step after one has practiced the narrower way. The idea is that, having reached enlightenment after long years of meditation, one has no choice but to live in and through others, just as Siddhartha, having reached enlightenment after sitting under the bodhi (rose-apple) tree for forty days and nights, declined to remain in nirvana, feeling he must share his bliss with everyone else and teach them how to be as serene as he was.

In the time of Siddhartha the world had many troubles, but there were no global conditions of today's dimensions, no continual outbreaks of terrorism, no everyday fears that disaster is omnipresent and waiting to happen anywhere, anytime. Were he alive today, he would very likely have been at Ground Zero on September 11, 2001, asking what he could do to help. For most of the rest of us, doing what is necessary may have a narrower definition: obligations to family, friends, and work. There are children to meet at the corner school bus stop, an aging parent or other relative to care for, and a host of personal tasks to be done, such as pursuing a degree, learning a new trade as a means of rising above tough economic times, supporting a family. Most of us cannot become buddhas or live as Siddhartha did, wandering from place to place without a family, eating very little, paying scant attention to personal needs. Yet Mahayana Buddhism does not expect quite this much. However far you go on the Path is better than not taking that first step. This is the Buddhist view of happiness.

The Dalai Lama

The Dalai Lama, the acknowledged leader of Tibetan Buddhism, is a role model for thousands who seek to emulate his serenity as well as his Mahayana efforts to help bring about world peace. Those who admire him and flock to his lectures often are curious about what it means to do without many of the pleasures that others of his stature and following usually enjoy—particularly pleasures of the flesh.

> *I am sometimes asked whether this vow of celibacy is really desirable and indeed whether it is really possible. Suffice to say that its practice is not simply a matter of suppressing sexual desires. On the contrary, it is necessary to fully accept the existence of those desires and to transcend them by the power of reasoning. When successful, the result of the mind can be very beneficial. The trouble with sexual desire is that it is a blind desire and can only give temporary satisfaction. Thus, as Nagarjuna said: "When you have an itch, you scratch. But not to itch at all is better than any amount of scratching.*[10]

The Dalai Lama's writings are full of wise sayings and aphorisms in short entries that remind one of the *Tao Te Ching* of Lao-tzu. And with their publication and dissemination throughout the globe, the Dalai Lama must, of course, hope that he will lead thousands, even millions, to the path of serenity. Knowing how to live a serene existence would make a good many people desist from doing their utmost to spread terror and hatred and continually renew the cycle of war and broken peace accords. He cannot, however, wish that the peace (and hope for happiness) of the entire world would come about only when all sides are of one mind.

> *All the waters and rivers of different lands and climes have their ultimate meeting point in the ocean. So, too, the differing viewpoints of society, the varieties of economic theories, and the means to their attainment benefit mankind itself. There is no point in indulging in dissension-creating discussions on differing ideologies. No possible result has accrued from attempting to convert all men of different temperaments and likings into one common ideology and mode of behavior.*[11]

In his view, serenity—or, as he calls it, tranquility—has to be achieved through acceptance of, not the burning need to change everyone else.

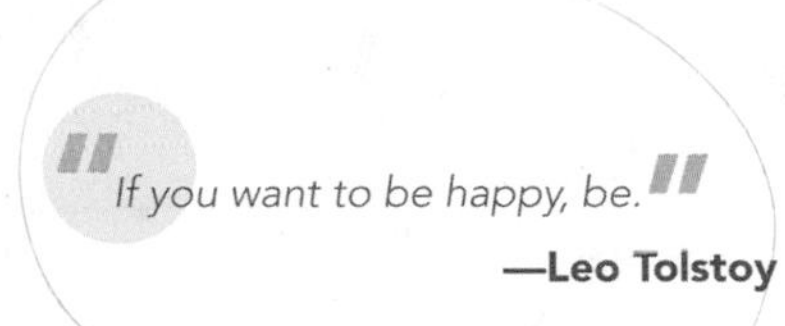

"If you want to be happy, be."
—Leo Tolstoy

> *The essence of all spiritual life is your emotion, your attitude toward others. Once you have sincere and pure motivation, all the rest follows. You can develop the right attitude toward others on the basis of kindness, love, and respect, and on the clear realization of the oneness of all human beings.*[12]

Whether we call it bliss, moksha, or nirvana, or go with the hedonists and insist that it is having as much as possible of life's pleasures—plenty of money, sex, fast cars, a showcase for a home, the nature of the good life remains open to debate. This chapter has not promised an easy solution, a neat summing up. Happiness is but one of the colors we apply to the canvas of "human."

The terms *winner* and *loser* are strong in our vocabularies. Frequently they lead us to an either-or approach to living. Blithely we describe someone as a loser and resolve that only *winner* will ever apply to *us*. But if a loser is someone who fails at everything, must a winner be the exact opposite? Is it possible to win continually? Do we always know what it *means* to win? And what is *loss*? The absence of money, health, love? Can these be absent continually?

We do not wish to leave you with the impression that Aristippus, Epicurus, Aristotle, or Siddhartha discovered the best and only road to happiness. Our advice is to carefully map out your requirements for the good life, bearing in mind some of the options discussed in this chapter. Once you recognize that you are in control of defining happiness and can make it mean what is possible for you, not what you can never hope to achieve, then you may experience a measure of contentment.

Musée des Beaux Arts

About suffering they were never wrong
The Old Masters: how well they understood
Its human position, how it takes place
When someone else is eating or opening a window

or just walking dully along;
How, when the aged are reverently, passionately waiting
For the miraculous birth, there always must be
Children who did not especially want it to happen, skating
On a pond at the edge of the wood:
They never forgot
That even the dreadful martyrdom must run its course
Anyhow in a corner, some untidy spot
Where the dogs go on with their doggy life and the torturer's horse
Scratches its innocent behind on a tree.
In Brueghel's Icarus, for instance: how everything turns away
Quite leisurely from the disaster; the ploughman may
Have heard the splash, the forsaken cry,
But for him it was not an important failure; the sun shone
As it had on the white legs disappearing into the green
Water, and the expensive delicate ship that must have seen
Something amazing, a boy falling out of the sky,
Had somewhere to get to and sailed calmly on.

W. H. Auden[13]

LEARNING OBJECTIVES

Having read and carefully studied this chapter, you should be able to:

1. Define and give two examples of hedonism.
2. Define epicureanism relative to Hemingway's "In Another Country."
3. Define stoicism relative to Rome and Christianity.
4. Summarize Aristotle's theory of happiness.
5. Explain why both Viktor Frankl and Anne Frank were happy even in disastrous circumstances.
6. Distinguish between Hinayana and Mahayana Buddhism as paths to happiness.
7. Explain which theory of happiness best applies to the Auden poem which concludes the chapter.

KEY TERMS

big earnings theory from the hedonist view that people who work hard or who make sacrifices for others deserve material rewards.

carpe diem Latin phrase meaning "seize the day"; a major hedonist creed advising us to live for the moment and amass all the pleasures we can.

epicureanism based on teachings of Epicurus, the belief that happiness is freedom from pain.

hedonism from the Greek for "delight," the belief that happiness consists of the sum of all the pleasures we can experience.

Hinayana one of the two major schools of Buddhism; from the Sanskrit meaning "little ferryboat," the narrow path to personal happiness attained by serenity through meditation.

Mahatma from Sanskrit meaning "great soul," a title of love and respect for one known to be wise and good; applied to Gandhi.

Mahayana one of the two major schools of Buddhism; from Sanskrit meaning "big ferryboat," the wider path to happiness, attained by helping others find the way.

moksha early Hindu term for the highest state of happiness possible, a condition of pure bliss and freedom from all desire.

stoicism belief that happiness consists of coping rationally with sources of unhappiness.

TOPICS FOR WRITING AND DISCUSSION

1. If you had to choose one theory of happiness discussed in this chapter as dominant in our society, which would it be? Explain. Then indicate whether it represents your own view.
2. Create and then describe three television commercials for the same product, each directed toward a different audience: (a) a hedonist, (b) an epicurean, and (c) a Buddhist.
3. Choose one of the following options for discussion or a short paper:
   - **a.** A gambler who has lost all evening makes one last bet with money that has been saved for the down payment on a house and wins back twice the sum. Could you justify the risk? Or take the gambler to task regardless of the win? Is life a matter of taking risks anyway? Is it worth playing close to the vest?
   - **b.** In a children's game of musical chairs, one child is clearly the winner. Should the organizers of the game give each child the same prize in order not to hurt anyone's feelings? Or should children be taught at an early age how the world usually works? Which of these two approaches is likely to produce the happier child?
   - **c.** The big earnings theory, discussed in the chapter, maintains that people who work hard or sacrifice for each other deserve substantial rewards. Pretend you have found somebody's wallet containing $1,000 as well as the name and phone number of the owner. You return it and receive a "thank you very much" and that's all. You ask Aristippus, Epicurus, and Aristotle how you should feel. What do they answer?
4. Write a toast you would make for a newly married couple, as if you were (a) a stoic and then (b) the Dalai Lama.
5. Andrew Carnegie wrote: "While the law of competition may be sometimes hard for the individual, it is best for each race, because it insures the survival of the fittest. We accept and therefore welcome great inequality of environment, the concentration of business in the hands of a few, and the law of competition between them as being essential for the future progress of the race." On which theory of happiness is this idea based? Do you agree with it? Why or why not?
6. Which theory of happiness in your opinion is most helpful to the world and which the least? Explain your answers.
7. The mother in a very poor family once made fried dough with powdered sugar for Thanksgiving dinner and told everyone they were going to have a real treat. Which philosophy of happiness would be most likely to say this was a lie? Which would be most likely to agree with the mother? Think carefully before you answer, then explain your choices.
8. Both Gandhi and King were assassinated. In your opinion, does this fact alter the view that, in Aristotelian terms, they led happy lives?
9. The English philosopher Bertrand Russell said work is a major component of happiness. Which kind of work do you anticipate doing? Which kind of work do you think offers the best chance of leading you to happiness? Are they the same?
10. A philosopher said, "Take care that your happiness does not depend on what happens to you." To which theory of happiness is this statement most closely related? Is it, in your opinion, a reasonable or even possible approach to living? What can be said in favor of and against it?

Study and **Review** on **MyHumanitiesKit.com**

Picasso 23

Chapter 13

Love

We can scarcely overestimate the importance of love, yesterday and today, in our lives, in the world, and in the humanities. One of the world's most beautiful buildings, the glorious Taj Mahal mausoleum in Agra, India, is evidence of the love of one man, Shah Mumtaz, for his favorite wife. Without the theme of love, all of the arts would be diminished. Even the successive marriages of the frequently divorced give evidence that people believe so strongly in love they keep looking for it and that, no matter what their other achievements, they probably believe they have wasted their lives if they cannot say they have loved and been loved at some point. In countless poems, novels, operas, films, and plays, love is shown as the source of both pleasure and pain, often at the same time.

Love is hard to describe scientifically; it may be solely the invention of the human imagination without objective existence. Even the attempt to describe it has been dismissed, as in "Some Enchanted Evening" from Rodgers and Hammerstein's *South Pacific.* The lover sings that fools give you reasons but wise men never try.

Nevertheless, this chapter will analyze ways in which humanity has been affected by the myth or the mystery of love as it has been depicted in different cultures and different times. We note that artists are not united in their depictions of love: some have glorified it; others have emphasized its pain; some have even tried to imagine a society whose leaders ban it entirely. Recognizing this obsession and its possible impact on our beliefs is crucial to the art of being human.

◀ **Pablo Picasso, *The Lovers*, 1923**

Picasso's famous lovers, before Cubism.

> "Love: any form of relationship between human beings when used in conjunction with the phrase "falling in love" or "being in love.""
>
> —Morton M. Hunt

Eros

Despite the sentiments in poems and songs that love is timeless, it must be considered in the context of history. Love has meant different things at different times and in particular places, including its relative unimportance for people in desperate circumstances.

Cultural anthropologists once discovered that people in a certain remote area of Africa had no word that translates as "love," though parents probably showed affection for their young by teaching them how to survive in a hostile environment. As you may have guessed, their vocabulary was filled with words that relate to survival strategies, all with favorable connotations. They seemed, however, to have little need for words that refer to tight family bonds and none for words indicating romance between adults.

Imagine the difficulty of having a meaningful discussion about love between people from totally different backgrounds—one waiting for romance and passion, with a wide choice of partners, the other obediently preparing to marry a stranger in a match arranged by the parents of the couple. If they are fortunate, they will enjoy their marriage without necessarily talking about love, even as Golde, the wife in *Fiddler on the Roof*, objects to Tevye's question "Do you love me?"

Physical passion and its consummation in the pleasures of the flesh found their share of glorification in the ancient world. The Hebrew Bible, for example, contains the Song of Solomon (Song of Songs), which, though variously interpreted, appears to be a lyrical idealization of physical ecstasy. Its inclusion among sacred writings suggests that to the Hebrews passion was a glorious experience, not at all inconsistent with the love of God. In this work the lover speaks to his beloved in sensual terms. Her physical splendors fill him with joy. He compares her breasts to clusters of fruit and her breath to wine.

In the classical world of Greece and Rome the word *love* can be found in poetry, philosophy, and mythology, but a citizen of that world, alighting from a time machine in our era, might not understand axioms such as "Love is blind" or "Love is the answer." The time traveler, having caught the latter sentence, might retort, "To what question?"

> "Couples work themselves into hypnotic states daily by repeating to each other over and over again that they love each other . . . They also say they love a certain brand of toothpaste."
>
> —Charles Willeford

The Greeks made a distinction between **eros**, or love as physical lust (named after the god of passion), and **agape**, or a spiritual and intellectual relationship that is more important than a strictly physical one. Though the Romans are famous for their wine-filled orgies, they recognized the distinction as well, and that distinction is still with us.

Lust in Classical Myth

In the classical world passion was dangerous, responsible for endless misery. This poem by the Roman Petronius Gaius (c. 100 C.E.) offers a warning about lust and an invitation to something better.

Doing, a filthy pleasure is, and short;
And done, we straight repent us of the sport:
Let us not then rush blindly on unto it,
Like lustful beasts, that only know how to do it:
For lust will languish, and that heat decay.
But thus, thus, keeping endless holiday,
Let us together closely lie and kiss,
There is no labour, nor no shame in this;

> *This hath pleased, doth please, and long will please; never*
> *Can this decay, but is beginning ever.*[1]

> "Men have died from time to time and worms have eaten them, but not for love."
> —William Shakespeare

The debate continues over whether what we call "love" can mean anything more than lust. Francine Prose, a contemporary author and cultural satirist, is convinced that lust is crucial to our survival.

> *Unlike the other deadly sins, lust and gluttony are allied with behaviors required for the survival of the individual and the species. One has to eat in order to live; presumably the race would die out if lust were never permitted to work its magic.*[2]

The destructive, often tragic, effects of physical desire have been the source of some long-lasting stories emerging from classical mythology. Typical is the account of someone—mortal or divine—caught in the grip of uncontrollable passion. In Roman myth, the figure of Cupid, child of Venus, is often the mischief-maker as he aims his arrow at some unfortunate creature who is no longer able to think rationally.

In classical mythology and literature, nothing good ever comes from love.

One of Cupid's victims is his own mother, the goddess of love herself, who, after being wounded by his arrow, becomes overcome by attraction to a mortal, Adonis. After enjoying passion with a divine being, Adonis announces his intention to go hunting. Venus pleads with him not to go in search of dangerous game. Such advice being distinctly non-Roman, Adonis understandably ignores it and is promptly killed by a wild boar. To perpetuate his memory, Venus transforms his blood into a dark red flower called the anemone. But like passion itself, the anemone is short-lived. The wind blows the blossoms open and all the petals suddenly are gone.

The story of Venus and Adonis lives on in powerful words and pictures. Many artists, especially the Flemish painter Peter Paul Rubens (1577–1640), have been inspired by the myth of an impossible love between a mortal and the immortal goddess who could not follow him to the grave. This story would not be the last to show that physical desire has a very brief existence and that death alone can insure what human beings dream of and sing about: love that never ends.

akg-images/Newscom

Peter Paul Rubens, *Venus and Adonis*, mid to late 1630s

In Rubens's painting, Venus is entreating Adonis not to hunt boar. His obstinacy kills him.

In Shakespeare's dramatic poem about the pair, Venus is very definitely the aggressor, pursuing and seducing the reluctant Adonis:

> *Thrice-fairer than myself, thus she began*
> *The field's chief flower, sweet above compare,*
> *Stain to all nymphs, more lovely than a man,*
> *More white and red than doves or roses are;*
> *Nature that made thee, with herself at strife,*
> *Saith that the world hath ending with thy life.*[3]

In this version, after the young man dies, the goddess puts a curse on love. Henceforth it shall never make anyone happy. Henceforth love shall be passion unfulfilled or passion turned bitter.

> *It shall be fickle, false, and full of fraud,*
> *Bud and be blasted in a breathing-while;*
> *The bottom poison and the top o'erstrawed.*[4]

The Art Gallery Collection/Alamy

Antonio Allegri da Correggio, *Jupiter and Io*, c. 1530

In Correggio's painting, Io is transformed back into a human being so that she can be enjoyed by Jupiter.

Venus and Adonis goes on to say that love will be the cause of war and dire events. Fathers and sons will fight each other over the same woman. If any lovers are lucky enough to escape the decay of their passion for each other, that passion will nevertheless make them miserable.

Adonis was not alone in being radically changed following an erotic misadventure. Other mythic mortals who attract the attention of Olympian gods and goddesses either died or were changed into vegetation or heavenly bodies. In a Greek myth, it is a woman who must die because of a god's attraction to her.

Persephone, daughter of Demeter, the earth mother, is so beautiful that Pluto, god of the underworld, falls in love (lust) with her, then captures and transports her to his dark kingdom. Demeter so grieves over her loss that Zeus, king of the gods, takes pity on her and allows her to share custody of the lovely daughter. During the six months that Persephone is gone, the earth mother mourns, and thus winter came to the world. When she returns, however, the earth is reborn in spring.

In classical mythology, human beings are not responsible for their tragic passions. Outside forces, personified as the gods, toy with them for amusement or the satisfaction of their own physical needs. Occasionally, the afflicted mortal is rewarded for having been the target of a god's lust, but only after undergoing physical and mental torment.

One myth inspired a masterpiece of visual art, *Jupiter and Io* by the Italian artist Antonio Allegri da Correggio (1494–1536), known in art history by his last name only. Io is an innocent young girl who stirs the sexual longings of Jupiter, king of the Roman gods. When she runs away, she is transformed by Jupiter into a heifer for her protection. Juno, the chronically jealous wife of Jupiter, does everything she can to rain destruction upon the girl, but fails to kill her. Instead Jupiter finally makes love to Io, the heifer now transformed back into a girl, and the result is a son, whose own descendants would include the great hero, Hercules. This tale probably does not make a statement that lust is guaranteed to have happy consequences. Rather, it suggests—as do many classical myths—that human beings are related to the gods and in many respects are more than their equals. This relationship explained why the gods are jealous of mortals and often affect them tragically, even if Io's fate is better than that of most women who wander into a lustful god's field of vision.

Medieval Lust

During the late Middle Ages, though Europe was strongly Christian, secular and erotic themes began to creep into poems and songs, often written by young men studying for the priesthood.

If they did not turn from their faith, they could nonetheless be irreverent in their praise—or at least defense—of sexual pleasure. Groups of rebellious students known as **goliards** frequented the taverns in their leisure hours singing the praises of secular life. The most famous of these is "*Gaudeamus Igitur*" ("Let us rejoice while we are young"), which is still played at countless college commencement ceremonies minus the lyrics that urge people to eat, drink, and be merry before the inevitable happens: "Then the dust shall claim us." Many of the goliard songs as well as others have been discovered within the past century, including "In Trutina . . ." ("I am suspended

> *Lust's passion will be served; it demands, it militates, it tyrannizes.*
>
> —**Marquis de Sade**

between chastity and lascivious love"), which, along with other student songs, was given a modern setting by composer Carl Orff and recorded by innumerable artists including Sarah Brightman and Barbra Streisand. The narrator of the poem is probably a novitiate about to take her final vows—and wishing she were not.

The most famous secular author of the fourteenth century was Geoffrey Chaucer (1340–1400), who was fond of creating lusty stories and characters that shocked church authorities. In his masterpiece, *The Canterbury Tales,* he recognizes the weakness of the flesh in both laypersons and clerics. Among the lust-driven men and women is his most unforgettable character: the aging Wife of Bath, married five times (but always "at church door") and as lusty a creature as can be found in the pages of literature. She sings the praises of youth and glorious sex, culminating with a misty-eyed recognition that as we grow old and unattractive we bid farewell to the joys that have made life rich and happy.

But lord Christ! When I remember
My youth and joyful times,
It tickles me to my heart's roots.
Even now it does my heart good
To know that I have had my world
In my own time.[5]

The Canterbury Tales notwithstanding, whatever indiscreet acts may have been taking place in the privacy of cloisters, monasteries, and rectories, medieval writings generally steered clear of the subject of lust. As the Middle Ages waned, however, and the Renaissance began to spread over much of western Europe, bringing with it the lost glories of the classical world, the ancient theme of lust awakened a sympathetic response from writers. Some treated it compassionately as a human tragedy, and others, like Shakespeare in his sonnets, ardently wished their lady friends would be a bit more obliging.

Lust on the Shakespearean Stage

In what is probably the most popular love story ever written, *Romeo and Juliet,* it is quite clear that physical desire initially attracts the pair. This desire makes Juliet fearful. Before encouraging Romeo's suit, she warns that such an attraction is "too like the lightning," because it "ceases to be ere one can say it lightens." Their sexual attraction causes them to forget family duty, forget the fact that Juliet is promised to someone else—in short, to commit themselves to each other with total abandon. Though their love is couched in the language of pure romance, they too are destroyed by the curse of Venus.

Listen on **MyHumanitiesKit.com**
Romeo and Juliet

The darts of the mischievous Cupid are a popular plot device, whether for ill or good; and with or without him, we still have stories of people stricken with sudden, blinding passion—as if they *were* sporting arrows in their chests. Shakespeare also saw the humorous side of the affliction in his comedy *A Midsummer Night's Dream* (1594), when Titania, Queen of the Fairies, finds herself irresistibly drawn to a man she would never have looked at if she were in her right mind. But she is far from being in her right mind because a magic love potion has been administered to her that causes her to desire the first creature she looks at—in this case, a bumbling rustic would-be actor wearing the head of a donkey and responding to the queen's passionate endearments with a typical donkey's bray, a sound that drives her into absolute sexual frenzy. This scenario is the comic flip side of the

"Some Cupid kills with arrows, some with traps."
—William Shakespeare

Hedonism enjoyed much favor in Shakespeare's time, urging people to enjoy life to the fullest because who knew what lay beyond the grave?

"love coin" for Shakespeare. Whether you laugh or cry, passion doesn't bring much good fortune.

Nonetheless, Shakespeare's time was one in which passion took center stage. In England, the philosophy of hedonism, discussed in the previous chapter, enjoyed much favor. It urged people, as the songs of the medieval goliards had, to enjoy life to the fullest because who knew what lay beyond the grave? The time of Queen Elizabeth I, who reigned until the very beginning of the seventeenth century, was the heyday of celebrating the pleasures of the flesh, but usually with the darker implication that death can strike at any time. Remember that Epicurus (Chapter 12) denounced hedonism on the grounds that its underlying obsession with death was more than enough to offset the fleeting pleasures of loving.

Eros in Eastern Culture

"We are all like Scheherazade's husband in that we want to know what happens next."

—E. M. Forster

A Thousand and One Nights is usually, and inaccurately, referred to simply as *The Arabian Nights*. In truth, however, this vast collection of more than four hundred tales, put together from the ninth to the thirteenth centuries, came from India and Persia as well as from Arabia and so represents a blending of different cultures. In the decade of the 1880s, the stories were finally translated into English by Sir Richard Burton (1821–1890), an author and explorer, and have remained classic ever since.

The central character is Scheherezade, the latest wife of a much married Sultan, who looks upon women as sexual playthings, with no other function than to be available at any time of the day or night. Because he is all-powerful and can have any woman he desires, he has each bride executed after the wedding night. Scheherezade faces the same fate as her predecessors unless she can find a way to entertain the Sultan—other than through the customary lovemaking, which would guarantee her death.

The resourceful heroine decides to start telling stories, and they prove so engrossing that she dazzles her husband for a thousand and one nights, by which time we can presume that the Sultan begins to see her as a human being rather than as a temporary bed partner. We can never know whether the long book was hugely popular with Victorian readers because the ending satisfied the moral standards of the time or because the ending was overlooked in favor of the exotic tales of harem intrigues. Perhaps it offered the perfect escape into an imaginary land of brilliant colors, fragrant spices, scrumptious feasting, and nights of delirious sex. Its musical counterpart, the symphonic poem *Scheherezade* by the Russian composer Nicolai Rimsky-Korsakov (1844–1908) remains a standard in the repertoire of all major orchestras and continues to enthrall listeners with its lush and sensuous tones.

Listen on **MyHumanitiesKit.com**
Khayyam, *The Rubáiyát*

The Rubáiyát (which means quatrains, or four-line verses, in Persian) was translated by the English scholar Edward Fitzgerald (1809–1883). Attributed to Omar, called Khayyám (tent maker), a Persian poet and philosopher who lived around 1100, it is a collection of verses that celebrate both the glory and the short-lived pleasures of life, especially those of physical love. The poems tell us that this love is at once the thing that makes life exciting and the thing that, because it cannot endure, makes life ultimately a sad, futile enterprise.

Ah, Love! Could you and I with Him conspire
To grasp this sorry Scheme of Things entire,
Would we not shatter it to bits—and then
Re-mould it nearer to the Heart's desire.[6]

Though a philosopher, Omar appears to have abandoned the life of reason in favor of the life of the senses. Making love and drinking steadily were far more satisfying than spending sleepless nights trying to understand existence.

You know, my Friends, with what a brave Carouse
I made a Second Marriage in my house;
Divorced old barren Reason from my bed,
And took the Daughter of the Vine to Spouse.[7]

The twelfth-century Sufi poet Rumi, while recognizing and praising physical delight, is also subtle and internal:

When I am with you, we stay up all night,
When you're not here, I can't get to sleep.
Praise God for these two insomnias!
And the difference between them.[8]

Another poem by Rumi is even less direct:

The minute I heard my first love story,
I started looking for you, not knowing how blind that was.
Lovers don't finally meet somewhere,
They're in each other all along.[9]

Adultery

The eighteenth century, on both sides of the English Channel, was a time of polite society. Manners were extremely important, but under the surface the lusty life continued to be celebrated. One historian of the period observed that though the drawing room was elegant and proper in all respects, behind the gilded bedroom door the rules were abandoned. Infidelity was rampant. It was expected that every well-bred gentleman of means would keep at least one mistress. Though religion kept denouncing flagrant immorality, even pious church-goers could look the other way, especially at their own behavior.

Bygone though these eras may have been, the fact remains that the theme of masculine domination and women-as-playthings—servants of Eros, if you will—has never gone entirely out of fashion. Two of the favorite Mozart operas remain hugely popular, and both center on roguish adulterers. The countess in the 1786 *The Marriage of Figaro* (analyzed in Chapter 8) is the long-suffering wife of a philandering husband who exercises his right to take to bed a female servant on her wedding night—*before* the husband does! The countess is, however, rewarded for her patience by getting to sing glorious musical laments—and by obtaining a promise from her philandering husband that he will be faithful, at least until the curtain falls.

Don Giovanni (1787) is actually a glorification of the most famous serial seducer of all time, Don Juan. One of his victims, Zerlina, is engaged to marry someone of her own station in life and has sworn fidelity to him, a fact that makes little difference to the Don—and presumably the audience. Though the hero dies at the end and is consigned to hell, we cannot imagine that the intent of Mozart and his librettist, Lorenzo da Ponte (both of whom were discussed in Chapter 8), was to make a strong case against male promiscuity.

> *"If love is often cruel or destructive, the reasons lie not in love itself, but in the inequality between people."*
>
> —**Anton Chekhov**

In certain circles today, sexual encounters are assumed to be of brief duration, and relationships with numerous partners are accepted as the norm. Freedom to engage in such relationships does not, however, mean that ending them is always painless. "Breaking Up Is Hard to Do" is the title of a song that finds many listeners nodding in agreement with its sentiments. One is tempted to conclude that during the eighteenth and nineteenth centuries tales of philandering outside of marriage were popular *because of,* not despite, the rigid moral codes prevailing. The relaxation of moral codes notwithstanding, physical passion and the pain of lost love remain dramatic subjects.

Agape

We should not think *love* in the humanities has always meant uncontrollable passion that makes people tragic victims or fools. In fact its opposite, *agape (ah-ga-pay),* is a Greek word meaning simply "love." In other words, in the classical world, *eros,* or lust, was not considered to be a form of love, but something else altogether.

> *"Love must be as much a light as a flame."*
>
> **—Henry David Thoreau**

The most famous discourse on the subject came from Plato (427–347 B.C.E.); thus *agape* is often called **Platonic love**. In popular usage the term "Platonic" has come to mean not only the opposite of lust, but a synonym for a totally nonphysical relationship, as in the expression "They're just Platonic friends." As you will see, a truly Platonic friendship involves much more than, say, having a classmate who studies with you while both save other relationships for the weekend!

The Platonic Ideal

In point of fact, Plato's ideal love may indeed include physical union with another, but the philosopher also believed the pleasures of the body can never be the highest possible good. There is no reason to believe he did not enjoy those pleasures, but he saw them as only the first rung on what we may call a ladder to the ideal.

In Platonic philosophy, each of us is born with a soul, the rational capacity for comprehending all of the eternal truths. The soul eventually discovers that it is imprisoned in a body, which is subject to deterioration, pain, and death. The soul, however, is immortal and will find a new home after the present body dies. The constant longing of the soul is therefore to escape from the body.

In his 1629 play *The New Inn,* Ben Jonson (1673?–1737) defined Platonic love as "A spiritual coupling of two souls/ So much more excellent as it relates unto the body." For Plato, a human being's attraction to another on a strictly physical level is at least a step in the right direction because it represents a preoccupation with something other than the self—our temporary home, which, being short-lived, is of no great importance. Besides, the goal of bodily attraction is reproduction, the generation of another life; generation is likewise closer to immortality than being trapped in the trivial, everyday details of the self. Bringing into existence another life offers us a glimpse of the eternal because we have for the time being substituted a fresh young life for a decaying, older one. Plato believed, therefore, that physical love can be construed as a good when it is an expression of the need for contact with what is not the self. It is not a good when physical attraction becomes obsession with the need to own, to possess, to make the other a part of oneself.

After a time, the soul glimpses higher visions. It longs for contact with other minds, with ideas, with art. One can therefore be in love–Platonically–with another person's mind, a painting, a sculpture, a symphony. One can fall in love with the face of another because it represents a perfect arrangement: in short, when it provides aesthetic pleasure, desirable for its own sake, not for the sake of possession. One can find a painting in a museum that strongly attracts the soul and sit before it for a long time, wanting only to remain in its presence, even as one might have, at another time, longed to remain in the exciting physical presence of another person. The difference? Why is one said to be a higher good than the other? The answer is that the painting will always be there. The painting is a window through which one sees a little piece of the eternal. With the painting the soul revisits its home beyond physical reality, where one is in the presence of pure beauty that cannot be tarnished like the things of the material world. Platonic love is a ladder that leads past physical pleasure and upward toward the experience of pure beauty, an experience that cannot be expressed in words, but only felt by the soul.

> *[T]he true order of going, or being led . . . to things of love, is to begin from the beauties of earth and mount upwards for the sake of other beauty, using these as steps only, and from one going on to two, and from two to all fair forms, and from fair forms to fair practices, and from fair practices to fair notions, until from fair notions he arrives at the notion of absolute beauty, and at last knows what the essence of beauty is.*[10]

For Plato, the highest form of love is therefore the love of the beautiful: in a mind, in art, in life itself.

Christians during the Middle Ages preferred Plato to Aristotle mainly because of his theory of *agape*. Christians believed the Platonic ladder leading from physical desire to a vision of the ideal was in actuality a ladder to God. Platonic love thus became God's love for humanity and, conversely, human spiritual, or holy, love divorced from base passions. Whether Christian-based or not, this idea continues to influence vast numbers and forms the basis for the popular notion that to love Platonically means to refrain from sexual contact.

Platonic Love Evaluated

Almost none of us can fail to be affected by this idealism that love transcends passions. During a long separation, lovers may imagine each other as they once looked, but in a reunion years later, they can face disappointment. Consider the major ideals of Plato's world: The Good, The True, and The Beautiful. Then consider how the world of the flesh conspires against them. To be alive, to be human, is to change, eventually to be different from before, just as a flower only briefly achieves its potential. The beautiful smiling child in a photograph is for its time the epitome of how a child should look. Part of the pleasure of seeing it is the knowledge that the child has the potential to become something else—larger, smarter, more agile—but different. The separated lovers may compare present reality with old photographs, noting with sadness how the actual person is no longer the ideal person.

> *"The beauties of the body are as nothing to the beauties of the soul, so that wherever one meets with spiritual loveliness, even in the husk of an unlovely body, he will find it beautiful enough to fall in love with and to cherish."*
>
> **—Plato**

Platonism carries with it an ideal worth striving for and yet intrinsically disappointing, even antilife. (An example is the famous aria "The Impossible Dream" from *Man of La Mancha*, the 1967 musical version of *Don Quixote*, in which the virtuous knight declares that he will devote his life to pure and beautiful causes. But we note that even he admits his dream is "impossible.")

For the confirmed Platonist a price must be paid for attempting to live in a world higher than the physical plane. In John Keats's "Ode on a Grecian Urn"

A mathematician's love of a perfect equation is an example of Platonic love: a reaching out for the ideal.

(1820), the poet envies the inanimate lovers pictured on the urn as being superior to human lovers because they will not suffer the pains of aging and death: "All human passion far above/ The burning forehead and the parching tongue." The pictured lovers will stay the same: "Forever wilt thou love and she be fair." The poem is just one of many, many works to make the Platonic statement that art is better than life because it does not change; one of many works to view the love of art as equivalent to the highest form of love.

The Platonic concept that love in its highest form takes us to the realm of pure beauty that rules supreme at the top of Plato's ladder may have sounded inspiring to lovers and the artists who depict them, but they have also been quick to recognize that few can withstand the rigors of the climb.

In his short story "The Birthmark," Nathaniel Hawthorne recognizes the impossibility of reaching pure perfection, of experiencing ideal beauty. In the story, a husband frequently remarks that his wife is beautiful, almost perfect in fact, except for the small birthmark on her cheek. He thinks he knows a way to remove it, but there may be danger. The wife begs him to try. She wants to appear completely beautiful for the man she loves. With the aid of his assistant, the husband performs an experimental operation and manages to take away the ugly blemish. As the birthmark disappears, the wife dies. Hawthorne is saying that we cannot expect perfection in this world. Humankind is born naturally flawed and can never attain an ideal state in which love is pure and untainted and beauty lasts forever. But is the Platonist injured by striving for it?

Family Love

The majority of us take for granted having siblings, cousins, and aunts. These are the close kin who sign letters, cards, and e-mail "with love," hug and kiss us at family gatherings, and expect loyalties and favors from us—even as we expect such in return—without asking why. All these actions are performed under the rubric of the word *love*. Loyalty to the family is so much taken for granted that juries tend to disregard a defendant's alibi that depends on a mother's testifying that her child couldn't be guilty because he or she never left her side.

Calendars are filled with reminders to demonstrate the kind of family love once called "togetherness." Advertisements exhort us to "show how much you care" with elaborate gifts and greeting cards. Supermarkets like to show a happy assemblage of relatives around a festive table, the implication being that if we would only shop at Food Stuff somehow all family ties will be restored and all guilt washed away.

Still, we know the truth is rarely as pictured. The French satirist and social reformer François Arouet, better known as Voltaire (1694–1778), once defined the family as a "group of people who cannot stand the sight of each other but are forced to live under the same roof." The American poet Robert Frost (1875–1963) in his narrative poem *The Death of the Hired Man* has one character observe

> *Home is the place where, when you have to go there,*
> *They have to take you in.*[11]

To be sure, this is not the final word on the subject in the poem, but these lines have become famous and often quoted as if they did indeed express his philosophy. Sometimes they express the thinking of those who quote them!

How important are blood ties? The concept of family love has changed over time. Movies and television programs can barely keep up with the new dynamics. Nowadays school children easily master a complicated family tree, with visits to and from grandparents, gifts of varying value from one branch or another, and different rules required for dealing with stepparents and former siblings, as well as the less well-defined zone of the "significant others" and their offspring.

An acclaimed film, *The Kids Are All Right* (2010), deals with two lesbians (played by Annette Bening and Julianne Moore) who have each borne a child from the sperm of the same donor. Now the grown children have sought out the man who is their biological father. Even though this man never knew them because laboratory technology assisted in conception, he and the children experience the fundamental need to create a family unit. Undoubtedly this modern version of the search for one's roots can be widely found. "Family ties" has undergone a change, or at any rate has expanded.

Even before the current fluid state of marriage and family, the humanities dealt extensively with family love and its discontents, if only because people enjoyed reading about or watching stories about unhappy, dysfunctional families. One college instructor of playwriting told her class that "if you come from a happy home life, you may never be able to write a play."

> *It is in the love of one's family only that heartfelt happiness is known.*
>
> —**Thomas Jefferson**

> *Children begin by loving their parents. After a time they judge them. Rarely, if ever, do they forgive them.*
>
> —**Oscar Wilde**

Family Conflicts

Think of the many unhappy children in literature and drama, eager to escape parents who don't appreciate them or stepparents who abuse them. In popular fiction there is usually a happy ending in which the runaways return, sometimes with a fortune. In more serious work, especially on the stage, there is seldom a happy ending. Theater features a host of disappointed fathers, mothers, and offspring who never manage to find themselves. The bewildered Willy Loman, hero of Arthur Miller's *Death of a Salesman* (1949), wants his son to be more successful than his academically gifted friend, only to be told by the son in a wrenching confrontation scene he is only "a buck an hour" and is never going to be anything else. The son passionately adds that the family has never ever told each other the truth for one minute.

The revelation shocks Willy into a Don Quixote–like delusion that his son is still "going to be magnificent," impelling the poor salesman to crash his car into a wall so that the son will collect the insurance and become a business triumph.

The humanities are full of epic struggles for family fortunes and hatred between brothers who have had nothing to do with each other for years. Perhaps some people find solace in reading about and seeing portrayals of families a lot less loving than theirs. Particularly during holidays, these solace-seekers have the feeling that everyone else is enjoying a festive meal complete with harmony among the generations. Though TV commercials show Grandma setting a turkey on the table to the applause of her loving family, many are alone watching that old skinflint Scrooge, in a rerun of *A Christmas Carol* on cable, come to his senses and supply the poverty-stricken Crachits with enough food to sink a ship.

A not-so-wonderful holiday account of family life is found in Amy Tan's *The Bonesetter's Daughter* (2001). One scene takes place in a San Francisco Chinese restaurant during the Festival of the Full Moon. Because of last-minute acceptance of invitations, the party is larger than expected and guests are seated at two tables. The hostess, her mother, her live-in boyfriend, and his two daughters are at one. The boyfriend's ex-wife, her parents, her husband, and their children are at another. Everyone arrives at the same time so that unity is hard to achieve. One character, noticing the non-Chinese children, asks: "'Hey, are we in the white ghetto or what?'"

Following Chinese tradition, the hostess offers the first delicacy to her mother, but the non-Chinese children squeal their disapproval of the foreign-looking food with cries of "Take it away!" The mother's boyfriend pays particular attention to his ex-wife, and Grandma shows signs of dementia. A somewhat less than happy family get-together.

The Family in Religion

In The Republic, *Plato advises that in an ideal community children should be taken from their parents and raised by the state.*

The ancient Hebrews may have given the world its first idea of the family unit, the one that has survived for so many centuries. In developing the father-children relationship between God and humanity, Judaism also created a model for earthly existence. First came the tribe, the larger group comprised of interrelated families and governed by a patriarch, an older and presumably wiser man with great powers of judgment over all the members. The prominent biblical patriarchs Abraham and Moses are examples. Such an arrangement was logically paralleled by the idea of God the father with the same power over human children. The family circle became sanctified as a means of protecting the larger unit, the tribe. Rules against worshiping false gods or marrying outside the tribe helped to maintain coherence and unity.

Love for God, which included fear and respect, was also demanded for the father of the earthly family. Without obedience there would be no order, and without fear, awe, and respect there could be no obedience. Fear was the means by which the children of a patriarch and humanity as children of God showed their love. The sometimes wrathful imposition of discipline and punishment (as well as unexpected forgiveness) from both fathers was in turn *their* way of showing love.

Two biblical women, Ruth and Naomi, however, changed the traditional view of the family when, after the death of Ruth's husband, she chose not to return to her original roots but remain instead with Naomi, her husband's mother, thus forming the basis for a new family.

> *And Ruth said, Intreat me not to leave thee,*
> *or to return from following after thee:*
> *for whither thou goest, I will go; and where*
> *thou lodgest, I will lodge: thy people shall be*
> *my people, and thy God my God:*
>
> Ruth: 1:16

If biblical historians are accurate, a group of Hebrew elders got together hundreds of years after the historical events we read about in the earliest portions of the Bible, gathered up all known written accounts of Hebrew history and cultural practices and embarked upon the astonishing project of setting everything down in what they considered proper order.

The biblical concept of family love has created a model of human behavior that is beautiful to contemplate if not easy to achieve.

Even though the giving of the Ten Commandments to Moses is regarded as pivotal in Hebrew history, they have since been perceived as binding on all humanity, not merely those of the lineage of Abraham and Moses. One of the commandments—honor thy father and thy mother—is a restatement and an enlargement of early tribal requirements, but it has become universally accepted, whether acted upon or not.

To honor a parent may require specific instructions, and the Chinese sage Confucius provided exactly that. (A fuller discussion of Confucius is found in Chapter 10.) Almost every detail of living is covered by Confucius, but none in greater detail than the rules for the treatment of one's parents and in-laws. Assuming that most households included several generations, Confucius instructs children to eat whatever food is left over after their elders have finished. They must constantly inquire after the comfort of their parents, whether they are too warm or too cold, and whether they have an itch that needs scratching. There are prescribed visits morning and evening, and always obedience is foremost.

> *When sons and wives are ordered to do anything by their parents, they should immediately respond and reverently proceed to do it. In going forward or backward, or turning around, they should be careful and serious. While going out or coming in, while bowing or walking, they should not presume to belch, or cough, to yawn or stretch themselves, to stand on one foot, or to lean against anything. . .*[12]

The rules set down by Confucius may sound quaint to viewers brought up in a child-centered home and nurtured with the idea that individual happiness is more important than tradition or loyalty to the family. Audiences and readers cheer when the obedient (and therefore repressed) young adult leaves home to seek a fortune far from the restrictive rules of the tribe. Nonetheless, respect for the wisdom of the strong patriarch or matriarch remains alive and well in cultures throughout the world.

One of the reasons for the enduring popularity of the 1967 musical *Fiddler on the Roof* seems to be that its subject matter—the strength of the family unit and its ability to survive oppression—appeals to many who might accept the weakness of family bonds but secretly wish it were otherwise.

Matriarchs and Patriarchs

Two plays by Federico García Lorca (1898–1936) illustrate the tragic consequences of strong parental control. In both, mothers claim the right to steer the destinies of their daughters and to have the final say about when and whom they marry. In *Blood Wedding* (1935), the bride, promised to a man she does not love, runs off with someone else, a solution that cannot end happily in the repressed, traditional Spanish society of Lorca's plays. *The House of Bernarda Alba* (1936) explores the tragic effect of a fiercely dominating matriarch over her daughters in a cheerless household dominated by unbreakable rules of endless mourning, forced chastity, and waiting without joy for an arranged match to materialize.

In a similar vein, a dominating mother in the 1993 Mexican film *Like Water for Chocolate* demands that her daughter marry no one at all in order to continue to cook and otherwise take care of the household. All she can anticipate in life is becoming the caregiver of an aging parent.

John Steinbeck's *The Grapes of Wrath* gave the world one of the most memorable portraits of a matriarch named Ma Joad with responsibility for keeping her family together. In the 1930s, the Joad family suffers bank foreclosure on their farm in Oklahoma and joins hundreds of other displaced, scornfully labeled "Okies" on a grueling migration to the Promised Land of California, only to discover that the promise of abundant field work and high pay was a scam. Because there are so many of them, the impoverished Okies are forced to pick fruit from sunup to sundown for paltry wages. The four men of the family are paid *collectively* one dollar

Steinbeck's Ma Joad gave the world one of its most memorable portraits of the matriarch who struggles to keep the family together.

Bettmann/Corbis

Jane Darwell, Henry Fonda, and Russell Simpson, *The Grapes of Wrath*, 1940

Ma Joad has become an archetype of the strong matriarch.

for a day's work. Ma buys a dollar's worth of hamburger from the store operated by the company and watches as her men devour the few scraps of meat. When one of the sons asks if there is any more food, she says in a voice that tries to sound pleasant and hopeful but nonetheless tears at the heart: "No, son, they ain't." They made a dollar, and they ate a dollar's worth of meat. No one noticed that Ma ate nothing. The novel has attained the status of a classic, and Ma Joad who has taken her place among the great archetypes of the family protector, is heroic in the best sense of that word.

All strong parents in American literature are not as self-sacrificing as Ma Joad. One of the most overbearing fathers is the frightening creation of Henry James (1843–1915) in his 1881 novella *Washington Square*, later to become a play and film of the 1940s, both called *The Heiress*. This father makes no attempt to conceal his disappointment in his daughter, reminding her that she is far less attractive in every way than the mother who died giving birth to her. The daughter is told that she lacks grace and charm and the feminine ability to flirt and make small talk. In an age when a proper marriage is the only suitable future for a physician's daughter, she is continually reminded of her sad deficiencies.

The father in Henry James's Washington Square *is a memorable portrait of the dominating patriarch who doesn't know how to give love.*

At length a suitor appears, a handsome, charming young man, who woos her respectfully and begs her to be his wife. After meeting the man and appraising both his income and career aspirations (or lack of them), the doctor decides the suitor is nothing but a fortune hunter. Why else would such a handsome person take an interest in his daughter? The father announces his intention of bequeathing his money to a charitable institution if the marriage takes place, but the daughter is confident that her suitor will marry her anyway. The two plan an elopement, but the heroine is left broken-heartedly waiting for the man who claimed to love her and who never comes for her.

Years later, after she has inherited her father's wealth, the absent suitor, now full of apologies and renewed declarations of love, again asks the heiress to marry him. Again she agrees to an elopement, but this time she leaves him at the front door, pounding on it and begging her to forgive him. As his cries fill the empty street, she lights a lamp and goes upstairs to bed. When her aunt asks how she can be so cruel, the heiress replies with a stony face, "I have been taught by masters."

Nor should we believe that family domination of children's destiny has been limited to stage and fiction. In her 1984 study of the struggle for women's independence, *The Weaker Vessel,* Antonia Fraser writes about the arranged marriage.

> *During this period, the emotion we should now term romantic love was treated with a mixture of suspicion, contempt, and outright disgust by virtually all pundits. . . . that tender passion which has animated much of the great literature of the world . . . received a hearty condemnation. Nor was this a revolutionary state of affairs in seventeenth-century England, the arranged marriage as opposed to the romantic union having been preferred by most societies. . . .*[13]

Friendship

> *Love is blind; friendship closes its eyes.*
>
> **—Old proverb**

Unlike his teacher Plato, Aristotle does not speak about love, but he is a strong believer in friendship. He includes it among the highest goods of the happy life. For him, friendship is a strong bond between individuals sharing common interests and moral values, and it is thus suspiciously like Plato's ideal of the perfect nonphysical relationship, except that Platonic love need not involve interaction with another person at all.

If *kinfolk* is the traditional word for people related by blood, there ought to be a designation for the friendship that replaces the bonds of family, "super kin," or "kin by choice." The international stage hit *Hair* (1969), subtitled "The American Tribal Love Rock Musical," ushered in the era of the family with a common bond that is not biological, focusing on a spontaneous family of young men and women bonded by a mutual hatred of the war in Vietnam. This family was also environmentally sensitive, singing a warning about the imminent death of our planet unless active measures are taken to save it. At a performance on Earth Day in Chicago in 1976, the audience, customarily invited to join the actors at the curtain call in a dance celebrating life and love, was inspired to pour onto the street and help the actors dispose of litter. Well-dressed ladies and gentlemen were photographed on their hands and knees, some even in the gutter, picking up candy wrappers and cigarette butts. The dancing continued on the street for hours, tying up traffic and attracting policemen, many of whom joined this impromptu family in the common cause.

> *Friendship is seldom lasting but between equals.*
>
> **—Samuel Johnson**

The sitcom *Friends* attracted millions of viewers each week during a ten-year period, and nearly that many years in reruns. In fact, it has been called the most successful TV show in history. Audiences ranged in age from the very young to the elderly. Clearly, it struck a responsive note; and that may have had something to do with alarming reports about the gradual eroding of the **nuclear family**. Once considered the foundation of our society, the nuclear family, comprising parents, children, and often one or both sets of grandparents, has given way to the *extended family,* which may include some blood relatives as well as lifelong friends and even recent acquaintances with whom quick bonds are established. *Friends* represented the kin-by-choice family in which no one was related. Perhaps its enormous popularity is evidence that Americans secretly fear the isolation that a swiftly moving, rapidly changing society can bring.

In times gone by, friendship may not have been as desirable as it now seems to be in our fragmented society. In *Hamlet,* for example, Polonius gives his son Laertes some advice before the young man sets out to discover his place in the world: "Neither a borrower nor a lender be;/ For loan oft loses both itself and friend. . . ." This advice is tough-minded, isn't it? The implication is that friendship won't withstand either borrowing or lending. If the loan isn't paid back, chances are neither will ever speak to the other again.

Far more cynical are two recommendations about friendship made two centuries apart. In the novel *Tom Jones* by Henry Fielding (1707–1754) we are told that "when you have made your Fortune by the good Offices of a Friend, you are advised to discard him as soon as you can." In other words, what is a friend if not someone you can use to better your own station in life? One wishes that particular definition were indeed a thing of the past!

Close in spirit to the super-kin idea of family is the buddy relationship, extolled in two classic novels: Cervantes's *Don Quixote* and Mark Twain's *Huckleberry Finn.* In both cases, we note a close bond between two men may have something to do with the fact that one outranks the other.

In *Don Quixote,* the buddies are the Don and his faithful servant, Sancho Panza, who knows exactly what his master is but who deeply loves his idealism, however misguided it may be. If love is sometimes defined as caring more for another than for oneself, Sancho Panza, in dedicating his entire life to a man who has lost all contact with reality, nurturing and protecting him from the jeers of the crude world, is the veritable icon of selfless devotion. Whether or not it can exist between friends in the real world, readers may decide for themselves. The servant's love for the master is the more admirable when we consider that the master is too far gone to appreciate it, and it may be that the fragile health of the master makes it easier for the servant to devote his entire being to him.

Photos 12/Alamy

Jessica Tandy and Morgan Freeman, *Driving Miss Daisy,* 1989

In this film version of *Driving Miss Daisy,* Morgan Freeman allows Jessica Tandy to think she retains her independence.

That relationship has contemporary parallels, as in Alfred Uhry's 1988 Pulitzer Prize–winning play *Driving Miss Daisy.* The master in this case is a feisty old woman who belongs to Atlanta's moneyed aristocracy. The servant is her African American chauffeur, who understands and accepts the racial barriers separating them but, like Sancho Panza, has a deep-rooted loyalty toward and genuine love for the woman. He does all he can to protect her from the knowledge that she is close to senility and will soon be utterly incapable of even feeding herself. The popularity of both the play and the movie version may be a testament to audience nostalgia for a vanished past in which such unquestioning devotion could exist.

Huckleberry Finn begins with a continuation from an earlier novel of the buddy adventures of Huck and Tom Sawyer, but the author must have realized that Tom was too middle-class, too much of a conformist to fully understand the rebellious Huck. That friendship is replaced by the bond that develops between Huck and Jim, a runaway slave. Once more we have discrepancy in rank and ethnicity. Jim is the stronger of the two, teaching Huck how to survive the hardships of life on the Mississippi River.

The age discrepancy between the 14-year-old Huck and the much older Jim also became the forerunner of many such relationships celebrated on film and television in our era. Italian film directors, in particular, have been fond of pairing an old man and a young boy. The man teaches the boy about the ways of the world, in perhaps a nostalgic glimpse of a past age when aging persons were less likely to be considered burdens on the young.

> *Love sickness needs a love cure.*
>
> **—Chinese proverb**

Romantic Love

We have seen how the behavior of people said to be in love is strongly influenced by time period and cultural values. Most probably, when you the reader first looked at the title of the chapter, you thought of one kind of love in particular, one that has yet to be discussed: **romantic love**. For many, the words *love* and *romance* are synonymous. Perhaps we like to think that the need for such love is inborn. When friends advise that a current suitor is not the right boy/girl for you, the implication is that such a person must surely exist and will come along eventually. How many people have become lost in self-pity because Mr./Ms. Right has never shown up?

The "right" person is a mythic archetype indigenous to our culture, but not necessarily universal. The prototype of romantic love is, undeniably, Shakespeare's *Romeo and Juliet,* performed almost continuously throughout the world. It is the first work that comes to mind when someone is asked to name a great love story.

Still, as we have pointed out, the famous star-crossed lovers *are* smitten by passionate physical desires in the classical tradition. Near the end of the balcony scene, Juliet tells Romeo she must go inside now, and the anguished young man cries out, "O, wilt thou leave me so unsatisfied?" There is no mistaking what he means. Juliet answers, "What satisfaction canst thou have tonight?" The key word is *tonight*.

But there is more. Shakespeare wrote at a time when women, at least of the upper classes, were no longer mere commodities. Yes, Juliet is destined for an arranged marriage, and yes, its purpose is her financial security as well as the social advantages of uniting two prominent families; but Romeo, after all, is willing to have Juliet despite the fact that if they were to marry both would be cut off without a penny. Hence Juliet is not property in his eyes. The play tells the world there is something more important than financial security or social approval. And that has come to be called romantic—or true—love. The language of the lovers is the language of romance as far as subsequent eras have been concerned. Nobody is saying that romance is an experience entirely separate from sexual passion, but most of us would agree that romance has something more that transcends obsession with sexual union alone. Shakespeare's lovers indeed seem to believe in, to share that something more, and to give up their lives for it.

Bridgeman/SuperStock

Frank Dicksee, *Romeo and Juliet*, 1884

The language of the lovers is the language of romance for all time.

Cynics believe the language of romance is all a facade and that lust is always the reality. Yet the archetype of romantic love still exerts such a strong influence on our lives—as do many other archetypes—that one must be cautious about calling it a lie or a delusion. Why would romance novels constitute a billion-dollar industry? Why would so many readers be lost without those heroes and heroines who think of nothing but being with each other? Poetry and songs are filled with accounts of the all-consuming emotion defined by the word *romance,* with hearts being won, lost, broken, and crushed. The despairing lover in a classic Cole Porter song cries "You took my heart and threw it away." The heart, not some other part of the body, is the location of romantic feelings.

Romance continues to be talked or written or sung about in terms that exclude all mention of physical desire. Lovers long for one glance, for the touch of a hand, for an ascent to paradise. Romeo and Juliet elevate their passion through verse. The *West Side Story* lovers in their version of Shakespeare's play do so by thrilling audiences with "Maria" and "Tonight." Even if so many of the pop tunes of today deal with the torments of finding that one's true love is cheating, even if romance is considered a *tragic* state, the fact remains that it is the basis of hopes and dreams for millions, the thing most worth striving for. It must therefore be a real force. And, if it comes from the humanities, why, what better testament to the power of myth, art, and literature? Where would we be without them?

The language of romance is exactly what we do not find in the writings of Greeks and Romans. Except for Plato they were strictly earthbound; they saw love as an affliction, often terrible, which drives people into desperate fires of longing. Love may be fun for a time, but unless one is willing to suffer, one is better off without it. Plato, with his ladder that leads to the ideal, paved the way for the eventual emergence of the belief that ideal love transcends the flesh.

Three sources for the romantic ideal of love:

- *the cult of the Virgin Mary*
- *the literary genre called the romance*
- *the code of chivalry*

The notion of the love that transcends lust and lasts through and beyond time may have been glimpsed by Plato, but it grew firm roots in the Middle Ages. We can cite these sources for its growth and spread, and its continued hold on our emotions:

- The cult that grew up around the poets and artists who celebrated the glory of the Virgin Mary
- The *romance* itself, a sophisticated genre of literature about a (usually highborn) young man or woman for whom physical union is not allowed; one partner may be married or have obstinate parents
- The code of chivalry, a set of generally elegant actions performed by a knight to honor his lady fair including, if need be, laying down his life for her in jousting tournaments

Mariolatry

The writings of the Christian Bible do not say much about Mary, but as the religion spread and the Christian tradition grew during the Middle Ages, the subject of the mother of Jesus became a matter of increasing fascination. Madonna and Child were favorite subjects for medieval and, later, Renaissance painters (see Chapter Five). Poets waxed eloquent about Mary as the perfect woman, and particularly about her chastity. Though the virgin birth was not always easy to comprehend, no one doubted the purity of Mary; and since Mary was mortal, not divine, her purity and glory encouraged reverence for other women as well, women deemed to be superior to men—virtually "above" them, as if they were on a balcony or in a tower, from which they could wave and provide inspiration to the adoring men below.

Idolatry of Mary, or **Mariolatry**, led to innumerable kinds of artistic expression, and it carried over into secular literature as writers borrowed the idea of the virginal heroine, worshiped for her purity as the poets worshiped Mary. Earthly love was thus presented in spiritual terms, even if lust were secretly there as well.

The same period saw a rebirth of interest in Plato's theory of love. It now became readily understood as the pursuit of an ideal love—pure, chaste, true, and undefiled by lust—that cannot be destroyed, even in the grave. This ideal is still very much with us despite attacks by an all-pervasive cynicism.

Romance and Chivalry

The **romance** is a literary genre popular during the eleventh and twelfth centuries. The word itself derives from the French *roman,* a long fictional narrative. Today the word is translated as "novel." Early romances were told rather than written, since there was no printing press and storytelling had become an art form. Though they usually revolved around a man-woman relationship, the stories were not always about love but might include perilous journeys to distant Eastern lands at the time of the Crusades. Told from the Christian point of view they presented dangers lying in wait for noble knights in combat with "infidels." Many of the best-loved romances were stories about King Arthur, Camelot, and the knights of the Round Table.

The word *chivalry* also had its origin in France, coming from the word *cheval* (horse). The dashing knight on his horse had many admirable qualities, including a willingness to fight to the death in the name of his lady. All that was required of her was that she allow him to risk his life, perhaps while wearing a scarf she had given him as a token of the honor she bestowed. Thus was born the tradition of placing the lady on a pedestal and of expecting nothing in return, should she be disposed to offer nothing. Chivalry, the knight's code, was the ancestor of the polite gestures that are often performed and expected, such as opening doors, pulling out chairs, and in general placing the lady first in any order of events. (The gentlemanly practice of walking nearer to the curb is a latter-day version of chivalry, originally meant to spare the lady from being splattered with mud from carriages racing by.)

> *So faithful in love, and so dauntless in war,*
> *There never was a knight like the young Lochinvar.*
>
> **—Sir Walter Scott**

In many of the stories, even if the lady were willing to offer herself to the gallant man, they could not form a lasting union because one of them was already married or otherwise unavailable. Typically such marriages were arranged by families more interested in property and financial gain than in the happiness of the offspring. Perhaps the loving couple experienced a few moments of physical gratification in secret, but on the surface was the assumption that love denied was nobler than a loveless marriage. Love outside of marriage was made to seem as chaste.

A second assumption was that true love was made in heaven and was therefore elevated above earthly concerns such as bodily pleasure and marriages of convenience and the wealth they brought. The belief that heaven destines each of us for someone else and that this someone is the right and only mate has persisted through the centuries. Even if no union ever takes place between two right people, the rightness lasts forever.

Dante and the Divine Comedy

One of the enduring romantic and unconsummated relationships in the Middle Ages was that of Dante (Chapter 3) and the woman he called Beatrice, whom he presumably first saw when he was nine years old and whom he later immortalized in *The Divine Comedy.*

> *At that moment, I say most truly that the spirit of life, which hath its dwelling in the secretest chamber of the heart, began to tremble so violently that the least pulses of my body shook therewith; and trembling it said these words "Here is a deity stronger than I; who, coming, shall rule over me..." I in my boyhood often went in search of her, and found her so noble and praiseworthy that certainly of her might have been said those words of the poet Homer, "She seemed not to be the daughter of a mortal man, but of God."*[14]

Dante's overwhelming attraction toward Beatrice was, he said, the inspiration behind the hundred **cantos** of *The Divine Comedy*. It is the reason he as narrator of the poem is willing to undertake the arduous journey through the Inferno and Purgatory before reaching Paradise. It is understood that they will never be able to enjoy their love in any mortal way.

In Canto V of his poem, Dante visits the circle of hell (the Inferno) in which are the souls of damned, carnal sinners, who must suffer eternal punishment for their unsanctified lust. Because illicit passion had swept them off their feet, they can now find no rest. Still, in the tragic tale of Paolo and Francesca, two of the doomed lovers, the poet, while not justifying their sin, nonetheless is compassionate toward them. In fact, the reason he does not place them in lower circles where punishment is far more severe is that, even though they were misguided, at least they *loved*. The lowest circle is reserved for Satan, who represents the total absence of love.

Paolo is the brother of a man in an arranged marriage to Francesca sent to inform the lady of the parents' wishes. One day, however, they are so strongly affected by reading about the passion of an Arthurian knight that they fall into each other's arms, unable to keep from enjoying the strong sexual feelings that overwhelm them. Francesca explains to the poet-narrator:

> *We were alone and without any dread.*
> *Sometimes our eyes, at the word's secret call,*
> *Met, and our cheeks a changing color wore.*
> *But it was one page only that did all.*
> *When we read how that smile, so thirsted for,*
> *Was kissed by such a lover, he that may*
> *Never from me be separated more*
> *All trembling kissed my mouth...*[15]

Yearning and aspiration toward an unreachable beloved is a feature of romantic love. Domesticity is not. Stories about romantic love tend, rather, to feature not wedding anniversaries and visits from in-laws and grandchildren, but the death of one or both lovers. Lovers of music are the beneficiaries of their suffering, as, for example, in the erotic yet also spiritual "Liebestod" (Love-Death) from the opera *Tristan and Isolde,* composed between 1857 and 1859 by Richard Wagner (see Chapter 8) to celebrate his love for a married woman. As in the story of Paolo and Francesca, Isolde, the heroine, has been promised to another, in this case King Mark, and is escorted to the wedding by the king's nephew Tristan. On the ship they drink a love potion that creates feelings too powerful to resist.

Like much romantic art, the opera carries the implied message that illicit love is short-lived but wonderful enough to make early death worthwhile. Ordinary mortals who live by the rules are shown to live safe but dull lives. True love is therefore often combined with death. In the final scene, Isolde kneels by the body of her lover and sings the "Liebestod," perhaps the most sexually explicit as well as passionately romantic music ever written. Its rising melodic line and crescendo, its sonorous chords becoming a musical parallel to the sex act itself (according to many interpretations) reach a glorious high note of ecstasy before resolving in a serene aftermath, which brings peace and death to Isolde as she rests on the body of her lover.

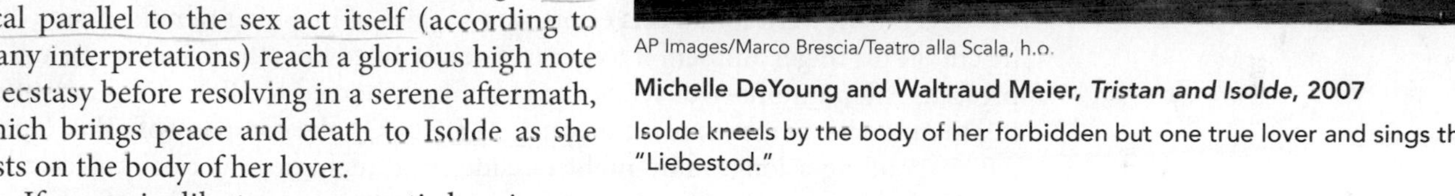

AP Images/Marco Brescia/Teatro alla Scala, h.o.

Michelle DeYoung and Waltraud Meier, *Tristan and Isolde*, 2007

Isolde kneels by the body of her forbidden but one true lover and sings the "Liebestod."

If, as cynics like to say, romantic love is pure balderdash, we must be proud of a human tradition that can so nobly celebrate and create its reality.

Love as Amusement

During the twelfth century Queen Eleanor of Aquitaine, wife of England's King Henry II and mother of Richard the Lion-Hearted, inaugurated a form of entertainment that eventually spread to other royal courts and became known as **courtly love**. In order to amuse themselves, Eleanor and her circle of aristocratic friends would hold mock trials in which the defendant, a young man who had declared his passionate longing for a reluctant young woman, was given a series of difficult tasks to perform in order to win her approval. The "jury" would hear the case—that is, the young man's account of all he had done to win the lady's favor—and then decide whether such favor should be granted. Most of the time it was not, an outcome that was in no way expected to diminish the plaintiff's devotion.

Courtly Love

Becoming known more precisely as a set of rules for the proper conduct of courtship, Courtly Love was based on the recommendations of Eleanor and others as they developed this "harmless" diversion. The idea that a high-bred woman was born to be adored and a man to be her virtual slave was implicit, if not directly stated, in the romances so that by the time rules were actually set down, there was little objection from the masculine side.

Earlier in this chapter we mentioned Cervantes's *Don Quixote* and the deep friendship between the hero and his servant. In addition, Cervantes created his own version of courtly love. The mad hero, who imagines himself to be a courageous knight, invents a fair lady he names Dulcinea, who is actually a peasant girl named Aldonza. He has no contact with her, but in his delusion he imagines she is pure and unreachable and makes himself her slave. The don invites her to ask anything of him, even his very life.

A real knight, Ulrich von Lichtenstein, spent 15 years trying to please his lady, who rewarded his devotion with scorn and derision.

The model for Don Quixote's lady may well have been a real person described in a relatively obscure book of the thirteenth century called *Freudenliest* (The Service of Women) by an actual knight, Ulrich von Lichtenstein. The book contains 30,000 lines of narrative verse, all claiming to constitute the autobiography of a man who sacrificed nearly his entire existence for a princess who for years did not know he existed.

When he was 12, Ulrich, knowing that if he were to become a knight he must adopt the role of a courtly lover, became a page in the court of a certain princess. He was so much in love that he would steal a basin of water in which the lady had washed her hands, then reverently drink it. Later, he fought in tournaments, developing a reputation as a brave knight willing to defeat all others in the name of his all-consuming obsession.

His only reward for all this effort was a series of insulting rebuffs. Even when he cut off his finger and sent it to her in a velvet-lined box, the princess was unimpressed. After a number of years, the lady finally agreed to allow the poor suffering man to visit her, but only if he came as a leper in the company of other lepers. After spending a long, rainy night outside in a ditch, he was finally allowed to climb a ladder and peer into the window of the lady's chamber, only to find a hundred candles burning and eight maids standing by her bed. After making a few crude remarks about his appearance and stupid devotion, she then pushed him and the ladder back into the moat surrounding the castle. *Freudenliest* concludes with some pretty cynical observations about women—rare for the time but perhaps understandable in this case.

> "*Love is merely a madness.*"
>
> **—William Shakespeare**

In 1507 the long-standing rules of Courtly Love were altered in a book called *The Courtier* by Baldassare Castiglione (1478–1529), in which the tempering effect of the Renaissance begins to be felt. The woman, though still powerful, is now less cruel; instead, she is well-educated, charming, witty, and sophisticated, and she requires a suitor to be her match—or nearly so. She still refuses to lose control no matter how much she secretly admires the man, and while he is expected to sue for a physical encounter, she is not supposed to grant it. The rules, however, have changed. To surrender to him would coarsen what was thought to be an entirely civilized relationship. She anticipates some of Shakespeare's wittiest and most independent heroines, who adore privately but hurl insults publicly!

Love as a Game

> "*And when we meet at any time again,*
> *Be it not seen in either of our brows*
> *That we one jot of former love retain.*"
>
> **—Michael Drayton**

The Roman poet Ovid (43 B.C.E.–18 C.E.), who specialized in writing about the subject, defines love as "a game of seduction." Whether readers of Castiglione agreed and privately enjoyed physical encounters behind bedroom doors we cannot be entirely sure. During the seventeenth century—again, among the highborn and well-bred—the game of seduction became quite fashionable, often as a way of making the satisfaction of lust more delicious. Courtship began as a verbal match between educated and witty partners and ended in a physical or physical-romantic union, only if preceded by stylish playfulness. The game of love has provided us with some of literature's most memorable dialogue and charming characters. (Whether it will continue to do so depends on the willingness of authors, playwrights, and scriptwriters to provide clever talk—and whether audiences and readers will have the patience to listen.)

Love Amid Conflict

In England, especially during the period known as the Restoration (beginning in 1661, when monarchy was reinstated after twenty years of unsuccessful democracy), the sexes reached an equality exceeding even that of the late Middle Ages. Charles II adored women and encouraged them to show their strength. In this period women took two steps forward—before the nineteenth century would take them three steps back.

Mirabell and Millamant

English theater sparkled with plays about the game of seduction carried off in high style and delightful banter. Mirabell and Millamant were the most glittering couple to grace the stage of that time in William Congreve's *The Way of the World* (1700). They manage to hide their feelings for each other behind a dazzling display of linguistic skill, yet also manage not to hide the truth of their deep feelings for each other. The play combines the purity of romantic love with the sophistication of courtly love.

Rules of the love game are observed by the couple, who openly scorn sentimentality and sincere vows. They speak in mutually curt tones and throw challenges to each other that would never be understood by people unaware of the game they are playing. Millamant sounds downright cruel when she laughs at her lover's serious face and talks of using his letters to roll up her hair. She is reluctant to entertain a proposal of marriage, despite the fact that she has never wanted to marry anyone else. Yet, according to the fashion of the day, she declares that she really would not want to surrender her cherished solitude. Besides, she has a host of other admirers. (Her name *means* "a thousand lovers.")

For his part, Mirabell is no saint, and she knows it. He has been the lover of other women in the play, one of whom has accused him of fathering her child (which he probably did). Nor is he foolish enough to suggest to Millamant that they elope without the approval of her aunt and guardian, who would withhold the lady's fortune if marriage were to take place without her consent. Instead, he uses his wits and ingenuity to embarrass the guardian and gain both her approval and her fortune. Neither Millamant nor the audience would have expected Mirabell to be morally perfect. In this sophisticated, essentially hard-boiled society one had to be a tough survivor; and true love had to accommodate the fact that it can exist only when love is a game played for high stakes by skillful players.

The play is over three centuries old and yet audiences today would find it way ahead of its time when it comes to the scene in Act IV in which the lovers draw up a marriage contract, or prenuptial agreement, as it is now called. Millamant demands that after the wedding her husband must respectfully request sexual favors from her, not regard them as automatic rights. She will sleep as late as she wants in the morning; she will not endure being called pet names such as joy, jewel, sweetheart "and the rest of that nauseous cant" when they are in public. She insists on her privacy and refuses to be "intimate with fools, because they may be your relations."

Mirabell insists that she limit what she drinks (no strong liquor) and the confidences she shares with her female friends. He commands her not to smear her face with creams and oils at bedtime and reminds her not to squeeze her body into corsets when she becomes pregnant as a result of their "endeavors"—to which Millamant cries "Odious endeavors!" (But there is every indication that both are

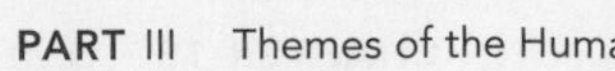

looking forward to them.) "These provisos admitted," he concludes, "I may prove a tractable and complying husband." She replies, "These articles subscribed, if I continue to endure you a little longer, I may by degrees dwindle into a wife." The underlying devotion between the lovers is clearly there.

Allowing for changes in language during the three centuries since *The Way of the World* first appeared, couples determined not to make public parade of their strong feelings for each other no doubt can still enjoy the banter of Congreve's famous lovers. They stand as icons of how sophisticated people can hold their own in an unsentimental environment and yet not forego the pleasures of romance. Despite today's high divorce rate and the competition between men and women for success and recognition, there may currently be more Mirabells and Millamants—closet romantic lovers so to speak—than we might suppose.

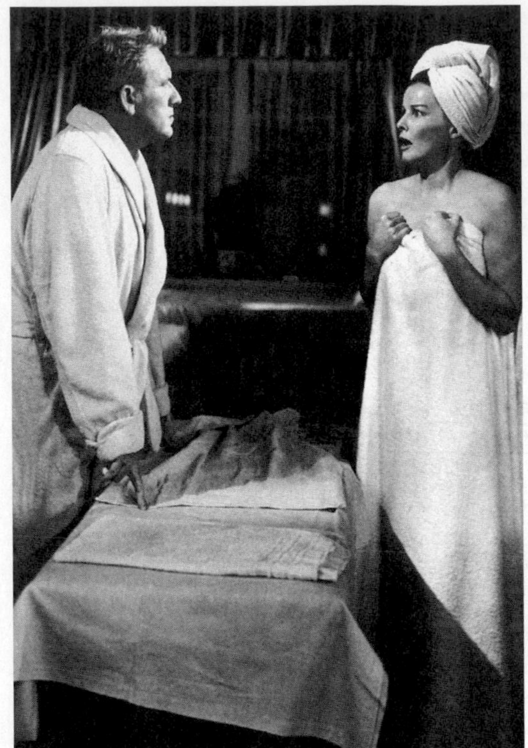

Digital Press Photos/Newscom

Spencer Tracy and Katharine Hepburn, *Adam's Rib*, 1949

In the film classic *Adam's Rib*, a modern Mirabell and Millamant show that romantic love can exist between competing professionals.

Tracy and Hepburn

A newer version of love-as-a-game was popular during the late 1940s in a series of classic films starring Spencer Tracy and Katharine Hepburn, whose screen chemistry has perhaps never been equaled.

A Tracy-Hepburn classic is *Adam's Rib* (1949). Their married characters play successful lawyers—he as a prosecuting attorney, she as a defense attorney—who are arguing opposite sides in the trial of a woman who has shot and seriously wounded her unfaithful husband. Tracy's character insists that, despite his wife's efforts to convince the jury that the woman was only defending her home, no one has the right to violate the law and therefore the defendant must be sent to prison. The married lawyers go at it stormily in court (but in one priceless scene, they wave to each other under the table). Hepburn wins, and Tracy is furious with her *on the surface.* Underneath, both are modern Mirabells and Millamants, closet romantic lovers.

Love and Marriage

You may have noticed that marriage has been mentioned sparingly thus far in the chapter. Marriage deserves its own special treatment because sometimes convenience or pre-arrangements outweigh love as the reason to marry; sometimes romantic love is present at the outset but diminishes as time goes on; and often, quite often, differences of opinion about gender roles interfere with the course of true love. And yes, true love can remain throughout the course of a lifetime. Clearly, no institution, especially in modern society, is quite so complex.

The Victorian Model

A strong moral code emerged on both sides of the Atlantic during Queen Victoria's reign (1837–1901). The Victorian era was the heyday of the upper-middle class, which decided to forget its humble past and start living "correctly" in what it believed to be the manner of the aristocracies of old. It created the most stringent code of behavior any society had ever known.

Erich Lessing/Art Resource, NY

Georges Seurat, *A Sunday Afternoon on the Island of La Grande Jatte*, 1884
Seurat's pointillist work suggests the stiffness of Victorian society.

As it was first conceived, the Victorian model saw marriage as not only the goal but the duty of respectable men and women, the prime—really, the only—source of true happiness. Specific **gender roles** were assigned. The husband was to be the breadwinner. The status of men became thus elevated, and women now saw their importance diminished. Even when the wife's inheritance was the original source of a family's income, the husband was still the dominant figure in the household, making the big decisions about where the family would live, what kind of education the children would receive, and, of course, when and whom they would marry. If daughters were likely to be married off to promising future executives, sons were frequently earmarked for wives who would bring with them generous dowries.

The wife's job was to run a good household, to deal with the servants, to choose the menus (always with an eye to pleasing her husband's tastes), and on appropriate occasions, to show off her husband's net worth. The still prevalent phrase **conspicuous consumption** was coined in 1901 by economist Thorstein Veblen (1857–1929) to describe the spending habits of this money-conscious society, which included the wife's costly apparel and display of fine jewelry as demonstrations of her husband's success.

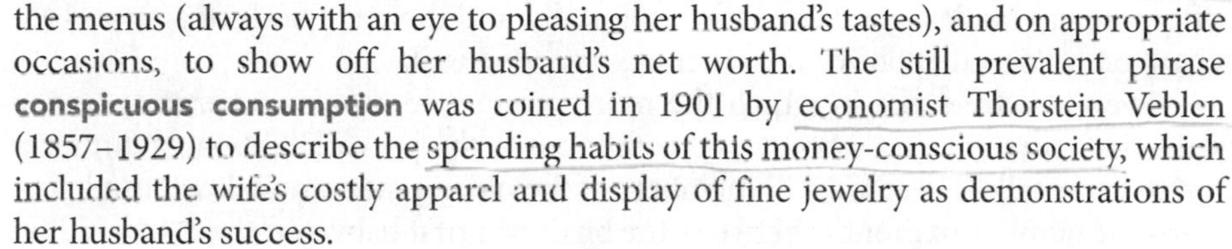

Out of this society emerged a **double standard** by which the woman, not the man, was expected to remain a virgin until the wedding night. The groom had the right to wed a bride untouched by other men, regardless of his own past (or present) escapades. An adulterous wife was ostracized forever from polite society, but a husband suspected of indulging in extramarital affairs usually incurred only mischievous winks from other men. Wives were not supposed to mention the subject. Novel after novel, play after play during the Victorian age showed the disasters that befell women who broke the moral code.

One of the best visualizations of the Victorian middle class can be found in *A Sunday Afternoon on the Island of La Grande Jatte,* shown above, painted by Georges Seurat in what was considered a revolutionary and controversial style known as *pointillism.* Instead of brushstrokes, the artist creates his images by dabbing at the canvas with the tip of a tightly rolled brush dipped in the desired colors. The effect gives the scene an almost unearthly appearance that can suggest the lack of substance in this stiff society in which proper manners were everything.

Remnants of the double standard remain today in varying degrees of acceptability. They continue to be influential, even admired, especially among those who value traditional institutions such as carefully specified gender roles that provide clear rules about the obligations of each member of the household. Throughout the world today, in some societies, the patriarchal system remains in place. Marriages are arranged for toddlers, educational opportunities are minimal or nonexistent for girls, women are prevented from showing their face in public, and in custody disputes, children are expected to remain with their father.

> *"Men marry because they are tired; women because they are curious. Both are disappointed."*
>
> **—Oscar Wilde**

In the 1930s, when the family unit was in danger of splitting apart because of economic instability, an American play set in the Victorian era was a long-running success. *Life with Father,* adapted in 1938 by Howard Lindsay and Russell Crouse from the memoir by Clarence Day, provided a genial and nostalgic visit to what many considered the Good Old Days. Father Day, stubborn and tyrannical, is the acknowledged ruler of the family domain, believing that his word is law, almost by divine right. Mother Day—perhaps for the pleasure of the modern wives—*appears* to accept her subordinate role while managing by devious strategies to get her way, but never by bickering or direct confrontation. Sometimes she pretends not to understand what her husband is saying and talks in a disorganized manner that spins Father's head until he backs down. The play became a successful movie in 1947, perhaps because in post-World War II marriage and the family were threatened by shifting gender roles and nostalgia for a more stable past grew even stronger than it had been a decade earlier. And what about now? The film version, released on DVD, received this Internet comment from a young viewer: "This movie is too stupid for me to relate to."

New Versions

Despite current cynicism about the way family life used to be shown, differing attitudes toward love that we have reviewed in this chapter, *including* the Victorian model, continue to influence our hopes and expectations. In discussing a recently announced engagement, overtly or discreetly, friends usually want to know if a bride or groom has made a good choice economically, and there are nods of approval (or envy) on hearing that one or the other has "married well."

Even in a freer age in which the more productive moneymaker may be the wife, the househusband who takes the children to the park and prepares dinner is apt to cause talk. There are still members of the older generation who count backward the number of months between the birth of a first baby and the day wedding vows were exchanged.

At the same time, the twenty-first century has brought greater freedom to choose. Newspaper announcements of recent weddings (or commitment ceremonies) are not confined to members of the same ethnic group, class level, or even gender. Accounts of how the couple met and were attracted to each other may often include shared trips and apartments long before a public exchange of vows.

Love without marriage can sometimes be very awkward for all concerned; but marriage without love simply removes that institution from the territory of the humanly admissible.

Feminist thinking sees no reason not to be frank and open in matters of intimate relationships, even if it means denying that love alone makes life complete. The heroine of Wendy Wasserstein's Pulitzer Prize–winning play *The Heidi Chronicles* (1988) learns that love need not be the pivotal event in anyone's life. After a disappointing relationship with a gay doctor, Heidi, in a final scene that is anything but poignant, feels totally free to continue her life without a long-term commitment to anyone.

Playwright Edward Albee (b. 1928) has written bitingly of marriage, parenthood, and relationships between the sexes. The characters in what many consider his masterpiece, *Who's Afraid of Virginia Woolf?* (1962), are products of a modern sophisticated society from which the Victorian model is notably absent, though it has not been replaced with other strict codes. Consequently, they are unable to find a secure and stable footing in any kind of relationship, marital or otherwise.

Who's Afraid of Virginia Woolf? is the story of a modern marriage between two insecure people: George is a history professor at a small liberal arts college in New England; his wife Martha is the alcoholic daughter of the college president, childless, bored with her life, disappointed that her laid-back husband has never used his intellect to make a name for himself.

AP Photo

Elizabeth Taylor and Richard Burton, *Who's Afraid of Virginia Woolf*, 1966
Martha pleads with George not to kill off their fantasy child.

At a faculty party they meet a young biology teacher named Nick and his wife Honey. Everyone has been drinking to excess, and Martha, who is attracted to Nick, invites the young couple to continue the party at their home. As increasing amounts of liquor are consumed, the hostility between George and Martha intensifies. The latter makes an unsuccessful attempt to seduce Nick, who has some remnants of Victorian morality in him. He wards off Martha's persistent advances by asking her to tell them about a mysterious son, supposedly coming home for his twenty-first birthday. George warns her of dire consequences if she talks about the young man. She defies her husband's orders, describing the son in passionate terms. George makes good on his threat, informing her that while she was out of the room they received a telegram telling them that their son has been killed driving his car on a country road, where he "swerved to avoid a porcupine" and smashed into a tree.

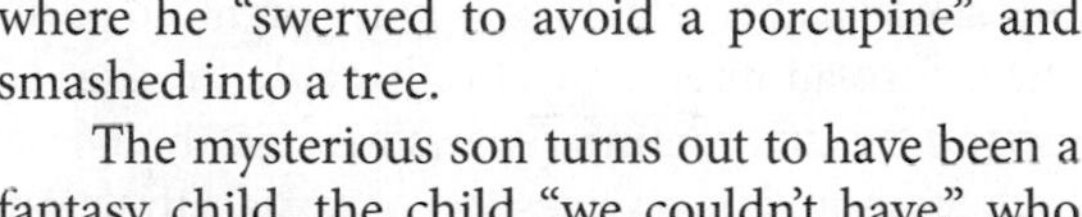

The mysterious son turns out to have been a fantasy child, the child "we couldn't have," who became central to the game of parenting they have been playing for years; and George has decided to make an end of the game, partly to punish Martha for verbally abusing him in front of their guests. Albee, adopted when he was eighteen days old, seems, according to his biographer Mel Gussow, to be obsessed with the subject of parents and children. Is the playwright longing for a different society, one in which the home is once more the core unit? Or is he writing the tragedy of alienation within a society of broken homes—as broken as the people who inhabit them?

Love in a Time of Health Hazards

The pairing of love and disease has a long history in the humanities. Some new works may remind us of the romantic operas of the nineteenth century, such as Verdi's *La Traviata,* in which heroines die, usually from tuberculosis or consumption (as it used to be called). At their deaths they achieve a beautiful spiritual union with their lovers. We have already discussed Jonathan Larson's *Rent,* a modern adaptation of Puccini's *La Bohème,* in which AIDS substitutes for consumption.

At one time AIDS had a tremendous effect on the entertainment world. Many actors and dancers succumbed quickly to the disease, especially during the 1980s, when medical treatments were less advanced than they are now. Writers gave us plays and films about love that strengthens and deepens under the shadow of inevitable death, about dying men cared for by lovers who might otherwise have never shown the ability to care more for another than they do for themselves.

Perhaps we can say that the health hazards of the world today have unexpectedly turned many writers away from the cynical attitude toward love that flourished in less troublesome times.

Larry Kramer's play *The Normal Heart* (1985), revived in 2011, contains a powerful and heartbreaking scene. The caregiving lover of a man near death from AIDS returns home with a bag of groceries, hoping to induce his dying partner to eat something, only to find him on the floor shaking from an unstoppable fever. The caregiver's profound grief suddenly erupts into anger at death and at his lover for leaving him and at the whole complacent society that pretends none of this is happening. In his rage he hurls groceries at the pitiable figure on the floor, screaming invectives through his tears. An equally memorable scene occurs at the end of Craig Lucas's *Longtime Companion* (1990) when a man holds his dying lover in his arms and gives him permission to "let go," even though it means leaving him forever.

Love and Older People

If thousands upon thousands of younger people have been lost to AIDS, thousands of older people have found their life spans greatly lengthened with the emergence of once unavailable drugs and medical treatments. In addition to experiencing unexpected and continued health, many senior citizens now face a different kind of problem: how to overcome society's and their own stereotyped notions of what is and is not acceptable behavior for people past sixty. Years ago one never heard, "Sorry. I have to babysit tonight because grandmother has a date."

According to Colombian-born Nobel-Prize winner Gabriel García Márquez (1928), one is never too old to love and be loved. His 1988 novel *Love in the Time of Cholera*—made into a 2007 film of the same title—deals with both disease and aging. In the beginning of the story, Florentino Diaz, a rather unattractive and awkward young man, is overwhelmingly attracted to Fermina Daza. The lady, however, marries a successful doctor, partly because she finds her relentless suitor Florentino peculiar, if not repulsive. Nonetheless, the ardent admirer is loyal to his lady for over 50 years. When at length Fermina's husband dies, Florentino renews his suit, though by now both have reached an age when there should be no question of sexual attraction.

Nonetheless, Fermina agrees to marriage, if only out of weariness from having repelled Florentino's advances for so long. At first she has no intention of sharing her body with him as they set sail on a long voyage to escape the cholera epidemic that is ravaging the country. One night, however, Fermina submits to his ceaseless demands:

> *Then he looked at her and saw her naked to the waist, just as he had imagined her. Her shoulders were wrinkled; her breasts sagged, her ribs were covered by a flabby skin as pale and cold as a frog's. She covered her chest with the blouse she had just taken off, and she turned out the light. Then he sat up and began to undress in the darkness, throwing everything at her that he took off, while she threw it back, dying of laughter.*[16]

So what is love in this instance? We cannot say the word is inappropriate or has no sexual connotations, for this geriatric couple indulge in passionate sex incessantly after their wedding night. It is their saving grace. Their love is not Platonic, for, having lost touch for over half a century, they know almost nothing of each other's mind. What they have, however, is assuredly good and seems to be the author's almost mystic answer to the world's problems.

It certainly beats hate, doesn't it?

Imagining a World in Which Only Sex Exists

Warnings about separating love and sex are evident in three works of fiction that attack **utopianism**, the belief that there are ideal ways to plan and run a society. This belief goes all the way back to *The Republic* of Plato, who describes a society in which parents give their newborns into the care of the state, which will raise them to become rational human beings, free of emotional ties, understanding that marriage is for reproduction only.

In Aldous Huxley's novel *Brave New World* (1932), there are no emotional quandaries that cannot be solved by popping a pill called "soma." Sex is easily available for pleasure alone, without guilt or responsibility. Couples get together briefly, enjoy themselves, and move on to other partners. This behavior is not only condoned but demanded by the state. Skilled scientists take care of reproduction through in vitro fertilization. Children are thus conceived and born in the laboratory. The babies have no connection with parents; they all immediately become wards of the state, to be carefully conditioned and monitored as productive citizens of the future.

The only taboo is affection for another person: in other words, sex yes, love no. In a world carefully engineered for efficiency, love would only get in the way. Something inside Huxley's main character, however, tells him that there is more to life than this, that he is missing out on something. He manages to escape this utopia and wanders far away, where he finds and joins a group of people living as a nuclear family. For the first time in his life he is happy.

In George Orwell's *1984* (written in 1948), love is again forbidden on grounds of being contrary to the interests of the state ruled by the unseen Big Brother, who watches everybody constantly. The novel gave rise to the immortal phrase "Big Brother is watching you," now used to describe surveillance technology in public buildings, the monitoring of protest marches, and the proliferation of bugging devices. Two of the citizens break all rules by falling in love and indulging in sexual relations, only to have their most intimate moments and private conversations discovered and exposed. Their punishment is to be sent for brainwashing at a rehabilitation center, called ironically the Ministry of Love. When Orwell wrote the novel, World War II had just ended and Soviet communism was being declared the next great enemy. The book remains a powerful anti-utopian statement, but more than that, a powerful warning against government intrusion into the right of individual privacy.

In Margaret Atwood's novel *The Handmaid's Tale* (1986), all rights except that of reproduction have been taken from women. They are denied education, careers of their choice, and the ability to choose a mate based on love. The handmaid of the title is a slave who must always wear an identifying garment; her name, Offred, means she is owned by a man named Fred. When they have sex, as is required when a woman is in her fertile period, Fred's wife is present to oversee the process. The child will then belong to the husband and wife. Atwood shows that the powers of the state, even in a democracy, can be used as instruments of oppression against those deemed undesirable.

The theme that runs through all of the novels we have discussed in this section is that love is a natural instinct and cannot be denied or controlled by outside forces. Some may argue that *this* version of love is ultimately based on the sexual drive. Or is there more to it than that?

> *"Everything is, everything exists, only because I love."*
>
> **—Leo Tolstoy**

One of the major lessons the humanities teach us is that all of us are free to choose, and that includes the freedom to define love in a way that is most meaningful for us. Will chivalry be an important component? Or a return to the stability of unbreakable family ties? Or a game that is not expected to last? Or an ad in the Personals column?

We may choose to remain single without feeling the need to travel with or arrive at a social event with a recognizable lifetime partner. We may be comfortable behaving according to the traditional rules requiring us to marry someone from a background acceptable to our family and friends and fitting into accepted gender roles. We may make our own rules, unconcerned about which partner earns more money, which one is considerably older or younger than the other, or even whether a relationship that seems so right at the moment will or must last a lifetime.

Or we may decide love is not to be defined, only to be experienced, as the poet Hannah Kahn would have us believe.

Signature

If I sing because I must
being made of singing dust,

and I cry because of need
being made of watered seed,

and I grow like twisted tree
having neither symmetry

nor the structure to avert
the falling axe, the minor hurt,

yet of one thing I am sure
that this bears my signature

that I knew love when it came
and I called it by its name.[17]

LEARNING OBJECTIVES

Having read and carefully studied this chapter, you should be able to:

1. Contrast, with an example for each, *eros* and *agape*.
2. Define Platonic love, distinguishing it from how it is generally understood.
3. Show how the concept of the family was developed in the Hebrew Bible.
4. Give three examples of alternate concepts of the family.
5. Explain the origins of romantic love, including the influence of Mariolatry.
6. Define and present an example of courtly love.
7. Explain the Victorian model of marriage and indicate ways in which this concept has changed.
8. Describe how Orwell's *1984* and Atwood's *The Handmaid's Tale* explore the death of love as a major theme.

KEY TERMS

agape Greek term defining actions of the spirit or soul (in an intellectual or aesthetic sense) including love for another's mind; adopted by Christianity as love for God and one's fellow beings; generally understood as the opposite of sexual love.

canto a division of a long poem, such as in *The Divine Comedy,* corresponding to a chapter in a book.

conspicuous consumption phrase coined by Thorstein Veblen to explain the economic habits of the Victorian-era middle and upper classes, connoting the desire to make a public display of one's wealth.

courtly love an artificial and codified set of rules governing the mating behavior of the upper classes during the late Middle

Ages and the Renaissance; principal among these was the right of the lady to make any demands she wished in order to test the loyalty and devotion of her suitor.

double standard originally a reference to the right of the husband, but not the wife, during the Victorian period to have had sex before, and often outside as well as during, marriage.

eros Greek term used as the opposite of agape, referring to the appetites of passion and the flesh.

gender role the way society defines the rights and responsibilities of each sex, especially within marriage.

goliard a medieval troubadour, usually a young man training for the priesthood, who sang songs extolling the hedonistic life and encouraging others to enjoy themselves before entering austere holy orders.

Mariolatry the idealization of the Virgin Mary as practiced by a late medieval cult of poets and painters; not only did the practice ennoble the life and characteristics of the mother of Jesus but it also tended to elevate the status of upper-class women and women in holy orders.

nuclear family the traditional family unit of father, mother, and children; once including grandparents but less apt to now.

Platonic love originally an ideal relationship between two compatible minds, one that may have begun as physical passion but moves to a higher plane that includes mutual intellectual and aesthetic interests; it can also define one's love for an idea or work of art or the physical beauty of another divorced from any desire to possess it; in popular usage, it connotes simply a relationship without sex.

romance a genre of fiction originating in the Middle Ages, then featuring the exploits of a dashing knight and his pure love for a lady fair for whom he is willing to die—and often does.

romantic love a relationship that may or may not include sex, which is less important in any case than tender feelings and a desire to be with the other person for the sake of that person, not for the satisfaction of personal desires.

utopianism a belief that the ideal society can be planned and rationally administered.

TOPICS FOR WRITING AND DISCUSSION

1. One of the ways Platonic love has been defined is as a ladder beginning with delight in a physical union and leading upward to the oneness of two minds. Do you believe the concept is still valid? Or is love only a fancy word for lust?
2. Is genuine friendship more or less important to you than a satisfying, if temporary, physical relationship? Pretend you are forced to choose because you cannot have both.
3. Parents, unhappy because they believe their children show them insufficient gratitude, have been known to say, "After all, look what we have done for you. Don't you think you owe us something back?" Is "owe" a verb that should be used in discussions of family love?
4. Today there are feminist liberation movements, male breadwinners who frequently need assistance from working wives, and househusbands in increasing numbers. Cite evidence that the Victorian model is still around or appears to have vanished altogether.
5. Tap your creative energies. Write a little story in which two of the characters you have met in this chapter meet each other and have a conversation about love. What would Romeo, for example, say to Ulrich von Lichtenstein? How about Mirabell and Juliet on the balcony?
6. Still tapping your creative energies, write a dialogue between two people who both use "love" when they refer to their relationship, yet who somehow make it clear to us that each is operating according to a different definition of the word.
7. If, when some people declare love for each other, they really mean they have physical desires and nothing else, would it help matters if one simply said to the other, "I am in lust"? Or do we need to disguise the actual meaning? If we do, explain why.
8. Does romantic love still figure in your expectations of a relationship? Or a marriage? Or both? Or is it only a figment of the imagination?
9. Watch two or three television sitcoms that deal, in one way or another, with relationships that can be classified under the heading "love." Report on the different meanings you find. Talk about the handling of gender roles.
10. Imagine you are living next door to an elderly single man or woman, who suddenly takes on a live-in companion and the two of them party nightly into the wee hours. Suppose, further, that the neighbors, including your parents, sign a petition asking the police to put an end to this disgraceful blight on the neighborhood. Write a speech that you would make either to the partying couple, explaining why their behavior is inappropriate, or to the petitioners, explaining why their attitude is inappropriate.

Chapter 14

Life-Affirmation

According to one way of looking at art, life must be shown to be good. Even if most of the story has been filled with destructive forces like vampires, the ending for the heroic characters will be what we would want for ourselves. Why read, view, or listen to material that is depressing?

A contrary belief is that art should reveal the truth of human experience, some of it life-affirming, some of it not; and we harm ourselves by hiding from the truth. Insisting on never-ending optimism and refusing to acknowledge mortality may bring temporary comfort, but we cannot ignore it forever. The subject of death informs some of the most glorious works of visual art, music, drama, and literature. The reason? Because the omnipresence of death, even at its most tragic, can enhance the appreciation of being alive. Death and life affirmation often are found in the same work.

In this chapter we explore how thinking about mortality has affected artists and philosophers; how their works tend to be either life-affirming or life-denying; and how the popular arts have capitalized on both our fear of and fascination with death. How do we benefit from death as a subject? First, experiencing intense creativity is in itself life-affirming for *us*. Second, we benefit from the reminder that we too may face problems as our lives unfold and ignoring them is life-denying in itself. Once recognized and accepted, sorrow and death lose some of their terror.

Inconsistency of belief is one kind of death-in-life. Some beliefs are at cross purposes with each other: for instance, a belief in the happiness to come in an afterlife struggles against the belief that one cannot bear to leave the pleasures of *this* life. Many of us would not mind having both a rich, exciting life with fame and wealth and then an eternity of bliss.

One reason for despising the thought of life's termination is the importance placed on the self. It seems impossible that there should ever come a time when that self is nonexistent. For some people, the next best thing to immortality is the thought of their own funerals. In their fantasy they are actually present, listening to what is being said about them. Facing up to the reality that each of us is only a temporary resident of this world and that the world will continue without us may be difficult at first but more and more acceptable once we get used to the thought.

The idea that life is temporary, however, can be another form of self-preoccupation. Asked whether growing old was unpleasant, one person said: "*I don't mind getting old and facing death when I think about the terrible things to come on this earth.*" This sentiment can be rephrased to read: "*The one compensation for my death is that I won't be around to face the awful future. I'll leave that to the people who keep on living.*" This statement is not an example of the courage to face life. It is a comment by someone who allows death to cast its shadow each day and who tries to escape from fear by believing that life for the survivors will be worse than death.

It is our hope that this consideration of death in the humanities will encourage you to take stock of where you are at present in the matter of life-denying thoughts and actions. You may discover that death is not

◀ **Laura Linney, *The Big C*, 2010**

In the Showtime TV series, a suburban mother deals privately with an incurable illness.

Jordin Althaus/© Showtime Network/Courtesy Everett Collection always something that happens only once. Unfortunately, many people needlessly die over and over.

Images of Death

> *We humanize what is going on in the world and in ourselves only by speaking of it, and in the course of speaking of it, we learn to be human.*
>
> **—Hannah Arendt**

Death can be thought of in a number of ways. It may be an enemy out to get us; a force that makes us all equal; a glorious finale to the lives of the pious and the brave; a preordained end destined for everyone (but not till our "number is up"); a beautiful woman or handsome man, welcoming arms extended, inviting the dying person to a haven of peace and joy; or as a natural event, part of the universal cycle. Or it can be something that happens only to people who deserve it.

Death is often portrayed by pictures of candlelit tombs, skulls, masked killers, and the black-hooded Grim Reaper holding a long scythe. Businesses thrive on such images, believing that if we didn't enjoy being safely frightened, we wouldn't look at them or attend Halloween parties where many are wearing ghoulish costumes. The thought of possible death provides excitement for people who love to ride roller coasters and stand up shouting "No hands!" or those who love boat rides through dark tunnels with skeletons popping up unexpectedly and bodies moving out of coffins.

Sometimes death is celebrated in a life-affirming fashion to honor the memory of those who have departed. In Hispanic cultures such as Mexico and Puerto Rico the Dia de los Muertos, or Day of the Dead, is an annual occurrence. Originally an Aztec custom that took place earlier in the year, it was moved to the beginning of November to coincide with the Catholic All Saints' Day. The holiday is now more often celebrated in rural areas than in the big cities, but, wherever it is observed,

The Print Collector/Alamy

Jan de Provoost, *Death and the Miser*, c. 1500

Popular image of Death as something that happens only to people who deserve it.

people tend and decorate the graves of loved ones, after which there is a fiesta, with large quantities of food, including cakes and candies in the shape of skeletons.

In the following sections we shall be looking at varied possibilities for thinking about death taken from art, literature, the popular media and our own imaginations. The aim is to find the means of affirming life without refusing to consider the inevitable.

Moviestore collection Ltd/Alamy

Kenneth Branagh, *Henry V*, 1989

Henry with the troops on St. Crispin's Day in the film version.

A Memorable Heroic Image

Shakespeare's King Henry V, in the history play of that title, encouraged his outnumbered English soldiers as they awaited battle with the French. Reminded that their side would benefit from more troops, the King is defiant:

> *. . . he which hath no stomach to this fight,*
> *Let him depart . . .*
> *We would not die in that man's company*
> *That fears his fellowship to die with us. . . .*
> *We few, we happy few, we band of brothers;*
> *For he to-day, that sheds his blood with me*
> *Shall be my brother; be he ne'er so vile,*
> *This day shall gentle his condition;*
> *And gentlemen in England now-a-bed,*
> *Shall think themselves accurst they were not here,*
> *And hold their manhoods cheap whiles any speaks*
> *That fought with us upon Saint Crispin's day.*
> *[IV: iii, 35–39; 60–67]*

But poet Wilfred Owen (1893–1918) described military sacrifice in far less glorious terms as he detailed wounds suffered on a World War I battlefield:

Dulce et Decorum Est

> *Bent double, like old beggars under sacks,*
> *Knock-kneed, coughing like hags, we cursed through sludge,*
> *Till on the haunting flares we turned our backs*
> *And towards our distant rest began to trudge.*
> *Men marched asleep. Many had lost their boots*
> *But limped on, blood-shed. All went lame; all blind;*
> *Drunk with fatigue, deaf even to the hoots*
> *Of disappointed shells that dropped behind.*
> *GAS! Gas! Quick, boys!—An ecstasy of fumbling,*
> *Fitting the clumsy helmets just in time;*
> *But someone still was yelling out and stumbling*
> *And floundering like a man in fire or lime.—*
> *Dim, through the misty panes and thick green light*
> *As under a green sea, I saw him drowning . . .*

To children ardent for some desperate glory,
The old Lie: Dulce et decorum est
Pro Patria mori.[1]

Death in the Popular Arts

An unexpected source of life-affirmation may be the way death (including all acts of violence, of murder, suicide, and other kinds of self-destruction) is treated in popular arts and entertainment. The public that lines up to buy tickets for horror movies, murder mysteries, and perhaps even automobile races may not *know* these events are life-affirming, but in fact they are to the extent that they turn death into an unreality.

Death at a Distance

During the nineteenth century the horror story established the ghoulish images of death that have stayed with us.

In the nineteenth century, the popular arts were magazines, pulp fiction, stage melodramas, and tented spectacles like the circus and Wild West shows. Monthly journals with mass circulation ran serialized horror tales. Sentimental tearjerkers featuring the deaths of young children and frail maidens were the staples of melodramas. (Audience members were advised to bring three or four hankies with them.) Pulp fiction, called "Penny Dreadfuls" by the British press, allowed readers to gorge themselves on lurid tales set in haunted houses, dreary castles, remote inns, all with spider webs, bodies hanging on closet hooks, distant shrieks of terror, and thunderstorms raging outside.

Bram Stoker's *Dracula* (1897) seized hold of the public imagination, and its subject matter has never let it go. We continue to be fascinated by stories about the walking dead stalking the living. In our own time, the novels of Anne Rice, revolving around the centuries-old vampire Lestat, are surefire best sellers. Her hero's insatiable thirst for blood has even led him to Miami Beach, where he jumps out of dark alleys and kills innocent old people—a subject one would *think* would be too horrible for readers to enjoy. Vampires are ingrained in our culture. From the popular television series *True Blood* to Hollywood's *Twilight* saga, bloodthirsty characters have become cult idols.

Circuses, rodeos, and similar spectacles continue to lure crowds that evidently love the element of danger faced by performers, auto races with their death-enticing speeds and the unacknowledged but always present possibility of a fiery crash. Drivers, trapped inside burning vehicles, are at such a remove that spectators can readily distance themselves from the actual horror. Confronting death at a safe distance, whether at a racetrack or in a movie house, can make us feel that we are strong enough to withstand the real thing. Nonetheless, we tend to glamorize the real thing, endowing it with exotic terrors it usually lacks in order to give us the illusion that we have faced death fearlessly.

One popular approach to dealing with death is to show how people would change their lives if doctors told them they had a finite amount of time to live. Would a timid, obedient housewife turn on the people she had been obeying? Would she stop saving money for the rainy day that has already come? Would she share her news with her family or boldly and inexplicably do whatever she felt like, leaving them bewildered by her sudden change?

A television series that dealt with these questions in a way that would have been unheard of in earlier times was *The Big C.* The title refers to a once commonly used term for the word "cancer," which people avoided, as if saying it would cause it. The series starred actress Laura Linney as a woman in a late stage of melanoma who has been told she has a short time to live. She decides to share the news with as few people as possible. Instead, she will live as she sees fit, without being treated differently as someone whose medical condition is all anyone would notice about her. The actress said the role interested her because the story was about "time and what do you do with time."

Catastrophes

Some popular novels herald the near destruction of the world and the salvation of the good. These tend to balance apocryphal books and movies in which the earth is wiped out by meteors or comets. Both spring from the same source: the assurance that death can be overcome, either because it is happening to actors who are being paid to die on the screen or because a last-minute rescue is possible for those who are pure of heart, or at least not completely evil.

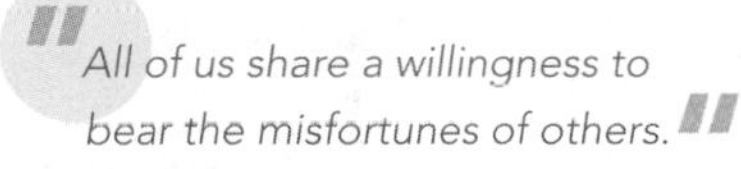

"All of us share a willingness to bear the misfortunes of others."
—François de La Rochefoucauld

Hugely popular, also, are novels, films, and television programs about the disasters awaiting humanity from global warming and the unpredictable effects of climate change. It is probably just a matter of time before we are treated to a succession of tales about people huddled together in seacoast communities, waiting to be engulfed by monstrous waves caused by sea levels rising to unthinkable heights.

Why would people seek escape from their fears by immersing themselves in stories in which life seems cheap? The answer is that in stories and films involving murders and global disasters deserving people are usually not the ones who die. In one of the early disaster films, *Earthquake*, a street suddenly opens and swallows hundreds of people—except the hero and heroine. In *Titanic* (1997), which became the biggest box-office success in cinema history up to that time, the hero (played by Leonardo di Caprio) freezes to death in the water, but the lovely heroine (played

***The Day After Tomorrow*, 2004**

Manhattan is destroyed in a new ice age, in what has become a cult classic for all who find disaster entertaining.

by Kate Winslet) survives the tragedy while floating on a piece of debris. Both lovers could not possibly be lost!

In 2004 Hollywood released a disaster film called *The Day After Tomorrow* in which global warming has caused catastrophic climate reversals. A new Ice Age sweeps over the east coast of the United States, burying Manhattan under a hundred feet of snow. The rationale, endorsed by many environmentalists, was to sound a dire warning that this could happen unless nations of the world realize that saving humanity is more important than carbon-emitting industrial growth. Indeed, a significant percentage of viewers undoubtedly took the message to heart, but an equally significant percentage undoubtedly went to the cineplex to enjoy another spectacle of suffering and death happening to all except most of the film's stars—and, in any case, to no one in the comfortable safety of stadium seating.

> *"They cut me down and I leap up high:*
> *I am the life that'll never die:*
> *I'll live in you if you'll live in me.*
> *I am the Lord of Dance, said he."*
>
> **—Anonymous folk song**

Horror tales, murder mysteries, and disaster films seem to have one thing in common, regardless of the period in which they were written or produced: deadliness is not random. In the classic murder mysteries there are apprehended culprits with clear motives. Most stories of the apparently supernatural end with rational explanations. Climate-change thrillers offer the "comforting" underlying message that reasonable people can still do something to avert the tragedies that engross audiences for two hours before the message is delivered.

The eternal fascination with lurking terror and sudden, violent death and the reassurance that it is not random or personally threatening may not completely strengthen us for the hard chore of facing up to reality. If we are to be strong and skillful in being human, we must still explore meaningful ways to say Yes to life without trying to escape from truth.

Strategies for Dealing with Death

The real thing, as described by Dr. Sherwin B. Nuland in his book *How We Die,* is

> *. . . not a confrontation. It is simply an event in the sequence of nature's ongoing rhythms. Not death but disease is the real enemy, disease the malign force that requires confrontation. Death is the surcease that comes when the exhausting battle has been lost.*[2]

A realistic encounter with approaching death is found in Randy Pausch's "Last Lecture," as seen on YouTube and in many television interviews. Pausch (1960–2008) was a professor of Computer Science at Carnegie Mellon. In the video, aware that he faces imminent death from an incurable disease, Pausch does push-ups in front of a large audience—one-armed push-ups at that. He tells them, with a twinkle, that he probably can do exercises better than most who watch him. In 2007 a magazine named him Person of the Year. Pausch's heads-up approach to death seems to have helped countless numbers facing a similar destiny.

Another approach to terminal illness is by author Christopher Hitchins, who insists there is nothing to be learned in trying to match his recent success with the moment he learned the bad news. The universe simply doesn't care:

> *Of course my book hit the best-seller list on the day that I received the grimmest of news bulletins, and for that matter the last flight I took*

> *as a healthy-feeling person (to a fine, big audience at the Chicago Book Fair) was the one that made me a million-miler on United Airlines, with a lifetime of free upgrades to look forward to. But irony is my business and I just can't see any ironies here; would it be less poignant to get cancer on the day that my memoirs were remaindered as a box-office turkey, or that I was bounced from a coach-class flight and left on the tarmac? To the dumb question "Why me?" the cosmos barely bothers to return the reply: "Why not?"*[3]

Avoidance of Death Talk

For many "death" is a word to be avoided, unless used for purposes of exaggeration, as in "I was so embarrassed I thought I'd die!"

Directly confronting even the *idea* of death is considered "morbid." Insurance sellers agree that life insurance is a sensitive issue. The salesperson must employ euphemisms such as "In the event that something happens to you. . . ." Married couples are urged to make out their wills as soon as the first child is born, but attorneys will tell you how seldom they do so. The very words "death" and "die" are considered poor taste in conversation. Instead, we speak of "passing on" or use other evasions.

> *Rather than live on in the hearts and minds of my fellow men, I'd prefer to live on in my apartment.*
>
> **—Woody Allen**

Among those who avoid talk of death are people who believe they have plenty of time before they must be "serious" about such matters as wills and burial arrangements. Audiences that munch their popcorn, entranced by a screen full of blood, love the terror of anticipating what is going to happen to the innocent walker on the lonely street. They must certainly have a fear of death concealed in their unconscious even as the vampire is concealed in the doorway, but it is a fear that can wait a little while before it is realistically confronted. No one who goes to horror movies appears to want the triumph of life over death. Sometimes improbable happy endings are tacked on so the ratings will allow minors into the theater, yet the irony is that minors are the *last* people who want happy endings. After all, the younger you are, the more immortal you feel.

Those who are a little older and therefore apparently less immortal may enjoy the spectacle of violent death, or the many films and television shows about terminal illness, because the disaster is happening to *other* people. As the philosopher La Rochefoucauld cynically remarked, "All of us share a willingness to bear the misfortunes of others."

Humor

Would-be funeral directors studying for state boards that will license them as embalmers often exhibit a sense of humor about their profession.

One joke is about the golfer who is asked why her husband is not playing with her that day.

"He died," she replies.

"Oh, I'm sorry," comes the reply. "When was the funeral?"

Looking up at a procession of cars on the road above them, she says, "That must be it now."

Another is about the dying man whose son says, "Pop, what can I do for you? Is there anything you want?"

"Yes," says the man, "I'd like a piece of your mother's apple strudel."

The son leaves the room, goes into the kitchen, then comes back empty-handed, saying, "Ma says it's for after the funeral."

Aubrey Beardsley

Aubrey Beardsley, *The Pestilence*, c. 1890s

Christoph Neimann

Christoph Neimann, from *The New Yorker*, c. 1990s

Left, Victorian image of Death as Grim Reaper; right, a humorous treatment of same theme, showing Death as budget-minded.

Is it better to confront death in a humorous story than to suppress not only the fear but the very mention of it? Suppressed, the idea of death becomes magnified, and the more terrible is the anticipation of it. Laughing—when appropriate, of course—may be better than becoming addicted to the murder tales that actually *deny* the truth of death despite the multiplication of corpses and the darkened streets down which the unsuspecting walk to their doom.

Magnifying and Beautifying Death

We magnify in direct proportion to an emphasis on the self. Most of us want to be recognized, singled out for special achievements; and so few of us can think of death in casual terms as a natural event to be accepted whenever it comes. To magnify death—to mark it as a special event that happens only after a person has achieved high status—is to create a mythology for ourselves.

> *"They sang alternate measures, not louder than the twittering of the awakened wood-lark before it goes up the dewy air, but dolorous and full of the desolation of death . . . in a few moments the greensward was smooth as ever—the very dews glittering above the buried Fairy."*
>
> **—Christopher North**

We mask our fears about our own mortality in the importance we place on the death of celebrities. Perhaps many of us, consciously or otherwise, identify with the pomp and majesty surrounding their funerals. Noted personalities, revered authors, and heads of state pay eloquent tribute to the lifetime achievements of the deceased. We are moved, as if this extraordinary homage were being paid to *us*. Empathizing with graveside eulogies often stands as the ultimate summing up of an individual's worth and can—at least for a time—dispel our secret insecurities, our hidden doubts about our own value to the world.

In magnifying the role of death, we also become aware of the pain of death, the stroke of the scythe, and so we need to invent strategies for shielding ourselves. The best thing we can say of someone who has just died is that the end was peaceful or that death came during sleep, these representing everyone's fondest hopes.

Greek mythology offers two versions of finality. One is well known as the dark place ruled by Hades, god of the underworld. But the Greeks also had their own kind of Avalon: the Elysian Fields, a bright and sunny land of eternal happiness, where heroes who fall in battle are spared pain in death. Parisians, wanting to make their major thoroughfare seem like a place of perfect joy, named it the *Champs-Elysées*; and, significantly enough, it leads to the tomb of the Unknown Soldier.

In Chapter 3, the passing of the myth hero is described as unlike that of other mortals. His death is shown to be not one of physical pain, but rather a beautiful passage into a mysterious, nonthreatening realm. Frodo, the tiny hobbit hero of J. R. R. Tolkien's popular trilogy *Lord of the Rings*, meets a peaceful end after a wonderful if brief lifetime of facing up to grave dangers, including a terrifying dragon, in order to save others. Yet he is never shown to have died at all. He outfits his own little ship and sets sail for the Grey Havens.

> *And the ship went out into the High Sea and passed on into the West, until at last on a night of rain Frodo smelled a sweet fragrance on the air and heard the sound of singing that came over the water. . . . And he beheld white shores and beyond them a far green country under a swift sunrise.*[4]

The question remains: Even if magnifying or beautifying death helps to diminish, temporarily, our fear of it, are we better off facing it as the natural termination of our time here and not masking it in mythology?

Of course, there is nothing like opera to beautify death. Mimi, a beloved operatic heroine in *La Bohème* (Chapter 8), dies beautifully as Puccini's music enhances our pleasure. In *La Traviata,* Verdi's opera based on Dumas's *La Dame aux Camélias* (Chapter 8), the dying heroine nobly extracts a promise from her lover that he will one day marry someone else and know she is observing and blessing them from the heaven she will soon inhabit. Again, the music eases the heartbreak.

The Medicalization of Death

New drugs and medical technology have raised life expectations; but when they don't work, they add to the sense that death is intolerable. The medical profession has made the conquest of death a priority. Medical research has devoted itself to finding cures for cancer and ALS, prominent among the still unconquered afflictions, and much progress has been made in at least prolonging life or making it as pain free as possible. For this reason, members of the profession are not only saddened but *outraged* when patients die. Physicians believe they have a duty to save lives at all costs. Sometimes this sense of responsibility continues even when a patient is beyond medical help.

> *"In the midst of the current technological emphasis on the success story of healing the patient whose disease cannot be cured, the human being who is dying is inexorably perceived to be a failure to the health profession."*
>
> **—Elisabeth Kübler-Ross**

The doctor shows on television have enjoyed almost unbroken popularity since the early years of the medium when physicians like Dr. Kildare, Dr. Gillespie, and Dr. Welby were always ready to put aside their personal lives and sit by the bedside of the sick and dying. Images of death were abundant, but they were usually gentle, photographed through special lenses that obscured the stark realities of the medical surroundings.

Medical shows with death themes have become less sentimental over the years, yet shows like E.R. *have reassured, not depressed, viewers possibly because the realistic struggle to save lives is comforting.*

One of the most popular medical shows of recent years, *E.R.*, was less romantic in its approach. Its medical staff was far more pressured. Mistakes were made. On one occasion a head nurse inadvertently caused a patient to die after giving him the wrong blood type. Egos were wounded, conflicts between medical personnel erupted over proper procedures—all in an attempt to make the stories truer to real life and to avoid the sentimentality of the show's predecessors. A good many episodes revolved around the torment and guilt experienced by doctors who do not always triumph over death. Nonetheless, the show aimed to reassure, not depress, us. The staff of the emergency room were always there, willing to forget personal problems and grief as soon as they heard the ambulance outside. Despite the deaths that occurred, *E.R.* was life-affirming, administering to our need for a way to erase the fear of dying.

The fact that *E.R.* lasted more than ten years with strong ratings indicates that sophisticated viewers were tired of the formulaic affirmation of life regardless of the quality of the material. The artistic success of a different kind of hospital show, *House*, which premiered in 2004, indicates that the time had come for an antihero kind of doctor. Gregory House is described by a TV critic as

If famous actors play cameo roles as dying patients, we know in the back of our minds they will be revived in a different show.

> *an almost sociopathic genius who is given to muttering bitter comments such as "Humanity is overrated." He's a mess of a man, filled with open disdain as well as Vicodin, which he takes to stop the pain of "muscle death" in his leg. And yet he is a brilliant diagnostician, a last-ditch doctor who cures people the rest of the medical world has written off.*[5]

Gregory House is, in a sense, a medical detective and much like the cynical antiheroes of the film noir school: he is a hard-nosed realist, obsessively

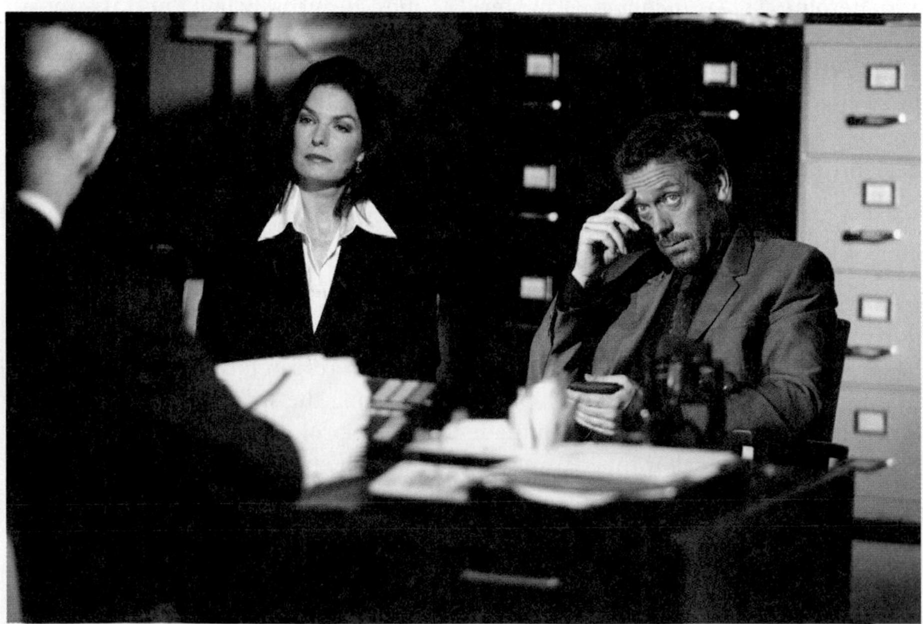

Chris Haston/NBCU Photo Bank via AP Images

***House*, 1994–2011**

Hugh Laurie as Dr. House in a darker hospital show that takes a sobering path to life-affirmation.

unsentimental. But a good many fans of this dark show would rather have a serious illness treated by someone like him, who may have no bedside manners whatever but can be depended on to find a solution—no matter how obscure. This is life-affirmation at a high price, but perhaps worth the money.

Some critics point out, however, that shows like *E.R.*, a pioneer in deromanticizing hospitals, and even the more intellectually appealing *House*, are always going to be *seemingly* but not *actually* real. If we recognize, as we often do, that a famous actor is doing a cameo bit as a dying patient, we know in the back of our minds that he or she will be revived in a different show. The wise course is to approach the viewing in the knowledge that the story isn't real but the subject matter *is* real, and we are preparing ourselves for the truth by "practicing" with the fable.

Death in Literature

Death is generally easier to take on the printed page because there are neither skilled actors nor realistic scenery. Yet some of the most potent insights into the meaning of death have come from novelists and poets. It would take many volumes to do justice to the vast literature. Here are a few representative samples.

Death and Children

A Death in the Family (1938) by poet and novelist James Agee (1900–1955) remains an American classic that should be read by anyone concerned with the effect of death on children. It is especially timely in Western society, where death has been removed from the home. Years ago—including the period of Agee's novel—the viewing (or wake) always took place in the living room, with neighbors and friends coming by to pay their respects and offer a support network to the grieving family. The sight of death was thus unavoidable for the youngest family members. The book shows how a child approaches death when its reality is not kept hidden.

Rufus, the young protagonist, has never known about death or had it explained to him before his father is suddenly killed in an auto accident. Agee analyzes every minute detail of the little boy's thoughts, feelings, and confusion. At one point the boy even experiences a sense of pride and achievement because he is undergoing something denied to the other kids on the block. A memorable passage (among many) is this account of Rufus's first sight of the casket and body in the living room of his grandparents' home.

> *Rufus had never known such stillness. . . . Rufus had never seen [his father] so indifferent; and the instant he saw him, he knew that he would never see him otherwise . . . an indifference which would have rejected them . . . in this self-completedness which nothing could touch, there was something else, some other feeling which he gave, which there was no identifying even by feeling, for Rufus had never experienced this feeling before; there was perfected beauty. The head, the hand, dwelt in completion, immutable, indestructible: motionless.*[6]

It could be argued that what a mature writer feels about death is not what an actual little boy would feel. But we can trust the instincts and compassion of a poet and trust his assurance that children are able to handle early tragedy in their own way and that the exposure will only fortify them for the pain of loss in later years.

Asked about when a child is ready to learn the facts about death, psychologists generally advise that children can deal with loss when they fully understand the concept of time: not how to *tell* time, but time as the unending agent of change.

> *For certain is death for the born*
> *And certain is death for the dead;*
> *Therefore over the inevitable*
> *Thou shouldst not grieve.*
>
> **—The Bhagavad Gita**

And children may be more sophisticated than we suppose, even though they may not have the words to express their knowledge.

In the following poem by Gerard Manley Hopkins a young girl is staring sorrowfully through a window at autumn's change of leaves. Instead of asking why she is so glum (as many an adult probably would), instead of telling her to come away from the window and cheer up (as many adults probably *do* in order to force gaiety on a child rather than taking the time to probe to the heart of the sadness), the poet interprets the emotion she is experiencing and, in so doing, will fortify her for sorrows yet to come.

Spring and Fall

To a Young Child

Margaret, are you grieving
Over Goldengrove unleaving?
Leaves, like the things of man, you
With your fresh thoughts care for, can you?
Ah! as the heart grows older
It will come to such sights colder
By and by, nor spare a sigh
Though worlds of wanwood leafmeal lie;
And yet you will weep and know why.
Now no matter, child, the name:
Sorrow's springs are the same.
Nor mouth had, no nor mind, expressed
What heart heard of, ghost guessed:
It is the blight man was born for,
It is Margaret you mourn for.[7]

Facing the Inevitable Before It Happens

In a poem called "Terence, this is stupid stuff," A. E. Housman (1859–1936) is speaking to a friend who writes cheerful but bad poetry. Housman takes him to task for his blind optimism about life. He denounces the literature of false hope, when it's much better to expose oneself little by little to the fact of sorrow and death, as he explains to Terence in this fable:

There was a king reigned in the East:
There, when kings will sit to feast,
They get their fill before they think
With poisoned meat and poisoned drink.
He gathered all that springs to birth
From the many-venomed earth;
First a little, thence to more,
He sampled all her killing store;
And easy, smiling, seasoned sound,
Sate the king when healths went round.
They put arsenic in his meat
And stared aghast to watch him eat;
They poured strychnine in his cup
And shook to see him drink it up:

They shook, they stared as white's their shirt:
Them it was their poison hurt,
—I tell the tale that I heard told.
Mithridates, he died old.[8]

Housman faces death with humor as well as a profound resignation. Rational acceptance of death as well as other afflictions is also life affirming.

Death in Music

We associate certain kinds of music with life's final moments and the rituals that follow: hymns played slowly on an organ; a somber march played in drawn-out cadences; a solo voice solemnly assuring the mourners that the deceased is at rest in a better land. The effects of the music vary, depressing some listeners, uplifting the spirits of others.

> *Out of the earth, I sing for them*
> *A horse nation, I sing for them.*
> *Out of the earth, I sing for them.*
> *The animals, I sing for them.*
>
> **—Teton Sioux chant**

Sometimes music seems to be an exact translation into external sound of the way we feel inwardly; and sometimes it seems to impose a mood of its own. The jazz funeral, still conducted in New Orleans, has a dual personality. On the way to the cemetery, mourners follow the casket and walk in time to a slow and sad march; but the return trip absolutely *defies* those in attendance to be consumed with sorrow. The musicians throw off the mantle of grief and break out into joyous jazz. What it says is that the deceased is better off now, is free of life's pain, worries, debts, tangled relations, and the pettiness and hypocrisy of others. The jazz funeral echoes Milton's famous line from *Samson Agonistes:* "Nothing is here for tears."

Great composers have explored through music the tangle of conflicting emotions that all must experience when the end is in sight, when no escape is possible

Philip Gould/Corbis

Funeral march, c. 1990

New Orleans jazz musicians on their way to the cemetery.

other than to transcend the fear of losing a personal identity and merging with what is timeless.

Richard Strauss (1864–1949), one of those responsible for the transition from romantic to modern opera, is equally famous as the composer who brought the genre of the symphonic poem to new heights. The symphonic or tone poem is an elaborate work that tells a story through sound, belonging to a category known as **program music**, in which the composer has a definite scenario in mind. Repeated melodies represent major characters and events, as in the operas of Wagner. At the age of 26, Strauss contributed *Death and Transfiguration* to the permanent concert repertoire, showing a premature concern for what happens as a person dies. The program notes to an early recording of the work make clear how the composer translates the experience into orchestral instruments, melodies, and rhythms.

Listen on **MyHumanitiesKit.com**
Strauss, *Death and Transfiguration*

> *A muted string figure in a softly pulsing rhythm, heard at the beginning, sets the scene. A sick man lies dying in a dark room, except for the ticking of a clock. The flickering of a candle is represented by an upward flick on the flutes, while the stifled moans of the sufferer are heard on the strings. Presently a wistful phrase on the oboe, known as the motif of childhood, indicates that, with a stirring of consciousness, the innocent happiness of youth is being recalled.*
>
> *(Strauss, "Death and Transfiguration," Artur Rodzinsky conducting; Seraphim Records, 1958)*

In the next section of the music, the dying man rebels against the coming of death and asserts the will to live. Two melodic lines—one representing the fierce demands of death, the other a desire for life—struggle against each other in a massive and richly textured orchestration, out of which emerge the strands of what will be the beautiful Transfiguration theme played on cellos, trombones, and horns.

As these fragments of the final theme begin to come together, the protagonist slides peacefully into what we presume to be a coma, in which he returns to his childhood and then his young adulthood, revisiting as well the trials he undergoes as he matures, the pangs of lost love, the anger that wells up when one crisis after another begins to overwhelm him, leading to the worst of all—the onslaught of his final illness. The figure of death finally appears as the strings tremble and fade slowly away and the dramatic stroke of a gong is heard.

The Transfiguration theme now begins, building from near silence to a majestic musical statement of the human spirit freeing itself from the pains of the flesh and the tribulations of the world and ascending into what we have been taught to call the Unknown. But through the great gift that music is able to give us, the Unknown is heard while visual imagery floods the mind of the listener. If the fear of dying is indeed present in the unconscious of most of us, great works of the humanities, such as those we have been dealing with, can support and comfort.

Death in Philosophy

Unforgettable images of how some actual people faced death can be as life-affirming as the tone poem of Strauss. Exemplary lives are as much a part of the humanities as works of art. They are in fact *living* works of art, even as death neared. This aspect of the humanities offers shining images of people who endured the continual presence of death without the natural instinct to save themselves at all costs. What all of these people had in common is the ability to bear the thought of not existing. Preoccupation with the loss of personal identity can underlie the fear of death. An old folk song expresses an attitude shared by many people:

Nothing was here before I came;
All that is here now bears my name.

Socrates provided a philosophical way to transcend the fear of death. The father of philosophy may have had selfhood, but there is no evidence that he was preoccupied with self*ness*. In all the accounts of Socrates that Plato has given us, the mentor seems out of touch with himself in our sense of what *himself* means. His choice of death by poison rather than life in exile without being able to teach indicates that the freedom to think and communicate rational thought was more important to him than simply being alive. In the accounts Plato has written, Socrates, in his final days, is shown to be a man genuinely interested in seeking wisdom and not at all in making people feel sorry or afraid for him. After he has drunk the hemlock prescribed by law, surrounded by the young students who adore and are weeping for him, he shows a singular absence of self-consciousness.

> *I covered my face and wept, not for him, but at the thought of my own calamity in having to part from such a friend.*
>
> **—Plato (on the death of Socrates)**

When one of those students, Phaedo, observes that the master drank his poison "cheerfully," we have no reason to believe Socrates was struggling to put on a brave act in front of his young friends. And then comes a most telling statement:

> *No pessimist ever discovered the secret of the stars, or sailed to an enchanted land, or opened a new doorway for the human spirit.*
>
> **—Helen Keller**

And hitherto most of us had been able to control our sorrow; but now when we saw him drinking, and saw too that he had finished the draught, we could no longer forbear, and in spite of myself my own tears were flowing fast; so that I covered my face and wept, not for him, but at the thought of my own calamity in having to part from such a friend.[9]

The passage reminds us that the loss of someone we love can also be tinged with self-interest. Phaedo has not learned from the selfless behavior of his teacher.

One reason loss is hard to separate from self-interest is that only very strong people do not need others to reinforce their identity. You can miss those who die, but you should be able to survive without them. Insecure lovers sometimes test each other with questions like "If I should die, would you ever get over it?" A reply like "Surely you would want me to find someone else and be happy" would not be understood, or there would not have been a question to begin with.

Tomas Abad/Alamy

Jacques-Louis David, *The Death of Socrates*, 1787

In this famous French painting, Socrates appears to be the only one who is not sorrowful over his impending death. Note that even the jailer who has administered the poison is in tears.

Death and an Afterlife

A prevalent idea about death is that it doesn't really exist, that life continues beyond the grave. The arts as well as some religions offer concepts of an afterlife, a place where the dead retain their earthly identities and will one day be reunited with loved ones. Immortality has a different meaning for those who define it as living on in the memory of family and friends or achieving eternal life through the works they leave behind.

An argument against believing life continues beyond the grave is that it prevents us from accomplishing all we might during this one chance given to us. Another is that belief in an afterlife is simply a weak excuse to minimize our failures in this life.

Christianity speaks of heaven as a reward for virtue and hell as a punishment for sin, but the Christian next life has always had an ambiguous nature. Is it an actual place with a geography of its own? Or are the Inferno and Paradise, so vividly described in Dante's *Divine Comedy* (written between 1302 and 1321), purely *literary* inventions? An afterlife is implied, if not defined, in the Christian Bible. On the cross, Jesus promises one of the thieves that he will be in paradise that same day, but paradise can mean many things, including a state of release from pain rather than a place of eternal life. Many believe that Jesus appeared to the disciples after his resurrection. This story may be partly responsible for the idea that physical identity continues beyond death. The idea is reinforced by reports from those who have attended séances and claimed to have actually seen their loved ones. A popular element in films of the 1930s was the after-death appearance of the departed, looking just as they did in life, except for being transparent.

In the Hindu faith there is not only moksha, the blissful state the soul attains when it is released from the cycle of death and reincarnation, but also a heavenly paradise enjoyed by the souls of those who died with a preponderance of good karma but who must still undergo at least one more stay on earth. They are allowed to remain in this paradise for a certain length of time before revisiting the earth. When they achieve perfection, however, they are not in paradise but become reunited with Brahman, the soul of the universe.

An eighteenth-century illustration from India depicts Krishna, believed to have been the god Vishnu (second in the Hindu trinity; see Chapter 10) in his mortal incarnation. Krishna continues to have many followers who see him in much the same light as Christians see Jesus: as a mortal incarnation of God. He is the god-hero of the Hindu epic *The Mahabharata*, discussed in Chapter 4. In illustrations, Vishnu is shown in a geographical paradise, dancing to music played by three young women. Buddhism has no such concepts of a physical afterlife.

"In remembrance is the secret of redemption."

—Jewish proverb

In Judaism, the afterlife is traditionally the memory of a good person who lives on in charitable works and the broad impact of a life well-lived. The ancient Hebrews were a realistic, survival-bound people, and in their Bible is the hope of a better life *here*, free of persecution and despair. Canaan, the Promised Land of Abraham and the covenant, is a real place in a highly desirable fertile area over which violent struggles are still being waged. In contrast to the arid desert, it offers green pastures and may possibly have influenced agricultural images of the next world. The depiction of God as a shepherd providing green pastures for his flock reinforces the image.

The Christian vision of the afterlife is often accompanied by feelings of apprehension and fear. In the Book of Revelations the Christian Bible contains vivid, even frightening imagery of the world's end and tells about the violent war against the Antichrist and the terrible suffering that awaits the sinner. Hell, especially as described by Dante, has a tenacious hold on the human imagination. If the perpetuation of the body in heaven is often a vague concept, not so Dante's accounts of the physical torments to be endured in hellfire. The sermons of early New England Puritan ministers are particularly filled with flesh-crawling warnings of the agony to come.

The need to believe that life is somehow, if not some*where,* perpetuated beyond death is deeply ingrained in the human tradition. In the humanities of many periods we keep finding the theme of survival through love. If two people are so close that they consider themselves to be one person, then death cannot take away the identity of *that* person. It matters not who dies and who lives on: the survival of one ensures the survival of the other.

John Donne, whose sonnet "Batter My Heart" was discussed in Chapter 4, was death-conscious throughout his life, the more so as love for his wife deepened with each passing year. The thought that so ideal a relationship could end was unbearable to him. In 1612 he was asked to accompany his patron, Sir Robert Drury, to the continent, despite strong protests from a wife who feared that something tragic was going to happen during his absence. Her premonition was accurate. While Donne was away, his wife gave birth to a stillborn child. To reassure her before leaving, Donne wrote one of his major poems, "A Valediction Forbidding Mourning," giving posterity the gift of an amazing metaphor for life beyond death.

Our two souls, therefore, which are one,
Though I must go, endure not yet
A breach, but an expansion.
Like gold to airy thinness beat.
If they be two, they are two so
As stiff twin compasses are two;
Thy soul, the fixed foot, makes no show
To move, but doth if the other do.

Other artists have found that art itself is the gateway to immortality. John Keats, the nineteenth-century romantic poet, was death-conscious throughout his life. It was a very short life, marked by ill health and the fervent need to believe that death would not be final. In one of his sonnets he links death (his own?) to the rebirth of life in the spring—in three startling and immortal words that close the poem.

AFTER DARK VAPOURS

After dark vapours have oppress'd our plains
For a long dreary season, comes a day
Born of the gentle South, and clears away
From the sick heavens all unseemly stains.
The anxious month, relieved its pains,
Takes as a long-lost right the feel of May;
The eyelids with the passing coolness play,

Like rose leaves with the drip of summer rains.
And calmest thoughts come round us; as, of leaves
Budding,—fruit ripening in stillness,—Autumn suns
Smiling at eve upon the quiet sheaves,—
Sweet Sappho's cheek,—a sleeping infant's breath,—
The gradual sand that through an hour-glass runs,—
A woodland rivulet,—a Poet's death.

John Keats

Death and Fate

> *"Tell him that we shall all bear his memory in the most precious part of our hearts. Tell him he is only before us on the road as he was in everything else, and that we are coming after him."*
>
> **—Leigh Hunt (on John Keats)**

Fatalism—the belief that all events, including the nature, time, and place of one's death have been predetermined—is found throughout history, religion, and literature. It is a popular way of thinking about and accepting misfortune and death. It was the foundation of Greek mythology in which great and powerful families are doomed by events beyond their control. Without the concept there would have been far less tragic theater in ancient Athens.

Greek myths saw fate as a mysterious, universal force that preceded the birth of the gods and the creation of the world. Sometimes fate was represented as three women spinning, measuring off, then cutting the thread of life. The snipping of the scissors appears arbitrary and capricious. On the other hand, with the coming of urban society and the establishment of law, people (even the Greeks) were held responsible for their actions, no matter how much they insisted their deeds were preordained. The opposing forces of fate and free will have been a source of confusion for thousands of years. Fatalism in the courts nowadays takes the form of arguments that defendants were driven to commit crime because of a bad family background, a bad neighborhood, or temporary insanity which has robbed them of free will. Fatalism is also involved in religions that stress God's omnipotence. In Chapter 10 we discussed one of the ongoing questions: Does the fact that the deity knows in advance what will happen mean that it *must* happen? Does God therefore will it to happen?

For some, fatalism is the inevitable conclusion that must be drawn from the belief in God's omnipotence. But people of faith adopt different attitudes toward fatalism: 1) depression because a disaster can be just waiting to happen and nothing can be done about it; 2) a willingness to accept the inevitable no matter how unsettling. Besides, if what happened *had* to happen, then it's really nobody's fault, is it? Nothing could have changed the outcome.

> *"To die is to go into the Collective Unconscious, to lose oneself in order to be transformed into form, pure form."*
>
> **—Hermann Hesse**

Still, some have said, it is difficult, if not impossible, to accept dreadful calamities, especially the death of the young, with serenity. In his popular book *When Bad Things Happen to Good People,* Rabbi Harold Kushner has a personal reason for discussing the subject. He himself lost a young son to incurable disease. In his search for answers, he considers possible errors in the way people think about and attribute motives to God. Perhaps fatalism is a human construct not in any way connected to God. Kushner suggests that instead of asking "Why me?" we say "Why *not* me?" In this, he echoes what was written long ago in The Book of Job: that God gives and God takes away and humanity must accept either action without complaint.

A popular brand of fatalism is one that can be accepted or rejected as circumstances dictate. A believer in free will may explain sudden death in terms of fate ("It was his time"). Some may say they don't mind flying because "if your number is up, there's nothing you can do about it." (The reply may be, "Suppose the pilot's number is up, not yours?") Yet the same fair-weather fatalist might avoid taking unnecessary risks, such as joining a parachute club or refusing to undergo a delicate operation with a fifty-fifty survival rate on the grounds that the odds are not favorable enough.

Islam has traditionally maintained a strong belief in the will of Allah, allowing for the peaceful acceptance of all that happens. Eastern thought has its own versions of fatalism. Hindus believe karma determines the circumstances of the next cycle of life, but they also believe the individual is responsible for leading a better life and proving worthy of a brighter future. This outlook surely implies that the will is free to accumulate good or bad karma, but, once the choice is made, there is no escaping the consequences.

To the Buddhist and the Taoist, the Dharma or the Way is a controlling force that operates through the choices people make. There is no conscious deity arranging the future. The universal order is a dynamic, flowing force that changes as people change. The death of anyone is part of the natural way of the universe and is to be accepted without anger.

Symbolic Death

However we approach death, we need to remember that we have to die only once. Unfortunately, we often *barely* live because the shadow of symbolic death continually crosses our paths. This shadow is psychological rather than biological, but it is all the more terrible because it *can* be avoided. Here the life-affirming gifts of the humanities would help us if only we would seek them out. In this section we examine prevalent ways of dying psychologically.

Unworth

An inner sense of unworth is the most obvious form of symbolic death. We hang back from taking risks that could have beneficial results. We worry continually about what others are saying, though chances are they have troubles of their own and are not buzzing about *us*. A woman once attended a two-week group therapy workshop hoping to overcome paranoid feelings that people were talking about her behind her back. After days of exhaustive persuasion by the trainer and fellow group members, the woman smiled and announced she had made a real breakthrough: "I see now that my neighbors aren't always gossiping about me behind my back. After all, who am *I* that they should do that?"

The sense of unworth can affect the body's condition and appearance. Often people believe they are not popular because of the way they look. Consequently, they overeat as an escape, become overweight, and can bring about the very unpopularity they feared. In rare instances, people suffering from an acute case of unworth may harbor a secret wish to escape from living altogether, and sometimes their bodies heed the message. There is a will to live, as we all know. Who has not observed it in action? Who has not witnessed startling recoveries that seemed to defy medical science? But there is also the will to die.

Envy of others is a sign that one has contracted the affliction of self-perceived unworth. To wish for another's looks, financial resources, beautiful possessions, or talent is to overlook or devalue one's *own* resources. The British philosopher

Bertrand Russell tells the story of a painter who produced fewer works than he might have because of his fear that they would turn out badly. On one occasion Russell asked him how he was feeling. The reply: "I spent a horrible morning comparing myself to Raphael." Envy of others can also mean believing *they* deserve what they have and *we* deserve not to have anything. The self-destructive cycle continues.

Symbolic Suicide

> "You only live once, and usually not even then."
>
> —Michael O'Donoghue

Literature and drama have given us many stories of people who beat themselves up inside, or who long to die, even imagining what it would be like. James Thurber's short story "The Secret Life of Walter Mitty" appeared in 1942. Its hero has become a modern archetype for someone whose life is synonymous with a leading cause of symbolic suicide: *the need to escape from a reality that does not give one a significant identity*. Walter spontaneously, and with no warning, disappears mentally and emotionally into a fantasy world. His shrunken self-image is encouraged by a nagging wife, who tells him how fast to drive, when to see a doctor, and even where to sit while waiting for her in a hotel lobby. On one occasion Walter explains that he has forgotten some errand because "I was thinking." Mrs. Mitty responds: "I'm going to take your temperature when I get you home."

In his perpetual escapes from reality, Walter Mitty lives as an airplane pilot making a perilous landing in a hurricane, a world-famous surgeon, a defendant in a murder trial, a war hero, but, in the saddest fantasy of all, as a man about to be executed:

> *He took one last drag on his cigarette and snapped it away. Then, with that faint, fleeting smile playing upon his lips, he faced the firing squad; erect and motionless, proud and disdainful, Walter Mitty the Undefeated, inscrutable to the last.*[10]

> "Death is not the worst evil, but rather, when we wish to die and cannot."
>
> —Sophocles

Just as there are martyrs who have died for a cause and may be said to have committed a kind of suicide, not surprisingly there is also *symbolic martyrdom*. When life appears hopeless, one recourse is to become its victim and completely evade responsibility for what has happened. Such "victims" derive a measure of comfort from having others say, "Oh, you poor thing." They eagerly seek out ways to keep the pity going: volunteering for tasks nobody else wants to do; making sacrifices of time and money whenever possible and making sure everyone knows about it; reciting misfortunes in great detail, hoping their listeners will make an extravagant show of sympathy. On the whole, however, listeners tire of feeling sorry for someone who demands such a response. For this reason, acting teachers warn students they must never feel sorry for themselves in the roles they play because audiences will lose interest in them.

A subtle form of symbolic suicide is compulsive gambling, at least according to psychologists. Compulsive gamblers secretly want to punish themselves by losing. They suppress guilt over what they perceive as past wrongdoing, and, supposedly, do not want to win. Even if they do, even if they gamble because of debt or the desire to improve their lifestyles, chances are that in losing they will experience the guilt that will restart the cycle, leading them to gamble more in the unconscious hope of further failure. The 1998 film *Oscar and Lucinda* featured a pair of ostensible lovers who were linked by the need to gamble and who found themselves trapped in a vortex of self- and mutual-loathing.

Victims of social prejudice can develop strong feelings of unworth causing self-inflicted symbolic death. Of course, the very opposite result can occur, whereby at some point the victim refuses to be victimized any longer and rebels, performing an act we may call *symbolic resurrection*. Mark Medoff's play *Children of a Lesser God* (1981) gave us a heroine who undergoes both experiences.

The central character, Sarah, was born without hearing and, though she is extremely bright and has mastered American Sign Language, she resists efforts to make her talk. Like so many others in her predicament, she harbors deep-seated feelings of inferiority. She knows that others who attend her "special" school and who speak cannot sound like normal people and therefore are undoubtedly derided behind their backs. Nonetheless, she falls in love with and eventually marries the new speech teacher, who seems to understand her completely and to treat her as a full equal. His plan, however, is to induce her to talk, believing this would be the final proof that she is *not* a child of a "lesser god," but is capable of functioning as an accepted member of society.

In a harrowing confrontation scene, when the teacher-husband taunts and goads her into speaking—hoping thereby to prove to her that she can do anything—the woman screams out her resentment in a high-pitched wail that doesn't sound normal at all and runs off in a convulsive outpouring of tears. The hope that he has engendered in her has died, as she herself symbolically dies when faced once again with the glaring truth about herself. Yet in this fierce assertion of will, Sarah finds that she has not, in fact, died. If she is not able to function as a normal member of society, she will function as herself. Free of dependence on her husband's hollow support, she has proved that alternatives to symbolic destruction *do* exist.

Symbolic suicide is sometimes the consequence of feeling unworth because of the aging process. Our society is in the throes of the greatest antiaging campaign in human history. Fitness is not only a fad but a multibillion-dollar industry. Almost any new diet makes the best-seller list. Cosmeticians and plastic surgeons charge exorbitant fees to impart the illusion of youth. Television commercials exhibit product after product guaranteeing the user will look like the obviously younger models employed to demonstrate product effectiveness. Older people are shown playing golf, kicking up their heels on a cruise ship, or rehearsing in the clubhouse for a musical comedy. No one ever advertises the quieter pleasures of age. Quiet features such as a well-stocked library are seldom found in ads for retirement homes. Everyone is conditioned to believe that resisting age, not accepting the biological and sociological changes that age inevitably brings, is life-affirming and the sign of a healthy society.

To enjoy looking dapper for one's age, to exercise and maintain a sensible diet, to avoid excessive use of life-shortening pastimes like drinking and smoking . . . these *can* be called life-affirming and can be the signs of a creative approach to one's existence. Having attained the age of, say, 75, one is not automatically required to consider oneself *old* or to obey the rule our society has adopted for its senior citizens: *look young and act young so that the rest of us will not be intimidated by the thought of aging.*

The humanities not only consider the universal fear of aging but have supplied us with memorable images and prototypes. In the final moments of the film *Dangerous Liaisons* (1989), Glenn Close, as an aging aristocrat whose only pleasure in life has come from the game of love, finally accepts the fact of her advanced years and works up the courage to confront herself in a mirror. Without speaking one word, the aristocrat removes every bit of her makeup and stares at the reflection of her true physical image: past middle age, wrinkled, and gray-toned. But the image in the mirror brings no acceptance—only misery and contempt for herself.

Alan Parker's 1994 darkly comic film *The Road to Wellville* makes diabolic fun of today's obsession with stay-young health fads and cults. Based on a novel by T. Coraghessan Boyle, it disguises its contemporary relevance by pretending to be a period piece about the beginnings of the health craze a century ago. The arch villain is John Henry Kellogg, a physician and nutritionist, who founded the famous (and, as we find out, infamous) Battle Creek Sanatorium catering to the very rich who are willing to spend fortunes to look and feel young again. Dr. Kellogg—who, incidentally, invented cornflakes—subjects his patients to daily sessions of excruciatingly painful exercises and imposes strict rules, forcing them to abstain from meat, tobacco, alcohol, and even sex. In addition, they must soak for hours in boiling-hot water. One man dies after a wiring malfunction in the water heater electrocutes him.

> *"Aging, fatal disease, and dying are not seen as part of the life process but as the ultimate defeat."*
>
> **—Stanislav Grof**

The classic literary treatment of the burning need to stay young is provided by Oscar Wilde in his 1891 novel *The Picture of Dorian Gray*. The hero is a slim, incredibly handsome young aristocrat who is totally committed to a life of sensuality, leisure, and extravagance. In the opening scene he is observing his portrait, just finished by a major artist of the day:

> *How sad it is! . . . How sad it is! I shall grow old and horrible and dreadful. But this picture will remain always young. It will never be older than this particular day of June. If it were only the other way! If it were I who was to be always young, and the picture that was to grow old! For that—for that—I would give everything! Yes, there is nothing in the whole world I would not give! I would give my soul for that!*[11]

Like Faust, another famous character who barters his soul, Dorian has his wish granted by a mysterious power. He thus remains young while the man in the portrait grows older, but he loses his innocence. He becomes cruel and sadistic; develops an addiction to every conceivable pleasure, knowing he cannot do harm to his body; and ultimately, he even commits murder. The possession of eternal youth suggests he must be immortal—and perhaps out of the law's reach. In a grisly finale, however, the hero, both sickened by the knowledge of what he has become and now despising the portrait with its wizened face that shows every evil action he has ever committed, seizes a knife and plunges it into the heart of the painting. His servants find him "withered, wrinkled, and loathsome of visage." He has become the very thing he feared most; on the wall, however, the servants see a splendid portrait of their master in all the wonder of his exquisite youth and beauty. Immortality exists in art, but not in life.

The Eastern mind, with its acceptance of the natural cycle of life and death, youth and age, has no literature of symbolic suicide, though the physical act is often performed by people wishing to avoid dishonor. What is taught is to surrender to that cycle and let happen what must. The way of life is soft, the way of death is hard, say the Taoists; and the death to which they refer is the one we inflict on ourselves. There is in actuality only life, only existence. The individual self just borrows that existence during its brief stay, only to pass it on to someone else. Knowing this, the individual comes to understand that existence is always young. The *Tao Te Ching* gives this wisdom:

> *The student learns by daily increment.*
> *The Way is gained by daily loss,*

Loss upon loss until
At last comes rest.
By letting go, it all gets done;
The world is won by those who let it go!
But when you try and try,
The world is then beyond the winning.[12]

For the young who have not yet learned how life works, who are involved in day-to-day struggles to find a secure place for themselves, each day brings new knowledge; and with new knowledge comes tension and bewilderment. The older person gains wisdom by realizing that everything passes. Since this is so, what makes that person think he will not also pass? The tragic mistake is to hold out for what is impossible.

Symbolic Murder

There are two ways to win a race. One is by being the fastest runner. The other is by tripping your opponent. Too many deal with their insecurities by killing others symbolically, especially those who appear self-confident and are successful and much admired. The joke, of course, is that the majority of symbolic murder victims are busy committing symbolic suicide.

> *"When you're younger, people forget your birthdays. When you're older, they remember every one."*
> **—Meridith Vieira**

An often noted form of symbolic murder is the verbal knife thrust. There is a famous anecdote in the New York theater about the visit by one actress to another after the latter's opening. The "friend" embraces her and tells her that the performance was just marvelous: "I argued with everyone."

Molière, discussed in Chapter 7 as possibly the greatest of all comic dramatists, was fond of eliciting smiles from the audience with scenes in which one person, professing to be well-meaning, destroys another verbally by pretending to be "merely" reporting what others are saying. In *The Miser* (1668) the tight old codger's cook tells him off indirectly.

> *"I'm too old to do that."*
> *"What will they think of me?"*
> *"Nothing ever turns out right."*

Harpagon: *I'm glad to hear what the world says of me.*

Master Jaques: *Sir, since you will have it, I tell you frankly that people everywhere make fun of you; they are never more delighted than when they tell stories without end of your stingy tricks. . . . One tells a story that you ordered a cat of one of your neighbors to be cited in court, for having eaten the remains of a leg of mutton. Another that you were caught one night stealing your horses' oats. . . . You are the laughing stock of all the world, and you're never spoken of, but by the names of miser, skinflint, penny-pincher, and extortioner.*[13]

Molière, who dared not speak out directly and risk angering his aristocratic patrons, often used the device of loose-tongued servants to make fun of their supposed "superiors."

> *"Darling, I loved your performance.*
> *I argued with everyone."*

Symbolic murder can also spring from subterranean hostility that the "killers" do not even see in themselves. Often such "murder" takes place within the family circle. The British author Katherine Mansfield (1888–1923) pioneered the literature of the suppressed self—of people who can never be free to express how they really feel, but whose emotions, including those of hostility and resentment, nevertheless find other ways to come to the surface.

The title character of her short story "The Man Without a Temperament" is constantly at the beck and call of his invalid wife confined to a wheelchair. All day long he wheels her about the garden, responding in monosyllables to her comments. He has become devoid of all personality and interest in life. The wife senses he is keeping everything inside and at one point asks him: "I sometimes wonder—do you mind awfully being out here with me?"

> *He bends down. He kisses her. He tucks her in, he smoothes the pillow. "Rot!" he whispers.*[14]

Models of Life-Affirmation

A DEATH MODEL
"I've already taken the qualifying exam for the third time. Now I'm out for good. I'll never amount to anything
A PHOENIX MODEL
"I'm obviously not suited for that kind of work. Let me see . . .

If negative attitudes and negative internal imagery act to dampen people's lives, causing them to die many times before the actual and unique moment of their physical death, it should be possible—and indeed it is—to reverse the depression and be driven by positive attitudes and positive imagery. We are not talking here of shallow optimism. The issue is the profound realization that the potential for a productive, exciting life belongs to each of us. *We* control our attitudes, as Zeno the stoic would be quick to remind us. **Life-affirmation** is recognizing not only that life is worth living but that real death happens only once and, in a sense, does not happen to us at all. In this final section we will look at ways of refusing to allow the shadow of death to eclipse the sunlight of living.

The Phoenix

An ancient symbol of life-affirmation is that of the phoenix, a mythological bird of rare and exotic plumage and supernatural powers. The Greek historian Herodotus reported that the phoenix actually existed and was known to have visited the Egyptians every five hundred years. The Roman belief was that each era bears witness to the birth of one phoenix, that it lives for a very long time, and that at the moment of its death it generates a worm that becomes the phoenix for the next age.

Yet another version of the legend is that the phoenix is a bird from India which lives for five hundred years and then flies to a secret temple where it is burned to ashes upon the altar, only to rise from the ashes three days later, young and resplendent.

In folklore, poetry and song, in literature and drama, the phoenix has endured through time as a symbol of rebirth, new growth, regeneration, and redemption. Religions have counterpart symbols: gods who die or descend into the underworld, there to remain for a time and then to rise, reborn and renewed.

The **phoenix model** gives structure to many masterworks, such as Dante's *Divine Comedy,* in which the poet, seeking a vision of God in Paradise, must first travel through the very depths of hell before his wish is granted. The phoenix model has suggested to many people certain ways of thinking about events. Thus "I've been through hell" often prefaces an account of some happier turn of events, or at least invites the listener to effect a happy change for the sufferer through lavish sympathy and compassion. People say, "I'm going to pull myself out of this."

Even the popular exhortation "Lift yourself up by your own bootstraps" has underlying suggestions of phoenix imagery.

The epic poem *Faust* (published in sections beginning in 1790) by the greatest of all German poets, Johann Wolfgang von Goethe (1749–1832), makes inspiring use of phoenix mythology. In the Christian Middle Ages, Faust was an alchemist—someone who attempts to transform ordinary metal into gold—and gives up his soul in exchange for the ability to discover *all* of earth's secrets. Goethe turns the old legend into his own version of the phoenix myth, one that echoes nineteenth-century German romanticism and its strong belief in the power of individuals to reinvent themselves.

There are two distinct parts to Goethe's masterpiece, but only Part One is widely read. In it, the protagonist, having wearied of his intellectual efforts to probe the secrets of life, is willing to part with his soul in exchange for a lifetime of unlimited sensory pleasures without having to think. He bargains with Mephistopheles, an agent of the devil, who promises to grant his every wish, but on one condition: *He must never be so satisfied within a given moment that he would want time to stop.* He must live from day to day at a frantic pace, never looking back, never wishing to hold onto anything or anyone.

Faust falls in love with an innocent maiden called Gretchen, then seduces and abandons her. (Charles Gounod's opera *Faust* centers on the poignant story of Gretchen, now called Marguerite, and the eventual loss of the hero's soul as punishment for what he has done to her.)

Courses in world literature seldom assign Part Two (published after the poet's death). It is less dramatic, as the term is generally understood, and requires many hours of reading as well as studying many complex passages. It eventually rewards the patient reader with the true meaning of the entire work: not the triumph of the devil, but the triumph of humanity. In its entirety, Goethe's *Faust* offers the perfect phoenix model, a work of ringing life-affirmation in the very confrontation of life's harshest realities.

In Part One, Faust readily agrees to the condition laid down by Mephistopheles. He has decided that life has no meaning beyond the enjoyment of each passing moment. There is no truth. There is only continual change. Why should anyone ever want to hold onto a moment? In Part Two, the protagonist is older and has grown tired of a life that offers nothing but a variety of sense experiences without thought. He is beginning to long for some accomplishment, something to show for his having lived. He is also tired of serving only himself, and so he becomes the mayor of a seaside village situated on land so low that the waves threaten to engulf it and render life there intolerable. His project as mayor is to build a seawall, but he finds that each time the wall is extended a little further, the sea has already begun to erode what was already built. He sees that he faces an impossible task; the wall will *never* be finished. Yet this realization fills him with a raging passion to challenge the sea. He will continue putting up the wall, then going back to repair the damage. He will keep on,

Lebrecht Music & Arts/Alamy

Advertisement featuring Faust and Mephistopheles, 19th century

Mephistopheles agrees to give Faust a life of constant pleasure, but he must never wish to make any moment last.

knowing that each day a little more land will be made suitable for agriculture, and, though inevitable floods will come, the people will have raised food—perhaps a little more each year.

The thought that the human courage to accept continual change and to meet challenges head-on regardless of whether one succeeds or not is greater than success itself—the thought that things are worth doing even if the work of one individual's life is unfinishable—hits him with the force of lightning. If he cannot ultimately win, he shall not ultimately lose.

He only earns both freedom and existence
Who must reconquer them each day.
And so, ringed about by perils, here
Youth, manhood, age will spend their strenuous year.
Such teeming would I see upon this land,
On acres free among free people stand.
I might entreat the fleeting minute:
Oh linger awhile, so fair thou art![15]

Mephistopheles warned Faust when the bargain was made that "when to the moment thou shalt say 'Oh linger awhile, so fair thou art'" his doom will be sealed and hell will have triumphed. Faust has asked time to stop so that he can enjoy the beauty of his realization—and has lost the bargain. In a sense, all of us lose the bargain in that we eventually run out of lifetime. Yet it is within our power not to believe we have lost anything, *provided* we know that we reconquer our freedom and existence every day. Faust's original pact is made because he wants it all—wants to experience every sensation life has to offer. His victory is recognizing that "it all" is present completely in every moment and that it is far more than sensory pleasure. It is knowing that one has confronted every challenge and done all that was possible, and thus has not wasted one precious second. Faust knows he has given everything for the good of his people, and what one gives is what one also *has*. To give nothing to life is to have nothing from life.

There Is Only Now

The late Uta Hagen, giving a workshop to several young aspiring actors, asked a girl to prepare a certain scene in which she would play a 50-year-old woman. At the appointed time, the girl made her entrance in a wheelchair and spoke in a cracking voice, sounding much like the witch in *Snow White*. "What in the world are you doing?" the actress interrupted her. "Trying to physicalize the character's age," was the answer. "Do you feel as though you are 50?" the girl was asked. "No, of course not." Hagen told her to play 50 as she would play 16—the girl's actual age—because, barring unfortunate accidents of fate, she would feel no different inwardly when she really *was* 50 and therefore there was no reason to indulge in external and false signs of aging *now*.

Time is physical in the contemporary world of science. It forms part of Einstein's fourth dimension and can be measured. Time for us human beings is a habit, a social construct, something on the hands of a watch that lets us keep appointments. In terms of actual experience, what is it? Can one experience yesterday? In memory, to be sure, but we can also choose *not* to remember. Can one experience tomorrow? Only in imagination, and again we can decide against it.

> *"For me, thinking finally came late that night as I wandered through the shattered house by flashlight. I looked up through where the kitchen ceiling had been and saw a clear sky filled with more stars than I ever knew were possible. I realized that those stars were only visible now because there was darkness all around; they were no longer lost in the wash of light from Earth."*
>
> **—Leonard Pitts, Jr. (After Hurricane Andrew)**

What we cannot control is the presence of the present moment, and regrettably, too often we are so busy with our inner thoughts we lose the sense of that moment. The more we actually experience, the less significant is the myth of time. It has been wisely said: "Time is important only when you're doing it—in prison." Even at that, prisoners can choose not to keep marking their calendars.

Ways of thinking about time are well within our power. The poet William Wordsworth, to whom we return again and again for his quiet wisdom, has left us with this definitive statement about living in the eternal Now:

MY HEART LEAPS UP

My heart leaps up when I behold
A rainbow in the sky:
So was it when my life began;
So is it now I am a man;
So be it when I shall grow old,
Or let me die!
The Child is father of the Man;
And I could wish my days to be
Bound each to each by natural piety.

Did you ever think that life can run a course that is the complete opposite of the popular way of depicting it? Your childhood can be your tomorrow. The future has not yet even begun, and you can choose never to have it. Like Merlin in the musical play *Camelot,* you can live backwards and "youthen" as the years unfold. The great Picasso urged us to remain as children, filled with wide-eyed wonder.

Internal imagery can be adjusted. To break the illusion of time rushing by to an inevitable aging and death, we can replace pyramids with circles. In pyramid imagery, we visualize ourselves rising through the ranks (in school, in athletics, on the job), reaching a peak or a crest ("Ah! At last I've made it!" or, negatively, "This is as far as I'm going!") and then feeling we are "over the hill." In circle imagery, on the other hand, life is like a Ferris wheel, rising, cresting, going back down, and then starting up all over again. This is a particularly effective image because riders of Ferris wheels know that moving around is preferable to being stuck on top for very long.

Jack Benny, one of the great comics of the twentieth century, always gave his age as 39. Audiences laughed every time he did, reacting to the apparent absurdity of persisting in such a lie. Yet, up to the time of his unexpected death at 70, Benny exhibited the imagination and energy of the pretended age.

Einstein showed that time is absolute only with respect to bodies moving at uniform speed. If A is traveling in a train side by side with B on an adjacent train and both trains have the same speed, A and B could wave to each other whenever they wished; and for both the length of the trip would be the same. The theory of relativity also demonstrates that as one travels faster and faster time slows down. If astronauts could travel at the speed of light, they would never grow old. Though it is unlikely that this particular part of the relativity theory will be tested anytime soon, it does nonetheless remind us that time—absolute time—is a variable even in the universe of science.

> *"In the depths of winter I finally learned there was in me an invincible summer."*
>
> **—Albert Camus**

One way to explain relativity is to think of identical twins, one of whom takes off in a spaceship that will travel at the speed of light (186,282 miles per second), while the other remains on earth. The mission lasts 20 years as measured on earth by the homebound twin. When the space twin returns, he will find his brother 20 years older, while he himself looks the same as when the mission began. It is possible to live your life as if moving at the speed of light because, unless you *want* to feel old inside, you need be conscious only of where you are *now* and what you are doing.

The most famous work by the French author Marcel Proust (1871–1922) is titled *Remembrance of Things Past* in its customary English translation, but literally the title is *In Search of Lost Time.* Memories are pleasant diversions for a rainy afternoon, but to actually wish we could go back in time (time travel mythology notwithstanding) is not life-affirming.

In Eastern thought mind, or consciousness, is infinite. Awareness is always with us. Even memories of past events are alive within us in the everlasting moment. We carry time with us. There is no such thing as the past, and therefore no reason to lament that it's gone. Those who try to hold onto time are the ones suffering the most, for they come to recognize how quickly it flies by. Those who do not try to seize it are living vividly in the Now.

Eastern philosophers tell us that we become dismayed by the passing of time because we create the illusion of *beginning,* which we date from the instant of our birth, and of *ending,* which is death. Books end, movies end, the party is over—always the same pattern, so that ending becomes ingrained in us. The Chinese poet and philosopher Chuang Chou, who lived over 2,000 years ago, had fun with verbal dazzle that is also profound:

> *. . . there is never beginning to have a beginning, there is never beginning to never begin to have a beginning. There is existence, there is nonexistence. There is never beginning the existence of nonexistence . . .*[16]

How can the beginning begin? Where was it before? If the beginning cannot begin, then it cannot end either. In this philosophy all of us live between the two poles, but where that is cannot be precisely defined, can it?

Reinventing Ourselves

> *"The world cannot be discovered by a journey of miles, however long, but by a spiritual journey, a journey of only one inch, very arduous and humble and joyful, by which we arrive at the ground at our feet, and learn to be at home."*
>
> **—Wendell Berry**

It's easy enough to say that memory imprisons us in time, but not so easy to erase memory. Memory is a distinguishing attribute of our species. It can brighten the darkest of days, offer consolation for loss, and link us to the past so that we don't have the sense of drifting aimlessly through life. But memory can also exert a ferocious hold over us, triggering negativity. Too many of us accumulate self-determined bad karma from the past; we refuse to let go of it and thus see no way of ever changing. What is desirable is that we learn to put memory in proper perspective, to recognize that things we have done or that have been done to us in the past may have relevance to the present but *not in the same form.* We do ourselves harm when we act and react *now* as if it were still *then.*

There are those, however, who carry the pain of yesterday into the way today is experienced and finally decide to terminate their existence. Committing even symbolic suicide is in its own way a termination of existence.

Psychologists who treat suicidal patients usually try first to convince them to reaffirm life, to consider what is good in it. Often their counseling fails, and in retrospect, some of them have said that self-inflicted death can be a highly rational act, a meaningful, if somber, way of reinventing oneself that is not to be recommended—only, on occasion, understood.

The Greeks and Romans generally believed self-inflicted death served four purposes: to show bereavement; to preserve honor; to avoid pain; and to benefit the state. Socrates disagreed, warning that human beings did not create themselves and therefore were not at liberty to dispose of their bodies as they willed. Most religions which oppose suicide do so on similar grounds.

Jewish law forbids self-inflicted death, but many Jews did in fact kill themselves to avoid capture by the Romans. Early Christians, also oppressed by Romans, frequently took their own lives, apparently without fear of God's retribution. Christianity now expressly forbids the act, but the deaths of the following may be regarded as suicides: Thomas à Becket, Archbishop of Canterbury, who refused to say the king was greater than the pope and was slaughtered on his altar; Joan of Arc, who refused to sign a paper confessing she did not hear heavenly voices urging her into battle and was burned at the stake; and Bernadette of Lourdes, the peasant girl who, having discovered a spring that was said to have cured many hopelessly ill pilgrims, suffered from a terminal disease which she never mentioned until medical help was no longer possible, and who maintained that heaven would not allow her to use the water for herself.

What seems sad, however, is that artists sometimes end their lives prematurely, overlooking the fact that, of all people, they possess the creativity to reinvent themselves. Sometimes the reason is, tragically, the very excess of their own genius. Compulsively driven to create what we now acknowledge as masterpiece after masterpiece, van Gogh was increasingly victimized by lack of recognition and the thought that his work must, after all, deserve its obscurity. Earlier in his short life he *was* able to tell himself, defiantly, that he would paint as he liked no matter what others thought. This attitude was reinvention, but van Gogh ultimately lost the power to do it.

Compulsively driven to create masterpiece after masterpiece, van Gogh was victimized by the thought that his work must deserve its obscurity. He ultimately lost the power to reinvent himself.

Two major poets of the twentieth century also took their own lives, thus depriving us of the full flower of their genius. Whereas Hamlet had seen a choice in "to be or not to be," these poets said emphatically "not to be"; and in both cases the decision appears to have been calculated, inevitable, and not the result of a sudden, uncontrollable impulse. Both women were feminists. Both were married to intelligent, productive men who may have—or ought to have—understood their creative needs, at least at some points in the marriage. Yet those needs were finally incompatible with the demands that even a flexible marriage can impose.

Sylvia Plath (1932–1963) had two small children and a husband, the poet Ted Hughes, who had his own creative and emotional needs. Many such literary marriages are full of tension, and Plath had a history of emotional breakdowns. Apparently she tried at first to make the marriage work, but found that it was stifling her creativity and her personality. As she neared her thirtieth birthday, she began to fear that she could no longer write, and the inner anxiety brought her to a final breaking point, a condition that only worsened when her husband left her.

Robert Lowell, a fellow poet, once described Plath as being "a little like a racehorse, galloping recklessly with risked outstretched neck, death hurdle after death hurdle topped." While the description makes Plath seem quite out of control—and there is little doubt she suffered from at the very least a profound depression—the signs she gave of approaching suicide in her writings tend to be calm and deliberate. There is no reason to believe she did not know exactly what she was doing when she made her final decision.

The following lines, written when Plath was 27 and pregnant, say a great deal about the frustrations she was experiencing:

> *I'm a means, a stage, a cow in calf,*
> *I've eaten a bag of green apples,*
> *Boarded the train there's no getting off.*[17]

It's just speculation, of course, but were there no other options? In using the metaphor of the train, might Sylvia Plath have forgotten that there are stations all along the way, and trains travel through many different landscapes?

Anne Sexton (1928–1974) lived in a sophisticated eastern seaboard world of martinis, smart talk, broken marriages, abortions, and tranquilizers. A wife and mother like Plath, she found she could not balance all of the conflicting strands of her life and decided the rewards were simply not enough to offset the pain. Her decision to end her life was also not a momentary impulse. Sexton struggled for a long time (note that she reached middle age), often quite determined to live. In fact, she even wrote a poem called "Live." At this stage of her life she may have been trying to find a way to reinvent herself. Apparently, in the long run, the "excitable gift," as she called life in the poem, was not enough. Yet it is tempting to wonder why a poet who had at least once decided that the sun was reason enough to live could not recapture the feeling again.

> "I postpone death, by living, by suffering, by error, by risking, by giving, by losing."
>
> —**Anaïs Nin**

Perhaps the best known literary suicide of the last century was that of Ernest Hemingway. Suffering from ill health and a dramatic loss of creativity, he ended his life with a violent blast from a shotgun. Most of his novels and short stories deal with men who exist without fear on the borders of violence and death. Throughout his work there is admiration for *machismo,* masculine pride and daring: that of the so-called great white hunter in Africa, that of the bullfighter, and that of Robert Jordan, the American hero of *For Whom the Bell Tolls,* who dies fighting with guerillas in the Spanish Civil War of the 1930s. Perhaps when he acknowledged the truth that his life of heavy drinking, prolific sexual activity, and long sessions at the writing desk was no longer working, Hemingway decided to bow out in a heroic way, as if his readers would expect nothing less. A drastic way to reinvent himself, perhaps, but for the writer, it must have made complete sense.

Ibsen's *A Doll's House*, the play about the woman who realized she had been denied the truth about life and was therefore unfit to be a mother and a wife before leaving her husband and children, slamming the door behind her—a sound effect that shocked many in the original audiences, but can now be seen, in retrospect, as the very model of self-reinvention.

Guilt and Forgiveness

Life-affirmation cannot happen until we do something about guilt. First, we must discover that hidden guilt is indeed responsible for anxiety, fear, the sense of unworth. Second, we must determine what is causing the guilt. Is it really deserved? Too many of us suffer from unexplained depression because of supposedly wrongful actions that, if brought to light, can turn out to be sheer fantasy—or at the very most, deeds that were not as bad as we thought, or were led to believe.

A classic case is that of the only child of parents who are getting divorced. One parent agrees to leave while the other agrees to take care of the child, with the usual explanation: "Mommy [Daddy] is going away for a while and wants you to be good in the meantime." The explanation is like a time-release capsule: effective for as long as it works. Eventually the child wants to know when the parent is in fact coming home and why the parent hasn't even called. The time has come for the more difficult answer: "He [she] is not going to come home anytime soon. The new job is very hard." After a few weeks the question is now: "Doesn't Mommy [Daddy] love me anymore?"

Our parents are an integral part of us, consciously or not, and they are talking inside us all the time. Close behind them might be a teacher, a minister or priest, an older sibling. The existentialist (Chapter 16) advises us we are free to carve our own destinies, but sometimes we cannot find the key to remove the shackles of our early lives.

> *Good, to forgive;*
> *Best, to forget!*
> *Living, we fret;*
> *Dying, we live.*
>
> **—Robert Browning**

Many people spend hours, weeks, months, even years on the psychiatrist's couch willing to confront their guilt only to have it revived, starting up the whole cycle again. Or else they find that original guilt has been joined by a lot of new guilt. After all, *I'm a terrible person, and I know that everything bad that happens is my fault*. The result can be a decidedly neurotic individual.

What is known as "survivor guilt" is among the most common sources of depression, whether conscious or not. Testimony from those who escaped death in Nazi concentration camps during World War II indicates that their suffering did not cease just because they were still alive. D. M. Thomas's celebrated 1981 novel *The White Hotel* is a fictionalized account of an actual case in which Sigmund Freud psychoanalyzed a woman afflicted with hysteria, a mental disorder with external physical symptoms traceable to this woman's buried survivor guilt, her sorrow at not having gone to the gas chamber. Many confronted with the truth of such depression have cried, "Why was *I* not the one?"

> *What did it matter if he existed for two or for twenty years? Happiness was the fact that he existed.*
>
> **—Albert Camus**

Too frequently natural disasters such as earthquakes, mudslides, raging wildfires, tsunamis, and cyclonic winds and seas abruptly terminate existence for thousands of men, women, and children. Television reports show anguished survivors walking amid the rubble, dazed and tearfully searching for a wife, a husband, a child. Who knows how many of them may harbor the secret feeling that the punishment for past sins is their being forced to live without their loved ones? It is hard for those of us fortunate enough not to have experienced such unbearable losses to isolate ourselves from the recognition that human existence is fraught with perils and that little can be said to comfort the unlucky. Or it should be. To hope that saying "Life goes on" will take care of the problem is unrealistic and often unkind.

Yet something *can* be done by those whose guilt has been buried for a long time, who suffer needlessly when nothing is able to change the past. A suggestion is to have a Goodbye to Guilt party. Make sure the invitation states clearly what the party is for and require that attendees show up with a large piece of paper on which, using letters clipped from magazines, they have spelled out the most terrible thing they have ever done or been responsible for. The paper is to be folded into a small wad and deposited in a receptacle of some kind. (The hosts of one party made a tiny casket out of cardboard and decorated it with flowers.)

A forgiveness ritual follows that should be developed spontaneously rather than planned in advance. Participants have made up hymns on the spot, engaged in a ritual dance, conducted a funeral service as they buried the receptacle, and even formed a torchlight procession to a nearby lake, where they set the receptacle ablaze and cheered as they watched it drift away and finally consume itself.

Geo Images/Shutterstock

The Phoenix, c. 2000

Like the ancient phoenix bird, we have the power to reinvent ourselves.

> *The past and present wilt—I have fill'd them, emptied them*
> *And I proceed to fill my next fold of the future.*
>
> —**Walt Whitman**

Hebrew tradition has for centuries encouraged a forgiveness ritual.

> *[T]he Jewish practice known as tashlikh (Hebrew for "throw") is derived from a verse from the prophet Micah, "And You [God] shall throw their sins into the depths of the sea" (7:19). Based on the prophet's words, a Jewish custom arose during the Middle Ages. On the first day of Rosh ha-Shana . . . Jews go to a river and symbolically cast their sins into the water. In many communities, people pull out their pockets and shake them, emptying them of the sins they contained.*[18]

Alternatively, we can create a private ritual, which involves sitting quietly in a corner, concentrating very hard on the guilt we don't want to share, gathering up all of it into a tight ball, and then—calmly and deliberately—imagining ourselves hurling the ball straight up into the sky. See? There it goes. The ball of guilt suddenly becomes a bird winging its way over a cloud, becoming lost in an azure infinity, and never being heard from again.

Death itself—biological death, the single stroke that happens only once to each of us—will come as it may. In this chapter we have not really been discussing that event. We have been talking about *other* kinds of death and how the resources in the humanities can, except in cases of overpowering disasters, help us to affirm the value of life.

The most distressing aspect of a death-denying culture is the fact that we die (or cause others to die) *symbolically*: that is, psychologically experiencing the death of self-worth and the loss of the power to reinvent ourselves. We may laugh heartily at the guilt-ridden, anxiety-filled neurotics in movies or on television, but they can also be looked upon as tragic examples of how to waste a life.

We end the chapter, however, on a positive note. The humanities are sources of life-affirming models, such as the myth of the phoenix bird, that we have the power to use as we reinvent ourselves and continue to be born anew.

LEARNING OBJECTIVES

Having read this chapter, you should be able to:

1. Summarize the many forms of death beside the final moment itself.
2. Indicate life-affirming and life-denying elements in your own life.
3. Discuss three images of death in the chapter as being life-affirming or life-denying.
4. Explain the popularity of disaster films.
5. Restate in your own words La Rochefoucauld's famous remark that "all of us share a willingness to bear the misfortune of others."
6. Explain what the text points out as being shared by Greek mythology and Tolkien.
7. Compare two views of children's reactions to death.
8. Indicate the function of the New Orleans jazz funeral.
9. Explain why Socrates showed no fear of his imminent death.
10. Compare views of an afterlife in Hinduism, Judaism, and Christianity.
11. Explain the meaning and give two examples of symbolic death.
12. Show why the phoenix has become a symbol of life-affirmation.

KEY TERMS

fatalism the belief that all events, including the nature, time, and place of one's death, have been predetermined.

life-affirmation the belief that life is essentially good and worth living; the ability to free oneself from unnecessary burdens of guilt and a lack of self-esteem as well as fears of growing older and eventually having to die and substituting the realization that death happens only once, not every day.

program music musical genre, represented in this chapter by Richard Strauss's *Death and Transfiguration,* an orchestral poem telling a story or following a scenario in the composer's mind, knowing which adds to listener's enjoyment.

TOPICS FOR WRITING AND DISCUSSION

1. Identify and explain three of the images of death discussed in this chapter.
2. People not only enjoy watching horror movies but they will invariably slow down every time they see what looks like a terrible accident. These tendencies can be either life-affirming or life-denying; make the case for both.
3. What is symbolic, as opposed to actual, death? Explain by giving a specific example. Then indicate how one can be saved from such a death.
4. Reread Wordsworth's "My heart leaps up" on page 467. Explain the line "The child is father of the man." Then indicate in what way it relates to the subject matter of this chapter.
5. Much of the artwork depicting people's reaction to death shows them grieving. In your own words define *grief* and indicate whether it is life-affirming or life-denying.
6. Laura Linney's smiling face is the opening image for this chapter. The text indicates her character is suffering from an incurable disease but that she doesn't want it widely known. Is concealing such a fact life-affirming? Why or why not?
7. The film *The Road to Wellville* is a satire on the lengths (and expense) to which people will go to stay (or think they are staying) young. Do you think the desire to stay young is life-affirming? Why make fun of it?
8. Write a short paper on this question: Is it life-affirming or life-denying to say that one ought to have as much fun as possible whenever one can because life is so short?
9. Read the account of the Forgiveness Ritual described by Rabbi Telushkin. Then create your own ritual and describe it to the class. Or better still, volunteer to arrange the ritual in which the entire class may participate.
10. We live in perilous times: global warming, rising poverty levels, seemingly endless conflicts in the Middle East, nuclear threats, and much more. Is it life-affirming to take the attitude that "There's nothing I can do about it, so why be concerned?" Explain your answer.

Chapter 15

Nature

On the whole, the humanities have been friendly toward **nature**, even though some artists and philosophers have been indifferent to the natural world. Key figures in the Greek cultural explosion, which began in the sixth century B.C.E., focused on the mind and its powers. Theirs was a city-oriented society. Yet Greek civilization is not to be taken as the absolute norm when it came to an interest—and even a concern—for Nature. Nor is Rome, which believed its mighty city was the true measure of humankind.

Long before those two civilizations, Eastern philosophers were reverent toward the force that ruled the universe, the force the West ultimately called nature and that philosophers in India, called *Brahman*; in China, the *Tao*; and to Buddhists, the *Dharma*. In both East and West this force had an outward appearance (trees, mountains, and so on), but also an inner soul or rationality operating in accordance with unchanging principles that either were always there or were created by a divine power. In our time, scientists in both hemispheres continue to probe the natural world for its secrets, guided by the belief that such rationality must indeed exist.

◀ Stream, Olympia, Washington, c. 2010

Nature in a pristine state.

Corbis/SuperStock

"Those who dwell as scientists or laymen, among the beauties and mysteries of the earth, are never alone or weary of life."

—Rachel Carson

Romantic Views of Nature

During the nineteenth century, on both sides of the Atlantic, the humanities were dominated by a vast movement in art, literature, music, and philosophy called *romanticism.* (We have already discussed this term as it applies to the music of Mozart and of Beethoven in Chapter 6.) The philosophy of those who brought the United States into being, influenced in part by the romantic movement, equated the words "natural" and "free." Natural rights are still the cornerstone of democracy. Before the coming of civilization, human beings living in nature were free to roam where they wanted, settle where they wanted, and create a social order that suited their needs. Implicit in the Declaration of Independence is the equation of human and natural rights.

Today popular use of the word "natural" has any number of meanings. Natural foods are supposed to be free of chemicals and laboratory-injected ingredients, though it is often hard to pronounce whatever is taking their place. Those opposed to gay rights brand homosexuality as "unnatural." Those who put business interests ahead of environmentalism say that nature seems to know what it is doing—leave it alone. Environmentalists, however, are hastening to say that nature has been ruthlessly tampered with and may soon reach a point of no return.

In 1836, Ralph Waldo Emerson wrote a long essay entitled "Nature." What he said still has the power to move those of us who have ever stood on a mountain and gazed in awe at the surroundings.

> *Nature, in the common sense, refers to essences unchanged by man space. . . . The stars awaken a common reverence, because they are always present. They are inaccessible, but all natural objects make a kindred impression when the mind is open to their influence.*

Emerson taught that all of us should look for nature in ourselves (a traditional Eastern philosophy), should feel that we and "it" are parts of the same whole. To love ourselves is to love the world that enfolds us. The belief that nature and humanity are separate entities may be one of the causes of the present crisis: the belief that humankind has the right to impose its will on nature.

A major voice in romanticism was William Wordsworth (1770–1850), one of whose masterpieces is modestly titled "Lines Composed a Few Miles Above Tintern Abbey on the Banks of the Wye." Here is a passage from the work that can still inspire reverence toward nature.

> *And I have felt*
> *A presence that disturbs me with the joy*
> *Of elevated thoughts; a sense sublime*
> *Of something far more deeply interfused,*
> *Whose dwelling is the light of setting suns,*
> *And the round ocean and the living air,*
> *And the blue sky, and in the mind of man;*
> *A motion and a spirit, that impels*
> *All thinking things, all objects of all thought,*
> *And rolls through all things.*

"Man has been endowed with reason, and the power to create, so that he can add to what he's been given, but up to now he hasn't been a creator, only a destroyer. Forests keep disappearing, rivers dry up, wildlife's become extinct, the climate's ruined, and the land grows poorer and uglier every day."

—Anton Chekhov

Early Warnings

Despite his country's urban orientation, the Roman poet Lucretius (c. 99–55 B.C.E.) wrote a vast poem entitled *Of the Nature of Things* in which he attributes the beginning of the natural world to a mighty collision of atoms. He predicts that eventually this primal atomic energy will reassert itself and the world will end in a violent explosion. His prediction is not early environmentalism; but Lucretius does suggest that we respect nature not as a loving, kind mother who will always be there for us, but as an awesome power that is dangerous to trifle with.

Some **environmentalists** refer to Genesis when placing blame for the increasing deterioration of Nature, citing this passage:

> *So God created man in his own image, in the image of God he created him; male and female he created them. God blessed them, and said to them, "Be fruitful and increase in number; fill this earth and subdue it. Rule over the fish of the sea and the birds of the air and over every living creature that moves on the ground."*
>
> Genesis, 2: 4-5, 7–8

Museum of Fine Arts, Budapest

Eugenè Delacroix, *Horse Frightened by a Storm*, 1828

Wordsworth's wonderful use of "rolls" also suggests that Nature, in all its magnificence, can also be a devastating power.

But environmentalists hasten to add the biblical passage does not mean that humankind has inherited the right to trash the garden. Perhaps the perception of God as an absentee owner may encourage some to think *they* are the owners. Suppose a building's owner hires a superintendent but never visits the property. How long before the superintendent grows cocky and believes the property is actually his? Perhaps a good case could be made for the belief that some have conveniently forgotten another line from Genesis (2:15): "And the Lord God took the man, and put him into the Garden of Eden to dress it and keep it." Thousands of years after Genesis, the Islamic Qu'ran echoed the same sentiments.

Centuries after the Qu'ran was written, John D. Rockefeller I, founder of globe-spanning Standard Oil, also cites God. In his autobiography he states his assurance that God was responsible for his financial success. Since much of that success involved the large-scale depletion of fossil fuel, was Rockefeller implying that God approved of this depletion? Or that a God-fearing man who benefitted humanity through the employment he provided and the fuel to drive cars and run factories was an instrument through whom God's plans were carried out?

But not so fast. Perhaps Rockefeller read or reread the admonition that humanity must dress and keep the Garden. Perhaps he saw that too much of Nature was being despoiled, and he was in a position to do something about it. At any rate, late in his life, Rockefeller purchased a good portion of Wyoming wilderness and willed it to the United States with the proviso that it be kept forever as a natural reserve. This land, of course, became the Grand Teton and Yellowstone National Parks.

> *"Humankind's great challenge is not so much to build the perfect mousetrap, but to subdue and transform its worst instincts."*
>
> **—Joel Achenbach**

The Forest of Arden

During the early Middle Ages—from the sixth to the eleventh centuries—Nature must have been in a pristine, unspoiled state. Yet for the most part, medieval people probably did not venture very much outside their villages or their walled fortresses or the monasteries. Medieval Nature must have been something "out there," with little direct relationship to human beings. Besides, why spend time looking at clouds and flowers when nothing in this vale of tears mattered as much as preparing oneself for salvation in the next world?

During the eleventh and twelfth centuries, there appeared a new kind of literature written by rebellious young men studying for the priesthood but objecting to the rigors of their austere training and to the otherworldly bent of their elders. Poems by the young rebels urge their fellow students to discover the natural world outside.

Cast aside dull books and thought,
Sweet is folly, sweet is play;
Take the pleasure Spring hath brought
In youth's opening holiday!
Right it is old age should ponder
On grave matters fraught with care,
Tender youth is free to wander,
Ever to frolic, light as air.

Here was the earliest stirring of what would become a great poetic theme, one that still resonates today: the identification of unspoiled Nature with youth and joy and all good things.

As the walled fortresses turned into walled cities, as plague and pestilence and poverty snaked along insidiously behind those walls, many looked on the city as a place of death, decay, and evil. Crime was prevalent. The countryside became a place of blessed escape. But everyone did not share this view. For the religious traditionalists, one could find God without frolicking in the spring air. Centuries later, the philosopher Baruch Spinoza (1632–1677) argued that God and Nature were one and the same.

Like other Renaissance poets, the young William Shakespeare wrote about imaginary, unspoiled countrysides, where the joys of love were abundant. By the time he came to London in the late sixteenth century, that city was already a den of filth, poverty, and crime. Aristocrats who patronized poets and bought their work could ignore the truth of the city. Why worry about the wretched poor, gasping for breath in their crowded rooms, when there isn't anything we can do about it? The patrons of art in their airy, comfortable homes enjoyed the literature of escape, subsidizing handsomely those who could please their taste.

I90/Zuma Press/Newscom

Helen Mirren, *The Tempest*, 2010

In the film version, director Julie Taymor turns Prospero into a woman without sacrificing the play's magic.

The popularity of idealized country settings—far away from the reality—led Shakespeare to capitalize on this form of escapism. *A Midsummer Night's Dream* (1594) is set in a Disney-like woodland, with charming fairies and lovers who will stay young forever. Shakespeare's presumed final play, *The Tempest* (1611), takes us to a faraway desert island, a "brave new world" far away from urban reality, where a magician named Prospero controls everything.

In 1598 Shakespeare had written *As You Like It,* one of his most enduring comedies, containing a decidedly premature environmentalism. An aristocrat identified only as Duke Senior has been exiled by his evil brother. He and a small band of followers move to the Forest of Arden, the author's version of the Garden of Eden, where they enjoy a simple existence free of the corruption found in court.

> *Sweet are the uses of adversity;*
> *Which like the toad, ugly and venomous,*
> *Wears yet a precious jewel in his head;*
> *And this our life, exempt from public haunt,*
> *Finds tongues in trees, books in the running brooks,*
> *Sermons in stones, and good in everything.*[1]

"Reading about nature is fine, but if a person walks in the woods, he can learn more than what's in books."

—George Washington Carver

This would not be the last time a writer would suggest that one can receive a better education in Nature than in the library.

The Duke's followers, however, are urbanized men, accustomed to the food of city-bred people. Instead of leaving their paradise the way they found it, they begin to kill the wild deer, which sorely grieves one of the Duke's attendants, Jaques, a brooding, melancholy individual. Jaques, the Duke is told, "swears you do more usurp/ Than doth your brother that hath banished you."[2] In fact, Jaques angrily denounces what they're doing to Nature, insisting it is worse than the court corruption that exiled them in the first place. At one point Jaques witnesses the excruciating death throes of a wounded stag:

> *"Poor dear," quoth he, "thou mak'st a testament*
> *As worldlings do, giving thy sum of more*
> *To that which had too much."*[3]

"Eating meat is primitive, barbaric, and arrogant."

—Ingrid Newkirk

Then he cries out to the herd of still-surviving deer that they should hide themselves from the tyrants who have come to destroy the animals in their "assigned and native dwelling place."

In Shakespeare's time, Nature and humanity were not considered part of each other. Humanity should therefore not try to meddle with a natural universe in which everything has its rightful place and function. The tragedy of Jaques is that he *feels* the agony of animal destruction without being able to do anything to help. All he can do is be seen "weeping and lamenting/ Upon the sobbing deer." His misanthropy, fueled by the corruption of the forest, drives him almost mad. Despite his true helplessness, he develops the delusion that he can reform the world.

> *Invest me in my motley, give me leave*
> *To speak my mind, and I will through and through*
> *Cleanse the foul body of th' infected world,*
> *If they will patiently accept my medicine.*[4]

We know he will never be successful. At the play's conclusion, when the exiled and usurper brothers are reconciled and the four young lovers are to be happily married, Jaques wishes everyone peace and joy, but then declares that he cannot stay in their midst; he is "for other than dancing measures." When they beg him to return to their urban civilization, he refuses. "To see no pastime I. What you would have/ I'll stay to know at your abandoned cave."

The Decay of Nature

"Nature is the art of God."

—Dante Alighieri

During the eighteenth century, many decades after Newton published the laws of motion and gravity and followers were echoing his idea that Nature was as finely tuned as a clock, a number of writers and philosophers presented a pessimistic view of the "grand machine" view of Nature derived from Newton. Central to their view was the certainty that even the most well-crafted clock would eventually stop running.

The principal architect of the **"Decay of Nature Theory"** was Sir William Temple, a distant cousin and one-time employer of Jonathan Swift, author of *Gulliver's Travels*. As a young man newly graduated from college, Swift worked as Temple's private secretary, becoming familiar with his cousin's pessimistic outlook. Temple and his circle were strongly interested in **deism**, the philosophy held by the authors of the Declaration of Independence, according to which Nature, the finely tuned clock, had been created by God, who left it to run unchanged forever and saw no need to intervene.

Temple's circle, however, expressed the belief that as the clock slowed down Nature would wither and die and all life would perish. Swift, deeply influenced by Temple, believed not only Nature but humanity itself was decaying—*morally* decaying. Moral decay, it followed, leads to physical decay: drunkenness, overindulgence in food and sex, and a general indifference to the natural world and human responsibility toward it. Physical nature and human nature were both deteriorating.

In *Gulliver's Travels*, the hero, finding himself in the land of Brobdingnag peopled by a race of giants, is asked to tell the king about his country and the human beings who inhabit it. Gulliver is proud and believes the king will be impressed. Instead the horrified king declares that "by what I have gathered from your own relation, and the answers I have with much pain wringed and extorted from you, I cannot but conclude the bulk of your natives to be the most pernicious race of little odious vermin that nature ever suffered to crawl upon the surface of the earth." Though the work has endured for centuries as a much loved children's classic, this tale of a young Englishman's misadventures in various lands is also a cynical condemnation of moral corruption.

"Study nature, stay close to nature. It will never fail you."

—Frank Lloyd Wright

Later in the century, many artists and writers perceived that options existed. The word Nature began to signify not the total Newtonian system, not the clock Temple believed would eventually stop, but the countryside, the out-of-doors, with fresh, clean air. Nature took on the connotation of a part of the world not destroyed by factories, vermin-infested housing, and garbage-strewn streets.

The Urban Attitude

The Athenians of the fifth and fourth centuries B.C.E. were partly responsible for developing the attitude that civilization meant the urban world. When asked why he never went for walks in the countryside, Socrates simply stared and replied that being by himself in lifeless Nature could never take the place of stimulating conversation with his companions. The city meant for him culture, sophistication, the arts, and philosophy—life itself. The urban attitude persists today in Los Angeles, Chicago, Manhattan, and many other places. A love of New York is shared by those whose world is bounded by theaters, art galleries, museums, concert halls, Lincoln Center, Fifth Avenue, elegant restaurants, and expensive apartment houses with uniformed doormen.

The mythology of our country is essentially urban. Early settlers were the "trailblazers," brave pioneers who "fought and tamed a wilderness"—so cried the trailers for endless films about the subject. In these Hollywood Westerns, the pioneers and cowboys, aided by the U.S. Cavalry, "righteously" killed the uncivilized, marauding red men, whose sole purpose (so went the myth), was to prevent the spread of "civilization."

In 1845, a journalist named John Louis O'Sullivan, defending the annexation of Texas, coined the phrase **Manifest Destiny**, the underlying implication of which was that the superior nation was *obliged* to spread the gospel of civilization to the "less developed world." Despite his love of the natural world, Walt Whitman (1819–1892) was also caught up in the excitement of American urbanity, which for him was New York.

Rich, hemm'd thick all around with sailships and steamships, an island
sixteen miles long, solid-founded,
Numberless crowded streets, high growths of iron, slender, strong, light
splendidly uprising, toward clear skies,
Tides, swift and ample, well-loved by me, toward sundown,
The flowing sea-currents, the little islands, larger adjoining islands,
the heights, the villas,
The countless masts, the white shore steamers, the lighters, the
ferry-boats the black sea-steamers well model'd,
The downtown streets, the jobbers' houses of business, the houses of
business of the ship-merchants and money-brokers, the river-streets,
Immigrants arriving fifteen to twenty thousand in a week,
The carts hauling goods, the manly race of drivers of horses, the
brown-faced sailors.
A million people—manners free and superb—open voices—hospitality—
the most courageous and friendly young men,
City of hurried and sparkling waters/city of spires and masts!
City nested in bays! My city![5]

> *"Great things are done when men and mountains meet. This is not done by jostling in the street."*
>
> **—William Blake**

The Chicago Attitude is famously represented by Carl Sandburg (1878–1967), who in 1914 wrote this about *his* city.

They tell me you are wicked and I believe them, for I have seen your
painted women under the gas lamps luring the farm boys.
And they tell me you are crooked and I answer: Yes, it is true I have seen
the gunman kill and go free to kill again.
And they tell me you are brutal and my reply is: On the faces of women
and children I have seen the marks of wanton hunger.
And having answered so I turn once more to those who sneer at this
my city and I give them back the sneer and say to them:
Come and show me another city with lifted head singing so proud to
be alive and coarse and strong and cunning.
Flinging magnetic curses amid the toil of piling job on job, here is a
tall bold slugger set vivid against the soft little cities;
Fierce as a dog with tongue lapping for action, cunning as a savage
pitted against the wilderness.[6]

Sandburg and Whitman are not museum pieces. Their respective attitudes bring millions of tourists each year into the sprawling cities, where hordes

Hall Grout II

Hall Grout II, *Times Square*, 2010

The Manhattan attitude shared by millions of tourists worries environmentalists.

continue to gaze in awe at the skyscrapers. With all its growing pollution and suspect water supply, the city continues to be, in the opinion of many, the proper abode of civilized humanity: the attitude that worries environmentalists.

Henry David Thoreau

The most famous American environmentalist of the nineteenth century was Henry David Thoreau (1817–1862). He was also something of a political activist, but not for an environmental reason. In fact, he called himself a **naturalist**, meaning someone who chooses to live far from society in a natural environment. His political activism landed him in jail overnight for refusing to pay a poll tax levied on people who wished to exercise their right to vote. Thoreau called voting a *natural* right.

His environmentalism stemmed from a lack of need to enjoy companionship and conversation in urban surroundings. In his great work *Walden, or Life in the Woods* (1854), he observes he "could easily do without the post office" because he "never received more than one or two letters . . . that were worth the postage." He did not organize marches to protest what greedy factory owners were doing to the environment, but he *did* equate urbanity with a sad way to live. He pitied those who were imprisoned in daily city labor and never saw birds feeding or hatchlings emerging. His animosity toward urban society gave rise to his most famous, often quoted observation.

> *"Each moment is absolute, alive, and significant. The frog leaps, the cricket sings, a dewdrop glitters on the lotus leaf, a breeze passes through the pine branches, and the moonlight falls on the murmuring stream."*
>
> **—D. T. Suzuki**

> *The mass of men lead lives of quiet desperation. What is called resignation is confirmed desperation. . . . A stereotyped but unconscious despair is concealed even under what are called the games and amusements of mankind. There is no play in them, for this comes after work. But it is characteristic of wisdom not to do desperate things.*[7]

Nature for Thoreau is not a universal cause. It is the road to personal happiness. Let those who choose to toil in the city do so. It's their business. Instead, he migrated into a deep woodland surrounding Walden Pond in western Massachusetts, not far from Concord, where he built himself a one-room hut for $23.44. [A TV spoof had the hut costing $75,000 at today's prices. One doubts he could have gotten a mortgage!] His book based on his experiences there is comprised of short chapters with titles such as "Sounds," "The Ponds," "Solitude," "The Pond in Winter," and "Spring." Thoreau's naturalism is a prescription for *noticing things*, something he believed was impossible in what he thought was crowded Concord.

> *Thoreau built his hut for $23.44. A recent TV spoof put today's cost at $75,000 and wondered where Thoreau would find a mortgage.*

> *I did not read books the first summer; I hoed beans, Nay, I often did better than this. There were times when I could not afford to sacrifice the bloom of the present moment to any work, whether of the head or*

hands. I love a broad margin in my life. Sometimes, in a summer morning, having taken my accustomed bath, I sat in my sunny doorway from sunrise till noon, rapt in a revery, amidst the pines and hickories and sumachs, in undisturbed solitude and stillness, while the birds sang around or flitted noiseless through the house, until by the sun falling in my west window, or the noise of some traveller's wagon on the distant highway, I was reminded of the lapse of time.[8]

Reading Thoreau makes us realize that, even if a woodland retreat with its solitude and perfect stillness is not readily available, we are still free to notice things. There are birds in the backyard. Even in a depressingly rundown area, there are probably some wildflowers trying to assert themselves from a sandy stretch of soil.

Nature as Awesome Force

In his sonnet "The World is Too Much with Us," Wordsworth speaks of the "getting and spending" which cause us to lose touch with the natural world. Nature for him was a force capable not only of healing itself but of healing the troubled hearts of those who were willing to flee urban society. Many today may believe that they need do nothing to help in the healing process, that it will take place magically, as it did for the romantic poets. Not everyone agrees, including a modern poet named David Kwiat.

Many believe they need do nothing to help in the healing process, that it will take place magically.

Hurricane Season, the Nature of War

The winds like war have wreaked
their havoc once again,
Upturned, bent, crushed and crushing,
bringing along roots, grass, concrete and
God help us, coffins.
These giants, so many of them a century in the
making; sprung from this brackish earth and water,
these once towering, yawning canopies
are reconciled to their befallen state—
duly pacified in the knowledge of their role
in the greater scheme;
the one that is incomprehensible
in the here and now.
The one that says the winds are nature's
cleansing power and that these
earthly steeples have not died in vain.
The reasoning of an ecological 'sound bite'
as buzz-sawed trunks rot
and limbs still quiver
in a calmer wind.[9]

Romantic artists invested Nature with the awesomeness that Dante and Michelangelo attributed to God. The vast canvases of nineteenth-century English painter J. M. W. Turner (1775–1851) depict Nature as a force that is both terrifying

SuperStock

Winslow Homer, *Gulf Stream*, 1899

Winslow Homer advised young artists to look at Nature for their inspiration. This famous depiction of the Gulf Stream shows Nature as beautiful but terrifying.

and majestically beautiful. The most comprehensive collection of his work is in the recently added wing of London's Tate Gallery. There the viewer will find landscapes and, especially, seascapes, in which the furious energy at the heart of Nature bursts forth in riotous colors and monstrous ocean waves—an elegy that seems impossible to comprehend and never to be ignored, but always worshiped by humanity that is part of but in no way superior to its grandeur.

The early work of American artist Winslow Homer (1836–1910) depicts calm seas and families enjoying themselves on a day at the beach. He studied in Paris, where his work was influenced by the soft colors of the Impressionists. Then he returned to live out his life in Maine. His work, under the influence of Turner, displays the sea as an awesome power to be respected but never tamed.

In the work of Turner and Homer we find early environmentalism of a kind that cries "Love it, worship it, but keep your distance!" In the very year of Turner's death, Herman Melville published his epic novel *Moby-Dick,* written in a sweeping, breathtaking style that is the verbal equivalent of Turner and Homer. In Melville, Nature is God, but not benevolent and caring. *Moby-Dick* is about the tragic attempt of one human being to destroy a white whale that has taken off his leg in a previous encounter and symbolizes all of Nature's, therefore God's, unreasonable power. But Melville, raised in the conservative Dutch Reformed Church, has an ambiguous relationship with God, and therefore Nature. It is a sin to meddle, but it is also frightening that such power exists at all.

> *"Only in the profoundly unbounded sea can the fully invested whale be truly and livingly found out."*
>
> **—Herman Melville**

Moby-Dick has been compared to the great Greek tragedies as well as to the Book of Job, and called a warning against moral pride, or *hubris*. Earlier in the nineteenth century, another novel also warned against pride, rooted in science.

The Frankenstein Monster

Many attempts have been made by science to control Nature—in particular, to destroy or at least to weaken Atlantic hurricanes and Pacific cyclones. On one occasion the experiment went so badly that one hurricane split into two. A few centuries before this unfortunate incident, Mary Wollstonecraft Shelley (1797–1851), wife of the famous poet, wrote *Frankenstein,* or *The Modern Prometheus,* a fantasy novel that warned against meddling with Nature. Her fable has since become a classic and added terminology to our vocabularies. We speak of anything that goes terribly awry as a "Frankenstein monster" and the creator of a product that backfires as a "regular Doctor Frankenstein." The novel also spawned innumerable films.

The youthful novelist based her story on the ancient myth of Prometheus, one of an early species of human being that was half human, half god. His godly nature caused him to seek unlimited power, a power equal to that of the gods. He attempted to steal fire from them but was caught in the act and sentenced to an eternity of anguish in which he was chained to a rock while a vulture ate his liver, a torture that could never end because the devoured liver always grew back.

Mary Shelley's version of the myth has for its central character Victor Frankenstein, who is not the mad scientist of the well-known movie adaptations but a sensitive, gentle person intrigued from childhood by science (then called "natural philosophy") and eager to learn everything that could possibly be learned in order to create a better life for all people. As he matures, he finds himself particularly concerned with the way the body functions.

> *Wealth was an inferior object, but what glory would attend the discovery if I could but banish disease from the human frame, and render man invulnerable to any but a violent death.*[10]

Yet, he asked himself, how am I to find the secret of immortality unless I first learn where life comes from?

Like her husband and other romantic writers, Mary Shelley saw Nature as a wondrous mystery full of almost divine secrets. She and Percy Bysshe Shelley, whom she married at the age of sixteen, especially loved the grandeur of lakes and mountains. Switzerland, the locale of the novel, was her favorite spot on earth. For her, Nature was to be admired, adored, worshiped, but never analyzed, always to be left alone. The tragic flaw of Victor Frankenstein is that he wants to be more than a *part* of Nature. Not content with understanding how the spark of life enters lifeless matter—from electricity, he is convinced—he must take a further step. He will assemble parts of cadavers into an eight-foot superman who will represent the perfection of the species and live forever.

The outcome of his experiment is, as everyone knows, not what he expected.

> *I had selected his features as beautiful. Beautiful—Great God! His yellow skin scarcely covered the work of muscles, and arteries beneath; his hair was of a lustrous black, and flowing; his teeth of a pearly whiteness; but these luxuriances only formed a horrid contrast with his watery eyes, and seemed almost of the same colour as the dun white sockets in which they were set.*[11]

Nonetheless, the **"daemon,"** as the author calls him, is at first kind and gentle. He is a creature of Nature; and the author believes Nature, undisturbed, is good at heart—a fervent attitude shared today by those who believe that gashouse emissions, offshore drilling, and other humanly engineered projects are not harmful to the environment. Yet society will not leave the daemon alone. Because of his frightening appearance, he is rejected, scorned, and ultimately becomes a vicious killer. Before his transformation, he has shown the noblest of feelings. He is a vegetarian, believing it immoral to eat animal flesh. Overhearing an account of how America was discovered, he weeps at the fate of the original inhabitants. Hiding out in a farmhouse, he stops stealing the food for which he desperately hungers when he observes how little food the family has for itself.

In an extraordinary finale, anticipating *Moby-Dick* by over thirty years, the doctor pursues the daemon to the ends of the earth, insanely believing, as does Captain Ahab, that once the monster is destroyed all evil will vanish from the

> *"Numerous archetypes are present here. The basic fear of what evil technology may bring along with the good is a central theme, as is the warning against playing God."*
>
> **—Ian Fowler**

> *More than anything else,* Frankenstein *is a novel of ethics and of ideas about ideas, with Mary Shelley's themes arranged in multiple layers throughout: God, self, society, science . . . these are ideas and issues that predominate the book, and anyone expecting a horror novel pure and simple is out of luck.*
>
> **—Gary F. Taylor**

earth. In the end it is Frankenstein, not the daemon, who dies. The daemon is reclaimed by Nature, his true and only parent. Dwarfed by the frozen mountains of the polar circle, he sails on a raft of ice into a mist, there to meet who knows what destiny. We feel that he belongs in this primordial limbo outside of time, deep within which lie the ultimate secrets glimpsed and even unleashed but never grasped or fully controlled by human intelligence.

If Mary Shelley were alive today, she might advise us to hold on to—or acquire—the sense of mystery that the romantic writers attributed to Nature. A mystic reverence for the power of Nature is well understood by our greatest scientists, Einstein among them. Victor Frankenstein was a scientist also, but one who lost sight of his own limitations. Who was the "daemon" in this great novel? Frankenstein ultimately pursued his own glory, did he not? The humanities have not been afraid to face the grim possibility that such pursuits are in conflict with the primal innocence of the natural world. That world, as we pointed out earlier, can also be violent and terrifying, but storms, tsunamis, and devastating floods are indigenous to that innocence.

Nature and Native Americans

> *The wind keened, the grasses hissed as they bent and flowed; the hills rolled endlessly toward the horizon like an amber sea. Far above, in the cobalt sky, a hawk circled and floated. In this world of whisperings and unseen forces, it was easy to imagine that it was watching us and had come to bear witness to the burial of a fellow human being.*
>
> **—Kent Nerburn**

Native Americans enjoy a long tradition of a deeply spiritual relationship with Nature. Their gods watch over Nature's varied aspects: rivers, the hunting of animals, the cycles of birth and death, and so on. They have rituals with songs and dances to intensify this relationship. Their language is filled with the understanding of Nature's deepest secrets, as in this observation from a 90-year-old Lakota elder named Dan. Kent Nerburn, a specialist in Native American thought and customs and close friend of Dan, has just asked about the depth of water in a certain creek.

> *I'd have to sit and listen. If the creek giggled, it was shallow because it meant there were rocks close to the surface. If it whispered, it was deeper, but not so deep you couldn't walk across it. If it was silent, you had to be careful. That's how you knew where to cross in the darkness—by listening to how the creek talked.*[12]

Crowfoot (1821–1890), of the Blackfoot nation, sees all existence from Nature's viewpoint:

> *What is life? It is the flash of a firefly in the night. It is the breath of a buffalo in the winter time. It is the little shadow which runs across the grass and loses itself in the Sunset.*[13]

The difference between those who identify with Nature and those who either deny that bad things are happening to it or believe it is their privilege to bend Nature to their will is expressed by a venerable holy woman of the Winter nation:

> *The white people never cared for land or deer or bear. When we Indians kill meat, we eat it all up. When we dig roots we make little holes. When we burn grass for grasshoppers we don't ruin things. We shake down acorns and pinenuts. We don't chop down trees, kill everything. The tree says, "Don't. I am sore. Don't hurt me." But they chop it down and cut it up. The spirit of the land hates them.*[14]

In *The Wolf at Twilight* (2009), in which Kent Nerburn recounts his travels with Dan, the latter asks him, "You got a house, Nerburn?" The former replies that, of course, he has a house. Whereupon Dan makes an analogy that blames biblical teachings for the white man's arrogance with respect to Nature:

> *Well, think about it. Someone comes into your house for a visit, you feed them and treat them right, and pretty soon they say they're staying and that they're going to make all the rules. They eat all your food and break up all your furniture and tell you which rooms you can go in and which rooms you can't. They say it's all written down in a book they've got and that you've got nothing to say about it. That's how it was, and we didn't much like it.*[15]

Courtesy of the Rockwell Museum of Western Art, Corning, NY

Alfred Jacob Miller, *Crow Indian on Horseback*, 1844

An early American impression of a Native American lifestyle.

There is, however, another side to this. Some Indian nations, such as the Miccosukee and the Seminole, have decided that if capitalist enterprise is the name of the game they can play it as well as anyone else. Taking advantage of their exemption from state control of gambling venues, they have netted huge profits from casinos. These nations have built luxurious hotels on their land so that gamblers can play blackjack and roulette all night if they so desire and not have to drive home.

Regardless of how much urban society has wrought changes in some Native American quarters, the fact remains that they *have* a long history of oneness with Nature, and much of their traditional wisdom can be seen in the proud displays of Native clothing and the performances of traditional dances and songs, most of which have roots in the natural world.

> *"Whenever, in the course of the daily hunt the red hunter comes upon a scene that is strikingly beautiful or sublime—a black thundercloud with the rainbow's glowing arch above the mountain, a white waterfall in the heart of a green gorge, a vast prairie tinged with the bloodred of sunset—he pauses for an instant in the attitude of worship."*
>
> **—Ohiyesa**

Joseph Conrad

Native American resentment at being dispossessed is quite understandable when their history is considered. Dan, Crowfoot, and the venerable holy woman of the Winter nation seem to have had a right to express anger. Who would not have felt as they, considering they were confined? But a major literary figure of the established culture wrote long ago of the moral bankruptcy of a white man who believed he had godlike powers and could do whatever he wished to what we now call "developing populations."

In 1889, during a period of economic growth in the so-called civilized world, a slender volume appeared called *Heart of Darkness*. It was the work of a Russian-born writer of Polish ancestry, Teodor Jozef Konrad Korzeniowski, who ultimately changed his name to Joseph Conrad after becoming a British subject. The novel remains one of the strongest indictments of arrogance in the dominant culture ever written.

Conrad (1857–1924) spent his formative years working on ships that took him to remote corners of the globe, including the then Belgian Congo, a relatively unexplored, largely impenetrable land that nonetheless promised untold wealth in ivory for the intrepid elephant hunter. The narrator of the story is Charlie Marlowe, a thinly disguised alter ego of Conrad himself. Conrad used the same character performing the same function—that of the impartial observer—in many of his tales. In *Heart of Darkness* Marlowe is hired by a trading company that sends him into the Congo to find out whether the company's principal trader, an Austrian named Kurtz, is still alive. Kurtz has not been heard from in some time.

Early in the narrative, Marlowe describes what it felt like to enter the eerie, forbidden land, a region truly primal:

> *Going up that river was like travelling back to the earliest beginnings of the world, when vegetation rioted on the earth and the big trees were kings. An empty stream, a great silence, an impenetrable forest.*[16]

> *"As a central device, the parallel journey into the heart of Africa and the dark centre of the human experience, remains as powerful as ever."*
>
> **—Hugh Riminton**

On the way he hears legend after legend about the extraordinary Kurtz, reported to be a wilderness tamer and a god in the eyes of the natives. White men in outlying posts refer to Kurtz as "a prodigy . . . an emissary of pity and science and progress." What we gradually learn, however, is that Kurtz represents all that went wrong with civilization, beginning with the myth that humanity was the noblest achievement of evolution. Armed with the belief in the infallibility of his civilization and in the inherent rightness of "taking over," Kurtz believed that his way of dealing with the natives was in their best interest. What he did not know—and what Marlowe comes to see—is that the mythical aura in which Kurtz has enveloped himself serves only to mask the real heart of darkness.

> *But the wilderness had found him out early, and had taken on him a terrible vengeance for this fantastic invasion. I think it had whispered to him things about which he did not know.*[17]

In one of the most dramatically anticipated confrontations in all of literature, Marlowe and the reader as well finally meet Kurtz after the latter has been mortally wounded during an explosive and bloody revolution. "I had immense plans," Kurtz insists. "I was on the threshold of great things." What these were to have been, we never find out. Perhaps in his madness the man thought he was going to impose the order and discipline of a great civilization upon a people who would otherwise never have seen the light of human progress. Were the many murders committed by Kurtz the result of "savage" resistance to his plan? Or were they evidence of power run wild?

> *There was nothing either above or below him, and he knew it. He had kicked himself loose of the earth. Confound the man! He had kicked the very earth to pieces.*[18]

Conrad does not give a full account of the sins committed by Kurtz, but we do learn that the man presided "at certain midnight dances ending with unspeakable rites"; that he has probably stolen a native woman from her husband; that he has been party to the wanton killing of elephants for their ivory; and that he has murdered anyone who stood in his way. In *Apocalypse Now*, Francis Ford Coppola's

1979 film version of *Heart of Darkness*, a memorable moment comes when the camera pans along rows of shrunken heads on poles outside of Kurtz' house. This terrifying image is also in the novel. As he dies in Marlowe's presence, Kurtz at last looks deep into his soul and whispers "*The horror! The horror!*" Returning to his home in London, Marlowe visits the grieving widow of Kurtz. When she asks whether her husband had spoken any final words, Marlowe lies and tells her that "his last words were of you."

One characteristic of a classic, as we pointed out in Chapter 4, is that it continues to resonate from one period to another. If one reads *Heart of Darkness* as an allegory of the present conflict between those who say we needn't worry about Nature (even as the genteel society Marlow left behind him would do today) and those who say there is plenty to worry about, one is astonished at Conrad's prophetic vision. Is the novel saying that we have gone too far along the course we have chosen to admit our mistakes and so must live our own lie? Is the lie itself a sign of civilized progress?

Kelly Shannon Kelly/Alamy

Headhunter spears, 2008

A row of heads on poles reminiscent of the terrifying image from the novel.

Inconveniences

The environmental movement began in the 1960s. In 1962 Rachel Carson's *Silent Spring* warned about the deadly effects of the pesticide DDT. During the 1980s, when the central government was predicting a new wave of economic prosperity, bookstores were selling such grim works as *The Fate of the Earth* and *The End of Nature*. Scientists began issuing stern warnings that if the levels of carbon emissions were allowed to continue building up in the atmosphere a chaotic change in climate would follow, and this change would prove devastating to our civilization as we know it. They warned about the deforestation caused by big business interests that failed to realize the atmosphere needs an abundance of trees to absorb carbon dioxide and respire oxygen. They warned people not to drive unnecessarily because the carbon emissions from automobiles alone could ruin the planet.

In 1990, Jonathan Weiner's *The Next Hundred Years: Shaping the Fate of Our Living Earth* predicted the tree problem could be solved if every man, woman, and child on earth would plant a tree tomorrow and never cut it down. One finds optimism somewhat difficult when confronting the unlikelihood of such action. Yet, if all hope is gone, why write books like *The End of Nature* at all?

> *"The debate over whether or not humanity is contributing to global warming is over."*
>
> **—Ronald Bailey**

A 2006 documentary film written and narrated by Al Gore, who jokingly refers to himself as the former next-president of the United States, gives a strong and sobering message to all who choose to listen. *An Inconvenient Truth* won multiple awards and much praise, at least from those who were already convinced that global warming was real and posed irreversible damage to the planet if it were not dealt with now.

The film features a slide show with graphic photographs of disasters that have already taken place, including the melting ice sheets in Greenland, the Arctic Circle, and Antarctica. It also contains the picture seen around the world of a polar bear clinging desperately to a slender piece of ice in its desperate search for food. It contains opinions from eminent environmental scientists, who point out that carbon levels in the Antarctic are higher than in any of the last 650,000 years and that if the ice sheet that has enshrouded Greenland continues melting (and they are certain it will), sea levels could rise at least twenty feet, flooding coastal areas and producing one hundred million refugees. Animal life, adapted to current climatic

> *"With these lectures he [Al Gore] only considered one point of view, and did not consider the other side of the story (warming being natural)."*
>
> **—Kristen Byrnes**

Jan Martin Will/Shutterstock

Jan Martin Will, polar bear in Arctic Sea

A favorite image of environmentalists, a polar bear on an isolated ice floe.

conditions, would be severely affected; innumerable species would vanish. The food supply for the entire world's population would greatly diminish, as would drinkable water.

The film concludes, however, with a slight ray of hope. The situation *is* reversible if every industrial nation would cooperate and agree to lower its carbon emissions. But, one wonders, will people alter their driving habits? Will a nation such as China, which depends on carbon-producing industries to provide employment for its teeming population, have any incentive to intensify its concern for the environment?

The problem is staggering. If you asked people on the street whether they worry about the health of the planet, the answer would probably be yes, but they might add, "What can I do about it? I have to commute a long way to my job." Summit meetings on global warming have resulted in much agreement and little change. Like Conrad's Marlowe, we may all have to be content with the lie. Or we can hope that the scientists are right who assure us that global warming is part of a natural cycle that has repeated itself time and again. We may have to cling to a tiny ice floe and hope for the best.

LEARNING OBJECTIVES

Having read and carefully considered this chapter, you should be able to:

1. Supply at least three definitions of "nature."
2. Summarize arguments both for and against environmentalism.
3. Explain the romantic view of nature.
4. Explain why Shelley's daemon is called a child of Nature.
5. Show how Conrad's *Heart of Darkness* can be read as an allegory relevant to the present environmental crisis.
6. Summarize the "inconveniences" discussed in the final section of the chapter.

KEY TERMS

environmentalist one who believes that greenhouse gases cause global warming, which in turn endangers all life on the planet; as well as one who is concerned about all actions by people that adversely affect the planet.

daemon term by which the creature in the novel *Frankenstein* is sometimes called. Unlike "demon," it has no diabolic connotations.

Decay of Nature theory advanced by Sir William Temple, according to which the universe would slow down and eventually come to a complete halt.

deism eighteenth-century philosophy, held by Thomas Jefferson and others who created the Declaration of Independence, that God created Nature and then left it alone to run by itself.

Manifest Destiny popular phrase coined in 1845 by John Louis O'Sullivan to support the annexation of Texas. It came to mean, for some, that the United States has an obligation to become a world leader and a role model for "less advanced" nations.

naturalist one who prefers to live apart from society, in the country, observing day-to-day events taking place in Nature. Henry David Thoreau was such an observer.

nature a term with multiple meanings: a reference to the nonurban world; the system of laws governing the universe; an indwelling spirit or mind governing the universe; and the environment and the ecosystem within it.

TOPICS FOR WRITING AND DISCUSSION

1. Eastern philosophers believe in the wisdom of Brahman, the Tao, or the Dharma. How do you think those who use such terms might respond to the present environmental crisis?
2. Explain how romanticism links the terms "natural" and "free."
3. Many Shakespearean scholars maintain that Jaques in *As You Like It* was intended to be a darkly comic figure and that it is sheer nonsense to consider him an early environmentalist. What is your take on the subject?
4. What is Manifest Destiny? Where and how did the phrase originate? Is it still applicable to the present environmental crisis?
5. The section titled "Nature as Awesome Force" begins with a poem by David Kwiat. Explain the title and then explain what the content of the poem has to do with the subject matter of the section.
6. Write a brief speech you would give to Congress in which you use the phrase "Frankenstein monster."
7. What is meant when the text says that the daemon was "reclaimed by nature"?
8. What do you think is the reason some Native American nations, once with strong natural bonds, now operate gambling casinos and luxury hotels?
9. Discuss *Heart of Darkness* as an allegory applicable to the present environmental crisis.
10. Single out and then discuss the "inconveniences" mentioned in the final section.

Chapter 16

Freedom

Humanists believe freedom is vital to the art of being human: the freedom to create and to enjoy what others create; the freedom to think and listen to the thoughts of others, whether in agreement or not; the freedom to examine one's options and then decide upon the wisest course of action.

In a 2010 article he wrote for *The New York Times*, Stanley Fish, an American literary theorist and legal scholar, describes an educational movement in Britain that would allow students to choose their own subjects *provided* that they lead to a "comfortable living." His concern is that such a program will find supporters on this side of the Atlantic and that it could mean the end of learning about art, literature, and philosophy. Would that also be the end of freedom?

As with other important ideas, freedom has not had the same meaning in every historical context. The Greeks, for example, invented the concept of democracy and passed on as their legacy the model of the democratic state in which citizens are free to think, to question, and to speak out. Ironically, at the time free citizens comprised only about five percent of the population; the rest were slaves and women, who were generally deemed too irrational and irresponsible to be trusted with political decisions.

The Roman state also denied freedom to the majority of the population and held many thousands in slavery. Rome believed it had the right to enslave the conquered in the name of civilization, which it was bringing to the barbarian world. In other words, why give freedom to barbarians, who would not know what to do with it? But Rome also had its famous forum, where duly qualified citizens had the right to exchange ideas and debate the laws, even if an emperor such as Caligula ruled with an iron hand.

Still, there was Epictetus, whose teachings on Stoicism were discussed in Chapter 12, Happiness. A Greek philosopher held in captivity by the Romans and at first tortured, he was finally recognized for his brilliance and became a tutor. Surely during his early years as a slave, Epictetus was free to think.

Christianity struggled for centuries with the complexity of freedom. Did human beings have free will or not? If God was all-powerful, he must be all-knowing; and that meant having advance knowledge of what people will do. If human actions had already been determined, in what sense, then, could free will exist?

In Chapter 10, Religion, we discussed Augustine's solution: God possessed foreknowledge, but still this did not mean humanity was not held responsible for its sins. On the divine level, there was no free will; on the human level, there was. Augustine believed in predestination (the divine level), but since humanity did not have this foreknowledge, it was actually free to do as it pleased, free by God's grace and predestined because of God's power. Detractors,

◀ **Pablo Picasso, *Woman Ironing*, 1904**

The artist depicts a woman who may or may not be limited by her circumstances. The slight smile suggests she is either content or calmly resigned to her fate.

> *Man is free. This is at once a heady luxury and also the source of his discontent.*
>
> **—Carlton Beck**

however, argue that Augustine cannot have it both ways. We are either free or we are not free. The Augustine problem is only one of many recognized by the humanities in relation to that highly valued human state—being able to do what one feels like doing. For centuries, writers and philosophers, whether invoking God or not, have been asking: How free *are* we? Can we really do what we please—on *any* level?

When we argue that we should be free to do what we really want to do, how do we know what we really want? Perhaps many forces are pushing us in one direction or another. How much of what we are, what we think, and what we do was determined long before we ever entered this world and reached an age when making choices was possible? A great many scientists, philosophers, sociologists, economists, and psychologists maintain that total freedom is an impossibility, even in a free society.

> *In all this he always acts according to necessary laws, from which he has no means of emancipating himself.*
>
> **—Baron d'Holbach**

Some have equated free will with natural rights. William Blake, who wrote "The Lamb" and "The Tiger," analyzed in Chapter 4, was a strong believer in the rights of the individual. In the very proper eighteenth century, he and his wife demanded the right to go naked in their own garden. Blake loved nature and loved being out of doors in his original state. He viewed clothing as a symbol of society's oppression. He saw the right to do as one pleased as nature's bequest, and he believed nature (or heaven, which had the same meaning for him) responded ferociously when that right was denied. In "Auguries of Innocence," he put the matter succinctly:

A robin redbreast in a cage
Puts all Heaven in a rage.

This chapter focuses on the question of *whether or not the will is truly free*. If it is not, then what does it mean to be a truly free individual? We will look into the two major sides of the debate. **Determinism** holds that freedom of the will does not exist, that there are too many factors governing our choices. **Libertarianism** holds just the opposite: that there are ways to prove the existence of free will. Determinist arguments outnumber libertarian arguments, but readers must resolve the issue for themselves.

Determinism

First, we will consider the many arguments claiming that we are not, or at least not completely, free. Only when we offer a meaningful challenge to these arguments do the words *I am free* acquire true and powerful significance. Growing up and constantly hearing the phrase *free country* is likely to put our rational faculties to sleep, to lull us into the unexamined assumption that because we are told we live in a free country we must obviously be free.

Freedom of will can be defined as the ability to choose between alternatives: obeying the speed limit or driving faster than we should down the highway; spending an entire paycheck on unneeded luxuries or saving a substantial portion; deciding on marriage, living together, or staying single. Listing the number of options with which we are faced each day might cause us to think we are indeed free.

Yet stop a moment and reflect on even one of these options. Without an automobile, the first alternatives are reduced to just words. There is a limitation right off. Without the money or adequate credit, we cannot buy the automobile—another limitation. Without a job, we cannot have either money or credit. What kind of job? It has to be a good one if we seek a certain kind of automobile. If we do not have sufficient training, many jobs are out of the question. Of course, money to buy ten cars can be inherited, but to qualify, we have to be born into the right circumstances.

Economic considerations encompass only one class of limitations. Suppose one is born without the coordination that makes driving possible at all: a genetic limitation. In order to go 55 miles per hour in a 40 mph zone, one must be willing to risk being stopped by the police. Even if this were a first offense, one would be forever deprived of the opportunity to commit a first offense again—a legal limitation. As the offenses mount, the limitations on choice become imposing.

Rigid determinists believe the limitations integral to our lives are too numerous for there to be any question of making a *free* choice ever. Our social class lays down the parameters of our lifestyle. Responsibilities incurred by marriage and family tell some they must continue reporting to jobs they may not like or tell homemakers they must put a career on hold in order to care for children. Switching roles results not in greater freedom but in different limitations.

Determinism emerged from the eighteenth-century revolution in philosophy triggered by science—in particular, the impact of the view that every effect must have a cause. Taking this scientific law and applying it to human behavior, some philosophers argued that all choice is limited by a prior condition—limited so severely that it cannot be considered a free choice. Each of us is in fact the product of a chain of cause and effect stretching back to the very dawn of existence.

Major arguments challenging free will include these: limitations on freedom of action, past and present; institutional determinism; economic determinism; character consistency; behaviorism; genetics; and sociobiology.

Past and Present Limitations

The issue of freedom has haunted philosophers for a long time, and it appears there are more arguments against freedom than for it.

Obstacles to freedom of choice and action are the restrictions imposed on the individual by groups in power. It is hard to imagine that when people are aggressively denied freedom of action freedom of thought is readily available to them.

An independent film titled *Chinese Dreams* (2004) dealt with uneducated, poverty-stricken young men in China who are lured into signing up for work in the United States with promises of unlimited opportunities but who are smuggled into the country, brought to New York without being told where they are, forced into menial labor for long hours every day in the stifling heat of a restaurant kitchen, and made to live in dirty, crowded, airless dormitories, never seeing sunlight. The sensitive young protagonist asks only for cigarettes and a magazine showing pictures of New York, the promised land of his dreams. Finally escaping one night, he is penniless and bewildered by the roaring traffic and frenetic pace of the big city, a vast neon wasteland in which he will never be free to create his own destiny.

Millions exist in countries that deny freedom to all but a privileged few. Azar Nafisi, now a professor at Johns Hopkins University and author of *Reading Lolita in Tehran* (2004), formerly taught literature at a university considered the most liberal in her country of Iraq. It did admit some women, but they were not treated as the equals of the male students.

> *I felt helpless as I listened to their endless tales of woe. Female students were being penalized for running up the stairs when they were late for classes, for laughing in the hallways, for talking to members of the opposite sex.*[1]

Thwarted in her attempts to enlarge the scope of her students' reading background and their critical-thinking skills, Nafisi decides at one point she will never be allowed to teach books that invite a free exchange of ideas and so offers her resignation, which is promptly refused on the grounds that only the university has the right to decide when employment is to be terminated. At length she does manage to leave, but not without regret that she has been unable to fulfill completely her mission as a teacher dedicated to opening the minds of her students so that they might think for themselves.

Facing up to the reality of freedom denied to a large portion of the world's population can be unpleasant to those who sigh, then shrug their shoulders, as if to say, "But what can I do about it? Let's just be glad *we're* free." Yet understanding that "free" is not a word to be tossed about lightly or to be simply *assumed* is the first, absolutely essential step we must take. Even if we are lucky enough not to be penalized for laughing in the hallway, so goes the determinist argument, too many other forces must at some point be recognized, all the more frightening because they have no human face.

> *"I am as free as Nature first made man,*
> *Ere the base laws of servitude began,*
> *When wild in woods the noble savage ran."*
>
> **—John Dryden**

Institutional Determinism

Though he is known as one of the staunchest advocates of freedom from oppression, Jean-Jacques Rousseau (1712–1778), whom many consider the major architect of the French Revolution, is also famous for his analysis of the forces that limit freedom. Since these forces are still at work, he must be considered, in part at least, a determinist. If he could be asked, his answer might well be: "I wish I were not, but the conditions under which we live require me to adopt this belief."

Rousseau's thinking was as radical as that of any activist of the modern era. He was vehemently against any repressive government with the power to limit human choice; for, he reasoned, the ideal form of government is something we *should* be free to create. Total freedom, however, was for him impossible, given the uncontrollable forces stacked against everyone. But to take what freedom remained and surrender it to one human being or group of human beings was an affront to all civilized people. He believed the ideal government was answerable to the entire population rather than existing for personal power or prestige.

Reunion des Musées Nationaux/Art Resource, NY

Jan Breughel, *The Garden of Eden*, 1612

An imaginative depiction of a pristine world with no environmental worries and with no hostilities.

In fanning the revolutionary flames beginning to sweep through a France increasingly outraged at the decadence of the aristocracy and the injustices suffered by the common people, Rousseau constructed a mythical account of the origin of the human species to back up his claim that freedom was both a natural condition and a natural right. Called *A Discourse on the Origins of Inequality,* the myth draws a romantic picture of a lost age of innocence when early people lived in peace and harmony, sharing the fruits of the abundant earth through a common realization that nature provided equal bounty for everyone. In this age of innocence, no laws or government existed because, obviously, law and government are not necessary when everyone is happy and there is no crime.

Many artists, poets, and religions have been inspired by the idea of a pristine state of innocence. Judaism, Christianity, and Islam all share the belief that our earliest ancestors lived in the Garden of Eden before their fall. A famous painting about that time is *The Garden of Eden* (opposite page) by Flemish artist Jan Breughel (1568–1625).

In his "Discourse on Inequality," Rousseau says one day *a man with a stick* decides to grab more than his natural share of things. He is the first person to *abuse* nature's gift of freedom by putting it to his own advantage. With his stick he carves out a private piece of territory for himself.

> *The first man, who, after enclosing a piece of ground, took it into his head to say, "This is mine," and found people simple enough to believe him, was the true founder of civil society.*

The man with the stick was the founder of society as Rousseau knew it because, by creating the model of the exploiter, he and his followers became an ever-present threat to the rights of the others. The exploiters therefore had to be suppressed by the gradual development of law, government, and all other institutions dedicated to the curtailment, or the limitation, of natural rights. But these safeguards of liberty, once in place, become despotic.

The man with the stick was the founder of society as Rousseau knew it. By creating the model of the exploiter, the man with the stick and his followers became an ever present threat to the rights of others.

It is here that Rousseau's position becomes revolutionary. The philosopher asserted that revolution, even if violent, is a genuine alternative to exploitation and may often be the only means by which to deal with it. Rousseau explains and justifies revolution in the name of natural rights belonging to all, but he does *not* in his myth account for the *origin* of the man with the stick. What made this one man decide to become possessive, when the others were joyously bobbing for golden apples in an age of sun and fun? Or was he merely the first to manifest himself? Did the potential for exploitation lie deep within *every* member of that "innocent" society? If so, when were institutional safeguards ever *not* needed?

Rousseau's anti-institutional bias is based on the assumption that in the *state of nature* (a phrase hotly debated then and since) humankind is decent, tame, moral, and benevolent. Only when held in check, only when threatened with punishment for disobedient acts, do people become hateful, aggressive, and violent—particularly when rebelling in a just cause. But what Rousseau did not know, because he died a decade before the revolution he predicted, was that Napoleon Bonaparte would rise from the ashes of France and, sword in hand, create a new age of exploitation, perhaps even more oppressive than the one it supplanted. History shows us that this cycle of oppression, liberation, and further oppression has been repeated many times over.

Rousseau justifies revolution in the name of natural rights but fails to account for the origin of the man with the stick.

A tragic example of a revolutionary cause turned lethal occurred on November 18, 1978, when over 900 members of a religious sect called People's Temple were ordered to commit suicide by drinking cyanide-laced Kool-Aid. From all accounts, their leader, Jim Jones, was earnest in the beginning about establishing a communal agricultural society, which, had it come to pass, would have resembled Rousseau's free and benevolent community. But when many became disillusioned and tried to defect, the community turned into a prison.

One member was able to secretly contact outside sources and describe Jones's manic, self-absorbed leadership, forced sexual intercourse, and brutal beatings administered to those who disobeyed his rules. Four Americans, including U.S. Representative Leo Ryan and several relatives of Jones's prisoners, visited the camp but were gunned down before they could reboard their plane. With time running out, Jones ordered the mass suicide. Among the dead were 270 children. A memorial service was held, and one speaker said: "Remember the people of Jonestown, not for their horrible deaths, but for who they were—people in search of a better world."

If a strong-willed person leads a once-benevolent cause, Rousseau might have said, it sometimes turns in to "forced benevolence," which then must be autocratically monitored. Is the stick inborn in certain people, who become a menace to civilized life and must in turn be controlled? Are the institutions of control inevitable? And can *they* in turn become oppressive, acting as curtailments on everyone's freedom?

> *"They are not free who drag their chains after them."*
>
> **—French Proverb**

Rousseau believed he had solved the problem when he advanced the theory of the *social contract*. By this he meant that the only way to guarantee the protection of human rights was not through unlimited freedom but through each citizen's willingness to hand over some rights to institutions dedicated to the maintenance of order within society. The social contract is a cornerstone of **institutional determinism**, which holds that government controls are needed to protect people from other people. Yet what happens when institutions insist they must have more and more power in order to do their job? Will the man with the stick suddenly reappear?

Economic Determinism

The philosophy of Karl Marx (1818–1883) profoundly influenced the Bolshevik Revolution of 1917 in Russia and the subsequent spread of **socialism** throughout much of the world. Despite the failure of the socialist experiment in the Soviet Union and its satellite nations, communism continues to be strong in other countries, notably China, Cuba, and North Korea.

Not nature, not humanity, but *money* calls the tune, so believed Marx. As an economist, he developed a theory explaining that our behavior, our hopes and aspirations, our career choices are all determined by the social class into which we are born. The rich want to hold onto their money and tend to favor legislation designed to keep their holdings intact. The poor desire to better themselves, and in some cases, this desire becomes an obsession, eclipsing everything else in their lives. People dream of becoming rich. Lacking money, some who might have been decent neighbors are driven to a life of crime. If we are middle class, we want to climb to the top while making sure that those below are not following too closely.

> *". . . only romantic fools and children of affluence can suppose that being poor is anything but hard."*
>
> **—Irving Howe**

Marx believed that **economic determinism**—the quest for money and property that controls thinking and dictates actions—would inevitably lead to a society divided into two classes: the affluent **bourgeoisie**, that controls means of production, and the **proletariat**, or workers. Sooner or later, however, the proletariat, made furious by the unfair distribution of wealth, would unite, rise up, and seize the means of production for themselves. Marx believed this radical change could take place without violence—but not necessarily.

His theory was influenced by the thinking of an earlier German philosopher, Georg Wilhelm Friedrich Hegel (1770–1831), who had developed a theory of knowledge which stated that we reach philosophical certainty through a method he called the **dialectic**, which involves analyzing opposing views and combining them into a *synthesis*. Marx took Hegel's abstractions and applied them to the concrete realities of the class struggle. The opposition of the bourgeoisie, who want to hold onto money and power, and the proletariat, bent on seizing some of it, would lead to a synthesis Marx called the *classless society.*

Communism, a social system based on the idea of the classless society, was the banner of the 1917 revolution in Russia. The revolutionists agreed with Marx that violence would sometimes prove to be the only way to bring about the workers' paradise. They had grown tired of waiting. Vladimir Lenin (1870–1924) had redefined Marxism to make violent revolution a necessity. The first dramatic, worldshaking event was in February of 1917 with the execution of the Czar and his family. In October of that same year, the Bolshevik Revolution occurred and with it came the establishment of the Soviet Union and a new social order, communism, whereby most private property would be state-owned and the private sector nearly abolished.

"We don't allow our enemies to have guns. Why should we allow them to have ideas?"

—Joseph Stalin

The Communists were careful to say "public" not "state-owned" while socialism is nearly the same thing, except that in the latter system a limited amount of private business is considered a necessity. For example, the Soviet Union soon realized that public ownership of all farm lands was not practical. Could farmers be induced to raise crops and livestock for society as a whole rather than for themselves and their families? Since the answer seemed to be no, they were given small farms (about one acre) and told they could answer their own needs first and then sell what was left over. As a result, farmers were better off than factory workers in the city. The vast majority of the population under communism was given assigned jobs, and everybody was paid what was considered a modest, but decent, wage. The housing program was also administered by the state under the strictest of guidelines: so many square feet per person.

"The freedom and independence of the worker during the labor process do not exist."

—Karl Marx

As time went on, more and more capitalism became necessary. The classless society never really materialized, and, because the private sector grew, a few people prospered while the mass of workers looked on with envy. Propaganda was strong, constantly assuring the people that their sacrifices were for the good of all; but as time went by, workers began to wonder when the "paradise" was coming. It began to look as though the Marxist separation of the rich and the poor was still there. Without being able to satisfy their self-interest, most workers could not be motivated to produce more goods or provide more efficient service.

A serious consequence of the Communist experiment was that the majority of workers, unlike the farmers, were unable to see the products of their labor. (Much the same is true of assembly-line workers everywhere.) Salespeople in department stores, without the incentive of commissions, failed to go out of their way to sell goods.

The coming of television was a boon to bored workers crammed into tiny apartments. They scrimped to buy even the tiniest set, which enabled them to see how their counterparts in the West were supposedly living. Many of the viewers probably did not realize the sitcoms they loved to watch were not telling the whole truth. The illusion, however, must have been powerful indeed: Workers in a free society, with the help of labor unions, were shown to be more than comfortable. Modest, but decent, wages eventually did not suffice for a population tired of scrounging around in grocery stores for a few vegetables and the limited supply of meat farmers were able to provide.

There remains the question: To what extent do economic needs control us and therefore set limits on freedom?

Whether or not the classless society could ever exist, Marxist theory is still invoked by many as a way of explaining, at least partly, what motivates human behavior. Whether or not the theory works in practice, there remains the question: to what extent do economic needs control us and therefore set limits on freedom?

"When the state exists, there is no freedom. When there is freedom, there will be no state."

—Vladimir Lenin

In Chapter 11 we discussed Adam Smith's theory that capitalism is the natural driving force behind human life. Smith argues that greed, natural to humanity, is good because it ensures a free market system. If businesses are allowed the freedom to do what they like, they will provide employment, which in turn gives people disposable income, which in turn moves the economy upward. When there is too much money to spend, businesses raise prices until a point is reached at which buying slows down and prices begin to fall.

Marxism and capitalism share a common underlying assumption: Economic needs dominate. Some economists believe both philosophies are flawed because there are never enough material resources to satisfy everybody. In a communist society, workers may not be motivated to produce abundantly. In a capitalist society, the affluent can afford to buy whatever they want regardless of price, but inflated costs eventually harm those less fortunate. The case for determinism at this point becomes very strong. Can anybody escape the desire for more money? The more one has, the less one is likely to be satisfied. The less one has, the need for more becomes obsessive. According to economic determinists, all human behavior can be understood in terms of how much money is or is not available.

> *"The inherent vice of capitalism is the unequal sharing of blessings; the inherent virtue of socialism is the equal sharing of miseries."*
>
> **—Winston Churchill**

Traditional humanists object. They find it degrading to suppose that money alone should be the source of well-being. Finding pleasure in other than material resources is one thing; however, denying that economic concerns underlie much of our behavior is quite another.

The art of being human does not entail making a choice between the humanities and money. It *does* require that we observe ourselves in action. If economic motives are not the sole reasons that we do what we do, they *are* sometimes the major ones.

Creative artists, once romantically thought to be "above" the vulgarity of seeking money, retain agents, negotiate contracts, charge high fees for television interviews and college lectures, and go on promotional tours to boost the sales of their latest film or publication.

Whether we like it or not, economics often dominates our lives, such as when our only options are staying in a job we hate or not being able to make our car payments. Still, to be economically determined is not the same as being either a Marxist or a crass materialist. The important thing is at all times to recognize the roots of our behavior (or try to, anyway). We become chronically unfree the more we remain blind to reality when it confronts us. We take a step on the path to freedom when we begin to see the things that limit us—or when we impose the limitations on ourselves.

Character Consistency

> *"A foolish consistency is the hobgoblin of little minds. With consistency a great soul has simply nothing to do."*
>
> **—Ralph Waldo Emerson**

Enduring characters in memorable works of fiction—Don Quixote, Becky Sharp, Huckleberry Finn, and Scarlett O'Hara, for example—stay in our minds not because they are amorphous, fluid, and unpredictable, but because they have specific character traits that can be summarized and readily explain what they do. If they were real people, the determinist would say they lack free will, that they are bound by the very traits that make them come alive to us.

We think of each other as we think of literary characters. We characterize our family, friends, and associates as we interpret what they say and do. This person is witty and intelligent; that person is arrogant and pretentious; another is totally amoral. Of course, due reflection tells us that real-life people, unlike many characters in books, are unfairly placed in rigid categories. At the same time, when someone does something unexpected and atypical, we are likely to say, "He isn't himself" or "That is so unlike her." We expect predictability. We expect consistency. A determinist argument often advanced is that the more people are consistent and predictable, the less they are free. A frequently heard determinist pronouncement is that because insane people are totally unpredictable, *only the insane are totally free.*

Suppose someone stops a stranger in the street and strikes that person in the face. Imagine a panel of experts on human behavior being told this story and asked to predict what the response of the stricken person would be. Their predictions would surely be based on some cause-and-effect view of human interaction, which they would call *rational behavior.* But what does this mean? Does it not mean that the stricken person is expected to respond in one of certain ways that are accepted and shared by all "rational" persons? Thus, the assaulted person may be projected as (1) striking back out of righteous anger; (2) not striking back, because of pacifist beliefs, but attempting to leave without undergoing further harm; (3) voluntarily deciding against the use of force on his or her own, preferring to call a police officer; (4) turning the other cheek, because of a strong religious upbringing; or (5) simply staring in disbelief at the assailant, not quite knowing what to do.

But now suppose the victim does not respond in any of these predicted ways, instead suddenly producing a sword and bidding the attacker kneel down and be knighted. There is a good chance that not the assailant but the assailed would be hauled away for observation. Such a response would not fall within any *meaningful* category of behavior. The determinist is likely to argue that, of the responses considered, the King Arthur action is the only one rightfully labeled *free.* Under these circumstances, how many of us live in a free world? Or would *want* to if everyone were unpredictable?

Comments like "He isn't himself" or "That is so unlike her" indicate how predictable people are expected to be.

Some indeterminists and libertarians not only criticize the character-consistency argument but urge us not to be bound by the character traits instilled in us during the so-called acculturation process. They tell us we can be rational without being continuously predictable. If such were not the case, how could we explain the creative and the imaginative, the divergent thinkers whose oddball notions have in one way or another altered the shape of human experience? Are all of them insane? And, come to think of it, does any of us want to acquire a hard-and-fast reputation for being always and tiresomely the same?

The determinist would argue that only the insane are truly free because their behavior can't be predicted.

Behaviorism

Founded on the work of B. F. Skinner (1904–1991), **behaviorism** is a school of thought that says we are what we do, and how we behave is determined by a series of rewards and punishments that begins to weave its web as soon as we are born.

If humanity has a nature, it lies in *the capacity to be conditioned.* Everything we do is the result of a reinforcement of behavior. Those actions that are followed by pleasant consequences tend to be repeated; those followed by unpleasant or painful consequences tend to be avoided. Behaviorism is both a philosophy and a method used by some psychologists to alter patterns of human behavior that need to be changed according to individual wishes or institutional commands. In both theory and practice, behaviorists believe that what people do is determined by responses to the consequences of their actions. The child who repeatedly drops dishes on the floor is scolded or otherwise punished until the unacceptable behavior is at last avoided.

> *"Physics does not change the nature of the world it studies, and no science of behavior can change the essential nature of man, even though both sciences yield technology with a vast power to manipulate their subject matters."*
>
> **—B. F. Skinner**

According to Skinner, freedom is nothing but the effort to escape from the unpleasant consequences of certain actions. We slap at a mosquito that's about to attack to prevent the itching that will follow a bite if we don't. A child who throws a tantrum and is sent to bed without supper may cry so loudly that the parents will change their minds in order that *they* in turn may escape the sound of the crying. Whatever the motive for escape, say behaviorists, the fact remains that the *desire* to escape is a determining force; moreover, if freedom is defined as escape, no such thing as pure and absolute freedom exists because freeing oneself from all unpleasantness is impossible.

People, says Skinner, identify the state of absolute freedom as one in which "aversive control" is absent: that is, if there is no apparent oppression, then people imagine themselves to be free. Skinner calls such people "happy slaves." They are molded by hidden controls and don't know it. Their freedom is an illusion. Victims of oppression are in a sense better off. At least they know where they stand. Skinner adds that "the literature of freedom has been designed to make men 'conscious' of aversive control, but in its choice of methods it has failed to rescue the happy slave."[2] Activists who fight against oppression are concerned solely with obvious victims, not enlightening those who believe they are free but in fact are not.

Skinner's position is that the desire to hold fast to the ancient and honorable abstraction "freedom" is tied in with the belief that human dignity is lost if it is shown that humanity is not nor ever can be considered free. What happens to the great artists, writers, and philosophers if they are considered only products of conditioning forces? "We are not inclined to give a person credit for achievements which are in fact due to forces over which he has no control," says Skinner.[3]

> *Science can point out dangers, but science cannot turn the direction of minds and hearts. That is the province of spiritual powers within and without our very beings—powers that are the mysteries of life itself.*
>
> **—Chief Oren Lyons, Faithkeeper of the Turtle Clan of the Onondaga Iroquois**

But, he argues further, people do not vibrantly experience an inner something called "dignity" at the thought of being free. Like every other human condition, dignity is a very specific response to a particular kind of stimulus: It is the positive reinforcement given to one who has behaved properly or who has performed some achievement deemed notable. Dignity equals praise. Dignity equals recognition. Robbing people of their dignity is taking away recognition they believe they have rightfully earned.

Praise and recognition represent very positive reinforcements and, as such, are among the most pervasive of conditioning forces. We may push Skinner's idea even further and point out that to win praise and recognition some people would do just about anything required of them. Many forgive their own lapses of artistic or intellectual integrity when the emotional or economic stakes are high enough. How many writers and composers have said a fond farewell to the novel in the desk drawer or the sonata in the piano bench in exchange for fame and fortune in the world of popular entertainment?

Some believe dignity is personal integrity; those who hold fast to their dignity in this sense of the word are indeed free. For them, the tortured van Gogh possessed *both* dignity and creative freedom.

Skinner would not agree. The title he gave to one of his most influential works is, in fact, *Beyond Freedom and Dignity*. We need, says Skinner, to take broad terms that mean very little in themselves—like "freedom" and "dignity"—and redefine them in strictly behavioral language. We need to concentrate on creating what Skinner calls a "technology of behavior." Since people are going to be conditioned anyway, the focus should be on the good controls that *can* exist. He maintains that "the problem is to free men, not from control, but from certain kinds of control, and it can be solved only if our analysis takes all consequences into account."[4]

Skinner is also a modern utopian thinker, believing that eventually an ideal society can be designed in which people develop their abilities to the maximum through carefully preplanned reinforcements. In such a society there would be no crime, no aggression, no exploitation. *But would we want such a society?*

Genetics

Genetics developed from a study of the role played by biological factors in determining how plants, animals, and human beings develop their characteristics. Exhaustive research has found the way to look inside the infinitesimal cells that comprise the various forms of life, discovering, in effect, the very secret of life itself.

There are an estimated 3 trillion cells in a human body. Within each cell are two **genomes** (one from each parent), which are sets of genetic instructions that determine gender, hair and eye coloring, height, and certain tendencies, such as susceptibility to a disease that runs in the family. Instructions are transmitted through **chromosomes**, discovered more than a century ago. Inside these long, stringy bodies in the cell's nucleus are the **genes**. The genes are made up of granular substances containing DNA (deoxyribonucleic acid) molecules: long strands of sugar and sulphate that are the actual carriers of the genetic code determining how we will look and how we will sound.

The sequence:
two genomes in each cell (one from each parent)
chromosomes—transmitters of genetic instructions genes (inside chromosomes)
DNA molecules (inside genes)

We now know that diabetes, Alzheimer's disease, cystic fibrosis, and certain forms of cancer can be inherited. Arguments, though far more tentative, have been advanced that one can inherit alcoholism and other dependencies once thought to have been socially acquired. The details of genetic research can change almost weekly. Now that the strands of DNA have all been identified and labeled, gene replacement therapy has become a major goal in medical science. Researchers claim the time may not be far off when expectant parents will be able to decide on the sex of their offspring or when an inherited birth defect can be stopped in its tracks by locating and replacing the gene responsible.

Opinions are sharply divided about the advisability and the ethics of investing in medical science the power to use such therapy. Many are afraid of where it could lead. Predetermining the gender of a child is one thing. But suppose a gene is discovered that governs intelligence. Will science be able to produce a "super" child? Some say that nothing is wrong with making the race smarter. Others say that gene specialists would have too much power.

On the other hand, what happens if society demands that genes must be left alone to do whatever they are biologically suited to do? Preventable birth defects and inherited disease would continue unchecked. Yet some are disturbed by the idea of interfering with nature or producing a super race. For certain religious sects such practices substitute the will of science for the will of God.

In the social sciences, the role of genetics becomes intertwined with the long debate about heredity versus environment, also known as the nature-nurture dispute, which asks whether we owe our personalities and behavioral patterns to the influence of family, peers, education, and the social structure around us. Replacing a faulty gene is one thing; replacing external influences at will is quite another.

In addition, no one can say for sure how much of what we are is determined by more than the DNA molecule or by the nurturers. Other factors, including—yes!—a person's will can affect even one's genetic destiny. There are documented cases of people with supposedly incurable diseases who have refused to accept a death verdict and whose determination to live has thwarted medical predictions.

Still, despite all the debates, genetic science continues to make powerful strides and seeks to probe ever deeper into once unimagined possibilities for assuring the human race of a brighter and longer future. Many medical researchers want unrestricted access to stem cells that may, as the technology develops, grow healthier hearts and organs that eliminate diabetes and other genetically transmitted diseases. Powerful religious sects lobby against the use of human embryos for the research, but recently a way has been found to extricate stem cells from skin alone. Yet even so, debates over the ethics of interfering with natural process are likely to continue.

Gene replacement has already been amazingly successful, particularly in mice and chimpanzees. Using their knowledge of genetic codes, scientists have cloned animals. This means they already have in their hands the process of bringing about prearranged genetic results.

Manipulation of genes in the sports world is already taking place. Athletes have been found to use or are suspected of using so-called "gene doping." Foreign genes are injected into cells of the muscles; they carry a "growth code," and the muscles become strengthened. Theodore Friedman, director of the human gene therapy program at the University of California, San Diego, told the National Institute of Health that those "intent on subverting the gene therapy will do so. The technology is too easy."

On the other hand, successful gene therapy, performed with the intention of curing once fatal illness or prolonging human life span, may silence those who denounce genetic science. If people can live longer, healthier lives, may not they be free to maximize their potential?

Sociobiology

Sociobiology redefines love in terms of how much genetic investment people are willing to make.

A discipline combining biology and social science, **sociobiology** assumes the absence of free will and studies human behavior in terms of *genetic investment*. Its beliefs are closely related to those of the self-interest philosophies. The basic assumption is that everything we do pertains to our genetic strain. Love between two people is a matter of genes. If a single male wants unlimited sex with different partners, he is showing that he is not ready to make a genetic investment; he has no immediate need to continue his genetic line. A single female may also want unlimited sex, but, even with birth-control devices, she has to think about the possibility that she is making more of a genetic investment than her partner. Marriage and family are viewed as a mutual agreement to make the investment. Married people who do not wish to have children are showing that genetic investment is not necessary for their happiness. Everyone is not the same, but everyone can be studied in relation to a "genetic attitude." How we feel about genetic propagation determines how we conduct intimate relationships.

Traditional definitions of love are thus displaced. People who share the same genetic attitudes are likely to attract each other. Even family ties result from sharing a similar gene pool. Altruism, or self-sacrifice, is also redefined. A mother sacrifices for her children because they represent the continuing life of her own genes. She would face death to save her own child, but not someone else's—except for cases in which she has become close to another's child she considers part of her family, or in which she unconsciously believes the child in danger is her own. Soldiers who die to save their battalion do so because the battalion has become a substitute family.

The sociobiologist contends that not just romantic but *all* decisions—political, religious, educational, financial—relate in one way or another to genetics. If nothing else, genes determine *who* we are, and who we are determines what we stand for, and apparently we cannot decide to walk a different path.

But all of this is only half the story. There are many who advance contrary arguments and say freedom is a reality that can be attained.

Free Will

Thus far in this chapter we have reviewed a great many determinist views, from ancient times to the present. Determinist arguments are too powerful to be ignored because much of what determinists say does indeed apply to many, but perhaps not all, people. The state of being a free person may well be a gift not equally shared. Perhaps the art of being human includes the art of being free, where that is possible. Yet like any art, freedom needs to be very delicately and carefully fashioned and preserved. We need to begin our investigation into possibilities for free will on a cautionary note, reminding ourselves that we cannot simply *assume* we have it.

> *I have no friends*
> *I make my mind my friend*
> *I have no enemy*
> *I make carelessness my enemy*
> *I have no armor*
> *I make benevolence my armor*
>
> **—Fourteenth-century Japanese samurai**

A Pessimist's View of Free Will

Many have argued that the phrase "free will" is redundant; that, in fact, if one *has* a will at all it must be free. The existence of will implies freedom. But is there in fact such a thing as the will? Or is what some philosophers have called "will" nothing but causation working through our conscious level, making us *think* we are doing what we want, not what we must? B. F. Skinner, for example, argues that the will cannot be detected, cannot be felt. We cannot say "I have free will" with reference to a specific sensation or emotion. So *where* is will? Not everyone agrees on an answer.

The German philosopher Arthur Schopenhauer (1788–1860) had no doubt that the will existed, but the fact did not fill him with joy. He tells us how to *see* the will objectified in an action: Stand in front of a mirror and observe yourself. Think you would like to raise your left arm; then do it. One instant the desire to raise the arm is locked inside the mind, the consciousness, the next instant the will is visibly present in the action perceived in the mirror.

Schopenhauer believed that free will was the will to live and could be used for selfish purposes.

Whereas many have thought that having discovered the will is enough to dignify the human condition, Schopenhauer went on to ask: *What is the will for?* It is obvious, one might respond. The will makes free choices among available options. Here is an imaginary conversation:

SCHOPENHAUER: *Indeed, but is making free choices enough to justify optimism about the human condition?* (We say we do not understand.)

SCHOPENHAUER: *Is a free choice always a good choice? Suppose the choice is to kill someone. Does the fact that it was a free choice in any way soften the horror of the crime? Do we take a measure of comfort in knowing that the decision to murder was determined solely by the will of the murderer? Would it not be far better had the potential killer been conditioned by a religious upbringing that taught benevolence toward one's fellows?*

Schopenhauer believed the will is actually the will *to live*. The will drives us to actions that we think will benefit us, will ensure our survival. Often these are downright evil.

> *Unjust or wicked actions are, in regard to him who performs them, signs of the strength of his affirmation of the will to live, and thus how far he still is from true salvation, which is denial of this will.*[5]

In other words, while not denying our freedom to act, Schopenhauer is saying that everyone is constrained, is *forced*, to use the power of will to further their own cause, even if that means harm to others. The freedom of not acting also exists, but too often this results from the fear of being caught—or at least, of not profiting from the act—and cannot be construed as a true denial of will.

Schopenhauer seems to believe freedom is possible in the denial of will. While remaining pessimistic about human nature in general, he entertains the hope in his books that a rare few will understand and curb their own aggressive drives.

In a dialogue between Man and the World Spirit, Schopenhauer thinks of what he might say to the Spirit: "Should I tell him that the value of life lies precisely in this, that it teaches him not to want it?"[6] The philosopher is not recommending suicide here. He is talking about willfully turning aside from the pleasures and successes life appears to offer because the free pursuit of them only makes us evil in our intentions: that is, solely self-centered. Yet he believed few were capable of abandoning the pursuit of success-regardless-of-cost. A disillusioned idealist, Schopenhauer longed for a world of peace and *good* will, but he saw little chance that it would ever come about.

Feminists disapprove of Schopenhauer's seemingly blatant put-down of women. In truth, what he said about women tends to be condescending and insulting. He called them "incurable philistines." He said, "The entire sex have proved incapable of a single truly great, genuine and original achievement in art, or indeed of creating anything of lasting value."[7] Yet, in backhanded fashion, he pays women a compliment by pointing out that their will for power is much less aggressive and destructive than that of men, and that, while fathers train their children to exercise their wills for evil purposes, mothers impart softer values. For Schopenhauer, in a sense, women are more apt to deny their wills, and by his own definition, are better for the world than men.

Regret and Relief as Signs of Free Will

"Each roll of the die . . . is totally unrelated to events that were before it. . . . Yet our brains simply refuse to accept this fact. This is randomness: insisting that there is order where there is only chaos."

—Charles Seife

The American philosopher William James (1842–1910) reviewed the case for pure determinism as set forth by European philosophers and concluded they were wrong. In fact, James developed a theory he pointedly called **indeterminism**, which presents the world as a random collection of chance happenings. Determinism, for James, was too coldly logical: Cause A leads to effect B. Determinism made people seem like well-run, well-oiled machines. James said people, on the contrary, were indecisive and unpredictable, exactly the opposite of machines.

Take regret, he said. Regret is a universal phenomenon. At any given moment people are able to think back over a hundred choices they wish they had not made. But at the same time, regret cannot be meaningfully experienced unless there exists an opposite—satisfaction—that gives regret its identity. In other words, within the random collection of happenings, people sometimes make what they consider the right move and many times make what they consider the wrong move. If everything were predetermined—that is, if the will were not free—looking backward could not reveal missed chances. We could not see them unless they had existed, though we may have been blind to them at the moment of choice. How often do murderers think back and realize that they did not *have* to carry a pistol when confronting their eventual victim? For James, hindsight is proof that genuine alternatives always exist. The determinist would reply that alternatives not chosen have no real existence; something always makes us choose one—and only one.

If we were to extend the philosophy of indeterminism, we could say that another revealing exercise is to sit back and think of all the terrible things we might have done last week but refrained from doing, such as

Having a confrontation with a friend that could have threatened the relationship.

Lying about something that would have involved a whole series of other lies.

Dropping a course in an impulsive moment, a course required for graduation.

Taking a chance and driving the old car with two bald tires.

We would probably feel relieved we had not done these things. Thus the experience of *relief* is another sign of freedom of will. When we consider the wrong moves that might have been made but were not, we are aware of having chosen wisely. We were free to do so because we *could* have made the wrong decision. Nothing except our own intelligence determined the choice.

Our lives are probably split down the middle, with good moves on one side and bad moves on the other. That we can say we have made many mistakes is an admission that we know ourselves to be free agents. That we have sometimes chosen wisely may cause us to think, "If the good choice was predetermined, then I freely embrace determinism!"

Psychoanalysis and Free Will

Certain schools of psychology are based on the premise that whatever we think or do is impelled by a previous cause which is not always of our own choosing. **Psychoanalysis**, in examining a patient's dreams, the thought processes evidenced in their conversation, and their free association of ideas, seeks to free people from acting without the knowledge of why they do what they do. It aims to lead people to a rational state of mind in which free choice is possible, to help people integrate their behavior by learning the causes of deviant, antisocial, or uncharacteristic actions. The theory is that once the cause is discovered the subterranean forces driving their actions can be fully or at least partially controlled. For people who undergo treatment because they don't like who they are or what they do, therapists hold out the hope that through understanding and proper guidance they can change and become less "determined" than they were before.

Psychoanalysis has had a tremendous influence on theater, films, television, and literature. It has replaced the "who done it?" with the "what made him do it?"

Psychoanalysis, invented by Sigmund Freud (1856–1939) to assist people toward mental health, is based on the assumption that painful past events hidden away in the unconscious minds cause some people to have bizarre dreams, make odd statements, and perform incomprehensible actions. In other words, their lives are determined by unconscious prior causes: sometimes by guilt-ridden emotions they have refused to deal with; often by desires of the *id*, that primitive, animal self human beings possessed long before they developed the rational *ego*. Controlled only by the *id*, one does not possess free will.

Bjanka Kadic/Alamy

Signmund Freud's couch, c. 1930s

Freud used this famous couch to help free clients from bondage to hidden guilt and shame.

In the Freudian view, the ego is the Apollonian conscious mind, and the id, the Dionysian self. In the id are sexual and aggressive drives that society has taught us to suppress. Freud called the values imposed upon us by family, education, religion, the law, and the opinions of others the *superego:* the voice inside the mind that tells us what we may or may not do. Yes, the will is free to disobey this voice, but chances are those who do so will be plagued by guilt. And yes, we are free *not* to think about our guilt, but, for Freud, denying it only makes matters worse.

The aim of the Freudian therapist is to analyze the patient's dreams, characteristic use of language, and free associations; to uncover the hidden self responsible for neurotic—that is, disordered—behavior; and to lead the patient to a happier life dominated by the ego. Presumably the successfully psychoanalyzed patient comes to possess freedom of the will, having been released from the determining phantoms of the past. Will thus resides in the fully conscious ego.

In recent years Freud's theories have been reevaluated. There is growing skepticism about two of his basic assumptions: the first, that all behavior can sooner or later be traced back to significant early experiences, often in childhood; and the second, that the ego, or the conscious self, is capable of rational, sustained thought once the suppressed secrets of the past are brought to light. His critics believe human behavior is far more complex than Freud suggests, and freedom is not attainable only in the therapist's office.

World History Archive/Alamy

John Henry Fuseli, *The Nightmare*, 1781

An eighteenth-century painting, uncharacteristic of its time, amazingly anticipates the Freudian view that dreams have a powerful hold on our unconscious.

Another objection is that the role of the superego, as defined by Freud, is far less pronounced than it was in his day. Sexual mores, in particular, are far less rigid, violations less apt to instill guilt. In much **psychotherapy** of today, there are a counsellor and a client, and a willingness to listen with less likelihood of a search for dreadful skeletons in closets.

Nevertheless, Freud has received much recognition in the study of the humanities for having created one of the most prominent and influential myths of the twentieth century: *the myth of the liberated self.* Novels, plays, and films, especially in the first half of the century, display the overwhelming impact of Freud. A popular plot centers on a man or a woman haunted by nightmarish dreams and held prisoner by past guilt, which the conscious mind refuses to confront. He or she then meets a benevolent, wise (and often attractive) analyst, who forsakes all personal concerns and works solely to free the patient from the shackles of tormenting guilt.

The structure of this generic therapy plot is similar to that of a detective story. The old question "Who done it?" is replaced by "Why was it done?" or "What is someone afraid to face?" Sometimes we learn that the victim as a young child killed one or the other parent in a terrible accident. Or (very often indeed) that the victim was responsible for the death of a sibling, as in

Alfred Hitchcock's 1945 film *Spellbound* in which the victim of suppressed guilt is a therapist himself, troubled by nightmarish dreams involving snowstorms. At lunch one day, another therapist, a beautiful woman in his employ, quietly observes him unconsciously using a fork to make parallel lines on a white tablecloth. The subordinate becomes the mentor, forcing him to confront his buried past in which he had slid down the wrought-iron railing on his parents' front steps unaware that his younger brother was perched at the bottom. An inevitable collision caused the boy to be impaled on a spear-like post, a trauma that the therapist has locked deep in his unconscious for many years. As expected, the recognition liberates him from guilt and steers him straight into the waiting arms of his beautiful employee.

Psychoanalytic films were extremely popular during and just after World War II. The endings were usually happy (often with marriage in the offing between patient and therapist); audiences seemed never to tire of the familiar plot structure. Interestingly enough, the popularity of Freudian-based entertainment coincided with the recovery of the American economy from the dismal depression of the 1930s as well as the recognition that the United States had to enter World War II to help free those overrun by fascist forces. The need for the literature and drama of freedom was apparently an insatiable one. Whether on the battlefield or in the therapist's office, characters struggled against overwhelming odds and in most cases emerged victorious.

Writers unconvinced that anybody can readily be freed from a suppressed past show little optimism, and a few have given us memorable modern tragedies. Tennessee Williams's milestone work *A Streetcar Named Desire* (1947) presents audiences with a harrowing study of mental illness culminating in madness. The heroine, Blanche DuBois, tries to give the impression that she is a genteel Southern belle, carrying on the elegant traditions of the Old South, but as the play deepens, she exhibits unmistakable signs of an unstable mental condition that causes her to denounce her sister's uncouth husband while she is at the same time driven by a fierce sexual attraction to him. Recognizing this attraction and thinking of his own sexual gratification, the husband rapes her violently. The abuse causes Blanche to retreat into a fantasy world from which she will never escape. The author himself was in therapy for a good part of his life, apparently unable to free himself from the demons of his own past.

Dennis Lehane's novel *Mystic River* (2001) is a dark tale about a troubled man who has attempted all his life to absolve himself of the guilt he suffered when, as an innocent child, he was repeatedly abused sexually by a high-ranking clergyman. So often as a consequence of such childhood traumas, the boy grows up with feelings of worthlessness and an inability to communicate his feelings, even to his wife. His suppressed passion for revenge becomes his tragic flaw when he murders a man he believes to be a child molester, an act that leads to his own violent death at the hands of his best friend. In 2003, Clint Eastwood directed a powerful screen adaptation of the novel, which won Oscars for Tim Robbins as the troubled protagonist and Sean Penn as the friend. In his review of the film in the *New Yorker* magazine for October 13, 2003, David Denby declared the film "is as close as Hollywood has ever come to creating true Greek tragedy."

First airing in 2008, the television series *In Treatment* shows in semidocumentary style a psychotherapist's technique. The therapist in turn goes to his own psychoanalyst, presumably to achieve rational control of his ego. Freud-based entertainment appears destined for a very long life. If nothing else, it serves as escapism for those who have no wish to ponder their own hidden selves.

Of course, determinists can always argue that the liberation of the unconscious and the confrontation with reality may provide the illusion of freedom but only for a time. Stamping a patient's chart CURED does not guarantee freedom from all determining influences. Just as physicists discovered that matter is composed of particles within particles within particles, so too may the self be a circular staircase leading down into an infinity of shadows. Freud understood this and was generally cynical about human existence, but his theories provided hope that many could ascend that staircase into the clear light of day.

Studying the humanities of the past century would be difficult indeed without recognition of Freud's role. Many schools of psychotherapy continue to be rooted in his thought, and millions have been restored to mental health through psychoanalytical methods. That Freud's views may not represent an all-inclusive means to human freedom from the determining past should not eclipse the importance of these views to both the arts and to modern psychology.

Existentialism

> *"I know of no more encouraging fact than the unquestionable ability of man to elevate his life by a conscious endeavor."*
>
> **—Henry David Thoreau**

After the armistice ended the First World War in 1918, older beliefs were swept out the door. European countries exhausted from years of turmoil and a staggering loss of life eagerly sought new ways of thinking and living. Then Roman-style nationalism, the belief that one's country was superior to all others and had a right to subjugate the rest of civilization, reared its head once more.

A maniacal dictator named Adolf Hitler decided to take advantage of the chaos that usually follows a large-scale conflict. Thousands were enslaved, tortured, and executed. The freedom to be whatever they wished to be was denied to thousands more.

Hitler and his allies were defeated in 1945. Once again came a call for new approaches, new values, and a new way of defining freedom that if difficult to attain was nonetheless within the reach of anyone prepared to work for it. That definition was provided by the philosophy called **existentialism**. Born in the middle of the nineteenth century, the philosophy was little known until postwar cynicism spread throughout Europe, especially France, a nation that once prided itself on being the cultural center of Western civilization but had been brought to its knees by Nazi occupation. After the war, France found itself without a guiding philosophy, and its art reflected hopelessness and despair. But then existentialism was rediscovered, and with it, a strong light that could be seen at the end of a long, dark tunnel. Existentialism taught that people are free to be anything they want—but that freedom came with a price.

Religious Existentialism

The first official existentialist was a Dane, Søren Kierkegaard (1813–1855), who was raised in an austere religious environment, rebelled against it for a time, then returned to it as a matter of conscious choice, without the need of mystic revelations. For Kierkegaard, religion became a psychological reality freely accepted rather than a revealed truth with required acceptance. When one reached a point of absolute despair (as indeed he did) and felt ready to turn to God, one could take a **leap of faith**.

In that leap, however, lie undeniable anxieties. The leap must be made over many counterarguments, especially scientific evidence that seriously questions religious beliefs. On one's knees in the darkness of a church, one might feel one's prayers soaring heavenward and have a sense of union with God, but one can never *know* if God is listening—or is even there at all.

To dramatize the plight of the believer, Kierkegaard recounts the biblical tale of Abraham and Isaac in his book *Fear and Trembling*. An angel appears to

Abraham and tells him God demands the sacrifice of his son Isaac. Abraham is appalled, but what can he do? If God wants the sacrifice and he is God's servant, he must obey. His unquestioning willingness to do as God commands is a leap of faith. In that leap, in that raising of the knife, must not Abraham experience unutterable anguish? Suppose the message was not really from God—what then? The anguish of Abraham represented for Kierkegaard the existential dilemma of all people. An existential dilemma is knowing that one is free to make a choice, but who knows whether it is the right, or even the best, choice?

The contemporary philosopher Martin Buber (1878–1965), like Kierkegaard, found his way to religion through nontraditional means. He is most famous for defining two kinds of relationships a person can have. The first is the "I/it"—or the objective relationship with objects and events with concrete reality. Here there is no God, but only the existential moment. The second relationship is "I/Thou," representing a bridge to God. For Buber, an "it" must be defined; it has to be justified as concrete reality, otherwise there can be no relationship. A "Thou" is not defined, but addressed. The difference is clear. If you can address someone (whether a person standing in front of you or God, unseen), objective definition is beside the point. The fact that you are addressing anyone means that for you, at least, they exist. When it comes to "I/it," objective proof is possible. The "it" is out there for all to see. When it comes to "I/Thou," the experience of God comes through feeling, through intuition, through an overpowering sense of God's presence, and is not out there for all to see. Hence there can be no challenging it. Buber and Kierkegaard are very close on this point.

"So long as the heaven of Thou is spread out over me the winds of causality cower at my heels, and the whirlpool of fate stays its course."

—Martin Buber

Early in his adult life Buber approached religion intellectually. He was a scholar of sacred Hebrew texts concerned with the interpretation of traditional religious history as being a matter of myth and legend; yet he sought the fundamental truth behind them. He did not address God personally. God was not a "Thou" until the reading of one particular text—just a few sentences, really—changed his life forever.

> *I opened a little book entitled the* Zervaat Ribesh*—that is the testament of Rabbi Israel Baal-Shem—and the words flashed toward me: "He takes unto himself the quality of fervor, for he is hallowed and become another man and is worthy to create and is become like the Holy One, blessed be He, when he created his world." It was then that, overpowered in an instant, I experienced the Hasidic soul.*[8]

In Chapter 2 we would have called this a Dionysian religious experience. Buber discovered that truth in religion comes from irresistible feeling, not analytical thought. From that moment on he became a Hasid—a member of a sect that emphasizes joy in God's closeness to humanity and the warm fellowship with other members of God's family.

Buber was then led to a passionate concern for the sacredness of human relationships, for in human contact he also found God. Every person with whom one connects was for him a "Thou," and every "Thou" contained the spirit of God. In one of his books he tells of greeting a visitor perfunctorily; though he showed the man ordinary courtesy, he was eager to return to a

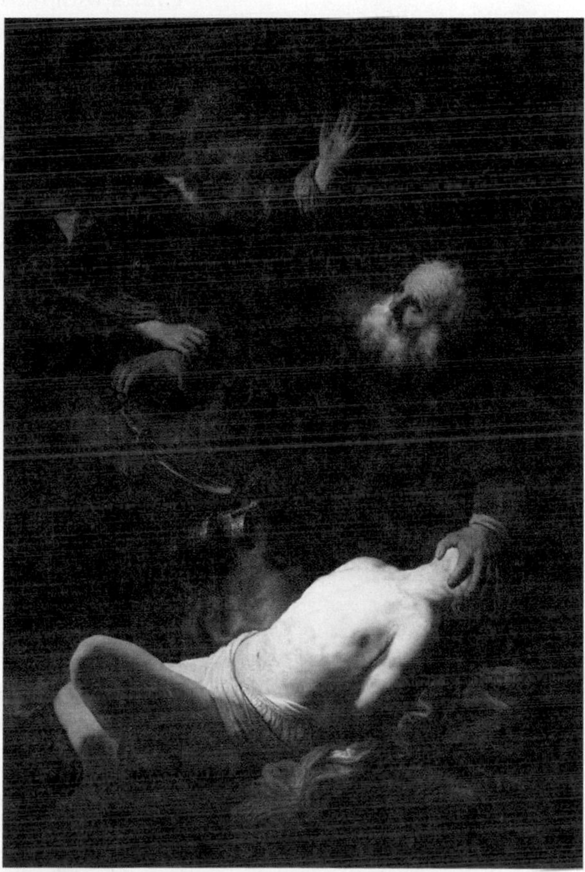

Interfoto/Alamy

Rembrandt van Rijn, *The Sacrifice of Issac*, 1635

Rembrandt's famous painting shows an angel stopping the sacrifice of Isaac. For Kierkegaard, Abraham's leap of faith was filled with anguish.

According to Buber, if you can address someone (including God), they must exist at least for you. Objects have objective reality, but since you don't address them, they have no actual existence.

scholarly manuscript he was editing. Upon learning that his visitor later committed suicide, Buber recognized that human beings are more important than any task.

"I/Thou" created a revolution in modern ethics, for here was a philosopher who dispensed with the rules, who challenged the moral absolutes of both the Socratic and major religious traditions, but still found a way to affirm that moral goodness was there in every human heart, provided it was sought. Not everyone would find it, but each of us was free to search for it.

Secular Existentialism

A different kind of existentialism swept over Europe after World War II. Secular existentialism fitted the depressed mood of countries that had been devastated by fighting and loss. At the same time, its belief in freedom as a natural condition helped to stir up some optimism.

Secular existentialism does not seek to address a God whose existence we cannot prove. Belief in God entails obeying commandments as well as believing that one is put here for the purpose of deserving God's love and mercy. Secular existentialism opposes a religious teaching that human beings have an *essence* which defines their humanness. All we can be sure of is *existence*. Once we recognize that fact, we can begin to work our way out of the sense of abandonment that comes with the understanding that human beings are alone in a bewildering universe that exists for no known reason. Of course, this knowledge means that each of us is free in the sense of having no obligation to a higher force or indeed to anything else; but this brand of freedom is at first confusing if not terrifying. Most people, say the secular existentialists, choose religion or some other authority that lays down guidelines for them. Even if they don't obey them, they have at least a perspective. They know what they are *supposed* to be doing.

"Freedom is fragile and must be protected. To sacrifice it, even as a temporary measure, is to betray it."

—Germaine Greer

Central to the secular existential movement is the thought of three French philosophers: Jean-Paul Sartre (1905–1980), Simone de Beauvoir (1908–1986), and Albert Camus (1913–1960). Sartre, the most influential of the three, bases his belief in the human right of self-definition on the absolute certainty that God cannot exist. He is opposed to the acceptance of God as a matter of psychological necessity. Deep down we know that each of us is alone in a world that makes no sense—something that must have seemed all too true to many war-weary survivors in Europe.

Sartre maintains there is no such thing as human nature. People *talk* about human nature, but who has ever seen it? We cannot assume people are fundamentally good *or* bad, when in fact they are *neither* at birth. No one comes into this world to serve any purpose whatever or to fulfill some preexisting definition of what it means to be human.

> *If man, as the existentialist conceives him, is indefinable, it is because at first he is nothing. Only afterward will he be something, and he himself will have made what he will be. Thus, there is no human nature, since there is no God to conceive it.*[9]

Saying that humankind is born without any identifying nature is in direct conflict with earlier philosophies that describe everyone as having an essence. In Christianity, for example, that essence is the soul. For Aristotle, it is rationality. In short, existentialism says you have to work at developing an essence that can be defined as human, an essence that includes good will and a strong, clear sense of moral responsibility to one's fellows. For the religious existentialist, one creates an essence that is spiritual and longs for union with God. Thus the ringing declaration of both religious and secular existentialism is *Existence precedes essence.*

According to Sartre, only natural phenomena and manufactured objects have essences from the beginning. A paper cutter was "born" to cut paper. If it doesn't cut paper, you have the right to demand your money back. A storm was "born" to bring wind and rain (or snow) and maybe knock down a few buildings in its path. Even animals have essences, for they too are natural phenomena. A tiger has to growl and be carnivorous. But human beings somehow escaped *having* to be anything.

> *"Freedom is what you do with what's been done to you."*
>
> **—Jean-Paul Sartre**

Ah, but there is a bright side to the picture. We *are* capable of reason, a faculty we develop through experience. Some choose to exploit this capacity more than others do. Some decide they cannot live without an essence, without a purpose, without a way of defining themselves. The bad news is that each person must find the definition all alone. If one borrows an essence from the past, from the traditions and beliefs of one's ancestors, or is influenced by peer pressure or educational or religious institutions, the right to define oneself is forfeited. One's essence has already been predefined.

Once we realize we have no essence, we have to create one freely; or, as Sartre puts it, we are "doomed to freedom." Each of us, having declared our essence, must then take responsibility for it. You cannot decide you are going to be such-and-such, only to deny, when your actions harm someone else, that you ever made that decision. No one is free to be morally unaccountable. True freedom carries a hefty price tag, reason tells us. You cannot argue that reason guarantees the right to behave any way you want to, unless, as Kant (Chapter 11) would say, you can accord that right to everyone else. In that case, you'd have to be careful not to turn your back on anyone. Do we *really* want to live in a society in which no one is responsible for anything?

Sartre says that many prefer to believe they serve a purpose and what they do was meant to be. He relates the tale of a young man who could not pass the examinations for various professional careers and decided he was meant to fail because he was truly destined to become a priest. Nonsense! declares Sartre. The young man was always in charge of his own life and should not have turned to the priesthood solely on the hunch that destiny was forcing him into it. Freedom is a painful thing sometimes. If we fail, we try to blame others or circumstances, thus denying the truth of our freedom.

Sartre argues that to avoid difficult choices most people prefer to become things and believe they serve a destined purpose, like a paper cutter. Whatever a *thing* does, it must do in order to fulfill its thingness. Things have no moral responsibility. If we cut our finger on the paper cutter, we cannot blame *it* for our clumsiness. People would rather renounce freedom than blame themselves for what happens to them.

The true existentialist—like Abraham—has to make choices and is always confronted with anguish. An existential ship's officer, faced with the awful decision of having a dangerously overcrowded lifeboat or having to kill some of the survivors, might decide to shoot certain people to save the others; but he would not be able to argue that he was a victim of circumstances. Of course, he *could* do so, but, if he does, he cannot be considered *authentic.* An authentic person is one who defines himself or herself, stands behind the definition, and willingly accepts either praise or blame.

Simone de Beauvoir (1908–1986), a feminist writer and close associate of Sartre, urged women to create bold new essences. Her route to existentialism was the feminist rejection of male rules and the essences males imposed on females.

By the time humankind reached the stage of written mythology and law, the patriarchate was definitely established:

> *the males were to write the codes. It was natural for them to give woman a subordinate position, yet one could suppose that they would look upon her with the same benevolence as upon children and*

> *cattle—but not at all. While setting up the machinery of woman's oppression, the legislators were afraid of her.*[10]

If not the most influential of the French existentialists, Albert Camus has surely been the most poetic—and dramatic. In his three major essays, "An Absurd Reasoning," "The Absurd Man," and "The Myth of Sisyphus," he makes the existential case that rationality is found not in the universe but in the human mind. The intellect, attempting to make sense out of reality, realizes it is not to be understood. Why then are we rational? To what end? Reason leads us to the conclusion that living is absurd, meaningless.

Having said this, he begins "An Absurd Reasoning" with his most often quoted statement: "There is but one truly serious philosophical problem, and that is suicide." Where Sartre believed that abandonment in a meaningless universe opened the door to freedom, Camus goes deeper, analyzing that condition of abandonment and insisting that life is not worth living if we cannot assign a value to it. Yet, if life is absurd, what value *can* it have?

> *"Real generosity toward the future lies in giving all to the present."*
>
> **—Albert Camus**

Camus's answer is that it has an absurd value. What we think and do may not make any ultimate sense, but perhaps "ultimate sense" ought never to have been the goal. That there is only this existential moment, this here and now, does not imply that the moment is not worth experiencing. Unlike his colleagues, Camus talks about the colors, the sounds, the continually unfolding wonders of the universe. Absurd, yes, in that they have no meaning beyond themselves, but this fact does not make suicide the inevitable, the *only* recourse.

If we do not, as Hamlet does not, choose suicide, then we must have a purpose. That is, if we *had* chosen suicide would it not be said that our purpose was to do away with ourselves? People don't kill themselves for no reason. Choosing life rather than death is, therefore, purposeful as well. But if the world is absurd and we choose to remain in it, it must follow that we accept the absurdity and move on from there. In that lies our freedom, and with freedom comes an infinite number of possibilities.

To dramatize his point, Camus recounts the Greek myth of Sisyphus, "the wisest and most prudent of mortals," who also questioned the meaning of life. To find the answer, he stole secrets from the gods. They retaliated by condemning him to roll a heavy rock up a steep hill. When, through exhausting labor and physical pain, he reached the top, the rock rolled back down, and Sisyphus had to start all over again. This was to continue for eternity.

> *I leave Sisyphus at the foot of the mountain! One always finds one's burden again. But Sisyphus teaches the higher fidelity that negates the gods and raises rocks. He too concludes that all is well. This universe henceforth without a master seems to him neither sterile nor futile. Each atom of that stone, each mineral flake of that night-filled mountain, in itself forms a world. The struggle itself toward the heights is enough to fill a man's heart. One must imagine Sisyphus happy.*[11]

There are American existential writings as well. In *Mother Night* (1972), a novel by Kurt Vonnegut, Jr., an American newspaper columnist ostensibly defects to Germany during World War II and gets a job writing anti-Semitic propaganda for a German newspaper. After the conflict is over, he is tried as a war criminal, the charge being that the message of hatred in his inflammatory columns played a part in the Holocaust. The man's defense is that he was actually an American spy sent on an undercover mission by President Roosevelt himself. Of course, since

Roosevelt is dead, the journalist cannot prove what he claims. The author's message is that we are what we say we are and thus we need to be very careful about defining ourselves. In the author's eyes, the journalist was guilty because he had created for himself an essence which led, however indirectly, to the deaths of many innocent people. Whether he was secretly anti-Semitic or merely carrying out orders can never be known. He narrates his story from an Israeli prison, his freedom denied. Had he made a responsible use of freedom before?

The view of freedom expressed in much existential philosophy and literature has been widely questioned. Is it the freedom to behave without regard for others? The Norwegian philosopher Dagfinn Follesdal asked whether anyone who creates his own values can do anything that is morally wrong. True, the existentialists insist that one be held accountable for speech and actions, but are people free to lie? To behave toward others in a way that will draw praise and make it easy to manipulate them? And if people use their freedom for their own profit, are they *really* free, or are they victims of their own selfishness?

Freedom within Limitations

> *Keep in mind always the present you are constructing. It should be the future you want.*
>
> —**Alice Walker**

By now it may have occurred to the reader that the philosophies of freedom we have been discussing were all generated by Western thinkers living in comparatively open societies in which freedom of thought and expression were and are taken for granted. Even Augustine, within the confines of Christianity, was at liberty to express his doubts. Determinists like Marx and Skinner were not threatened with jail for saying that our choices are not freely made.

Sometimes a philosopher of freedom is in fact living under an oppressive government: Rousseau, for example, in a rigid monarchy; Sartre, during the Nazi rule in France. Both fought against tyranny: Rousseau through his pen, and Sartre through his work in the French Underground, an organized covert attempt to help those being sought or persecuted by the Nazis. Neither philosopher abandoned his belief that freedom was the natural condition of humanity. That belief tends to be echoed throughout the humanities in different ways.

What does freedom mean to those who grow up in societies which have been or are now embroiled in bitter religious and territorial disputes that severely limit choices? Or do those who are born into centuries-old ways of being human resign themselves to some form of slavery? Is freedom a narrowly Western idea? Or may we now extend its possible meanings?

For the Japanese, strongly influenced as they are by Western capitalism and the urgent need to do well financially, there is as well the strong tradition of family honor, a severe limitation that many of us, accustomed to open pathways, would see as an impediment to the exercise of will. Succeeding in business is often the way for a Japanese son or daughter to win family approval, but in the West, one may well decide that a business career was not the right choice. There is the heartbreaking story of the Japanese girl attending an Ivy League university who killed herself when she received less than an "A" grade in one subject and thought her family would be disgraced. She left her roommate a note, saying that because she had not studied hard enough there was no other course of action open to her.

Japanese society is nothing if not rule-driven, Western influences notwithstanding. We have already studied the principles of Zen Buddhism, a dominant practice in Japan. Zen requires long hours of meditation. To excel in any of the martial arts demands many years of training in body coordination and muscular development.

These arts are also products of a civilized society in which ethics and good manners are essential. Opponents must bow to each other as a mark of deep respect.

The Japanese love of the beautiful dictates how tea is prepared and served and how flowers are arranged in a vase. All of these requirements might strike some in the West as cumbersome impositions, as jailers imprisoning the will. Yet it is doubtful that the Japanese would agree.

One of the foremost modern spokespersons for Buddhist thought and practice was Chögyam Trungpa, who fled Chinese persecution in his native Tibet and founded a still thriving American Buddhist community in Boulder, Colorado. Among those who came there to absorb his teachings was poet Allen Ginsberg, a major voice of the Beat Generation, post-World War II writers, artists, and composers who found themselves disillusioned with the greed they saw on all sides and what they took to be the goal of rebuilding America as a more materialistic version of what it had once been. The so-called Beats proclaimed themselves social dropouts, adrift in a land that called itself the cradle of liberty where people could be whatever they wanted to be yet were really slaves to its shoddy values.

Many, like Ginsberg, saw in Buddhism the one true path to freedom from this enslavement through the discipline of meditation and the renunciation of materialistic desires. In *The Myth of Freedom* Trungpa explains that Western definitions of the word imply an absence of external control and the right to disobey the rules whenever it suits—or the right to become the chief and impose whatever rules one wants. Trungpa maintains that, in order to be free in the Buddhist sense of the word, one must first wake up to the reality of pain and suffering. It is absurd to suppose that following the American Dream and striving for wealth and the pleasures it can buy will avoid pain and suffering. If anything, wealth and pleasure only add to the pain because, as Epicurus points out (Chapter 13), there is never enough pleasure to satisfy us; and, even if we had all the money we could ever want and spent our life doing whatever we pleased, there would be the excruciating pain of recognizing that death will bring an end to our holiday. According to Trungpa:

> *. . . we must begin by seeing the experience of life as it is. We must see the truth of suffering, the reality of dissatisfaction. We cannot ignore it and attempt to examine only the glorious pleasurable aspects of life. If one searches for a promised land, a Treasure Island, then the search only leads to more pain. We cannot reach such islands, we cannot attain enlightenment in such a manner. So all sects and schools of Buddhism agree that we must begin by facing the reality of our living situations. We cannot begin by dreaming.*[12]

Trungpa defines true freedom as surrendering to reality and, by accepting things as they are, liberating oneself from pain, which is, after all, a goal of the free person. In his view, one can be free though tightly shackled. Even in a narrow prison cell, freedom is possible because no one can put chains on our thoughts and feelings. This doctrine of freedom through personal choice despite limitations has inspired hundreds of Trungpa's followers. However, a critic has said it is doubtful that it would bring solace to the many who still live in slavery or under severe autocratic rule.

Perhaps all one can say at this point in time is that there are many paths to freedom and that some of them still have impassable barriers. All the more reason to be grateful if you have the right to choose.

It seems appropriate to close this book with a theory—and it is just that—by means of which we can apply the word *free* to ourselves. According to this theory, derived from a number of sources, freedom is achieved *only* when we place limits on our options.

> *He who bears in his heart a cathedral to be built is already victorious. He who seeks to become sexton of a finished cathedral is already defeated.*
>
> **—Antoine de Saint-Exupéry**

People who jog know all about the relationship between freedom and limits. They will tell you about a consciousness of freedom in running, pushing against the wind and feeling their arms and legs equal to the demands made by the will; for runners, in contrast to what Skinner has said, *do* feel their will. When there is a sharp incline, runners must draw upon reserve strength. On the downward slope, they know that power needs to be conserved. If they run flat-out, they may not have enough left for the final mile. If they are running against others and there is a need to win, they accelerate. If all they want to do is complete the course, they adopt a more leisurely pace.

But the vivid experience of will does not happen all of a sudden. In the beginning, jogging is a distinct effort accompanied by pain and soreness. There is the inevitable pulling of muscles, the labored breathing, the tendency to overheat rapidly. In the beginning, joggers often stop running for the slightest excuse. After a time they set a goal: to the end of the road and then back; one mile; two miles; down to the county line. Self-imposed limits are crucial; the goal must be met. Even wind and rain are not likely to keep the determined runner at home. The ultimate feeling of liberation—the sense of floating, the so-called runner's high—occurs when the runner's body is equal to the task set by the will. And the will is experienced when runners feel at ease within the limitations they impose on themselves.

In Chapter 4, we talked about the sonnet form in which the poet's choices are determined by the requirement of fourteen lines. It would be easy for the poet to complain that the length limitation prevents the free expression of an idea; and indeed many poets have chosen to write in free verse for which no restrictions exist. The romantic poet William Wordsworth did not see the rigid sonnet rules as constraints upon freedom.

NUNS FRET NOT

Nuns fret not at their convent's narrow room;
And hermits are contented with their cells;
And students with their pensive citadels;
Maids at the wheel, the weaver at his loom
Sit blithe and happy; bees that soar for bloom,
High as the highest Peak of Furness-fells,
Will murmur by the hour in foxglove bells:
In truth the prison unto which we doom
Ourselves, no prison is: and hence for me,
In sundry moods, 'twas pastime to be bound
Within the Sonnet's scanty plot of ground;
Pleased if some Souls (for such there needs must be)
Who have felt the weight of too much liberty,
Should find brief solace there, as I have found.

Why, one asks, is freedom so vital? If Sartre is right in saying that most people prefer not to be free, why should we *have* to be free? Or, if freedom and liberty are not the same thing, what's wrong with seeking liberty for its own sake? What's wrong with going through life unfettered by rules and behaving in any way one desires? Why do we need to define ourselves at all and then be responsible for what we do?

When you put a tight lid on a pan of boiling water, the energy inside will become intense. So too will the joy of living be intense to the degree that we face a limited number of choices. Liberty is bewildering. Liberty does not know what to choose. Defining oneself as a certain kind of person is the first limitation. Unless we can do that, we become scattered to the winds, at the mercy of every gust. Narrowing the range of possibilities and *then finding the best way to work within that range* might, after all, be the answer. And what is the question? It is: *How can I do the most with the one life I have after I take inventory of how much freedom of choice is available to me?*

Of course, determinist arguments are powerful, and one has the right to believe there is no free will and thus one cannot be held responsible for anything. If one adopts that view, one must accept the fact that no one else is responsible either. Determinism is the only logical course for some. Many artists and philosophers do not agree. If a painting is decried by those who fund the exhibit, we don't hear the artist saying, "But I came from a bad environment that forced me to paint that way." Instead, the artist defends the work and decries the funders. Without *this* kind of freedom, there can be no pride in any accomplishment.

"Without freedom, no art; art lives only on the restraints it imposes on itself, and dies of all others."

—Albert Camus

If determinism is chosen, is the chooser forced to make that choice? Surprisingly enough, many *do* choose determinism without realizing it. How many people do we know who seem to be happy only when they find someone who will listen to their tragic tales of victimization—by other people, by the law, by the government, by their parents, and on and on? Never by themselves. As Jean-Paul Sartre continually reminds us, the only way to be an authentic person is to admit that you're free and to take responsibility for the bad choices you make. We have conceded many times that not everyone is lucky enough to have the right to choose. Those who do and who prefer to see themselves as helpless victims without responsibility would do well to recognize that they were nonetheless free to reject that responsibility.

Authentic people advertise their natures. We always know what to expect from them. Inauthentic people, backed into a corner after being blamed for something, try to plead their innocence by saying something forced them to make a wrongful choice. If free will is a fact of life it cannot be accepted here and rejected there at one's convenience.

In the final analysis, true freedom may reside in the limitations we impose upon ourselves freely. To believe that freedom means having unlimited options is to be trapped in infinity. Only by deliberately narrowing our range of options can we experience the exhilarating sense of being truly our own persons. It is freedom to say we can do this or that. It is not freedom to say we can do this, or that, or perhaps that other thing, or even its opposite, and on and on forever. When we come to this realization, we also see we need not trap ourselves by always choosing the easy way. At a sumptuous buffet we can gorge ourselves or decide to enjoy fully a limited amount of delicious food.

Those who achieve the strength of inner control are not only authentic persons; they are *good people*. They never want to harm others, for doing so would mean being at the mercy of uncontrollable passions, becoming the victims they choose not to be.

A study of the humanities looks into the minds and hearts of creative and thoughtful human beings and reveals many innovations in art and philosophy. Countless artists and philosophers have changed the course of human consciousness and given us options our ancient ancestors could not have dreamed of: options for experiencing the beautiful, the different, even sometimes the shocking, and, of course, the thought-provoking. How predetermined were *they* when the greatest of them did what nobody else had ever done? If they were predetermined, why was there not more than one Beethoven or Shakespeare or others who might have been similarly directed? The humanities would seem to be the study of the free spirit, and from this study each of us can know that more can be done with our lives. It is your birthright as a human being to reach up and mentally redo the Sistine Chapel ceiling if you don't happen to like it. Once you have investigated the past, it is your birthright to let go of it, but knowingly and with full awareness of what you want the present to be. It is your birthright to reach into the darkness and from it pull forth a new lantern, however unfamiliar the shape, however irregular the beam of light.

Reaching beyond ourselves is a natural right. Without the risk of failure, there can be no possibility of success. The American novelist and poet Stephen Crane sums it all up:

I SAW A MAN PURSUING THE HORIZON

I saw a man pursuing the horizon;
Round and round he sped.
I was disturbed at this;
I accosted the man.
"It is futile," I said,
"You can never—"
"You lie," he cried
And ran on.[13]

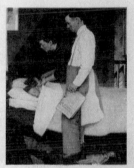

OURS... to fight for

Freedom of Speech — Freedom of Worship

Freedom from Want — Freedom from Fear

Pictorial Press Ltd./Alamy

Norman Rockwell, *The Four Freedoms*, 1943

LEARNING OBJECTIVES

Having read and carefully studied this chapter, you should be able to:

1. Discuss two arguments for determinism and two for free will.
2. Explain how and when science influenced the development of determinism.
3. Explain the difference between the philosophy of Karl Marx and communism.
4. Define and give two examples of B. F. Skinner's "aversive control."
5. Discuss Sigmund Freud's contribution to the understanding of the mind.
6. Distinguish between religious and secular existentialism.
7. Show why Arthur Schopenhauer thought the will was dangerous.
8. Explain why regret and relief, according to William James, are indications that the will is free.
9. Relate William Wordsworth's sonnet "Nuns Fret Not" to the final section of the chapter.

KEY TERMS

behaviorism both a philosophy and a school of psychology that believe people are what they do and what they do is determined by systems of rewards and punishments.

bourgeoisie in Marxism, refers to the affluent upper class.

chromosomes long, stringy bodies in the nucleus of the cell containing the genes.

communism a system of governing in which nearly all property is state (or publicly) owned and there is very little entrepreneurship in the private sector.

determinism philosophy that believes everything has a prior cause and consequently free will cannot exist.

dialectic philosophical method of Georg Hegel, involving the presentation of one idea, followed by an analysis of its opposite, and then arriving at a synthesis that combines the two; adopted by Marx to describe the conflict between the proletariat and the bourgeoisie and the eventual synthesis of a classless society.

DNA abbreviation for *dioxyribonucleic acid,* which forms long strands of sugar and sulphate within the gene and carries the genetic codes throughout the body.

economic determinism another name for the philosophy of Karl Marx, maintaining that our behavior is controlled by the need for money.

existentialism a philosophy with either a religious or a secular foundation, that maintains humanity is free to create its own essence.

genes granular substances within the chromosomes that contain the DNA molecules.

genome genetic codes inside each cell, one from each parent, that determine physical features and susceptibility to certain diseases.

indeterminism philosophy expounded by William James that whatever happens does so randomly, without a clearcut prior cause, and therefore we have free will to make choices.

institutional determinism name given to Jean-Jacques Rousseau's belief that the will is governed by restrictive forces of law, education, and religion, all necessary because of the inborn depravity of a few people.

leap of faith phrase invented by Søren Kierkegaard to indicate that religion can be freely chosen, but to do so one must bypass reason and thus can never be sure if the choice is right.

libertarianism political and philosophical belief in unrestricted freedom.

proletariat in Marxism, the working classes that will eventually rise up against the affluent bourgeoisie, leading to the classless society.

psychoanalysis a technique invented by Sigmund Freud that examines a patient's dreams and patterns of free association of ideas in an effort to diagnose the causes of neurotic behavior and mental illness.

psychotherapy clinical treatments of mental and emotional disorders.

socialism a system of governing in which more property is owned and there is more entrepreneurship in the private sector than in communism.

sociobiology a social science that believes human behavior can be analyzed in terms of genetic investment or the lack of it—that is, the extent to which one is motivated by the need to propagate his or her genes either directly through a sexual relationship, or indirectly through the need to survive physically, socially, or economically.

TOPICS FOR WRITING AND DISCUSSION

1. Freedom is a term we all take for granted, but, as the text points out, whether one is free or not depends on what is meant by "free." What is *your* definition?
2. Define and describe determinism. Do the same for two philosophies that oppose it.
3. Of the determinist philosophies discussed in the chapter, which one(s) do you believe has (have) the most bearing on your life? Which the least? In view of your answer, would you call yourself a complete determinist? Partial? Not at all?
4. Whether or not people agree with B. F. Skinner, most do concur that all of us are subject to a certain amount of aversive control. What is it? Describe one or two present or past aversive controls in your own life.
5. As the chapter points out, great strides have been taken in the science of genetics, and genetic research aims to contribute more and more to the way life is lived—and even to the prolongation of life. In 2001 the president of the United States said there would be limited federal funding of stem cell research using cells taken from fetuses. Opponents of any funding at all maintain that dissecting fetal stem cells to learn more about genetic diseases is tantamount to murder. Advocates of funding say that the research will result in extraordinary medical breakthroughs. Support your argument for or against federal funding.
6. Jean-Jacques Rousseau's famous position was that if it were not for the necessary but oppressive limitations imposed by social institutions people would be naturally benevolent toward each other. Do you agree that in a state of nature, without any limitations, people would get along? Or is aggression inherent in human nature?
7. On what does William James support his argument to support free will? We can't deny that the conditions he cites do actually exist, but do they prove we act freely?
8. The gist of Arthur Schopenhauer's free-will theory is that it would probably be better if the will were not free. Why does he believe this?
9. The chapter discusses two schools of existentialism. On what do they agree? Where do they disagree?
10. Stanley Fish's article on a British educational movement to allow students to choose their own subjects of study provided these would lead to a comfortable living raises interesting questions. If this movement gained popularity in the United States, would you be for it? Do you believe that a program devoid of humanities would create a truly valuable college education? Explain your views.

Endnotes

Chapter 1

1. Taylor Mali, "Totally like, whatever, you know?" www.TaylorMali.com.

Chapter 2

1. William Wharton, *Dad* (New York: Avon, 1981), 419–420.
2. Daniel Mendelsohn, "But Enough about Me," *New Yorker*, January 25, 2010, 68–74.
3. e.e. cummings, "somewhere I have never travelled, glady beyond." *Complete Poems, 1904–1962* (New York: Liveright Publishing Corp.).
4. Alex Ross, *The Rest Is Noise* (New York: Farrar, Straus and Giroux, 2007), xii.
5. Alistair Macauley, "Review of Joffrey Ballet Production of *Cinderella*," *New York Times*, Monday, February 22, 2010.
6. William Wordsworth, "The World Is Too Much with Us," *The Major Poets, English and American* (New York: Harcourt Brace, 1954), 257.

Chapter 3

1. Anthony Lane, "Review of 'Eternal Sunshine of the Spotless Mind,'" *New Yorker* (March 22, 2004), 103.
2. June Singer, *Boundaries of the Soul: The Practice of Jung's Psychology* (New York: Doubleday, 1972), 79.
3. Ibid., 79.
4. Joseph Campbell, *The Myths of God: Oriental Mythology* (New York: Viking Penguin, 1976), 243.
5. Ibid., 342.
6. Ibid., 9–10.
7. Edith Hamilton, *Mythology* (New York: New American Library, 1969), 63.
8. *Paradise Lost*, Book VII, ll. 211–217.
9. Hamilton, *Mythology*, 89.
10. Rose Anna Mueller, "La Llorana, The Weeping Woman," *Community College Review* 20, no. 1 (1999): 28–33.
11. J. R. R. Tolkien, *The Return of the King* (New York: Ballantine Books, 1966), 384.
12. Paraphrased from R. H. Blythe, *Zen and Zen Classics* (Tokyo: Hokuseido Press, 1960–1970).
13. Walter de la Mare, *Memoirs of a Midget* (New York: Knopf, 1921), 379.

Chapter 4

1. John Steinbeck, *The Grapes of Wrath* (1940; reprint, New York: Penguin Books, 1992).
2. *The Iliad*, translated by Augustus Taber Murray.
3. Sappho, "Ode to Aphrodite," trans. J. Addington Symonds, in *Our Heritage of World Literature*, ed. Stith Thompson and John Gassner (New York: Dryden Press, 1942), 258.
4. Catallus, trans. Walter Savage Landor, *Our Heritage of World Literature*, 268.
5. Jaron Lanier, "Jaron's World. The Meaning of Metaphor," *Discover*, February 2007.
6. *Collected Sonnets of Edna St. Vincent Millay*, eds. Ruth Bornschlegel and Norma Millay (New York: Harper & Row, 1987).
7. *Red Dragonfly on My Shoulder*, trans. Sylvia Cassedy and Kunihiro Sustake (New York: HarperCollins, 1992).
8. Ibid.
9. Campbell McGrath, *Seven Notebooks* (New York: HarperCollins, 2008), 99.
10. Georgia Douglas Johnson, "Black Woman," in *The Portable Harlem Renaissance*, ed. Daniel Levering Lewis (New York: Penguin Books, 1995.)
11. *The Collected Poems of Archibald MacLeish, 1917–1982* (Boston: Houghton Mifflin, 1995).
12. Billy Collins, *Sailing Alone Around the Room* (New York: Random House, 2001).
13. Campbell McGrath, 206–207.
14. F. Scott Fitzgerald, *The Great Gatsby* (New York: Scribner Paperback Edition, 1995), 160–161.
15. Carson McCullers, *The Member of the Wedding* (Boston: Houghton Mifflin, 1973), 3.

16. Ibid., 23.
17. John Updike, *My Father's Tears and Other Stories* (New York: Knopf), 89.
18. Ibid., 112.

Chapter 5

1. William Fleming, *Art and Ideas* (New York: Henry Holt, 1958), 307–308.
2. Bruce Cole and Adelheid Gealt, *Art of the Western World* (New York: Summit, 1985), 271.
3. Jan Garden Castro, *The Art and Life of Georgia O'Keeffe* (New York: Crown, 1985), 25.
4. Amy Helene Kirshke, *Aaron Douglas: Art, Race, and the Harlem Renaissance* (Jackson: University Press of Mississippi, 1995) 10, 77.
5. Jonathan Lipman, *Frank Lloyd Wright and the Johnson Wax Building* (New York: Rizzoli, 1986), xii.

Chapter 6

1. Abraham Veinus, Syracuse University, liner notes for Beethoven, Symphony No. 3, Vanguard Records.
2. Joan Baez, "Joe Hill," http://www.ilyric.net/Lyrics/J/JoanBaez/JoeHill.html/.
3. Alan Bullock and R. B. Wooding, eds., *20th Century Culture (*New York: Harper & Row, 1983), 212.
4. Charlie Gillett, *The Penguin Book of Rock and Roll Writing*, ed. Clinton Haydin (London: Penguin, 1992), 11.
5. Ibid., 14.
6. Ibid., 212.

Chapter 7

1. *Henry V*, IV, Prologue, 1–9, 22–28.
2. Sophocles, *Antigone*, trans. Dudley Fitz and Robert Fitzgerald.
3. *Othello*, V, ii, 338–344.
4. *King Lear*, V, ii, 306–308.
5. *Aristotle*, trans. Philip Wheelright (New York: Odyssey, 1951), 296.
6. *Othello*, V, ii, 91–97.
7. *Romeo and Juliet*, II, ii, 2–3; 5–6.
8. *Hamlet*, III, iv, 162; 164–165.
9. *Hamlet*, III, ii, 1–8.
10. *Hamlet*, V, ii, 217–222.
11. *Macbeth*, V, v, 17–28.
12. *Phædra*, by Jean Racine; translated by Robert Bruce Boswell. The Harvard Classics series. Charles W. Eliot ed. New York: P.F. Collier & Son, 1909–14.
13. Henrik Ibsen, *A Doll's House*, trans. Rolfe Fjelde, in *Literature of the Western World*, ed. Brian Wilke and James Hurt (New York: Macmillan, 1988), 1303.
14. *Henry IV, Pt. II*, V, v, 47–50.
15. Harold Bloom, *Shakespeare and the Invention of the Human* (New York: Riverhead, 1996), 271–272.
16. Ibid., 272.
17. *Twelfth Night*, II, iv, 14–19.
18. Molière, *Tartuffe*, trans. Richard Wilbur (New York: Roundhouse, 1997).
19. Tom Stoppard, *The Real Thing* (New York: Faber and Faber, 1983), 53.
20. Eugene O'Neill, *Long Day's Journey into Night* (New Haven, CT: Yale University Press, 1955), 165–166.

Chapter 8

1. John D. Drummond, *Opera in Perspective* (Minneapolis: University of Minnesota Press, 1980), 15.
2. Ibid., 278.
3. William G. Hyland, *Richard Rodgers* (New York: Yale University Press, 1998), 127.
4. Ibid., 131–132.

Chapter 9

1. Gerald Mast, *A Short History of the Movies* (New York: Macmillan, 1986), 68.
2. Ephraim Katz, *The Film Encyclopedia*, 3rd ed. (New York: Harper Perennial, 1998), 121.
3. David Denby, *New Yorker* (July 23, 2007).

Chapter 10

1. Walt Whitman, *Leaves of Grass* (New York: Heritage Press), 25.
2. John A. Hutchinson, *Paths of Faith*, 2nd ed. (New York: McGraw-Hill, 1975), 79.
3. Justice Thomas Berger, "Mackenzie Valley Pipeline Inquiry," Briefs and Transcripts, October 1976, gateway.uvic.ca/micro/.
4. *Buddhist Scriptures*, trans. Edward Conze (London: Penguin Books, 1959), 51.
5. A. A. Milne, *The Complete Poems and Tales of Winnie the Pooh* (New York: Quality Paperback Book Club, 1997), 81.
6. Ibid., 82.
7. *The Republic and Other Works by Plato*, trans. B. Jowett (New York: Doubleday Anchor Books, 1989), 470.
8. Ibid.,
9. *Aristotle*, ed. and trans. Philip Wheelright (New York: Odyssey Press, 1951), 4–5.
10. Rabbi Joseph Telushkin, *Jewish Literacy* (New York: William Morrow, 1991), 102.
11. *The Confessions of Saint Augustine*, Book VI (New York: Airmont Publishing Company, 1969), 213.
12. Jeffrey Long with Paul Perry, *Evidence of the Afterlife* (New York, Harper Collins, 2010), 3–6.
13. Edwin Arlington Robinson, "The Man Against the Sky," in *American Poetry and Prose*, ed. Norman Foerster (Boston: Houghton Mifflin, 1947), 1275–1276, ll. 305–314.
14. Charles S. Peirce, "How to Make Our Ideas Clear," *Popular Science Monthly*, 1878.
15. Charles S. Peirce, "The Fixation of Belief," in *The Search for Meaning*, ed. Robert F. Davidson (New York: Holt Rinehart Winston, 1967), 259.
16. Peirce, Ideas.

Chapter 11

1. Plato, *The Republic*, trans. Benjamin Jowett (New York: Doubleday, 1973), 44ff.
2. Ibid., 44ff.
3. John Rawls, qtd. in Donald Palmer, *Does the Center Hold?* (Mountain View, CA: Mayfield, 1996), 262.
4. Mitchell Cohen, "Argument: Should Opera Be Subsidized?" *Dissent*, summer 1999, 96.
5. Ibid., 98.
6. Huston Smith, *The World's Religions* (San Francisco: Harper, 1991), 290–291.
7. John A. Hutchinson, *Path of Faith*, 2nd ed. (New York: McGraw-Hill, 1973), 121–122.
8. Studs Terkel, *Working* (New York: Pantheon, 1974), 48ff:
9. Nicholas D. Kristof, "In Japan Nice Guys (and Girls) Finish Together," *New York Times*, April 15, 1998.

Chapter 12

1. Kurt Vonnegut, "Joe Heller," *New Yorker*, May 10, 2005.
2. Epicurus, *The Extant Remains*, trans. Cyril Bailey (London: Oxford Universirty Press, 1926), 64.
3. Ibid., 65.
4. *The Collected Poems of Archibald MacLeish, 1917–1982* (Boston: Houghton Mifflin, 1995).
5. *The Complete Short Stories of Ernest Hemingway* (New York: Scribners, 1982), 289–290.
6. Viktor Frankl, *Man's Search for Meaning: An Introduction to Logotherapy*, preface by Gordon W. Allport (New York: Washington Square, 1998), 90.
7. Anne Frank, *The Diary of a Young Girl*, ed. Otto J. Frank and Miriam Pressler, trans. Susan Massotty (New York: Doubleday, 1991), 28.
8. Ibid., 54.
9. Ibid., 190.
10. Dalai Lama, *The Path to Tranquility* (New York: Viking Arcana, 1999), 163.
11. Ibid., 303.
12. Ibid., 395.
13. W. H. Auden and Edward Mendelson, *Collected Poems* (New York: Modern Library, 2007).

Chapter 13

1. Petronius Gaius, "Doing, a Filthy Pleasure Is, and Short," trans. Ben Jonson, in *99 Poems in Translation*, eds. Harold Pinter et al. (London, Faber and Faber, 1994).
2. Francine Prose, *Gluttony* (New York: Oxford University Press, 2003), 8.
3. William Shakespeare, *Venus and Adonis*, in *The Annotated Shakespeare*, ed. A. L. Rowse (New York: Clarkson N. Potter, 1978), ll. 7–12.
4. Ibid., 1141–1144.
5. Trans. from the Middle English by the authors.
6. *The Rubáiyát of Omar Khayyám*, trans. Edward Fitzgerald, *The College Survey of English Literature*, rev. ed. (New York: Harcourt, Brace & World, 1951), ll. 393–396.
7. Ibid., ii. 217–220.
8. *The Essential Rumi*, trans. Coleman Barks (New York: HarperCollins, 2004).
9. Ibid.
10. Plato, *The Symposium*, trans. B. Jowett (New York: Doubleday, 1989).
11. "The Death of the Hired Man," in *The Poetry of Robert Frost*, ed. Edward Connery Lathern (New York: Holt, Rinehart and Winston, 1969).
12. Confucius, "Classical Rites," in *Anthology of World Literature*, ed. Robert E. Van Voort (Belmont, CA: Wadsworth, 1999), 152–153.
13. Antonia Fraser, *The Weaker Vessel* (New York: Knopf, 1984), 26.
14. Dante, *La Vita Nuova*, trans. D. G. Rossetti (New York: Viking, 1947), 547–548.
15. Dante, *The Divine Comedy*, trans. Lawrence Binyan (New York: Viking, 1947), 30.
16. Gabriel García Márquez, *Love in the Time of Cholera* (New York: Knopf, 1988), 339.
17. Hannah Kahn, "Signature," in *Eve's Daughter* (Coconut Grove, FL: Hurricane House, 1962), 17. Reprinted by permission of the poet.

Chapter 14

1. *Peace Prayers*, eds. staff (San Francisco: Harper, 1963).
2. Sherman B. Nuland, *How We Die* (New York: Knopf, 1994), 10.
3. Christopher Hitchens, "Topic of Cancer," *Vanity Fair*, November, 2010.
4. J. R. R. Tolkien, *The Return of the King* (New York: Ballantine, 1966), 849.
5. Matthew Gilbert, "Review of *House*," *Boston Globe*, November 16, 2004.
6. James Agee, *A Death in the Family* (New York: McDowell, Obolensky, 1957), 307–308.
7. Gerard Manley Hopkins, "Spring and Fall," *The Experience of Literature*, ed. Lionel Trilling (New York: Holt, Rinehart and Winston, 1967), 1213.
8. *The Collected Poems of A. E. Housman* (New York: Henry Holt, 1965), 88.
9. *The Republic and Other Works*, trans. Benjamin Jowett (New York: Doubleday, 1989), 551.
10. James Thurber, *My World and Welcome to It* (New York: Harcourt, Brace, 1942), 61–62.
11. Oscar Wilde, *The Picture of Dorian Gray* (New York: Dell, 1977), 33.
12. *Tao Te Ching*, trans. R. B. Blakney (New York: New American Library, 1955), 101.
13. Molière, *Four Plays*, trans. Carl Milo Pergolizzi (Boston: International Pocket Library, 1999), 234.
14. Katherine Mansfield, "The Man without a Temperament," *Ten Modern Masters*, ed. Robert Gorham Davis (New York: Harcourt, Brace, 1953), 61–62.
15. Johann Wolfgang von Goethe, *Faust*, trans. Walter Arndt (New York: Norton, 1976), 294.

16. *The Essential Tao*, trans. Thomas Cleary (San Francisco: Harper, 1991), 75.
17. Sylvia Plath, "Metaphors," *Collected Poems*, ed. Ted Hughes (New York: HarperCollins, 1981).
18. Rabbi Joseph Telushkin, *Jewish Literacy* (New York: Morrow, 1991), 566.

Chapter 15

1. *As You Like It*, II, i: 12–17.
2. Ibid., 20–27.
3. Ibid., 47–49.
4. Ibid., II: vii, 58–62.
5. "Manhatta," in the Calamus section of *Leaves of Grass*.
6. "Chicago," in *The Complete Poems of Carl Sandburg* (New York: Harcourt, Brace, Jovanavich, 1969).
7. Henry David Thoreau, *Walden and Civil Disobedience* (New York: Barnes & Noble Classics, 2003), 11.
8. Ibid., 90.
9. David Kwiat, *A Traveler in Residence* (Miami: Three Star Press, 2010), 144.
10. Mary Wollestonecraft Shelley, *Frankenstein, or The Modern Prometheus* (Berkeley: University of California Press, 1989), 24.
11. Ibid., 51.
12. Kent Nerburn, *The Wolf at Twilight* (Novato, CA: New World Library, 2009), 161.
13. T. C. McLuhan, *Touch the Earth* (New York: Promontory Press, 1971), 12.
14. Ibid., 15.
15. Nerburn, 189.
16. Joseph Conrad, *Heart of Darkness* (New York: Norton), 34.
17. Ibid., 69.
18. Ibid., 67.

Chapter 16

1. Azar Nafisi, *Reading* Lolita *in Tehran* (New York: Random House, 2004), 9.
2. B. F. Skinner, *Beyond Freedom and Dignity* (New York: Bantam Books, 1972), 37.
3. Ibid., 41.
4. Ibid., 39.
5. Arthur Schopenhauer, *Essays and Aphorisms*, ed. and trans. R. J. Hollingdale (London: Penguin Books, 1970), 65.
6. Ibid.
7. Ibid., 86.
8. Martin Buber, *Tales of the Hasidim* (New York: Schoken Books, 1992), viii.
9. Jean-Paul Sartre, *Existentialism and Human Emotions*, trans. Bernard Frechtman (New York: Philosophical Library, 1947), 15.
10. Simone de Beauvoir, *The Second Sex*, ed. and trans. H. M. Parchley (New York: Knopf, 1969), 79.
11. Albert Camus, *The Myth of Sisyphus and Other Essays*, trans. Justin O'Brien (New York: Vintage Books, 1995), 123.
12. Chögyam Trungpa, *The Myth of Freedom* (Berkeley, CA: Shambala, 1976), 1–2.
13. Bonnie Szumski, ed., *Readings in Stephen Crane* (San Diego: Green Haven Press, 1998), 194.

Credits

Haiku, "Detestable crow!" by Matsuo Bashō, translated by Sylvia Cassedy and Kunihiro Suetake, from *Red Dragonfly on My Shoulder*, New York, HarperCollins Publishers, 1992. By permission of Ellen Cassedy.

Haiku, "Oh, don't strike the fly!" by Kobayashi Issa, translated by Sylvia Cassedy and Kunihiro Suetake, from *Red Dragonfly on My Shoulder*, New York, HarperCollins Publishers, 1992. By permission of Ellen Cassedy.

"Joe Heller Poem" by Kurt Vonnegut from the *New Yorker*, May 14, 2007. Reprinted by permission of Donald Farber, Esq., Secretary and Trustee for Estate of Kurt Vonnegut.

Excerpt from *Night Mother*: A Play by Marsha Norman. Copyright © 1983 by Marsha Norman. Reprinted by permission of Hill and Wang, a division of Hill and Wang, a division of Farrar, Straus and Giroux, LLC.

Reprinted by permission of the publishers and the Trustees of Amherst College from *The Poems of Emily Dickinson*, Thomas H. Johnson, ed., Cambridge, Mass.: The Belknap Press of Harvard University Press. Copyright 1951, © 1955, 1979, 1983 by the President and Fellows of Harvard College.

"Terence, this is stupid stuff" from "A Shropshire Lad" authorized edition from *The Collected Poems* by A. E. Housman. Copyright 1924, 1965 by Henry Holt and Company. Reprinted by permission of Henry Holt and Company, LLC.

Excerpt from "The Death of a Hired Man" from *The Poetry of Robert Frost*, edited by Edward Connery Lathem. Copyright © 1958 by Robert Frost. Copyright © 1967 by Lesley Frost Ballantine. Copyright 1930, 1939, 1969 by Henry Holt and Company. Reprinted by permission of Henry Holt and Company, LLC.

Excerpt from "You, Andrew Marvell" from *Collected Poems 1917–1982* by Archibald MacLeish. Copyright © 1985 by The Estate of Archibald MacLeish. Reprinted by permission of Houghton Mifflin Harcourt Publishing Company. All rights reserved.

"Ars Poetica" from *Collected Poems* 1917–1982 by Archibald MacLeish. Copyright © 1985 by The Estate of Archibald MacLeish. Reprinted by permission of Houghton Mifflin Harcourt Publishing Company. All rights reserved.

Excerpt from *Tartuffe by Moliere*, English translation copyright © 1963, 1962, 1961 and renewed 1991, 1990 and 1989 by Richard Wilbur, reprinted by permission of Houghton Mifflin Harcourt Publishing Company. CAUTION: Professionals and amateurs are hereby warned that this translation, being fully protected under the copyright laws of the United States of America, the British Empire, including the Dominion of Canada, and all other countries which are signatories to the Universal Copyright Convention and the International Copyright Union, are subject to royalty. All rights, including professional, amateur, motion picture, recitation, lecturing, public reading, radio broadcasting, and television, are strictly reserved. Particular emphasis is laid on the question of readings, permission for which must be secured from the author's agent in writing. Inquiries on professional rights (except for amateur rights) should be addressed to Peter Franklin, William Morris Agency, 1325 Avenue of the Americas, New York, NY 10019; inquiries on translation rights should be addressed to Harcourt, Inc., Permissions Department, Orlando FL 32887. The stock and amateur acting rights of *Tartuffe* are controlled exclusively by the Dramatist Play Service, Inc., 440 Park Avenue South, New York, NY. No amateur performance of the play may be given without obtaining in advance the written permission of the Dramatists Play Service, Inc., and paying the requisite fee. This material may not be reproduced in any form or by any means without the prior written permission of the publisher.

"somewhere i have never travelled, gladly beyond." Copyright 1931, © 1959, 1991 by the Trustees for the E. E. Cummings Trust. Copyright © 1979 by George James Firmage, from *Complete Poems*: 1904–1962 by E. E. Cummings, edited by George J. Firmage. Used by permission of Liveright Publishing Corporation.

Billy Collins, "My Number" from *The Apple that Astonished Paris*. Copyright © 1988, 1996 by Billy Collins. Used by permission of the University of Arkansas Press, www.uapress.com.

"The Chaser" by John Collier. Originally appeared in the *New Yorker*, 1940. Copyright 1951 by John Collier. Renewed 1978 by the estate of John Collier. Permission to reprint granted by Harold Matson Co., Inc. All rights reserved.

"Musee des Beaux Arts," copyright 1940 & renewed 1968 by W. H. Auden from *Collected Poems of W. H. Auden* by W. H. Auden. Used by permission of Random House, Inc.

Courtesy of Taylor Mali, Words Worth Ink.

Excerpt from *Long Day's Journey into Night* by Eugene O'Neill. Copyright © 1955 by Carlotta Monterey O'Neill. Copyright renewed 1984 by Yale University. Reprinted by permission of Yale University Press.

"A Doll's House" (18 lines from Act I) from *The Complete Major Prose Plays of Henrik Ibsen* by Henrik Ibsen, translated by Rolf Fjelde. Copyright © 1965, 1970, 1978 by Rolf Fjelde. Used by permission of Dutton Signet, a division of Penguin Group (USA) Inc.

"La Vita Nuova," translated by D. G. Rossetti, copyright 1947, renewed (1975) by the Viking Press, Inc., from *The Portable Dante* by Dante, edited by Paola Milano, translated by Laurence Binyon. Used by permission of Viking Penguin, a division of Penguin Group (USA) Inc.

"Requiem" from *Death of a Salesman* by Arthur Miller. Copyright 1949, renewed © 1977 by Arthur Miller. Used by permission of Viking Penguin, a division of Penguin Group (USA) Inc.

"I'm a means, a stage, a cow in calf/. . ." from "Metaphors" in *Crossing the Water* by Sylvia Plath. Copyright © 1960 by Ted Hughes. Reprinted by permission of HarperCollins Publishers and Faber and Faber Limited.

"5 a.m.: the frogs" (haiku) from *Seven Notebooks* by Campbell McGrath. Copyright © 2008 by Campbell McGrath. Reprinted by permission of HarperCollins Publishers.

"Then" (29-line poem) from *Seven Notebooks* by Campbell McGrath. Copyright © 2008 by Campbell McGrath. Reprinted by permission of HarperCollins Publishers.

Excerpt from "Joe Hil." Music by Earl Robinson. Words by Alfred Hayes. Copyright 1938, renewed by Music Sales Corporation (ASCAP) and MCA Music Publishing. International copyright secured. All rights reserved. Reprinted by permission.

"Joe Hill" by Alfred Hayes and Earl Robinson. Copyright 1938 by Universal Music Corp. (ASCAP). Copyright renewed. Used by permission. All rights reserved.

"American Pie" by Don McLean. Copyright © 1971 by Songs of Universal, Inc. and Benny Bird Co., Inc. Copyright renewed. All rights administered by Songs of Universal, Inc. (BMI). Used by permission. All rights reserved.

"Signature" by Hannah Kahn from *I Hear My Sisters Saying*: Poems by Twentieth Century Women by Carol Konek, ed. by Dorothy Walters. Copyright © 1976. Reprinted by permission of Hannah Kahn Poetry Foundation and Heirs to Hannah Kahn.

"Hurricane Season: The Nature of War" (p. 144) from *A Traveler in Residence* by David Kwiat. Copyright © 2010. Reprinted by permission of David Kwiat.

Index

Italicized page numbers show the location of illustrations.

B.C.E.	HISTORY	HUMANITIES
c.7000	Native Americans May Have Migrated from Northern Asia	
c.3200	Egyptian Civilization Established	
c.1500	Hinduism Develops in India (p. 317)	The Vedas (p. 317) The Upanishads (p. 317)
c.14th century	Amenhotep IV Establishes Monotheism (p. 316) Tutenkhamen Reestablishes Polytheism (p. 317)	
c.13th century	Moses Leads Exodus from Egypt (p. 332)	
c.1200	Presumed Period of Trojan War (p. 71)	
c.l027–256	Golden Age of Chinese Philosophy	Lao-tzu, 6th century (p. 326) Confucius (557–479) (p. 329)
c.700	Age of Homer and Greek Mythology (p. 71)	*The Iliad* (p. 71)
6th century	Buddhism in India (p. 322) Festivals of Dionysus in Athens	Siddhartha Gautama (564–483) (p. 322) Sappho (early 6th century) (p. 74) Aeschylus (525–456) (p. 13)
5th century	Golden Age of Athens	Sophocles (496–406) (p. 196) Euripides (484–406) (p. 199) Socrates (469–399) (p. 360) Plato (c. 427–347) (p. 360)
4th century	Alexander the Great	Aristotle (c. 382–322) (p. 198)
C.E.		
1st century	Christianity in Rome	
c.400	Fall of Rome to the Goths	Augustine (354–430) (p. 337)
6th century		Mohammed (571–632) (p. 342)
8th century	Moors Occupy Spain	
10th century		Lady Murasaki Shikibu (978–1031) (p. 91) *Tale of Genji*, Japan, earliest known novel (p. 91)
11th century	Norman Conquest of England in 1066 (p. 112)	Bayeux Tapestry (p. 112)
12th century	Japanese Feudal Period, Rise of Samurai	Angkor Wat (p. 145) Moses Maimonides (1135–1204) (p. 340)
13th century	High Middle Ages in Western Europe	Notre Dame Cathedral (p. 344) Thomas Aquinas (1225–1274) (p. 341) Dante Alighieri (1265–1321) (p. 377)
14th century	Renaissance Begins to Emerge	Geoffrey Chaucer (1340–1400) (p. 413)
15th century	High Renaissance Starts in Italy 1492, Columbus	Leonardo (1451–1519) (p. 115) Michelangelo (1475–1564) (p. 117) Raphael (1483–1520) (p. 119)
16th century	1517, Martin Luther's Reform Proposals (p. 345) 1519, Conquest of Mexico by Cortes 1533–1603, Reign of Elizabeth I	Sophonisba Anguissola (c. 1532–1626) (p. 120) Cervantes (1547–1616) (p. 92) William Shakespeare (1564–1616) (p. 76, 194)